THE ENGLISH HER

LONDON'S BLUE PLAQUES

The Lives and Homes
of London's Most
Interesting Inhabitants

Edited by HOWARD SPENCER

september

13 5 7 9 10 8 6 4 2

This revised and updated edition published in 2019 by September Publishing

Publisher: Hannah MacDonald
Project editor: Charlotte Cole
Design: Two Associates, Martin Brown
Picture research: Abigail Lelliott
Maps: Mark Fenton, Clifford Manlow
Proofreaders: Beth Hamer, Cathy Benson
Indexer: Stephen Blake

Printed in Poland on paper from responsibly managed, sustainable sources
by Hussar Books

ISBN 978-1-912836-05-5

September Publishing
www.septemberpublishing.org

English Heritage is a charitable trust; as well as running the capital's plaque scheme,
it looks after over 400 historic monuments, buildings and places across
England including Stonehenge, Hadrian's Wall, Dover Castle and Tintagel.
The blue plaques scheme is now entirely reliant on donations.
Please consider making a donation through our website.

www.english-heritage.org.uk

CONTENTS

FOREWORD

THE plaque is the most common form of public commemoration today, replacing the tombs and statues which fulfilled that role in previous centuries. It is the perfect one for a democratic age, in that all of the people honoured with one, irrespective of their social status, occupation or the decade in which they died, have their names and reason for fame inscribed upon an object of identical design. They thus take their places in an open-air pantheon, growing as the decades pass. Furthermore, they are intrinsically connected with a building of special significance to the life and work of the individual concerned, and some of that person's distinction is shared by the structure in which they resided or worked. As metal, in the form of a crown, confers a mystique when placed upon a human's head, so a piece of ceramic, called a plaque, can do the same to the building on which it is set. It brings together person, place and story in a way done in legends since human time began, but in a specially tangible and objective form. As well as informing passers-by and honouring the dead, it can also play a role in giving further appreciation to a solid structure.

The blue plaques scheme of London is the oldest in the United Kingdom. It belongs to the people, in that anyone is free to propose somebody for commemoration on a plaque; but the worthiness of the subject is determined by the panel that I chair, against very high standards of enduring fame. That panel is composed of experts in the British record of every branch of human activity, all bearing national and/ or academic honours, and serving for fixed periods to ensure freshness of approach. They are provided with further detailed information on each candidate, requiring intensive research currently undertaken or overseen by the scheme's resident historian, Howard Spencer. This book is infused with his unmatched knowledge, his profound love of the people and places concerned, and his eye for a sharp one-liner. My own sense of what London is, and what it is to be a Londoner, and has been, is immeasurably enriched by it.

Like the scheme of which it is a distillation, this book keeps

GREATER LONDON COUNCIL
SIR
ROBERT
WALPOLE
1676–1745
Prime Minister
and his son
HORACE WALPOLE
1717–1797
Connoisseur and
Man of Letters
lived here

faith with past, present and future. It keeps faith with the past, by recognising the Londoners whose lives and work have been of especial benefit to their fellow humanity, and who have made a lasting impact on history. It keeps faith with the present, because the choice of recipients for plaques involves a recognition of what the contemporary world values and thinks worthy of memory and of applause. It also keeps faith with the future, by holding up to it an image of what modern Britain has believed to constitute greatness. Those robust and beautiful ceramic circles – set into a wall, not screwed to it – will last as long as the buildings themselves. In a thousand years from now perhaps a visitor from Australia – or even Mars – will survey the ruins of London, see and read these plaques, and know from them what we were worth as a civilisation.

Professor Ronald Hutton
English Heritage trustee and Chair of the English Heritage Blue Plaques Panel

INTRODUCTION

BLUE plaques are as much a part of the London street-scape as red telephone boxes, plane trees and terraces of stucco and stock brick. Their laconic inscriptions, telling of where famous figures of the past were born, lived, worked and died, have been informing, educating and entertaining passers-by for 150 years.

Lord Byron had the honour of being the recipient of the very first official London plaque, in 1867. The scheme was started by the Society of Arts (now the RSA) the year before, after a suggestion by the MP William Ewart*. In 1901 the plaques scheme was taken on by the London County Council (LCC), and a senior administrator at the council, Laurence Gomme*, was largely responsible for shaping the plaques scheme into a form we would recognise today.

From 1965 the Greater London Council (GLC) took blue plaques into a wider geographical area, reflecting the suburban spread of the capital. Somewhat confusingly, the London blue plaques scheme does not cover the square mile of the City, where the Corporation of London operates its own scheme. (The plaque to Dr Johnson in Gough Square is the single exception to this rule.)

In 1986 the GLC was abolished and the scheme passed to English Heritage, then a government agency, and which became a charitable trust in 2015.

The blue plaque has become, to employ an over-used term, a design icon – and has been much imitated and parodied. The plaques now used in London are 495mm (19.5in) round, but can be smaller if this better suits a particular building. Made of ceramic slipware, the plaques are inset into walls to a depth of about 50mm (2in). They are the work of skilled craft ceramicists, most recently the Ashworth family and Ned Heywood. Slightly domed so as to be self-cleaning, they are intended to last for as long as the buildings they adorn.

The design history, however, is complicated. Not all blue plaques are blue, for a start; many of the earlier 'tablets' – to use the term once favoured – were terracotta or brown. Green and grey ceramic has also been used, as have other materials, including bronze, lead, stone and enamelled steel. And just to add to the fun, plaques are not all round either: squares, rectangles and other shapes also feature.

Official plaques almost invariably feature the name of the responsible body in their inscription. The Society of Arts embedded its name discreetly in an intricate border, while the former London councils put their monikers on more prominent display. The same goes for English Heritage, which added its famous portcullis logo. The exceptions are a handful of plaques that were put up privately and later officially adopted. Some good examples of these may be found in Bloomsbury, where ornate bronze plaques – complete with cherubs – were put up by the landowner, the Bedford Estate.

WHO (OR WHAT) GETS A BLUE PLAQUE – AND HOW?

SINCE the early years of the 20th century the engine of the scheme has been public suggestions, from both individuals and institutions. Today, these are considered by the Blue Plaques Panel – a collection of experts in the broad areas of enterprise and achievement that the plaques commemorate. Similar assemblies, such as the GLC's Historic Buildings Sub-Committee, performed this task in earlier times.

For someone to be considered for a plaque, the present rule is that they need to have been dead for 20 years, so as to be as certain as possible of a figure's enduring reputation. This rule has been in place for some time, with certain variations; until 2013, deceased figures could also be considered if a century had passed since their birth.

One plaque per person is another important rule, but this has not always been the case, either. At one time Charles Dickens had no fewer than four official plaques in London and William Makepeace Thackeray can still boast three.

Careful preparatory work is undertaken before a plaque goes up. A high level of proof is needed of the connection between a person and building, involving the use of evidence culled from such sources as the census, electoral registers, rate books and directories, as well as correspondence and diaries. The widespread renumbering of streets in London is a particular hazard to be navigated.

CELEBRATION – AND CONSERVATION

FROM the mid-1950s, the most important selection criterion has been that a commemorated person must have made 'a positive contribution to human welfare and happiness'. Well before this, the design of the early-20th-century plaques featured a laurel wreath – a classical motif that signifies triumph and success. From the outset, the London plaques have been about celebration, rather than just simple matters of record.

Judging who is worthy, both in terms of 'positive contribution' and overall historical significance, is a tricky business. And a few of the plaques described in this book commemorate individuals whose reputation has not, it has turned out, entirely stood the test of time. On the other hand, there are cases such as that of the novelist Wilkie Collins: his writings, declared an LCC report of 1910, 'were not of a high order' – but by 1951, when he got his plaque, opinions on his work had moved on. History, as this shows, is an ongoing debate.

Turning from the person to the building, conservation has been part of the intention since the earliest days of the plaques. The Dickens Museum in Doughty Street, Bloomsbury, was under threat of demolition when the plaque went up in 1903: while we cannot say for sure that the plaque saved it, it may well have done so. Similarly, the survival of J. M. Barrie's old home on the Bayswater Road – now dwarfed by the modern blocks around it – must surely have been assisted by the blue roundel on its frontage.

Plaques are, however, a form of soft power – as distinct from the hard legal protection conferred by the listing of a building. This is an entirely separate process to the award of a plaque and is now overseen by Historic England. The listing of some London buildings, however, has been assisted – or even inspired – by the presence of a plaque indicating an important personal association.

In recent years, blue plaques have been sited only on buildings that survive in a form that would have been recognised by the commemorated figure – the thought being that once the original bricks and mortar have gone, so has the meaningful connection between person and place. In the past this line was not always followed, meaning that a number of blue plaques sit (often rather uneasily) on later structures, sometimes with a supplementary plaque to date the rebuilding.

The rule now in place ensures authenticity but it does have the unfortunate consequence that if a 'plaqued' house is demolished and no alternative London address exists for that individual, they will no longer be commemorated under the scheme. Such a fate befell Air Chief Marshal Lord Dowding as recently as 2009, after his house in Wimbledon fell to a wrecking ball.

Despite occasional losses such as this, there are now very nearly 950 official plaques across Greater London, commemorating people from an astonishing variety of human endeavours – from 'the emigrants' friend' (Caroline Chisholm) to the 'namer of clouds' (Luke Howard). The arts are well represented; science, technology and sport rather less so. Women account for about 14 per cent of those commemorated, and black and ethnic minority figures less than five per cent. Efforts to redress these imbalances are bearing fruit; more remains to be done. But it should be remembered that, as a 150-year-old project, the blue plaques scheme reflects the shifting perceptions over time of what constitutes 'historical significance' – not the consensus of today.

Something the plaques illustrate very clearly is London's long-held status as an international city. The foreign visitors represented range from Gandhi to Marx and from Van Gogh to Mendelssohn; numerous exiled emperors, kings, princes and ministers also feature, together with a president of the United States (Martin Van Buren). The rather large contingent from France includes the oldest surviving plaque: that to Napoleon III (put up in 1867).

One more caveat: not all the plaques covered here commemorate individuals. A handful record some other aspect of a building's history; for instance, there is the roundel on Alexandra Palace, which commemorates the first broadcast television transmissions, and the square plaque on Islington Green that denotes the former Collins Music Hall.

Over the past century and a half, blue plaques have embedded themselves in the public consciousness: their own 'positive contribution to human welfare and happiness' is clear enough. This book – the first portable and comprehensive guide to the plaques for many years – aims to inspire a deeper appreciation of the plaques, and of the people and buildings commemorated.

By some distance, the City of Westminster has the most blue plaques; it is nip and tuck between the Royal Borough of Kensington and Chelsea and the London Borough of Camden for second place.

HOW TO USE THIS BOOK

THIS book covers the 950-odd official London plaques. It is divided into 36 chapters, radiating out from Westminster; within each chapter, the plaques are laid out according to geographical logic. It is not a walking guide as such, but has been designed so that readers may easily trace their own tours. For reasons of space, the maps presented here are highly simplified, and it is suggested that the book be used with a smartphone mapping system, the (free to download) blue plaques app or a printed street map – remembering to add the area of London as well as the street address. References within entries to other figures with plaques are marked with an asterisk*; an asterisk after a name in a heading indicates a figure with more than one plaque.

WESTMINSTER AND PIMLICO

WESTMINSTER has been at the heart of national government since the 11th century. Here are the Houses of Parliament and the broad sweep of Whitehall where the business of state is carried out. Many of the office buildings date from the 19th century, but behind the arterial routes lie the 18th-century terraces of Smith Square and Queen Anne's Gate, which are dotted with blue plaques.

From the mid-1800s, a new commercial centre grew up between Parliament Square and Victoria Station. This quarter is characterised by tall blocks of mansion flats, department stores and modern offices, and by the Roman Catholic Westminster Cathedral, built to designs by J. F. Bentley* between 1895 and 1903.

Pimlico, to the west, was built up in the mid-Victorian era as a genteel suburb for professional men; it aspired to – but never quite matched – the social standing of neighbouring Belgravia. The area's stuccoed Italianate terraces and squares are now intermingled with post-war local authority housing and subsequent developments.

SCOTLAND YARD

(1829–90) first headquarters of the Metropolitan Police   3–8 Whitehall Place

NUMBERS 3–8 Whitehall Place is a government building, currently home to the Department for Business, Energy & Industrial Strategy. It stands on the site of a row of small houses built in about 1820 that became, in September 1829, the headquarters of the new Metropolitan Police force. The police's earliest nicknames – the 'blue army' and the 'raw lobster gang' – were soon replaced by 'Peelers' and 'bobbies'; both derive from the force's founder, Sir Robert Peel*, who lived at nearby 4 Whitehall Gardens. The back of 4 Whitehall Place was extended to form a police barracks, opening onto Great Scotland Yard. This entrance, used by the public and the press, caused the whole building to be known popularly as Scotland Yard from the early 1840s. By 1888, the police headquarters had overflowed into several adjacent buildings and in November 1890 the police moved into the purpose-built New Scotland Yard on Victoria Embankment, now called the Norman Shaw Building after its eminent architect. The Met HQ has since moved in 1967 to Broadway, off Victoria Street, and then back to Victoria Embankment in 2016 – but the name 'Scotland Yard' has stuck.

SIR HENRY MORTON STANLEY

(1841–1904) explorer and writer   6 (formerly 2) Richmond Terrace

STANLEY was born John Rowlands in Denbigh, north Wales, and spent much of his childhood in the workhouse. Emigrating to the United States in 1859, he was adopted by a cotton trader called Stanley, and became a journalist. Urged by the flamboyant proprietor of the *New York Herald*, Gordon Bennett, to 'find Livingstone', Stanley set off for Africa, and, having tracked down the famous explorer in 1871, greeted him with the famous line 'Dr Livingstone, I presume?' and a bottle of champagne. Stanley went on to author the hugely popular *How I Found Livingstone* (1872) and *Through the Dark Continent* (1878), and played a major, and now very controversial, part in opening up the Congo. Stanley resettled in England in 1890 and married the painter Dorothy ('Dolly') Tennant (1855-1926); they lived with Dolly's formidable mother Gertrude at this house, then numbered 2 Richmond Terrace. It was handy for Parliament when he became a Liberal Unionist MP in 1895 and he continued to travel, lecture and write. It was at Richmond Terrace – just after hearing the chimes of Big Ben – that Stanley died. The house forms part of a terrace built in 1822–5 to designs by Henry Harrison; since reconstructive work in the 1980s only the facade remains, on which the plaque may be glimpsed from Whitehall through the security barrier.

SIR MANSFIELD CUMMING
(1859–1923) first chief of the Secret Service   2 Whitehall Court **3**

AN eager experimenter with secret writing, disguises and gadgets, Cumming always signed himself – in green ink – as 'C': James Bond's boss 'M' is his fictional counterpart. Born Mansfield George Smith – he later changed his name – he enlisted in the Navy at the age of 12. He got the 'tap on the shoulder' to run the newly established Secret Service Bureau in 1909; two years later this split into home and foreign sections – the precursors of MI5 and MI6. Cumming led the foreign section, which from 1911 to 1922 had its headquarters – and a flat for the chief – at numbers 53 and 54, on the seventh floor of Whitehall Court – a vast Thames-side building resembling a Renaissance French chateau. The plaque is by the door to what is now the Royal Horseguards Hotel. Cumming's time there encompassed the First World War, so most of his work here related to intelligence-gathering in Germany. He lost a leg in a motor accident in 1914 that killed his son Alastair; afterwards Cumming used a scooter to propel him around the office, and would sometimes disconcert colleagues by jabbing a paper knife into his artificial limb to emphasise a point.

T. E. LAWRENCE
(1888–1935) 'Lawrence of Arabia'   14 Barton Street **4**

BARTON Street is a rare surviving example of early Georgian brown-brick terraced houses; it was developed by the actor Barton Booth in 1722. Two hundred years later, between March and August 1922, Thomas Edward Lawrence stayed at number 14, where he worked on the final draft of *Seven Pillars of Wisdom* (1926). With this colourful – some were to say fanciful – tale of his adventures as a soldier and diplomat during the Arab revolt against Turkish rule (1916–18) Lawrence became a legend, inspiring the David Lean film of 1962.

Lawrence worked in a simply furnished attic, which he declared 'the best-and-freest place I ever lived in', and where 'nobody has found me . . . despite efforts by callers and telephones'. His hideout was located above the office of architect Herbert Baker (1862–1946), who recalled that Lawrence was largely nocturnal, and 'refused all service and comfort, food, fire or hot water'; he 'ate and bathed when he happened to go out' and kept chocolate – 'it required no cleaning up, he said' – for emergency rations. Baker added: 'We who worked in the rooms below never heard a sound; I would look up from my drawing-board in the evening sometimes to see him watching, gnomelike, with a smile; his smile that hid a tragedy.'

LORD REITH

(1889–1971) first Director-General of the BBC   6 Barton Street **5**

BORN in Scotland, the son of a church minister, John Charles Walsham Reith was knighted on his appointment to the Director-Generalship in 1926, at which juncture the BBC became a public corporation. Reith had moved to Barton Street in June 1924 with his wife Muriel, and it was from his study here that he announced the beginning of the General Strike in 1926 – a 'very impressive performance', he noted in his diary, with a characteristic horror of false modesty. Tired of the 'dirt and confinement' of London, however, the Reiths left Barton Street, the birthplace of their son Christopher, for Buckinghamshire in March 1930. On the original plaque, which was unveiled in 1994, Reith's second forename had been omitted and as he was, in the words of his son, 'such a stickler for absolute correctness in every detail', it was decided to have a new plaque made with a simplified wording. It is sited on the side of the building facing Cowley Street.

SIR JOHN GIELGUD

(1904–2000) actor and director   16 Cowley Street **6**

WITH Ralph Richardson* and Laurence Olivier, Gielgud was one of a trio of theatrical knights who dominated the English stage for much of the 20th century. Onstage at the Old Vic, in the West End and later at the National Theatre, he took leading parts in plays by Shakespeare, Chekhov, Richard Brinsley Sheridan* and – later – Alan Bennett and Peter Shaffer; his film credits include *Oh! What a Lovely War* (1969), *Murder on the Orient Express* (1974), *Providence* (1976) *Arthur* (1981) and *Prospero's Books* (1991). Born in South Kensington, Gielgud was of Prussian and Polish ancestry on his father's side, while his maternal aunt was the actress Ellen Terry*. He moved to this early Georgian townhouse in 1945 and stayed for 31 years, sharing the place with a menagerie of pets – six dogs, two owls and a cockatoo, at one point – and his cook, driver and general manservant Bernie Dodge. Gielgud was famously otherworldly, once conversationally asking the Prime Minister Clement Attlee* where he was living, not being aware to whom he was speaking. The story of Gielgud's conviction for a homosexual offence, following police entrapment, is itself now the subject of a play – Nicholas de Jongh's *Plague Over England* (2009).

ELEANOR RATHBONE

(1872–1946) pioneer of family allowances   5 Tufton Court, Tufton Street

THE daughter of the philanthropist and politician William Rathbone, Eleanor Rathbone became the secretary of the Liverpool Women's Suffrage Society in 1897. In 1909 she became the first woman elected to Liverpool City Council; ten years later she succeeded Millicent Fawcett* to the presidency of the National Union of Societies for Equal Citizenship and moved to London, where she lived at 50 Romney Street – around the corner from Tufton Street – with her lifelong friend and companion Elizabeth Macadam (1871–1948), a fellow social reformer. Rathbone was elected to Parliament for the Combined English Universities as an Independent, and held the seat from 1929 until her death. Bombed out of Romney Street in 1940, Eleanor and Elizabeth moved to 5 Tufton Court – a flat on the ground floor of a recently built seven-storey block. Since the 1920s Rathbone had campaigned for a universal benefit payable to mothers, and the Family Allowances Act of 1945 owed much to her persistence. She also pressed for a more sympathetic policy towards refugees – especially Jewish refugees. In April 1945 Eleanor and Elizabeth moved to Highgate, where Rathbone died suddenly the following year.

STELLA, LADY READING

(1894–1971) founder of the Women's Voluntary Services   41 Tothill Street

This imposing early-20th-century office building, Queen Anne's Chambers, was the HQ of the Women's Voluntary Services from its foundation in 1938 until 1966; the 'shop' was on the ground floor, and the offices up on the fourth. The organisation was ably led by the equally imposing Stella Reading, the widow (and one-time secretary) of the politician Rufus Isaacs*, Marquess of Reading. From 'Totters', as the HQ was colloquially known, she issued a stream of injunctions to her million-strong green-uniformed army of women volunteers: 'Always have food for bombed out people that is easy to eat. The first thing people lose is their spectacles, and the second their teeth,' was one memorable wartime edict. The service assisted in many vital tasks, like looking after refugees and child evacuees, sewing and mending clothes, devising ration-book recipes and making endless cups of tea. As the (now unisex) Royal Voluntary Service, its work continues today.

SIR EDWARD GREY, VISCOUNT GREY OF FALLODON

(1862–1933) Foreign Secretary

B UILT in 1776, this house was the London home of Edward Grey, who as Foreign Secretary from 1905 to 1916 in the Liberal governments of Henry Campbell-Bannerman* and Herbert Asquith* was largely responsible for negotiating the pre-First World War defence agreements between Britain, France and Russia. In February 1906, facing a crisis over Morocco, he suffered the tragic death of his wife Dorothy in a coaching accident. She had just secured the lease on 3 Queen Anne's Gate, where Grey was installed by early spring. 'I am left alone and have no wish to live,' he told a friend; when time permitted, he found solace in birdwatching, which he and Dorothy had once

'The lamps are going out all over Europe; we shall not see them lit again in our life-time.'

Sir Edward Grey on the eve of the First World War

enjoyed together. He was the last person to use number 3 as a private residence. Having moved away from Queen Anne's Gate in 1913, Grey returned during the dramatic days leading up to the outbreak of war to lodge with his friend Viscount Haldane*, who wrote of him 'sparing no effort to avoid the catastrophe'. Others were more sceptical: Ramsay MacDonald*, the Labour leader, thought that Grey 'combined a most admirable intention with a tragic incapacity to drive his way to his own goal'. The name of Grey's Northumberland seat, Fallodon, is unfortunately misspelt on the plaque.

Queen Anne's Gate contains a total of seven plaques – one of the largest concentrations in London – many of them commemorating political figures. Until 1873 it was two separate streets: Queen Square was to the west and Park Street to the east; the former intersection is now marked by a statue of Queen Anne.

JAMES MILL (1773–1836)
JOHN STUART MILL* (1806–73)
philosophers   40 Queen Anne's Gate

A FATHER-AND-SON pairing, the Mills occupied this Grade I-listed early-18th-century house from 1814 to 1831. Scottish-born James Mill leased the house from Jeremy Bentham, a fellow member of the group of thinkers who became known as Philosophical Radicals. (The site of Bentham's house, just to the south, is marked with a green Westminster City Council plaque.) Mill senior completed his ten-volume history of India while living in Queen Anne's Gate, and – believing that schools promoted 'vulgar modes of thought and feeling' – set about home-educating his nine children

> John Stuart Mill was tutored in Greek from the age of three, history from four, and in Latin and advanced mathematics from eight. By the age of 14 he had written a treatise on logic – in French.

here; but John Stuart Mill grew up, as he remembered, 'in the absence of love'. Mistakes were punished with no lunch, and while the gruelling curriculum did eventually propel him to becoming the leading political thinker of his age, he suffered an almost catastrophic mental breakdown at the age of 20.

CHARLES TOWNLEY
(1737–1805) antiquary and collector   14 Queen Anne's Gate   **II**

B ORN to a Catholic landowning family in Lancashire, Townley had this house – originally 7 Park Street – built by Michael Barratt from 1775 to the designs of Samuel Wyatt, for the express purpose of displaying the collection of mostly Roman statuary that he had acquired in Italy. He moved into the house in 1778 and his treasures, which also included terracottas, bronzes, coins, gems and drawings, were put on permanent display,

with servants under instruction to admit 'all individuals of respectability who desired to see them'. Some of the 700 or so annual visitors were given guided tours by Townley himself, whose Sunday dinner guests included Joseph Nollekens*, Joshua Reynolds* and Johann Zoffany*. He continued to amass antiquities right up until his death, which occurred here in 1805. Much of Townley's collection is now on show at the British Museum.

WILLIAM SMITH

(1756–1835) pioneer of religious liberty   16 Queen Anne's Gate **12**

A UNITARIAN, and a Whig MP from 1784, Smith was a leading light in securing religious dissenters their full civil rights, culminating in 1828 with the repeal of the Test and Corporation Acts, which had effectively barred Nonconformists from Crown offices. Between 1805 and 1832 he was Chairman of the Dissenting Deputies, and secured the passage of the Unitarian Toleration Act (1813). Active in the anti-slavery movement led by his friends William Wilberforce* and Thomas Clarkson, Smith was himself among the founders of the London Society for the Abolition of Slavery in Our Colonies in 1823. Having lived for many years in Clapham, Smith moved in 1794 to this house, then 6 Park Street, with his wife Frances (1758–1840) and large family; their grandchildren included Florence Nightingale* and the women's rights campaigner Barbara Bodichon. Business reverses – including a disastrous fire at a Millbank distillery – forced the sale of the house in 1819, along with much of his library and art collection.

LORD FISHER, OM

(1841–1920) Admiral of the Fleet, First Sea Lord   16 Queen Anne's Gate

A SECOND plaque at number 16 commemorates Admiral Fisher, who had his official residence as First Sea Lord here, between October 1904 and January 1910; he returned to this post, though not to this address, between October 1914 and May 1915. The son of an army captain, John Arbuthnot Fisher – popularly known as Jacky – was a strong, confident personality who entered the Navy at the age of 13 and worked his way up through the ranks. As First Sea Lord he embarked on a programme of modernisation and commissioned the building of fast, heavily armed battleships; the first and most famous of these, HMS *Dreadnought*, was launched in 1906, while the world's first battlecruiser, HMS *Invincible*, entered service the following year. Appropriately, Fisher – awarded the Order of Merit in 1905 – chose the motto 'Fear God and Dread Nought' on his elevation to the peerage in 1909. He had a bellicose reputation, suggesting pre-emptive strikes against the German and Japanese navies, and yet it was his routine to walk to the Admiralty in Whitehall via Westminster Abbey each day for morning prayer. It was there that he was given a public funeral.

LORD PALMERSTON*

(1784–1865) Prime Minister   20 Queen Anne's Gate **14**

IT was once thought that Lord Palmerston, who was three times Foreign Secretary and twice Prime Minister, was born at Broadlands, the family estate in Hampshire. But when the LCC investigated they found a diary entry by his father, Henry Temple, the 2nd Viscount Palmerston, describing a journey to London, and soon afterwards – on 20 October 1784 – a joyful report: 'Lady P. brought to bed of a son at seven in the evening.' They therefore placed a blue wreathed plaque on this house, formerly 4 Park Street, which forms part of a terrace built between 1775 and 1778. Palmerston's father was its first occupant, and stayed until 1791; he was in London to sit for a portrait by Joshua Reynolds* when his second wife Mary, née Mee, went into labour. The younger Palmerston was baptised at St Margaret's, Westminster, on 23 November 1784. A magnificent ball was thrown at Winchester to celebrate his birth; four years later, he was described as 'quite stout, with a fine high colour'.

LORD HALDANE

(1856–1928) statesman, lawyer and philosopher   28 Queen Anne's Gate **15**

DATING from 1704–5 and an important early survival, this house was the London home of Richard Burdon Haldane, later Viscount Haldane of Cloan, from 1907 until his death in 1928. Born and educated in Edinburgh, he served as Secretary of State for War from 1905 until 1912, during which time he founded the Imperial General Staff and the Territorial Army, and introduced the concept of a British expeditionary force. Haldane then served as Lord Chancellor until 1915, and briefly held the same office again in 1924, having switched allegiance from the Liberals to Labour.

Kaiser Wilhelm II lunched with Haldane in May 1911 and chaffed him about the small size of ...

'28 Queen Anne's Gate, which he called my Dolls' House'.

A man with a wide range of intellectual interests, Haldane helped to establish the London School of Economics in 1895, translated works by Schopenhauer* and wrote a number of his own, including *The Reign of Relativity* (1921). Guests at the house included Lord Kitchener*, Lord Curzon*, Albert Einstein, Edmund Gosse* and the Emperor (Kaiser) of Germany.

WILFRID SCAWEN BLUNT

(1840–1922) diplomat, poet and traveller 15 Buckingham Gate **16**

THIS mid-18th-century terraced house opposite Wellington Barracks was the London home from about 1878 until 1887 of Wilfrid Scawen Blunt, who married Lord Byron's grandchild Anne King (1837–1917) – the daughter of Ada, Countess of Lovelace* – and shared Byron's passions for verse, travel, radical politics and women. He and Anne spent much time travelling in Spain, Turkey, North Africa and the Middle East, and Blunt campaigned for causes such as Egyptian and Irish self-determination; he also published works including *Sonnets and Songs by Proteus* (1875) and *Satan Absolved* (1899). In 1872 Blunt inherited Crabbet Park in West Sussex, where – six years later

> At Crabbet, it was said, Blunt's weekend guests played tennis in the nude.

– he and Anne founded a famous stud breeding Arab stallions. Blunt's mistresses included the famous courtesan Catherine Walters ('Skittles') and Lady Gregory. An entry in his private diary for 1880 records his renting a flat opposite Victoria Station as a love nest; his wife eventually left him in 1906. Blunt's dark good looks and bids for political martyrdom led one contemporary to observe: 'The fellow knows he has a handsome head and he wants it to be seen on Temple Bar.'

LORD HORE-BELISHA

(1893–1957) statesman 16 Stafford Place **17**

BORN in London, the son of a Jewish businessman, Leslie Hore-Belisha was elected Liberal MP for Plymouth Devonport in 1923, and held the seat – latterly as a National Liberal – until 1945. In 1937 Neville Chamberlain* appointed him Secretary of State for War; he piloted important army reforms, but his relations with the top brass – notably Viscount Gort* – were problematic, and he

> Leslie – later Lord – Hore-Belisha is best remembered for the Belisha beacon, the flashing orange crossing indicators brought in as a road safety innovation in 1934, while he was Minister of Transport. They had a significant impact on road safety, despite initial problems with vandalism.

resigned in 1940; he was raised to the peerage in 1954. Hore-Belisha bought this house in the summer of 1936 and lived here – after their marriage in 1944, with his wife Cynthia – until his death. He was only the third occupant of the early-19th-century terraced house.

Edwin Lutyens* remodelled the entrance hall for him and added panelling in the dining room: the politician 'Chips' Channon, writing in May 1938, described the décor as 'a horror ... Wedgwood plaques cover the walls ... old ones, small ones, good ones, bad ones'.

CARDINAL MANNING

(1808–92) Roman Catholic prelate

22 Carlisle Place

HENRY Edward Manning was ordained an Anglican deacon in 1832 and appointed Archdeacon of Chichester in 1840 – three years after the death of his young wife, Caroline. In 1851 he followed John Henry Newman* in converting to Roman Catholicism. As Archbishop of Westminster from 1865, Manning won regard for his social concerns, and was dubbed the 'Cardinal of the Poor'. The building which bears this unusual lead plaque (on the Francis Street elevation) is a vast brick Italianate palazzo designed by H. A. Darbishire in about 1867, and acquired by Manning in 1872 as part of the development plans for Westminster Cathedral (built 1895–1903). It had been built as the Guardsmen's Institute, but Manning found 'the austerity of its bareness' to his taste. He added a bedroom on the upper storey and worked in a large room on the first floor, surrounded by his books and papers on the floor and

tables. After his death in January 1892, his body lay in state here and the crowds who queued to see him brought traffic to a halt in Victoria Street. The building, then called Archbishop House, remained the residence of the archbishops of Westminster until 1901.

JOSEPH CONRAD

(1857–1924) novelist

17 Gillingham Street

CONRAD rented rooms in this modest 1820s terraced house from early 1891 until his marriage in March 1896 to Jessie Emmeline George. Born in Ukraine as Józef Teodor Konrad Korzeniowski, Conrad was exiled to a remote Russian province for his family's Polish nationalist beliefs before coming to Britain in 1878 to join the British mercantile marine. Conrad's first novel – *Almayer's Folly*, begun at his previous lodgings not far away at 6 Bessborough Gardens (demolished) – was completed in his 'snug bachelor quarters' in Gillingham Street in 1894 and published the following year. His famous *Heart of Darkness* (1902) was based on his nightmarish experiences of a trip up the Congo river in 1890, which left him with a life-threatening malarial fever, for which he was treated at the German Hospital in Dalston just before his arrival at Gillingham Street.

SIR MICHAEL COSTA

(1808–84) conductor and orchestral reformer

59 Eccleston Square

NAPLES-BORN Michael (originally Michele) Costa came to England in 1829, and rose to become the most prominent British conductor of his generation. An early practitioner of authoritative conducting by baton (hitherto, orchestras had been led from a piano or by the first violin), he is credited with having greatly improved the standards of orchestral playing and discipline in England. Costa moved to 7 Eccleston Square in 1846, 11 years later, crossing the square to number 59, where he remained for 26 years. By this time well established as a conductor at Covent Garden and elsewhere, his later years also saw him conducting at triennial festivals at the Crystal Palace devoted to the music of Handel* (whose work he was prone to 'improving' by adding extra brass, timpani and even cymbals). Costa was also a composer, but his works have not stood the test of time.

JOMO KENYATTA

(*c.*1894–1978) first President of the Republic of Kenya   95 Cambridge St. **21**

KENYATTA stayed at this address for a short spell in 1930 and then resided here again between 1933 and 1937. Born Kamau wa Ngengi in East Africa, the son of a Kikuyu farmer, he took the name Kenyatta – after the Kikuyu word for a type of beaded belt he wore – during his twenties. In 1928 he became General Secretary of the Kikuyu Central Association (KCA), a body that sought to represent the community's grievances. This was Kenyatta's role while he lived in Cambridge Street, when he also worked on the book *Facing Mount Kenya* (1938). Money was very tight; he often owed rent to his landlady, Mrs Hocken, and sold the stamps from mail he received from Kenya in order to buy penny buns. In 1934 Kenyatta supplemented his income by working as an extra on *Sanders of the River,* which starred Paul Robeson*. Kenyatta returned to Africa in 1946, where in 1953 he was unjustly convicted for involvement in the Mau Mau rebellion and imprisoned for almost nine years. When Kenya won self-government in 1963 he became Prime Minister, and President of the new independent Kenyan republic the following year. He died in office in 1978.

AUBREY BEARDSLEY

(1872–98) artist   114 Cambridge Street **22**

BEARDSLEY lived in this house with his sister Mabel and mother Ellen between June 1893 and June 1895. Its lease was partly bought with the proceeds of Beardsley's precocious successes; his commissions from this time included the celebrated illustrations for Thomas Malory's *Morte d'Arthur* (1893–4) and Oscar Wilde's *Salome* (1894). The two connecting rooms on the first floor in Cambridge Street were used by Beardsley as a drawing room-cum-studio, where he worked by candlelight, among exotic furnishings and behind heavy curtains. Visitors to the house included Max Beerbohm*, Walter Sickert* and Oscar Wilde*. In 1894 Beardsley was employed by John Lane as art editor of *The Yellow Book,* but he was dismissed in the aftermath of Wilde's downfall; the resultant loss of income prompted his departure from Cambridge Street. By the close of 1896, he was recuperating on the south coast from the consumptive attacks that claimed his life two years later, at the age of just 25.

SWAMI VIVEKANANDA

(1863–1902)
Hindu philosopher

63 St George's Drive
(formerly St George's Road) **23**

BORN in Calcutta as Narendranath Datta, the monk (or swami) Vivekananda became a leading spokesman for modern Hinduism and an early proponent and apologist for the faith in the West. He embarked upon his first Western Mission in 1893 and later, on his lecture tour of 1895–6, stayed at several London addresses, including – from early May until mid-July 1896– this house in St George's Drive, part of a stucco terrace built in about 1870. The house was let to him furnished by Mortimer Reginald Margesson and his wife Lady Isabel, who was interested in the Swami's teachings. Vivekananda held regular classes in the first-floor double drawing room, while the hub of everyday life was the street-facing ground-floor parlour, and he slept in a windowless room immediately to the rear; other parts of the house were given over to his entourage, which included Swami Saradananda who was – like Vivekananda – a disciple of the leading proponent of the Hindu revival, Sri Ramakrishna. Back in India, Vivekananda established the Ramakrishna Mission; still based in Calcutta (Kolkata), it seeks to propagate Ramakrishna's principles and translate them into social action.

DOUGLAS MACMILLAN

(1884–1969) founder of Macmillan Cancer Relief

15 Ranelagh Road **24**

MACMILLAN moved from Somerset to London at the turn of the 20th century, and worked as a civil servant. A Strict Baptist convert, he started a monthly periodical, *The Better Quest*. In the issue for August 1911, Macmillan wrote about the death of his father from cancer, and the following year founded the Society for the Prevention and Relief of Cancer. Macmillan shared the mid-19th-century stuccoed terraced house in Ranelagh Road – built by Thomas Cubitt* – with his wife Margaret; she had initially been his landlady there. They were married in 1907 and ran the society from their home virtually unassisted until their move to Sidcup in 1924. The offices of the charity – which changed its name to the National Society for Cancer Relief that year – stayed in Ranelagh Road until 1936. Since the plaque went up, the charity has changed its name to Macmillan Cancer Support, but a key priority remains the training of specialist cancer nurses.

MAJOR WALTER CLOPTON WINGFIELD

(1833–1912) father of lawn tennis 33 St George's Square

WHILE Wingfield did not invent the principles of lawn tennis, it was he who patented the game in 1874 by formalising rules and standardising and marketing a tennis set that included racquets, balls, posts and a net. Wingfield called these sets 'Sphairistike', derived from the Greek for ball-game, a name which never caught on; the sets were sold at five guineas a throw by Messrs French & Co. at nearby 46 Churton Street. Lawn tennis – the supplementary name given to it by Wingfield as an after-thought – quickly became a popular and sociable open-air pursuit for the middle classes. By 1877 the All England Croquet Club at Wimbledon had added lawn tennis to its title, and many croquet lawns were turned into tennis courts. The game developed rapidly from Major Wingfield's original rules, which envisaged an hour-glass-shaped court and a higher net than modern players would recognise. Later in life, Wingfield tried, less success-fully, to promote group bicycle riding in time to martial music, as described in his book *Bicycle Gym-khana and Musical Rides* (1897). He lived for the last ten years of his life in St George's Square, in part of a stuccoed terrace built in about 1850 by Thomas Cubitt*.

HARRY MALLIN

(1892–1969) policeman and Olympic boxing champion in 1920 and 1924

Peel House
105 Regency Street

DESCRIBED as 'the copper that no-one could lick', Mallin retired from amateur boxing undefeated in some 350 bouts, and was British amateur boxing champion at middleweight for five years running. He was the first – and until 1956 the only – boxer to win Olympic gold medals at consecutive games. At Antwerp in 1920, Mallin out-pointed the Canadian George Prud'homme to take the title. Four years later in Paris, his defence was mired in controversy after his quarter-final opponent – local lad Roger Brousse – was disqualified for biting. Mallin eventually beat fellow Briton Jack Eliot on points. Born in Hoxton and raised in Hackney Wick, Mallin's early homes are gone, as is the Eton Manor club where he learned to box. Hence he is com-memorated at Peel House, a former police section house where he occupied spartan bachelor quarters from 1923 until at least 1939.

MILLBANK PRISON

ON the Thames Embankment side of Millbank, nearly opposite the entrance to Tate Britain, is a large cylindrical granite block with a bronze plaque commemorating Millbank Prison. It is unique among London's official plaques in marking a fragment of a structure: the stone, which was moved from its original position, was formerly a bollard at the head of the river steps to Millbank Prison or Penitentiary. It was from Millbank Prison, between 1843 and 1867, that prisoners sentenced to transportation to penal colonies in Australia and elsewhere embarked on their journeys. Millbank Prison, completed in 1821 by the architect Robert Smirke*, was the first national prison, and when built was the largest of its type in Europe. It was founded on the humane and rational principles of classification, employment and reason, and its design drew on the ideas of the philosopher Jeremy Bentham and the prison reformer John Howard*. After 1843 it was used as a military gaol and a general-purpose prison for both male and female convicts. It closed in November 1890, and most of the buildings had been demolished by 1893.

ST JAMES'S

IN the 1660s Henry Jermyn, 1st Earl of St Albans, created a high-class residential area adjacent to St James's Palace. A grand, French-style piazza – St James's Square – was developed for 'Noble men and other Persons of quality' and is dominated to the north by Sir Christopher Wren's church of St James's, Piccadilly (1676–84).

St James's has one of the highest concentrations of listed buildings in England. Throughout the 18th and 19th centuries, its proximity to Court and government ensured that St James's was home to many public figures, a fact reflected in the remarkably high number of plaques to politicians.

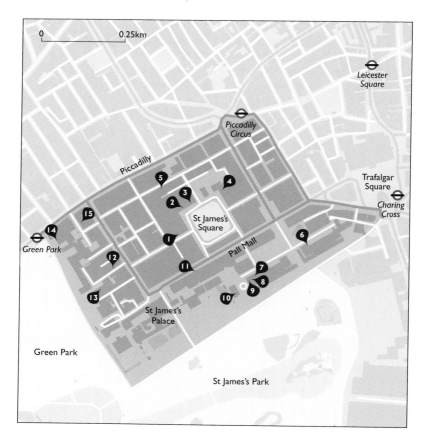

NAPOLEON III

(1808–73) Emperor of France

PRINCE Louis-Napoléon Bonaparte was born in Paris and, like other members of his family (he was Napoleon I's nephew), was exiled from France after the Battle of Waterloo (1815). On his return to France in 1840, he was imprisoned for life, but six years later he managed to escape and fled to England. In February 1847 he took a lease on this house, then newly built, and transformed its interior into a shrine to the Bonapartes, installing a portrait of Napoleon I by Delaroche, uniforms worn by his uncle and other relics that survived the fall of the dynasty. The prince became a leading figure in London society: he was given honorary membership of some of the most celebrated clubs in St James's, and enrolled as a special

Napoleon seems to have left King Street in some haste in 1848; his landlord found

'the Prince's bed unmade and his marble bath still full of water'.

constable during the Chartist riots of 1848. Greater disturbances across the Channel in this year of revolutions led to the overthrow of the French monarchy, and in September 1848 Louis-Napoléon departed for France, becoming President of the French Republic in December; within four years he was crowned Napoleon III. When he was exiled to England once more following the disastrous Franco-Prussian War, he moved with his wife and son to Chislehurst, Kent, where he died two years later.

This is London's earliest surviving blue plaque. Manufactured by Minton Hollins & Co. and put up by the Society of Arts in 1867, it is the only plaque to have been installed during the lifetime of the person commemorated, and is notable in bearing the imperial eagle, used as a symbol of empire by both Napoleon I and his nephew and heir, Napoleon III.

ADA, COUNTESS OF LOVELACE

(1815–52) pioneer of computing

BORN in Piccadilly, Augusta Ada was the only legitimate child of the poet, Lord Byron. She was brought up by her mother Annabella who supervised her education and encouraged her interest in mathematics and science. In 1833, Ada met Charles Babbage, the inventor of the first general computer, a calculating machine or 'analytical engine': 'I do not believe that my father was (or ever could have been) such a Poet as I shall be an Analyst; (& Metaphysician),' she told him. At once, she began to collaborate with him and mixed in his circle of friends and acquaintances. In 1843, while she was living here, she translated a paper by an Italian, L. F. Menabrea, on Babbage's analytical engine, and added her own extensive notes; this work, published in September of that year, has led to her being described as one of the world's first computer programmers. Her house was built in 1836 for her husband, William, Lord King (created Earl of Lovelace in 1838), and is an early example of the Italianate style of Thomas Cubitt*.

WILLIAM PITT, EARL OF CHATHAM (1708–78)
EDWARD GEOFFREY STANLEY, EARL OF DERBY (1799–1869)
WILLIAM EWART GLADSTONE* (1809–98)

Prime Ministers

THE house – now home to a global think-tank – was built as one of three in 1735–6 to the designs of the architect Henry Flitcroft. It was owned by the Heathcote family from 1736 until 1890 and is a fine surviving example of a Palladian townhouse; the principal feature of its interior, which would still be recognised by its three most famous residents, is its full-height staircase. Pitt the Elder – created an earl in 1766 – occupied the house from 1759 until late 1761, when at the apogee of his power and glory, nominally as Secretary of State for the Southern Department but in effect leading the government. During this time, Pitt presided over a series of military victories that effectively marked the beginning of the British Empire and ensured Britain's success in the Seven Years' War (1756–63). He left St James's Square at about the time of his resignation as Secretary of State in October 1761, and went on to serve as Prime Minister between 1766 and 1768.

Lord Derby, three times Prime Minister, was in opposition when he took up residence here in late 1837. While living here, in 1852, he had his first, fleeting, taste of the top job; in about 1854 he moved to 23 (now 33) St James's Square, his final home.

Gladstone lived here during the parliamentary session of 1890, while leader of the opposition; he went on to serve his fourth, and last, term as Prime Minister in 1892–4.

NANCY ASTOR

(1879–1964) the first woman to sit in Parliament   4 St James's Square

VIRGINIA-BORN Nancy Witcher Langhorne came to England in 1904 and two years later married fellow American Waldorf Astor, the politician and newspaper proprietor. In 1912 they acquired this house, built in 1726–8 for the 1st Duke of Kent and the oldest to survive on the square (it is now the Naval and Military Club). Its magnificent reception rooms provided a glittering setting for entertainment: the house's first-floor ballroom could hold as many as 1,000 people.

Nancy, according to her *Oxford DNB* entry, 'liked to pose at the top of the staircase, sparkling with jewels, to welcome her guests'. Originally promoted as a stop-gap candidate for her husband's seat when he succeeded to a peerage, she was Conservative member for Plymouth Sutton for over 25 years (1919–45); her most notable achievement was in banning the sale of alcohol to minors. The house, bomb-damaged and requisitioned during the Second World War, was sold in 1946.

SIR ISAAC NEWTON

(1642–1727) natural philosopher and mathematician   87 Jermyn Street

NEWTON moved to London – and to Jermyn Street – in 1696, on his appointment as Master of the Mint. He lived at number 88 until 1700, before moving next door to a larger house which stood on this site until the early years of the 20th century; here he remained until autumn 1709. During this time Newton held a series of important appointments: he was Lucasian Professor at Cambridge until 1702 and President of the Royal Society, 1703–27. His knighthood arrived in 1705. In 1704 he published *Opticks*, drawing upon earlier research, and in 1713 came the second edition of *Principia*, in which Newton set out his three laws of motion and his law of universal gravitation.

WILLIAM EWART GLADSTONE*

(1809–98) statesman 11 Carlton House Terrace

LIVERPOOL-BORN, Gladstone moved to London in 1833, on taking his seat in the Commons, and moved to this address in April 1856, having previously lived at two other houses in Carlton House Terrace (4 and 13). He began his second stint as Chancellor of the Exchequer in 1859, was Leader of the House of Commons in 1865–6 and became Prime Minister in 1868. Defeated over proposals for Irish Home Rule in 1874, Gladstone resigned as Liberal Party leader the following year and left Carlton House Terrace for Hawarden Castle in north Wales, though he was to return three times as Prime Minister, before finally retiring in 1894. Gladstone preferred living in this John Nash* terrace of 1827–32 to any of his official residences: 'I had grown to the house, having lived more time in it than in any other since I was born, and mainly by reason of all that was done in it,' he said. He occasionally used it for Cabinet business and entertained here extensively: his breakfast parties were celebrated, and in 1865 he gave a ball for the Prince of Wales. Gladstone installed a 'modest' picture gallery here, and displayed his collection of Wedgwood and other china.

GEORGE NATHANIEL CURZON, MARQUESS CURZON OF KEDLESTON

(1859–1925) statesman and Viceroy of India 1 Carlton House Terrace

AN MP from the age of 27, Curzon acquired this house in 1898, shortly before he left England to take up the post of Viceroy of India. He settled permanently here, soon after his return, in March 1906; sadly, his ailing wife Mary – to whom he was devoted – died here that July. Out of office until 1915, Curzon devoted himself to the arts and conservation: he restored Bodiam Castle, East Sussex, and Tattershall Castle, Lincolnshire, and drafted reports that shaped the future of the National Gallery and the Tate Gallery. He was also a leading opponent of women's suffrage. In May 1914 the coming-out ball of Irene, one of his three daughters, was held in the house; a supper room 21m (70ft) long was erected in the garden, and the Robert Adam* silver was brought from Kedleston, Derbyshire, Curzon's ancestral home. He returned to office in 1915 in the coalition Cabinet, and four years later became Foreign Secretary under Lloyd George*. Curzon remained at the Foreign Office until 1924, and died at his home here the following year.

LORD PALMERSTON*

(1784–1865) statesman   4 Carlton Gardens

HENRY John Temple, 3rd Viscount Palmerston, was one of the most colourful and commanding of Victorian politicians. He lived from late 1846 until January 1855 at a house on this site. An MP from 1807, Palmerston sat in 16 parliaments, at first as a Tory, later as a Liberal. He became Foreign Secretary – for the third time – in the year he moved here. Palmerston's maverick approach to the niceties of diplomacy often brought him into conflict with Queen Victoria and Prince Albert, and the Court seized the pretext of his unofficial recognition of Napoleon III* to secure his dismissal from office in 1851, though he was subsequently appointed Home Secretary (1852–5). In 1855 he began the first of two spells as Prime Minister, and left for 94 Piccadilly. When the plaque was erected in 1907, the house was the residence of the former Prime Minister, Arthur Balfour, who had acquired the property in 1870. The site is now occupied by an office block of 1933–4 by Sir Reginald Blomfield & Son.

GENERAL CHARLES DE GAULLE

(1890–1970) President of the French National Committee   4 Carlton Gdns

DE Gaulle set up the HQ of the Free French Forces here in late July 1940; his private office was next door, at number 3. On 18 June 1940, the day after his arrival in London, de Gaulle had used the BBC radio service – with the support of Winston Churchill* – to deliver his famous address, encouraging his countrymen to continue to fight the occupation; the broadcast was concluded with the words, 'Whatever happens the flame of French resistance must not and shall not be extinguished.' Sentenced to death *in absentia*, de Gaulle set about organising the Free French Forces, which by the end of 1944 numbered one million individuals. Following liberation, he led the French Provisional Government, and in 1958 became the first President of the French Fifth Republic, a post he held until 1969.

FIELD MARSHAL EARL KITCHENER OF KHARTOUM, KG

(1850–1916) senior army officer — 2 Carlton Gardens **10**

HORATIO Herbert Kitchener was born in Ireland to English parents, and spent his military career abroad, coming to public attention as Commander-in-Chief (Sirdar) of the Egyptian Army (1892–9) in which capacity he saw victory at the Battle of Omdurman (1898), avenging the death of General Gordon at Khartoum and earning himself a barony – the earldom followed in 1914. He was lent this splendid semi-detached house, with views over The Mall and St James's Park and complete with domestic staff, by his friend Harriet, Lady Wantage, and he lived here, with his personal secretaries Captain Oswald Fitzgerald and George Arthur, towards the end of his long and distinguished career, from August 1914 until February 1915. On the outbreak of war in 1914, he had been appointed Secretary of State for War, and while living here advised the Cabinet on military strategy and prepared plans for the expansion of the British Army. This laid the foundations for the victory he did not live to see: Kitchener drowned when the ship carrying him on a special mission to Russia struck a German mine in June 1916.

THOMAS GAINSBOROUGH

(1727–88) artist — Schomberg House, 80–82 Pall Mall **11**

REBUILT for the 3rd Duke of Schomberg in 1698, the building was subdivided into three properties in 1769; Gainsborough occupied the westernmost portion. Born in Suffolk, he received the patronage of George III in 1774 and immediately became the most fashionable portrait painter of the age. At his home here, he built a large painting room over the garden, above which was a salon used as another studio and also for the display of paintings; here, the artist produced works such as the portraits of the Duke and Duchess of Cumberland (1777) and Mrs R. B. Sheridan (1785), and his series of 'fancy pictures', the name given to his genre pieces such as *The Cottage Girl* (1785). After Gainsborough's disagreement and then break with the Royal Academy – headed by his great rival, Joshua Reynolds* – in 1783, the display of pictures at Schomberg House assumed greater importance, and patrons and critics were regularly admitted to his galleries. He held his first private exhibition here in 1784.

FREDERIC CHOPIN

(1810–49) composer

4 St James's Place

BORN near Warsaw to a French father and Polish mother, Chopin was a child prodigy. In 1848, in flight from revolutionary Paris, he travelled to England with his Scottish pupil, Jane Stirling. He first took lodgings in Mayfair and then in October, following a trip to Scotland, and already seriously ill, he settled in this house, which dates from the development of 1685–6, was originally part of a brown-brick terrace but was stuccoed in the early 19th century and refaced in the 1970s. It was from here, as the plaque records, that Chopin travelled to the Guildhall to give what turned out to be his final performance.

WILLIAM HUSKISSON

(1770–1830) statesman

28 St James's Place

HUSKISSON moved to this late-17th-century house, which was rebuilt by Henry Holland in 1794, in 1804, the year he became MP for Liskeard and was appointed a Secretary to the Treasury; he went on to be variously President of the Board of Trade, Colonial Secretary and Leader of the House of Commons, and was tipped as a potential Prime Minister in succession to his ally, George Canning*. Sadly, Huskisson's political successes as a promoter of free trade tend to be overshadowed by the circumstances of his death. Always accident-prone, he was Britain's first railway casualty, killed by a train at the ceremonial opening of the Liverpool and Manchester Railway on 15 September 1830.

HENRY PELHAM

(1694–1754) Prime Minister

Wimborne House, 22 Arlington Street **14**

THIS house, of considerable significance as a survival of William Kent's work in London, was begun in 1740, but was only finished shortly before Pelham's death here in March 1754; its interiors are among the most magnificent in St James's, and were used as a setting for Pelham's many levees (meaning receptions). The first part of the house was sufficiently complete for Pelham and his wife, Lady Katherine, to take up residence in May 1743; shortly afterwards, Pelham's near neighbour, Horace Walpole*, commented that Arlington Street had become 'absolutely the ministerial street'. Shortly after moving in, Pelham – a Whig, and a protegé of Robert Walpole* – became First Lord of the Treasury, Chancellor of the Exchequer and Leader of the House of Commons; he died in office, and was succeeded as Prime Minister by his elder brother, Thomas, Duke of Newcastle. The house, a testament to Pelham's architectural passion, was altered in the 20th century. The plaque is to the rear, facing Green Park.

SIR ROBERT WALPOLE, EARL OF ORFORD
(1676–1745) Prime Minister
HORACE WALPOLE
(1717–97) connoisseur and man of letters   5 Arlington Street

REGARDED as the first British statesman to hold the office with which the title of Prime Minister is now associated, Walpole left 10 Downing Street, which had been granted to him by George II after his fall from power in 1742, and moved back to Arlington Street, keeping his London house here until his death. Earlier in his career, between 1715 and 1732, Sir Robert had lived at 17 Arlington Street (demolished in the 1930s to make way for Arlington House); it was there that his son Horace was born, the youngest of Walpole's children with his wife Catherine.

Renowned as an author, aesthete and wit, Horace is remembered especially for the creation of the 'little Gothic castle' of Strawberry Hill, Twickenham (1749–66), a striking contrast to the magnificence of Houghton Hall, Norfolk, that had been built by his father in 1721–35. Horace filled Arlington Street with part of his collection. Paintings and antiquities jostled for space with his 'curious cabinets of limnings, enamels, and his collection of English heads &c', together with 'a number of antique coins, medals, medallions, etc'. Such wonders made the house a meeting place for London's dilettanti, but also attracted unwelcome visitors: in 1771 it was rifled by burglars. While living here, Walpole published his Gothic romance *The Castle of Otranto* (1764). A lifelong bachelor, he lived in Arlington Street until 1779, when he moved to 11 Berkeley Square, Mayfair (demolished).

Although both Walpoles are commemorated at number 5 it is now known that only Horace lived here, while his father lived in a larger house at number 4, a late-17th-century building partly refronted in 1786–7. After his father's death in 1745, Horace moved next door to number 4, the more spacious of the two houses. The house bearing the plaque was later rebuilt, in 1795–7.

COVENT GARDEN AND THE STRAND

THE Strand – on the north bank of the River Thames – forms a significant part of the route between the cities of London and Westminster, and was a prestigious place of residence for churchmen and aristocrats. Covent Garden to the north was developed in 1629–37, to designs by Inigo Jones, based around an Italianate piazza, with a church on its west side. Noted for its coffee houses, taverns, lodging houses, theatres and brothels, the area was especially popular with artists, writers and dramatists. Above all, Covent Garden is associated with its fruit and vegetable market, once the largest in England; the market house, constructed in 1828–30, served its original function until the market moved to Battersea, in 1974.

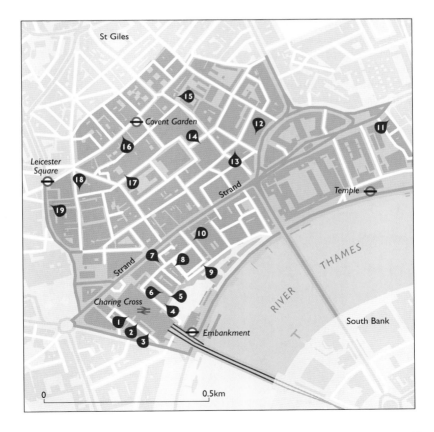

BENJAMIN FRANKLIN

(1706–90) American statesman,
writer and scientist

BORN in Boston, Massachusetts, Franklin trained
as a printer and by the 1730s had
become a highly successful writer
and newspaperman. His study of
electricity and his many inventions – including bifocal glasses
and the lightning rod – earned him
international acclaim. In the years
1757–62 and 1764–5, he lived in
London, an agent of the Pennsylvania Assembly, encouraging pro-
American sympathies, continuing
his scientific experiments and, still
active as a writer, mixing in circles
that included James Boswell* and
Joseph Priestley*. On his return to
Philadelphia, Franklin assisted in
the preparation of the Declaration
of Independence of 1776 and later

*Franklin was amazed by the 'dearness of
living' in the capital. In a letter, 19 February
1758, he wrote:*

'The whole Town is one great
smoaky House, and every
Street a Chimney, the Air
full of floating Sea
Coal Soot'.

became President of Pennsylvania
(1785–8). Franklin lived at a lodging
house here run by Margaret
Stevenson; he occupied four
comfortable rooms shared with his
son and assistant, William ('Billy')
– later Governor of New Jersey –
and their two slaves, Peter and
King. Now Benjamin Franklin
House, 36 Craven Street is open
to the public.

The Society
of Arts, not
appreciating that
the street had
been renumbered
since Franklin's
stay, put a plaque
to Franklin on a
house opposite.
This may now be
seen downstairs
at Benjamin
Franklin House.

HEINRICH HEINE

(1799–1856) German poet and essayist

THE great German poet Heine was born in Düsseldorf into a Jewish family, and studied law before converting to Protestantism and turning to a career in literature. His poetry inspired composers such as Schumann, Mendelssohn* and Wagner, though his works – like others of the Young Germany movement – were banned in Germany in the mid-1830s. Heine's visit to London in 1827 was not a success. He complained of the cost of living and of there being

'It is so fearfully damp and uncomfortable here and no one understands me, and no one understands German.'

Heine, writing in April 1827

'nothing but fog, coal-smoke, poets and Canning' (meaning the politician George Canning*). In 1831 Heine settled in Paris, where he became a major literary figure; he died there at the age of 58.

HERMAN MELVILLE

(1819–91) author of *Moby Dick*

MELVILLE, who was born in New York, spent much of his early life at sea; it was his experiences aboard a whaling ship in the Pacific that inspired many of his works. He came to London in autumn 1849 to secure a publishing deal for his new novel *White-Jacket, or, the World in a Man-of-War* (1850) and to gather material for an account of the American revolutionary Israel Potter (published 1855). Living in cheap lodgings in Craven Street, Melville was an indefatigable partygoer and sightseer; in his diary, he recorded seeing the Lord Mayor's Show, a public hanging, the British Museum, the National Gallery and London Zoo. On returning home to Massachusetts, Melville wrote his best-known work, *Moby Dick, or, The Whale* (1851), dedicated to his friend Nathaniel Hawthorne*; it became one of the first American novels to attain classic status, though on first publication it flopped. The failure of this work – and of its satirical successor, *Pierre* (1852) – brought about a mental breakdown from which Melville never entirely recovered. He became a New York customs inspector, and abandoned fiction for poetry, save for a final – unfinished – novel, *Billy Budd* (published posthumously in 1924).

RUDYARD KIPLING

(1865–1936) poet
and story writer

Embankment Chambers,
43 (formerly 19) Villiers Street

KIPLING was born in Bombay and schooled in England. He returned to India in 1882, becoming a successful journalist and writer. It was in 1889–91 that Kipling lived at Embankment Chambers – in three second-floor rooms above the establishment of Harris the Sausage King and opposite Gatti's music hall – 'small, not over-clean or well kept ... trains rumbled through my dreams'. While here, Kipling wrote

The Light that Failed (1890), a novel with passages recording his early impressions of London. The works for which he is most widely remembered – *The Jungle Book* (1894) and *The Second Jungle Book* (1895) – he wrote while living in Vermont, where the family of his wife Caroline were based. In 1897 Kipling settled in Sussex, where he produced *Stalky & Co.* (1899), *Kim* (1901) and the *Just So Stories* (1902).

SAMUEL PEPYS* (1633–1703) diarist
ROBERT HARLEY, EARL OF OXFORD
(1661–1724) statesman
WILLIAM ETTY (1787–1849) painter
CLARKSON STANFIELD
(1793–1867) painter

14 Buckingham Street

THE original late-17th-century building was so radically altered in the 1790s as to be unrecognisable today. Pepys lived here from around March 1688 while Secretary to the Admiralty until August 1701, when he moved to the Clapham home of his friend Will Hewer. He was immediately succeeded by Robert Harley, Speaker of the House of Commons and later Chancellor of the Exchequer (1710) and Lord Treasurer (1711). Harley remained here until 1714, building up the nu-

cleus of his manuscript collection, now part of the British Library. Etty and Stanfield both lived here after it had been rebuilt as residential chambers. Etty, wanting to be close to the river, moved to rooms on the first floor of the house in mid-1824, later moving to the coveted top floor in 1826, where he stayed for 22 years. In his rooms, 'of which I love in my heart every stick, hole, and corner', he painted works including *The Combat* (1825) and *The Sirens and Ulysses* (1837). Stanfield and his family moved into the first-floor rooms vacated by Etty in 1826 and stayed for six years. During this time, Stanfield was a scene painter at the Theatre Royal, Drury Lane, but also executed paintings such as *The Opening of New London Bridge* (1832), commissioned by William IV.

SAMUEL PEPYS*

(1633–1703) diarist

12 Buckingham Street

BORN near Fleet Street, Pepys worked at the Exchequer and the Navy Board before being promoted, in 1673, to Secretary to the Admiralty. In 1679, amidst accusations of 'Piracy, Popery and Treachery', he resigned and in May was imprisoned in the Tower of London. On his release that July, the widowed Pepys found refuge with his friend and former employer, Will Hewer. While living at number 12, Pepys was in his heyday: here he continued to amass his library (later bequeathed to Magdalene College, Cambridge) and in 1684 began his second stint as Secretary to the Admiralty. It seems that this building was used as an office in connection with this post, and in 1688 – possibly due to the consequent reduction in living space – Pepys moved next door to 14 Buckingham Street, a larger house with a fine prospect of the river. As the latter has since been rebuilt, this house, completed in 1677 – which features an original oak staircase – is the only one of Pepys's London residences to survive.

THOMAS ROWLANDSON

(1757–1827)
artist and caricaturist

16 John Adam Street
(formerly John Street)

FOR the last 27 years of his life, Rowlandson lived in attic rooms in an 18th-century corner house on this site then numbered 1 James Street (now Durham House Street) and demolished in 1904. He kept a printing press here and worked at this time chiefly as an illustrator of books, most notably those produced by Rudolph Acker-mann's firm, the Repository of Arts. They included *The Microcosm of London* (1808–10), a collaboration between Rowlandson and the artist A. C. Pugin. In his day, Rowlandson's animated and satirical drawings in *The Three Tours of Doctor Syntax* (published in three volumes in 1812, 1820 and 1821, with verses by William Combe) were hugely popular.

ROBERT ADAM (1728–92) architect
THOMAS HOOD* (1799–1845) poet
JOHN GALSWORTHY* (1867–1933) writer
SIR JAMES BARRIE* (1860–1937)
novelist and dramatist
1–3 Robert Street **8**

SINCE the early 20th century numbers 1–3 Robert Street have been conjoined, and known as Adelphi Terrace House. Long before this, Robert Adam moved to 3 Robert Street in 1778 and remained until his move to Mayfair, in 1785. Numbers 1–2 are early examples of purpose-built, high-status flats. Thomas Hood lived here with his wife Jane between 1828 and 1830, when they moved to Enfield. Galsworthy lived here in 1917–18, after all three houses were conjoined as Adelphi Terrace House, as did his friend and fellow dramatist J. M. Barrie, whose flat was just across from Bernard Shaw* and his wife, from November 1909 until his death. He wrote *Peter and Wendy* (1911) here, along with several plays.

THE ADELPHI
various former residents
Adelphi Terrace **9**

THIS unusual 'plaque' commemorates several former residents of this vanished development (*see box opposite*). The Beauclerks lived at 3 Adelphi Terrace in 1772–6 and Garrick* at number 5 from 1772 until his death here. D'Oyly Carte* lived at number 4 from the time of his marriage in 1888 to Helen Lenoir until his death in 1901; during this period, he was famously in partnership with Gilbert* and Sullivan. Their works were performed at the nearby Savoy Theatre, Strand, which D'Oyly Carte opened in 1881; he also built the Savoy Hotel, completed in 1889. Thomas Hardy* worked as a draughtsman in the office of the architect Arthur William Blomfield, based on the first floor of number 8, in 1864–8, and G. B. Shaw* lived at number 10 from 1898 until 1927 with his wife Charlotte, who had leased the two upper floors of the property in 1896 from the London School of Economics and Political Science, co-founded the previous year by a group including Bernard Shaw. The LSE was based at number 10 until 1900, when it moved to its present site. The Savage Club, a gentlemen's club founded in 1857, met at numbers 6 and 7 from 1890.

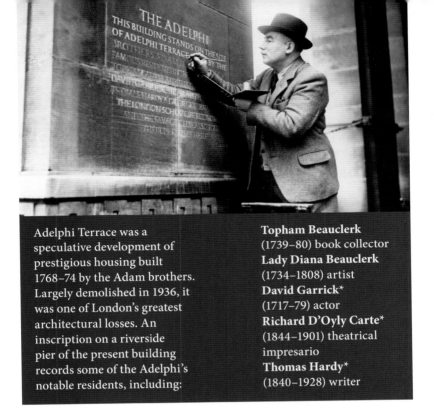

Adelphi Terrace was a speculative development of prestigious housing built 1768–74 by the Adam brothers. Largely demolished in 1936, it was one of London's greatest architectural losses. An inscription on a riverside pier of the present building records some of the Adelphi's notable residents, including:

Topham Beauclerk
(1739–80) book collector
Lady Diana Beauclerk
(1734–1808) artist
David Garrick*
(1717–79) actor
Richard D'Oyly Carte*
(1844–1901) theatrical impresario
Thomas Hardy*
(1840–1928) writer

SIR RICHARD ARKWRIGHT

(1732–92) industrialist and inventor

8 Adam Street

ARKWRIGHT was born in Preston, Lancashire, the son of a tailor, and began his career as a barber and wigmaker, settling in Bolton in 1750. In 1767 he co-invented a roller spinning machine that revolutionised the manufacture of cotton. Putting his pioneering device into operation, he set up mills in Nottingham and Cromford, Derbyshire, becoming known as the 'father of the factory system'. From about 1780, Arkwright became involved in a series of trials regarding his various patents, which drew him to London, where he spent much of the last five years of his life. He found Adam Street ideally situated, being close to the Inns of Court and the law courts at Westminster Hall. Arkwright died at his home in Cromford. His splendidly furnished London residence was sold by his son in 1794.

ESSEX STREET

ESSEX Street was laid out by Nicholas Barbon (*c.*1637–*c.*1698) in 1675 on the grounds of Essex House, formerly the home of Elizabeth I's favourites Robert Dudley, Earl of Leicester, and Robert Devereux, 2nd Earl of Essex. Of those named on the plaque, Bridgeman was the earliest resident; he lived in the part of Essex House that survived Barbon's development from 1651 until his death – its site is now represented by Essex Hall, on which the plaque is sited. Fielding lived at 24 Essex Street for a brief period from 1739 to 1740, when he was called to the Bar. Bonnie Prince Charlie was an even more short-term resident: during a six-day visit to London in September 1750, he stayed with Lady Anne Primrose in a house here. Brass Crosby moved to 17 Essex Street in about 1773, three years after he was elected Lord Mayor; he remained until about 1780. Theophilus Lindsey founded a meeting house in the surviving portion of Essex House, which was altered for use as a chapel; the first service was held in April 1774, when over 200 people were present, including Joseph Priestley* and Ben-

> **Residents include:**
> **Sir Orlando Bridgeman**
> (1609–74) Lord Keeper
> **Henry Fielding***
> (1707–54) novelist
> **Brass Crosby** (1725–93)
> Lord Mayor of London
> **James Savage**
> (1779–1852) architect
> **Prince Charles Edward Stuart**
> (1720–88) the Young Pretender
> **Revd Theophilus Lindsey**
> (1723–1808) Unitarian minister
> **Dr Samuel Johnson***
> (1709–84) writer

jamin Franklin*. Lindsey remained in an adjacent house until his death. The chapel itself was remodelled in 1886 as Essex Hall, a venue used by groups including the Fabian Society*; it was completely rebuilt after being destroyed by a flying bomb in 1944. On the opposite side of the road, at what was – by the late 19th century – 40–41 Essex Street, Dr Johnson* established a club; James Savage, known for buildings such as St Luke's, Chelsea (1820–24), lived at 31 Essex Street from *c.*1827 until *c.*1852.

IVOR NOVELLO

(1893–1951) composer and actor-manager

DAVID Ivor Davies, as he was born in Cardiff, inherited his love of music from his mother Clara Novello Davies, a singing teacher.

In 1927 he changed his name to Ivor Novello, having begun to make his mark with works such as the 1914 song 'Keep the Home Fires Burning (Till the Boys Come Home)'. He is best known for his musical shows, most of which starred Novello himself and were staged at the Theatre Royal, Drury Lane; they included *Careless Rapture* (1936) and *King's Rhapsody* (1949). Novello and his mother ('Mam') settled in this top-floor flat in 1913, part of a block built in 1905. It remained his London base until his death here, in the presence of his lifelong companion, the actor Bobbie Andrews. Novello loved to entertain and 'The Flat' was the setting for many sparkling parties.

THOMAS DE QUINCEY

(1785–1859) writer   36 Tavistock Street (formerly 4 York Street) **13**

DE Quincey was born in Manchester, and according to his *Confessions*, first tasted opium, then readily and legally available, in London in 1804. In 1807 he met Coleridge*, Wordsworth and Robert Southey, and dedicated himself to literature. He spent a significant – if miserable – part of his career in London, where he arrived in mid-1821, leaving his wife Margaret and their family at home in Grasmere, Westmorland, and moved into lodgings in what was then an insalubrious thoroughfare. Here – reputedly in a small room at the rear of the property – he completed his *Confessions*, published in the *London Magazine* that autumn, a work which established his reputation. Beset by debt, De Quincey frequently went into hiding from his creditors, though it seems that his lodgings here remained his base for much of the period 1821–5. Thereafter he resided largely in Edinburgh.

DR SAMUEL JOHNSON* (1709–84) author
JAMES BOSWELL* (1740–95) biographer   8 Russell Street ⓮

ON the evening of Monday 16 May 1763, after Boswell had finished drinking tea in the back parlour of a bookshop with Thomas Davies, a former actor turned bookseller, and his wife, Johnson unexpectedly came into the shop. Mr Davies, 'having perceived him through the glass-door in the room in which we were sitting, advancing towards us', announced 'somewhat in the manner of an actor in the part of Horatio, when he addresses Hamlet on the appearance of his father's ghost, "Look, my Lord, it comes."' Despite an initial snub from Johnson, who was prejudiced against Scots,

> In his *Life of Johnson* (1791) Boswell noted that he had never since passed by 8 Russell Street 'without feeling reverence and regret'.

Boswell – then just 22 – made an immediate impression; the pair talked for three hours, and Davies noted, when seeing Boswell out, 'I can see he likes you very well'. Shortly afterwards, Boswell called on Johnson at his lodgings at 1 Inner Temple Lane (demolished), on the south of Fleet Street, beginning the friendship that would last until Johnson's death.

BOW STREET
19–20 Bow Street ⓯

BUILT from 1637, Bow Street was home to a number of illustrious individuals. Henry Fielding* moved to a house here in December 1748 – just as his literary masterpiece, *Tom Jones*, was being printed. The following year he became magistrate for Middlesex at the Bow Street office, based at number 4 (until a purpose-built police station and courthouse on the street's east side replaced it in 1880). Here he established the Bow Street Runners, a precursor of the modern police force. In 1751 Henry's blind half-brother, John Fielding, became a magistrate

> Residents include:
> **Henry Fielding***
> (1707–54) novelist
> **Sir John Fielding**
> (1721–80) magistrate
> **Grinling Gibbons**
> (1648–1721) woodcarver
> **Charles Macklin**
> (*c.*1699–1797) actor
> **John Radcliffe**
> (1650–1714) physician
> **Charles Sackville, Earl of Dorset** (1643–1706) poet
> **William Wycherley**
> (1641–1716) dramatist

for Westminster, and succeeded him as court justice in 1754. Grinling Gibbons was an earlier resident, living at a house on the east side of the street from about 1678 until his death. This period saw his greatest work accomplished, including the carving at St Paul's Cathedral. Among Gibbons's neighbours were Charles Sackville, who lived here in 1684–5,

and John Radcliffe, who lived here from 1684 until 1702. Wycherley – author of such successful comedies as *The Country Wife* (1675) – lived in Bow Street from *c.*1678 until his death. Macklin, a regular performer at the Drury Lane Theatre, lived on the west side of the street in about 1743–8. All of these buildings have been demolished.

DAME MARGOT FONTEYN

(1919–91) prima ballerina assoluta 118 Long Acre **16**

AMONG the stars of ballet, Fonteyn towers high: the title of 'Prima Ballerina Assoluta' at the Royal Ballet was awarded in 1979. Born Peggy Hookham in Reigate, Surrey, she grew up in Ealing: the flat in Long Acre was her first independent home. The four years that she spent here from the late 1940s encompassed some career-defining lead roles at the Sadler's Wells (later

Royal) Ballet, in Frederick Ashton* productions such as *Daphnis and Chloë* (1951) and *Sylvia* (1952). The flat was conveniently close to Covent Garden, but she often took a cab home in order to give over-ardent fans the slip. Fonteyn passed the flat on to her sister-in-law, who apparently lent it back to her for romantic trysts. The plaque was unveiled by Darcey Bussell (*pictured*).

THOMAS ARNE

(1710–78) composer

THE son of an upholsterer, Thomas was born here; in 1712 the house – newly built – was destroyed by fire, and the present building was put up on its site the following year. It remained the Arne family home until 1733. Arne loved music but, as his father disapproved, he is said to have practised secretly at home, muffling the strings of his spinet with cloths. It was only when his musical studies had reached an advanced stage that his father discovered Thomas's subterfuge and sanctioned his chosen career. He composed music for some 90 theatrical works, many for

> Arne's unusual 'cropped' plaque was so designed to fit the tight space between the windows.

the Drury Lane and Covent Garden theatres. He worked frequently with his sister Susannah – a singer and actress who married the successful playwright Theophilus Cibber in 1734 – and his brother Richard, also a singer and actor; Arne married an actress, Cecilia Young, in 1737. He is best known for 'Rule, Britannia', a poem written by James Thomson* which Arne set to music for his opera *Alfred* (1740).

THOMAS CHIPPENDALE (1718–79)
THOMAS CHIPPENDALE (1749–1822/3)

cabinetmakers

THE elder Thomas Chippendale was born in Yorkshire, the son of a joiner, and moved to London in the late 1740s. In late 1753 he set up shop at the substantial premises in St Martin's Lane that his firm would occupy for 60 years. He moved into the buildings with his new business partner, James Rannie, in 1754, the same year that he published his furniture pattern book *The Gentleman and Cabinet-Maker's Director* (1754), which made

his name a byword for beautiful furniture. Chippendale sold copies from his house, number 60, to the rear of which was a yard enclosed by workshops and warehouses accommodating a team of cabinetmakers, upholsterers, gilders and polishers. The firm's shop stood adjacent at 61 – the site marked by the rectangular bronze plaque, which is so discreetly sited on a doorway entrance pillar that it is easy to miss. The younger Thomas Chippendale, who was active in the firm at the time of his father's retirement in 1776, lived from 1793 to 1813 at number 62, the only original building to survive. The Chippendale firm carried out lavish furnishing programmes at country houses such as Nostell Priory, Newby Hall and Harewood House, all in Yorkshire. Thomas junior took over some of these projects along with the firm's management in 1779, working with the bookkeeper Thomas Haig until the mid-1790s. A distinguished designer in his own right, Chippendale junior stayed at St Martin's Lane until he and the business moved to Haymarket in 1813.

AL BOWLLY

(1898–1941) singer   Charing Cross Mansions, 26 Charing Cross Road **19**

BORN in Mozambique to a Greek father and Lebanese mother, Bowlly became the pre-eminent British jazz singer of the early Thirties; he rented Flat 5 here in 1933 at the height of his fame. One of his best-known songs was 'The Very Thought of You', recorded with Ray Noble's New May-fair Orchestra. Bowlly also sang with the ensembles directed successively by Roy Fox and Lew Stone at the Monseigneur Restaurant in Piccadilly, then London's hippest night spot. He was one of the first vocalists to use the microphone effectively, and was an early exponent of 'crooning', though he disliked the term. Helped by his good looks and personal magnetism, Bowlly was the first singer to get the kind of star treatment that, hitherto, had been accorded to band leaders. He died after a wartime bomb exploded in the street outside his later place of residence in Duke Street, St James's, on 17 April 1941.

SOHO AND LEICESTER SQUARE

THIS area – at the heart of the West End – has, perhaps more than any other in London, experienced a radical transition in character from residential to commercial. Developed in the late 17th and early 18th centuries, Soho and Leicester Square were desirable places to live for the titled and successful. By the mid-1700s, however, residents had begun to move to grander houses elsewhere – in recently developed Mayfair, for example. In Soho, a new wave of residents arrived – artists, craftsmen, tradesmen and immigrants from the Continent, especially French Huguenots, who settled here from the 1680s. By the middle of the 19th century, the area had become one of the most overcrowded and densely populated in the capital, with its once-neat terraces turned into slum tenements. The 19th and 20th centuries brought further change. Leicester Square – invaded by theatres, shops, restaurants and hotels – gained its reputation as London's centre of entertainment. Soho became synonymous with the sex industry, but is now increasingly gentrified.

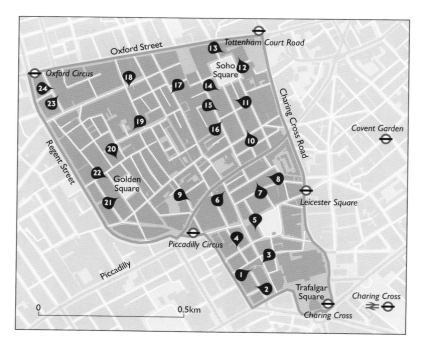

RICHARD DADD

(1817–86) painter   15 Suffolk Street **1**

THE Dadd family home was in part of a terrace designed by Lewis Wyatt in about 1823, and which was rebuilt in a neo-Regency style in the mid-20th century. Dadd's father, Robert, ran his gilding and ormolu manufacturing business from here. Dadd entered the Royal Academy Schools in 1837, and exhibited paintings nearby at 6½ Suffolk Street, the galleries of the Society of British Artists. He established his reputation as a fairy painter with two scenes from *A Midsummer Night's Dream*: *Titania Sleeping* and *Puck* (both 1841). Soon after, he began to suffer from mental delusions, and in 1843 achieved notoriety for murdering his father. Dadd fled to France, but was arrested, brought back and certified insane. Although institutionalised for the rest of his life, his artistic output was undiminished.

RICHARD COBDEN

(1804–65) statesman   23 Suffolk Street **2**

COBDEN was born in Sussex, but with his friend John Bright led the Manchester-based campaign to repeal the Corn Laws. In 1841 he entered Parliament as a Liberal MP; he played a major part in the repeal of the Corn Laws in 1846, and campaigned tirelessly for free trade and liberal reforms. In November 1864, after addressing a Rochdale constituency meeting, Cobden was taken ill, and he was confined to his home in Dunford, Sussex. The following March, he took lodgings at number 23 while attending the House of Commons. On arrival in London, however, he had an asthmatic attack and he died here on 2 April. The following year, the Cobden Club was founded in his honour, its motto being 'Peace, free trade and goodwill among nations'.

SIR MORTIMER WHEELER

(1890–1976) archaeologist   27 Whitcomb Street **3**

WHEELER was instrumental in establishing archaeology as a popular subject, and in the 1950s became well known as a television and radio personality. With his wife Tessa, who died in 1936, he excavated sites including Caerleon, Verulamium (St Albans) and Maiden Castle, Dorset; inspired by the work of Pitt-Rivers*, he set new standards for excavation and recording. He established, with Tessa, the Institute of Archaeology, and subsequently became Director-General of the Archaeological Survey of India and Secretary of the British Academy. Wheeler's devoted secretary, Molly Myers, chose 27 Whitcomb Street (said to be a former brothel) for him in 1958 while he was excavating in Pakistan. He lived here until shortly before his death. Wheeler's flat – on the upper floors – was furnished with his oriental rugs and Persian plates, and yellow curtains from Liberty.

TOM CRIBB

(1781–1848) bare-knuckle boxing champion 36 (formerly 26) Panton St.

CRIBB entered his first public bout in Wood Green in 1805. His most famous fight was with the black American champion Tom Molineaux in 1811 at Thistleton Gap, Leicestershire; it was watched by around 20,000 people, and the victorious Cribb was received back in London as a public hero. From about 1819 to 1839 he ran the Union Arms pub in Panton Street – which became known as 'Cribb's Parlour', and has since been officially renamed in his honour. It became a

'The action's still there but the steam's all gone.'

Tom Cribb's reported last words, after throwing a final punch

popular meeting place for both the aristocracy and for prize-fighters. Cribb retired from boxing in 1821 but was allowed to keep his champion's belt for the rest of his life. His last years were marred by financial and domestic problems, and gambling debts forced him to give up the pub to his creditors.

SIR JOSHUA REYNOLDS

(1723–92) painter 47 Leicester Square

BORN in Devon, Reynolds moved to London in 1740. In summer 1760 he moved to 47, a grand late-17th-century house on the square's west side (the site of his house is now occupied by a 1930s office block). He immediately set about modernising it, building an extension to accommodate a series of studios and a picture gallery; his painting room was octagonal in shape and lit by a single window, positioned high up in the wall. It was during his time here that

'Everybody in the house painted ... the coachman and the man servant Ralph and his daughter, all painted, copied and talked about pictures.'

Theophila Gwatkin, Reynolds's niece

Reynolds enjoyed his greatest success, and established himself as the leading portrait painter of the day. Appointed first President of the Royal Academy in 1768 – a position he held until his death – Reynolds was knighted in 1769 and in 1784 became Principal Painter in Ordinary to George III. His home was the centre of Reynolds's social life: regular visitors included Dr Johnson*, with whom he founded the Literary Club (also known simply as 'The Club') here in February 1764. He was looked after by a

Reynolds's former home, demolished in 1937.

housekeeper, a role fulfilled first by his sister Fanny and, from the late 1770s, by his niece, Mary Palmer, both of whom were talented artists.

WILLY CLARKSON
(1861–1934) theatrical wigmaker

41–43 Wardour Street **6**

THESE premises were designed for Clarkson's expanding wig business by H. M. Wakley and completed in 1905. Clarkson's origins are obscure, but he seems to have been born in London, the son of a perruquier – possibly of Jewish ancestry – and inherited his father's business at the age of 12. At the height of his success, Clarkson was hiring out 10,000 wigs each

Christmas. It was to these premises that the most famous actors of the day came for their costumes, while others hired clothes for the military tournaments and fancy-dress balls popular at the time. A small, thick-set man, with curly hair and a beard, Clarkson spoke in an accent that 'was at once Cockney, Jewish and guttural French'; it has been said that he 'was hardly real, in the sense of ordinary, everyday humanity, but was something essentially of the theatre'. By the time of his death his living quarters in Wardour Street were, according to one later profile, 'crammed with the junk of a make believe life time'. A recent book on gangland Soho alleges that Clarkson was notorious as an insurance fraudster and a blackmailer.

EDMUND BURKE
(1729–97) author and statesman   37 Gerrard Street **7**

DUBLIN-BORN, Burke entered Parliament as a Whig MP in 1766. An outstanding orator, he is said to have been 'gentle, mild and amenable to argument in private society', but 'was often intemperate and even violent in Parliament'. Burke lived with his wife Jane at a house on or near this site between 1787 and 1790, by which time his long friendship with fellow Whig Charles James Fox* was on the rocks. In *Reflections on the Revolution in France* (1790), Burke condemned the French Revolution – which Fox supported – and set out his belief in the values and virtues of the British constitution. The book provoked enormous controversy; one response was Tom Paine's *Rights of Man* (1791). Burke transferred allegiance to the Tory William Pitt the Younger*, and died a few years later at his Buckinghamshire estate. Number 37 forms part of a terrace built in 1737. By 1974 the house was in such poor condition that all but the ground floor was demolished. Opposite at 9 Gerrard Street, the former Turk's Head pub – used by Burke, Dr Johnson* and Joshua Reynolds* – survives.

JOHN DRYDEN
(1631–1700) poet   43 Gerrard Street **8**

THE plaque to Dryden was erected here in 1870, but subsequent research has established that he in fact lived, with his wife Elizabeth, in a house on the site of neighbouring number 44 from about 1687 until his death. Born in Northamptonshire, Dryden settled in London in about 1660. Three years later, his first play, *The Wild Gallant*, was staged at the Theatre Royal, Drury Lane. For much of his career Dryden was known for his dramatic works – including satires such as *Marriage à-la-mode* (1671) and the tragedy *All for Love* (1678) – but he is now best remembered for his poetry and translations.

Dryden's years in Gerrard Street were difficult: his conversion to Catholicism in *c.*1685 meant that he was unable to take the oath of allegiance after the Glorious Revolution of 1688 and lost his 20-year-old position as Poet Laureate. He nonetheless remained active in London's literary world. Number 44 was built in about 1681, refronted in 1793, and redeveloped in about 1901 at which time number 43 was also demolished – a deed described in the press as an 'act of vandalism'.

Dryden usually worked in the front ground-floor room of the house, and it was here that he completed his last play, *Love Triumphant* (1694), the poem *Alexander's Feast, or, The Power of Musique* (1697) and translations such as *The Works of Virgil* (1697); in its preface, Dryden likened himself to Virgil in his 'Declining Years, struggling with Wants, oppress'd with Sickness'.

DR WILLIAM HUNTER
(1718–83) anatomist Lyric Theatre, Great Windmill Street

THE rear facade of the Lyric Theatre, Shaftesbury Avenue is all that remains of Hunter's home and museum; the stage door is the entrance through which bodies were once taken for dissection. Scottish-born William and his younger brother John Hunter* were two of the greatest physicians and anatomical collectors of their time. Moving in 1740 to London, William Hunter ran a popular anatomy school in Covent Garden and, later, in Jermyn Street. He was also an accomplished male midwife, and in 1762 was appointed Physician-Extraordinary to Queen Charlotte, becoming Professor of Anatomy at the Royal Academy six years later. In 1767 he built a house at 16 Great Windmill Street, designed by the Scottish architect Robert Mylne, who was related to Hunter by marriage. The building incorporated a lecture theatre, dissecting room, library, and a museum at the rear – described in 1812 as 'a room admired for its proportions, of great size, with a handsome gallery running round'. Hunter gave his first anatomical lecture here in October 1767, and took up residence the following year. Following his death here in 1783 his collection was bequeathed to Glasgow University, later becoming the Hunterian Museum. Hunter's house passed to his nephew and pupil, Matthew Baillie, and continued in use as a school of anatomy until 1831. In 1888 the property was greatly altered as part of its incorporation into the Lyric.

JOHN LOGIE BAIRD*

(1888–1946) engineer

22 Frith Street

BAIRD rented two attic rooms here as his laboratory between November 1924 and February 1926 and it was here, in 1926, that he first demonstrated television. Born in Scotland, Baird studied electrical engineering in Glasgow, and began to formulate ideas about how to transmit and receive pictures. In March 1925 he began a three-week series of demonstrations of moving silhouette images at Selfridge's in Oxford Street. On 2 October, working from Frith Street, he transmitted the first television picture with tone gradation, first using the head of a ventriloquist's dummy and then a human face. Baird repeated the feat in front of 40 members of the Royal Institution the following January. The first television broadcasts followed in 1929.

Baird's first human subject was William Edward Taynton, a 20-year-old office boy. Taynton, who attended the unveiling of the plaque, recalled that 'Mr Baird rushed downstairs in baggy flannels, a pair of carpet slippers, and no socks. He almost dragged me into his workroom and sat me in front of his machine, a mass of wires and enormous electric light bulbs.'

A cameraman films the unveiling of Baird's plaque in 1951.

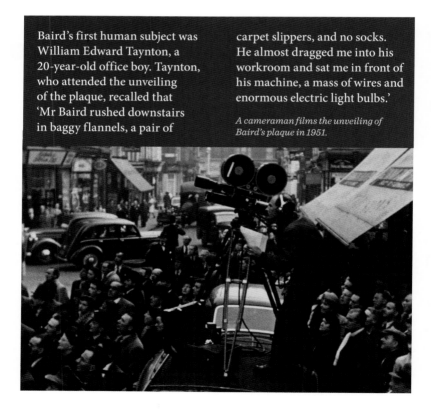

WILLIAM HAZLITT
(1778–1830) essayist

6 Frith Street

HAZLITT was born in Kent into an Irish dissenting family; moving to London in his teens, he decided to become a painter – like his elder brother John – and mixed in the circle that included Wordsworth, Coleridge*, and Charles and Mary Lamb*. In 1812 he turned to lecturing and journalism. Hazlitt had his greatest success with *The Spirit of the Age, or, Contemporary Portraits* (1824), a collection of biographical studies of such figures as Lord Byron and Jeremy Bentham. By the time of his move to lodgings in Frith Street in early 1830, however, he was living in consider-able poverty, and had been briefly arrested for debt. The appearance of the third and fourth volumes of his magnum opus, a biography of his hero Napoleon, had been delayed owing to the publisher's bankruptcy – they appeared shortly after his death – and his health was also failing. In September Hazlitt was confined, dangerously ill, to his bed – in a small room at the back of the house. There he died, with his son William and Charles Lamb at his bedside. The frontage of the house was rebuilt in approximate facsimile in 1909; the plaque, unusually, is green in colour.

ARTHUR ONSLOW
(1691–1768)
Speaker of the House of Commons

20 Soho Square
(formerly King Square) **12**

ONSLOW was Speaker from 1728 to 1761, a record 33 years. The house in which he lived (now demolished) was built in the 1680s for Earl Fauconberg and was one of the finest in the square. Onslow lived here with his wife Anne from about 1753 until his retirement from Parliament in 1761; he held parliamentary levees here, and entertained contemporaries such as the printer and novelist Samuel Richardson. Born in Kensington, Onslow had initially trained in law, but in 1720 became a Whig MP. Eight years later he was elected Speaker, becoming the third member of his family to hold the position. A close friend of Robert Walpole*, Onslow has been described as 'a man of rare integrity in an age of corruption'; he was the first 'career' Speaker, and the concept of the office as an impartial one dates from this period. The present building on the site was built as the offices of Crosse and Blackwell and dates from 1927, as does Onslow's bronze plaque.

MARY SEACOLE

(1805–81) Jamaican nurse, heroine of the Crimean War   14 Soho Square

MARY Jane Grant was born in Kingston, Jamaica, the daughter of a Scottish army officer and the mixed-race proprietor of a military boarding house; she went on to marry one of the occupants, one Edwin Seacole. Soon widowed, Mrs Seacole gained nursing experience during cholera and yellow fever epidemics, using knowledge of herbal medicine gained from her mother. In 1855, not having been chosen to join the nurses led by Florence Nightingale* to the Crimean War, she set up her own establishment behind the lines – a 'British Hotel' for the rest and recuperation of soldiers. Afterwards, financially embarrassed, she came to London; an open letter to the magazine *Punch* in May 1857, urging recognition for her endeavours, told of her 'poor little room' at 14 Soho Square. Strong sales of her autobiography helped to enable Mrs Seacole to spend the rest of her life in relative comfort; she had a home in Paddington.

SIR JOSEPH BANKS (1743–1820)
botanist, President of the Royal Society
ROBERT BROWN (1773–1858) botanist
DAVID DON (1799–1841) botanist
THE LINNEAN SOCIETY 32 (formerly 30) Soho Square

THE inscribed stone tablet on the modern office block marks the site of Joseph Banks's house. Born in nearby Argyll Street, the son of a Lincolnshire landowner, Banks returned to the capital after leaving Oxford, and soon became a Fellow of both the Royal Society and the Society of Antiquaries. In 1766 he set sail as naturalist on an expedition to Labrador and Newfoundland and, from 1768 to 1771, accompanied Captain James Cook* to the Pacific, a voyage that brought both men international acclaim. Banks acquired what was then 30 Soho Square in 1777 and it was his London home for the rest of his life, with his wife Dorothea and his sister Sarah, who was also a collector. It also housed his library and his extensive botanical collections.

Robert Brown first met Banks in about 1798, and was naturalist on the Australian expedition led by Matthew Flinders* in 1801–5. On his return, he was appointed librarian of the Linnean Society, and from 1810 was Banks's personal librarian at Soho Square. When Sir Joseph died, he bequeathed Brown a life interest in his collections, which subsequently passed to the British Museum. Brown lived at 17 Dean Street – the building to the rear, which housed Banks's library and collections – until his death, by which time he had amassed one of the world's greatest herbariums. Born into a family of botanists and gardeners, David Don succeeded Brown as librarian of the Linnean Society in 1822. He was later Professor of Botany at King's College London (1836–41), and died at number 32.

The Linnean Society was founded in 1788 by James Edward Smith (1759–1828) – a friend of Banks – for the study of natural history, and named after the 18th-century Swedish naturalist Carl Linnaeus, whose collection Smith had acquired in 1784. Brown (who was President of the society, 1849–53) leased the front part of number 32 to the society from summer 1822, although the group had met at the house since May of the previous year. It remained the society's headquarters until 1857, when it moved to larger premises at Burlington House, Piccadilly.

KARL MARX

(1818–83) political philosopher

28 Dean Street

BORN in Prussia into a Jewish family, Marx made his first visit to England in 1845, arriving with his friend and collaborator, Friedrich Engels*. He came again two years later – shortly before the publication of their *Communist Manifesto* (1848) – and, having been expelled from his homeland, settled permanently in London in 1849 with his wife Jenny, née von Westphalen (1814–81), and their family. Marx moved here from lodgings elsewhere in Dean Street in the winter of 1850-51; his income as London correspondent for the *New York Daily Tribune* was small and he lived here in considerable

'The evil frightful rooms which encompassed all our joy and all our pain.'
Jenny Marx on their Dean Street home

poverty. Two of his young children died during their time here, though the period also saw the birth of a daughter, Eleanor* (1855–98), later to become a socialist campaigner. They initially had only two rooms on the second floor of the house; at the back was a bedroom, used by the whole family, while the front room served as a kitchen and living room. Marx later rented a third room for use as a study. Despite the cramped conditions, friends and fellow radicals and refugees visited the family here; he also wrote the first volume of *Das Kapital* (1867) here, carrying out research at the reading room of the British Museum. In September 1856, with the help of Engels and an inheritance received by Jenny, Marx and his family moved to Kentish Town, where he remained until his death. This house, in Maitland Park Road – now demolished – first bore Marx's plaque.

DR JOSEPH ROGERS

(1820–89) health care reformer — 33 Dean Street

ON qualifying as a doctor, Rogers joined his brother's practice in Soho in 1844 and set up his own surgery here seven years later. In 1855 he became medical officer to the Strand Union Workhouse in Cleveland Street, Fitzrovia, and was appalled by the state of medical provision for the poor. Rogers's Assocation for the Improvement of London Workhouse Infirmaries, launched in 1866, secured the opening of

what were, in effect, the first public hospitals in the capital. With the support of Charles Dickens* and Florence Nightingale*, the association's lobbying led in 1867 to the Metropolitan Poor Bill, which provided for 20 hospitals for workhouse inmates. These were in effect the first public social hospitals built in London, and were absorbed into the National Health Service in 1949.

THOMAS SHERATON

(1751–1806) furniture maker   163 (formerly 106) Wardour Street

A CABINETMAKER from
County Durham, Sheraton
moved to London in about 1790; the
following year, he began to publish
*The Cabinet Maker and Uphol-
sterer's Drawing-Book* in weekly
parts. Intended as an aid to craftsmen, the book explained proportion,
perspective and geometry, and also
included a number of Sheraton's
own designs. These designs were to
become widely influential, both in
Europe and North America though
Sheraton did not enjoy the rewards
during his lifetime: he struggled to
make a living as a draughtsman,
author, publisher and teacher of
drawing – all of which he fitted in
with work as a Baptist minister –
and died in poverty. While lodging at

The plaque pictured in 1982.

what was then 106 Wardour Street,
he published the second edition of
his *Drawing-Book* (1794), as well
as *Scriptural Subjection to Civil
Government in an Exhortation to
Real Christians* (1794).

PERCY BYSSHE SHELLEY

(1792–1822) poet   15 Poland Street

S HELLEY and his friend
Thomas Jefferson Hogg took
rooms here in 1811, having been
sent down from Oxford for writing the pamphlet *The Necessity of
Atheism* (1811). 'We came to Poland
Street; [which] reminded [Shelley]
of Thaddeus of Warsaw and of freedom. We must lodge there, should
we sleep even on the step of a door,'
recalled Hogg. On the first floor
there was a sitting room, 'somewhat

dark, but quiet', and, opening off
it, a bedroom, which Shelley took;
Hogg's was on the floor above. The
pair were particularly impressed
with the 'delightful' wallpaper,
which bore a pattern of grape vines
and trellises. Touching it, Shelley
declared, 'We must stay here; stay
for ever!' Just over a month later,
however, he left for Sussex, but not
before meeting 16-year-old Harriet
Westbrook, who he later married.

CHARLES BRIDGEMAN

(d.1738) landscape gardener   54 Broadwick St. (formerly 19 Broad St.)

IT was while engaged in creating one of the most important landscape gardens of the age for the 1st Viscount Cobham at Stowe, Buckinghamshire, that Bridgeman and his wife Sarah moved to a Broad Street terraced house built by his brother-in-law, John Mist, in 1722–3. He was appointed Royal Gardener five years later, responsible for properties including Hampton Court, St James's Palace and Windsor Castle; he worked for Queen Caroline at Kensington Gardens, designing the Round Pond (1728) and the Serpentine (1731). Although Bridgeman had a series of official residences, it seems likely that he produced designs for many of his works at number 54; the inventory made of the property's contents at the time of his death – which occurred at his official residence in Kensington – records two drawing boards, a theodolite and 'a wooden Case for taking Prospects'. The house was rebuilt following bomb damage, and restored in 1983–4.

ANTONIO CANAL (CANALETTO)

(1697–1768) painter   41 Beak Street (formerly 16 Silver Street) **20**

BORN in Venice, the son of a painter, Canaletto made his name with the views he painted of his native city from about 1725; many of these were commissioned by English aristocrats making their Grand Tour of Europe. When the outbreak of the War of the Austrian Succession (1740–48) restricted the ability of potential English patrons to travel to Venice, Canaletto decided to visit them instead, arriving in London in May 1746; he stayed for about nine years. He exhibited his work at his lodgings here; the house dates from the 1680s. The show held here in summer 1749 included his *View of St James's Park*.

There is a second blue plaque to Canaletto, in Little Venice, which purportedly bears the authority of the London County Council. It is a fake!

THE PORTUGUESE EMBASSY
SEBASTIÃO JOSÉ DE CARVALHO
E MELLO, MARQUESS OF POMBAL

(1699–1782) Portuguese statesman and ambassador   23–24 Golden Square **21**

NUMBERS 23 and 24 were used as the Portuguese Embassy between 1724 and 1747. From 1739 to 1744 the two houses also served as the residence of the Marquess of Pombal. As chief minister under Joseph I, Pombal ruled as effective dictator from the time of the Lisbon earthquake of 1755 until the King's death in 1777. He oversaw Lisbon's reconstruction – featuring some of the world's first earthquake-proof buildings – and enacted reforms that were aimed at establishing an English type of commercial system, of which he had learned during his stay in London.

Number 24, dating originally from *c.*1675, was one of the earliest houses to be built in Golden Square; it was refronted in about 1730 and rebuilt behind its facade in 1959. The adjacent number 23 was built in about 1684 and, though it retains its original staircase, has been much altered internally since the 1700s. The two buildings backed onto a Catholic chapel, specifically established for the use of the Portuguese Embassy.

JOHN HUNTER

(1728–93) surgeon   31 (formerly 30) Golden Square **22**

HUNTER moved to London in 1748, and studied surgery and anatomy while assisting his elder brother William*, then served as a surgeon during the Seven Years' War (1756–63). He lived here from 1765–8, during which time he was elected a Fellow of the Royal Society, became a member of the Company of Surgeons and joined the surgical staff of St George's Hospital, Hyde Park Corner. He also began to collect anatomical specimens; the rapid expansion of this collection, and the success of his private practice, led him to move house, first to Jermyn Street, then to Leicester Square. Following his death, his natural history collection was purchased by the government and presented to what became the Royal College of Surgeons; in 1813 a purpose-built Hunterian Museum was opened at the college's head-quarters in Lincoln's Inn Fields, where it can still be found today.

WASHINGTON IRVING

(1783–1859) writer   8 Argyll Street **23**

IRVING lived in this 1730s house from about 1830 until he returned to the United States in 1832. He had arrived in London in 1829 as Secretary to the American Legation at 9 Chandos Place, just off Oxford Street. By this time he was already an established author, having had his first major success with *The Sketch Book of Geoffrey Crayon* (1819), a collection that includes 'Rip van Winkle' and 'The Legend of Sleepy Hollow'. It was at this address that Irving put the finishing touches to *The Alhambra* (1832) – published in London under the Geoffrey Crayon moniker – a book inspired by a trip to Spain in 1826–9. One of his last journeys in England before returning to the US was to visit the Nottinghamshire home of his hero Lord Byron, which he described in *Abbotsford and Newstead Abbey* (1835).

MAJOR-GENERAL WILLIAM ROY

(1726–90) founder of the Ordnance Survey   10 (formerly 12) Argyll St. **24**

BORN in Lanarkshire, Roy started working for the military survey of Scotland in 1747, by which time he was an accomplished surveyor and map-maker. Moving south in 1755, he joined the Army and carried out a reconnaissance survey of southern England. In 1765, he was put in charge of military surveys in Britain. At this time Roy was already urging the establishment of a national survey, and got his chance to lay the foundations for this when in 1783 it was proposed that the trigonomic connection between the observatories of Paris and Greenwich be established accurately, to determine their difference in longitude. The President of the Royal Society, Joseph Banks*, commissioned Roy to take charge of the English part of the survey. By 1789 he had completed the triangulation work; he died the following year at the Argyll Street house he had occupied since 1779. Roy's fieldwork – the starting point for which was a 5-mile straight line on Hounslow Heath – provided the foundations for the Ordnance Survey, set up in 1791 by the Board of Ordnance. Originally termed the Trigonometrical Survey, it produced its first map – of Kent – in 1801.

MAYFAIR

BOUNDED by Oxford Street, Regent Street, Piccadilly and Park Lane, Mayfair takes its name from the annual fair held until the mid-1700s in what were then open fields. The largest and most important high-class London development of its time, Mayfair was built up from the early to the mid-18th century on six principal estates: Burlington, Millfield, Conduit Mead, Berkeley, Curzon and – the largest of all and the only one to survive – Grosvenor. Its grand, luxurious houses represented the height of fashion,

'More intelligence and human ability, to say nothing of wealth and beauty, than the world has ever collected in such a space before.'

Sydney Smith*, on early-19th-century Mayfair

and their designers included several renowned architects. Mayfair attracted professional men and the aristocracy; its long association with figures of significance is reflected in one of the capital's highest concentrations of plaques.

RICHARD BRIGHT

(1789–1858) physician   11 Savile Row **1**

BRISTOL-BORN Bright was a physician at Guy's Hospital from 1820 until 1844. He moved here in September 1831 – the year of publication for the second volume of his acclaimed *Reports of Medical Cases* (1827–31) – and stayed for the rest of his life. Some of his most significant work dates from his time here; in 1837 he was appointed Physician-Extraordinary to Queen Victoria, and the following year was honoured for his identification

The tailors for which Savile Row is renowned are relatively recent arrivals, from the mid-19th century. Even in 1870 it was better known for 'eminent physicians and surgeons'.

of the kidney ailment that became known as Bright's disease. Like its neighbours, number 11 was built in 1732–5; the fourth storey was added during Bright's occupancy, in 1836.

GEORGE GROTE

(1794–1871) historian   12 Savile Row **2**

A NEIGHBOUR of Bright and a friend of the philosophers Jeremy Bentham, James Mill* and John Stuart Mill*, Grote first came to prominence as a politician; in the 1830s he was a leading spokesman for the philosophic radicals, authoring the *Essentials of Parliamentary Reform* (1831), and between 1832 and 1841 was MP for the City of London. He was also – according to a friend, the psychologist Alexander Bain – 'a Greece-intoxicated man'. He completed, among other works, his magnum opus, the 12-volume *History of Greece* (1846–56), while living here. Grote's wife Harriet was a noted hostess and woman of letters, and celebrated for her

musical receptions; visitors to the house included Frederic Chopin* and Jenny Lind*. The Grotes found number 12 'a convenient, roomy house, in a quiet situation'; it was George Grote's home for the last 23 years of his life and he died here.

RICHARD BRINSLEY SHERIDAN*

(1751–1816) dramatist 14 Savile Row **3**

SHERIDAN, born in Dublin, penned a number of brilliant comedies including *The Rivals* (1775) and *The School for Scandal* (1777), and was a leading Whig politician too. From 1776 he managed the Theatre Royal, Drury Lane, but its rebuilding in 1791–4, followed by its destruction by fire in 1809, effectively bankrupted him. Having long left his grander home in Hertford Street (*see p.75*), he hit rock bottom in Savile Row; a visitor found 'all the reception rooms bare, and the whole house in a state of filth and stench that was quite intolerable'. In his final days, Sheridan

'They are going to put the carpets out of the window, and break into Mrs S's room and *take me.*'

A desperate Sheridan, in fear of the bailiffs

narrowly avoided the bailiffs and a sponging house (a debtors' prison). The dramatist died here on 7 July 1816, in the presence of his second wife, Hecca, who was herself seriously ill. Against Sheridan's name in the rate-book is the following bureaucratic distillation of despair: 'Goods distrained by Sheriff, Distraint resisted. Dead and Insolvent.'

GEORGE BASEVI

(1794–1845) architect 17 Savile Row **4**

BORN in London into a Jewish family, Basevi became a pupil of John Soane in 1810, and completed his training six years later. His family connections – Benjamin Disraeli* was a cousin – brought him a steady stream of commissions, including work at Gatcombe Park, Gloucestershire (*c.*1820), the country home of David Ricardo. In 1825 William and George Haldimand, to whom he was also related, took over the development of Belgrave Square from Thomas Cubitt* and appointed

Basevi as surveyor. He went on to work in South Kensington, including Pelham Crescent (1833) and Thurloe Square (1840–45). The work for which he is best remembered is the Fitzwilliam Museum in Cambridge, begun in 1837; it was completed after the architect's death by C. R. Cockerell*. Basevi lived here from 1829 until the time of his unfortunate demise: while supervising repair work in Ely Cathedral's bell tower, the architect slipped through a hole in the scaffolding and fell to his death.

CHARLES ROLLS

(1877–1910) pioneer of motoring and aviation 14–15 Conduit Street **5**

THE Rolls family motto of *Celeritas et Veritas* ('Speed and Truth') certainly fitted the young Charles, who was fascinated by the mechanics of fast vehicles: first bicycles, then cars, then aeroplanes. His flair for driving was matched by his talents as a publicist; he was behind the wheel of the Rolls-Royce Twenty that set the London to Monte Carlo time trial record in May 1906. At that point the ink had not long dried on the contract between Rolls and the engineering genius Henry Royce, and Rolls had been established for about a year at an office and motor showroom in Conduit Street (at which his attendance was, according to his secretary Miss Caswell, 'erratic'). These premises remained the West End headquarters of Rolls-Royce until 1996. Rolls was the first to fly to France and back non-stop in June 1910, but achieved an unwanted distinction a month later by becoming the first British fatality of powered flight, when his plane crashed during a flying tournament at Bournemouth. A vegetarian and anti-vivisectionist, Rolls was also an adept impersonator of music-hall stars.

HORATIO, LORD NELSON

(1758–1805) naval commander and
hero of the Battle of Trafalgar, 1805

147 (formerly 141) New Bond St.
103 (formerly 96) New Bond St. **6**

NORFOLK-BORN, Nelson entered the Navy in 1771, and came to prominence as a commander in the 1780s; encounters of the following decade included that at Santa Cruz, Tenerife, when Nelson was wounded in his right arm. It was in order to convalesce following its amputation that he returned to London, in low spirits, and in mid-September 1797 moved to number 147, then a lodging house run by a Mr Jones. Happily, by 11 December he could describe himself as being 'perfectly recovered'. After spending a month or so in Bath, Nelson and his wife Fanny returned to Bond Street in early February 1798, taking up residence at number 103. This building is the only one of Nelson's London residences to remain intact, number 147 having been rebuilt. On 16 March, two days after taking his leave of George III, Nelson received orders to proceed to Portsmouth and left Bond Street, sailing to rejoin the British fleet near Cadiz. On 1 August that year he led a crushing naval victory against the French at the Battle of the Nile.

SIR HENRY IRVING

(1838–1905) actor   15A Grafton Street **7**

JOHN Henry Brodribb, born in
Somerset, took Henry Irving
as his professional name. He found
fame after joining the company at
London's Lyceum Theatre in 1871
and, having triumphed in roles
including Hamlet and Shylock, took
over the management of the theatre
in 1878. Under him, the Lyceum became renowned and in 1895 Irving
became the first actor to be knighted. Irving moved to Grafton Street
in 1872 after separating from his
wife, Florence, and lived a bachelor
existence in rooms on the first and
second floors, somewhat sombre
due to their stained-glass windows.
The dining room, overlooking Bond
Street, featured busts of John Philip
Kemble and Dante; there was also
a cigar room, a drawing room and a
study, where the actor planned his
performances. On medical advice,
Irving moved to sunnier quarters at
nearby 17 Stratton Street in 1899,
and stayed there until his death.

Irving as Cardinal Wolsey in Shakespeare's
Henry VIII, *c.1892.*

'Nowhere could be found a
more perfect example of the
confusion and neglect of order
in which the artistic mind
delights.'

A contemporary view of Irving's apartment

DANIEL O'CONNELL

(1775–1847) Irish leader and champion of civil rights   14 Albemarle St. **8**

'**S**CUM condensed of Irish bog/
Ruffian, coward, demagogue',
ran a verse about O'Connell that
appeared in *The Times* in 1836. This
typified much of the contemporary
British establishment's attitude
towards a man who, by creating a
mass political movement in Ireland,
had forced the Duke of Wellington's
government to grant full civil rights
to Roman Catholics in 1829. This
allowed O'Connell to take his seat

as MP for County Clare; four years later, his parliamentary supporters sometimes held their meetings at his London base in Albemarle Street, during a parliamentary session that saw slavery outlawed in British jurisdictions – another cause to which O'Connell was deeply committed. O'Connell's non-violent, insurgent campaign for Catholic emancipation was an inspiration to, among others, Mahatma Gandhi*. O'Connell nursed no doubts about his own place in the pantheon: asked to name Ireland's 'leading man' he plumped for Henry Grattan, another great parliamentarian, 'next to myself'.

BERT AMBROSE

(c.1896–1971) dance band leader

May Fair Hotel, Stratton Street

LONDON-BORN Benjamin Baruch Ambrose came to prominence as a musical director in New York (1917–20), before making his mark in London with his orchestra at the Embassy Club in Old Bond Street. In March 1927, he became musical director at the newly opened May Fair Hotel – a building begun in 1924, to designs by W. H. White. From here he broadcast on the radio on Saturday nights and made some 80 records a year, gaining national fame; singers and musicians he worked with included Sam Browne, Vera Lynn, Lew Stone and Ted Heath. The deal also included a flat at the hotel. Ambrose (he was mostly known by his surname alone) performed here for most of the next 13 years until, fed up with wartime air raids, he retired to Hertfordshire. He spent much of the rest of his career managing other performers, notably the singer Kathy Kirby.

SIR NORMAN HARTNELL

(1901–79) court dressmaker

26 Bruton Street

BORN in a public house in Streatham Hill, Hartnell became one of the most famous of British couturiers. His fabulous dresses were renowned for their glamour and ability to reflect the personality of the wearer. Highlights of his career included commissions to design Princess Elizabeth's wedding dress (1947) and the dress for her coronation (1953); other clients included Vivien Leigh*. In 1923 he opened a couture establishment at 10 Bruton Street (demolished) and moved to this address in the same street in

1935, after having the mid-18th-century house altered by the architect and designer Gerald Lacoste. From at least the mid-1950s, it also served as his London residence. The showrooms were on the ground floor, the main salon was at first-floor level and the workshops were to the rear.

Hartnell and models in the mirrored salon at 26 Bruton Street, 1955.

LORD CLIVE OF INDIA

(1725–74) soldier and administrator   45 Berkeley Square

THE son of a Shropshire squire, Robert Clive is best remembered as the victor of the Battle of Plassey (23 June 1757), in which the French were driven out of Bengal. This victory paved the way for British rule in India, and catapulted Clive to wealth and fame. Returning to Britain in summer 1760, he was created Baron Clive of Plassey, and in early 1761 he moved with his wife Margaret into this grand house in Berkeley Square, built *c*.1744–5 to the designs of Henry Flitcroft. They had it redecorated in the height of fashion and though Clive was often abroad his wife continued to live here; in 1765 she held a musical reception at which the young Mozart* made an appearance. Clive, however, had made some powerful enemies: on his return from India in 1767 he was accused of bribery and corruption. Although acquitted in 1773, he was left broken in heart and health, and the following year Clive died here, having taken a large dose of opium.

GEORGE CANNING

(1770–1827) statesman   50 (formerly 3) Berkeley Square

BORN in London to Irish parents, Canning – who was seldom out of public office between 1796 and 1827 – moved house frequently: this is one of only two surviving London addresses for him, and was later reputed to be haunted. Canning kept this town house for several months in 1806, not long before his appointment as Foreign Secretary in March 1807; his two years in post were marked by his determined handling of foreign policy relating to the Napoleonic Wars, and he became the effective leader of the House of Commons. In 1822, on the death of Viscount Castlereagh* – whom he had famously fought in a duel in 1809 – Canning was appointed Foreign Secretary for a second time; he held the post for five years, before briefly becoming Prime Minister in 1827, heading a coalition of Tories and Whigs. He held power for just 119 days before succumbing to fatal pneumonia.

WILLIAM PETTY, 2ND EARL OF SHELBURNE, 1ST MARQUESS OF LANSDOWNE

(1737–1805) Prime Minister and supporter of American independence
9 Fitzmaurice Place

LANSDOWNE (formerly Shelburne) House is one of the most important houses to survive in Mayfair. It was begun in 1762 for the 3rd Earl of Bute, to designs by Robert Adam*, and was sold, incomplete, three years later to Dublin-born Shelburne, who lived here from 1768 until his death, and oversaw its completion. While detractors found him arrogant and deceitful, and referred to him as the 'Jesuit of Berkeley Square', Shelburne was a significant figure, a patron of the arts and a consistent opponent of the war on the American colonists. During his time as Prime Minister (1782–3), he oversaw the signing of a provisional peace treaty with the United States – the so-called Treaty of Paris – which he and Benjamin Franklin* drafted at Lansdowne House in November 1782. Joseph Priestley* was employed as librarian and philosopher both here and at Shelburne's Wiltshire seat, Bowood.

HARRY GORDON SELFRIDGE

(1858–1947) department store magnate
9 Fitzmaurice Place

BORN in rural Wisconsin, Selfridge joined the Chicago department store of Field, Leiter & Co. at the age of 21, rising to be a junior partner. Eager to go it alone, he moved in 1906 to London, where he opened his pioneering 130-department store three years later; it included a library, roof garden, restaurants and a 'bargain basement'. With the fruits of success Selfridge bought racehorses, Rolls-Royces and Highcliffe Castle in Dorset; he leased Lansdowne House from 1921 until 1929 at a cost of £5,000 a year, and held famously lavish parties here. It was not to last: he got into debt and spent his last years in poverty, dying in a small flat in Putney.

FANNY BURNEY (MADAME D'ARBLAY)

(1752–1840) author   11 Bolton Street

BORN in King's Lynn, the daughter of the musician and writer Dr Charles Burney, Fanny moved with her family to London in 1760. She was fêted following the publication of her novel *Evelina* (1778) by Samuel Johnson* and David Garrick*, and, having consolidated her literary reputation with *Cecilia* (1782), spent five eventful years (1786–91) as Second Keeper of the Robes to Queen Charlotte. Virginia Woolf* described Burney as the 'mother of English fiction'. She moved here on 8 October 1818, following the death of her husband, the French émigré Alexandre D'Arblay. She intended the house to provide a London home for her son Alexander and described it as 'my new and probably last dwelling'; in the event, she stayed for a decade, and moved a further three times within Mayfair. Much of her time here was spent assembling the three-volume *Memoirs of Doctor Burney* (1832).

CHARLES JAMES FOX

(1749–1806) statesman   46 (formerly 44) Clarges Street

FOX was born in Mayfair, the son of Henry Fox, later 1st Baron Holland, and became an MP at the age of 19. A powerful orator, he supported the French Revolution and the cause of American independence. Antipathy between Fox and George III damaged his political opportunities; his most senior position was Foreign Secretary, a post he first held in 1782. In the following year, the King conspired to undermine Fox's coalition with Lord North, paving the way for their rival, William Pitt the Younger*, to begin his long stint as Prime Minister. By 1803, Fox – doyen of the Whigs – was living largely in retirement at St Anne's Hill, Surrey, and was only prompted to make his brief return to London by talks surrounding the resumption of the war between Britain and France, during which time he lived in this 1730s terrace. In 1806 he returned to office, becoming Foreign Secretary, but died shortly afterwards.

NANCY MITFORD

(1904–73) writer   10 Curzon Street **17**

THE eldest of the six Mitford girls, Nancy is best remembered for her novels *The Pursuit of Love* (1945) and *Love in a Cold Climate* (1949). During the Second World War, she worked at the fashionable Curzon Street bookshop run by Heywood Hill and his wife Anne. In December 1942 Mitford, assisted by Mollie Friese-Green, took over the running of the shop – a favourite haunt of writers including Evelyn Waugh*, Anthony Powell and Osbert Sitwell. The building has mid-18th-century origins, and remains largely as it was when Mitford last worked here in 1945, with a fine bowed early-19th-century shopfront.

LORD PALMERSTON*

(1784–1865) Prime Minister and Foreign Secretary   94 Piccadilly **18**

LORD Palmerston, like some other Prime Ministers of his era, never lived at 10 Downing Street: his own house was rather grander. During his residence at Cambridge House – named after another former resident, Adolphus, Duke of Cambridge (1774–1850), a younger son of George III – Palmerston served as Liberal Leader of the House of Commons and Prime Minister, a position he held for all but one year of the period 1855–65. Previously three times

Only a few of the great houses that once faced onto Piccadilly now remain, the most notable being Burlington House (which now houses the Royal Academy of Arts), originally built in *c.*1664–8. Another survivor is Cambridge (or Egremont) House at 94 Piccadilly, occupied from 1866 to 1999 by the Naval and Military Club and familiarly known as the 'In and Out' from the lettering on the gatepost.

Foreign Secretary, he was notable for his tough approach to foreign policy, and was committed to the suppression of the international slave trade. While living here Emily, Lady Palmerston, continued to hold the celebrated social 'assemblies' that had become such a famous feature of their home* in Carlton Gardens. Number 94, later the 'In and Out' club, had – then as now – two gateways that served to direct the flow of guests, who included politicians, ambassadors and society beauties.

GENERAL JOHN BURGOYNE

(1723–92) soldier, politician and dramatist　　　10 Hertford Street

NICKNAMED 'Gentleman Johnny', Burgoyne is best known as the general who surrendered to the Americans at Saratoga, New York, on 17 October 1777, one of the turning points of the War of Independence. Returning to Britain the following year, he re-entered Parliament and became a fierce critic of the war. He served as Commander-in-Chief of Ireland in 1782–4 but his later years were dedicated chiefly to literary work; Horace Walpole* described his play *The Heiress*, staged at the Drury Lane Theatre in 1786, as 'the best modern comedy'. He acquired this house in 1769, and commissioned Robert Adam* to carry out alterations. He moved here two years later with his wife Lady Charlotte, and it was here that he died in 1792.

RICHARD BRINSLEY SHERIDAN*

(1751–1816) dramatist and statesman　　　10 Hertford Street

SHERIDAN moved to this address in 1795, three years after the death of General Burgoyne*, and remained here until 1802. Irish-born, Sheridan came to live here on the occasion of his second marriage, to Esther ('Hecca') Ogle; their son Charles was born the following year. By this time, Sheridan was well established as a politician; famed for his parliamentary oratory, he was a leading Whig and a friend of Charles James Fox*. He was also a highly successful dramatist and theatre manager. While here, Sheridan wrote his last work, the tragedy *Pizarro* (presented in 1799), and continued to manage the Theatre Royal, Drury Lane, until he overstretched himself financially with the rebuilding of the theatre in 1791–4, and in 1802 the bailiffs seized his Hertford Street home – the start of a spiralling descent.

SIR GEORGE CAYLEY

(1773–1857) scientist and pioneer of aviation   20 Hertford Street **21**

CAYLEY laid down the principles of heavier-than-air flight and is widely regarded as the father of aeronautics. He was born in Scarborough and succeeded to the family estates in 1792, thereafter living mainly at Brompton Hall, Yorkshire, where he carried out his researches. By 1799 he had already sketched the basic configuration of the modern fixed-wing aeroplane. His studies, published in *Nicholson's Journal* in 1809–10, form the basis of modern aerodynamics. In 1853, half a century before the first powered flight by the Americans Orville and Wilbur Wright, Cayley built the first man-carrying glider, supposedly piloted by his coachman. He also invented the caterpillar tractor, the hot-air engine and the tension wheel (the forerunner of the modern bicycle wheel), and carried out original work on land reclamation, railway engineering, acoustics, optics and electricity. In addition, he was the first Chairman of the Polytechnic Institution from 1838 until his death. This was his town house from 1840 until *c*.1850. Dating from the 18th century, the building was heavily refaced *c*.1890.

BENJAMIN DISRAELI, EARL OF BEACONSFIELD*

(1804–81) Prime Minister   19 Curzon Street **22**

DISRAELI died in this 1760s terraced house on 19 April 1881. The writer Francis Espinasse, who visited him shortly before this, described the reception rooms as having 'a look of spick and span newness'. Disraeli acquired the house in November 1880 – using part of the proceeds of his recently published novel, *Endymion* – and moved in on 15 January 1881. By this time, he had retired from politics and hoped to spend his time writing novels; a work now known as *Falconet*, a sequel to *Lothair*

'No, it is better not. She would only ask me to take a message to Albert.'

The dying Disraeli declining the offer of a visit from Queen Victoria

(1870), was left unfinished at his death. His plans were thwarted due to a sharp downturn in his health. On 31 March – three weeks before his death – Disraeli corrected his last speech for *Hansard*, asserting that he would 'not go down to posterity talking bad grammar'.

LORD FITZROY SOMERSET, 1ST BARON RAGLAN

(1788–1855) Commander
during the Crimean War

5 Stanhope Gate
(formerly Great Stanhope Street)

LORD Raglan spent most of his long military career in the service of Arthur Wellesley, Duke of Wellington, who held him in high regard and whose niece Emily Wellesley-Pole he married in 1814. He was with him at Waterloo (1815), where he sustained a wound that caused his right arm to be amputated. At the age of 65, Raglan was appointed British Commander in the Crimea, and in April 1854 – a month after the outbreak of war – he left Mayfair for Turkey. Although he saw victory at the battles of

'Hey, bring my arm back. There's a ring my wife gave me on the finger.'

Lord Raglan keeping a stiff upper lip

Alma and Inkerman, he came under increasing censure, especially for his part in the disastrous Charge of the Light Brigade that October. The following year, shortly after the failure of an assault made as part of the Siege of Sebastopol, Raglan died at camp, worn out by anxiety and disappointment.

RUFUS ISAACS, 1ST MARQUESS OF READING

(1860–1935) lawyer and statesman

32 Curzon Street

ISAACS was born in the City of London, the son of a Jewish fruit merchant. Having enjoyed a highly successful career as a barrister, he served as Solicitor-General and Attorney-General in quick succession before becoming Lord Chief Justice in 1913. A close associate of Lloyd George*, he also had spells as Ambassador to the United States (1918–19) and Viceroy of India (1921–6). In 1926 he was created Marquess of Reading, taking his title from the

Berkshire town he had represented in Parliament for nine years from 1904. In 1931 he was briefly Foreign Secretary under Ramsay MacDonald*. Isaacs moved to Curzon Street in mid-1910 and lived here until his death 25 years later. He loved the late-18th-century house, which he shared with his wife Alice and their son Gerald, and – after Alice's death – with his second wife, Stella, Lady Reading* who went on to found the Women's (Royal) Voluntary Service.

BEAU BRUMMELL

(1778–1840) leader of fashion   4 Chesterfield Street

THE son of a private secretary to the Prime Minister Lord North, George Bryan ('Beau') Brummell moved to Chesterfield Street in 1799, having inherited money on coming of age, and lived here until 1804. Always smart and self-assured, Brummell set a new standard for his friends and contemporaries by scorning ostentatious dress. His style – which became known as dandyism – relied on fine-quality cloth, precise cutting and understated elegance, and was epitomised, above all, by the starched cravat. Brummell's house thronged with members of the aristocracy and the so-called 'Dandiacal Body', who anxiously hoped to gain access to the inner sanctum, Beau's front

BEAU BRUMMELL AND THE PRINCE REGENT

Brummell first met George, Prince of Wales, when he was 16, and the two later became close friends. The association famously ended in 1813: while walking with Lord Moira in St James's, shortly after being snubbed by the Prince, Brummell – known for his cutting wit – asked his colleague, 'Pray, who is your fat friend?' He was not forgiven.

dressing room. In 1816 mounting gambling debts forced him to flee to France, where he died in a paupers' lunatic asylum at the age of 62.

WILLIAM SOMERSET MAUGHAM

(1874–1965) novelist and playwright   6 Chesterfield Street **26**

BORN in Paris, Maugham qualified as a doctor in London in 1897 but – having written his first novel while still a student – chose to make literature his career, and became well known as a satirist of British society. Maugham moved house regularly and spent long spells abroad even before he left London for France in 1927. While based in Chesterfield Street, from 1 April 1911 until 31 March 1919, he enjoyed great success, writing *Of Human Bondage* (1915), and holding supper parties for the casts of plays such as *Caroline* (1916). During this period he also began his long relationship with Gerald Haxton, an Anglo-American with whom he served for a time in the First World War, before working for British Intelligence. In 1917 he embarked on his ill-fated marriage to the interior designer Syrie Wellcome (daughter of Dr Barnardo* and former wife of Henry Wellcome*). The couple were divorced in 1929, by which time Maugham was living in France with Haxton. The Second World War left numbers 5 and 7 Chesterfield Street gutted; they were incorporated with number 6, which survived intact.

ARCHIBALD PHILIP PRIMROSE, 5TH EARL OF ROSEBERY
(1847–1929) Prime Minister and first Chairman of the London County Council

20 Charles Street

ROSEBERY, who lived here for the first year of his life, was the first chairman of the LCC (1889–90); Rosebery Avenue in Clerkenwell, the first of the council's street improvements, was named in his honour and was opened by him in 1890, and in 1903 he unveiled the first of the council's blue plaques. He enjoyed greater success in this role than in national politics. Despite being one of the richest and most celebrated figures in Britain, he was a disappointment as premier and felt himself unsuited to the position. A Liberal, Rosebery became Prime Minister on the resignation of Gladstone* in 1894 but resigned the following year, having suffered electoral defeat and enormous personal strain, including the fear that his name would be mentioned in connection with the trial of Oscar Wilde*: Lord Drumlanrig, the elder brother of Lord Alfred Douglas, had been Rosebery's private secretary.

ALBERT HENRY STANLEY, LORD ASHFIELD
(1874–1948) first Chairman of London Transport

43 South Street

BORN in Derbyshire, Albert Henry Knattriess – he took the name Stanley in the mid-1890s – returned to England from the United States to work for the Underground Electric Railways Company of London (UERL). He moved to this house, part of an imposing terrace designed by J. J. Stevenson and built in 1896–8, while President of the Board of Trade (1916–19), a job which earned him a peerage. Together with Herbert Morrison* and Frank Pick* he masterminded the inauguration in 1933 of a unified transport system for the capital, the London Passenger Transport Board (later simplified to London Transport), of which he served as chairman until 1947.

J. ARTHUR RANK

(1888–1972) industrialist and film producer

BORN in Kingston upon Hull, Rank transformed the family milling business into the international conglomerate Rank Hovis McDougall (now part of Premier Foods). He was equally successful in the film industry, creating a business empire that encompassed both production and distribution: among the films produced by Rank were *The Red Shoes* (1948) and Ealing comedies such as *Kind Hearts and Coronets* (1949). This was the headquarters of the Rank Organisation from 1947; the large 'Wrenaissance' building dates from 1920. J. Arthur Rank decreed that, even for executives, the working day started at 8.30. Devout Methodist though he was, he had a ready command of swear words, picked up during his First World War army days – and despite the objections of some co-religionists to any form of gambling, he had few qualms about turning under-achieving cinemas into bingo halls.

SIR RICHARD WESTMACOTT

(1775–1856) sculptor

BY the time of his death, Westmacott was celebrated as Britain's foremost official sculptor. He produced a large body of work, including *Achilles* in Hyde Park (1814–22; *pictured*) and the group in the pediment of the British Museum (1851). The son of a sculptor of the same name, Westmacott spent his youth at 25 Mount Street, and moved next door at the age of 21. Needing larger premises to accommodate his expanding business and large family he moved here with his wife Dorothy and their children (his eldest son Richard was also to become a successful sculptor) in 1818.

Westmacott had the house, which was built in *c*.1736 by a carpenter named Roger Blagrave, altered to serve as combined residence, studio and gallery, and remained here until his death. During his time here he completed some of his most notable works, and in 1827 succeeded John Flaxman as Professor of Sculpture at the Royal Academy.

CHARLES X
(1757–1836) the last Bourbon King of France   72 South Audley Street

CHARLES-PHILIPPE, Comte d'Artois, was the younger brother of Louis XVI and Louis XVIII and the grandson of Louis XV. A devout Roman Catholic, the comte was also a notorious womaniser, known for his wit, charm and good looks. Following the storming of the Bastille in 1789, Louis XVI ordered him to leave France, and he eventually settled in Britain. After three years at Holyrood House, Edinburgh – lent to him by George III – he moved in 1799 to London. While at this address (between 1805 and 1814) he lived a mostly quiet and retiring life, saddened by the death in 1804 of his beloved mistress, Louise de Polastron. He returned to France on the restoration of the monarchy and succeeded to the throne in 1824 as Charles X. An unpopular, reactionary monarch, he was forced to abdicate in 1830 and exiled again.

CONSTANCE SPRY
(1886–1960) artist in flower decoration   64 South Audley Street

SPRY is renowned as the floral designer who took the art form – a status upon which she was most insistent – into the 20th century, using berries, fruits, vegetables, lichens, moss and twigs in her highly creative mixed arrangements. She was in charge of the flowers for the present Queen's wedding and coronation, having served a fashionable clientele since 1934 from her South Audley Street shop – premises which continued to bear her name into the 1990s. Born Constance Fletcher in Derby, her first career was in health education and teaching; for a time she was Principal of a London County Council school in Homerton. At the age of 42 she took up flower design as her main profession in 1928; within six years she was employing 70 people. Spry authored several books, including a self-sufficiency cookbook – a contribution to the war effort, entitled *Come into the Garden, Cook* (1942).

JOHN GILBERT WINANT

(1889–1947) United States Ambassador 1941–6   7 Aldford Street **33**

DURING his years in London, Winant made a great impact on the British public and press. People from all walks of life were impressed by his energy and his promotion of justice, freedom and truth; during night-time air raids, he walked the streets offering support and encouragement. Winant moved to this 'small house down the street' from the American Embassy in June 1945, also taking a lease on the neighbouring 9 Rex Place; the house was originally part of a stable building built in 1896–7 to serve 14 and 16 Park Street. But by the time he moved here, Winant was a broken man; the death of his friend President Roosevelt in April 1945 had come as a blow, and in March the following year he resigned as ambassador, left Mayfair, and in May returned to the US. Winant took his own life in 1947.

FLORENCE NIGHTINGALE

(1820–1910) nurse and heroine of the Crimean War   10 South Street **34**

FLORENCE Nightingale's father bought 10 (formerly 35) South Street (the site of which is now occupied by a block of 1930s flats) for her in 1865, five years after she had founded the Nightingale School of Nursing at St Thomas's in London and some nine years after her return as a heroine from the Crimean War. Nightingale, who was unmarried, lived here with five servants to attend to her but spent almost all her time in her bedroom, at the back of the second floor, only receiving visitors by appointment. She continued her campaigns for reform while living here, however, largely by letter, including the improvement of training for midwives and home-nursing for the poor and infirm.

Nightingale, probably in her bedroom at South Street, 1910.

During these years, she was, wrote a biographer, 'treated with an almost religious deference – ministers, kings, princesses, statesmen waited at her door, and her utterances were paid the respect due to an oracle'.

SIR ROBERT PEEL (1750–1830) manufacturer and reformer
SIR ROBERT PEEL (1788–1850) Prime Minister
and founder of the Metropolitan Police   16 Upper Grosvenor Street

THIS house, completed in c.1730 and stuccoed in 1881, was leased from 1800 to 1822 by the first Robert Peel. Originally from Oswaldtwistle, Lancashire, Peel senior was the owner of a successful and innovative calico-printing business and a pioneer of the Industrial Revolution, who went on to be an MP. His son, who was born in Bury, Lancashire, was brought up for a career in politics and the two are said to have resembled each other in many ways. The younger Peel spent intermittent but significant periods of his life in this house. He followed his father into politics at the age of 21, continuing Peel senior's efforts to reform working conditions in factories. His long and successful career was crowned by two periods as Prime Minister (1834–5 and 1841–6), ending in the repeal of the protectionist Corn Laws, which split the Tory party that Peel headed. In 1829, as Home Secretary, Peel had established the Metropolitan Police Force, based at Scotland Yard*, giving his name to the 'Peelers' or, more enduringly, 'Bobbies'.

SIR MOSES MONTEFIORE

(1784–1885) philanthropist   99 Park Lane
and Jewish leader   (formerly 7 Grosvenor Gate and 35 Park Lane)

MONTEFIORE was the first occupant of this house, which was completed in 1825 to the designs of John Goldicutt; he moved in the following year and remained here until his death 60 years later. Together with the Rothschilds, Montefiore was pre-eminent among England's 19th-century Jewish leaders, whose abilities and work brought the Jewish community into the mainstream of public life. Through his marriage in 1812 to Judith Cohen he became the stockbroker of her brother-in-law, Nathan Mayer Rothschild, and by the time of Rothschild's death in 1836, he had become exceedingly rich, having retired from active business at the age of 40. Knighted during his term as Sheriff of London (1837–8), Montefiore devoted his energies to philanthropic work on behalf of oppressed Jews both at home and abroad, visiting Palestine several times, as well as Russia and Morocco, and he became an internationally respected figure. He died aged 101 at East Cliff Lodge, his home in Ramsgate.

GEORGE SEFERIS

(1900–71) Greek Ambassador,
poet and Nobel Laureate

BORN Georgios Seferiadis in Smyrna (now Izmir, Turkey) and educated in Athens and Paris, Seferis came to prominence in 1935 with the publication of *Mythistorema*, a fusion of ancient Greek epic and modernism. He was awarded the Nobel Prize for Literature in 1963. Seferis was also a diplomat and a great Anglophile; it was while he was Greek Ambassador to Britain (1957–62) that he lived here with his wife Maro. The building of 1905–6, designed by R. G. Hammond, has been the official residence of the Greek Ambassador since 1921.

P. G. WODEHOUSE

(1881–1975) writer

BORN in Guildford, Pelham Grenville ('Plum') Wodehouse became Britain's best-selling author in the 1920s, with the creation of his brilliantly crafted and superbly comic novels featuring Bertie Wooster and Jeeves, Blandings Castle and the rest. Wodehouse and his wife Ethel lived in what was then Norfolk Street – in a neo-Georgian house built in 1897–8 to the designs of Sidney R. J. Smith – between early 1927 and summer 1934. This was the height of his success, and they were looked after by servants. Of Wodehouse's typical daily routine, his stepdaughter Leonora wrote: 'He writes in the afternoon, when he must on no account be disturbed. It is understood that he is thinking deep thoughts and planning great novels, but when all the smoke has cleared away it really means that he is either asleep or eating an apple and reading Edgar Wallace.' While here, he wrote ten books, usually in his bedroom, which he found 'really jolly'.

SIR THOMAS SOPWITH

(1888–1989) aviator and aircraft manufacturer 46 Green Street

SOPWITH'S name has been immortalised by the aircraft produced by the firm he headed after 1912: the Sopwith Aviation Company Ltd. During the First World War, more than 18,000 Sopwith aircraft served with the Allied air forces. Later Sopwith was involved with the Hawker Siddeley Group

Ltd, which produced the Hurricane, the Typhoon, and the revolutionary Harrier, capable of vertical take-off and landing. The Kensington-born Sopwith lived from 1934 to 1940 with his second wife Phyllis in this substantial neo-Georgian property, designed by Wimperis, Simpson and Guthrie (1913–15).

SIR FREDERICK HANDLEY PAGE

(1885–1962) aircraft designer and manufacturer 18 Grosvenor Square

HANDLEY Page lived in Flat 3, in a block built in 1933–5, from 1952 until his death here ten years later. His company, Handley Page Ltd, the first in Britain to be registered specifically to manufacture aeroplanes, was founded in 1909, and produced bombers during both world wars, including the Halifax, the first of which flew

in September 1939. In 1919 Handley Page Transport Ltd was founded; five years later this became part of Imperial Airways, Britain's first national airline service. Handley Page also lectured in aeronautics and in 1946 was involved in the foundation of the College of Aeronautics at Cranfield, Bedfordshire. He also had a home at Stanmore.

COLEN CAMPBELL

(1676–1729) architect and author of *Vitruvius Britannicus* 76 Brook St. **41**

SCOTTISH-BORN Campbell is closely associated with the development of Mayfair and in 1726 was the first occupant of this house, which he designed himself. Appointed architect to the Prince of Wales in 1719, his other patrons included Robert Walpole*, for

whom he designed Houghton Hall, Norfolk (1722–35). Other commissions included Stourhead, Wiltshire (c.1720–24); in London he remodelled Burlington House, Piccadilly. The three-volume *Vitruvius Britannicus* (1717–25) sets out his Palladian architectural principles.

ANN OLDFIELD

(1683–1730) actress

60 (originally 59) Grosvenor Street

OLDFIELD was – as the plaque records – the first occupant of this house, which was built in 1723 and damaged by fire in 1897; a shopfront was inserted at ground-floor level in the 20th century. Oldfield's time in Mayfair marked the culmination of her career, and reflected her status as the respectable mistress of General Charles Churchill, nephew of the 1st Duke of Marlborough. Having first joined the Drury Lane company in 1699, when she was barely 16, Oldfield appeared in more than 100 roles, embracing both tragedy and comedy; these included Lady Betty Modish in *The Careless Husband* (1704), a part written for her by Colley Cibber. A legendary beauty, Oldfield was buried in Westminster Abbey, the only actress to be so honoured.

SIR ALEXANDER KORDA

(1893–1956) film producer

21–22 Grosvenor Street

BORN Sándor László Kellner in Hungary, of a Jewish family, Korda – who had already established himself as a major figure in the film industry internationally – moved in November 1931 to London, where in February the following year he founded London Film Productions. This house, originally built in 1898–9 to the designs of Balfour and Turner, was the headquarters of London Films from February 1932 until the move to Denham Studios in autumn 1936. Korda had his first major hit with *The Private Life of Henry VIII* (1933). This was followed by the films that brought him worldwide fame, including *The Third Man* (1949), directed by Carol Reed. It was partly for his wartime undercover intelligence work that Korda was knighted in 1942.

ERNEST BEVIN

(1881–1951) trade union leader and statesman

Stratford Mansions,
34 South Molton Street

THE illegitimate child of a midwife from a village on the edge of Exmoor, Bevin went on to walk the corridors of power. One of the most powerful trade union leaders of the 20th century, he became General Secretary of the Transport and General Workers' Union in 1922.

In 1940 he was effectively head-hunted by Winston Churchill* to be Minister of Labour and National Service in the wartime coalition government, and a parliamentary seat was found for him; the 'Bevin boys' – conscripts who, by lottery, were sent to work down the mines – were named after him. After the war Bevin served as Foreign Secretary in the Labour government headed by Clement Attlee*, and was highly valued by both the Prime Ministers he worked under. He lived at Stratford Mansions from 1931 to 1939.

SIR JEFFRY WYATVILLE

(1766–1840) architect   39 (formerly 49 and then 50) Brook Street

THE Staffordshire-born Wyatt changed his surname in 1824 in order to distinguish himself from his illustrious relatives, the Wyatt family of architects and artists. He enjoyed the greatest years of his career during his residence in this house, from 1799 to 1840. During this time, his work included the alterations of 1820–41 at Chatsworth, Derbyshire, for the 6th Duke of Devonshire, and a spectacular reconstruction of Windsor Castle for George IV from 1824; the work at Windsor continued until about 1840, and earned him a knighthood.

This house, the core of which dates from 1720–23, served as his home and London office, and remained the residence of his daughter Emma Knapp until 1876. After the Tyburn brook, which runs beneath Avery Row, caused damage to the property, he remodelled it in 1821–3. The exterior of the house survives much as Wyatville intended, with the exception of shopfronts added in 1926–7; as such it is one of the very few houses in London designed by a pre-Victorian architect for his own occupation which still survives relatively unaltered.

GEORGE FRIDERIC HANDEL

(1685–1759) composer   25 (formerly 57) Brook Street

BORN in Halle in what is now Saxony-Anhalt, Germany, Handel settled in London in 1712, becoming a naturalised British citizen in 1727. He moved to Brook Street in July 1723, when the property was newly built, and stayed for the rest of his life. Here, in what is now his museum, he wrote masterpieces including *Israel in Egypt* (1739), 'Zadok the Priest' (composed for the coronation of George II, 1727), *Messiah* and

Samson (both 1741) and 'Music for the Royal Fireworks' (1749). From the house, Handel could walk to the King's Theatre, Haymarket, where many of his operas were performed, and to St James's Palace, where he served as Composer of Music for the Chapel Royal. A bachelor and a lover of good food and wine, he held frequent dinner parties, but suffered from blindness and poor health in his later years.

JIMI HENDRIX
(1942–70) guitarist and songwriter   23 Brook Street

JAMES Marshall Hendrix spent his most successful years in London, arriving in September 1966, three months after having been 'discovered' by the British musician Chas Chandler, who had been impressed by Hendrix's innovative guitar style and dynamic stage presence. In 1968, after an extended tour and the release of the album *Are You Experienced?*, Hendrix joined his girlfriend Kathy Etchingham at the flat she had taken on the top two floors of number 23. Jimi lived here for some months – assisting in its refitting and redecoration – before leaving to tour his native US in March 1969. The flat is now part of the Handel House Museum and its 1960s appearance recreated. Hendrix died of an overdose at a hotel in Notting Hill at the age of just 27.

PRINCE TALLEYRAND
(1754–1838) French statesman and diplomatist   21 Hanover Square (formerly known as Downshire House)

CHARLES-MAURICE de Talleyrand-Périgord spent two periods in London: the first was in 1792–4, when he attempted to dissuade the British government from fighting France. The other was in 1830–34, when he served as French Ambassador under Louis-Philippe, and shared a Hanover Square mansion with his niece, Dorothée, Duchesse de Dino, whose charm and intelligence assisted him 'in conciliating that very exclusive English society': she was described as Talleyrand's 'confidante, counsellor, and private secretary'. The pair held many sumptuous receptions here, where visitors included the Duke of Wellington; Dorothée told a friend that her dinners 'were making gastronomic history in London'. The house, built in *c*.1718, was refaced in stone in the late 19th century.

BELGRAVIA

SOCIALLY and architecturally, Belgravia has always been one of London's grandest districts, and thanks to the stewardship of the Grosvenor Estate it remains one of the most complete examples of late Georgian and early Victorian town planning in the capital.

The Grosvenor family owned the land from 1677, but development remained piecemeal until the 1820s when Robert Grosvenor, 1st Marquess of Westminster – whose statue gazes across Belgrave Square – commissioned the master builder Thomas Cubitt* to provide an ambitious plan based upon a grid enlivened by magnificent squares and terraces. The area's streets take their names from the Grosvenor estates in Cheshire, and are characterised by handsome, stucco-fronted houses. Proximity to Buckingham Palace, the Royal Parks and the Palace of Westminster has ensured that Belgravia attracted a mix of fashionable, aristocratic and, more recently, plutocratic residents; it has, in particular, long been popular with leading politicians.

GEORGE BENTHAM

(1800–84) botanist   25 Wilton Place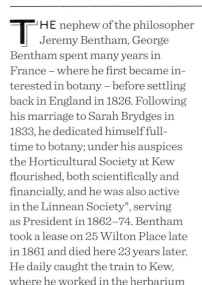

THE nephew of the philosopher
Jeremy Bentham, George
Bentham spent many years in
France – where he first became interested in botany – before settling
back in England in 1826. Following
his marriage to Sarah Brydges in
1833, he dedicated himself full-
time to botany; under his auspices
the Horticultural Society at Kew
flourished, both scientifically and
financially, and he was also active
in the Linnean Society*, serving
as President in 1862–74. Bentham
took a lease on 25 Wilton Place late
in 1861 and died here 23 years later.
He daily caught the train to Kew,
where he worked in the herbarium
from ten until four
in the afternoon;
returning home
he would write up
his notes and dine
quietly. The fruits
of Bentham's
labours included
the *Genera Plan-
tarum* (1862–83),
compiled with
Joseph Hooker*,
which gave a
revised definition
of every genus of
flowering plant.
It remains a
standard work.

EARL MOUNTBATTEN OF BURMA (1900–79)
COUNTESS MOUNTBATTEN OF BURMA

(1901–60) the last Viceroy and Vicereine of India   2 Wilton Crescent

PRINCE Louis of Battenberg
abandoned his German title
during the First World War and
the family name was anglicised; to
relations, he was known as 'Dickie'.
Mountbatten followed his father
into the Navy and served from 1942
as Chief of Combined Operations.
In 1946 he was appointed Viceroy
of India to oversee the country's
independence and, as it turned out,
partition. Mountbatten later became Admiral of the Fleet and Chief
of Defence Staff; he was killed by an
IRA bomb. His marriage to Edwina
Ashley was a tempestuous one,
but he was devastated by her early
death, which took place in Borneo
while she was on an inspections
tour as Superintendent-in-Chief
of the St John Ambulance Brigade.
The couple acquired 2 Wilton Crescent after their return from India
in 1948, and it was their London
home from 1950. Here, following his
appointment as First Sea Lord in

1955, the Earl held working breakfasts with the Board of Admiralty, amid the many treasures that Lady Mountbatten had inherited from her grandfather, Ernest Cassel. In the mid-1960s Mountbatten moved into the mews property at the rear, 2 Kinnerton Street.

SIR HENRY CAMPBELL-BANNERMAN

(1836–1908) Prime Minister   6 Grosvenor Place

C AMPBELL-BANNERMAN, originally from Glasgow, represented Stirling Burghs in Parliament from 1868 until his death, first achieving Cabinet rank under Gladstone* as Secretary of State for War. He lived in Grosvenor Place from 1878 to 1904: elected Liberal leader in 1899, he moved to 10 Downing Street as Prime Minister in December 1905, at the age of 69. Campbell-Bannerman was the first Prime Minister to be so called, the formal title having hitherto been First Lord of the Treasury. In early 1906 the Liberals were confirmed in office by a landslide election win, though heart problems prompted 'C-B' to give up the premiership in April 1908, and he died less than three weeks later. His period in power saw the foundations laid for House of Lords reform and the introduction of old-age pensions.

FIELD MARSHAL VISCOUNT GORT, VC

(1886–1946) Commander-in-Chief at Dunkirk   34 Belgrave Square

J OHN Standish Surtees Prendergast Vereker, later Viscount Gort, enjoyed an outstanding military career. During the First World War, he was awarded the Victoria Cross for his remarkable bravery at the Canal du Nord in September 1918. In 1937 he was made Chief of the Imperial General Staff, and two years later was given command of the British Expeditionary Force in France. His greatest moment came in 1940, when – in defiance of orders – he conducted the withdrawal of the BEF to Dunkirk, allowing the evacuation of nearly 340,000 British and French troops. Gort also masterminded the heroic defence of Malta in 1942, and proved an able diplomat in Gibraltar and Palestine. Belgrave Square was his London base from 1920 until 1926. He lived here with his wife Corinna, known as 'Kotchy', and three children; their departure was prompted by the couple's divorce in 1925, following Kotchy's affair with an official from the nearby Spanish Embassy.

JOHN RUSSELL, 1ST EARL RUSSELL

(1792–1878) Prime Minister   37 Chesham Place **5**

RUSSELL moved to this newly built four-storey townhouse in 1841, the year that he married his second wife, Lady Fanny Elliot, and was returned as an MP for the City of London. The newly-weds were joined here by Russell's two daughters and four stepdaughters from his previous marriage; John Russell, later Viscount Amberley, the eldest of his four children with Fanny, was born here. Russell was Foreign Secretary (1852–3 and 1859–65) and Prime Minister (1846–52 and 1865–6); among the liberal measures he introduced were the

According to his wife, Russell:

'never but once worked after dinner ... he always came up to the drawing room with us, was able to cast off public cares, and chat and laugh'.

extension of poor relief provision in famine-hit Ireland, and a legal limit on factory working hours. In 1847 Queen Victoria offered him the use of Pembroke Lodge in Richmond Park, which became his main residence. Russell was created an earl in 1861; the philosopher Bertrand Russell* was his grandson.

THOMAS CUBITT

(1788–1855) master builder   3 Lyall Street **6**

BORN near Norwich, the son of a carpenter, Cubitt followed his father's trade before setting up as a building contractor in London with his brother, William. In 1824 he developed part of the Bedford Estate in Bloomsbury, and went on to create Belgravia and Pimlico, the latter being known to contemporaries as 'Mr Cubitt's District'. While working from Lyall Street he built two separate additions to Buckingham Palace (1846–50 and 1852–6); he had earlier worked on the remodelling of Osborne House on the Isle of Wight, and Queen Victoria

and Prince Albert referred to him as 'our Cubitt'. He transformed the building trade from the haphazard employment of a mass of individual craftsmen to the system of centralised contracting known today. Cubitt had a large office in this, his last London base – it was divided into Law Business, General Office and Confidential; the house then incorporated the adjacent property, now number 4, and the stables and workshops in the mews behind. Cubitt continued to work here until two months before his death, which took place at his Surrey home.

WILLIAM WALTON

(1902–83) composer — Lowndes Cottage, 8 Lowndes Place **7**

LANCASHIRE-BORN William Walton won early praise from Hubert Parry*, who told his Oxford tutors 'there's a lot in this chap; you must keep your eyes on him'. He duly went on to become one of the 20th-century's leading British composers – in spite of the hostile critical reception at first given to the jazz-influenced *Façade* (1921), a setting of poetry by Edith Sitwell*. The success of the overture *Portsmouth Point* (1926) secured Walton a publisher, and though never prolific, he went on to write two coronation anthems, two symphonies, choral pieces – among which *Belshazzar's Feast* (1930–31) is a highlight – and numerous virtuoso orchestral works. In Twenties London Walton lived among the 'Bright Young Things', lodging with the Sitwells in Carlyle Square, Chelsea. When his flat in South Eaton Place was blitzed in 1941, he moved into Lowndes Place to live with his patron and lover, Alice Wimborne. On her death in 1948 Walton inherited the house; he sold the place in 1960 to finance a new house on the Italian island of Ischia, where he spent most of his later life.

SIR JOHN LUBBOCK, BARON AVEBURY

(1834–1913) politician — 29 Eaton Place **8**

LUBBOCK'S long and distinguished career embraced the worlds of banking, politics, science and archaeology. He spent much of his early boyhood at Eaton Place before his father inherited High Elms, Bromley, in 1840. He was behind important reforms of the banking system, and wrote numerous popular books on science. A Liberal MP, Lubbock was also President of the London Chamber of Commerce (1888–93), chaired the LCC (1890–92) and founded the organisation that became the Electoral Reform Society. When raised

> Lubbock drafted the bill of 1871 that brought about the first secular bank holiday; at that time this was the first Monday in August and popularly called St Lubbock's Day.

to the peerage in 1900, he took his title Baron Avebury from the Wiltshire prehistoric site that had featured in his campaign to preserve ancient monuments. His second wife was Alice Fox Pitt, daughter of his fellow archaeologist Augustus Pitt-Rivers*.

LORD KELVIN
(1824–1907) physicist and inventor   15 Eaton Place **9**

THOUGH William Thomson came from Belfast, he is more closely associated with the city of Glasgow where for over 50 years he was the university's Professor of Natural Philosophy. From his laboratory came a stream of epoch-making papers on heat, the movements of fluids and thermometric scales; he gave his name to that which measures absolute temperature. Kelvin acquired this house as a London base upon his elevation in 1892 to the House of Lords. He spoke mostly on maritime matters, and served on an Admiralty committee on the design of battleships in 1904–5; he had once been a keen yachtsman, and a marine sounding device and a compass featured in his long list of patents. Kelvin was appointed to the Order of Merit and sworn of the Privy Council in 1902. He was elected Glasgow University's Chancellor in 1904, and continued to publish papers at a prolific rate until his death at Netherhall, his Scottish country seat. Kelvin was buried in Westminster Abbey, alongside Isaac Newton*.

WILLIAM EWART*
(1798–1869) reformer   16 Eaton Place **10**

THE first occupant of 16 Eaton Place, William Ewart moved here early in 1830 after his marriage to Mary Lee, his first cousin. In September that year, his friend William Huskisson*, MP for Liverpool, died and Ewart was elected in his place. While in office, Ewart succeeded in carrying a bill that abolished the penalty of hanging in chains, and another that did away with capital punishment for cattle stealing and sacrilege. He also began, in 1836, to become involved in the promotion of education and public libraries, which became a major part of his work thereafter. In 1837, Ewart's wife – who bore him five children in six years – died and Ewart moved to Hampton, where he is also commemorated.

ALFRED, LORD TENNYSON

(1809–92) Poet Laureate   9 Upper Belgrave Street  11

TENNYSON'S works, such as *Maud, and Other Poems* (1855) and *Idylls of the King* (1859–85), drew deep at the well of High Victorian emotions. He lived in this rented property in 1880 and 1881 with his wife Emily, their son Hallam – his father's secretary, and later Governor-General of Australia – and ten servants. It was while here that Tennyson was painted by John Millais*, who reportedly regarded the portrait as among his finest.

Tennyson told Thomas Hardy*, who visited him here, that he and his family spent a month or two every year in London – though he essentially disliked the capital – because they all 'got so rusty' on the Isle of Wight.

WALTER BAGEHOT

(1826–77) writer, banker and economist   12 Upper Belgrave Street 12

BAGEHOT is best remembered today for *The English Constitution* (1867), which continues to influence interpretations of the role of the monarchy, and which he wrote while living here. Bagehot became editor in 1861 of *The Economist*, founded in 1843 by his father-in-law, James Wilson. This appointment – together with Bagehot's work for the London office of Stuckey's Bank, owned by his family – prompted his move from Cleveden, near Bristol, to Belgravia, where he lived with the family of his wife Eliza. Bagehot entertained extensively in Upper Belgrave Street; during his time here he counted Gladstone*, Thackeray* and Matthew Arnold* among his friends, and stood unsuccessfully for Parliament three times.

HENRY GRAY

(1827–61) anatomist

8 Wilton Street **13**

GRAY'S early life is obscure but he is thought to have been born in Windsor and to have lived in Wilton Street – his father was a messenger in the King's service – from about 1830 until his untimely death here 31 years later. While still a medical student, in 1848, Gray won a prize from the Royal College of Surgeons for a pioneering study of the eye. He was admitted a Fellow of the Royal Society at the age of just 25, and held various surgical posts – including lecturer in anatomy – at St George's Hospital, London. *Gray's Anatomy, Descriptive and Surgical,* notable for its fine illustrations and painstaking detail, was published in 1858; perhaps no medical text has ever been so extensively used by medical students and surgeons. Gray was working on a second edition in 1861 when he became fatally ill with smallpox, contracted while attending the sickbed of his nephew.

FELIX MENDELSSOHN

(1809–47) composer

4 Hobart Place **14**

MENDELSSOHN was a frequent visitor to London, and once said that there was 'no question that that smoky nest is my preferred city and will remain so. I feel quite emotional when I think of it.' He had a galvanising influence on music in Britain and some major works, such as his *Capriccio Brilliant* (1832) and *Elijah* (1846), were premiered here. Conversely, the influence of Britain – or specifically, Scotland – on Mendelssohn is apparent from the title of *The Hebrides* overture (1830), otherwise known as 'Fingal's Cave'. The lyricism of this piece is at odds with the composer's actual experience; when he visited the cave, he was violently seasick. Mendelssohn's personal charm was such that he even managed to get Queen Victoria to sing for him. On five of his ten visits to London, he stayed here, at the home of his friend Carl Klingemann, a Hanoverian diplomat.

LIEUTENANT GENERAL AUGUSTUS HENRY LANE FOX PITT-RIVERS

(1827–1900) anthropologist and archaeologist   4 Grosvenor Gardens

BORN Augustus Henry Lane Fox, Pitt-Rivers owed his fortune – and the name by which he is usually known – to an enormous inheritance from his cousin Horace Pitt, 6th Baron Rivers, who died in 1880. This provided him with the means to exchange a house in Earl's Court for a mansion in Belgravia and provided the resources for the excavations he carried out over the succeeding 20 years. During the 1870s Pitt-Rivers and his son-in-law – John Lubbock, later Lord Avebury* – introduced legislation that resulted in the Ancient Monuments Protection Act of 1882; Pitt-Rivers was the first holder of the office of Inspector of Ancient Monuments, and transacted much of his official business here. His extensive collection of ethnographic material formed the core of the Pitt Rivers Museum in Oxford, which opened in 1884, and his archaeological fieldwork set the pattern for modern excavation methods and techniques.

F. E. SMITH, 1ST EARL OF BIRKENHEAD

(1872–1930) lawyer and statesman   32 Grosvenor Gardens **16**

FREDERICK Edwin Smith, or 'FE', was one of the most successful barristers of his time, celebrated for his successful defence of Ethel le Neve, mistress of the murderer Dr Crippen, and renowned for his maverick approach to public life. He lived in this aptly exuberant house with his wife Margaret and their children from 1913 until his death. As Attorney-General from 1915 to 1919, Smith was responsible for the prosecution for treason of Roger Casement and, as Lord Chancellor from 1919 to 1922, he made a name for himself as a legal reformer. 'FE' took the

> After a long and boring introduction at one public meeting, concluding with the words 'Mr Smith will now give his address', 'FE' stood up and announced '32 Grosvenor Gardens', before leaving abruptly to catch a train.

title of Baron Birkenhead from his birthplace, and was elevated to an earldom in 1922. He became Secretary of State for India two years later, but left politics in 1928, unable to support his lavish lifestyle on a minister's salary.

IAN FLEMING

(1908–64) creator of James Bond   22B Ebury Street

FLEMING took over the lease here in late 1936, while working as a stockbroker in the City, and transformed the apartment – in a Greek Revival-style building of 1830, once Pimlico Grammar School – into an appropriate setting to entertain his gang of Old Etonian friends, known as 'Le Cercle Gastronomique et des Jeux de Hasard', and his numerous girlfriends. The living room, converted from the top half of the chapel-like interior, was painted grey with concealed lighting, a lavatory was fitted into an alcove, and the gallery became his bedroom. Plans to include an autobiographical diorama were abandoned. Fleming, who served with the Naval Intelligence Division during the Second World War, moved out because the dark blue roof skylight did not conform to blackout restrictions; he stayed at clubs and hotels until settling in late 1941 at Athenaeum Court (now the Athenaeum Hotel), Piccadilly. 'So the orchid has left the orchid house,' noted the writer Peter Quennell. In 1952 Fleming married Ann Rothermere and moved to Victoria Square, where he wrote the 14 Bond books.

MATTHEW ARNOLD

(1822–88) poet and critic   2 Chester Square **18**

ARNOLD had no fixed abode in London until he moved here in late 1858 with his wife Frances Lucy, known as 'Flu', and their family; he wrote that the house was 'a very small one, but it will be something to unpack one's portmanteau for the first time since I was married, now nearly seven years ago'. By the time he moved here, Arnold was already a noted poet. Between 1851 and 1856, he subsidised his literary efforts with work as an Inspector of Schools. While living here, Arnold had great success with the collection *Essays*

Arnold told his sister in 1858 that the house in Chester Square was:

'delightful inside, and very pleasant to return to, though at present I cannot quite forgive it for not being twenty miles out of London'.

in Criticism (1865), a landmark of its genre, and was also a noted social and religious critic, producing *Culture and Anarchy* in 1869. He left 'the dear little house' in March 1868 for Harrow, in pursuit of better schooling for his sons.

MARY SHELLEY

(1797–1851) author of *Frankenstein*   24 Chester Square **19**

THE daughter of Mary Wollstonecraft, the champion of women's rights, and the political philosopher William Godwin, Mary was, said her father, 'singularly bold, somewhat imperious, and active of mind'. The poet Percy Bysshe Shelley* left his wife for her; much of their life together was spent in Italy and Switzerland and in 1818, Mary wrote her masterpiece, *Frankenstein*, while in Geneva. After Shelley's death in a sailing accident in 1822, Mary returned to England, where she continued to write novels and to edit and promote Percy Shelley's works. She moved here in 1846, the house's first resident, but spent much time in Sussex. Plagued by ill health, Mary died here of a brain tumour, leaving behind an uncompleted biography of her husband.

VIVIEN LEIGH

(1913–67) actress   Flat D, 54 Eaton Square **20**

BORN Vivian [*sic*] Hartley in India, Leigh began acting professionally in her twenties, making her screen debut in *Things Are Looking Up* (1934). While making *Fire Over England* (1937), she formed an intense relationship with her co-star, Laurence Olivier, and the pair were married three years later. Leigh came to international attention for her Oscar-winning portrayal of Scarlett O'Hara in the film *Gone with the Wind* (1939). At the time she moved here in 1958 – alone, for though she furnished a study for Olivier, their marriage was ending – Vivien Leigh was suffering from bipolar disorder. The last decade of her life brought continued acclaim as a star of stage and screen but she died of tuberculosis here in July 1967, with her beloved pet cat, Poo Jones, by her side, and a portrait of Olivier on her bedside table.

PRINCE METTERNICH

(1773–1859) Austrian statesman   44 Eaton Square **21**

THE son of a diplomat, Klemens Wenzel von Metternich was born in Koblenz and held a series of senior diplomatic and political posts, culminating in his appointment as Chancellor in 1821. Metternich was made a Prince of the Austrian Empire in 1813 and the following year oversaw the formation of a new European order at the Congress of Vienna. The Metternich system was, however, oppressive and illiberal and in 1848 it collapsed in Europe-wide revolutions. Fleeing Vienna, Metternich arrived in London in April, taking a four-month lease from the Earl of Denbigh and moving here on 6 May. He liked England,

44 Eaton Square was, wrote Metternich's third wife Melanie:

'très-jolie, mais horriblement chère'.

which he thought 'the freest country in the world because it is the most orderly', and was astounded at the growth of London since his previous visit some 50 years before.

NEVILLE CHAMBERLAIN
(1869–1940) Prime Minister   37 Eaton Square

NEVILLE Chamberlain, son of Joseph Chamberlain*, was born in Birmingham where he enjoyed a long career in business. Soon after his marriage in 1911 to Anne Vere Cole he became active in local government, in 1915 becoming Lord Mayor of Birmingham. At the ripe age of 49, in 1918, Chamberlain was elected to Parliament and his rise thereafter was rapid. He served in the Conservative ministries of Stanley Baldwin* as Minister of Health and Chancellor of the Exchequer. The achievements of these years have been overshadowed by Chamberlain's reputation as the Prime Minister (1937-40) who appeased Hitler. He lived here from 1923 to 1935 and died in Hampshire in 1940.

STANLEY BALDWIN, EARL BALDWIN OF BEWDLEY
(1867–1947) Prime Minister   93 Eaton Square

BALDWIN bought this house in 1912 as an aspiring politician in need of more reception rooms. He became a junior minister at the Treasury in 1917, and it was here that the Prime Minister, Andrew Bonar Law*, informed him of his appointment as Chancellor of the Exchequer in 1922. Baldwin became Prime Minister in May 1923, having assumed the leadership of the Conservative Party ahead of the more experienced Foreign Secretary, Lord Curzon*. That December, Baldwin resigned as premier following a poor election showing – and briefly returned to live here – but he went on to be Prime Minister twice more, in 1924–9 and 1935–7. He sold this house in November 1924. Latterly, Baldwin, who cultivated the image of a pipe-smoking, tweedy country-man, spent much time at his country home, Astley Hall, Worcestershire, though after his retirement in 1937 he lived at 69 Eaton Square.

EDWARD WOOD, 1ST EARL OF HALIFAX
(1881–1959) Viceroy of India and Foreign Secretary   86 Eaton Square **24**

HALIFAX inherited 88 Eaton Square (since incorporated into number 86) in 1905 and it remained his London base until the outbreak of the Second World War. As British Ambassador in Washington in 1940 (a crucial posting at that juncture of the war), Halifax saw the United States join the Allies in late 1941, and held the post until 1946. His efforts to cement Anglo-American relations won him admirers; more controversial was

his spell as Viceroy of India (1926–31), which saw him jail Gandhi* and other Congress leaders. He was raised to the peerage as Baron Irwin in 1925, inherited his father's viscountcy in 1934 and was created an earl in 1944. As Foreign Secretary between 1938 and 1940, Halifax is strongly associated with the ill-omened strategy of appeasing Hitler, although he is credited with having inspired the firmer line taken from early 1939.

GEORGE PEABODY
(1795–1869) philanthropist   80 Eaton Square **25**

ON 4 November 1869, while on his way to the South of France for a recuperative holiday, Peabody died here, at the home of his friend Curtis Miranda Lampson, an American-born businessman; he had also stayed here in 1867. His last words were 'It is a great mystery, but I shall know all soon'. Born in South Danvers (renamed Peabody in 1868), Massachusetts, Peabody made his fortune trading in dry goods and settled in London in 1837.

By the mid-1840s he was a successful merchant banker, specialising in American securities. Lord Shaftesbury persuaded him to fund better housing for the working classes and through the Peabody Donation Fund – established in 1862 and today administered by the Peabody Trust – he applied much of his fortune to the construction of the estates that bear his name. The first, in 1864, was in Commercial Street, Spitalfields.

VISCOUNT CECIL OF CHELWOOD

(1864–1958) founder of the League of Nations 16 South Eaton Place

EDGAR Algernon Robert Cecil lived here from 1922 until his death in Kent 36 years later. The son of the 3rd Marquess of Salisbury*, the Conservative Prime Minister, Cecil entered Parliament in 1906. His service with the Red Cross in the First World War persuaded Cecil that the prevention of armed conflict was 'the only political object worth while'. Following the war, Cecil served as adviser to Britain's delegation at the Paris peace conference where he played a vital part in establishing the League of Nations, later constituted by the first part of the Treaty of Versailles, signed in June 1919. Cecil later won the Nobel Peace Prize (1937). For all its promise, the League did not prevent the outbreak of the Second World War, and at its final session in 1946 Cecil declaimed, 'The League is dead; long live the United Nations'.

PHILIP NOEL-BAKER

(1889–1982) Olympic sportsman and peace campaigner 16 S. Eaton Place

AN Olympic athlete, Captain of the British Olympic team and silver medallist in the 1920 1500m race, Philip Noel-Baker lived here with his friend Viscount Cecil* – to whom he acted as private secretary for a spell – from the time of the Second World War, taking over the lease on Cecil's demise and remaining here until his own. Born Philip Baker (he adopted the additional surname on marriage), Noel-Baker held a profound belief in the positive role of sport in fostering good international relations. He was elected to Parliament in 1929 and held several ministerial posts, including Secretary of State for Commonwealth Relations (1947–50). He wrote *The Arms Race: A Programme for World Disarmament* (1958) and won the Nobel Peace Prize.

WOLFGANG AMADEUS MOZART

(1756–91) composer 180 Ebury Street (formerly Five Fields Row)

MOZART, his father Leopold and his elder sister Maria Anna, 'Nannerl', were in London on a European grand tour when Leopold was taken ill. This then semi-rural lodging, owned by a Dr Randal, was chosen as a suitable place for his convalescence and the family moved here on 6 August 1764. It was decreed that no instrument could be played to disturb the invalid: so it was that, in the words of his sister, 'in order to occupy himself, Mozart composed his first symphony for all the instruments of the orchestra, especially for trumpets and kettledrums'. The work she referred to is lost, but the symphony now known as Mozart's first (K.16 in E flat major) was also written at this time, being one of the precocious works aired at the Haymarket Little Theatre in February 1765. From September 1764 the family lodged at 20 Frith Street, Soho, remaining there until the following July.

HAROLD NICOLSON (1886–1968)
VITA SACKVILLE-WEST (1892–1962)

writers and gardeners   180 and 182 Ebury Street **29**

I N 1914, 180 and 182 Ebury Street were combined into one house by the architect Edwin Lutyens* and occupied by Harold Nicolson and Vita Sackville-West. The house belonged to Vita's mother, Victoria, Lady Sackville, and here the couple laid the foundations of their literary careers, Harold with *Paul Verlaine* (1921) – the first of his six literary biographies – and Vita with her first novel, *Heritage* (1919), and the poem *The Land* (1926). After the First World War, their marriage nearly foundered on Vita's infatuation for fellow writer Violet Trefusis, and in 1922 Virginia Woolf* first dined here, beginning her long

Harold considered Ebury Street 'rather stern and prim and quiet'; his wife thought it haunted, having once felt 'a warm feminine hand close gently over her own as it rested on the banister rail'.

intimacy with Vita. Harold also had homosexual affairs, and by the time they left Ebury Street in 1927 their relationship was one of affectionate companionship, one fruit of which was the gardens at Sissinghurst Castle, Kent. In Ebury Street, Lutyens's garden dining room was destroyed by bombs in 1941, and the two houses are now again separated.

GEORGE MOORE

(1852–1933) author   121 Ebury Street **30**

BORN in County Mayo, Moore studied art before turning to writing, a move prompted partly by a meeting in Paris with Emile Zola*. He moved to this house in London in 1911 when his hopes of leading the Irish literary revival foundered. It was conveniently close to his lover Maud Cunard, the society hostess who lived in Grosvenor Square. Moore was a prolific man of letters and completed some dozen works while living here, including the three volumes of his autobiography, *Hail and Farewell* (1911–14), the novel *The Brook Kerith* (1916) and a volume of literary criticism, *Conversations in Ebury Street* (1924). He was accustomed to write in the dining room on the ground floor and had the front bay window put in for better light, though its external appearance did not accord with his intentions. He died here in 1933.

DAME EDITH EVANS

(1888–1976) actress   109 Ebury Street **31**

THIS was the childhood home of Edith Evans and she was living here in 1912 when she made her professional stage debut in a production of the sixth-century Hindu classic, *Sakuntala*. Before this, she had been apprenticed to a milliner, Mr Blackaller, in Buckingham Palace Road. The daughter of a minor public servant, Evans's upbringing was unmarked by either privilege or privation: she recalled that 'I always had a bedroom to myself'. Noël Coward*, whose mother ran a boarding house, lived next door. Evans was appointed DBE in 1946 and enjoyed a long and successful career, appearing on stage and screen until the mid-1970s. She is perhaps most widely remembered for her incredulous enunciation of two words – 'A handbag!' – as Lady Bracknell in the stage (1939) and film (1952) productions of *The Importance of Being Earnest*, an association that she came to abhor.

MARYLEBONE

MARYLEBONE takes its name from the medieval parish church of St Mary-le-Bourne, which was built in the heart of Tyburn village in about 1400. Bounded by Portland Place to the east and Edgware Road to the west, it lies to the north of Oxford Street. The whole area was open countryside – and a notorious haunt of highwaymen – when, in 1708, John Holles, Duke of Newcastle, bought part of the manor; within ten years his son-in-law, Edward Harley, 2nd Earl of Oxford and Mortimer, began developing a new residential quarter that fanned out from Cavendish Square. Building in the west of Marylebone began when the Portman family laid out Portman Square in 1764, and continued with the creation in the early 19th century of Bryanston, Montagu and Dorset Squares. Having shaken off its early disreputability, this largely Georgian townscape attracted many pioneering and reforming figures in the fields of politics, literature, architecture and medicine, as well as a host of cultural institutions. Since 1867, when Marylebone received the capital's first blue plaque – that to Lord Byron (lost through demolition in c.1889) – more than 60 plaques have been erected in the district.

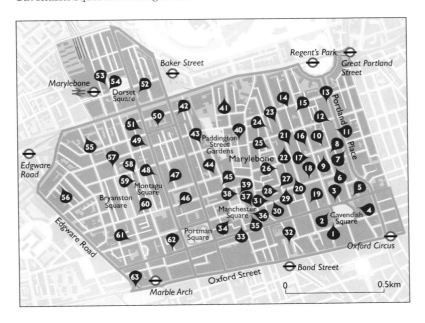

HERBERT HENRY ASQUITH, IST EARL OF OXFORD AND ASQUITH

(1852–1928) statesman   20 Cavendish Square

AN MP from 1886, Yorkshire-born Asquith moved here in 1895, following his marriage the previous year to his second wife, Margot. Their life here, with their two surviving children, Elizabeth and Anthony, proved happy. These years saw Asquith rise to the top of the Liberal Party: he was appointed Chancellor of the Exchequer in 1905, and then Prime Minister in April 1908, when he left Marylebone for Downing Street. His lasting achievement was the Parliament Act of 1911, which ended the House of Lords' veto on financial legislation, and the subsequent introduction of National Insurance. He resigned in favour of Lloyd George in December 1916 and returned to 20 Cavendish Square, which remained his home until 1920, when a shortage of funds forced a move to Bloomsbury; Asquith died at The Wharf, Sutton Courtenay, Oxfordshire, his country home since 1912. Although number 20 dates from 1729, it was refronted to designs by Edwin Cooper after being bought in 1922 by the Cowdray Club.

SIR RONALD ROSS

(1857–1932) discoverer of the mosquito transmission of malaria

18 Cavendish Square **2**

BORN in India to a Scottish family, Ross trained as a doctor in London and pursued a career in the Indian Medical Service. In 1894, while on leave in London with his wife Rosa, he met the great expert on tropical medicine, Patrick Manson*, who inspired him to research the possible link between mosquitoes and malaria. On his return to India, he discovered that the malarial parasite was transmitted to human beings by the blood-sucking *Anopheles* mosquito. In 1902, in recognition of this vital breakthrough, Ross – by then lecturer at the Liverpool School of Tropical Medicine – became the first Briton to receive the Nobel Prize, an honour that soured his friendship with Manson. Ross lived here between 1913 and 1916, while working as a consultant at King's College Hospital and for the War Office. In 1926 he founded the Ross Institute and Hospital for Tropical Diseases in Putney, and it was there that he died; the Institute was subsequently incorporated into the London School of Hygiene and Tropical Medicine.

SIR JONATHAN HUTCHINSON

(1828–1913) surgeon, scientist and teacher   15 Cavendish Square **3**

FROM a Yorkshire Quaker family, and educated at the York School of Medicine and St Bartholomew's Hospital, Hutchinson first came to attention as a surgeon and professor of surgery at the London Hospital in Whitechapel. He worked there from 1859 to 1883, specialising in ophthalmology, dermatology, neurology and venereology. He moved to this early-19th-century house in 1874, acquiring the freehold three years later – something that severely tested the family finances. Hutchinson stayed until 1907, when he moved permanently to Haslemere, Surrey. He held, among other posts, the Hunterian Professorship of the Royal College of Surgeons.

The first postgraduate medical college in London had its origins in Hutchinson's 'polyclinic' at 22 Chenies Street, Bloomsbury, where he stored his medical collections and gave public lectures and demonstrations. Hutchinson's research into syphilis was significant – unlike his theory that leprosy was chiefly caused by eating rotten fish, which has not stood the test of time. Hutchinson held strongly to the view that women should not be doctors, and dismissed as 'too absurd' the notion of Elizabeth Garrett Anderson* practising medicine.

QUINTIN HOGG

(1845–1903) founder of the Polytechnic, Regent Street   5 Cavendish Sq. **4**

HAVING made a fortune as a sugar merchant and businessman, the London-born Hogg devoted his life to educational philanthropy. He is best known for transforming the Royal Polytechnic Institution, originally founded in 1838, into the new Polytechnic. The building at 309 Regent Street opened in September 1882 to 2,000 students, offering instruction and recreation to men and women of working and trade backgrounds;

it became part of the University of Westminster in 1992. With his wife Alice and their five children, Hogg moved into this 1740s house, which backs onto the Polytechnic, in 1885, and built a bedroom and bathroom in the passage connecting the two buildings. When they moved out in 1898 Hogg retained use of the modest rooms to the rear; it was here that he died in January 1903, accidentally asphyxiated by fumes from the gas heater in the bathroom.

GEORGE EDMUND STREET

(1824–81) architect

ONE of the great champions of High Victorian Gothic, Street learned his craft in the office of George Gilbert Scott* in the 1840s; a fellow pupil was G. F. Bodley*. Street, who settled permanently in London in 1856, excelled in building subtly monumental churches, such as St James the Less, Pimlico (1859–61), which was influenced by the eclectic range of styles observed during his travels on the Continent. Street moved to this mid-18th-century house while engaged on his grandest and most important project, the Royal Courts of Justice, built between 1871 and 1882. During the decade he lived

'I felt as if I had been reprieved after a sentence of death. All my happiest associations are with these rooms, and I begin to think I should be less happy anywhere else.'

Street to his son, on the joys of not moving house

here, Street suffered the death of his first wife Mariquita in 1874, and of his second, Jessie, in 1876. He reluctantly considered moving to a smaller and more manageable house, but was relieved when the deal fell through. Street died here in 1881.

SIR ROBERT MAYER

(1879–1985) philanthropist
and patron of music

MAYER lived in Flat 31 of this 1923 mansion block from 1953 until his death. Born and educated in Mannheim, Germany, he settled in Britain in 1896 and forged a career in the metal industry; as a naturalised British citizen, he served in the British Army during the First World War. A talented musician, he was encouraged by his first wife Dorothy, a soprano singer, to use his private wealth to institute a concert series for children. The first season, conducted by Adrian Boult*, opened in 1923, and the concerts – mostly under the baton of Malcolm Sargent* – became an annual fixture in London as well as in provincial cities. With Thomas Beecham* he founded the London Philharmonic Orchestra in 1932, and five years later was knighted for services to music.

SIR ARTHUR PEARSON

(1866–1921) founder of St Dunstan's
(Blind Veterans UK)

POPULAR magazines were the basis of Sir Arthur's fortune, with the 'missing word' quiz in *Pearson's Weekly* being a notable hit with the public. Some of his early philanthropy went to the nascent scout movement founded by Robert Baden-Powell*, but after glaucoma robbed Pearson of his sight, his focus shifted to blind people, and in particular to the care and rehabilitation of blinded servicemen. The first hostel opened in Bayswater in 1915, but soon shifted to more spacious accommodation at St Dunstan's, Regent's Park: this mansion, destroyed by fire in the 1930s, gave its name to Sir Arthur's charity. He leased 21 Portland Place from fellow philanthropist Sir John Stirling-Maxwell from about 1915 to 1920 for the accommodation of officers, but also lived there with his wife Ethel – their established London home, nearby 15 Devonshire Place, being occupied by nursing staff. The charity founded by Pearson is now called Blind Veterans UK and has a purpose-built facility at Ovingdean, East Sussex.

CHARLES STANHOPE, 3RD EARL STANHOPE

(1753–1816) reformer and inventor

STANHOPE married Hester, the sister of William Pitt the Younger*, in 1774, and was elected an MP six years later. He inherited the earldom on his father's death in 1786 and used his seat in the House of Lords to campaign for parliamentary reform, the abolition of the slave trade and religious liberty, in particular for Roman Catholics. He was dubbed 'Citizen Stanhope' for sympathising with the revolutionaries in France, even after Britain declared war on that country, a stance that was not universally popular. On the night of 11 June 1794 this house, which he shared with his second wife, Louisa, a cousin of Hester, was set on fire by the mob; fortunately there was no lasting damage. Stanhope became disillusioned with politics and, in 1795, left this house to live principally at his estate at Chevening in Kent. He also conducted scientific experiments, his most successful invention being a stereotype process of printing (1805), which was taken up by Oxford University Press and *The Times*.

JOHN LOUGHBOROUGH PEARSON (1817–97)
SIR EDWIN LANDSEER LUTYENS (1869–1944)
architects   13 Mansfield Street

PART of a speculative build by the Adam brothers, the house dates from about 1773. Pearson, who moved here in May 1881, designed intricately crafted pieces of furniture to suit its Adam interiors, rather than try to impose his own Gothic aesthetic. He was then at the height of his powers, having established himself as one of the foremost proponents of Gothic architecture with a large number of church commissions, including St Augustine's, Kilburn (1870); this and other works brought him the prestigious commission to design Truro Cathedral in 1878. Pearson died here at the age of 80.

Lutyens, who moved here with his wife Lady Emily in 1919, had made his name designing country houses that blended vernacular styles with classicism. Despite running an internationally renowned architectural practice, Lutyens struggled to maintain this large London town house, with its complement of ten servants. In the early 1930s he created a more convenient layout by moving the kitchen and dining room to the first floor, which enabled the couple to manage with fewer staff and live more economically; he also transferred his studio to a building at the rear of the property and converted the basement into a flat for their daughter, the composer Elisabeth Lutyens. Edwin Lutyens died here on New Year's Day, 1944.

Lutyens's many country houses include Castle Drogo, Devon (1912–30), while his most ambitious commission was the creation of an Indian capital city, New Delhi (1913–31), with Herbert Baker. In July 1919 he was engaged to design a 'catafalque' to commemorate the British war dead; the resulting stone Cenotaph (*opposite*) in Whitehall was unveiled on Armistice Day 1920. From his studio here, Lutyens also masterminded the construction of Queen Mary's Dolls' House, which involved the work of 60 artists and over 250 craftsmen; it was unveiled to the press in 1924 in the drawing room here, and is now on display at Windsor Castle.

ALFRED WATERHOUSE

(1830–1905) architect   61 (formerly 8, then 20) New Cavendish Street **10**

AFTER buying the house – one of a pair built by John Johnson in 1776 – in 1864, Waterhouse remodelled the upper floors, adding iron verandas and balconies, to create a family home, and converted the ground floor into his office. Liverpool-born, he began his career in Manchester, where he designed a succession of public buildings including Strangeways Prison (1866–8) and Owens College (1870–1902, later Manchester University). He established both his home and his architectural practice here in 1865. It was from here that he designed

his two most famous buildings – Manchester Town Hall (1867–77) and the Natural History Museum at South Kensington (1872–81). His lavish rebuilding of Eaton Hall, Cheshire, for the 1st Duke of Westminster in the 1870s attracted a number of other country-house clients, but Waterhouse is especially known for his institutional and commercial work, most notably the 27 buildings he designed for the Prudential Assurance Company, including its headquarters in Holborn (1876–1901), now known as Waterhouse Square.

THOMAS GAGE

(1719/20–87) commander of
British forces in North America

41 (formerly 22, then 29 and
54) Portland Place **11**

GAGE was the first resident of this large terraced house, which was built in about 1776; the square was laid out for the 3rd Duke of Portland by the Adam brothers. Gage served from 1754 and throughout the Seven Years' War (1756–63) in North America, where, despite suffering a series of defeats, he won the respect of his fellow officers, including General James Wolfe*. Promoted Commander-in-Chief of British forces in North America in 1763, with headquarters in New York, he spent the next ten years failing to contain the growing discontent of the American colonies. He was discharged from his duties after full-scale rebellion broke out in 1775 and returned to England with his American wife, Margaret, and their children. Gage lived at this house from 1779 until his death here eight years later, during which time he briefly commanded the defences of Kent against French invasion (1781) and was promoted to full general (1782). It is now accepted that Gage was born in 1719/20, rather than in 1721, as is stated on the plaque.

EARL ROBERTS

(1832–1914) field marshal

47 Portland Place **12**

THE introduction of khaki uniforms and the Enfield rifle are both associated with Frederick Sleigh Roberts, who was born in Cawnpore, India, and had followed his father into the service of the East India Company. He rose to become Commander-in-Chief of all India (1885–93), and was honoured for his service during the Second Afghan War. Returning to England in 1893, he was promoted to field marshal in 1895; four years later, he was sent to South Africa with Lord Kitchener* to bolster the British Army, which had suffered defeats by the Boers. Within ten months, Roberts had gained control of the Orange Free State and the Transvaal. He returned to serve as Commander-in-Chief of the British Army (1900–04). He is commemorated with a rectangular stone plaque at the London home he shared with his wife Nora Henrietta from 1902 until 1906.

FRANCES HODGSON BURNETT

(1849–1924) writer   63 Portland Place

MANCHESTER-BORN Frances Hodgson spent her early adulthood in the United States. Her reputation as a children's author was established with *Little Lord Fauntleroy* (1886). Following her marriage in 1873 to Swan Moses Burnett, an American ophthalmologist, Frances divided her time between Washington and London, but they divorced in 1898.

She rented this large 1770s house in autumn 1893; its long chilly passages and cavernous cellar provided the inspiration for her historical novel, *A Lady of Quality* (1896). But she struggled to pay the bills and manage her servants, and in 1898 moved to Maytham Hall, Rolvenden, Kent, the grounds of which inspired *The Secret Garden* (1911).

SIR ARTHUR PINERO

(1855–1934) playwright   115A Harley Street

THIS delightful Queen Anne villa dating from 1898 was Pinero's home from 1909 – the year he was knighted – until the time of his death. Born near Sadler's Wells, Arthur Wing Pinero took up acting while in his teens, and performed in provincial repertory before being engaged in 1876 at London's Lyceum, where he supported

Henry Irving*. As a writer, he forged his reputation with a series of comedies – the so-called 'Court' farces – which included *The Magistrate* (1885) and *Dandy Dick* (1887). He had further success with *The Second Mrs Tanqueray* (1893), a bold denunciation of the sexual double standards that were then commonly applied.

GEORGE FREDERICK BODLEY

(1827–1907) architect   109 Harley St. (formerly 49 Upper Harley St.) **15**

A SUPERB proponent of late-Victorian Gothic, Bodley served a five-year apprenticeship (1845–50) in the office of George Gilbert Scott*, where he worked with G. E. Street*. He went on to be

Britain's leading ecclesiastical architect of the late 19th century. The son of a Hull doctor who ended up practising in Harley Street, Bodley spent much of his life in Marylebone. He lived here with his mother

Mary from 1862 until his marriage to Minna Reavely in September 1872, whereupon the newly-weds moved to Hampstead. During his years at number 109, which served as both home and office, Bodley worked on some important early commissions, including St Salvador's, Dundee (1865–74), and St John the Baptist, Tuebrook, Liverpool (1867–70). Following a serious illness in 1868–9, Bodley went into partnership with Thomas Garner, a collaboration that lasted until 1897.

SIR CHARLES LYELL (1797–1875) geologist
W. E. GLADSTONE*
(1809–98) statesman   73 (formerly 53) Harley Street

THE original number 53 was built in the 1770s and demolished in 1905; the present house was designed by W. H. White. Lyell – who was born in Scotland, the son of a botanist – moved here in autumn 1854, from elsewhere in Harley Street. While living here, he wrote *The Antiquity of Man* (1863) and prepared new editions of his most influential works: the three-volume *Principles of Geology* (1830–33) and *Elements of Geology* (1838). Despite his growing physical frailty, Lyell – a mentor and close friend of Charles Darwin* – continued to make geological tours both at home and abroad and, after the death in 1873 of his wife Mary, he dedicated himself wholly to his studies in order to forget his grief. He died here two years later.

Lyell was succeeded at the house – renumbered 73 in 1866 – by William Ewart Gladstone who, having lost the premiership and resigned as leader of the Liberal Party in 1874, moved here in May 1876. During his four years at this address, Gladstone at first distanced himself from politics, taking refuge in literary pursuits in his sparsely furnished study, with its fireplace tiled with Homeric subjects. But the issue of the 'Bulgarian atrocities' – a series of outrages committed by the Turks against Balkan insurrectionists – saw him renew his attacks on Disraeli*, culminating in the famous Midlothian campaign (1879–80), which took Gladstone back into 10 Downing Street for his second term as Prime Minister (1880–85).

SIR STEWART DUKE-ELDER

(1898–1978) ophthalmologist   63 Harley Street

WHEN Scottish-born Duke-Elder moved here in 1934 he entirely rebuilt the house to accommodate his home and flourishing practice, allowing room for two medical student lodgers and his secretary. While living here with his wife and fellow ophthalmologist, Phyllis, he wrote the bulk of his seven-volume *Text-book of* *Ophthalmology* (1932–54), known to students as the 'Ophthalmologists' Bible'. Knighted in 1933, Duke-Elder played a lead role in the foundation in 1947 of the Institute of Ophthalmology; his students were nicknamed 'Duke-Elderberries'. He moved to St John's Wood in 1963, but ran his practice from number 63 until his retirement in 1976.

SIR GEORGE FREDERIC STILL

(1868–1941) paediatrician   28 Queen Anne Street

THROUGH his work as a private practitioner and as physician for diseases of children (1899–1906) at King's College Hospital, Still established child health as a distinct branch of medicine, becoming the first professor of paediatric medicine in England (at King's College London). A somewhat reserved bachelor, he enjoyed a special rapport with children. His pioneering research into childhood arthritis – Still's disease is named after him – was followed by seminal texts on other childhood conditions and a *History of Paediatrics* (1931). Still led a successful campaign to found what is now the Royal College of Paediatrics and Child Health, and presided over the association's first meeting, held at this house in 1928. He retired four years later.

SIR FREDERICK TREVES

(1853–1923) surgeon   6 Wimpole Street **19**

A BRILLIANT student at the London Hospital, the staff of which then included John Hughlings Jackson* and Jonathan Hutchinson*, Treves initially practised in Derbyshire before qualifying as a surgeon and returning to work at the hospital where he had trained. He stayed until 1898, enjoying great celebrity as the foremost practitioner of anatomy and abdominal surgery in the country. Treves once boasted that his operating coat 'was so stiff with congealed blood after many years of use that it would stand upright when placed on the floor'. His consulting rooms here – at a house he shared with his wife Anne and their two daughters – were among the most famous in England. Treves famously rescued Joseph Merrick from being exhibited as 'the Elephant Man'

in freak shows and found him, in 1886, a permanent residence at the London Hospital. When Merrick asked to see inside a family home, Treves brought him here. After 1908 Treves , who counted three monarchs among his patients, lived at Thatched House Lodge in Richmond Park, and abroad.

Sir Frederick Treves's drawing room.

HENRY HALLAM

(1777–1859) historian   67 Wimpole Street **20**

BORN in Windsor into a clerical family, Hallam abandoned a legal career in order to concentrate on historical scholarship. Politically a Whig, he enjoyed a high reputation throughout the 19th century for his two-volume *Constitutional History of England from the Accession of Henry VII to the Death of George II* (1827), which was written while he was living here. His home, where he lived from 1819 to 1840, was immortalised by Tennyson* since the poet's *In Memoriam* (1833) was written in memory of Arthur Henry Hallam (1811–33), Henry's eldest son, who died suddenly while the family were in Vienna. Hallam's time here was also marked by the deaths of his daughter Eleanor in 1837 and his wife Julia in 1840, after which he moved to Belgravia.

EVELYN BARING, 1ST EARL OF CROMER

(1841–1917) colonial administrator   36 Wimpole Street **21**

BORN into a family of bankers at Cromer Hall in Norfolk – the name of which he adopted as his title when he was created an earl in 1901 – Baring spent much of his long career in Egypt and was appointed Consul-General in 1883, with orders to reform the civil administration there. An advocate of British withdrawal from Egypt, Baring only reluctantly supported General Gordon's mission to Khartoum, and devised the eventual peace settlement between France and Britain (1904). He retired to Britain in May 1907, and while living here – from 1908 until his death – wrote several books, including a defence of his policies, *Modern Egypt* (1908), and *Ancient and Modern Imperialism* (1910). In the summer of 1916 he was invited to preside over the Dardanelles Commission. He collapsed and died here the following January.

ELIZABETH BARRETT BARRETT*

(1806–61) poet   50 Wimpole Street **22**

BARRETT – who usually signed her name 'EBB' and was familiarly known as 'Ba', lived in an 18th-century house on this site, demolished in 1935, with her widowed father, the plantation owner Edward Barrett Moulton Barrett. Having moved here in May 1838, she was grief-stricken at the death of two of her brothers two years later. She was confined by chronic illness – which, it is now thought, may have been hypokalemic periodic paralysis (HKPP) – to her room on the third floor at the back of the house, which was gloomily decorated with dark green wallpaper and heavy curtains, while a large ivy blocked out the light from the window. It was here that she completed her highly successful two-volume collection of *Poems* (1844) and where, on 20 May 1845, she first met Robert Browning; the pair had corresponded about poetry. Soon they embarked on a passionate love affair, but Mr Barrett's disapproval compelled them to elope; they were married in old St Marylebone Church on 12 September 1846. 'EBB' was never reconciled with her father, who returned all her letters unopened.

ETHEL GORDON FENWICK

(1857–1947) nursing reformer 20 Upper Wimpole Street **23**

AFTER training in Nottingham and Manchester, Ethel Gordon Manson worked as a sister in the London Hospital before being appointed Matron and Superintendent of Nursing at St Bartholomew's Hospital. She resigned her post on marrying Dr Bedford Fenwick in July 1887, at which point the couple moved here; it was their home for nearly 40 years. Mrs Bedford Fenwick, as she became known, devoted her energies to improving the status of British nurses. At a meeting of matrons and doctors held in the drawing room of her house in November 1887, the British Nurses' Association was established; in 1891 it became the first women's professional body to receive a royal charter. Fenwick's most important achievement was the state registration of nurses, enacted in 1919. Fittingly, hers was the first name listed in the Register of Nurses in England and Wales, and she was appointed to the new statutory body, the General Nursing Council.

JOHN RICHARD GREEN*

(1837–83) historian 4 Beaumont Street **24**

FORMERLY a vicar in Stepney, Green moved to a house on this site in spring 1869. He wrote happily to a friend: 'I enjoy even the cleaner streets, and above all my morning's trot through the Parks. It is such a change too to get a chat when one likes, to be able to get a peep at good pictures, and to have one's mind free for the things one cares about ... I am getting on with work as well ... in fact, I am getting into the literary rut pretty well.' It was while living here that Green wrote *A Short History of the English People* (1874), which outsold all similar works except the *History of England* by Thomas Babington Macaulay* and helped shape a generation's understanding of history. Green moved in 1876, the year before his marriage to Alice Stopford, also a historian, and spent his last years writing *The Making of England* (1882).

CHARLES WESLEY (1707–88) divine and hymn writer
CHARLES WESLEY (1757–1834) musician
SAMUEL WESLEY (1766–1837) musician
1 Wheatley Street   (formerly 1 Chesterfield St., later Great Chesterfield St.) **25**

LIKE his elder brother **John***, Charles Wesley senior spent much of his life as a peripatetic Methodist preacher, and was also an active poet and writer; it is said that he could compose hymns on horseback in shorthand. In 1771 he and his wife Sarah, an accomplished amateur musician, moved from Bristol to a house on this site. Here they lived with their two sons and daughter, another Sarah. Both boys were musical; Charles was a fine harpsichordist and organist, and Samuel became one of the most important English composers of the period, producing works such as the *Ode to St Cecilia* (1794). The brothers gave subscription concerts here, attracting fashionable audiences, and continued to live here with their mother after their father's death.

VICTOR WEISZ, 'VICKY'
(1913–66) cartoonist   Welbeck Mansions, 35A Welbeck Street **26**

BETTER known by his pen name of 'Vicky', Weisz's personal experience of Nazi brutality gave his cartoons – in the *News Chronicle*, among other papers – a particular keenness and urgency. Between 1949 and 1953 he lived, as it transpires, not in the building commemorated by the plaque but in a maisonette flat on the upper floors of the neighbouring property, 35 Welbeck Street, which has since been rebuilt as 33 Welbeck Street. Vicky shared his flat with, in turn, the second (Lucielle) and third (Zlata) of his four wives. By 1954 he had moved to Upper Wimpole Street, where he took his own life 12 years later.

THOMAS YOUNG

(1773–1829) man of science 48 Welbeck Street **27**

AN extraordinarily precocious child, Young developed a lifelong fascination with languages; he was one of the first to attempt to understand Egyptian hieroglyphics, and successfully deciphered some 200 characters of the ancient Egyptian Rosetta Stone, discovered by the French in 1799. After completing his medical training at Cambridge – where he earned the sobriquet 'Phenomenon Young' – he set up in practice in early 1800 as a physician here, where he remained until 1825, sharing the house with his wife Eliza. During these years, he

> 'He knew so much that it was difficult to say what he did not know.'
> *Sir Humphry Davy on Young*

was briefly Professor of Natural Philosophy (1801–3) at the newly founded Royal Institution. Today, he is regarded as the founder of physiological optics, owing to his research into the mechanics of the eye, which also led him to pioneering attempts at formulating a wave theory of light and sound. His most recent biography is sub-titled 'The Last Man who Knew Everything' – not without some justification.

SIR PATRICK MANSON

(1844–1922) father of modern tropical medicine 50 Welbeck Street **28**

MANSON'S discovery of the intermediary role played by bloodsucking insects in transmitting disease paved the way for the breakthrough made by Ronald Ross* in deducing that the malarial parasite developed in the mosquito. A Scot, Manson spent most of his life working as a doctor in China and Hong Kong, but he returned to Britain in 1889 and resumed private practice in London. For the next 20 years he lived and worked at 21 Queen Anne Street, Marylebone (since demolished), and,

from there, successfully lobbied the government to improve its colonial medical service. In 1899 he founded the London School of Tropical Medicine, where he worked as administrator, lecturer and physician. His *Tropical Diseases: A Manual of the Diseases of Warm Climates* (1898) remained the principal authority on the subject for many years. Knighted in 1903, Manson lived in Welbeck Street from 1910 until his retirement in 1912, and died in London ten years later.

HECTOR BERLIOZ

(1803–69) composer

BORN near Lyon, Berlioz devoted himself to composition from the 1820s; it was during the following decade that he produced his most popular works, including *Symphonie Fantastique* (1830), *Harold en Italie* (1834) and *Roméo et Juliette* (1839), while he also made his name as a conductor, and in 1843 published the important *Grand traité d'instrumentation et d'orchestration modernes*. In 1851 he made the second of five trips to London, lodging here in an apartment above the New Beethoven Rooms, in the recently altered 18th-century house where the Beethoven Quartet Society held its meetings from 1845. On the occasion of this visit he was entrusted with the job of examining the musical instruments sent to the Great Exhibition. Early each morning he walked across Hyde Park to the Crystal Palace at South Kensington, and on some evenings he listened to the concerts held in the drawing room below his room at number 58. Berlioz returned

'I could easily hear the whole performance by simply opening my door. One evening I heard Beethoven's Trio in C minor being played. I opened my door wide, Come in, Come in, welcome proud melody! How fine and beautiful it is.'

Berlioz, on living above a concert room

to London in 1852, 1853 and, for the final time, in 1855, conducting a series of performances of his works.

EDWARD GIBBON

(1737–92) historian

7 Bentinck Street

GIBBON lived at a house on this site from early 1773 until his move to Switzerland in 1783, years during which he published the first three volumes of his masterpiece, *The History of the Decline and Fall of the Roman Empire* (6 vols, 1776–88). Before moving in, Gibbon had the house redecorated, paying particular attention to his library: 'the paper of the Room will be a fine shag flock paper, light blue with a gold border, the Book cases painted white, ornamented with a light frize [*sic*]: neither Doric nor Dentulated ... but Academic.' He was delighted with the results: ' ... absolutely the best house in London', he judged.

JAMES SMITHSON

(1764–1829) scientist, founder of the Smithsonian Institution

9 Bentinck Street

BORN in Paris, Smithson was an illegitimate son of the first Duke of Northumberland. He was admitted a Fellow of the Royal Society in 1787 on the strength of his work as a chemist and mineralogist: Smithsonite (zinc carbonate) is named after him. But it was for his foundational bequest for the Smithsonian Institution in Washington DC that he is best known – and his generosity is all the more remarkable since he never set foot in the US.

Childless, Smithson left his entire fortune to a nephew, with provision that if he died without heirs (which is what happened, in 1835) the money should go to the foundation of 'an Establishment for the increase and diffusion of knowledge among men'. Why he chose the United States as the site of this new institution is not clear, though it was always his belief that 'the man of science is of no country, the world is his country and all mankind his countrymen'.

MARTIN VAN BUREN

(1782–1862) eighth US President

7 Stratford Place 32

AS American Minister to Great Britain from September 1831 to April 1832, Van Buren lived in this elegant pilastered terrace, part of a grand cul-de-sac built in around 1771 to 1780 by Richard Edwin on the site of the Lord Mayor's banqueting house. His stay here was a happy and formative period in his career, and Van Buren, known for his charm, gained the close friendship of his Legation Secretary, Washington Irving*. A lawyer of Dutch descent, Van Buren – nicknamed 'Old Kinderhook' after the town of his birth – was President of the United States from 1837 to 1841, but his hard-headed attitude to the deep economic depression of 1837 put paid to his chances of re-election.

SIMÓN BOLÍVAR
(1783–1830) liberator of Latin America   4 (formerly 27) Duke Street **33**

BOLÍVAR enjoyed a privileged upbringing on his family's plantation in Caracas, and in his youth travelled extensively in Europe, where he imbibed the post-revolutionary principles of national self-determination. In June 1810 he landed in England, as part of a deputation from Caracas seeking British support in the fight for Latin American independence – Andrés Bello* was with him. Bolívar and Bello lodged at Morin's Hotel at what was then 27 Duke Street from July to mid-September, during which time they met Francisco de Miranda*.

Returning home in late 1810, Bolívar went on to liberate Caracas from the Spanish in 1813. Over the next 12 years he won independence for Colombia, Venezuela, Ecuador, Peru and Upper Peru, which changed its name to Bolivia in his honour. Declared President of the federation known as Greater (Gran) Colombia in 1821, Bolívar proved to be dictatorial in peace-time, fuelling conflict with neighbouring states and alienating his erstwhile supporters. He survived an assassination attempt in 1828 and died two years later, soon after resigning his presidency.

ALFRED, LORD MILNER
(1854–1925) statesman   14 Manchester Square

MILNER was a controversial figure whose reputation today is overshadowed by his imperialist and racist views. After coming under the influence of Arnold Toynbee* and helping to set up Toynbee Hall in the East End, he entered politics in 1884 as secretary to the Liberal Unionist politician, G. J. Goschen. An able administrator, Milner served in Egypt and as High Commissioner in South Africa (1897–1905), where he took a hard line against the Boers. During the Boer War of 1899–1902, he worked with Lord Roberts* to bring Orange

Free State and the Transvaal under British rule and served as Governor (1901–5) after the war. Milner was among the authors of the Balfour Declaration (1917), and was Secretary of State for War (1918–19) and for the Colonies (1919–21). He moved to 14 Manchester Square in 1921, shortly after marrying the widowed Violet, Lady Edward Cecil; he divided his retirement between this house and Sturry Court, Kent.

JOHN HUGHLINGS JACKSON
(1835–1911) physician   3 Manchester Square **35**

JACKSON moved here in 1871 with his wife (and cousin) Elizabeth and died here in October 1911. After training in York and at St Bartholomew's Hospital, Jackson was helped by Jonathan Hutchinson* to obtain a position at the Metropolitan Free Hospital in 1859. Within a few years he was working as a physician at the London Hospital in Whitechapel and the National Hospital for the Paralysed and Epileptic in Queen Square, Bloomsbury. In his clinical practice, Jackson investigated diseases of the nervous system that caused fits and paralysis, most notably epilepsy, and transformed contemporary understanding of how the brain controlled voluntary movements of the body. For this pioneering work, Jackson has been hailed as the 'father of modern neurology'.

SIR JULIUS BENEDICT
(1804–85) composer   2 Manchester Square **36**

THE son of a rich German banker, Benedict studied music with Johann Nepomuk Hummel in Stuttgart and with Carl Maria von Weber in Dresden, through whom he met Beethoven and Mendelssohn*. He came to London in 1835, and became conductor first of the Italian Opera at the Lyceum and then at Drury Lane, where he premiered his own compositions; these included *The Gipsy's Warning* (1838) and *The Bride of Venice* (1843). His oratorios and his later opera, *The Lily of Killarney* (1862), met with some success, but he was renowned more for his performances of works by his contemporaries, especially those by Balfe* and Mendelssohn; he was also an accomplished pianist. A naturalised British citizen, he was knighted in 1871, in recognition of the leading role he took in popularising classical music.

ROSE MACAULAY

(1881–1958) writer

11–14 Hinde Street **37**

BORN in Rugby, Emilie Rose Macaulay – a descendant of the historian Thomas Babington Macaulay* – was educated at Oxford and published her first novel, *Abbots Verney*, in 1906. She first moved to Marylebone in 1913 after winning a literary competition with her novel *The Lee Shore* (1912), and was introduced into London's literary circles by her childhood friend, Rupert Brooke. A string of successes followed during the 1920s. After being bombed out of her flat in Luxborough Street in March 1941,

'"Take my camel, dear," said my Aunt Dot, as she climbed down from this animal on her return from High Mass.'

The famous opening line of The Towers of Trebizond

Macaulay moved here to Flat 20. Here she wrote perhaps the best known of her 23 novels, *The Towers of Trebizond* (1956). Macaulay died in her flat in October 1958, leaving fragments of a novel, *Venice Besieged*, which was published with her *Letters to a Sister* in 1964.

CAPTAIN FREDERICK MARRYAT

(1792–1848) novelist

3 Spanish Place **38**

A TEARAWAY in his youth, Marryat joined the Navy at the age of 14. Over the next 24 years he proved an able and courageous officer, who saved over a dozen lives at sea; he also designed a new lifeboat. Marryat exploited his naval experiences to good effect in a stream of best-selling adventure stories; while living in this 1780s house, he ventured into writing for children, though his best-known novel, *The Children of the New Forest* (1847), was written after moving to Langham, Norfolk, following his marriage in 1843 to Catherine Shairp. He died there five years later.

GEORGE GROSSMITH

(1874–1935) actor-manager

3 Spanish Place

BORN in London, Grossmith devoted his life to the theatre, first appearing on stage at the age of 18 in his father, George Grossmith senior's*, operetta *Haste to the Wedding* (1892). It was his creation of the 'dude' role of Bertie Boyd in the comedy *The Shop Girl* (1894) that established him on the London stage, and he went on to star in numerous light comedies. He also wrote and produced shows, including some of the first revues to be performed in Britain. In 1919 he and Edward Laurillard opened the Winter Garden Theatre in Drury Lane, which scored a number of musical hits and pioneered cabaret in London in the 1920s. He continued to act, both on stage and in film, and enjoyed great success as Billy Early in the musical *No, No, Nanette* (1925). He lived here from 1909 until 1935, sharing the house with his wife Elizabeth, known during her acting career as Adelaide Astor.

OCTAVIA HILL

(1838–1912) housing reformer,
co-founder of the National Trust

1–3 Garbutt Place
(formerly Paradise Place)

OCTAVIA Hill was born in Wisbech, Cambridgeshire. Following her family's move to central London in 1852, she came into contact with a circle that included F. D. Maurice* and John Ruskin*. A loan from Ruskin enabled Hill to acquire, in spring 1865, this small terrace of early-19th-century cottages, then known as Paradise Place. Here, as the plaque's inscription records, she began her reforming work, transforming these cramped slum dwellings into neat, well-maintained lodgings for seasonal and casual workers, and created a playground for their children in the surrounding space. She managed the buildings and acted as a social worker and counsellor for her tenants, helping them find work and arranging classes; in this, she was assisted by, among others, Emma Cons*. Hill rescued other properties in nearby Freshwater Place and St Christopher's Place as well as in Walworth and Southwark, and campaigned to preserve precious open space in London, crucially saving Parliament Hill Fields from developers. She pioneered the idea of a 'green belt' in her article 'More Air for London' (1888), and together with Hardwicke Drummond Rawnsley and Robert Hunter founded the National Trust in 1893.

CHARLES EAMER KEMPE

(1837–1907) stained-glass artist   37 (formerly 28) Nottingham Place **41**

INITIALLY a student of the architect G. F. Bodley*, the ardently Anglo-Catholic Kempe turned to stained glass in 1864, working as an apprentice to the renowned firm of Clayton & Bell; two years later he founded his own business – the Kempe Studio for Stained Glass and Church Furniture – at 47 Beaumont Street, Marylebone, and made his name in 1869 with his decoration of Bodley's St John the Baptist, Tuebrook, Liverpool. He moved his flourishing studio here from Camden Town in 1886 and remodelled the building to create a small flat in the rooms above, where he lived when in London. The exterior of this late-18th-century house – together with the rest of the terrace – was embellished with bay windows, red-brick trimmings and a gable in 1891–2 by E. Keynes Purchase. In the first-floor studio, Kempe worked with his assistants – who included Arthur Hughes* – to produce the large-scale cartoons for the glass made at the factory he had established in Camden Town. Kempe died here in 1907.

WILLIAM PITT THE YOUNGER

(1759–1806) Prime Minister   120 Baker St. (formerly 14 York Place) **42**

BORN in Bromley, Pitt became – at the age of 24 – Britain's youngest Prime Minister. During his 17 years in office he took the country to war against revolutionary France, and made a lasting impact on domestic politics with his introduction of income tax in 1799 and the union with Ireland of 1800. His failure to persuade George III to agree to grant civil rights to Catholics forced his resignation on 3 February 1801. He moved from Downing Street to Park Place, St James's, and then to this house, built in 1789, in April 1802 (not 1803 as on the plaque). Here, the

Between 1801 and 1804, Pitt was replaced as Prime Minister by Henry Addington. 'Pitt is to Addington, as London is to Paddington', ran a contemporary couplet; Paddington was then a small village.

parlous state of Pitt's own finances were alleviated by the generosity of his friends and by the sale of his country seat in Kent. Pitt returned to office as Prime Minister in May 1804, but chronic ill health and the strains of wartime office led to his early death in January 1806.

SIR HENRY SEGRAVE

(1896–1930) world speed record holder　　St Andrew's Mansions, Dorset St.

IN 1926, the Baltimore-born Segrave set the first of his three land speed records at Southport, Lancashire; he was the first to take the land speed over 200mph. The newly knighted 'Sir Harry' then turned his attention to water, and set a new world record of 98.76mph on Windermere in March 1930, but died on a further run the same day. His plaque marks the flat – number 6 – where Segrave lived between 1917 and 1920, with his wife Doris and their bulldog, Laddie. It was during this period that he started to race at the Brooklands racetrack.

MICHAEL FARADAY

(1791–1867) man of science　　48 (formerly 2) Blandford Street

FARADAY lived and worked here as an apprentice to the bookbinder George Riebau from October 1805 to October 1812. Here he first encountered books on science, in particular Jane Marcet's *Conversations on Chemistry* (1805). Riebau encouraged his young apprentice, and provided space at the back of his shop for Faraday to make scientific instruments. In spring 1812 he introduced himself to the chemist Humphry Davy, who arranged for him to be appointed laboratory assistant at the Royal Institution in 1813. Faraday went on to discover electromagnetic rotation (1821) and electromagnetic induction (1831), which laid the foundation of all present-day applications of electricity. He was an extremely popular lecturer, and in 1826 founded Friday Evening Discourses and the Christmas Lectures for children, which are still the mainstay of the Royal Institution's education programme. Faraday has given his name to both the unit for measuring electrical charge (faraday) and that for measuring capacitance (farad).

SIR FRANCIS BEAUFORT

(1774–1857) admiral and hydrographer　　52 Manchester Street **45**

BORN in Co. Meath, Beaufort joined the Navy aged 15 and started to write a daily weather diary on his very first voyage. He served throughout the wars with France, rising to the rank of commander in 1800. In May 1829, he was appointed Hydrographer to the

Navy. In 1831 he commissioned the *Beagle*, under the command of Robert Fitzroy*, to survey the western shores of Patagonia, and arranged for a naturalist, the young Charles Darwin*, to accompany him. During this expedition, Beaufort's 12-point scale for measuring the strength of wind, which he had devised in 1805, was used for the first time; the Beaufort scale remains the internationally accepted measurement of wind force. He moved away from here in the summer of 1832.

TOM MOORE

(1779–1852) poet · 85 (formerly 44) George Street **46**

MOORE, a Dubliner, took lodgings here when he first arrived in London in spring 1799 to study law at the Middle Temple. It is likely that this remained his London home until 1801, during which time he began publishing poems and songs. His poetry proved extremely popular – in particular, his exotic romance *Lalla Rookh* (1817) and his verse satire *The Fudge Family in Paris* (1818) – though one reviewer denounced him as 'the most licentious of modern versifiers'. He also wrote biographies of Richard Brinsley Sheridan* (1825) and Lord Byron (1830), and a pioneering *History of Ireland* (1835–46). In 1812 he and his wife Elizabeth (Bessy) left London, before settling in Wiltshire.

SIR JOHN ROBERT GODLEY

(1814–61) founder of Canterbury, New Zealand · 48 (formerly 11) Gloucester Place **47**

BORN in Ireland and educated at Oxford, Godley became deeply interested in colonisation, and in 1847 joined forces with Edward Gibbon Wakefield – the co-founder of Wellington – to plan a new settlement on the South Island of New Zealand. Intended as an Anglican colony, the settlement was named Canterbury in honour of the eponymous Archbishop; its capital city, Christchurch, took its name from Godley's Oxford college. As chief agent of the Canterbury Association, Godley travelled in 1849 to New Zealand; after teething troubles, the fledgling colony became a self-governing province in 1852. On his return to London, Godley worked for the Inland Revenue and at the War Office, and championed the cause of colonial self-sufficiency. He moved here in 1858 and died in this house in November 1861.

WILLIAM WILKIE COLLINS

(1824–89) novelist · 65 (formerly 90) Gloucester Place

COLLINS moved here in 1867, and in his first year of residence wrote *The Moonstone* (1868), now hailed as one of the first detective novels in the English language. Named after his godfather, the painter Sir David Wilkie, Collins lived in or near Marylebone for most of his life. While at this address, he was at the height of his powers, having made his reputation with a string of 'sensation novels', among the best known of which is *The Woman in White* (1860). This, however, proved a turbulent period in his private life, for his mistress, Caroline Graves, left him in 1868 on discovering his affair with another woman, Martha Rudd. Although Collins had three children with Martha, Caroline returned to live with him here in 1870, and her daughter Harriet Graves continued to supervise the running of his household; he maintained his relationships with both women until his death. Collins wrote ten novels here, together with numerous short stories, plays and stage adaptations. In April 1888 he moved to nearby 82 Wimpole Street, where he died the following year.

ELIZABETH BARRETT BROWNING*

(1806–61) poet · 99 (formerly 74) Gloucester Place

ELIZABETH Browning lived here with her family from December 1835 to May 1838. The plaque places ready public understanding before strict historical accuracy; during her time here, she was known by her maiden name, Barrett Barrett, or – as she signed herself – 'EBB'. The family – headed by Edward Barrett Moulton Barrett, who had been widowed in 1828 – moved here from Sidmouth, Devon. At first Elizabeth desperately missed the countryside, and described how she had grown 'a double rind thicker and thicker on my spirit'. In May 1836, however, she met Wordsworth and struck up a close friendship with Mary Russell Mitford, who introduced her to the work of Robert Browning, her future husband. While living here, she worked on a collection of ballads and verses that was published in June 1838 as *The Seraphim, and other Poems*, the first work to bear her name on the title page. By the time of its appearance, she had moved to Wimpole Street, which became her family's permanent London residence, and where she is also commemorated with an official plaque.

GEORGE RICHMOND

(1809–96) painter 20 (formerly 10) York Street **50**

THE son of a miniature painter, Richmond trained at the Royal Academy Schools, where he was taught by Henry Fuseli*; in about 1825 he joined the circle of young artists around William Blake* and Samuel Palmer*, known as 'The Ancients'. His first major commission was a portrait of William Wilberforce* (1833), which launched his career as one of the most popular portrait painters of his day. Richmond, who moved here in February 1843, worked at a phenomenal rate: in 1847 he produced nearly 100 portraits, yet was

'Few houses in London can have been visited by a greater variety of interesting people, ranging from F D Maurice [and] the Duke of Wellington to Mrs Manning, the murderess, who came as lady's maid to the Duchess of Sutherland!'

John Richmond, recalling his father's house

rarely satisfied with the results and longed to concentrate on his original and greatest passion: landscape painting. He died here, aged 86.

GERALD KELLY

(1879–1972) portrait painter 117 (formerly 65) Gloucester Place **51**

THE grandson of Frederic Festus Kelly – the founder of Kelly's Post Office Directories – and the son of a curate, Gerald Kelly was born in Paddington and grew up in Camberwell. He studied art in Paris, where he came under the influence of Monet, Degas, Sargent and Sickert*. A year in Burma inspired him to paint his first series of oriental dancers, which were highly popular as prints. Kelly moved here in 1916 and exploited his flair for creating likenesses, turning his house into 'a portrait factory'. In 1945 he completed portraits of George

VI and Queen Elizabeth; he later proved to be an enterprising President of the Royal Academy (1949–54). Kelly worked in the studio he built in the garden, entertaining his sitters with a wide repertoire of songs. He and his wife Jane were greatly attached to their home, and when the lease was due to expire in 1955 Kelly sold manuscripts, proofs and first editions given to him by his great friend Somerset Maugham* in order to buy the freehold; thereafter he lived on the top floor and rented out the rest of the house. He died here in January 1972.

MICHAEL POWELL (1905–90)
EMERIC PRESSBURGER (1902–88)
film-makers   Dorset House, Gloucester Place

EMERIC Pressburger was of Hungarian-Jewish origins; he started writing film scripts while living in Berlin and then Paris, before the politics of continental Europe brought him to London in the mid-1930s. Michael Powell, the son of a Kentish hop farmer, had worked in the film business in London and Nice since 1925. With the encouragement of the film mogul J. Arthur Rank* they came together in 1941 to form 'The Archers' – arguably Britain's most creative and successful film-making partnership – and were together responsible for celluloid classics such as *The Life and Death of Colonel Blimp* (1943), *Black Narcissus* (1947) and *The Red Shoes* (1948). Martin Scorsese unveiled the plaque on what was their company's office between 1942 and 1947 – part of what Scorsese called 'the longest period of subversive filmmaking in a major studio ever'. The decor of the office was spartan, in keeping with the austerity of the period, and there were camp beds in case air raids forced an overnight stay.

SIR LAURENCE GOMME
(1853–1916) folklorist and historian   24 Dorset Square

AS Clerk to the London County Council from 1900 until 1914 Gomme oversaw the transfer of the blue plaques scheme (as it later became known) from the Society of Arts to the LCC in 1901, and the scheme's longevity and success is due in no small part to him. As the LCC's chief administrative officer Gomme oversaw huge transfers of authority to the council in such areas as housing and education. He was also a historian of London, antiquarian and writer; this inevitably fed into his day job, and led to a new reverence for things of the past, especially historic buildings. In 1878 he co-founded the Folklore Society; he was also closely involved in the early history of the Survey of London, an ongoing street-by-street history of the capital – the first volume of which was published in 1900 – and played a part in founding the Victoria County History (1899), a similar endeavour on a wider canvas. Gomme lived here with his wife Alice, also a notable folklorist, from 1895 until 1909. This early-19th-century house has since been thrown together with the neighbouring number 25.

GEORGE GROSSMITH

(1847–1912) actor and author 28 Dorset Square **54**

A T this house, which dates from 1815–20, Grossmith co-authored *The Diary of a Nobody* with his brother Weedon, starring the suburban archetype Charles Pooter. It was as an actor and entertainer that George first found fame, however. After making his name with solo shows, he was engaged in 1877 by Richard D'Oyly Carte*,

and created many of the leading comic roles in the Savoy operas by Gilbert* and Sullivan. In the 1890s he toured Britain and America with his highly successful 'humorous and musical recitals'. He lived here with his wife Emmeline Rosa and their children, among whom was George Grossmith junior*. It remained the family's home until 1902.

EMMA CONS

(1837–1912) philanthropist and founder of the Old Vic 136 Seymour Place **55**

T RAINED as an artist, Cons volunteered in the housing projects of Octavia Hill*. In 1879 she founded the South London Dwellings Company, which in 1884 built model dwellings in Morton Place, Lambeth, known as Surrey Lodge (demolished). A lifelong temperance campaigner, in 1879 Cons founded the Coffee Music Hall Company, with the aim of developing the coffee tavern as a non-alcoholic alternative to pubs. Her first venture was the Old Vic in

Waterloo Road, which opened as the Royal Victoria Coffee Music Hall in 1880, and later became the venue for Morley College's evening classes. She passed its management to her niece, Lilian Baylis* in 1899, and in the same year she took her seat as one of three female members of the new London County Council. Cons acquired this building – till then the Walmer Castle pub – in 1879 and converted it into a coffee tavern; she occupied rooms here until 1889, when she moved to Surrey Lodge.

CATO ST. CONSPIRACY

1A (formerly 6) Cato St. **56**

T HE plaque marks a former stable building in a mews, which is entered via an archway from Crawford Place. The Cato Street

Conspiracy was a plot by a group of insurrectionist London radicals to assassinate the British Cabinet. It was led by Arthur Thistlewood,

but – unknown to him – his second-in-command was a government spy, George Edwards. The conspiracy was foiled when, on the evening of 23 February 1820, the police raided the loft above the stables where the plotters met; a constable was killed in the ensuing fracas (*above*). Ten conspirators were arrested and tried for high treason; five were publicly executed at Newgate on 1 May, and the others were transported. By using an *agent provocateur* Lord Liverpool's government successfully discredited the radical movement and bolstered public support for the repressive legislation passed in the wake of the Peterloo Massacre of 1819. Crowds came here to view these notorious premises; the street's name was soon changed to Horace Street, which it remained until 1937.

SIR FABIAN WARE

(1869–1949) founder of the Imperial
War Graves Commission   14 Wyndham Place

A FORMER newspaper editor and civil servant, Fabian Ware volunteered for the Red Cross in the First World War, and was struck by the complete absence of provision to mark the graves of those who died in action. He began recording these with his own mobile unit, which was given the name of the Graves Registration Commission in 1915; in 1917, placed under the Army's wing, it became the Imperial (and later Commonwealth) War Graves Commission. It now looks after 1.7 million war graves. Ware lived at this Georgian townhouse from 1911 to 1919; it was later the home of the art collector Brinsley Ford.

JOHN LENNON

(1940–80) musician and songwriter 34 Montagu Square

I N July 1968, John Lennon moved into a basement and ground-floor maisonette here and stayed for around five months, a period during which he worked on the Beatles' *White Album*. It was the first home he shared with Yoko Ono – who unveiled the plaque – and it was here too, downstairs, that the controversial naked photograph was taken for the cover of their first album together, *Unfinished Music No. 1: Two Virgins* (1968). The apartment has multiple musical associations; Ringo Starr bought it in 1965, and it was briefly tenanted by

All four Beatles used a flat at 57 Green Street, Mayfair, as a crash-pad in 1963. It was equipped with a record player, but had no kettle.

Paul McCartney and Jimi Hendrix* in turn. Lennon and Ono's time here was brought to an end when, on 18 October 1968, the flat was raided by police, and the attendant publicity destroyed any hope of privacy. Lennon's subsequent conviction for possession of cannabis later became the basis for efforts to deny him residency in the United States.

ANTHONY TROLLOPE

(1815–82) novelist 39 Montagu Square 59

T ROLLOPE moved here with his wife Rose in 1873. An employee of the Post Office from the age of 19, Trollope made his most significant contribution to the organisation in 1852, when he pioneered the use of roadside pillar boxes, which were soon set up throughout the United Kingdom. He began writing his first novel while stationed in Ireland on Post Office duties, and followed it with the six-part *Barchester Chronicles* (1855–67). Trollope's portrayal of clergy and gentry in the fictional county of Barsetshire proved to

be phenomenally popular. Able to command fees of up to £3,000 for his novels, Trollope resigned from the Post Office in 1867 to concentrate on his writing, having already started a second series, the Palliser novels. While living in this house of *c*.1810–11, he completed the last three novels in the Palliser series and wrote the longest and most serious of his novels, *The Way We Live Now* (1875), which is partly set in nearby Welbeck Street. In 1880 he moved to Sussex, but later returned to Marylebone, where he died in a nursing home.

MUSTAPHA RESCHID PASHA

(1800–58) Turkish statesman and reformer

1 Bryanston Square

RESCHID, who was born in Constantinople, entered public service at an early age, and served as ambassador in Paris – a post he later held twice more – before travelling to Britain to perform a similar role in 1836. By April 1839 he and the Turkish Embassy had moved to 1 Bryanston Square, a magnificent five-storey stuccoed house built in 1811 to designs by Joseph Parkinson; he stayed here for the next four and a half months, and it continued as the embassy until the late 19th century. Reschid's diplomatic work was directed towards improving relations between Britain and Turkey but he failed to secure the aim of his second mission, which was to form an alliance (though he did help to embroil Britain in the Crimean War). After returning to his homeland in August 1839, he held the office of Grand Vizier six times between 1845 and 1857, and is regarded as one of his country's great statesmen. His most notable reform was the Tanzimat, a wholesale remodelling of Turkish administration and legislature, which brought about an end to slavery and enshrined the principle of equality.

ELIZABETH GARRETT ANDERSON

(1836–1917) the first woman to qualify as a doctor in Britain

20 Upper Berkeley Street

AFTER meeting Elizabeth Blackwell, an Englishwoman who had gained an MD in the United States, Elizabeth Garrett became determined to train as a doctor. She sidestepped the ban on female medical students at universities and hospitals by studying privately, and exploited a loophole that allowed her to qualify as a Licentiate of the Society of Apothecaries in 1865. Later that year, she set up in practice here in Upper Berkeley Street, giving lectures on physiology to a female audience. In June 1866 she moved her practice

around the corner to 69 Seymour Place. This subsequently became the New Hospital for Women, the first hospital in Britain to be staffed entirely by women; having moved to Euston Road, it was renamed after its founder in 1918. She married the ship owner J. G. S. Anderson in 1871 and three years later – the year of the founding of the London School of Medicine for Women, of which she served as Dean from 1883 to 1902 – moved to 4 Upper Berkeley Street, where she lived until 1902.

MICHAEL WILLIAM BALFE

(1808–70) composer   12 (formerly 7) Seymour Street

DUBLIN-BORN, Balfe first came to London in 1823 to study music under Charles Edward Horn, and travelled in the mid-1820s to Italy and France, where his career as an opera singer took off under the patronage of Cherubini and Rossini. While in Italy, he staged three of his own operas, and after returning to England in 1834 achieved notable success. His most popular opera, *The Bohemian Girl* (1843), with its well-known ballad 'I Dreamt that I Dwelt in Marble Halls', remained a hit for over a century. At this address – which he shared with his wife, the Hungarian singer Lina Roser – Balfe completed some of his last operas and wrote the cantata *Mazeppa* (1862). In 1864 he moved to Rowney Abbey, Hertfordshire, where he died six years later.

SITE OF TYBURN TREE

Junction of Edgware Road and Bayswater Road

THOUSANDS of public executions took place at these notorious gallows, which stood next to the Tyburn brook, the site of which is marked by a stone pavement plaque. The earliest recorded execution was that of William Fitz Osbert ('Longbeard') in 1196. The last hanging here – of the highwayman John Austin – took place on 3 November 1783. The lower branches of an elm tree formed the first gibbet, but in 1571 huge triangular gallows were built, capable of hanging up to 24 prisoners at once. Immense crowds would gather to watch the condemned die on the gallows and a raucous and carnivalesque mood gave way to silent sympathy if the crowd believed the individual to be innocent. Fear of public disorder and rioting persuaded the government to move executions to Newgate Prison in 1783.

PADDINGTON AND BAYSWATER

WHEN development of these districts began at the beginning of the 19th century, their starting-point was close to what is now Marble Arch – itself the former public execution site of Tyburn*. The area was dubbed Tyburnia as a result. Originally laid out by Samuel Pepys Cockerell, the father of the architect C. R. Cockerell*, the area developed rapidly, especially with the opening of the Great Western terminus at Paddington in 1854.

Districts south of the railway were entirely urbanised by 1870 and were popular, even if Tyburnia never quite matched Belgravia as a fashionable address. The journalist George Augustus Sala characterised the inhabitants as 'mushroom aristocrats, millionaires . . . people of that sort', an observation that resonates with some – but not all – of the figures commemorated in Paddington and Bayswater as a whole.

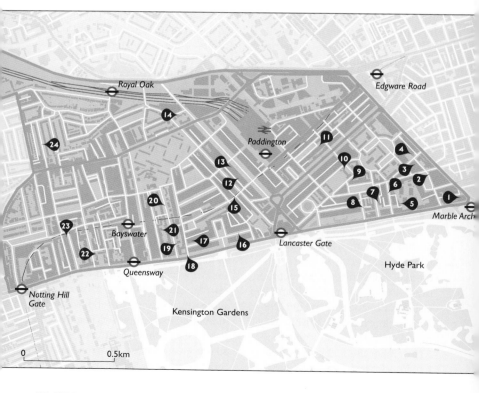

LORD RANDOLPH CHURCHILL

(1849–95) statesman

2 Connaught Place 1

ONE of the most flamboyant public figures of his era, Randolph Churchill was the father of Winston Churchill*, who lived here when he was young. Randolph became an MP in 1874 and took much credit for reviving the moribund Conservatives, thanks to his great oratorical skills. As Secretary of State for India, he was largely responsible for the annexation of Upper Burma – the final addition to British India. Churchill moved to Connaught Place, which is part of the early-19th-century Tyburnia development, early in 1883. The plaque is unfortunately sited on what used to be number 1: he lived at number 2. Churchill's American wife Jennie had it refurbished,

> A strong supporter of the union between Great Britain and Ireland, it was Randolph Churchill who coined the phrase 'Ulster will fight, Ulster will be right'.

installing electric lights (which she claimed to be the first in any London home), although the noise of the dynamo in the cellar 'greatly excited all the horses as they approached our door'. She wondered, being so close to the gallows at Tyburn, 'if the house would be full of wailing ghosts; but frankly I never saw or heard one'. By early 1893 the Churchills had moved to Grosvenor Square, Mayfair.

MARIE TAGLIONI

(1804–84) ballet dancer

14 Connaught Square 2

BORN in Stockholm into a family of choreographers and dancers, Taglioni made her debut in 1822. She was a pioneer of dancing *sur les pointes*, widely admired for the grace and lightness of her technique; among those who lionised her were Victor Hugo and William Makepeace Thackeray*. By the time of her first performance in London in 1829, Taglioni was already renowned; three years later,

she appeared at Covent Garden in the ballet for which she became best known, *La Sylphide*. She retired in 1847, and spent time in Italy before returning to London, where she worked as a teacher of deportment, her fortune having been dissipated through bad investment and the impact of the Franco-Prussian War. Taglioni lived in Connaught Square from 1875 to 1880, first at number 14 and then at number 6.

OLIVE SCHREINER

(1855–1920) author

16 Portsea Place **3**

SOUTH African by birth, Olive Schreiner was the daughter of a German-born missionary and his English wife. She drew on her tough upbringing in her most famous work, *The Story of an African Farm* (1883), a novel originally published under the pseudonym of Ralph Iron. She also wrote a collection of feminist and socialist allegories entitled *Dreams* (1890) and the treatise *Woman and Labour* (1911). Her free-thinking and anti-imperialist beliefs led to a breach with most of her family and friends in South Africa and she spent two long spells in England (1881–9 and 1913–20). Shortly after moving here in August 1885 she told her lover Havelock Ellis* that she was going through 'a very dark and bitter moment of my life', and was thinking fondly of her South African home. Schreiner returned there in 1889, and despite her failing health became increasingly involved in politics. Her brother, Will, was Prime Minister of Cape Colony in 1898–1900.

RICHARD TAUBER

(1891–1948) lyric tenor

297 Park West, Edgware Road **4**

TAUBER was the son of an actor and came from an Austrian-Jewish background. He was famous for his performances in the operettas of Franz Lehár; one such featured Tauber's best-known song, 'You Are My Heart's Delight'. From 1922 he worked for the Vienna and Berlin state operas but when the Nazis came to power in 1933 he fled Germany for his native Austria. Tauber first lived in London after his marriage to the English actress Diana Napier in 1936. He raised spirits during the Second World War with radio broadcasts of such tunes as 'We'll Gather Lilacs' by Ivor Novello* and composed several works, including the operetta *Old Chelsea* (1943). In 1940, Tauber became a naturalised British citizen, and moved to a ninth-floor flat in this vast 1930s block in the summer of 1947, telling his partly estranged wife Diana that 'My new flat is very sweet and cosy, very quiet and away from the noise'. Conveniently, his mistress, Esther Moncrieff, lived directly above him. As well as having a complicated personal life, Tauber was beset by financial and health worries. His performance of *Don Giovanni* at the Opera House in September 1947 turned out to be his last, and he died in a Marylebone clinic the following year.

LUCIE RIE

(1902–95) potter

LUCIE Gomperz, as she was born, trained in her home city of Vienna, and moved to London to escape the Nazi threat in 1938. She and her husband Hans Rie intended to continue to the United States; in the event, only he did so (they were later divorced), while she settled in the Bayswater mews studio that now bears her plaque. She was little known in London when she arrived, and at first made ceramic buttons for high-class fashion, together with simple items of jewellery; later she became known for domestic ware. A thoroughly modernist potter with a functional aesthetic, Lucie Rie pioneered the production of stoneware in an electric kiln. Her application of glaze to unfired clay – a technique adopted initially because she had no easy access to a kiln – became a signature of her work. For a time Rie shared her workshop with the German refugee Hans Coper. It was always her habit to rise early and bake Viennese cakes, which she served to her afternoon visitors. She died at Albion Mews, over half a century after first moving there. Part of Rie's studio has since been recreated at the V&A.

SIR CHARLES VYNER BROOKE

(1874–1963) the last Rajah of Sarawak

VYNER Brooke's great-uncle James founded the Brooke dynasty of white rajahs when he was granted the title in 1841 by Rajah Muda Hassim, uncle of the Sultan of Brunei, in acknowledgement of his help in quelling a rebellion in Sarawak, on Borneo. Charles succeeded as the third Rajah in 1917, though his appetite for the business of government was slender. He shared power with his brother Bertram and later with his nephew Anthony, and devolved many functions to his adviser, Gerard MacBryan, and a committee of administration. His major achievement was the establishment of Sarawak's first constitutional government in September 1941, the centenary of his family's rule. On the Japanese invasion three months later, Brooke took refuge in Australia before coming to London in 1943. Other than a brief return to Sarawak in 1946, he remained in London for the rest of his life. After the war he controversially ceded power to the British Crown. Brooke died in this 1830s terraced house – his home since 1949 – just a few months before Sarawak became part of the Federation of Malaysia.

W. H. SMITH

THE 'Son' of W. H. Smith & Son, William Henry Smith became a partner in his father's business in 1846. The firm's highly profitable station bookstalls – initially on the route of the London and North-Western Railway – were his idea. From his refusal to sell 'unsuitable' books, Smith – a devout Christian who had considered entering the Church – was dubbed the 'North-Western Missionary'. Using his position as a successful businessman to move into politics, Smith was elected Conservative MP for Westminster in 1868 and held several offices in the Cabinets of Disraeli* and Salisbury*, including First Lord of the Treasury and Leader of the House of Commons (1887–91). He was also a notable philanthropist and rendered a lasting service to Londoners by securing Victoria Embankment Gardens as a public open space in 1875. Smith lived in this house of about 1840 for 20 years, following his marriage to the widowed Emily Leach in 1858.

A kiosk at Waterloo Station in the 1960s.

SIR GILES GILBERT SCOTT

(1880–1960) architect Chester House, Clarendon Place **8**

UNTIL his death, Scott lived with his wife Louise and two sons in this 'restrained villa', which he designed in 1925–6. Born in Hampstead into a family of architects – his grandfather was George Gilbert Scott* – Giles won the competition to design a new Anglican cathedral in Liverpool, despite being aged just 22 and a Roman Catholic. Though consecrated in 1924, the cathedral was not completed until many years after his death. From his offices in Gray's Inn, Scott designed numerous other churches and acted as consultant architect for the power stations at Battersea and Bankside (now Tate Modern). He supervised the rebuilding of the House of Commons after the Second World War, and was also responsible for the most famous red British telephone boxes – the dome-topped Kiosk 2 design of 1926 and the squarer Kiosk 6 of 1935. Of his brick-built neo-Georgian home, Chester House, one critic commented that its design recalled Scott's exhortation 'to do all things in measure, even if in these commonplace times there is more money in being surprising'.

LADY VIOLET BONHAM CARTER, BARONESS ASQUITH OF YARNBURY

(1887–1969) politician and writer 43 (formerly 40) Gloucester Square **9**

THE daughter of one Liberal leader, Herbert Henry Asquith*, Violet Bonham Carter was the mother-in-law of another, Jo Grimond, and was the first female President of the Liberals (1945–7). She was a notable voice against the appeasement of Hitler; Churchill, a friend, made her a governor of the BBC, and she later wrote *Winston Churchill as I Knew Him* (1965). Twice defeated in pursuit of a Commons seat, Violet Bonham Carter was made a life peer in 1964 and campaigned for, among other causes, family allowances and an end to arms sales to Nigeria in the wake of the Biafran crisis. Her husband was Maurice Bonham Carter, 'Bongie', who was principal private secretary to her father. Together with their children, they lived in this substantial house of 1844 from 1935 until 1952; when it was converted into flats in 1953, they lived on the first floor. 'The flat is spacious & will be delightful when we get it straight. But oh for Cupboards!' remarked Violet in January 1953. She remained here for the rest of her life.

ROBERT STEPHENSON

(1803–59) engineer

THE son of the railway pioneer George Stephenson, Robert set up in business with his father and others at the age of 19. The firm, Robert Stephenson & Co., had its works in Newcastle – the first locomotive works in the world. In 1833 Stephenson was appointed Chief Engineer of the London to Birmingham Railway (1838), and moved to London. He moved to 34 Gloucester Square (now demolished) in 1847, the year of his election to Parliament for Whitby. The widowed Stephenson was a convivial host of Sunday lunches, entertaining 'many

Stephenson's drawing room had shelves 'so liberally stocked with works of curious contrivance, and philosophical toys, that they had almost the appearance of a museum. Singularly constructed clocks, electric instruments, and improved microscopes . . . were arranged on all sides.'

chiefs of literature and science', but he became prone to depression after the death of his brother-in-law and close friend John Sanderson in 1853. He died at this address.

HERTHA AYRTON

(1854-1923) physicist

PHOEBE Sarah Marks was born in Portsea, the daughter of a Polish-Jewish watchmaker whose family had fled pogroms. At Girton College she embraced her nickname of Hertha, and went on to make some important scientific and technological advances, filing 26 separate patents. For her work in tracing the hissing of an electric arc to the reaction of carbon and oxygen, she was admitted as the first female member of the Institution of Electrical Engineers (now the IET); Hertha was also the first woman to read a paper to the Royal Society.

She lived in Norfolk Square for the last 20 years of her life, initially with her husband and fellow scientist Will Ayrton. While living here, she developed the Ayrton flapper fan for dispersing poison gas from trenches, entertained Marie Curie, and – as an ardent supporter of votes for women – cared for suffragette hunger strikers, including Emmeline Pankhurst*. 'There are two or more detectives in front, two at the back, one at least on the roof of the nearest empty house; and a taxi waiting to pursue, if Mrs P. should get up and run away!' she recorded.

SUSAN LAWRENCE

(1871–1947) social reformer

LAWRENCE was born in this impressive terrace of 1840s stuccoed houses, the daughter of a successful solicitor, and lived here until 1917. She studied mathematics at University College London and at Cambridge, and was elected to the LCC in 1910. Two years later she abandoned her Conservative allegiance for Labour, and returned to the council under her new colours for Poplar. In 1921 she was one of the Poplar councillors imprisoned for refusing to pay what they regarded as unfairly weighted dues to the LCC (and was annoyed when she was forbidden to smoke in Holloway Prison). From 1913–45, Lawrence was a member of the executive of the Fabian Society* and became one of the first three women Labour MPs when she was elected for East Ham North in 1923. She held junior office in the first two Labour governments, and was the first woman to chair the party conference in 1930. With her upper-class accent, monocle and legendary indifference to dress, 'our Susan', as she was known, cut an unmistakable figure: Beatrice Webb, a critical admirer of Lawrence, wrote that she belonged 'to the old order of irreproachable female celibates'.

CHARLES MANBY

(1804–84) civil engineer

MANBY'S father Aaron owned the Horseley ironworks in Staffordshire, and the young Charles helped his father to build what is said to have been the world's first iron steamboat, the modestly christened *Aaron Manby*. This vessel sailed for France in 1822, with Charles Manby on board as Chief Engineer. The following year, Manby was given charge of the gas-supply company established in Paris by his father, and he went on to manage an ironworks in South Wales before establishing himself in London in 1835 as a specialist in heating and ventilation systems. As the first permanent Secretary of the Institute of Civil Engineers from 1839 to 1856, Manby was credited with raising the status of his profession. In 1856 he became the London representative for Robert Stephenson & Co., and was a member of the international commission on the feasibility of constructing the Suez Canal. He lived here from about 1870 to 1876 with his second wife Harriet and his stepson, Arthur Robert Hood.

ALEXANDER HERZEN

(1812–70) Russian
political thinker

1 Orsett Terrace
(formerly Orsett House) **14**

KNOWN as the 'father of Russian socialism', Herzen was exiled to London in 1852, in the wake of the revolutions of 1848. He intended to stay no more than a month, but was inspired by the indefatigability of Polish exiles and produced underground publications for circulation in his own homeland, the most influential of which was the journal *Kolokol* ('The Bell'). This was published from 1857–67 and attacked the autocratic tsarist regime, advocating the abolition of serfdom and censorship. As the son of a

'... about as boring as that of worms in a cheese'

Herzen's initial impression of life in London, 1855

nobleman, Herzen was better off than most refugees, and extended traditional Russian hospitality to visitors, many of whom were fellow exiles. He lived at this detached Italianate 1840s villa from November 1860 until June 1863, entertaining Tolstoy, Dostoevsky and Turgenev here, as well as the anarchist Michael Bakunin.

TOMMY HANDLEY

(1892–1949) radio comedian   Flat 1, Amersham House, 34 Craven Road **15**

HANDLEY was living here with his wife Rosalind, a singer, by autumn 1936 and remained there throughout the war years. A bomb blast of 1941 threw him out of bed, after which he is said to have dusted himself down and given an impromptu performance for a resting fire crew. Liverpool-born, Handley was in the Royal Naval Air Service in the First World War, and joined a concert party while on active duty. Soon he was a regular performer in variety programmes, both on stage and on the fledgling BBC Radio. Handley is widely

remembered as the star of *ITMA*, an acronym for 'It's That Man Again' – the 'man' being a veiled reference to Adolf Hitler. The show, scripted by Ted Kavanagh, ran for 310 episodes over the ten years from 1939; much of its innuendo-laden comedy centred on bureaucratic obstructiveness and incompetence, and relied heavily on memorable catchphrases, including the charlady's 'Can I do you now, sir?' and Handley's own 'TTFN' ('Ta ta for now'). The fun was cut short by Handley's untimely death: thousands turned out to pay their respects at his funeral.

SIR EDWARD FRANKLAND

(1825–99)
chemical scientist

14 Lancaster Gate
(formerly 56 Upper Hyde Park Gardens)

THE concept of valency – the combining power of a chemical element, in terms of the number of hydrogen atoms with which it is capable of bonding – is down to Frankland. On this rest all discoveries in structural chemistry made since, including the entire field of organometallic chemistry. In terms of public health, Frankland's greatest legacy lay in identifying the concentration of nitrates as a key indicator of water pollution: by this means were many contaminated supplies stopped, efficient filtration systems developed and legislative advances made. Having succeeded A. W. Hofmann* to the professorship at the Royal College of Chemistry in 1868, Frankland moved to this house, part of a richly ornamented mid-19th-century terrace, in 1870. Maggie, one of his four children, remembered that it had been 'most frightfully damaged by the extenants, who must have been a dreadful vulgar lot'. Unfortunately, Frankland's wife Sophie died of tuberculosis in 1874; he remarried the following year, had two further children and stayed at Lancaster Gate until 1880. Three years earlier he had become the first President of the Institute of Chemistry.

FRANCIS BRET HARTE

(1836–1902) American writer

74 Lancaster Gate

HARTE was born in Albany, New York State, and moved to California in 1854, where he turned to writing and journalism. He produced parodies of famous contemporaries such as Dickens* and Disraeli* but is better remembered for his stories of frontier life in the American West, such as 'The Luck of Roaring Camp' (1868). When his home audience tired of the formula, Harte found a new readership in Europe. He settled permanently in London in 1885, lodging at first with a Belgian diplomat, Arthur Van de Velde, and his wife Marguerite, who helped translate his works into French and to adapt several for the stage. Late in 1895 Harte moved alone to this end house of a grand terrace of 1865, where he remained for the rest of his life; he died at Marguerite Van de Velde's home near Camberley, Surrey. *Salomy Jane* (1898), based on an earlier story, was a posthumous West End hit in 1907, and his stories inspired many cowboy films of the silent era.

SIR JAMES BARRIE*

(1860–1937)
novelist and dramatist

100 Bayswater Road
(formerly Leinster Corner) **18**

BETTER known as J. M. Barrie, James Barrie worked as a journalist in Nottingham before settling in 1885 in London, where he first made his name with his sketches of life in his native Scotland, *Auld Licht Idylls* (1888). In June 1902 he moved to this house, one of a pair of 1824 villas – a rare survival in this immediate area – with his wife, the actress Mary Ansell. Barrie's play *Quality Street*, the name of which is perpetuated in a chocolate-box selection, was produced at the Vaudeville Theatre that September, and *The Admirable Crichton* premiered in November. It was here, in a study fitted out above a mews building at the bottom of the back garden (now demolished), that Barrie wrote *Peter Pan* (1904) and *Peter Pan in Kensington Gardens* (1906); the gardens, which lie opposite, were a place of inspiration and retreat for him. The models for the Darling family were the children of Arthur and Sylvia Llewellyn Davies, for whom Barrie later acted as guardian. With Sylvia – the sister of Gerald du Maurier* – Barrie became infatuated and this, alongside his wife's affair with a young actor, led to their divorce in October 1909. Barrie left for a flat at the Adelphi.

JOHN LOUDON (1783–1843)
JANE LOUDON (1807–58)

landscape gardeners

3 Porchester Terrace **19**

JOHN Claudius Loudon was instrumental in having the wall around Hyde Park replaced by a fence, to promote its enjoyment by the public as an open space. Numbers 3 and 5 Porchester Terrace were built in 1823–5 to his own design, featuring a prominent conservatory topped with a wrought-iron dome. To the rear was the office of his *Gardener's Magazine*, started in 1826.

J. C. Loudon's 'Hints Respecting the Manner of Laying out the Grounds of the Public Squares in London' (1803) led to the introduction of plane, sycamore and almond trees to the city – a fine legacy to London.

Lanarkshire-born Loudon lived here initially with his mother, Agnes, and after 1830 with his young wife Jane, author of the early science fiction work *The Mummy! A Tale of the Twenty-Second Century* (1827), a publication that had made Loudon anxious to meet her. Jane's later horticultural primers, such as *Instructions in Gardening for Ladies* (1840), were partly written from necessity, as Loudon's monumental *Arboretum et Fruticetum Britannicum* (1838) – in which he was assisted by John Lindley* – had saddled them with vast debts. Loudon, who had conquered laudanum addiction developed after the amputation of an arm, died at Porchester Terrace, collapsing into his wife's arms shortly after he had finished dictating *Self-Instruction for Young Gardeners* (1845) to her. Jane was granted a civil-list pension, and died here 15 years later.

JOHN LINNELL* (1792–1882) painter
CAMILLE SILVY (1834–1910)
photographer   38 Porchester Terrace **20**

NUMBER 38 was built by the painter John Linnell in about 1830 as his own residence and to his own design, hence its unusual proportions. Known for his landscapes, including local views such as *Kensington Gravel Pits* (1811-12), Linnell added a studio in 1837, which is now number 36. From 1859 he leased the studio (and from 1862 the house too) to the photographer Camille Silvy, who excelled in the lucrative art of the *carte-de-visite* portrait, the calling-card-cum-selfie of its day. He took over 17,000 carefully posed images here, with his sitters drawn from the upper echelons of society, including Prince Albert, Queen Emma of Hawaii, Harriet Martineau and even John Linnell: 'I little thought, when I built it, [the studio] would be used for such a purpose,' was his predecessor's comment. Sitters were carefully set against stylised backgrounds: the immaculately attired Silvy donned a fresh pair of white gloves for each assignment. Abruptly, he gave up the business in 1868, believing that exposure to chemicals had affected his health, and died in an asylum in his native France, having suffered from what may have been a bipolar condition.

SIR WILLIAM STERNDALE BENNETT
(1816–75) composer   38 Queensborough Terrace **21**

THE son of the organist of Sheffield parish church, Bennett was a musical prodigy, championed by Mendelssohn*, whom he visited in Germany. From 1837 he settled in London; among his early successes was *The Naiades* (1836), a popular orchestral work, and *Suite de Pièces* (1841) for piano. Bennett was an excellent pianist and many of his best compositions were written for the instrument. In 1856 he was elected Professor of Music at Cambridge and from 1866 he was Principal of the Royal Academy of Music, where his pupils included Arthur Sullivan. He moved to this mid-Victorian house in autumn 1865 after the death of his wife Mary, and stayed for five years. Bennett enjoyed a creative renaissance here, with such works as the sacred cantata *The Woman of Samaria* (1867) and the piano sonata *The Maid of Orleans* (1873). Knighted in 1871, he returned to this address briefly the following year.

SIR ROWLAND HILL*

(1795–1879) postal reformer

1 Orme Square **22**

HILL was instrumental in effecting vital reforms to a cumbersome and expensive postal system, where costs were charged to the recipient. He was living in Orme Square when the Penny Postage Act passed into law, having moved here with his wife Caroline in 1839; one of a pair of stucco-fronted houses, it had then not long been built. In 1840, as a result of Hill's work, the world's first official postage stamps were issued: the penny black and the twopenny blue. While overseeing these reforms he occupied a post at the Treasury at £1,500 a year, but lost it on a change of government in 1842 – an event that prompted 'vigorous retrench-ment' in his household expenses, for which Hill credited his wife Caroline. They moved to Brighton – where he worked for the London and Brighton Railway – in 1843, and finally on to Bartram House, Hampstead, where he died.

ALICE MEYNELL

(1847–1922) poet and essayist

47 Palace Court **23**

BORN Alice Thompson, Meynell spent much of her early life in Italy. She was a Catholic convert and religious themes imbue her poetry, the first volume of which – *Preludes* – was published in 1875, with illustrations by her sister Elizabeth. Among the admirers of her verse were Coventry Patmore* and George Meredith* but, although there was a suggestion that she might succeed Tennyson* as Poet Laureate, Alice considered that her best work was in prose. She wrote for numerous periodicals, and – together with her husband, the journalist Wilfrid Meynell – edited the *Weekly Register* and a monthly, *Merry England*. Their five-storey

house in Palace Court was designed for them by Leonard Stokes in 1890, and forms quite a contrast with its neighbours. The Meynells did most of their work at their dining-room table, so recorded their daughter Viola – herself a successful writer and one of their seven children to survive infancy. The couple's Sunday 'at homes' attracted figures such as Oscar Wilde*, Aubrey Beardsley* and W. B. Yeats*. A regular visitor, the writer Charles Lewis Hind, recalled 'arriving at about half-past three, staying till midnight, and meeting in the course of the year most of the literary folk worth knowing'.

GUGLIELMO MARCONI

(1874–1937) pioneer of wireless communications   71 Hereford Road

MARCONI was born in Bologna to an Italian father and an Irish mother. He came to London in February 1896, at the age of 21, and lived at a guesthouse run by a Mrs Sophia Gerstner here for some 18 months; while here, on 2 June 1896, he filed his famous patent for 'Improvements in Transmitting Electrical Impulses and Signals and in Apparatus therefor'. A fellow lodger recalled being shown Marconi's 'large room at the top of the house facing the road', with 'wires all round it' suggesting that Marconi actually conducted experiments here; he certainly brought from Italy

When Marconi died in Rome in July 1937 all radio transmitters in the world were silent for two minutes as a mark of respect.

his apparatus, which was damaged by the rough handling of HM Customs. In July 1897, while still in London, he founded the firm that became Marconi's Wireless Telegraph Company (later Marconi). Four years later he made the first transatlantic wireless transmission. Marconi, co-recipient of the Nobel Prize for Physics in 1909, settled permanently in Italy in 1914.

FITZROVIA

THE name 'Fitzrovia' to describe the area between Oxford Street and the Euston Road is relatively new. Dating from the mid-20th century, it is supposed to derive from the Fitzroy Tavern in Charlotte Street, rather than from Fitzroy Square, and has largely replaced the district's older name of 'North Soho' (though 'Noho' is sometimes used). Starting in about 1720, the area was developed in piecemeal fashion over the following century, mostly on a modest scale. An exception to this is the impressive Fitzroy Square, which was planned and partly built by Robert Adam* in 1790–94. The relentless move westwards of fashionable London meant that even these fine houses were soon subdivided, and the district became a favourite low-rent refuge for artists, craftsmen and writers. Fitzrovia has been extensively redeveloped since the Second World War, and the Post Office (now BT) Tower (1961–4) is a looming presence wherever you are.

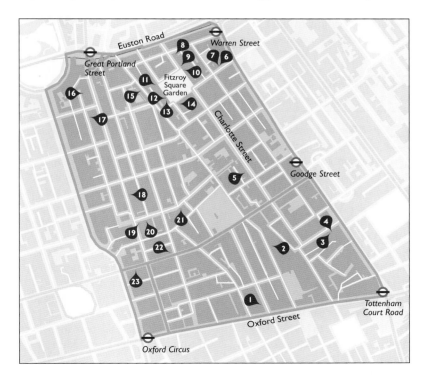

SAMUEL TAYLOR COLERIDGE*

(1772–1834) poet and philosopher   71 Berners Street

DEVON-BORN Coleridge lived in a house on this site for about 18 months in 1812–13, sharing it with his friend John Morgan and Morgan's family. Coleridge had, by this time, established himself as a writer; but his fortunes had taken a turn for the worse. Having separated from his wife Sara in 1808 he was suffering increasingly from poor health and had an addiction to opium; he was, moreover, in dire financial straits and had quarrelled with Wordsworth. In Berners Street, he made an attempt to pull himself together; he and Wordsworth were reconciled in May 1812 and, while here, Coleridge also began to give a series of lectures and had some success with his play *Remorse*, staged at the Drury Lane Theatre in January 1813. By the autumn of that year, Morgan's bankruptcy meant Coleridge had to leave Berners Street. He led a peripatetic existence until 1816, when he settled in Highgate, where he lived for the rest of his life. The plaque is a replacement of the original tablet, which adorned the building that Coleridge actually lived in for just three years before demolition claimed it in 1908.

THOMAS STOTHARD

(1755–1834) painter and illustrator   28 Newman Street **2**

BORN in Covent Garden, the son of a publican, Stothard trained initially as a silk weaver. In 1777 he entered the Royal Academy Schools, where he became friends with William Blake* and thereafter became a successful book illustrator. When Stothard bought a house here in 1793 the street was favoured by artists – he counted among his neighbours the sculptors Thomas Banks and John Bacon, as well as the President of the Royal Academy, Benjamin West. In his painting room at the house, where he lived with his wife Rebecca and their six children, Stothard produced a large and varied body of work, including *The Pilgrimage to Canterbury* (1806); engraved in 1817, it became one of the best-known prints of the 19th century. Stothard designed the magnificent silver shield presented to the Duke of Wellington by the merchants and bankers of the City of London to celebrate the victory at Waterloo, which may be seen at Apsley House. The Duke took a keen interest in the designs, visiting Stothard at his home here to inspect the drawings. The house was re-fronted in 1924.

COVENTRY PATMORE

(1823–96) poet and essayist

PATMORE is remembered chiefly for the four poems published between 1854 and 1863 known collectively as *The Angel in the House*. He had taken rooms at number 14 just before this, and made it his principal home in 1863. He was allowed leave from his post in the printed books department of the British Museum to go to Italy early in 1864, where he converted to Catholicism. Patmore moved out of Percy Street not long after marrying his second wife, Marianne Byles, in July 1864.

The Angel in the House **is a paean to the virtues of married love and, by extension, to Patmore's first wife Emily Augusta, who died in July 1862. He wrote** *The Victories of Love* **(1862–3) – the fourth and final part of the** *Angel* **series – while living here. Patmore was grief-stricken over his wife's death and would spend his evenings revisiting their old haunts.**

CHARLES LAUGHTON

(1899–1962) actor

RENOWNED for his portrayals of sinister villains, and for his definitive role of Captain William Bligh* in the film *Mutiny on the Bounty* (1935), Laughton was described by a friend of his youth as 'the ungainliest of schoolboys, very fat with a huge head'. He moved to Percy Street with the actress Elsa Lanchester (1902–86) – best remembered for playing the title role in *Bride of Frankenstein* (1935) – in 1928, and they were married the following year, though Laughton was, it seems, essentially homosexual. The couple kept a modest second-floor flat here in this 1760s

'It was high time, because an Indian restaurant had opened underneath and the smell of garlic and curry which rose up was getting stronger and stronger.'

Elsa Lanchester, on leaving Percy Street

terrace, knocking two rooms into one to maximise their living space, and also had a cottage in the Surrey Hills. They moved out in 1931, when a play they were both in transferred to New York. The couple settled in the United States in 1939, becoming American citizens in 1950.

SIR ROBERT SMIRKE

(1780–1867) architect   81 Charlotte St. (formerly 65 Upper Charlotte St.) **5**

THIS much-altered late-18th-century house was the residence of the painter Robert Smirke (1753–1845). His son, who was also called Robert (who was born in 1780 – not, as the plaque states, in 1781), lived here from about the age of six until 1804. During this time, the younger Smirke studied under John Soane and – more harmoniously – under George Dance the Younger*, who had a formative influence on the young architect. It was also while he was living here that he visited Italy and Greece with his elder brother Richard, travels which were inspirational for this architect of the Classical Revival. Smirke's most famous building is the British Museum (1823–46), which was completed after his retirement by his brother Sydney (1846–52).

FRANCISCO DE MIRANDA

(1750–1816)   58 Grafton Way (formerly
precursor of Latin American independence   27 Grafton Street) **6**

THE house forms part of a terrace dating from 1792. When Miranda lived here, the upper floors were given over to his collection of books, prints and paintings – he was a formidable classical scholar – and served as an informal embassy and headquarters for the cause of Latin American self-determination. He lived here between 1802 and 1810 (with a two-year absence in New York from 1805) with Sarah Andrews, the mother of his two sons, who stayed on until her death in 1847. Miranda, who has a statue nearby (*pictured*), died in gaol in Cadiz having been handed over to the Spanish. Now owned by the Venezuelan government, the 'Casa Miranda' is used as a cultural centre.

ANDRES BELLO

(1781–1865) poet, jurist, and Venezuelan patriot

LIKE Francisco de Miranda*, Bello was born in Caracas and collaborated with Simón Bolívar* in the cause of South American independence. He stayed here with Miranda soon after his arrival in Britain in 1810. He remained in the country until 1829, representing the new nations of Venezuela, Chile and Colombia to the British government; he married two Englishwomen in succession, fathered 15 children, got to know Jeremy Bentham and James Mill*, and also found time to write poetry. Regarded as early Venezuela's foremost man of letters, he also framed the civil code of Chile, which was widely imitated elsewhere in South America. As a philologist his greatest achievement was a grammar of Latin American Spanish, published in 1847.

CAPTAIN MATTHEW FLINDERS, RN

(1774–1814) 56 Fitzroy Street
explorer and navigator

FLINDERS'S pioneering survey of the coast of Australia, which he undertook between 1795 and 1803, was the basis for Admiralty charts for a century. He is credited with being the first to use the term 'Australia' (from the Latin for the 'Southern Country'). Returning to England in 1810 Flinders lived at several addresses in Fitzrovia, with creditors in hot pursuit. In 1813 he moved to this house, which he 'agreed for 6 months at £100 a year', but in February 1814 he moved again, to a house in nearby London (now Maple) Street. Copies of his account of his adventures, *A Voyage to Terra Australis* (1814), were delivered there by the publisher the day before his death.

'There have been many people calling at this house for money.'

Matthew Flinders's diary, May 1813

AUGUST WILHELM HOFMANN

(1818–92) chemist   9 Fitzroy Square **9**

BORN near Frankfurt, Hofmann studied at the universities of Giessen and Bonn, where he carried out investigative work into the organic chemistry of coal tar. Later he developed a lucrative sideline in the development of artificial dyes based on magenta; two shades of synthetic dye are still known as 'Hofmann violets'. Enjoying the patronage of Prince Albert, he was appointed Professor and Director of the newly established Royal College of Chemistry in London in 1845. In London, Hofmann initially rented rooms in George Street, Hanover Square, moving to Fitzroy Square in 1854. It was at this house that he recuperated after damaging an eye in a laboratory accident; at his insistence, students visited him here for tutorials during his convalescence. Hofmann is credited as a decisive influence on the teaching of laboratory science and chemical technology in Britain.

SIR CHARLES EASTLAKE

(1793–1865) painter, first Director of the National Gallery   7 Fitzroy Sq. **10**

EASTLAKE made his name with *Napoleon Bonaparte on Board the Bellerophon* (1815), the lucrative sale of which enabled him to travel to Rome, and he did not return permanently to England until 1830. Eastlake settled at 13 Upper Fitzroy Street, and enjoyed some of his most productive years as a painter, before moving the short distance to Fitzroy Square in 1842. Here he excelled in his second career as an arts administrator. As Secretary of the Fine Arts Commission, Eastlake worked alongside Prince Albert in supervising the interior decoration of the reconstructed Palace of Westminster (1841–63). He was elected President of the Royal Academy in 1850, was Keeper of the National Gallery from 1843 to 1847, and was appointed its first Director in 1855. He devoted the rest of his life to enlarging and improving the gallery's collection, and died while looking for new acquisitions in Italy.

ROBERT GASCOYNE CECIL, 3RD MARQUESS OF SALISBURY

(1830–1903) Prime Minister 21 Fitzroy Square

CECIL – a direct descendant of Robert Cecil, the minister of Elizabeth I and James I – moved here a year or so after his marriage to Georgina Alderson in July 1857. His father disapproved of the match on social grounds, and their consequent estrangement meant that money was tight for a while; Cecil, who had been elected as MP for Stamford in 1853, took to journalism to supplement his income. The Cecils moved to Duchess Street, Portland Place, in spring 1862, following the birth of their second child. Cecil was eventually reconciled with his father, to whose title he succeeded in 1868, and he went on to serve as Prime Minister for three terms between 1885 and 1902, twice combining the office with that of Foreign Secretary. Tall and luxuriantly bearded, it has been said that he was confused in the public mind with the cricketing hero W. G. Grace*, an association that probably rebounded to his political benefit.

GEORGE BERNARD SHAW*

(1856–1950) playwright and polemicist 29 Fitzroy Square

THE quotation on the plaque, 'From the coffers of his genius he enriched the world,' was written by Shaw's housekeeper, Mrs Laden, to announce his death. Shaw lived in the upper two storeys of this 1830s house – together with his mother Bessie, with whom his relations were cool – from March 1887 until his marriage to Charlotte Payne-Townshend in June 1898. During this time, Shaw cut his teeth as a theatre critic and playwright; among the works he wrote here was the collection *Plays: Pleasant and Unpleasant* (1898). In the 'unpleasant' category was *Mrs Warren's*

Profession (1893), which was banned by the censor; 'My reputation as a dramatist grows with every play of mine that is not performed,' he quipped. His future wife Charlotte was dismayed by the state of Shaw's small study at Fitzroy Square, which was in 'a perpetual state of dirt and disorder' and packed with ungainly furniture so that one was obliged 'to move sideways like a crab', and occasional clean-up operations 'took two full days' hard work'. After their marriage, the Shaws' London home was at the Adelphi, but his mother continued to live in Fitzroy Square until 1907.

'Heaps of letters, pages of manuscripts, books, envelopes, writing paper, pens ... butter, sugar, apples, knives, forks, spoons, sometimes a cup of cocoa or a half-finished plate of porridge, a saucepan and a dozen other things ... and all undusted, as his papers must not be touched.'

A description of Shaw's study at Fitzroy Square, by his wife

VIRGINIA WOOLF*
(1882–1941) novelist and critic   29 Fitzroy Square

VIRGINIA Stephen, as she was then known, moved to Fitzroy Square with her younger brother Adrian in August 1907, taking the former residence of George Bernard Shaw* on a five-year lease. 'We are having bright green carpets and I want to buy old furniture,' she told a friend excitedly. This was the siblings' first independent residence; despite their bohemian suppers of herrings and tripe, they still had servants to look after them. Virginia, who occupied the whole of the second floor, spent her time here writing articles for newspapers and began her first novel, *The Voyage Out*, published in 1915. This

period of her life was also marked by mental health troubles – in summer 1910 Virginia had her first experience of a sanatorium – and by an emotional entanglement with her brother-in-law, Clive Bell. Her trips to visit him and her sister Vanessa in St Ives caused her to wish that 'Bloomsbury was on the seashore', and provided the setting for Virginia's later novel, *To the Lighthouse* (1927). Finding the neighbourhood of Fitzroy Square to be noisy – Virginia complained of the vans 'which grind rough music beneath my window' – she was relieved to move to the quieter Brunswick Square in November 1911.

ROGER FRY

(1866–1934) art critic and artist   33 Fitzroy Square

MORE renowned as a critic than as an artist, Fry emerged as – and took plenty of flak for being – a champion of contemporary art; famously, he mounted London exhibitions in 1910 and 1912 of modern French painting, for which he coined the term 'post-impressionist'. In 1913, Fry set up the Omega Workshops here. While the Omega functioned, Fry kept a flat-cum-studio around the corner in Fitzroy Street, successively at the now-demolished numbers 21 and 18.

THE OMEGA WORKSHOPS
Fry set up the workshops to enable young artists to make a living from selling decorated homeware; he hoped, also, to blur the line between fine and applied art. Number 33 functioned as a workshop, a gallery and – on Thursday nights – a club, at which, Duncan Grant and Wyndham Lewis* were among the artists involved. With commercial success elusive, the Workshops closed in 1919, but its productions – all anonymously signed with the Greek letter 'Ω' – are now highly collectible.

SAMUEL MORSE

(1791–1872) painter and
inventor of the Morse code

141 Cleveland Street
(formerly 8 Buckingham Place) **15**

BORN in Massachusetts, the son of a Calvinist minister, Morse became a pupil of the painter Washington Allston in 1811 and accompanied him to England later the same year. In London, Morse studied under Benjamin West, the American-born President of the Royal Academy, and by August 1812 had settled with his fellow pupil Charles Robert Leslie (1794–1859) at Buckingham Place, 'in the very centre of all the artists in London'. Leslie described himself and Morse as 'very comfortable in our new lodgings', which became the setting for evening parties attended by other pupils of West. While living here, Morse studied at the Royal Academy Schools and became friends with William Wordsworth, J. M. W. Turner* and Coleridge*. Morse returned to the United States in 1815, where as well as painting he worked on the development of long-distance telegraphy. He first conceived the idea of his code of 'dots' and 'dashes' in 1832, and his system was universally adopted after 1851.

DANTE GABRIEL ROSSETTI*

(1828–82)
poet and painter

110 Hallam Street
(formerly 38 Charlotte Street) **16**

ROSSETTI was born in a 'dingy' and 'mostly unrespectable' but 'fairly neat' 18th-century house on this site to Gabriele Rossetti, a writer and teacher of Italian, and his wife Frances. His brother William Michael (all his siblings became writers, including Christina Rossetti*) wrote that it 'seems hardly an exaggeration to say that every Italian staying in or passing through London, of a Liberal mode of political opinion, sought out my father'. The house remained in the family until 1836, when they moved to a larger property opposite. Both

As a very young child Rossetti displayed a precocious interest in literature and art: he wrote his first poem 'towards the age of five', and at the age of about four 'he stationed himself in the passage leading to the street-door, and with a pencil of our father's began drawing his rocking-horse'; a passing milkman expressed great surprise at seeing 'a baby making a picture!'

houses have gone, and the plaque marks a 20th-century block of flats.

EDWARD R. MURROW

(1908–65) broadcaster   Flat 5, Weymouth House, 84–94 Hallam Street

NORTH Carolina-born Ed Murrow was European Director of the broadcaster CBS, but quickly assumed a front-line reporting role, making his first broadcast in Vienna during the *Anschluss* of 1938. He soon settled in London, where his news broadcasts – which famously began with the words 'This is London' – conveyed the horror of the Blitz, and helped to rally American public opinion to Britain's side. Murrow displayed courage in the pursuit of the best angle on a story; during raids, he regularly gave broadcasts from rooftops – including that of Broadcasting House – and also flew on a number of bombing missions.

At the height of the Blitz, he was one of only three occupants still listed at Weymouth House, where he lived with his wife and fellow broadcaster Janet. Murrow was frequently obliged to walk the short distance to the BBC and CBS offices in Portland Place in the blackout, sometimes while a raid was in progress; he would arrive 'often out of breath, occasionally dusty, very occasionally on all fours'. He returned to the United States in 1946 where he launched and hosted the influential documentary series *See it Now* (1951–8) – the vehicle for a celebrated attack by Murrow on Senator Joseph McCarthy, the virulently anti-communist senator.

JAMES BOSWELL*

(1740–95) biographer   122 (formerly 47) Great Portland Street

BORN in Edinburgh – the son of Lord Auchinleck, a successful judge – Boswell followed his father's wishes by pursuing a legal career, though he indulged his passion for literature whenever possible. In May 1763 while in London he was unexpectedly – but fatefully – introduced to Dr Johnson*, and shortly afterwards conceived the idea of the biography that would become his greatest work. Boswell moved permanently to the capital

'Convivial society became continuously more necessary to him, while his power of enchantment over it continued to decline.'

A contemporary on Boswell's last years

on being called to the English Bar in 1786 and, having been widowed in 1789, took up residence here in 1791, close to his friend and associate Edmond Malone*. His time at the house – which has now been completely rebuilt, as have all his other London homes – witnessed his greatest triumph: the publication on 16 May 1791 of the *Life of Johnson*. But the period was also marked by a deterioration of mind and body; by the time of his death, Boswell's notorious 'wine bibbing' and whoring had become the talk of the town, and he died at the house in May 1795.

DAVID EDWARD HUGHES

(1831–1900) scientist
and inventor of the microphone

94 Great Portland Street **19**

BORN in London, Hughes moved with his family to the US in about 1838. His early talent for music – which he taught from 1850 – soon gave way to experimental science; in 1856 he patented his printing telegraph, which was adopted throughout Europe. Hughes moved here in about 1878, in which year he made his most important invention: the microphone. Demonstrations of the device were given here before an audience of distinguished scientists. He also invented the induction balance – later used in metal detectors – and worked at developing a form of 'wireless' communication; walking up and down Great Portland Street, holding a microphone in one hand and a telephone to his ear in the other, he was able to hear at some distance the sounds made by a transmitter left at home. In February 1880 – shortly before his appointment as a Fellow of the Royal Society – he invited its president and secretaries to witness his early experiments in radio, but they 'pooh-poohed all the results' and, disheartened, he abandoned his researches; it was left to the likes of Hertz and Marconi* to pick up where he left off. Hughes also lived at 108 Great Portland Street, and at 40 Langham Street. This plaque was damaged by fire in 2018.

EDMOND MALONE

(1741–1812)
Shakespearean scholar

40 Langham Street
(formerly known successively
as 55 Queen Anne St. East, 58 Queen Anne St. and 23 Foley Place)

THE Irish-born Malone became a lawyer, writer and editor, and in 1777 – on the publication of his new edition of the works of Oliver Goldsmith – settled permanently in London. Malone was among the first scholars to base his research on Shakespeare on original documents, and drew widely on his celebrated library of Elizabethan literature, the greater part of which was presented to the Bodleian Library, Oxford, after his death. While living here, Malone – a lifelong bachelor – researched his monumental ten-volume edition of the works of Shakespeare, published in 1790 to great acclaim. He also provided invaluable assistance to James Boswell*. Malone held frequent dinner parties for his friends, among whom were Edmund Burke*, Joseph Banks*, Edward Gibbon*, Charles James Fox* and Joshua Reynolds*, whose collected works he edited in 1797 to 1798. The interiors of his late-18th-century house remain largely unaltered, although the facade was rebuilt and additional floors added in about 1900, possibly after the death of a later resident – David Edward Hughes*.

HENRY FUSELI

(1741–1825)
artist

37 Foley St. (formerly known successively as
72, 75 and 37 Queen Anne St. East)

JOHANN Heinrich Füssli was born in Zurich, Switzerland, and inherited a love of art from his father, though initially trained as a Zwinglian minister. In 1768, on his second trip to London, he met Joshua Reynolds*, who encouraged him to become a painter. He returned to England in 1779, where he began to establish himself as an artist. Upon his marriage in 1788 to society beauty Sophia Rawlins he moved to Queen Anne Street East and enjoyed a period of success here, completing a series of paintings for John Boydell's popular Shakespeare Gallery in Pall Mall, including *Titania and Bottom* (1790). In 1799 Fuseli was appointed Professor of Painting at the Royal Academy, and in 1803 moved briefly to nearby 13 Berners Street (demolished), before his appointment the following year as Keeper of the Royal Academy, upon which he moved to Somerset House.

JOSEPH NOLLEKENS

(1737–1823) sculptor 44 Mortimer Street

THE son of a painter, Nollekens was born at 28 Dean Street (later home to Karl Marx*), and began to work in the studio of the sculptor Peter Scheemakers at the age of 13. In 1762 he left London for Rome, where he made copies of antique sculptures and began to produce the portrait busts for which he became renowned: Dr Johnson*, William Pitt the Younger* and Charles James Fox* were among his famous subjects. On his return to England in 1770, he settled at what was then a substantial house on this spot, previously occupied by the portrait painter Francis Newton (1720–94). His modelling room was

'... small in stature, of grotesque appearance and eccentric in his behaviour'

A description of Joseph Nollekens

visited by some of the greatest and most fashionable figures of the time. Both he and his wife, despite the wealth they had accumulated, were notoriously parsimonious, to the extent of being squalid: old shaving lather was, for example, retained for use at home. Nollekens had his studio in a corner room, which featured – above the chimneypiece – his portrait painted by Lemuel Francis Abbott in c.1797. He died in the first-floor drawing room in 1823.

HECTOR HUGH MUNRO, 'SAKI'

(1870–1916) writer 97 Mortimer Street

BORN in Burma, Munro worked between 1902 and 1908 as special correspondent for the *Morning Post*, travelling to the Balkans, Warsaw, St Petersburg and Paris. On his return to London he moved to rented rooms on the third floor of this late-19th-century building, and entered the most creative phase of his career. The short stories he produced for periodicals were later collected and published between 1911 and 1924. While living here, he also wrote two novels, including

When William Came (1913), a parable about a German invasion ('William' being the Kaiser). Saki, a name thought to derive from a character in *The Rubáiyát of Omar Khayyám*, was smart, handsome and urbane. His pied-à-terre was convenient for his favourite haunts – the British Museum, Regent Street, the Cocoa Tree Club in St James's Street and the Turkish baths in Jermyn Street. Having enlisted, Munro left Mortimer Street in 1914; a sniper's bullet killed him two years later.

REGENT'S PARK

REGENT'S Park is ringed with palatial stuccoed terraces laid out from 1811, each constructed by a single builder under the supervision of John Nash*, the mastermind of the scheme and the Prince Regent's favourite architect. In spite of war damage so extensive that total redevelopment was mooted, the restored Nash terraces are still among London's most splendid architectural assets – intended, as they were, to conjure the illusion of living in a country mansion. Behind the Nash terraces lie more functional developments of the 19th and 20th centuries, including some impressively monumental apartment blocks.

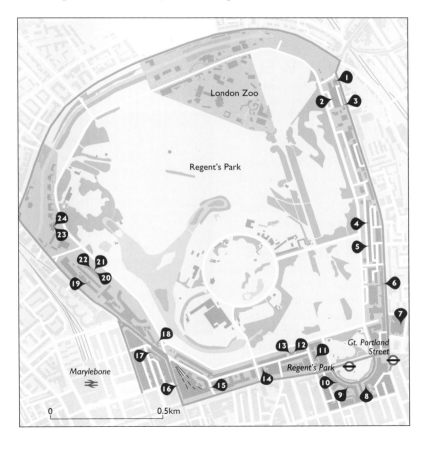

W. W. JACOBS

(1863–1943) author 15 Gloucester Gate **1**

BORN in Wapping, William Wymark Jacobs worked initially as a clerk in the Civil Service before the success of his fiction – notably *The Skipper's Wooing* (1897) and *Sea Urchins* (1898) – enabled him to devote himself to writing full-time. He is best remembered today for his macabre tales, especially 'The Monkey's Paw', which was later adapted for stage and screen. The plaque to 'W. W.', who lived in Gloucester Gate from 1928 to 1935, is actually located on the house's Albany Street frontage in order to mark the entrance to 15A, where Jacobs lived. This has now been reintegrated into the main body of the house, a detached villa of the late 1820s built to designs by John Joseph Scoles.

SIR HENRY WELLCOME

(1853–1936) pharmacist and founder of the
Wellcome Trust and Foundation 6 Gloucester Gate **2**

WELLCOME was born on a farm in Wisconsin; he began working in his uncle's drugstore and gave an early hint of entrepreneurial flair by marketing his own invisible ink. Coming to England in 1880, he established a hugely successful pharmacy business with fellow American Silas Mainville Burroughs. He leased 6 Gloucester Gate, part of an 1820s terrace of 11 houses, in about 1920. It was, writes Wellcome's biographer, 'not luxurious and he spent relatively little time there', though it remained his London base until his death. After the failure of his marriage to Syrie, the daughter of Dr Barnardo*, he became reclusive; Syrie had had several affairs including with

Wellcome ploughed his fortune into the establishment of medical research laboratories and museums, which were consolidated as the Wellcome Foundation in 1924. He also collected medical books, which form the basis of the Wellcome Library, housed by the Wellcome Trust, and anthropological artefacts, some of which are now on permanent loan to the Science Museum.

the author Somerset Maugham*, whom she later married. Wellcome became a British citizen in 1910 and was knighted, somewhat belatedly, in 1932.

CONSTANT LAMBERT

(1905–51) composer 197 Albany Street

THE son of a painter, Lambert won a scholarship to the Royal College of Music, where he studied under Ralph Vaughan Williams*. At the age of 21 he was commissioned to write a ballet score for Diaghilev, *Romeo and Juliet*, and the following year produced his most enduring work, *The Rio Grande* (1927), a jazz-based setting of a poem by Sacheverell Sitwell. Lambert also worked as a conductor and critic: the provocative book *Music Ho! A Study of Music in Decline* (1934) was, like his early musical work, infused with verve and wit, but the suicide of two close friends, the painter Christopher Wood and the composer Philip Heseltine (Peter Warlock*), affected Lambert's state of mind, which was not improved by his heavy drinking. As far as his relationships with women were concerned, Constant was misnamed: he was twice married, and numbered Margot Fonteyn* among his lovers. His life was correspondingly unsettled, and he is reckoned to have had 14 London addresses, most of short duration. Lambert lived at this 1830s terrace in Albany Street from 1947 until his death. It was here that he wrote his last work, the ballet score *Tiresias*; this was performed at Covent Garden in July 1951.

SIR JOHN MAITLAND SALMOND

(1881–1968) Marshal of the Royal Air Force
and RAF Commander 27 Chester Terrace

THE son of a general, 'Jack' Salmond followed his father into the Army but later transferred to the Royal Flying Corps. During the First World War, he reorganised air training at home, and was made Commander of the Flying Corps in France in January 1918. Promoted major-general three months later, he transferred to the newly formed Royal Air Force and resisted calls to disband the RAF after the war by promoting its use as an imperial policing force – most notably in Iraq, then a British protectorate. He lived at Chester Terrace, designed by John Nash* during the peak of his career, between 1928 and 1936, during which time he became Chief of the Air Staff and Marshal of the RAF.

C. R. COCKERELL
(1788–1863) architect and antiquary

13 Chester Terrace **5**

CHARLES Robert Cockerell was educated in the office of Robert Smirke*, a friend of his architect father. As a young man he toured the West Country and Wales with the artists Thomas* and William Daniell*, before spending seven years on the Continent. This had a profound effect upon his architectural style, which is unabashedly classical. His best-known surviving building is the Ashmolean Museum and Taylor Institution in Oxford (1841–5). Cockerell was Professor of Architecture at the Royal Academy from 1840 to 1857; he was also Surveyor of St Paul's Cathedral, and became the first professional President of the Royal Institute of British Architects in 1860. He moved to Chester Terrace in 1856 with his wife Anna, and later died here.

HENRY MAYHEW

(1812–87) journalist, social reformer
and founder of *Punch*

MAYHEW became part-proprietor and founding editor of *Punch* in 1841 – the engraver Ebenezer Landells is often credited as a co-founder, but Mayhew was largely responsible for setting the journal's humorous, satirical tone. His reputation as a social reformer rests on *London Labour and the London Poor* (1851), the definitive account of London street life of the era. Born in Great Marlborough Street, Westminster, Mayhew died in what is now Bedford Avenue, Bloomsbury, and – partly because he was perennially poor and occasionally bankrupt – lived at many different addresses in the intervening years. He lodged here between 1839 and 1840 with his brother Alfred, who threw him out of the house, so the story went, after he 'wrecked the kitchen and nearly killed the cook' after an amateur oxy-hydrogen experiment went badly wrong.

FABIAN SOCIETY

socialist organisation

RUNNING north from the Euston Road, Osnaburgh Street has been extensively redeveloped. Dominating its northern section is The White House, built in 1936 to designs by Robert Atkinson and now in use as a hotel; its main entrance faces on to Osnaburgh Terrace. The home of the solicitor Edward Pease (1857–1955) once stood here, at which a group of his friends met to discuss the ideas of the philosopher Thomas Davidson. The Fellowship of the New Life, as it was originally to be called, became the Fabians on 4 January 1884; its stated aim was 'the reconstruction of society in accordance with the highest moral possibilities'. The principles of the society were – and remain – broadly socialist, and its name was taken from the Roman general Fabius Maximus, who adopted a cautious approach to defeating Hannibal – hence 'Fabian tactics'. The founder members included the pioneer sexologist Henry Havelock Ellis*; George Bernard Shaw*, an early recruit, soon became its motive force, while Sidney Webb* and Annie Besant* joined in 1885. The society's influence in the Labour Party has been considerable, and it continues to publish pamphlets on a wide variety of political topics.

HENRY BROOKS ADAMS (1838–1918) US historian
UNITED STATES EMBASSY (1863–6)
98 Portland Place (formerly 5 Upper Portland Place)

8

THIS is the end house of the eastern half of Park Crescent, which was restored after severe bomb damage in the Second World War; the present facade is a close copy of the original. Adams was born in Boston into a political family; his great-grandfather was John Adams and his grandfather was John Quincy Adams, respectively the second and sixth Presidents of the United States. He arrived in London in 1861 as private secretary to his father, Charles Francis Adams, who had been appointed American Ambassador to the United Kingdom; the US Embassy was situated here for part of his tenure. While here Adams junior became friends with Charles Lyell* who inspired his enthusiasm for history. He was also the (anonymous) London correspondent to the *New York Times*. Returning to the United States in 1868, Adams became a professor at Harvard University and wrote a celebrated nine-volume history of his nation.

SIR CHARLES WHEATSTONE
(1802–75) scientist and inventor

19 Park Crescent **9**

WHEATSTONE is credited with numerous inventions and discoveries (including the concertina, which he patented in 1844 – he inherited a musical-instrument-making business from his uncle) but he is most famously associated with demonstrating the viability of mass communication by telegraph. He made his breakthrough at King's College on the Strand (where he held a professorship) by running four miles of suspended copper wire through the vaults beneath the building. His name is perpetuated in 'Wheatstone's bridge', an electric

PERSISTENCE AND RESISTANCE
Wheatstone was first proposed for a plaque, unsuccessfully, in 1906. The International Concertina Association had better luck when they revived the suggestion more than 70 years later.

circuit that measures resistance. This pioneer of mass communication was so afraid of public speaking that Michael Faraday* had to deliver his Royal Institution lectures.

DAME MARIE TEMPEST

(1864–1942) actress
24 Park Crescent

BORN Mary Susan Ethering-ton in the Marylebone Road, she took her stage name from a member of the aristocratic Vane-Tempest family whom she described as her godmother. Her early roles were in musical comedy when she gained a reputation for petulance (by her own admission she was 'a self-important little baggage, with a hot temper' in her youth). Tempest moved to Park Crescent in 1899 following her advantageous

Tempest's biographer wrote of her 'pretty chintz-covered boudoir where a little green parrot calls her "Marie"'.

marriage to Cosmo Charles Gordon-Lennox. While living here she took the title role in *Becky Sharp* (1901), which brought her to prominence as a serious actress. Marie Tempest's stage career lasted 55 years and she was a leading light in the foundation of Equity, the actors' union.

FREDERICK DENISON MAURICE

(1805–72) Christian philosopher and educationalist
2 Brunswick Place

JUST to the north of Maryle-bone Road lies Brunswick Place (formerly part of Upper Harley Street), which forms part of the grand entrance to Regent's Park – as conceived by John Nash*, and built in 1824. Maurice lived here between 1862 and 1866, before moving to Cambridge to take up a professorship. The son of a Unitarian minister, he was ordained an Anglican priest in 1834 and published one of his most significant works, *The Kingdom of Christ*, in 1838. His *Theological Essays* of 1853, however, led to accusations of unorthodoxy, and his academic career (he was then a professor at King's College London) was brought to a

temporary close. Chaplain of Lincoln's Inn from 1846 to 1860, Maurice was a leader of the Christian Socialist movement – his colleagues included Charles Kingsley* – which, in the wake of the Chartist agitation and European revolutions of 1848, sought to promote co-operation rather than competition. He put his educational theories into action by helping to establish Queen's College at 43–49 Harley Street, Britain's first higher education college for women, in 1846, and the Working Men's College at Red Lion Square, Holborn, in 1854. During his time at number 2, Maurice was Chaplain of St Peter's in nearby Vere Street, a position he held until 1869.

SIR CHARLES WYNDHAM

(1837–1919)
actor-manager

20 York Terrace East
(formerly 43 York Terrace) **12**

BORN Charles Culverwell in Liverpool, Wyndham qualified as a doctor, though his passion was always for the theatre. He made his name in London's West End as a handsome, seductive leading man with an outstanding talent for comedy, and afterwards excelled as a manager. He is distinguished in having a West End theatre named after him: Wyndham's Theatre in Charing Cross Road (*above*), which opened in 1899. Wyndham died at York Terrace, having taken up residence about a year before with Mary Charlotte Moore. Once his leading lady and mistress, she was, by this time, his business partner and second wife. The house is the eastern half of the Doric Villa by John Nash* (1822), which is, despite appearances, a pair of semi-detached villas.

DR ERNEST JONES

(1879–1958)
pioneer psychoanalyst

19 York Terrace East
(formerly 42 York Terrace) **13**

JONES grew up near Swansea, and first practised as a neurologist. He set up in private practice as a psychoanalyst in 1913, and in the same year co-founded the London Psycho-Analytical Society; in 1920 Jones established the *International Journal for Psycho-Analysis* and four years later co-founded the Institute of Psycho-Analysis in London.

He also wrote about his favourite hobby in *The Elements of Figure Skating* (1931). In 1938 he applied for leave for Sigmund Freud* and his family to settle in this country having earlier been responsible for bringing Melanie Klein* to England. Later Jones wrote the authorised, three-volume biography of Freud. He lived at Doric Villa from 1921 to 1940, along with his Austrian wife, Katherine, and their four children.

FRANCIS TURNER PALGRAVE

(1824–97) poet and compiler 5 York Gate

IT is as the compiler of *The Golden Treasury* (1861), an enduringly popular anthology of English verse, that Palgrave is best known, though he also wrote and published his own poetry. Palgrave conceived the idea of a collection of the best English verse while on a walking holiday in Cornwall with Alfred, Lord Tennyson*, who – despite finding Palgrave somewhat irritating – gave his blessing to the project. In December 1862 Palgrave married Cecil Greville Milnes and moved to York Gate. Their daughter recalled that their first year at the house was 'chiefly given up to seeing their many friends and relations', and the evenings to music, 'for my mother played the piano charmingly'. The house forms part of a Nash terrace of five built in the early 1820s.

KENNETH WILLIAMS

(1926–88) comic actor Farley Court, Allsop Place

ON moving to Flat 62 Farley Court, on the ninth and top floor of this post-war-rebuilt block, Kenneth Williams was 'elated ... my bedroom looks out over Regent's Park. The trees are turning now and the sight is beautiful. I can see all the traffic twinkling down the Marylebone Rd ... It's all so marvellous, I could cry.' The six and a half years he spent here were among his most successful; a regular on the radio show *Round The Horne*, and later on *Just a Minute*, Williams also took on some of his most memorable 'Carry On' roles, including the Khasi of Kalabar in *Carry On up the Khyber*, Dr Tinkle in *Carry On Doctor* and Julius Caesar in *Carry On Cleo* ('Infamy, infamy, they've all got it in for me!'). During a misanthropic turn in March 1967, he wrote in his famous diary of gazing from his flat upon 'the *nits* crowding round outside the waxworks. How I loathe them and Madame Tussaud.'

ERIC COATES

(1886–1957) composer Chiltern Court, Baker Street **16**

'TO write it is essential that I am high up, away from the ground,' the composer Eric Coates declared, adding that ideally, he would live 'in a balloon suspended a thousand feet above Regent's Park'. His top-floor flat in the monumental Chiltern Court block, above Baker Street station, was the next best thing: the view from its roof made up for any residual homesickness for his native Nottinghamshire, a sentiment he captured in his suite *From Meadow to Mayfair* (1931). Coates and his family lived here throughout the 1930s, and then moved to another airy eyrie atop Berkeley Court, just opposite; he drew inspiration from his morning walks to his publishers, Chappells, in New Bond Street, jotting musical ideas down

> Eric Coates and his wife Phyl were among the first in London to dance the Charleston.

in a pocket-book as he went. While living in Chiltern Court he wrote the march 'Knightsbridge' (1933) and *By the Sleepy Lagoon* (1930) – inspired by a summer sunset view of Bognor Regis from Selsey – which, with added seagulls, is still the theme for *Desert Island Discs*. *The Dam Busters March*, for which Coates is perhaps best known, came later (1954). His unapologetic flair for melody marked him out among his peers – on first meeting him, fellow composer Ethel Smyth greeted him with the question: 'You're the man who writes tunes?'

JOSÉ DE SAN MARTÍN, 'THE LIBERATOR'

(1778–1850) Argentine soldier and statesman 23 Park Road
(formerly 12 Park Place) **17**

BORN in Yapeyú, Argentina, San Martín spent his early life in Madrid, where he met and befriended Bernardo O'Higgins*. He returned to Argentina in 1812, and the following year led an army to victory against the Spanish at the Battle of San Lorenzo, the first victory of the Argentine War of Independence. He entered Santiago

'Estoy con comodidad y en buena situación'
(I am comfortable and in a good location)

San Martín on Park Place

in Chile with O'Higgins in February 1817, and subsequent victories helped to secure the liberation of

Peru. Following a meeting with Simón Bolívar* in 1822, however, he effectively relinquished all claims to authority. Returning to Argentina he learned that his wife had died, and he left with his daughter for Europe, where he spent the rest of his life. San Martín lived at Park Place in the summer of 1824; later that year he left for Paris where he spent much of his subsequent life. He died at Boulogne-sur-Mer, France.

ELIZABETH BOWEN

(1899–1973) writer   2 Clarence Terrace

THE Grade I-listed Clarence Terrace was built in 1823 by Decimus Burton, under the supervision of the architect of Regent's Park, John Nash*. The Anglo-Irish writer Elizabeth Bowen moved to number 2 in 1935 with her husband Alan Cameron. During the 17 years that they lived there, they entertained the London literati and Bowen wrote two of her finest novels, *The Death of the Heart* (1938) and *The Heat of the Day* (1949). The protagonists in the former book lived in a house on the edge of Regent's Park, and many scenes in the latter were drawn from her experiences of living in London during the Blitz – and in particular her tortured affairs with the writer Goronwy Rees and the Canadian diplomat Charles Ritchie. 'Writers do not find subjects; subjects find them,' Bowen once observed. So saying, she wrote a history of her now-demolished family home in County Cork, *Bowen's Court* (1942), and a novel, *The Last September* (1929), about the decline of the Anglo-Irish gentry – a film adaptation of which, featuring Maggie Smith and David Tennant, appeared in 1999.

E. H. SHEPARD

(1879–1976) painter and illustrator   10 Kent Terrace

SHEPARD is most celebrated as the illustrator of A. A. Milne's* *Winnie-the-Pooh*. Kent Terrace, which dates from 1827, and was designed by John Nash*, was Shepard's childhood home from the age of about four; and from the earliest age his parents encouraged him always to 'have a pencil in his hand, always have paper nearby and always be ready to draw anything that interested him'. He cheerfully described the house's garden as 'untidy, with some big trees and a lot of sooty shrubs, but it was an excellent place to play in'. The idyll ended when his mother fell terminally ill, and he was sent to live with an aunt in 1890. When researching his autobiography after the Second World War, Shepard was pleased to find the house intact – 'ornamented with stucco columns in front and a small balcony to each drawing room window' – though in a somewhat shabby condition, with the front railings removed; these have since been replaced.

RALPH VAUGHAN WILLIAMS, OM

(1872–1958) composer   10 Hanover Terrace **20**

VAUGHAN Williams's output ranged from sacred music to film scores. Although renowned as a collector of English folk songs, his range of musical influences was eclectic. He moved to Hanover Terrace in 1953 after his marriage to his second wife, Ursula Penton Wood. They 'enjoyed every minute of the time ... in that beautiful house', she recalled. 'A big study on the first floor at the back gave Ralph a pleasant place for work, and a Steinway piano ... allowed us to have plays-through of new works, parties with music and such luxuries.' The octogenarian Vaughan Williams was astonishingly productive: works composed here included a setting of the verse of William Blake* and his last three symphonies. His sudden death here came barely a month after he had attended the premiere of his Ninth Symphony.

ANTHONY SALVIN

(1799–1881) architect   11 Hanover Terrace **21**

SALVIN was a pioneering exponent of the Gothic and Tudor Revival; his best-known commissions were for country houses, such as the spectacular Harlaxton Manor, Lincolnshire (1831–7), and Scotney Castle, Kent (1835–43). He also undertook many well-regarded restorations, notably that of the Tower of London (1853–68), which secured him a commission to undertake similar work at Windsor Castle (1856–67). Salvin moved to Hanover Terrace in 1858, with his wife Anne, his architect son, also named Anthony, and two unmarried daughters. The move was prompted by medical advice: he had suffered a stroke and the omnibus commute from Finchley was proving arduous. After the death of his wife in 1860 Salvin built himself a new house – Hawksfold, at Fernhurst, Sussex – to which he moved in 1864.

H. G. WELLS

(1866–1946) writer

BORN in Bromley, Herbert George Wells had his first success with *The Time Machine*, published in book form in 1895; film and radio adaptations have made *The War of the Worlds* (1898) his most famous work. He moved to Hanover Terrace in 1936, and composed his own obituary the following year: 'He occupied an old tumble-down house upon the border of Regent's Park and his bent, shabby, slovenly and latterly somewhat obese figure was frequently to be seen in the adjacent gardens, sitting and looking idly at the boats on the lake, or the flowers in the beds, or hobbling painfully about with the aid of a stick.'

The house was in fact very comfortable – its luxuries included a private telephone exchange – and Wells continued to write almost until the day he died. Wells was one of the few residents of Hanover Terrace to stay put during the war, despite having windows shattered by flying bombs; he took particular delight in displaying a prominent '13' outside to deride superstition.

THOMAS COCHRANE, EARL OF DUNDONALD

(1775–1860) admiral Hanover Lodge, Outer Circle **23**

A CONTROVERSIAL figure, Cochrane won repute as a daring commander in the Napoleonic Wars, but his career was stymied by his inability to hold his tongue – especially when he encountered incompetence in the senior ranks. He also vented his grievances in Parliament, where he sat for the constituency of Westminster as a radical. After being implicated – unfairly, it appears – in a financial scandal of 1814, he served a prison sentence; subsequently he was a successful mercenary naval commander for the liberationists in South America – where he fell out with San Martín* – and in Greece. Cochrane inherited the family title in 1831 – the earldom of Dundonald – and in the following year was pardoned and awarded the rank of rear admiral. He took up residence at Hanover Lodge not long afterwards, and remained here until about 1845, devoting much of his time to researching the maritime applications of steam power; his work resulted in the warship HMS *Janus* (1848).

DAVID, EARL BEATTY, OM

(1871–1936) admiral Hanover Lodge, Outer Circle **24**

B EATTY, who was promoted rear admiral at the age of only 39, was appointed to command the Navy's battle-cruiser squadron in 1913, and took much credit for successful First World War engagements in the Heligoland Bight (1914). At the Battle of Jutland (1916), however, he saw the *Indefatigable* and the *Queen Mary* sunk before his disbelieving eyes, and his tactics have been criticised. Beatty acquired Cochrane's former residence in 1909, and had it altered and enlarged by Edwin Lutyens*. He

'There seems to be something wrong with our bloody ships today.'

Lord Beatty at the Battle of Jutland, 1916

filled the walls 'with portraits of old naval heroes and with pictures of the early battleships' and lived here with his wife Ethel until the mid-1920s. During this time Beatty was successively Commander-in-Chief of the Fleet (1916–19) and First Sea Lord (1919–27), a post he held longer than any other; his earldom and the Order of Merit came in 1919.

ST JOHN'S WOOD AND MAIDA VALE

BY the middle of the 19th century, St John's Wood had become an immensely popular residential area, noted for its clean air and for its detached and semi-detached villas set in substantial grounds. The relative remoteness of St John's Wood was an attraction for many – the area was known as a haven for mistresses, courtesans and exiled activists. Combined with its uninterrupted north light, this also provided a perfect setting for those connected with the arts, a point that is borne out by many of the area's blue plaques.

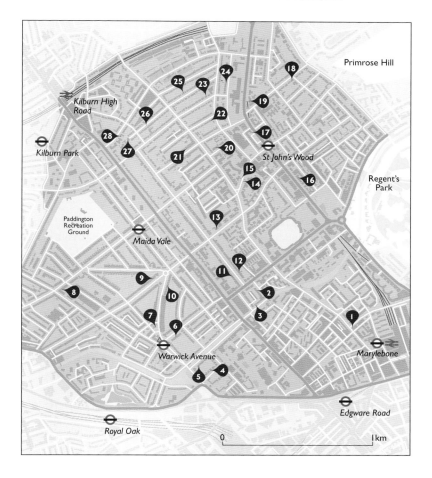

BENJAMIN HAYDON (1786–1846) painter
CHARLES ROSSI

(1762–1839) sculptor

116 Lisson Grove

(formerly 1 St John's Place, then 58 Lisson Grove) ❶

ROSSI built this house soon after 1808, and lived here – and probably also in the adjoining 112 and 114 – until his death. He was Sculptor to the future George IV from 1797, and then to his brother William IV. While living here he completed such works as the monument to Admiral Lord Rodney in St Paul's Cathedral (1810–15) and the caryatids of St Pancras New Church (1819–22). Haydon leased and occupied the Rossmore Road side of number 116 between 1819 and 1822, using as his studio a building on

'The quiet and peace of having a painting-room and a parlour to live in with my books around me was heavenly.'

An appreciative Benjamin Haydon

the site of the Evangelical church. Among the works Haydon produced here were the immense *Christ's Entry into Jerusalem* and *The Raising of Lazarus*. He was, however, imprisoned for debt in 1823 and had left by January 1824 for Connaught Terrace, near Edgware Road.

EMILY DAVIES

(1830–1921) founder of Girton College, Cambridge

17 Cunningham Place ❷

DAVIES, who was born in Southampton and raised in Gateshead, came with her recently widowed mother Mary to London in January 1862. The pair – with a cook and a housemaid – moved into this early- to mid-19th-century terraced house, found for them by Emily's brother Llewelyn. Emily considered the 'small but cheerful' house to be in an ideal position with 'a minute garden in which Mrs [Mary] Davies could potter about to her heart's content'. While here, she worked with her friends Barbara Leigh Bodichon, Frances Mary

Buss* and others to campaign for the opening of university courses and professional careers to women, and was also active in the women's suffrage movement. In 1866 she published *The Higher Education of Women*, and in the same year the London Schoolmistresses' Association was founded here, with Emily as Secretary. In 1869 – with Bodichon – she founded Girton College, a residential college for women. Based initially at Hitchin, Hertfordshire, and from 1873 on the edge of Cambridge, it survives as her greatest memorial.

GUY GIBSON, VC
(1918–44) pilot, leader of the Dambusters Raid   32 Aberdeen Place

GIBSON was at first rejected by the RAF for being too short but at Bomber Command he proved his worth as a pilot and was promoted to command 617 Squadron, which, in May 1943, he led in the famous air attack on the Ruhr dams. To say that the success of the raid – one dam breached, one damaged – lay mostly in its propaganda value is not to deny its importance; Gibson was awarded the VC and praised by Winston Churchill* as 'one of the most splendid of our fighting men'. (His ground crew were rather less in awe, nicknaming him 'bumptious

> As an early guest on Desert Island Discs Gibson chose Wagner's 'Ride of the Valkyries', saying, 'it reminds me of a bombing raid, though I don't say it's like one'.

bastard'.) Gibson's account of the Dambusters Raid was published as *Enemy Coast Ahead* (1946); the episode achieved legendary status thanks to the 1955 film. His plaque is on the house he shared with his wife from summer 1942. Gibson died on a further mission in 1944.

LOKAMANYA TILAK
(1856–1920) Indian patriot and philosopher   10 Howley Place **4**

BAL Gangadhar Tilak, known as Lokamanya – meaning 'beloved of the people' – was an ardent opponent of British rule in India. Towards the end of his life, he stayed in London, where he gave evidence to a parliamentary committee on behalf of the All Indian Home Rule League, and mixed with such figures as Ramsay MacDonald*, Arthur Henderson* and George Bernard Shaw*. His first plaque, unveiled in 1961 in Bayswater, provoked a stream of protests from those who felt him to be a 'seditionist'. Following the Bayswater house's demolition a new plaque was unveiled here, on the 1840s house where he lived for nine months after he first arrived in London on 29 October 1918. He and four colleagues had six rooms at their disposal, two on each floor, and were well looked after by a Mr and Mrs McNalty; such was the couple's mastery of curry preparation that they later opened an Indian restaurant. The Canaletto* plaque at the same address was not authorised by the LCC; there is no known connection between the artist and this area, which was open fields during Canaletto's London stint.

JOHN MASEFIELD, OM

(1878–1967) Poet Laureate   30 Maida Avenue (formerly Maida Hill West) **5**

MASEFIELD completed some of his finest work during the time he lived here with his Irish wife Constance, including his first novel, *Captain Margaret* (1908), *Ballads and Poems* (1910) and *The Everlasting Mercy* (1911). Masefield was perhaps attracted to this *c*.1830 house overlooking Regent's Canal because of his love of water; his teenage years were spent at sea, and it was his *Salt-Water Ballads* (1902) – which includes 'Sea-Fever' – that first brought him to literary attention. Masefield lived here from 1907 until 1912. After 1909, he split his time between London and a country home in Buckinghamshire.

SIR AMBROSE FLEMING

(1849–1945) scientist and electrical engineer   9 Clifton Gardens

BORN in Lancaster, Fleming worked as a science teacher before studying under James Clerk Maxwell* at Cambridge. In 1885 he was appointed Professor of Electrical Technology at UCL, where he remained until retirement in 1926. Fleming was closely involved with the development of the telephone, electric lighting and wireless telegraphy. The work which brought him worldwide fame was his invention in 1904 of the thermionic valve, used to detect (and later, to amplify) radio signals; this device was taken on and adapted by Marconi*, whom Fleming served as scientific adviser, and has a foundational role in modern electronics. Fleming lived in this mid-19th-century terraced house with his wife Clara from 1889 until 1896, a period that saw the publication of works on transformers and electric lighting.

ALAN TURING

(1912–54) code-breaker   Warrington Lodge,
and pioneer of computer science   2 Warrington Crescent **7**

TURING, who was born at a nursing home based in this mid-19th-century building, was interested in science from his youth and entered Cambridge University in 1931. By the age of 24, he had developed the concept of the 'universal Turing machine', now seen as embodying the principle of the modern computer. During the Second World

War, he worked as a cryptanalyst at Bletchley Park, Bedfordshire, where he made a vital contribution to the deciphering of the German Enigma code. After the war, at the National Physical Laboratory at Teddington, he was instrumental in the development of the Automatic Computing Engine (ACE), regarded as the world's first universal computing machine. In 1952, however, he was prosecuted for his relationship with another man and, despite having always been open about his sexuality, he came to be regarded by the authorities as a security risk. His ensuing depression ended in suicide by cyanide poisoning.

EDWARD ARDIZZONE
(1900–79) artist and illustrator   130 Elgin Avenue **8**

BORN in French Indo-China, to an Italian-French father and a British mother, Ardizzone became a naturalised Briton in 1922. Two years earlier, his father had acquired this house in Maida Vale, an area that inspired many of Ardizzone's early watercolours, and was his home for over 50 years. He set up his studio in the former drawing room on the first floor of this late-19th-century end-of-terrace house. In 1972 he left it for a home in Kent.

Ardizzone's distinctive work was variously adapted to war artistry and to illustration of books and magazines, including works by Anthony Trollope* and Eleanor Farjeon. Ardizzone produced his own series of children's books, starting with *Little Tim and the Brave Sea Captain* (1936), which drew on memories of a childhood spent partly on the East Anglian coast.

ANDREAS KALVOS

(1792–1869) Greek poet
and patriot

182 Sutherland Avenue
(formerly 7 Sutherland Gardens) **9**

ORIGINALLY from the island of Zakynthos and brought up in Tuscany, Kalvos spent most of his life in Italy and England. He is best known for his 20 patriotic odes, *The Lyre* (1824) and *New Odes* (1826), which helped to excite the upsurge of philhellenism that played an important role in the creation of the modern Greek state. Kalvos first came to England as the secretary of the writer Ugo Foscolo* in 1816, and married Theresa Thomas in London two years later. Following her death in 1820 he left England, but moved back in 1852 and married Charlotte Wadans; in partnership with her and Miss Georgina Keating, he established a school for young ladies at newly built Sutherland Gardens between 1857 and 1865. Kalvos and his wife then founded another school in Louth, Lincolnshire, where he died.

DAVID BEN-GURION

(1886–1973) first Prime Minister of Israel

75 Warrington Crescent **10**

BORN in what was Russian Poland, Ben-Gurion fought in the Jewish Legion of the British Army during the First World War. He first came to England with his wife Paula in 1920, and they rented this modest flat in Maida Vale, an area where many Jewish immigrants settled. While here, he worked for Poale Zion, an organisation of socialist Zionists, in the cause of attracting Jewish settlers to Palestine. In August 1920 their son Amos was born. The family subsequently moved elsewhere in London before returning to Palestine in 1921. Ben-Gurion came once more to London in 1940, and served as Prime Minister of Israel from its formation in 1948.

SIR JOSEPH WILLIAM BAZALGETTE

(1819–91) civil engineer 17 (formerly 48, then 83) Hamilton Terrace **11**

IT has been said that Bazalgette 'created more of London, above and below ground, than anyone else'. Born in Enfield, he moved to this new-built villa with his family in about 1831. He was later apprenticed as an engineer in Ireland, and entered the service of the Metropolitan Commission of Sewers in London in 1849. As Chief Engineer to the Metropolitan Board of Works from 1856 until his retirement in 1889, Bazalgette was responsible for the design and construction of some of the most important components of London's infrastructure, including a comprehensive new sewage system, following the 'Great Stink' of summer 1858. His treatment works, pumping stations and more than 80 miles of intercepting sewers

Bazalgette virtually defined his own career in his presidential address to the Institution of Civil Engineers in 1884; it was on 'those engineering works which promote the health and comfort of the inhabitants of large cities, and by which human life may be preserved and prolonged'.

remain in full use today. His many other works included the construction of the Albert (1868), Victoria (1870) and Chelsea (1874) embankments, the design of river crossings such as Hammersmith Bridge (1887) and the building of new thoroughfares, among them Shaftesbury Avenue (1886) and Charing Cross Road (1887).

WILLIAM STRANG

(1859–1921) painter and etcher 20 (formerly 7) Hamilton Terrace **12**

STRANG, a Scotsman, came to London in 1875, and studied art at the Slade. He made his name with illustrative etchings such as those for *The Pilgrim's Progress* (1885), *The Ancient Mariner* (1896) and *Don Quixote* (1902). While living here (from 1900 until his sudden death at a hotel in Bournemouth) he was active primarily as a painter, producing works including *Bank*

Holiday (1912) and his depiction of Vita Sackville-West*, *Lady in a Red Hat* (1918), and many portrait drawings, with subjects including Lord Kitchener* (1910) and John Masefield* (1912). The house, which dates from c.1830, also bears a plaque erected by the Society of Musicians in 1895 to the composer George Macfarren (1813–87), who lived and died here.

JOHN WILLIAM WATERHOUSE

(1849–1917) painter · 10 Hall Road **13**

WATERHOUSE was at the height of his fame when he moved to St John's Wood in 1900, along with his wife, Esther Kenworthy Waterhouse, who was also an artist. He remained here for the rest of his life. He was born in Rome, but his parents, who were both artists, lived in South Kensington from 1854. He studied at the Royal Academy Schools and became known in particular for his paintings of classical scenes and for his skilful depiction of women. From Primrose Hill Studios, which he leased from 1878, Waterhouse produced a stream of successful works in the romantic vein popular at the time; these include the much-reproduced *The Lady of Shalott* (1888), *Ophelia* (1889), and *Hylas and the Nymphs* (1896). While working from his studio here Waterhouse turned increasingly to non-narrative subjects, producing works such as *Song of Springtime* (1913). *The Enchanted Garden*, which stood on his easel at the time of his death, is believed to have been inspired by the garden at Hall Road.

SIR LAWRENCE ALMA-TADEMA, OM

(1836–1912) painter · 44 (formerly 17) Grove End Road **14**

DUTCH by birth, Alma-Tadema made his name as a painter of scenes from classical antiquity. He arrived in London in 1870, and moved here with his artist wife, Laura, in November 1886, having bought the house from the painter Jean-Jacques Tissot. His studio was a vast galleried room featuring a semi-dome lined with aluminium, providing the effect of silvery light so central to his work.

Rebuilt 'practically … from its foundations' to Alma-Tadema's own designs, the house – entered by a covered entrance (now number 44A) – was transformed into a sumptuous temple of the arts and a home to the painter's collection of antique and exotic furnishings. Alma-Tadema entertained widely here. 'His house is a glimpse of his work; it is his soul seen from the interior. Whoever understands his house learns to cherish his art,' said one visitor.

SIR THOMAS BEECHAM, CH

(1879–1961) conductor and impresario   31 Grove End Road **15**

BORN in St Helens, Lancashire – where his grandfather, also Thomas Beecham, set up his pill manufactory in the 1860s – Beecham made his debut as a conductor at the age of 20. During his long and successful career, he trained and conducted three new orchestras, the Beecham Symphony Orchestra (founded 1909) and the London Philharmonic (1932) and Royal Philharmonic (1946). This house, a handsome villa of about the 1820s, had six rooms, plus servants'

'The English may not like music, but they absolutely love the noise it makes.'

One of Thomas Beecham's many
bon mots

quarters, and was his home from 1950 to 1954. He lived here with his second wife, the pianist Betty Humby, who 'did what she could to cram a quart into a pint pot'. During his time at number 31, Beecham made a number of records at the nearby Abbey Road Studios.

MADAME MARIE TUSSAUD

(1761–1850) artist in wax   24 (formerly 12) Wellington Road **16**

MARIE Grosholtz – who was born in Strasbourg – learned her trade in Paris at the waxworks museum established by her mentor and guardian, Dr Philippe Curtius. Having lived for nine years at the Palace of Versailles, where she modelled Louis XVI and Marie Antoinette, Marie survived the Revolution by manufacturing death masks of victims of the guillotine. By the time of her marriage in 1795 to François Tussaud, a civil engineer, she had inherited Curtius's museum, with which she left France for England in 1802, spending the next 30 years touring Britain with her ever-expanding collection.

As well as the portraits in wax, this included a remarkable set of relics, including the blade from a guillotine, George IV's coronation robes and many items belonging to Napoleon. In 1835 the museum settled in the Bazaar, Baker Street, where it soon became one of London's most popular attractions, remaining here until 1884, when it moved to the Marylebone Road. Madame Tussaud lived in this early-19th-century villa in 1838–9 before moving to 58 (later 59) Baker Street (now demolished) where she lived until her death. The house in Wellington Road has been considerably remodelled since the plaque went up in 2001.

OSKAR KOKOSCHKA

(1886–1980) painter Flat 120, Eyre Court, 3–21 Finchley Road **17**

BORN in Austria to a Czech father, Kokoschka studied art in Vienna and first began to establish his reputation through portraiture. In 1938 he fled from Prague to London to escape the Nazi invasion of Czechoslovakia; he became a British citizen in 1947. Already an artist of repute in continental Europe, Kokoschka achieved prominence in Britain mainly in the post-war period, with works such as the two triptychs *The Prometheus Saga* (1950) and *Thermopylae* (1954) and his series of London panoramas, completed in 1970 with *London View with St Paul's Cathedral*. Kokoschka moved to Eyre Court – part of a block built in 1930 to designs by T. P. Bennett & Son – with his wife Olda in the winter of 1946–7. The flat had recently been vacated by Olda's parents, who had lived in London since 1940. It remained the Kokoschkas' main home until 1953, when they moved to Switzerland.

GEORGE FRAMPTON

(1860–1928) sculptor 32 Queen's Grove **18**

THE son of a stonemason, Frampton studied in London and Paris and enjoyed early success with works such as *An Act of Mercy* (1887) and *Mysteriarch* (1892). He produced a large body of public sculpture and architectural decoration, for example at the Victoria and Albert Museum (1909), but is best known for his statue of Peter Pan (1912) in Kensington Gardens. Frampton lived from 1894 to 1908 in this handsome 1830s detached villa with his wife the painter Christabel Cockerell and their son Meredith, who also became an artist. Here, in a studio and workshop at the rear, he executed the statues of the philanthropists Dame Alice Owen (1897) and Quintin Hogg* (1906).

THOMAS HOOD*

(1799–1845) poet 28 Finchley Road (formerly Finchley New Road) **19**

HOOD began a career in journalism in 1821, when he was appointed Sub-Editor of the *London Magazine*. A friend of Hazlitt*, Dickens* and Lamb*, he soon became known for verse, both serious and comic. He contributed to journals such as *Punch* and published collections of his work. He was often in debt, and – in order to economise – spent five years (1835–40) on the Continent. In winter 1841, soon after his return, he moved to 17 Elm Tree Road (demolished), close to Lord's cricket ground, calling himself 'Hood of the Wood'; there, he wrote the popular poem 'The Song of the Shirt' (1843), highlighting the plight of underpaid seamstresses. In January 1844, in increasing financial straits and declining health, he moved with his wife Jane and their two children to this recently built house. In a letter to Dickens, Hood described its location as 'just two or three doors short of the turnpike beyond the Eyre Arms'. Here, he launched *Hood's Magazine*, but publication ceased on his death in May 1845.

Hood named this house Devonshire Lodge, 'in remembrance of the exceeding generosity and kindness, which … he received from the late Duke of Devonshire'.

DAME LAURA KNIGHT (1877–1970)
HAROLD KNIGHT (1874–1961)
painters   16 (formerly 9) Langford Place

THE Knights met at Nottingham School of Art in 1890, and were married in 1903. After a period at Newlyn in Cornwall, they moved to London and in 1922 took a long lease of this substantial house of c.1890, where each had a studio. Harold was known for his portraits, while Laura – appointed DBE in 1929 – made her name with her paintings of ballet and circus life, such as *Charivari* or *The Grand Parade* (1928). In 1936 she became the first woman to be elected a full Royal Academician – the honour was extended to Harold a year later – and in 1946 was commissioned to produce a pictorial record of the war criminals' trials at Nuremberg. Following Harold's death in Colwall, Herefordshire – their country retreat for many years – Laura continued to live in Langford Place; she died here in 1970 at the age of 92.

THOMAS HENRY HUXLEY

(1825–95) biologist   38 (formerly 4) Marlborough Place **21**

HUXLEY was the first great populariser of science and did much to promote the theory of evolution, becoming known as 'Darwin's bulldog'. A St John's Wood resident since 1855, in December 1872 he moved with his wife and children to this early-19th-century villa and stayed for 18 years.

'[It] was built for comfort, not beauty ... to give each member of the family room to get away.'

Huxley's son Leonard* on their home in Marlborough Place

Huxley's laboratory was at what is now Imperial College. He was President of the Royal Society (1883–5).

SIR CHARLES SANTLEY

(1834–1922) singer   13 Blenheim Road **22**

DESCRIBED by George Bernard Shaw* as 'the best baritone singer with whom the London public is familiar', Santley was born in Liverpool and trained in Italy, making his debut in Pavia in 1857 and in London two years later. He remained active as an operatic performer until 1876, when he transferred his success to the concert stage, only retiring in 1911. In 1907, the year in which he celebrated his jubilee as a singer, Santley became the first of his profession to be knighted. He lived at five houses in St John's Wood, moving to Blenheim Road in 1911 and dying there 11 years later.

C. F. A. VOYSEY

(1857–1941) architect and designer   6 Carlton Hill **23**

CHARLES Francis Annesley Voysey was born near Hull and set up his own architectural practice in 1881, but was initially better known for his distinctive wallpaper and textile designs. Between 1890 and 1914 he enjoyed a flourishing career as an architect in the Arts and Crafts style, principally designing country and suburban houses, though there are examples of his work in Knightsbridge, Chiswick and Hampstead. While living at Carlton Hill between 1895 and 1899 he worked on commissions in his studio here, including New Place, Haslemere, Surrey, and Broadleys and Moorcrag, both in Windermere.

SIR BERNARD SPILSBURY

(1877–1947) forensic pathologist   31 Marlborough Hill

SPILSBURY had a hand in the conviction of many of the early 20th century's most notorious murderers – figures including the poisoner Frederick Henry Seddon and the 'Brides in the Bath' murderer, G. J. Smith. Born in Warwickshire, he first came to widespread notice for his persuasive evidence at the murder trial of Dr Crippen in 1910.

He moved to Marlborough Hill with his wife Edith and growing family in 1912; they remained here until 1940, when air raids forced their departure. Spilsbury equipped a back room on the top floor as a laboratory and had a study on the ground floor, where he wrote up some 6,000 case cards. Recently, concerns have been raised about his 'aura of infallibility'.

MELANIE KLEIN

(1882–1960) psychoanalyst and pioneer of child analysis   42 Clifton Hill

BORN to Jewish parents in Vienna, Klein first came to London in summer 1925 to give a series of papers on her work and settled permanently here the following year. She quickly established herself as a leading light of the British Psycho-Analytical Society, and her theories and approach, especially her play technique, attracted widespread attention; her most important

publication, *The Psychoanalysis of Children*, appeared in 1932. Klein lived in this semi-detached house of *c*.1840 from 1935 to 1953. Her professional rivalry with Anna Freud* was so divisive that it had a permanent impact on British psychoanalysis, but it was to Anna's brother Ernst that Klein turned to rework the interior of number 42, his first commission in England.

SIR WILLIAM REID DICK

(1878–1961) sculptor   Clifton Hill Studios, 95A Clifton Hill

REID Dick worked here from about 1908 until shortly before his marriage to Catherine Treadwell in 1914, initially in Studio 6 and, after 1910, in Studio 3. Born in Glasgow – where he was

apprenticed as a stonemason – he moved to London in 1907. He made his reputation as an exponent of the 20th-century classical school of sculpture with a number of memorials, including those to Field

Marshal Lord Kitchener* (1922–5) in St Paul's Cathedral and President Roosevelt (1948) in Grosvenor Square; he was also noted for his architectural sculpture, including that for Unilever House, Blackfriars (1932), and for his portraits: Harry Lauder* (1911) and a group piece, *Femina Victrix* (1913) were two such completed at Clifton Hill. A sometime President of the Royal Society of British Sculptors, Reid Dick wrote the introduction to a London blue plaques guide of 1953.

W. P. FRITH

(1819–1909) painter   114 Clifton Hill

BORN in Yorkshire, William Powell Frith entered the Royal Academy Schools in 1837 and is best known for his panoramas of scenes from contemporary life. His first painting of this type, *Life at the Seaside* or *Ramsgate Sands* (1854), was purchased by Queen Victoria; it was followed by *Derby Day* (1856–8) – of which it has been said that 'Few paintings have ever earned such universal acclaim'. These, and Frith's other most notable works, were painted at the now demolished 7 (formerly 10) Pembridge Villas, Bayswater, where he lived for more than 30 years (1854–88). Frith moved to this mid-19th-century property in Clifton Hill in 1896, and died here at the age of 90.

GILBERT BAYES

(1872–1953) sculptor   4 Greville Place

BAYES was born in St John's Wood and was greatly influenced by George Frampton*. His own work was adventurous in its use of materials, such as polychromatic stoneware and pre-cast concrete. The frieze *History of Pottery through the Ages* (1939), made for the ceramics firm of Doulton, is now in the Victoria and Albert Museum. Still *in situ*, over the entrance of Selfridges in Oxford Street, is the *Queen of Time* clock Bayes made for Harry Gordon Selfridge* in 1931. Always committed to public art, he also designed work for new housing estates, his *Four Seasons* clock in Somers Town being one surviving example. The three-storey stuccoed house in Greville Place was about a century old when Bayes moved here in 1931; it once featured his own terracotta exterior embellishments, of which only a tiny fragment has survived. Bayes remained here until just before his death.

BLOOMSBURY AND HOLBORN

THE name Bloomsbury has become most closely associated with the bohemian set of 20th-century artists, writers and intellectuals known as the Bloomsbury Group, several of whom have plaques. Much of the area remains part of the Duke of Bedford's estate, and the ornate, cherub-adorned bronze plaques erected by the estate in the early 20th century are a unique feature. The area has some of the finest Georgian houses in London. Further south, Kingsway is a modern thoroughfare – opened after slum clearances in 1905 – but High Holborn was a medieval road into the City. Either side of it lie two great Inns of Court – Gray's Inn and Lincoln's Inn – both founded in the late Middle Ages. Nearby, Lincoln's Inn Fields was first developed as a fashionable place of residence in the mid-17th century.

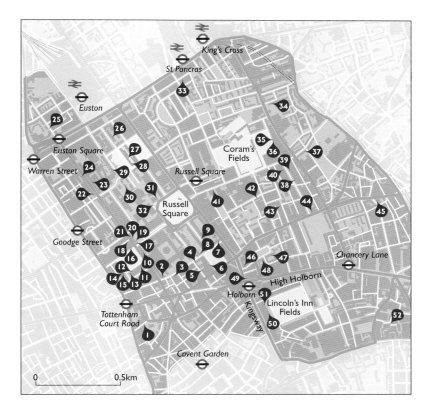

AUGUSTUS SIEBE
(1788–1872) pioneer of the diving helmet · 5 Denmark Street

SIEBE moved to London in 1814 from Saxony, having served in the Prussian Army. In 1828 he moved to these late-17th-century premises, where he both lived and ran an engineering firm. Siebe's closed diving-helmet design of 1840 – the first type where the helmet was sealed to a diving suit – remained in use for over a century; it was a vital enabling technology for many of the great Victorian civil engineering projects that required underwater foundation or investigative work, such as bridges, tunnels and lighthouses. Siebe also created the world's first commercially viable ice-making machine, which he built under licence. He retired in 1868; as Siebe Gorman, the firm he founded supplied diving equipment and submarine engineers until the 1990s.

GEORGE DU MAURIER*
(1834–96) artist and writer · 91 (formerly 46) Great Russell Street **2**

GEORGE Louis Palmella Busson du Maurier was born in Paris. He set up home here on his marriage to Emma Wightwick in 1863. They paid 25 shillings a week for the second-floor apartment: 'Our lodgings are very nice and the studio will be a beauty in time,' du Maurier told his mother. The studio in question cost him an additional £25 a year, and was on the ground floor, behind a shop selling Pears soap. In 1864, du Maurier became a staff artist at *Punch*, and there he drew the cartoon that spawned the expression 'a curate's egg'. Du Maurier was blind in one eye, and concern for his sight led him to embark upon a second career as a writer; among his gifts to the lexicon, taken from his novel *Trilby* (1894), were 'trilby hat' and 'Svengali'. Three children were born before the du Mauriers moved to Kensington in March 1868.

RANDOLPH CALDECOTT
(1846–86) artist and book illustrator · 46 Great Russell Street **3**

CALDECOTT had a great aptitude for creating pictures of animals and birds, though he is best known as an illustrator of children's books. He lived and worked here from 1872 to 1879, lodging with a Mrs Spencer; among the works he executed here were the drawings for his book *The House That Jack Built* (1878) and commissions for *Punch* and the *Illustrated London News*.

Thereafter Caldecott lived in Kent and Surrey, before travelling in 1885 to the United States, where he died.

JOHN NASH

(1752–1835) architect   66 Great Russell Street ④

THE Prince Regent's favourite architect, Nash laid out Regent's Park and Regent's Street, and designed Carlton House Terrace (1827–33) and the remarkable church of All Souls, Langham Place (1822–5). He substantially embellished both the Royal Pavilion at Brighton (1815–23) and Buckingham Palace (1825–35); the former featured onion domes, and the latter was eye-wateringly expensive. This terrace (numbers 66–71), along with its neighbour at 17 Bloomsbury Square, is Nash's earliest known surviving development, and a fine example of his pioneering use of stucco as a complete cladding. Ratebooks indicate that he lived in the corner house with what is now Bury Place from its completion in 1778 until 1781. However, the project – along with, so he claimed, the extravagance of his wife Jane at the milliners – brought ruin to Nash: five of the houses were unlet in 1781, and he was compelled to return to his native Wales. There he established a reputation as an architect of county gaols, before entering a successful partnership with the landscape designer Humphry Repton in remodelling country estates. Nash later had houses in Regent Street and Dover Street, both gone. When he died, the *Annual Register* noted that Nash had 'amassed a large fortune, but as an architect did not achieve anything that will confer upon him lasting reputation'. Posterity, being less prone to professional jealousy, may beg to differ.

BERTRAND RUSSELL

(1872–1970) philosopher
and campaigner for peace   34 Russell Chambers, Bury Place ⑤

RUSSELL, the best-known British philosopher of the 20th century, moved here in autumn 1911 in order to be close to Lady Ottoline Morrell*, who was then his lover. She enjoyed making the place 'pretty and nice for him' and supplied many of the furnishings. Russell's *Principia Mathematica* (1911–13), written with A. N. Whitehead and perhaps

Russell's most significant work, was published while he lived here, but mostly written in Cambridge. His pacifist stance during the First World War lost him his Trinity College fellowship and, to save money, in summer 1916 he let the flat. Back here in early 1917, Russell spent an unproductive few months 'brood- ing on the odiousness of the human race'; a spell in Brixton prison followed – for a libel on the US Army – and he finally moved out in 1922. The Russell Chambers block was built in the 1890s on the Duke of Bedford's estate, to whose family Bertrand Russell belonged – hence the coincidence of names.

DR ROBERT WILLAN

(1757–1812) dermatologist · 10 Bloomsbury Square **6**

YORKSHIRE-BORN Willan's reputation rests on his early classification of diseases of the skin, as described in *On Cutaneous Diseases* (1808), the first of its kind to feature colour illustrations. One of the first to link London's poor housing conditions to poor public health, Willan's *Reports on the Diseases in London* (1801) includes the luridly titled *An Account of the Dreadful Effects of Dram-Drinking.* Appointed physician to the Public Dispensary near Lincoln's Inn Fields in 1783, Willan lived in this terrace of five houses – built in the 1660s, but much altered – from 1800 to 1811, when he left for Madeira.

SIR HANS SLOANE

(1660–1753) physician and benefactor of the British Museum · 4 Bloomsbury Place **7**

SLOANE was born in County Down, and studied medicine in France before setting up his practice in London. It is as a collector, however, that he is remembered: his miscellanea of flora, fauna, manuscripts and some 30,000 books became the foundation of the British Museum collection, which was housed in nearby Montagu House from 1759. Sloane moved here in 1695, shortly after his marriage to Elizabeth Langley, an heiress to Jamaican property: a recent biography has highlighted that slave labour effectively funded much of Sloane's collecting mania. By 1708 he had accumulated so much that he needed to buy the house next door (number 5): both were refaced in about 1860. Sloane retired to Chelsea in 1842; Sloane Square was named after him.

THOMAS HENRY WYATT

(1807–80) architect   77 Great Russell Street ⬢8

WYATT belonged to a noted family of architects and was primarily a designer of country houses and churches – including St George's Garrison Church at Woolwich (1862–3), now a restored ruin after bombing, and a basilica-style parish church at Wilton, Wiltshire, which was inspired by the architect's sketching tours of Europe. That church was condemned as 'un-English', and many of Wyatt's later commissions were executed in the Gothic style. He lived in Great Russell Street from the late 1840s until his death here more than 30 years later. The house dates from the 17th century, but was remodelled in the mid-1800s; it is probable that the iron-roofed balcony on the Montague Street side was designed by Wyatt.

JOHN THELWALL

(1764–1834) political orator, writer and elocutionist   40 Bedford Place ⬢9

ONE of the leaders of the radical 'Friends of the People', Thelwall suffered imprisonment for his beliefs, which included the reform of parliament, universal suffrage, free speech and vehement opposition to the war with France; once, at Great Yarmouth, he was nearly press-ganged into the Navy. As a speaker he was compared by William Hazlitt* to a 'volcano vomiting out lava': more flatteringly, Samuel Coleridge* called him 'intrepid, eloquent and honest'. Born in Covent Garden, Thelwall grew up in Lambeth 'surrounded by fields'. He was apprenticed to an attorney and cut his teeth as a political orator at the public debates held in the Coachmakers' Hall, where he railed against the Fox–North coalition in 1783. Having himself overcome a lisp, Thelwall later lectured on oratory and elocution, and started a 'seminary' for the study and cure of speech impediments (he was one of the first to appreciate their physical origin) at his then-new home in Bedford Place in 1806. While living here Thelwall produced his *Vestibule of Eloquence* (1808), in which he summarised his educational plan; earlier publications included several volumes of poetry. In 1813 he moved both his home and 'Institution for the Remedy of Organic Defects, Cure of Impediments, and Preparation for the Pulpit, Bar and Senate' to 57 Lincoln's Inn Fields, a building which also survives.

JOHN SCOTT, LORD ELDON

(1751–1838) Lord Chancellor   6 Bedford Square

BORN in Newcastle upon Tyne and called to the Bar in 1776, Scott – ennobled in 1801 – was implacably opposed to almost all legal and political reform, from the abolition of slavery to the outlawing of the employment of boy chimney-sweeps. Yet the length of Eldon's tenure on the woolsack, which was almost unbroken between 1801 and 1827, has not since been equalled.

George IV called him 'Old Bags'; to Jeremy Bentham he was 'Lord Endless', on account of his lengthy deliberations before reaching judge-ment. Eldon lived here with his wife Elizabeth from 1798 to 1818; in March 1815 they were forced to flee out of the rear of the house, which was besieged by anti-Corn Law rioters; all the windows were broken and much furniture destroyed.

RAM MOHUN ROY

(1772–1833) Indian scholar and reformer   49 Bedford Square

RAM Mohun (otherwise rendered as Rammohun) was a pioneer of journalism in India, founding Bengali and Persian news-papers in 1822, and was one of the first to explore the shared ground between Christianity and Hindu-ism. He also campaigned against 'suttee': the self-immolation of Hindu widows. Arriving in England in April 1831 as an emissary of the Mughal emperor, Ram Mohun at-

tended the coronation of William IV and witnessed the passage of the 1832 Reform Act, as well as the renewal of the East India Com-pany's charter, the terms of which were a disappointment to him. He lodged here from January 1832 with Joseph Hare, brother of a Calcutta acquaintance, the watchmaker and philanthropist David Hare. From Bedford Square, he travelled to Bris-tol in 1833, and died soon after.

WILLIAM BUTTERFIELD

(1814–1900) architect   42 Bedford Square **12**

BUTTERFIELD established his reputation with All Saints, Margaret Street, just north of Oxford Street (1849–59). He went on to build

Keble College, Oxford (1868–83); its centrepiece, the chapel, features brick patterns that were designed, it is said, to lift the beholder's eyes heavenwards. A perfectionist, Butterfield is said to have put his umbrella point through stained glass that did not please him. A tall, ascetic bachelor, he lived between home, office and club – the Athenaeum – and resided at this house (dated *c*.1775), from 1886 until his death. Among his last commissions was restoration work on All Saints, Margaret Street, over which – quite characteristically – he clashed with the vicar.

SIR ANTHONY HOPE HAWKINS

(1863–1933) novelist   41 Bedford Square

ANTHONY Hope – to use his pen-name – wrote the swashbuckling bestseller *The Prisoner of Zenda* (1894), which gave us the word 'Ruritania' to denote a faraway romantic country. In summer 1903, Hope married Betty Sheldon and moved to Bedford Square that September. He enjoyed the 'spaciousness and dignity' of his new home, especially its billiard room and squash court. While he struggled to replicate the enormous success of his early novels, he still earned significant money, and achieved belated critical recognition for *Sophy of Kravonia* (1906). During the First World War, Hope worked for the Ministry of Information, and was knighted for his services in 1918. In March the previous year he had moved to a smaller house in Gower Street, thinking it prudent to have 'a smaller shell to carry on my back'.

THOMAS WAKLEY

(1795–1862) reformer and founder of *The Lancet*   35 Bedford Square

WAKLEY moved to London from Devon at the age of 20. He founded *The Lancet* in 1823, partly as a forum for medical innovation and partly to expose quackery and nepotism in medical appointments. As MP for Finsbury from 1835 he campaigned against punishment by flogging in the Army and supported the Tolpuddle Martyrs. He was the first qualified doctor to serve as West Middlesex coroner, a post previously reserved for lawyers. Wakley moved here in 1828, and remained for 20 years. His fortnightly whist or chess gatherings were attended by 'a large number of staunch friends who were attracted by his eloquence, his audacious defence of popular rights, his determination, self-confidence, and kindliness of manner'. It is thanks to Wakley's suggestion that all poison bottles are identifiable by touch.

THOMAS HODGKIN

(1798–1866) physician, reformer and philanthropist   35 Bedford Square **15**

A DEVOUT Quaker, Hodgkin was an opponent of slavery and a strong supporter of the rights of indigenous peoples, notably of North America. His work has had a lasting influence on our understanding of the body's immune system, and a disease of the lymphatic system is named after him. He lived here after his marriage in January 1850 to Sarah Scaife. Hodgkin died in Palestine, possibly of cholera, while investigating the plight of oppressed Jewish people.

SIR HARRY RICARDO

(1885–1974) mechanical engineer   13 Bedford Square **16**

THE only son of Halsey Ralph Ricardo, the Arts and Crafts architect, Harry Ricardo was born here and, when not away at school, lived here until his marriage in 1911 to Beatrice Hale. His interest in mechanics developed in the basement workshop at the house. He built his first internal combustion engine in 1902, and in 1907 joined the civil engineering company owned by his maternal grandfather. In 1915 Ricardo launched his own company, which was – and still is – based at Shoreham-by-Sea, Sussex. His petrol and diesel engines were used for aircraft, tanks and cars; he was responsible for an engine for London buses that halved fuel consumption, and for the design of a governor and fuel control for the first Whittle jet engine.

HENRY CAVENDISH

(1731–1810) natural philosopher   11 Bedford Square **17**

THE foremost experimental physicist of the age, Cavendish discovered hydrogen, nitric acid and the relative density of the Earth. He moved here in 1784, where he established his collection of minerals and a semi-public library of some 12,000 volumes. Cavendish retained the house – together with another, at Clapham Common, that held his laboratory – until his death. The staircase was of Portland stone, the floors of Norway oak and the interior decoration uniformly green. Cavendish usually communicated with his three servants by written note – because, it was said, he had such a high-pitched speaking voice.

THE PRE-RAPHAELITE BROTHERHOOD

founded 1848   7 (formerly 83) Gower Street

THE crucial meeting of the 'brotherhood', at which they drew up their manifesto, took place at this 1780s house – then the Millais family home – in September 1848. The group's first paintings were exhibited the following year, signed 'PRB'; colourful and naturalistic, they were inspired by the unaffected simplicity of early Italian art. Despite initial conflict with the art establishment, the three leading Pre-Raphaelites, John Everett Millais*, William Holman Hunt* and Dante Gabriel Rossetti*, went on to enjoy great success; the foundation of the group is now seen as a seminal moment in British art history.

DAME MILLICENT GARRETT FAWCETT

(1847–1929) pioneer of women's suffrage   2 Gower Street

MILLICENT Garrett – the younger sister of Elizabeth Garrett Anderson* – presided over the campaign leading up to the foundation of the National Union of Women's Suffrage Societies in 1897. Fawcett had an ambivalent attitude to the militant suffragettes led by the Pankhursts* and was a more conservative figure, opposed to Home Rule for Ireland and a strong supporter of the war effort in 1914–18. She moved here in 1884 – following the death of her husband, Henry Fawcett, a government minister – with her daughter Philippa, a fellow suffrage campaigner, to live with her sister Agnes, an interior designer who was responsible for two decorated ceilings at the house. Agnes proved a supportive companion for the widowed Millicent, who 'always loved the Gower Street house and all its associations'.

Fawcett addressing a rally in Hyde Park, 1913.

LADY OTTOLINE MORRELL

(1873–1938) literary hostess and patron of the arts   10 Gower Street **20**

OTTOLINE Cavendish-Bentinck married Philip Morrell, a Liberal politician and member of the Oxford brewing dynasty, at the age of 28. The marriage was not, conventionally speaking, a success – Philip was an incorrigible philanderer – but the couple became renowned for their literary and artistic parties both at Garsington, their Oxfordshire home until 1928, and in London. They moved to this house in 1927; here, Lady Ottoline spent the rest of her life and wrote her memoirs. Some of the artists and writers who benefited from her patronage included Jacob Epstein, Mark Gertler* and many of the Bloomsbury Group. She had a peculiar voice and manner, and was used as a literary archetype by, among others, D. H. Lawrence*, with whom – as with Bertrand Russell* – she had a tortured love affair.

JAMES ROBINSON

(1813–62) pioneer of anaesthesia and dentistry   14 (formerly 7) Gower St. **21**

ROBINSON wrote a groundbreaking text on dental treatments, *The Surgical, Mechanical and Medical Treatment of the Teeth* (1846), and was the first person to use anaesthetic in Britain on 19 December 1846 when, at the home of a Dr Francis Boott just up the street, he extracted a molar from a Miss Lonsdale while she slumbered under ether. Robinson, who had a prickly, intense personality, lived and worked here from 1842 until his death, which took place at his country house in Middlesex following an accident with a pruning knife. He founded a journal, *Forceps* (1844–5), helped to establish what became the Royal Dental Hospital and the University College Hospital Dental School, and was the first President of the College of Dentists.

GEORGE DANCE THE YOUNGER

(1741–1825) architect   91 Gower St. (formerly 29 Upper Gower St.)

AMONG Dance's commissions were the Church of All Hallows, London Wall (1765–7), Newgate Prison (1770–84; demolished 1902) and the Royal College of Surgeons building at Lincoln's Inn (1806–13). He was also responsible for the embellishment of the Guildhall (1788–9) and the layout of Finsbury Circus (1802); like his architect father, George Dance the Elder, he held the office of Clerk of Works to the City of London. Dance lived at this four-storey house (built in 1789) from 1790 until his death. The house was one of the many to owe its simple, elegant proportions to the standards set by the London Building Act of 1774 – legislation that Dance had helped to draft.

CHARLES DARWIN

(1809–82)
naturalist

Biological Sciences Building, UCL, 110 Gower Street (formerly 12 Upper Gower Street)

DARWIN lived in a house on this site between 1838 and 1842, during which time he wrote *The Structure and Distribution of Coral Reefs* (1842), inspired by his five-year voyage on the *Beagle*, and sketched out his developing evolutionary theories, later published as *On the Origin of Species* (1859). Darwin moved here during the last days of 1838, barely two weeks before he married Emma Wedgwood; her pleasure at his having secured a lease on the yellow-curtained house – which, from its riotous colour scheme, they nicknamed 'Macaw Cottage' – was tempered with the hope that the previous occupants had 'discarded that dead dog out the garden'. 'My father used to laugh over the surpassing ugliness of the furniture, carpets, etc.', recalled Darwin's son Francis. 'The only redeeming feature was a better garden than most London houses have ... thirty yards long.' On 14 September 1842 – for health reasons – Darwin and family moved to Down House.

SIR VICTOR HORSLEY

(1857–1916) pioneer of neurosurgery
and social reformer

129 Gower Street

A RECENT worldwide history of brain surgery states that Horsley 'may legitimately be called the first neurosurgeon'; he had numerous operating firsts to his name, and co-developed the Horsley–Clarke stereotaxic apparatus, which enabled precise areas of the brain to be pinpointed for treatment. Horsley's wax – a compound to stem bleeding – is still used today. In addition to this, Horsley chaired a government investigative committee into rabies, and his plan of strict quarantine laws and the muzzling of dogs was vital in securing its eradication from Great Britain. Horsley, who was the son of the artist John Calcott Horsley, was also an ardent advocate of temperance, women's suffrage and sex education. Although he was 57 when the First World War broke out, he – very characteristically – volunteered for active service, and died of heat exhaustion at a military hospital near Baghdad in July 1916. Horsley lived in Gower Street at the outset of his career (1882–5), while working at University College Hospital next door; the house is now a hostel for medical students.

GIUSEPPE MAZZINI

(1805–72) Italian patriot   183 North Gower St. (formerly 9 George St.) **25**

MAZZINI'S political aim of forming a single Italian republic led to his exile from his homeland. In 1837 he moved to England, living at this address from March of that year until March 1840. During this time, he earned a living from literary journalism and made contacts with, among others, John Stuart Mill* and several leading Chartists. In a large-hearted gesture, he took in a young foundling called Susannah, who became his house-keeper. Mazzini went on to lead a short-lived radical administration in Rome during 1849; after its demise he returned to London, where he spent much of the rest of his life.

HUGH PRICE HUGHES

(1847–1902) Methodist preacher   8 Taviton Street **26**

WELSH by birth, Hughes spent most of his life in London. In 1885 he founded the weekly *Methodist Times,* which he continued to edit until his death. He moved to Taviton Street in September 1887, on becoming Superintendent of the West London Methodist Mission, based in Holborn. Taviton Street was then gated: 'We might be in the midst of the most delicious rural retreat,' Hughes observed, comparing the distant sound of the Euston Road to 'the roar of advancing time'. Yet he refused to join a petition against the removal of the gates, on the grounds that Jesus would not have approved 'when hundreds of people have to go a mile out of their way because half a dozen of us do not want to be disturbed'. Hughes was behind the 'Forward Movement' in Methodism, which combined evangelism with social work, and he was strongly committed to Nonconformist unity.

JOHN MAYNARD KEYNES

(1883–1946) economist

46 Gordon Square **27**

KEYNES is remembered for the system of deficit finance that bears his name – Keynesianism – as described in his best-known book, *The General Theory of Employment, Interest and Money* (1936). He moved here in 1916 as a tenant of the art critic Clive Bell, who called the house the Bloomsbury Group's *'monument historique'*; earlier, it had been occupied by his wife, the artist Vanessa Bell, and her sister, Virginia Woolf*. Keynes, who worked for the Treasury during the first part of his time here, took over the lease in 1918, and remained here

> 'The old saying holds. Owe your banker £1000 and you are at his mercy; owe him £1 million and the position is reversed' – Keynes offers a sanguine view of Britain's gargantuan post-war debt.

until his death; his wife Lydia then stayed on until 1948. The spells of cohabitation with Clive Bell could be fractious: Bell once told Keynes that he should be the one to make do with an uncomfortable bed as he was far less sexually active.

LYTTON STRACHEY

(1880–1932) critic and biographer

51 Gordon Square **28**

STRACHEY is best known for *Eminent Victorians* (1918), his pungent account of the lives of Florence Nightingale*, General Gordon*, Thomas Arnold* and Cardinal Manning*, which contrasted with the uncritical biographies then much the norm. His mother, the suffragist Jane Strachey, secured this house (which dates from 1857) in 1919. Also based here were the unmarried Strachey sisters: Pippa, Marjorie and Pernel. The terrace was already home to many of the Bloomsbury Group; Strachey observed to Virginia Woolf*, 'Very

soon I foresee that the whole square will become a sort of college, and the rencontres in the garden I shudder to think of' (28 September 1919). It was Strachey's own chief London residence from 1921 and he had a self-contained flat on the ground floor from 1929 until his death. In 1963, his biographer Michael Holroyd discovered Strachey's lost dissertation on Warren Hastings in the basement, the family having given up the lease not long before. An 'In/Out' board still stood in the entrance hall: the deceased Stracheys were marked as 'Out'.

ROBERT TRAVERS HERFORD

(1860–1950) Unitarian minister, scholar
and interpreter of Judaism   14 Gordon Square **29**

HERFORD lived and worked here from 1914 to 1925: he was Secretary of Dr Williams's Library here, a collection devoted to religious Nonconformity. The library building – constructed in a Tudor revival style in 1848–9 – had been a university hall of residence, where Herford lodged in his student days. A pioneering scholar of Judaism, Herford explored the common heritage of the two traditions in works such as *Judaism in the New Testament Period* (1928) and *Talmud and Apocrypha* (1933); in lighter moments he referred to himself as a 'Jewnitarian'. His work confronted some of the deepest roots of anti-Semitism; this, especially at the time that he was writing, was of more than academic significance. After the war, Herford was fortunately able to trace many of his academic contacts on the Continent.

CHRISTINA GEORGINA ROSSETTI

(1830–94) poetess   30 Torrington Square **30**

THE sister of Dante Gabriel Rossetti*, Christina's reputation and influence as a poet have grown over time. Some of her earliest verses were published under the pseudonym Ellen Alleyn in the short-lived Pre-Raphaelite journal *The Germ*. Perhaps her best-known literary work is the poetry collection *Goblin Market* (1862), though Christina's name has come before a wider public through her Christmas carol 'In the Bleak Midwinter'. She moved here in 1876 sharing the house – which was built by James Sim in the early 1820s – with her widowed mother Frances Rossetti and two maternal aunts, Eliza and Charlotte Polidori. It was darkened

by soot-blackened trees that then stood in the square in front. Christina Rossetti's life was circumscribed by the needs of her elderly relations, who became bed-ridden: her nephew Ford Madox Ford* thought that her existence must have been 'extremely tragic' and detected in her poems 'a passionate yearning for the country'. A deeply religious High Anglican, her later verse was chiefly devotional, an exception being the sonnet sequence *Monna Innominata* (1881). Christina's health was failing by the time her aunt Eliza died in 1893, and her last companion was a Persian cat named Muff, who was invariably draped around her shoulders. Christina died in the front drawing room the following year.

SAMUEL ROMILLY

(1757–1818) law reformer   21 Russell Square **31**

ROMILLY strove to soften the savage 18th-century penal code; among his achievements was the abolition of the death penalty for pickpockets in 1808. A Whig, he was elected to Parliament in 1806, and served as Solicitor-General in the short-lived 'talents' ministry of 1806–7; Romilly was also an active campaigner for the abolition of slavery. He lived here for the most active part of his career, from 1805 – when the square was newly laid out – until his death by suicide here, in a fit of grief following the demise of his wife Anne. The imposing four-storey house dates from the early 19th century but has been much altered.

LILIAN LINDSAY

(1871–1960) the first woman dentist to
qualify in Britain   23 Russell Square **32**

LILIAN Murray, as she then was, won a scholarship to the North London Collegiate School – and defied its formidable headmistress, Frances Mary Buss*, who wanted her to teach deaf children. Instead she became Britain's first woman to qualify in dentistry – and to do so she had to train in Edinburgh, since no London-based training establishment would let a woman cross the threshold, even for an interview. For a time Lindsay practised in Hornsey Rise, not far from her Holloway birthplace, and worked in Russell Square at what was then the headquarters of the British Dental Association. Here she assembled a library and a collection of dental artefacts, and wrote on the history of dentistry – while sharing a flat upstairs with her husband Robert, from 1920 to 1935.

Lindsay was first commemorated in Hungerford Road, Holloway, but the house was lost to demolition.

PAUL NASH

(1889–1946) artist   Flat 176, Queen Alexandra Mansions, Bidborough St.

NASH moved here upon his marriage to Margaret Odeh in 1914, and it remained his London base for the next 22 years. One of his most famous pictures was *Northern Adventure* (1929), a surrealist take on the view of St Pancras Station from the small fifth-floor flat, a prospect now impeded by Camden Town Hall. A landscape painter of distinction, Nash was an official war artist in both world wars, and famously produced the stark battlescape *The Menin Road* (1918–19) and *Totes Meer* (1940–41), which depicts the twisted wreckage of German planes. He was dogged by asthma, and his search for a cure took him to country retreats on the borders of Sussex and Kent, and in Dorset. In 1936 Nash moved away to the fresher air of Hampstead.

THOMAS CARLYLE

(1795–1881) essayist and historian   33 (formerly 4) Ampton Street **34**

CARLYLE, best known for his history of the French Revolution, was venerated as an intellectual colossus by his contemporaries. He and his wife Jane – whose unhappy marriage lasted for nearly 40 years – lodged here for about six months from September 1831, the first London address that they shared; Carlyle reported to his mother that the house's owners, a family named Miles, were 'cleanly, orderly and seem honest: no noises, no bugs disturb one through the night'. He complained, however, of its *'hamperedness . . . I have a sort of* feeling as if I were tied up in a sack, and could not get my fins stirred'. While here he wrote the philosophical essay *Characteristics* (1831) and a piece on Dr Johnson*. In March 1832, the Carlyles returned to their native Scotland, returning briefly to Ampton Street in May 1834, before securing their long-term London residence at 24 (then 5) Cheyne Row, Chelsea, the following month. This house, now owned by the National Trust, became a museum to the couple; through her letters and journal, Jane Carlyle has achieved at least the fame of her husband.

R. H. TAWNEY

(1880–1962) historian, teacher
and political writer

A **CHRISTIAN** socialist and a professor at the London School of Economics, Richard Henry Tawney was one of the leading left-wing thinkers of the 20th century, and exerted a strong influence on the philosophy and policy of post-war Labour governments. His best-known books were a critique of contemporary capitalism, *The Acquisitive Society* (1921), and a historical investigation into its origins, *Religion and the Rise of Capitalism* (1926). Tawney always considered himself 'a displaced peasant' in the opulent surroundings of the Square – in which, over the years, he lived at four different addresses, including the surviving number 44. Slippers and an old First World War army tunic were his familiar attire, and he was constantly wreathed in pipe smoke. He and his wife Jeannette – sister of the social reformer William Beveridge, a friend of Tawney at Balliol College, Oxford – moved to the commemorated address from number 26 in 1951; here, Tawney remained until very shortly before his death.

SIR SYED AHMED KHAN

(1817–98) Muslim reformer and scholar

A **S** a magistrate in the service of the East India Company, Syed Ahmed saved thousands of British lives during the Great Rebellion or Indian Mutiny of 1857. He arrived in London in May 1869 and took furnished rooms at this house, which then belonged to a Mr and Mrs Ludlam. The notion of living as a tenant was unfamiliar to him, but he found the arrangement 'extremely comfortable' and his hosts charming yet unobtrusive. He and his sons Syed Mahmud and Syed Hamed – and another compatriot, Khudadad Beg – occupied six rooms and were attended by two servants. While here, he watched the Epsom Derby and witnessed the opening of the Holborn Viaduct; he also responded in print to hostile treatments of the prophet Muhammad and studied the English university system, being impressed by the general appetite for adult education, especially among British women. On his return to India, Khan founded the Muhammadan Anglo-Oriental College at Aligarh (1877), which continues today as the Aligarh Muslim University. Sir Syed Ahmed – he was one of the first Indians, and the first Muslim, to be knighted – was a pioneer of Islamic modernism, developing a theology that took account of European science, and founded a periodical called the *Mohammedan [sic] Social Reformer.*

WILLIAM RICHARD LETHABY*

(1857–1931) architect   20 Calthorpe Street

DURING his time at this early-19th-century house – where he lived from 1880 to 1891 – Lethaby worked in the office of Richard Norman Shaw* and assisted in the design of New Scotland Yard on Victoria Embankment, now known as the Norman Shaw Building. In 1883, he designed what was, by his later minimalist standards, a very ornate fireplace for Shaw's country-house masterpiece, Cragside in Northumberland. Lethaby set up his own practice in 1889, and completed five country houses and a church, All Saints, Brockhampton, Herefordshire (1901–2), before devoting himself to teaching and scholarship. He was joint director at the Central School of Arts and Crafts and art adviser to the LCC; from 1900 to 1918 he was the first Professor of Design at the Royal College of Art. Lethaby also served as Surveyor of Westminster Abbey from 1906 to 1928 and wrote on its history.

VERA BRITTAIN (1893–1970)
WINIFRED HOLTBY (1898–1935)

writers and reformers   58 Doughty Street

BRITTAIN'S autobiographical *Testament of Youth* (1933) deals with the devastating blow dealt to her generation by the First World War, in which she lost her fiancé and her brother. Holtby, a prolific author and journalist during her short life, is best known for *South Riding* (1936). The pair met at Somerville College, Oxford, both having worked as nurses during the war. Doughty Street, then a far more bohemian place than it is today, was their first London address; they moved here in September 1922 from elsewhere in the street; their top-floor flat was infested with mice, though its windows caught the afternoon sun, and it was cheerfully furnished in blue and mauve. Both women had their first novels published in 1923: Holtby's *Anderby Wold* and Brittain's *The Dark Tide*, an unflattering depiction of college life at Oxford; they worked as freelance journalists and took teaching jobs to make ends meet. In the autumn of 1923, the pair moved to Maida Vale. Brittain's biography of Holtby, *Testament of Friendship*, was published in 1940.

CHARLES DICKENS
(1812–70) writer 48 Doughty Street **39**

DICKENS moved here from Furnival Chambers, Holborn, in March 1837 on a three-year lease, paying the substantial sum of £80 a year in rent. He lived here with his wife Catherine and her younger sister, Mary Hogarth, who died suddenly at the age of 17 in Dickens's arms, prompting the only hiatus in his prolific writing career. While living here he nonetheless completed *The Pickwick Papers* (1837–8), *Oliver Twist* (1837–8) and *Nicholas Nickleby* (1838–9), and made a start on *Barnaby Rudge* (1841). Two daughters – Mary and Kate – were born in Doughty Street, and during his time here Dickens secured election to both the Garrick and Athenaeum clubs. Strong sales of *Nickleby* enabled him to move in December 1839 to a larger house, now demolished, in Marylebone.

The plaque of 1903 – one of the earliest put up by the LCC – pre-dates the opening of the house as a museum in 1925, prior to which it had been under threat of demolition.

SYDNEY SMITH

(1771–1845) author and wit · 14 (formerly 8) Doughty Street **40**

SMITH was a clergyman, but is remembered for his irreverent *bon mots*: the countryside, he averred, was 'a kind of healthy grave', and when it was proposed that St Paul's Cathedral be surrounded by wooden paving he replied, 'Let the Dean and Canons lay their heads together and the thing will be done'. He and his wife Catharine settled here shortly after their arrival in London in August 1803. Their first months here were marred by the fatal illness of their infant son Noel; Saba, their daughter, recalled the period as one of 'considerable anxiety and a severe and courageous struggle with poverty'. Smith eventually found a regular preaching engagement at the nearby Foundling Hospital in March 1805. The founder of the *Edinburgh Review*, he moved just north of Oxford Street in 1806.

WING COMMANDER F. F. E. YEO-THOMAS

(1902–64) secret agent · Queen Court, Queen Square **41**

FOREST Frederic Edward Yeo-Thomas was born in Marylebone but spent his early life in France. While underage, he fought in the First World War and after it, with the Polish Army against the Bolsheviks; captured, he evaded a death sentence by strangling his guard. 'Tommy' Yeo-Thomas joined the RAF in 1939 and escaped from France on one of the last boats out. Recruited by the Special Operations Executive (SOE), he was captured on his third mission into occupied France and subjected to torture. After several escape attempts, Yeo-Thomas was picked up by advancing American forces; afterwards, he returned for a time to his pre-war occupation, working for the Paris-based fashion house of Molyneux. Yeo-Thomas's plaque, which cites his *nom de guerre* of 'The White Rabbit', is on the six-storey inter-war Bloomsbury block where he shared a ground-floor flat (no. 5) with his partner Barbara Dean: he gave this as his address on joining SOE and eventually returned there.

JOHN HOWARD

(1726–90) prison reformer   23 (formerly 29) Great Ormond Street **42**

LEFT a fortune by his father, Howard found his calling as a result of being imprisoned by privateers in Brest, France. As High Sheriff of Bedfordshire, he was aghast to find many acquitted prisoners kept locked up until they had paid a release fee. Howard secured Acts of Parliament to prohibit this, and to improve health and sanitation in prisons. Despite ill health, he visited nearly every county gaol in England, and published his findings as *The State of the Prisons in England and Wales, with Preliminary Observations, and an Account of some Foreign Prisons* (1777). Howard's house here was left to him in August 1777 by his sister, and was his London base for the rest of his life. It dates from the early 18th century, with a stucco facing added later. A deeply religious man, Howard never sat for a portrait; the Howard League for Penal Reform perpetuates his name and his work.

DOROTHY L. SAYERS

(1893–1957) writer of detective stories   24 Great James Street **43**

SAYERS moved to these 'small but very pretty rooms' on Christmas Eve 1921. The newly decorated, white-panelled flat here cost her £70 a year. In January 1924, Sayers gave birth to an illegitimate son, a fact she concealed from most of her family; two years later, she married a journalist, Oswald Atherton 'Mac' Fleming, who – like her most famous literary creation, Lord Peter Wimsey – suffered from the after-effects of his First World War experiences. The couple kept cats to combat a mouse infestation. In 1929 they moved to Witham, Essex, but kept the flat as a pied-à-terre. Among the works Sayers wrote here was her first novel, *Whose Body?* (1923), which introduced the character of Wimsey; in her day job at Benson's, an advertising agency, she devised the slogan 'My Goodness, My Guinness'. The house dated from the early 18th century, but was rebuilt around 1970. Sayers's home would have been on the left-hand side of the faux-Georgian frontage.

BENJAMIN DISRAELI, EARL OF BEACONSFIELD*

(1804–81) Prime Minister 22 Theobald's Road (formerly 6 King's Road)

THE son of Isaac D'Israeli, a writer and historian, Benjamin Disraeli was a self-made man, and not averse to a little self-mythology: at various times he claimed to have been born in the Adelphi, where his father lived before his marriage; at 6 Bloomsbury Square, to which his family moved in 1817; and at his grandparental home in Islington. It is all but certain, however, that Disraeli was born here, in the early morning of 21 December 1804. Isaac D'Israeli and his wife Maria were living at the house by 1802, and it was here –

under the aegis of the Bevis Marks Synagogue – that the ceremony of circumcision took place. Disraeli attended a school in Islington kept by a Miss Roper, before moving on to another in Blackheath, run by the Revd John Potticary, where he was given separate instruction in Judaism; his baptism into the Church of England took place at St Andrew's Holborn in July 1817, just before the family left number 22. Disraeli dropped the apostrophe from the family name in 1822. The house is part of a terrace of five built in about 1775 and was restored in 1989.

SIR HIRAM MAXIM

(1840–1916) inventor and engineer Hatton House, 57D Hatton Garden

MAXIM designed the eponymous Maxim gun, the first fully automatic machine gun, capable of firing off a devastating 500 rounds a minute. He was born in the US state of Maine, arrived in England in 1881 and soon afterwards took a business lease on these workshop premises, which were built in 1880 and are outwardly

little changed. He perfected his gun by 1883 and set up the Maxim Gun Company the following year. The weapon soon attracted notice – Henry Stanley* carried one on his mission to 'rescue' David Livingstone in 1887 – and it was adopted as standard by the British Army in 1889 and by the Royal Navy in 1892. In 1888 Maxim's moved to Crayford,

Kent, following a merger and was absorbed by Vickers, the arms and aerospace firm, eight years later. Maxim became a naturalised British citizen in 1900 and was knighted in 1901, remaining a director of the company he had founded until 1911.

Among Maxim's other, more benign, innovations were pre-Edisonian electric lights, an improved mousetrap and an expensive aeroplane that refused to get airborne.

WILLIAM RICHARD LETHABY*

(1857–1931)
architect

Central School of Arts and Crafts
(now Central St Martins), Southampton Row

LETHABY served as first Principal of the school from 1896 to 1911. Born in Barnstaple, Devon, his teaching and books on art and architecture exerted enormous influence on the development of 20th-century British design; the college he headed was soon hailed as 'a school of University rank for the artistic crafts'. Lethaby defined art simply as 'a well made thing', and the teaching methods he promoted were correspondingly practical, with skilled craftsmen recruited to the college staff, among them the calligrapher

Edward Johnston*. An active principal, Lethaby made stately progresses through classrooms 'like a white moustached rabbit, with a quick, dark eye,' and his students felt themselves 'to be pioneers taking part in an exciting experiment'. In 1903 the school moved here from Regent Street. Lethaby stipulated that the college's new building should be 'plain, reasonable and well-built', and had a hand in its design, which was carried out by a former Central student, A. Halcrow Verstage.

DANTE GABRIEL ROSSETTI*

(1828–82) poet and painter

WILLIAM MORRIS* (1834–96) poet and artist

SIR EDWARD C. BURNE-JONES*

(1833–98) painter

17 Red Lion Square

ROSSETTI took a lease on the first floor of this house with the painter Walter Howell Deverell early in 1851, and stayed until May

that year. Five years later, he recommended the place to Morris and Burne-Jones, in spite of its increasing dampness and decrepitude. The pair moved in during the summer of 1856 and remained here until the spring of 1859. The first-floor room at the front served as their studio, with its central window cut to the ceiling to optimise the light for painting, a feature since removed. Burne-Jones ('Ned') worked here on his early commissions, including a collaboration with Rossetti and Morris on a scheme of murals for the Oxford Union building (1857–8). Meanwhile, Morris ('Topsy') embarked on his early ventures in interior decoration, producing rough-hewn 'medieval' furniture for their rooms: 'If you want to be comfortable, go to bed,' was his peremptory advice. The young artists were attended by a housekeeper, Mary Nicolson, known as 'Red Lion Mary', who was also an able needleworker and contributed to Morris's designs. The house, designed by Nicholas Barbon and dating originally from the mid-1680s, was refronted in the early 19th century. Unusually, the plaque is of Hopton Wood stone.

JOHN HARRISON

(1693–1776) inventor of the marine chronometer

Summit House, 12 Red Lion Square **48**

A SELF-TAUGHT clockmaker from Lincolnshire, Harrison designed a timepiece that maintained sufficient accuracy on a long sea voyage to enable a ship's longitude to be calculated accurately. The Admiralty had promised £20,000 for anyone who facilitated this but Harrison had to battle long and hard with them to obtain the full payment. He moved to a house on this site in 1752 from an address in Orange Street, a vanished thoroughfare nearby. The successful sea trials of his chronometers took place in 1761 and 1765 in which year, at this address, he made the final disclosure and explanation of his H4 prototype design. Harrison's room was on the second floor; his

Harrison's story was the subject of Dava Sobel's bestseller *Longitude* (1995). The anonymous LCC employee who proposed the plaque did so with a rhetorical flourish: 'surely an inventor who has saved hundreds or thousands of lives is as much worth attention as the scribblers whom the council delights to honour?'

first three experimental chronometers ticked away on the floor below, much as they do today at the Royal Observatory in Greenwich. Final settlement of his financial claims eventually came in 1773, just three years before he died here.

THOMAS EARNSHAW

(1749–1829) watchmaker and chronometer maker   119 High Holborn

EARNSHAW made significant refinements to the marine chronometer invented by John Harrison*. He lived variously in Clerkenwell, St Pancras, Kennington and Greenford, but was first apprenticed at a workshop on this site in High Holborn to one William Hughes. Earnshaw inherited the business in 1792 and carried it on until about 1815, when it passed to his son Thomas. Like Harrison, Earnshaw wrestled with the problems of how to compensate for the effects of motion and temperature change on the mechanism of a timepiece. He possessed a combative – even rebarbative – personality, and carried on a long-running feud by pamphlet with a fellow clockmaker, John Arnold, over which of them deserved credit for a particular innovation, the spring-detent escapement. The Board of Longitude eventually awarded Earnshaw £3,000, in response to repeated petitioning; Earnshaw's mechanism, which ran without lubricating oil, was still in use over a century later.

SPENCER PERCEVAL

(1762–1812) Prime Minister   59–60 Lincoln's Inn Fields

THIS imposing building was built in 1639–41 and is also known as Lindsey House, from the residence here in the early 18th century of the 4th Earl of Lindsey. The house was divided in two in 1751–2 and Perceval took up residence at number 59 in the early 1790s, reuniting the two halves in 1802. Short in stature, he was described by Sydney Smith* as having 'the head of a country parson, and the tongue of an Old Bailey Lawyer'. He became a King's Counsel and MP in 1796, and was Attorney-General in the Tory governments of Addington and Pitt (1802–6). He left Lincoln's Inn Fields in 1807, shortly after accepting the post of Chancellor of the Exchequer in the Duke of Portland's administration. In 1809, Perceval became premier but his time at the top was abruptly terminated on 11 May 1812, when he was shot at point-blank range in the lobby of the House of Commons by John Bellingham, a ruined merchant with a grudge. Perceval's dying words were reputed to have been, 'Oh, I am murdered!' Cynics acclaimed this as a rare example of an unambiguous truth being uttered within the walls of Parliament. Perceval's plaque is bronze, and easy to miss.

WILLIAM MARSDEN

(1796–1867) surgeon and founder of the Royal Free
and Royal Marsden hospitals   65 Lincoln's Inn Fields **51**

HAVING been unable to find a
hospital bed for a desperately
sick young woman he had found in a
churchyard, Marsden opened a free
dispensary at 16 Grenville Street,
Hatton Garden, in 1828. During
the 1832 cholera epidemic, this
dispensary was the only foundation
in London to admit sufferers; soon
after, Marsden wrote a treatise on
the disease. Thanks to the munificence of several rich backers,
the dispensary became the Royal
Free Hospital, which was situated
in Gray's Inn Road until its move
to Hampstead in 1978. In 1846,
Marsden's wife Elizabeth Ann died
from cancer and as a consequence,
Marsden founded in 1851 the Free
Cancer Hospital (based initially in
Cannon Row, Westminster), which
was dedicated to the study and
treatment of the disease. This became the Royal Marsden Hospital
in Fulham Road, the original part
of which was completed in 1862.
Marsden lived here from 1846 until
his death; the square was then a
popular address for surgeons, and
has been the location since the early
19th century of the profession's
Royal College. This four-storey
house, designed by Thomas
Leverton, dates from 1772.

DR SAMUEL JOHNSON*

(1709–84) author   17 Gough Square **52**

DR Johnson's House, as it is
known, is now a museum
dedicated to the great lexicographer.
It dates from the late 17th century,
and has three storeys, a basement
and a garret. Johnson worked on
his famous *Dictionary of the English
Language*, eventually published in
two volumes in April 1755, in the
attic rooms. This genre-defining
work was completed with the help
of five or six assistants who, despite
Johnson's well-advertised prejudic-
es, were mostly Scots; he presided
precariously over their endeavours
from a derelict armchair that was
missing an arm and a leg. Johnson
had moved here in 1746, just after
he was contracted to produce the
dictionary, in order to be closer to
his printers in Fleet Street. He suffered the loss of his wife Elizabeth
here and afterwards could not bear
to sit in the downstairs rooms that
he associated with her. By March
1759 Johnson, finding the house too
large, had moved into lodgings at
Staple Inn, Holborn.

Highgate Hill

20

19

Archway

18

17

16

15

Kentish Town

13   12

0   0.5km

14

10   11

Camden Road

8

9

Camden Town

7

6   5   Mornington Crescent

4

3   2

St Pancras   King's Cross

1

Euston

CAMDEN TOWN TO HIGHGATE HILL

CAMDEN Town was in existence by 1791, taking its name from the landowner Charles Pratt, 1st Earl Camden. The arrival of the railways in the mid-19th century led to a loss of social cachet, and the wider area was overwhelmed by people seeking cheap housing; West Kentish Town and Agar Town, a settlement to the east of St Pancras Way, were then among the worst slums in London. Low costs and intense industrial activity attracted entrepreneurs, businessmen, émigrés and artists.

Towards Highgate Hill, the desirability of the address seems to rise with the land – as noted by one local, John Betjeman*.

SIR NIGEL GRESLEY

(1876–1941) locomotive engineer   King's Cross Station, Platform 8

AS Chief Mechanical Engineer of the London and North Eastern Railway (LNER) from 1923 until his death in April 1941, Gresley worked from an office in the block on which the plaque has been placed. Born in Edinburgh, Gresley designed some of the fastest and most magnificent locomotives of the steam age. In 1934, the *Flying Scotsman* became the first steam engine to break the 100mph speed barrier, an achieve-ment bettered by the *Mallard*, which in 1938 clocked up a world record speed of 126mph. Perhaps Gresley's best-known design, the *Mallard* is on display at the National Railway Museum in York. Gresley pushed the technology of steam engines to its limit, but he recognised where the future lay, and had a hand in the plans for the electrification of the line between Sheffield and Manchester. He was knighted in 1936.

GEORGE CRUIKSHANK

(1792–1878) artist   263 Hampstead Road (formerly 48 Mornington Place) **2**

THE son of a caricaturist, Cruik-shank's own artistic abilities were well developed by the age of ten and he was widely celebrated by the time he reached his 20th birthday. He is remembered as the illustrator of *Oliver Twist* (1837–9) and other works by Dickens* but first made his name as a satirist. Cruikshank's time in this house of c.1830 – to which he moved on marrying his second wife, Eliza Widdison (1807–90) – was marred by persis-tent debt and, despite sporadic success, a failure to live up to his former successes. While here, Cruikshank seduced one of the young house-maids, Adelaide Attree, with whom he had a number of children. The scale of his double life – and his maintenance of two households, one here and the other close by at 31 Augustus Street – was not fully revealed until after his death.

WALTER SICKERT

(1860–1942) painter and etcher   6 Mornington Crescent **3**

SICKERT'S penchant for seedi-ness was commented on by contemporaries, and Camden Town certainly possessed that quality at the time he was living in a two-room lodging in this early-19th-century terrace (1905 to *c*.1908). In 1907 the 'Camden Town Murder' of the prostitute Emily Dimmock hit the headlines, and inspired him to create a series of paintings; other works produced here were the *Mornington Crescent Nude* series and studies of the model 'Little Rachel'. A founder member of the Fitzroy Street Group

> Sickert's artistic interest in low life and crime scenes has led to him being fingered, on doubtful grounds, as a Jack the Ripper suspect.

and the Camden Town Group, Sickert was based in the area until 1915.

SPENCER FREDERICK GORE

(1878–1914) painter   31 Mornington Crescent

A N early assimilator of French impressionism, 'Freddie' Gore was an inspiration to his friend, fellow Camden Town Group artist and near-neighbour Walter Sickert*. Gore was also important as an organising force in the Fitzroy Street Group and the London Group. He lived at this 1820s terraced house as a lodger of the Reverend Osmond Edward Archer from 1909 until his marriage in 1912. A number of his works were painted from the window of his room; others were done al fresco in the neighbourhood: *Nearing Euston Station* (1911), an evocative depiction of the railway artery that bisects Camden, is one such. Gore's enthusiasm for painting from life brought his own to a premature end after he contracted pneumonia after an outdoor session in Richmond Park. His father, Spencer William Gore, was the winner of the inaugural men's singles at Wimbledon in 1877.

GEORGE MACDONALD

(1824–1905) writer   20 (formerly 1A, then 4) Albert Street

M ACDONALD moved from his native Aberdeenshire to London in 1859, where he taught English at Bedford College. He is known especially for the 'fairy romance' *Phantastes* (1858) and for his children's stories, which include *The Princess and the Goblin* (1872). MacDonald and his wife Louisa lived in this handsome Gothic style house of 1843-4 – known as Tudor Lodge – from August 1860 until around July 1863. In the semi-autobiographical *The Vicar's Daughter* (1872), MacDonald described the house as 'stuck on like a swallow's nest to the end of a great row of commonplace houses, nearly a quarter of a mile in length'. He used the studio built for the house's first inhabitant, the artist Charles Lucy, as a study and lecture room.

JOHN DESMOND BERNAL

(1901–71) crystallographer   44 Albert Street

BERNAL was born in Ireland and studied physics at Cambridge, where he was nicknamed 'Sage' for his impressive knowledge. In 1938, he was elected to the chair of physics at Birkbeck College, London, and in 1963 became Professor of Crystallography, the science of analysing the crystalline structure of materials. Bernal transformed the understanding of the structure of genes, viruses, proteins, vitamins and hormones, and was also a pioneer of modern X-ray crystallography. During the Second World War, he contributed to the success of the D-Day landings, not least by co-inventing the Mulberry floating harbour. An ardent Marxist, and a friend of Mao, Khrushchev and Picasso, Bernal believed in sexual liberty; his wife Eileen and his two mistresses knew each other well. He lived in Albert Street from about 1967 until his death at the house four years later.

DYLAN THOMAS

(1914–53) poet   54 Delancey Street

THOMAS moved to London from Swansea in 1934, soon after the publication of his first collection of verse, *Eighteen Poems*. According to his biographer Paul Ferris, 'Thomas was a commuter – writing in Wales and travelling up to London to drink.' In Delancey Street he lived with his wife Caitlin – also a writer – and their young children in a three-room basement flat from about October 1951 until their departure for America in January 1952. At this time, his greatest work *Under Milk Wood* was in preparation; the final version was broadcast in January 1954, three months after his alcohol-related death in New York. The poet's daughter, Aeronwy, recalled that their home here was 'decorated throughout . . . in a riot of chintz, a real floral cornucopia'. The landlady was Margaret Taylor, wife of the historian A. J. P. Taylor*; she provided a Romany caravan in the garden for Thomas to write in.

TOM SAYERS

(1826–65) pugilist   257 Camden High Street **8**

SAYERS moved to London from Brighton in 1842 to work as a bricklayer, and made his first appearance in the boxing ring in 1849; weighing just under 69kg (11 stone), and standing 175cm (5ft 9in) tall, he relied on his strength, courage and his capacity to endure pain. His final, and most famous, bout was in Farnborough, Hampshire, in April 1860, against the American John C. Heenan, dubbed 'the fight of the century'. After over two hours and 37 rounds, it ended in a draw; Sayers was badly hurt, and retired from the championship. Having lived in Camden Town for about 20 years, his last days were spent here at the home of his friend John Mensley, above the Mensley boot factory. Sayers fell ill, and died here on 8 November 1865. His famous funeral procession, modelled on that of the Duke of Wellington, set out for Highgate Cemetery from this address.

RUTH FIRST (1925–82) & JOE SLOVO (1926–95)

South African freedom fighters   13 Lyme Street **9**

FIRST and Slovo met at the University of Witwatersrand in Johannesburg – where their fellow students included Nelson Mandela – and married in 1949. They both became prominent white activists in the Defiance Campaign, and helped to develop the Freedom

Nelson Mandela unveiling the plaque in 2003.

Charter of the African National Congress (ANC). First was imprisoned in 1963 and on her release fled to England, where the account of her experience, *117 Days* (1965), brought her fame. The Slovos lived here from July 1966 to the end of 1978, with Ruth's parents living in a self-contained basement flat. First taught and wrote during this period – the sound of her typewriter is said to have been heard day and night – while Slovo worked full-time for the ANC. In 1982, while she was living in Mozambique, First was killed by a letter bomb sent by South African government agents. Slovo continued the fight, and played a vital role in bringing about the peaceful transfer of power in South Africa.

WILLIAM DANIELL

(1769–1837) artist
and engraver

135 St Pancras Way
(formerly 7 Brecknock Terrace) **10**

IN 1785 William accompanied his artist uncle Thomas Daniell* to India, where he made drawings and sketches. These, worked up as engravings, were published in *Oriental Scenery* (1795–1808), the finest visual record of the subcontinent then available. William was a master of the aquatint, a process pioneered by Thomas, but refined by his nephew in works such as his *View of London* (1812) and *Voyage round Britain* (1814–25). Daniell lived at this house for a few months before dying here on 16 August 1837. The early-19th-century building was badly damaged during the Second World War and rebuilt in facsimile; Daniell's other homes, in Fitzrovia, have gone completely.

THEODOR FONTANE

(1819–98) German writer
and novelist

6 (formerly 52) St Augustine's Road **11**

FONTANE grew up in Brandenburg and Berlin. In 1844, he made the first of three journeys to England, home of his idols Dickens* and Thackeray*, which he described as the 'model or, better, the essence of the whole world'. Fontane's stay of 1852 resulted in his *A Summer in London* (1854). During his last trip, of 1855–9, he worked as a foreign correspondent for newspapers, and also kept a diary of observations on mid-Victorian London society. He and his family lived at this end-of-terrace house from August 1857 until their return to Germany at the end of 1858. Fontane, who turned the back drawing room into his study, described the house as having a 'pleasant' aspect.

FRANCES MARY BUSS
(1827–94) pioneer of education for women

Camden School for Girls, Sandall Road **12**

BUSS was born in Camden Street and worked as a teacher from her teens in order to help support her family. In the 1840s, she taught at a private school founded by her mother in Kentish Town, and in 1850 she decided to open a school of her own; this, the North London Collegiate School for Ladies (NLCS), provided the middle classes with good tuition at moderate fees. In 1871, Buss opened a second school, the Camden School for Girls, in Prince of Wales Road (transferring after the Second World War to the former site of NLCS on Sandall Road). The first to describe herself as a headmistress, she dedicated herself to the improvement of teacher training for women. Buss also campaigned for women to be allowed to sit public examinations and for women's admission to universities.

GEORGE ORWELL
(1903–50) novelist and political essayist

50 Lawford Road **13**

ERIC Arthur Blair was born in India and brought up in England. During the Spanish Civil War he fought with the republican forces, as described – under his pen-name of George Orwell – in *Homage to Catalonia* (1938). Further experiences modified his socialist convictions: wariness of tyranny and scepticism of dogma characterise his two best-known works, *Animal Farm* (1945) and *Nineteen Eighty-Four* (1949). Orwell lived on the first floor at the back at number 50, and stayed here from August

> The clacking of Orwell's mechanical typewriter was a source of aggravation to his neighbours in Lawford Road, who were not sorry to see him go.

1935 until January 1936, along with fellow writers Rayner Heppenstall and Michael Sayers: relations with the former were not always smooth, notably over Heppenstall's alleged reluctance to wash up. While here Orwell completed the novel *Keep the Aspidistra Flying* (1936).

'FATHER' HENRY WILLIS

(1821–1901) organ builder   9 Rochester Terrace   **14**

THE son of a carpenter, Willis was apprenticed in 1835 to John Gray, a London organ builder, and later set up in business on his own. His big break came with his 1847 commission to rebuild the organ of Gloucester Cathedral. A stream of commissions followed; they included the organ for the 1851 Great Exhibition, later moved to Winchester Cathedral, together with those for St George's Hall, Liverpool (1854–5), the Royal Albert Hall (1871) and St Paul's Cathedral (1872). Over the course of his career, Willis built or rebuilt over 2,000 organs, which are known for their richness and clarity of sound. His firm – based from 1866 at The Rotunda, 67–71 Rochester Place – also produced 'Scudamore' organs for small country churches. Willis – dubbed 'Father' in 1898 after the famous 17th-century organ builder 'Father' (Bernard) Smith – lived from 1867 until 1895 at this semi-detached property of *c*.1840; his organ works would have been visible from the rear of the house.

FORD MADOX BROWN

(1821–93) painter   56 Fortess Road (formerly 13 Fortess Terrace)   **15**

BROWN lived here with his second wife Emma, formerly his model, from 1855 until 1862. By this time, he was an artist of repute, closely associated with the Pre-Raphaelite Brotherhood*, whose leading lights visited him here. His most famous paintings include *The Last of England* (1852–5), and *Work* (1852–63), an innovative and complex image set in Hampstead that shows the effect of the work ethic on every level of society. In the 1860s, Brown also made a name for himself as an accomplished designer of furniture and stained glass, and was a partner in William Morris's* company – Morris, Marshall, Faulkner & Co. – from its foundation in 1861; some of his furniture was designed specifically for the house in Fortess Terrace. In 1878, he began his last major work: 12 paintings on a panel for Manchester's new town hall, illustrating the town's history.

KWAME NKRUMAH

(1909–72) first President of Ghana 60 Burghley Road

NKRUMAH moved to London in spring 1945 from the Gold Coast (now Ghana) to study philosophy and law. Academic work was soon eclipsed by his political activities; that October he became Vice-President of the West African Student Union, Regional Secretary of the Pan-African Federation, and joint Secretary of the organising committee of the fifth Pan-African Congress in Manchester. Initially, Nkrumah found it hard to find accommodation; countless doors were slammed in his face because of his colour. Eventually, he found a welcome in Burghley Road, his home from June 1945 until November 1947, where his landlady, Mrs Florence Manley, looked upon him 'as a member of my family', and made a point of opening her home to his friends. In 1957, Nkrumah became the first Prime Minister of independent Ghana; three years later, he became President. Controversially, he turned Ghana into a one-party state, but left a lasting legacy – in the provision, for example, of free elementary education.

RICHARD D'OYLY CARTE*

(1844–1901) opera impresario and hotelier 2 Dartmouth Park Road **17**

D'OYLY Carte was the business brains behind the musical partnership of W. S. Gilbert* and Arthur Sullivan; it was he who brought the pair together to write their first operetta, *Trial By Jury*, which he presented at the Royalty Theatre in 1875. In 1881 Carte opened his own London theatre, the Savoy, where Gilbert and Sullivan's subsequent, roaringly successful 'Savoy Operas' were staged. Eight years later, he opened the Savoy Hotel, next door, which soon became a favourite high-society haunt. Number 2 Dartmouth Park Road, then newly built, was Carte's family home during the 1860s, while he worked for his father, a woodwind instrument maker in Charing Cross. The family name was altered from 'Cart'; Carte's father also encouraged his offspring to speak French at home. D'Oyly Carte (D'Oyly being a first name, with origins in his mother's family) saw his own first opera – *Dr Ambrosias: His Secret* – performed in 1868, while living in Dartmouth Park.

SIR GEOFFREY JELLICOE

(1900–96) landscape architect

19 Grove Terrace **18**

BEING convinced that 'architecture was part of the environment and therefore incomplete when considered in isolation', Jellicoe played a major part in founding the Institute of Landscape Architects in 1929. Among his commissions were the Kennedy Memorial, Runnymede, Berkshire (1964–5), Shute House, Wiltshire (1970–80), the Royal Horticultural Society's gardens at Wisley, Surrey (1970–72), and the modern, pedestrianised form of Fitzroy Square (1972–7). A follower of Jung, Jellicoe developed ways to access the subconscious mind when framing his designs. He had offices in Bloomsbury and lived in Grove Terrace for nearly half a century from 1936, sharing the tall, narrow terraced house and garden with his wife and collaborator Susan; together, they wrote a wide-ranging historical survey, *The Landscape of Man* (1975).

SIR JOHN BETJEMAN

(1906–84) poet

31 Highgate West Hill **19**

'**D**EEPLY I loved thee, 31 West Hill', wrote Betjeman in his blank verse autobiography *Summoned by Bells* (1960). Memories of his childhood – he lived here with his family from 1908 until he went to the Dragon School in Oxford – suffuse his creative output; as late as 1972, when he was appointed Poet Laureate, he still owned his childhood teddy-bear, Archie. It was at West Hill, attending Byron House school, that Betjeman developed his first crush, on one Peggy Purey-Cust. A less happy memory was of being taunted for his Teutonic-sounding name after the outbreak of war. Betjeman's interest in architecture

> While at Oxford University – which he left without taking a degree – Betjeman invented a sherry and advocaat-based cocktail called 'liquid cake'.

and its conservation later manifested itself in books – starting with *Ghastly Good Taste* (1933) – and in television programmes such as *Metroland* (1973). These interests may be traced to his years at this three-storey mid-terrace house of about 1860: a keen social observer, he drew an analogy between its position on West Hill – about half way up – and his family's rung on the social ladder.

J. B. PRIESTLEY

(1894–1984) novelist, playwright and essayist

JOHN Boynton Priestley was born in Bradford. After war service and Cambridge, he established himself as a literary journalist and made his reputation with the novels *The Good Companions* (1929) and *Angel Pavement* (1930). A prolific playwright – no fewer than 50 plays flew off his pen – Priestley is most remembered for *Time and the Conways* (1937) and the enduring *An Inspector Calls* (1946). His social commentaries – in particular *English Journey* (1933) – won him considerable notice as a documenter of the state of the nation, and this led on to his becoming a principal broadcaster during the Second World War. Priestley was hugely successful though never quite taken into the literary establishment. With his wife Jane, he acquired this house of c.1688 in late 1931 – he thought it 'one of the loveliest things you ever saw' – and remained until bombing forced them out ten years later. The house was also the last residence of Samuel Taylor Coleridge*.

PRIMROSE HILL AND BELSIZE PARK

BEFORE the area was built up, Primrose Hill – so-named from at least the 16th century – dominated the landscape, while other local landmarks included Belsize House and Chalcot's Farm – known as Chalk Farm House by the mid-18th century. Throughout the middle decades of the 19th century, fields gave way to long terraces of semi-detached and detached houses. From the outset, the area proved attractive to artists and writers, as well as the professional classes.

Belsize Park

Kentish Town West

Chalk Farm

Primrose Hill

Regent's Park

0   0.5km

HUMPHREY JENNINGS

(1907–50) documentary film-maker   8 Regent's Park Terrace **1**

SUFFOLK-BORN Jennings joined the GPO Film Unit* – later the Crown Film Unit – in 1934, where he edited and directed short documentaries. In 1936, with Roland Penrose* and others, he organised London's International Surrealist Exhibition, and the following year co-founded Mass-Observation, a study of the everyday lives of ordinary people in Britain. During the war years he produced his most influential work for the Crown Film Unit including *London Can Take It* (1940) and *A Diary for Timothy* (1945). Jennings lived in this 1840s house from January 1944 until his death; he rented part of the property from his friend Allen Hutt, the journalist, who lived here with his family. Jennings originally lived in two rooms on the ground floor but after he was joined by his wife Cicely and two daughters in summer 1946, they moved to the top two floors of the house. It was, he said, 'rather noisy at times but extremely romantic'. While living here, Jennings also worked on *Pandaemonium*, a posthumously published anthology that charted the Industrial Revolution through contemporary texts.

ARTHUR HUGH CLOUGH

(1819–61) poet   11 St Mark's Crescent **2**

CLOUGH was born in Liverpool and raised partly in South Carolina: his father was a cotton merchant. Doubts about his Anglican faith caused him to give up life as an Oxford don, to which his narrative poem 'The Bothie of Tober-na-Vuolich' (1848) was a farewell. He and his new wife Blanche moved to St Mark's Crescent in 1854, shortly after the house was built. During their five years here, their first two children were born, and Clough worked on the poems 'Amours de Voyage' and 'Dipsychus'. He was a busy man, with a day job as an examiner at the Education Office, while he also worked as an unpaid assistant to his wife's cousin, Florence Nightingale*, in her campaign to reform military hospitals. Overwork seems to have been a factor in the breakdown of his health, and he died aged just 42; his friend and fellow poet Matthew Arnold* was moved to elegy in 'Thyrsis'. During the Second World War, Winston Churchill* invoked Clough's famous line 'westward, look, the land is bright' when seeking assistance from the United States – an appropriate choice, given the poet's transatlantic links.

A. J. P. TAYLOR

(1906–90) historian and broadcaster

TWO doors down from Clough's is a plaque to another one-time Oxford academic who was also the son of a Lancashire cotton merchant. Alan John Percivale Taylor, born in Birkdale, was one of the first 'TV dons', who enjoyed parallel careers as a broadcaster – he had an extraordinary ability to lecture without notes – and journalist. A left-wing maverick with a dry wit – he once told an Oxford interview panel that he had 'extreme views, weakly held' – he ranged widely as a historian. A recurring theme in Taylor's work was German expansionism and – as he outlined in his controversial book *The Origins of the Second World War* (1961) – he did not believe it was sufficient simply to blame the Nazis for what he saw as a manifestation of a longer-term phenomenon. Taylor's domestic life was complicated: he shared the house in Primrose Hill with his first (and by then already ex) wife Margaret and their four children, from 1955 to 1978. For the earlier part of this period he spent half his time in Fortis Green with his second wife, Eve, with whom he also had a family.

WILLIAM ROBERTS

(1895–1980) artist

ROBERTS studied at the Slade, where his fellow pupils included Mark Gertler* and Paul Nash*. With Wyndham Lewis* and others, Roberts was a founder in 1914 of the short-lived but influential Vorticist group, which set out to free England from the artistic legacy of the Victorian age. After serving as an official war artist from 1918, Roberts began the work for which he would become best known: studies of everyday urban life. Roberts and his wife Sarah moved to this mid-19th-century house backing onto Regent's Canal in 1946. At first, they lived in one room of what was a lodging house, but gradually took over the house as other tenants dispersed. Eventually, the owner offered to sell the property to them for £1,200; William and Sarah were offered the sum by a friend in exchange for some paintings. They set about decorating and furnishing the house; Roberts made many of the fittings. Working from his studio in the ground-floor front room, he completed works such as *Trooping the Colour* (1958–9) and *The Lake* (1964). He died here at the age of 84.

ROGER FENTON

(1819–69) photographer   2 Albert Terrace

FENTON lived in this imposing semi-detached house from 1847 for about 16 years, at the height of his career. Born near Bury, Lancashire, he originally trained as a lawyer, but on receiving a large inheritance turned to painting, which he studied in Paris and London. He was first drawn to the new art of photography in about 1852, and the following year helped to found the (Royal) Photographic Society; in the long term, he was to play a crucial part in promoting the standing of his profession. Fenton is remembered above all for his images of the Crimea; taken in 1855, these included *Valley of the Shadow of Death* and proved significant in educating the British public about the realities of war. His mastery of technique and his distinctive, imaginative style are also evident in his photographs of landscape, still-life, architecture and the British royal family, who were important patrons. Despite his success, Fenton suddenly and mysteriously abandoned photography in 1862, possibly disenchanted by the lowly status still accorded to the art form. He left his 'quiet nest in Albert Terrace' – at which his photographic studio was based – for Potters Bar, Hertfordshire, in about 1863, and returned to his career at the Bar.

WILLIAM BUTLER YEATS

(1865–1939) poet and dramatist   23 Fitzroy Road **6**

THE son of the painter John Butler Yeats, William and his family moved to London from Dublin in summer 1867 and lived in this house until 1872, when he went on an extended stay to the Sligo home of his grandparents. The Yeats family later settled in Bedford

Park in west London. Yeats's poetry, deeply influenced by mysticism and Gaelic legend, was to bring him international acclaim and, in 1923, the Nobel Prize for Literature; his best-known works include 'The Lake Isle of Innisfree' (1890) and 'Easter 1916' (1916). In London, where he lived for much of his life, Yeats was a prominent figure, and mixed with the likes of Oscar Wilde*, William Morris* and George Bernard Shaw*.

SYLVIA PLATH

(1932–63) poet   3 Chalcot Square ⑦

BORN in Boston, Massachusetts, Plath moved to England with her husband, the British poet Ted Hughes, in December 1959. In January the following year, through the efforts of the American poet W. S. Merwin and his wife, the couple found an unfurnished three-roomed flat here on the top floor; it was to be their home until August 1961, when they moved to Devon. Plath's time here was productive; she saw the publication of her first volume of poetry, *The Colossus* (1960), wrote her only novel, *The Bell Jar* (1963), and gave birth to her first child, Frieda. Later she lived – and died – at the house bearing Yeats's plaque.

DR JOSÉ RIZAL

(1861–96) writer and national hero of the Philippines   37 Chalcot Crescent ⑧

RIZAL was an early leader of the Filipino movement for political, economic and social independence from Spain. His first novel, *Noli Me Tangere* ('Touch Me Not'; 1887), quickly attracted the attention of the Spanish authorities, and was banned in the Philippines. Rizal was forced to travel abroad, and arrived in May 1888 in London, lodging with the Beckett family. During his stay here, which lasted until early 1889, Rizal was occupied largely in scholarly research; at the British Museum, he discovered Antonio de Morga's *Sucesos de las Islas Filipinas,* an early-17th-century account of the rich history of the Philippines before Spanish rule. In 1890 he published an edition of this work, and in 1891 followed it with *El Filibusterismo* ('The Subversive' or 'The Reign of Greed'), which further exposed the ills of the Spanish colonial government. In 1892, he returned to the Philippines; there, he was accused – unjustly – of associating with a secret revolutionary society, and was executed by firing squad on 30 December 1896.

FRIEDRICH ENGELS

(1820–95) political philosopher

THE son of a German textile manufacturer, Engels came in 1842 to England, where he worked for the Manchester branch of his father's business. During this period, his interest in radicalism and socialism intensified, and he wrote influential works including

The house 'delights us all with its wonderfully free setting'.

Jenny Marx on number 122

The Condition of the Working Class in England (1845). In 1844, Engels met Karl Marx*; thereafter, the pair's careers and writings were inseparably linked. Together, they wrote *The Communist Manifesto* (1848), and in 1849 both settled permanently in England, where Engels provided Marx – whom he named 'the greatest living thinker' – with both intellectual and financial support.

In 1869, Engels retired from the family firm and the following year moved here from Manchester. He chose the house, in a mid-19th-century terrace at the foot of Primrose Hill, because it was close to Marx's home on the other side of Haverstock Hill; it was Marx's wife Jenny who found the house for him. Engels lived here until December 1894, when he moved east along the street to 41 Regent's Park Road.

Engels (standing, left) with Karl Marx and Marx's daughters on Hampstead Heath, 1864.

SIR JOHN SUMMERSON

(1904–92) architectural historian 1 Eton Villas **10**

SUMMERSON must take much credit for the emergence of architectural history as a mature academic discipline. Having made his name as the biographer of John Nash* he went on to author landmark works such as *Georgian London* (1946) and *Architecture in Britain, 1530–1830* (1953), while also finding time to be a highly effective director of Sir John Soane's Museum in Lincoln's Inn Fields. His aim, he once said, was to produce histories that were 'comprehensible and, if possible, eloquent'. With his wife Elizabeth (sister of the sculptor Barbara Hepworth) and their triplet sons, Summerson moved to Eton Villas in 1949, where he remained until

> As a conservationist Summerson could be very selective, once stating that the demolition of Battersea Power Station would be 'no great loss'.

he died here 43 years later. The house dates from exactly a century before the family moved in, having been built by one Samuel Cuming, a Devon carpenter made good. Summerson paid £1,700 for a 17-year lease on the house and later bought the freehold from Eton College for £4,500. The knowledgeable affection with which he wrote about his home and its environs played a part in the listing of the house and its neighbours in 1974.

ALFRED STEVENS

(1818–75) artist 9 Eton Villas **11**

STEVENS gained his artistic training working with his father, a house painter and decorator, before studying in Italy from 1833 to 1842. The most important event in his career was the commission, in 1857, to design the Wellington Monument for St Paul's Cathedral. This work was to take up the remainder of his life, and was unfinished at the time of his death; it was later completed by John Tweed*.

Stevens was living in this terraced house, built about 1849, by the late 1850s and remained here until his death. During his time here, Stevens was something of a recluse; it was said that, 'Engrossed with his work, he never went into society', but 'ate when he was hungry, and not always then, and went to bed when fatigue drove him there'. Yet he kept up a formal appearance: strangers often mistook him for a Catholic priest.

LESLIE 'HUTCH' HUTCHINSON

(1900–69) singer and pianist   31 Steele's Road **12**

'HUTCH'**,** as he was usually
known, was born in Grenada
and began his musical career in the
United States; alarmed at the activities of the Ku Klux Klan, he left for
Paris. In 1927 he came to London,
where his lush baritone and accomplished piano-playing brought him
great success as a cabaret artiste,
performing such songs as 'Night
and Day', 'These Foolish Things'
and 'A Nightingale Sang in Berkeley
Square'. Hutch made up his own
raunchy verses to Cole Porter's
'Let's Do It', and evidently took the
song's essential message to heart:

his high-society lovers included
Edwina Mountbatten*. Having just
landed a recording contract with
Parlophone, he bought the two-
storey detached house in Steele's
Road – built in 1874 by the architect
J. M. Brydon – in 1929. The post-
war years saw a decline in Hutch's
popularity and his health. In 1967,
debts forced the sale of the property, which had grown increasingly
squalid since the death of his wife
Ella nine years earlier. In a phrase
from a lost world, Hutch's *Times*
obituary called him 'the ideal artist
for the relaxed hour after dinner'.

ARTHUR RACKHAM

(1867–1939) illustrator   16 Chalcot Gardens **13**

LAMBETH-BORN Rackham
turned to illustration full-
time in 1892. The publication of
his illustrations for *Grimm's Fairy
Tales* (1900) marked the beginning
of his success. He was in particular
demand as an illustrator of children's stories, including *Rip Van
Winkle* (1905), *Peter Pan in Kensington Gardens* (1906) and *Alice in
Wonderland* (1907), and his vivid
depictions of fairies, witches, elves
and other fantastical characters
were to be found in treasured books
in households across Britain and
the United States. Rackham lived in

'a most delightful place, cool,
airy and quiet'

Arthur Rackham's first-floor studio

Chalcot Gardens with his wife, the
painter Edyth Starkie. The house,
built in 1881 and enlarged in 1898 to
the designs of C. F. A. Voysey*, was
further altered by Maxwell Ayrton
before the couple took up residence
in 1906; Ayrton provided studios
for both husband and wife. The
Rackhams moved to Sussex in
1920, though Arthur retained a
workplace and pied-à-terre at
6 Primrose Hill Studios.

SIR HENRY WOOD

(1869–1944) musician · 4 Elsworthy Road **14**

WOOD was born in Oxford Street, and was to remain firmly connected with that area for much of his life; his greatest work, as a conductor and musical director, was carried out at the Queen's Hall, Langham Place (demolished). He lived in Elsworthy Road from summer 1905 until autumn 1937, though the house – built in about 1880 – was often let to friends, including Delius* who stayed here in 1918. Wood lived here with his first wife Olga (1868–1909), a Russian-born soprano, and later with his second, Muriel Greatrex.

It was at the Queen's Hall that, in 1895, Wood first conducted the Promenade concerts (the 'Proms'), conceived by the Hall's manager, Robert Newman. Wood was to conduct them for 50 consecutive seasons; his last Prom took place in 1944, by which time the concerts had transferred to the Royal Albert Hall. Knighted in 1911, Sir Henry hoped – through the Proms – to bring classical music to the masses. In this, he was eminently successful: by the time of his death, the Proms were a popular and successful British institution.

AGNES ARBER

(1879–1960) botanist · 9 Elsworthy Terrace **15**

ARBER researched the physical forms and microscopic structures of living and fossil plants, including cereals and grasses, as well as seed-producing and flowering plants. Over her long career, she published some 70 scientific articles and eight books. In her sixties she became the first woman scientist to win the medal of the Linnean Society and the third – and first woman botanist – to be admitted as a fellow of the Royal Society. Born Agnes Robertson, she lived here with her parents and sisters – appropriately, within sight of leafy Primrose Hill – from 1890, when the house was fairly new, until her marriage in 1909. She attended the North London Collegiate School for Girls and University College London, where she took a first degree in botany and held a research studentship. These came either side of further study at Newnham College, Cambridge, the city to which she moved upon marrying fellow botanist Edward Arber.

DAME CLARA BUTT

(1872–1936) singer   7 Harley Road

CLARA Butt's fine contralto voice was evident from her school years. In 1890, she won a scholarship to the Royal College of Music and moved from Bristol to London. She made her debut at the Royal Albert Hall in 1892, in Arthur Sullivan's cantata *The Golden Legend*. Most of Dame Clara's appearances were confined to the concert platform, where her powerful voice and striking presence – she was 188cm (6ft 2in) tall – made her one of the most popular singers of her day. She was particularly associated with the hymn 'Abide with Me', while Edward Elgar* composed *Sea Pictures* (1899) with Clara's voice in mind; in 1902, she became the first singer to perform Elgar's 'Land of Hope and Glory'. Butt lived here with her husband Robert Kennerley Rumford, a baritone singer with whom she performed regularly.

ROBERT POLHILL BEVAN

(1865–1925) Camden Town Group painter   14 Adamson Road **17**

BEVAN studied art in London, Paris and Brittany. Among the first to bring post-impressionism to Britain, he was a founder member of the Camden Town Group in 1911. It was while living at this tall late-19th-century brick studio house that he carried out much of the work he is best known for: paintings of urban and country scenes, including views of cab horses and horse sales, and many Hampstead and Belsize Park vistas, characterised by strong colour, broad brushwork and simplified definition. Bevan lived here from 1900 to 1925 with his wife, the Polish painter Stanislawa de Karlowska; the house became a rendezvous for artists, including Wyndham Lewis*.

HENRY NOEL BRAILSFORD

(1873–1958) writer, champion
of equal and free humanity

37 Belsize Park Gardens **18**

THE son of a Wesleyan minister, Brailsford started out as a journalist for Liberal newspapers such as the *Daily News*. Having joined the Independent Labour Party in 1907 he went on to edit its newspaper *New Leader* (1922–6), and contributed regular columns to the *New Republic, Reynolds's News* and the *New Statesman*. Brailsford was an insightful critic of British imperial and foreign affairs; publications included *The War of Steel and Gold* (1914) and *Rebel India* (1931), which supported Indian self-government. He moved to this imposing mid-19th-century villa in 1926, four years after separating from his first wife, and stayed for the rest of his life. During the 1930s he had a relationship with the artist Clara Leighton (1898–1989) and in 1944 married Evamaria Perlmann Jarvis, a widowed German refugee, who was still living here when the plaque was erected in 1983.

FREDERICK DELIUS

(1862–1934) composer

44 Belsize Park Gardens **19**

DELIUS was born in Bradford, Yorkshire, of German parents and was intended by his father to work in the wool trade, but his love of music prevailed. 'Fritz', as he was known in early life, eventually settled in France at Grez-sur-Loing near Fontainebleau, with the artist Helena 'Jelka' Rosen; the two were married in 1903. In the years that followed, Delius composed prolifically, working in a variety of musical

Delius's time in London was not a productive one – Jelka said that her husband could never 'compose living in a town'.

forms, including chamber, choral, orchestral and operatic works. Towards the end of the First World War, at the height of his powers and public acclaim, Delius was forced to flee France for England.

In early October 1918, he and Jelka moved into a large furnished flat here which featured 'a beautiful Bechstein grand'. The couple stayed until May 1919, when they returned to France.

RAMSAY MACDONALD

(1866–1937) Prime Minister — 9 Howitt Road

SCOTTISH-BORN, and the illegitimate son of a farm servant and a ploughman, James Ramsay MacDonald was introduced to political life in the late 1880s as private secretary to a Liberal parliamentary candidate. His own political career only began after his marriage in 1896 to the socialist and feminist Margaret Gladstone, whose private income brought him financial independence. In 1900, he became Secretary of the newly founded Labour Representation Committee (which in 1906 became the Labour Party), and entered Parliament as MP for Leicester. In January 1924 he formed the first Labour government, filling the office of Foreign Secretary as well as Prime Minister. In 1929, he

'One of those modest little villas favoured by middle-class English intelligentsia.'

Former Soviet Ambassador Ivan Maisky on MacDonald's house

regained the premiership as leader of another minority government and two years later, amid the economic crisis of the Great Depression, he formed a national government with Liberal and Conservative support. This kept him in office until 1935, but earned him the lasting enmity of most of his former Labour colleagues. MacDonald lived here, as a widower, from January 1916 to May 1925, a period encompassing his re-election as Labour leader in 1922 and his first spell as Prime Minister.

DAVID DEVANT

(1868–1941)
magician

Flat 1, Ornan Court
(formerly Ornan Mansions), Ornan Road

BORN David Wighton in Holloway, he made his stage debut in 1893 at the Egyptian Hall

in Piccadilly, England's 'Home of Mystery'. In 1905, he went into partnership with the great John Nevil

Maskelyne; the pair were to dominate the world of magic for the next decade and are remembered today as the founding fathers of English conjuring. Based at St George's Hall in Langham Place (demolished), *Maskelyne and Devant's Mysteries* wowed audiences with innovative and daring feats of illusionism. Devant lived in Ornan Road between 1915 and 1917, when he was at the height of his fame.

HENRY NEVINSON (1856–1941) journalist
C. R. W. NEVINSON
(1889–1946) artist

4 Downside Crescent **22**

The Nevinsons were father and son; Henry was a campaigning journalist, notably against the continuing evil of slavery and in support of independence for India and votes for women. In 1907 he was a founder-member of the Men's League for Women's Suffrage; both his wives, Margaret Nevinson and Evelyn Sharp, were suffragists too. Richard (or C. R. W.) Nevinson is best known for his depictions of the horrors of the Western Front (on which his father also reported) in such paintings as *La Mitrailleuse* (1915, now at Tate Britain), described by Walter Sickert* as 'the most concentrated and authoritative utterance on war'. Henry moved his family into number 4, then a new house, by 1903, and stayed until bombed out 40 years later; Richard lived here from age 13 until his marriage some 16 years later; he painted the view from the back window in *Suburbia* (c.1919).

WALTER GROPIUS (1883–1969)
MARCEL BREUER (1902-1981)
LÁSZLÓ MOHOLY-NAGY (1895-1946)
pioneers of modern design
at the Bauhaus

Lawn Road Flats
(Isokon Building) **23**

The Bauhaus, a vastly influential modernist German art school, was founded in 1919 in Weimar by the Berlin-born architect Walter Gropius. He was joined there by two Hungarian-born kindred spirits: Marcel Breuer, best known for his pioneering tubular steel chairs, and the filmmaker and photographer László Moholy-Nagy. All three came to England to escape the modernist-hating Nazis (for Moholy-Nagy, his Jewish heritage made the need to leave more pressing). All three men eventually pursued their careers in the United States but during the mid-1930s, each had an apartment in the Isokon – also known as Lawn Road Flats. The block was designed by Wells Coates* and was then new.

Its former garage now houses the Isokon Gallery, in which the history and significance of the building is presented in fascinating detail. Another famous former inhabitant was Agatha Christie*.

HENRY MOORE, OM

(1898–1986) sculptor

11A Parkhill Road

MOORE was born in Yorkshire, the son of a miner, and studied at the Leeds School of Art; there he met Barbara Hepworth, and the two went on to study together at the Royal College of Art. It was through Hepworth that Moore found number 11A, a two-storey extension to a Victorian house;

Henry Moore in his Parkhill Road studio, 1933.

it was his home from the time of his marriage in late July 1929 until 1940, when – after a few months at the Mall Studios (where Hepworth and Ben Nicholson* were based) – he and his wife Irina moved to Hertfordshire. Moore's time in Parkhill Road was one of productivity and innovation, during which he was greatly inspired by the local artistic circle, described by Herbert Read as 'a nest of gentle artists'. Moore produced 22 pieces in 1930 alone, most of them reclining figures and mother and child groups in a new and distinctive abstract style. He also produced his series of 'shelter drawings' here, inspired by a night spent in Belsize Park Underground station in 1940.

PIET MONDRIAN

(1872–1944) painter   60 Parkhill Road **25**

PIETER Cornelis Mondriaan, as he was first known, was a principal founding member of the Dutch art movement De Stijl ('The Style'). Between 1917 and 1920, he wrote a series of articles that introduced and discussed the artistic philosophy known as neo-plasticism, which advocated abstraction and a simplified, reduced use of colour and form. Piet Mondrian lived for many years in Paris, but in autumn 1938 the threat of war drove him to London, where he settled in a large first-floor room at the back of 60 Parkhill Road. Here, he became what Barbara Hepworth described as 'a most important focus'. Mondrian's

'We saw Mondrian nearly every day, communicating by the garden gates. He made his studio as exciting as the one in Montparnasse where he lived for so many years.'

Barbara Hepworth, writing to the GLC in 1972 to suggest a plaque for Mondrian

window overlooked a studio used by Ben Nicholson* while the garden connected via a gate to the Mall Studios. Number 60 was Mondrian's base until late 1940, 'when a nearby bomb brought down his ceiling'. He subsequently moved to New York, where he died four years later.

HAMPSTEAD

HAMPSTEAD was an ancient Middlesex settlement, its name meaning 'homestead'. The chalybeate springs that rise here brought droves of Stuart and Georgian visitors up the hill to find a cure for whatever ailed them through the iron-rich waters, and a growing number chose to retire here. From the later 1700s, the woods and sprawling heath – not to mention the ever-changing skies – were increasingly appreciated by artists and by town dwellers eager to reconnect with their dwindling links to the countryside. In the popular mind, Hampstead is peopled with the intelligentsia, and given over to left-leaning politics, the arts, opulence and émigrés. On the evidence of the blue plaques put up so far, which are legion and densely clustered, the popular view is not far off the mark.

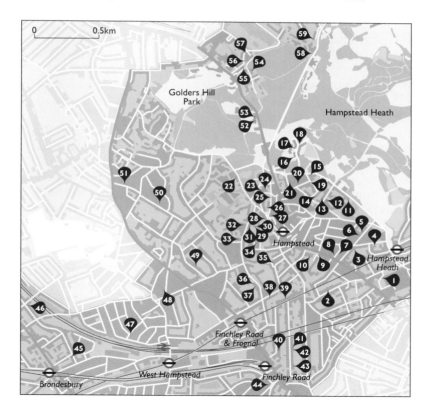

SIR ROWLAND HILL, KCB

(1795–1879) originator of
the Penny Post

Royal Free Hospital, Rowland Hill St.
(formerly Bartram House, Pond St.) **1**

HILL lived at the now-demolished Bartram House – the early chocolate-brown plaque marks its site – from 1849 until his death. He was already a national celebrity when he moved here: his lifetime's preoccupation became apparent with the publication of *Post Office Reform: Its Importance and Practicability* (1837), and the introduction in 1840 of the Penny Post established his success. While in Hampstead, he served as Secretary to the Postmaster-General (1846–54) and Secretary to the Post Office (1854–64). Hill died at Bartram House and was buried in Westminster Abbey, a remarkable accolade for a sometimes controversial public servant.

RICHARD BURTON

(1925–84) actor

6 Lyndhurst Road **2**

RICHARD Jenkins was the son of a South Wales coal-miner, and took the name of his teacher and acting mentor, Philip Burton. He first appeared on the London stage in 1944; early in 1949 he moved with his new wife Sybil to this semi-detached 1860s house, where they lived successively in two flats, firstly on the lower floors and latterly on the second. Burton's time here encompassed his major successes as a Shakespearean stage actor: writing of his Prince Hal, the critic Kenneth Tynan said he could 'make silence garrulous'. Meanwhile, his early screen career encompassed films such as *Waterfront* (1950), *My Cousin Rachel* (1952) and *The Desert Rats* (1953), while in 1954 he recorded his

'Home is where the books are.'
Richard Burton

famous version of *Under Milk Wood* by Dylan Thomas*. That same year he bought his first car, a Cadillac. Always acutely conscious of money, he is said to have kept a suitcase full of banknotes under his bed, and in 1956 he left Hampstead for tax exile in Switzerland (though he stayed in the area on subsequent sojourns). Later, his on-off marriage to the Hampstead-born Elizabeth Taylor, with whom he appeared in the films *Cleopatra* (1963) and *Who's Afraid of Virginia Woolf?* (1965), was the subject of intense media interest; *Equus* (1977) and *Nineteen Eighty-Four* (1984) were highlights of his more recent film career.

JOHN HEARTFIELD

(1891–1968) master of political photomontage   47 Downshire Hill

BORN Helmut Herzfeld in Germany, he anglicised his name during the First World War in a typical gesture of defiance. Together with Georg Grosz, he was one of the central figures in Berlin Dada. A committed communist, Heartfield used photomontage, a new art form in which cut-out photographs were superimposed to create radical and disturbing images, to express his political disaffection. His anti-Nazi posters are some of the best-known images of interwar political conflict; they include *Adolf the Superman: Swallows Gold and*

Spouts Junk (1932). Heartfield fled Germany when the Nazis came to power in 1933 and eventually came to London in December 1938. Fred Uhlman, a Jewish refugee, and his wife Diana, gave him an upper room at Number 47; they were much taken with 'Johnny', whom they found to be 'a charming, modest, meek and mild little man who only got excitable and fanatical when it came to politics'. Gertrud Fietz, who later became Heartfield's wife, was also staying here at the time; together, they moved to Highgate in 1943, returning to Germany in 1950.

JOHN KEATS

(1795–1821) poet   Wentworth Place, Keats Grove (formerly John St.) **4**

THIS house, now a museum to Keats, was built in 1815–16 as a joint enterprise and shared residence by the antiquary, writer and critic Charles Wentworth Dilke (1789–1864) and his friend Charles Armitage Brown (1789–1842). Dilke occupied the west half and Brown the east; Keats had been introduced to Hampstead in 1816 by Leigh Hunt* and on his brother Tom's death in December 1818 he moved in with Brown at Wentworth Place. A number of his finest poems were composed at this time, including *The Eve of St Agnes* and 'La Belle

Dame sans Merci'. In April 1819, the Brawne family rented Dilke's part of the house. Keats wrote 'Ode to a Nightingale' in May, seated beneath the plum tree in the garden, and by June, he was engaged to Fanny Brawne. Keats was already suffering from tuberculosis, and even the much-vaunted Hampstead air was not sufficient cure; his health declined sharply after a freezing ride on a stagecoach home from town in February 1820. That September he left London for Rome, where he died. Wentworth Place was altered by a later resident, and enlarged.

LEE MILLER (1907–77) photographer
SIR ROLAND PENROSE
(1900–84) surrealist

NEW York-born Miller started out on the other side of the lens as a successful model. In 1929 she went to Paris where she became Man Ray's pupil, lover and muse, joined the surrealist movement and established herself as a photographer. Back in the United States in the early Thirties, Miller was listed as 'one of the seven most distinguished living photographers'. In 1944 she became an official war correspondent, following the US Army across Europe. Her photo-journalism, covering such key events as the liberation of Paris and of Dachau, was among the hardest-hitting and most memorable of the war.

In 1937 Miller had met Roland Penrose, a painter and art patron, and later founder (in 1947) of the Institute of Contemporary Arts. A significant figure in the avant-garde British art scene, he had formed the British Surrealist Group in 1935 and organised the International Surrealist Exhibition in London in 1936, the year he moved here. Miller joined him three years later and the couple (*pictured below*) remained here until 1947, the year they married. Their hospitality (Miller later became a gourmet surrealist cook) made their home a focal point for artists, politicians and journalists: Man Ray and André Breton were both regular visitors.

SIR PETER MEDAWAR

(1915–87) pioneer of transplantation immunology   25 Downshire Road

MEDAWAR was born in Brazil, and was of mixed Lebanese and British background. At Oxford University, he undertook doctoral research into tissue growth and repair. In 1943, with Thomas Gibson, Medawar published a paper on 'homograft reaction' – the theory, which was later demonstrated, that the body's immune system was responsible for triggering the rejection of skin grafts. His subsequent work covered the effect of an individual's genetics on immunity, and the phenomenon of 'acquired immunological tolerance', for which he was jointly awarded the Nobel Prize for Physiology in 1960. Medawar's research kicked

'People who write obscurely are either unskilled in writing or up to mischief.'

Peter Medawar

off a search for immunosuppressive drugs and therapies, thus enabling the transplantation of human tissue and organs. Medawar held a professorship at University College London and served as Director of the National Institute of Medical Research at Mill Hill. He lived at two other addresses in Hampstead before settling here, his final home, in the mid-1970s. His autobiography was entitled *Memoir of a Thinking Radish* (1986).

BEN NICHOLSON, OM

(1894–1982) artist   2B Pilgrim's Lane

THE son of the artist William Nicholson*, Ben lived with his family at another house in Pilgrim's Lane – number 1 – from 1904 to 1906. During the 1930s, he occupied the Mall Studios, off Tasker Road, together with his second wife, the sculptor Barbara Hepworth, and their triplets. Nicholson was then in the vanguard of progressive art in Britain. He belonged to Unit One, a collective of artists and architects that included Paul Nash* and Henry Moore*, and was one of the

international pioneers of constructivism, editing the journal *Circle* with Naum Gabo and the architect Leslie Martin. His final period in Hampstead, from spring 1974 until his death, was spent at 2B Pilgrim's Lane; previously used as a studio by the abstract sculptor Robert Adams, it forms a 20th-century addition to a handsome late-Georgian house fronting on to Rosslyn Hill. The house was substantially altered soon after the installation of the plaque in 2002.

SIR WILLIAM NICHOLSON

(1872–1949) painter and printmaker   1 Pilgrim's Lane **8**

WILLIAM Nicholson first won renown for woodcut posters produced with his brother-in-law, James Pryde, under the name 'J. and W. Beggarstaff': these included advertisements for *Harper's Magazine* (1895) and Rowntree's Elect Cocoa (1896). In 1897, he produced an informal woodcut portrait of Queen Victoria for her diamond jubilee, which led to a string of commissions: Max Beerbohm* (1903), Walter Greaves* (1917) and Gertrude Jekyll (1920) were among his sitters. Nicholson and his young family (including Ben Nicholson*) moved here in October 1904 and stayed for 20 months, before they succumbed to his wife Mabel's 'mania for moving house'. In 1909 they settled in Rottingdean, Sussex, where Nicholson painted poetic landscapes – especially of the South Downs – and still-lifes. His son Ben wrote of his 'very simple direct painterly approach'. Nicholson senior also worked in the theatre: the year he moved to Pilgrim's Lane, he designed costumes and scenery for the first production of *Peter Pan*.

SIR HARRY VANE

(1613–62) statesman   Vane House, Rosslyn Hill **9**

HENRY Vane's early interest in republicanism prompted him to emigrate to the New World in 1635; within a year, at the age of 23, he was Governor of Massachusetts. He returned to England, and played a leading part in the prosecution of the Earl of Strafford in 1641. He helped Cromwell manage the House of Commons during the Civil War, up to the execution of Charles I in 1649, but won the sobriquet 'Sir Harry Weathervane' for his inconstancy thereafter. This shift of allegiance was not enough to save him after the Restoration; arrested at his Hampstead home in July

'He is too dangerous a man to let live, if we can honestly put him out of the way.'

Charles II on Harry Vane

1660, he was executed in 1662. The moral philosopher Bishop Joseph Butler (1692–1752) later lived here and in 1855 it became the Royal Soldiers' Daughters' Home. The house was demolished in 1969, although the gatepost – in which the plaque is set – was retained.

DAME EDITH SITWELL

(1887–1964) poet Flat 42, Greenhill, Hampstead High Street

THIS large neo-Georgian apartment block of 1936 at the top of Rosslyn Hill was rather an ordinary address for the singular-looking poet, who, with her equally celebrated brothers Osbert and Sacheverell, promoted progressive literary and aesthetic endeavours to a largely sceptical British public. Sitwell wrote the words of *Façade* (1923), set to music by William Walton*, and later won a reputation as a popular historian with works such as *The English Eccentrics* (1933); but it was as a poet that she wished to be remembered. Her time here was rather melancholy: when

'… just big enough for ghosts'

Edith Sitwell on her Hampstead flat

she arrived, in 1961, her health was failing, her reputation was being challenged and her finances were a cause of anxiety. The flat was small and was shared with her nurse, Doris Farquhar. Nonetheless many visitors trekked faithfully 'to that Greenhill far away' and the following year, aged 75, Sitwell published a historical fiction, *The Queens and the Hive*, and her final collection of poetry, *The Outcasts*. In spring 1964 she moved to nearby 20 Keats Grove and died soon after.

SIR ARTHUR BLISS

(1891–1975) composer East Heath Lodge, 1 East Heath Road

BLISS was born in Barnes, the son of an American business-man. He lived in this fine semi-detached house of c.1785 at the height of his career, between 1929 and 1939. One of the first works he completed here was the choral symphony *Morning Heroes* (1930), his tribute to the First World War dead.

Here, he also wrote the stirring music to the 1936 film *Things to Come* (produced by Alexander Korda*) and the music for the 1937 ballet *Checkmate*. Cosmopolitan and innovative, Bliss was seen as the successor to Elgar* as a late romantic composer; he became Master of the Queen's Music in 1953.

JOHN CONSTABLE

(1776–1837) painter   40 (formerly 6, later 26) Well Walk **12**

CONSTABLE first moved to Hampstead from Fitzrovia in search of fresh air for his growing family and ailing wife, Maria, in 1819. They moved to this late-Georgian terraced house of *c.*1820 in 1827; Constable called it 'comfortable'. While living here, he completed *Dedham Vale* (1828), as well as numerous *plein-air* sketches that capture the effects of weather and light on the Hampstead landscape. In November 1828, following the birth of their seventh child, Maria died of TB and the family returned to Fitzrovia, though their Hampstead house was kept up as an occasional residence until at least 1834.

HENRY MAYERS HYNDMAN

(1842–1921) socialist leader   13 Well Walk **13**

HYNDMAN shared the house for the last four years of his life with his wife Rosalind, a poet, renting it from John Masefield*. Born in London, the son of a rich merchant, Hyndman became a socialist on reading Marx's *Das Kapital* in 1880. The following year he published *The Text-Book of Democracy: England for All* and helped to establish the Social Democratic Federation (SDF), a precursor to the Labour Party. Hyndman was also involved in the formation of the British Socialist Party in 1911 – later folded in to the Communist Party – but left over its pacifist stance to found the unfortunately named National Socialist Party in 1916, which later reverted to the SDF name.

KARL PEARSON

(1857–1936) pioneer statistician   7 Well Road **14**

A PROTÉGÉ of Francis Galton*, Pearson bears a similar taint of association with eugenics, but is credited with establishing the modern discipline of mathematical statistics. He was instrumental in the development of correlation theory and – with W. F. R. Weldon – co-founded the discipline of biometry, the application of statistics to biology. 'KP' was Galton Professor of Eugenics at University College London (1911–33). His house, in which he lived from 1892 to his death, is one of a procession of semi-detached red-brick pairs built in about 1880.

KATHERINE MANSFIELD (1888–1923) writer
JOHN MIDDLETON MURRY
(1889–1957) critic   17 East Heath Road (formerly 2 Portland Villas) **15**

FELLOW Hampstead writer D. H. Lawrence* portrayed Mansfield and Murry in *Women in Love* (1920) as Gudrun and Gerald, a couple of intensely connected fellow spirits. Born and raised in Wellington, New Zealand, Mansfield's career was cut short by TB; it was in the vain hope that the Hampstead air might help her that she and Murry, her husband, moved here in late July 1918. They called this tall Italianate semi-detached house 'The Elephant' on account of its greyness and size, though it offered a superb view over the western heath. Ida Baker, Mansfield's lifelong friend and Hampstead housekeeper, stated that 'Katherine saw in the house her last chance of a home of her own'. The couple set up a press in the basement to print small editions of their works. Visitors here included Virginia Woolf*, Walter de la Mare*, T. S. Eliot* and Ottoline Morrell*. Mansfield died in France in 1923. Murry edited several literary journals, including *The Athenaeum* and *The Adelphi*; he was an influential critic from the 1920s onwards and a prominent pacifist.

J. L. HAMMOND (1872–1949)
BARBARA HAMMOND
(1873–1961) social historians   Hollycot, Vale of Health

MEETING at Oxford University, (John) Lawrence Hammond and (Lucy) Barbara Bradby were married in 1901; both were ardent Liberals. During most of their time at Hollycot, a semi-detached house of the late 19th century, Lawrence was employed as Secretary to the Civil Service Commission. The couple were also starting to work closely together on a jointly written sequence of studies of 18th-century workers; this trilogy began with *The Village Labourer* (1911), a seminal study of the effect

'They asked first not what would pay but what was true, what was right, and what was humane.'

The classical scholar Gilbert Murray on the Hammonds

of enclosure on rural life, and was completed with *The Town Labourer* (1917) and *The Skilled Labourer* (1919). The Hammonds' aim was to awaken public conscience, and to inject a note of corrective realism into the complacent view of the Georgian age that was then widely prevalent.

RABINDRANATH TAGORE

(1861–1941) poet

TAGORE, a Pirali Bengali Brahmin born in Calcutta, was a much-revered writer: he produced novels, short stories, dramas and essays, but is best remembered for his poetry, and for his sensitive plea for multiculturalism. This was his home for a few months in the summer of 1912, during Tagore's third visit to England. While here, he worked on translations of religious songs and lyrics, which were published in November 1912 by the India Society of London as *Gitanjali* ('Song Offerings'); the collection led to Tagore's becoming – in 1913 – the first non-European to win the Nobel Prize for Literature. Knighted in 1915, Tagore renounced the honour in protest at the Amritsar massacre of 1919.

D. H. LAWRENCE

(1885–1930) novelist and poet

1 Byron Villas **18**

THE only London address that Lawrence ever regarded as home (as opposed to temporary lodgings) was this ground-floor flat of an unremarkable Edwardian house of about 1903, where he lived with his German wife Frieda. Although only resident for a few months, his time here was significant: it saw the publication and suppression (on the grounds of obscenity) of *The Rainbow*, while Lawrence's experience of watching a Zeppelin raid from Hampstead Heath found its way into his 1923 novel *Kangaroo*. Shortly before Christmas 1915 – driven from London by depression following the ban of *The Rainbow* and the threat of air raids – Lawrence moved with Frieda to Cornwall, where he wrote *Women in Love* (1920).

SIR GERALD DU MAURIER

(1873–1934) actor-manager

Cannon Hall, 14 Cannon Place **19**

THE son of George du Maurier*, Gerald was born in Hampstead and made his stage debut in 1894. He was a highly successful actor, best remembered for his roles in plays by J. M. Barrie* such as *The Admirable Crichton* (1902). From 1910 he turned to theatre management, first at Wyndham's and from 1925 at the St James's. Du Maurier, who was knighted in 1922, was extremely fond of Cannon Hall. He shared it with his wife Muriel Beaumont, and his novelist daughter Daphne also grew up here – but as she was still living when the plaque was erected in 1967, her name does not appear on its inscription. The house dates from c.1720 and is one of Hampstead's most imposing early survivals of domestic architecture. It takes its name from the bollard outside, which is made from a piece of spent ordnance.

'He loved the garden and the view, and the rambling plan of the house – the lofty rooms, the old staircase, and especially the view from his bedroom window. He felt like a wanderer returned to the land of his birth ... He would never want to move from Hampstead again. He would be a fixture now and for ever, part of the soil.'

Daphne du Maurier on her father Gerald in London, 1912

SIR FLINDERS PETRIE

(1853–1942) Egyptologist

5 Cannon Place **20**

PETRIE came to this house of c.1875 from nearby Well Road in 1919, and remained until 1935, when he and his wife Hilda moved to Jerusalem. Born in Charlton – then in Kent – he was the son of an electrical engineer and the grandson of the explorer Captain Matthew Flinders*. He led a number of pioneering excavations in Egypt and Palestine and established the British School of Archaeology in 1906, leading the way in promoting the proper investigative recording of sites. Among his many famous discoveries was the Palace of Apries, Memphis (1909). Between 1892 and 1933, he served as the first Professor of Egyptology at University College London, a chair endowed by Amelia Edwards*. The college's Petrie Museum in Malet Place, Bloomsbury, houses a collection of some of his finds.

BARON FRIEDRICH VON HÜGEL

(1852–1925) theologian   4 Holford Road **21**

BORN in Florence, the son of an Austrian diplomat and a Scottish mother, von Hügel first settled in Hampstead in 1876. A pivotal figure in modern approaches to Bible studies, and – with Cardinal Newman* – one of the key Catholic thinkers of his day, von Hügel combined intellectual rigour with deep respect for religious faith. He went on to found the London Society for the Study of Religion in 1905, and to publish *The Mystical Element of Religion as Studied in St Catherine of Genoa and her Friends* (1908), generally regarded as his most important work. A devoted heath walker, he was often accompanied by disputatious friends who shared his inquisitive piety. In 1903 von Hügel left the large, gabled house in Holford Road – where he had lived since 1882 – for Vicarage Gate, Kensington, where he died.

PAUL ROBESON

(1898–1976) singer and actor   The Chestnuts, 1 Branch Hill **22**

ROBESON, one of the first black performers to achieve world renown, lived here in 1929–30, at the peak of his fame. His reputation was established with *Show Boat*, first performed in London in 1928, and his rendition of 'Ol' Man River'. London was important to Robeson's career: his performance of *Othello* at the Savoy Theatre in 1930 won many plaudits – the show moved to Broadway in 1943, where it became the longest-running Shakespearean production of all time – and he spent a number of years in the city in the latter stages of his career. Robeson combined outspoken opposition to the racial inequality of his native United States with wider left-wing sympathies and he consequently suffered during the 'red scare' of the early 1950s.

JOHN GALSWORTHY*

(1867–1933) novelist and playwright   Grove Lodge, Admiral's Walk **23**

GALSWORTHY'S earliest successful novel was *The Man of Property*, first published in 1906. This was the start of the renowned *Forsyte Saga* series, which continued with *In Chancery* (1920) and *To Let* (1921), both written during the author's time here.

His domestic chronicle attracted a huge following – Stalin being one of his less expected admirers. During his lifetime, Galsworthy was best known as a playwright, his works including *Strife* (1909), *The Skin Game* (1920) and *Escape* (1926).

He was awarded the Nobel Prize for Literature in 1932; a delegation was sent to Hampstead from Sweden in order to make the presentation to the ailing author here – at the house he had lived in since 1911, and in which he died the following year.

SIR GEORGE GILBERT SCOTT

(1811–78) architect Admiral's House, 21 Admiral's Walk

SCOTT lived here – in what was then known as The Grove, Upper Heath – between 1856 and 1864, at the height of his career; he shared the house with his wife Caroline and their sons (including the architect George Gilbert Scott junior). Scott was one of the most industrious and successful of High Victorian architects, a prolific architect and restorer of churches; he had a hand in one way or another in projects at practically every medieval cathedral in England and Wales; secular commissions undertaken during his residence here included the Foreign Office in Whitehall (1862–75) and the Albert Memorial in Hyde Park (1863–72). The house, largely Georgian, is not evidently that of so eminent a Gothic Revivalist. A later occupant was the noted historian of the British Army, John Fortescue (1859–1933).

Admiral's House, which dates from about 1700, is one of the substantial first-generation suburban houses to be built in Hampstead. It takes its name from Fountain North, a naval officer who once lived here and who added a 'widow's walk' to the roofline, enabling him to look out across London and fire cannon in salute; that he was a lieutenant, not an admiral, is incidental.

GEORGE DU MAURIER*

(1834–96) artist and writer New Grove House, 28 Hampstead Grove

BORN in Paris, George Louis Palmella Busson du Maurier is remembered for his highly successful 1894 novel *Trilby*, which he wrote while living here. He was also celebrated for his satirical book illustrations; the best known of these appeared in *Punch* during the 1870s and 1880s. He and his wife Emma moved here in 1874 (their fifth and last child Gerald* was born the previous year). George remained in this house, of 18th-century date with an early-Victorian 'Tudorbethan'

He 'was almost always sitting in the corner [of his studio] with the north light at his back, at work on his drawings, joining from time to time in the general conversation or interspersing a few comments'.

George du Maurier remembered by the writer C. C. Hoyer Millar

exterior, until 1895. His studio here was the centre of family life.

JOANNA BAILLIE

(1762–1851) poet and dramatist Bolton House, Windmill Hill **26**

BAILLIE was lionised in her day; Scott, Wordsworth, Edgeworth, Byron and Keats* all made the pilgrimage to Bolton House; Scott, in *Marmion* (1808), asserted that 'Avon's swans think Shakespeare lives again'. Hyperbole perhaps, but Baillie was genuinely seen as the successor to Shakespeare in terms of her ability to infuse historical drama with a fitting measure of psychological intensity. Her 1800 play *De Montfort* was produced at Drury Lane by John Philip Kemble and Mrs Siddons; there too was performed in 1815 her most successful work, *The Family Legend* (1810). The house is one of

The chocolate-brown plaque to Baillie was the fourth put up by the Society of Arts to commemorate a woman.

a row of three built in about 1730. Joanna first moved to Hampstead in 1791, but seems only to have taken up residence here in 1820: in March of that year, she wrote of 'our new house ... on what is called Holly Bush hill'. She shared the house with her sister Agnes (1760–1861), and lived here until her death at the age of 88.

GEORGE ROMNEY
(1734–1802) painter   5 Holly Bush Hill **27**

ROMNEY was born in what was then Lancashire and worked with his father as a cabinet-maker before being apprenticed to a painter in Kendal. His practical skills enabled him to design his own studio extensions, first at his London studio in Cavendish Square, and subsequently here in Hampstead. This house he extended by adding two huge rooms, the lower for teaching and painting and the upper for use as a studio and gallery, and took up residence in 1798. It had, said Romney's friend William Hayley, 'a very magnificent view of the metropolis', but he was not to enjoy it for long. In declining health, he only lived here a few months before returning north to be reconciled with the wife he had left behind in 1762. The house was used as assembly rooms from 1807, and later as a constitutional club. It was altered again by the architect, writer and creator of Portmeirion, Clough Williams Ellis (1883–1978), who owned the place from 1929 to 1939.

SIR HENRY DALE
(1875–1968) physiologist   Mount Vernon House, Mount Vernon **28**

DALE, whose specialism was the pharmacology of nervous impulses, was knighted in 1932, shared the Nobel Prize for Medicine in 1936 and received the Order of Merit in 1944. He was President of the Royal Society 1940–45; chaired the Scientific Advisory Committee to the War Cabinet, and was President of the British Council between 1950 and 1955. From 1914, he worked for what became the National Institute for Medical Research, serving as its Director between 1928 and 1942. His home, a late-Georgian building all but hidden by its boundary wall, lay conveniently close to the Institute, which was housed in the looming French Renaissance pile of Mount Vernon Hospital; this has now been converted for residential use.

SIR WALTER BESANT

(1836–1901) novelist and antiquary — Frognal End, 18 Frognal Gardens **29**

A T the top of a private drive and largely hidden from view, Besant's house, built for him in 1891–2, was laid out in the grounds of a much older building. Generous and sociable, Besant was a hugely popular writer; he founded the Society of Authors in 1884. He was also brother-in-law to the redoubtable reformer Annie Besant* and in his books heightened public concern over the state of east London slums. One direct result of his energetic campaigning was the opening in 1887 of the People's Palace in the Mile End Road, a huge complex devoted to popular entertainment and self-improvement.

HUGH GAITSKELL

(1906–63) statesman — Frognal End, 18 Frognal Gardens **30**

A FTER Oxford, Gaitskell won his political spurs as a Workers' Educational Association lecturer in the Nottingham coalfields. Entering Parliament in 1945, he became a minister in the government of Clement Attlee* two years later and was appointed Chancellor of the Exchequer in 1950. He remained here rather than move to 11 Downing Street, and Gaitskell's group of friends and allies became known as the Hampstead or Frognal Set. His feud with the left-winger Aneurin (Nye) Bevan* culminated with Gaitskell being elected Labour Party leader in 1955; he went on to fight (and lose) the general election four years later. Gaitskell lived here until shortly before his death.

TAMARA KARSAVINA

(1885–1978) ballerina — 108 Frognal **31**

B ORN in St Petersburg, Karsavina was the daughter of a dancer and trained at the Imperial Russian Ballet School. In 1909 she became one of the founder members of Diaghilev's Ballets Russes, taking leading parts alongside Vaslav Nijinsky. Karsavina was deeply influenced by the company's choreographer, Michel Fokine; she created a number of famous roles in Fokine's ballets, including the title role in *The Firebird* (1910) and the doll in *Petrushka* (1911). In 1917, she married an English diplomat – Henry J. Bruce – and the couple settled in London the following year. In 1920, she helped to found the Royal Academy of Dance and encouraged the development of British ballet, mentoring, among others, Margot Fonteyn*. She and her husband bought this early-18th-century house in 1950 and she left in 1974.

KATHLEEN FERRIER

(1912–53) singer   Flat 2, Frognal Mansions, 97 Frognal

LANCASHIRE-BORN, Ferrier's first job was as a telephone operator – not the best use of her remarkable contralto voice. In 1937, accepting a wager from her husband, she won the singing and piano competitions at the Carlisle Festival. Her professional career took off in 1946, when she was cast in the title role of Benjamin Britten's* *The Rape of Lucretia*. Under the baton of Bruno Walter she gained wide renown as an interpreter of Mahler. She lived in Frognal Mansions from late 1942 until shortly before her untimely death from cancer in 1953.

SIR HAROLD GILLIES

(1882–1960) plastic surgeon   71 Frognal

BORN and raised in New Zealand, Gillies put his surgical skills to work in seeking to make good the hideous damage done to soldiers' faces during the First World War. In so doing, he made considerable advances in the techniques of plastic surgery, which resulted in his 1920 work *Plastic Surgery of the Face*. During the Second World War, Gillies was responsible for setting up a network of plastic surgery units across the country. He lived at this unusual corner house from 1921 until he was driven out by bombing 20 years later.

ALASTAIR SIM

(1900–76) actor   8 Frognal Gardens **34**

SIM made his debut on the London stage at the comparatively late age of 30, at the Savoy in a production of *Othello*; he both starred in and directed several plays by James Bridie, including *Mr Bolfry* (1943). But he is best known to a wider public through his film roles, especially in Ealing comedies; these included *The Happiest Days of Your*

Life (1950) with Margaret Rutherford*, *Scrooge* (1951), *The Belles of St Trinian's* (1954) and *Blue Murder at St Trinian's* (1957), in which he played the hapless headmistress Miss Fritton. Latterly he enjoyed Chichester and West End stage successes with *The Magistrate* (1969) and *Dandy Dick* (1973). Sim's flat here was his London base from 1953 until the year before his death; he also had a home in Henley-on-Thames, shared with his wife and daughter. A private man who did not sign autographs, Sim was notably generous to emerging acting talents: among those he mentored was George Cole.

RICHARD NORMAN SHAW*

(1831–1912) architect   6 Ellerdale Road **35**

THIS detached red-brick house with its irregular facade was built in 1874–6 to Shaw's own plans, and was his home until his death here 36 years later. Born in Edinburgh, Shaw moved with his family to London at about the age of 14. The highlight of his long and busy architectural career is probably Cragside, Northumberland (1870–85), a spectacular country house in Queen Anne style. At Ellerdale Road, in his 'den' above the inglenook fireplace, Shaw designed many of his later buildings, including New Scotland Yard (1887–90).

KATE GREENAWAY

(1846–1901) artist   39 (originally 50) Frognal **36**

GREENAWAY'S asymmetrical studio-house was designed in 1884 by Richard Norman Shaw*. The huge north-facing studio contrasts with the intimate scale of her drawings. Her reputation rests on her illustrations for children's books; the Kate Greenaway Medal is still awarded for achievement in this field. Greenaway, who lived here from February 1885 until her death, was very attached to John Ruskin*, and he visited her here regularly.

DENNIS BRAIN

(1921–57) horn-player

37 Frognal

BRAIN, who died in a car accident while still in his thirties, was regarded internationally as the outstanding horn-player of his era. Born in London, the third generation of a distinguished family of horn-players, he studied at the Royal Academy of Music, where he was taught by his father, Aubrey Brain. He made his name in the RAF Central Band and Orchestra during the Second World War, and at the peak of his career was in huge demand for concerts and recordings. He lived here from 1952 until his untimely death.

TOBIAS MATTHAY

(1858–1945) teacher and pianist

21 Arkwright Road

BORN in London to German parents, Matthay was associated with the Royal Academy of Music for over 50 years, from his student days in the 1870s to 1925, when he retired as Professor of Advanced Piano Playing. Celebrated pupils of his included Myra Hess*, Clifford Curzon and Moura Lympany. Matthay lived here at the height of his career, from 1902 until 1909, when he left London for Surrey.

JOHN PASSMORE EDWARDS

(1823–1911) journalist, editor
and builder of free public libraries

51 Netherhall Gardens

PASSMORE Edwards was a Cornishman, the son of a market gardener and carpenter, who spent his last 65 years in London amassing (and disbursing) a fortune made from publishing. His early ventures were unsuccessful, and by the mid-1850s he was bankrupt and broken in health, but his fortunes were reversed by the acquisition of the architectural journal *Building News* in 1862, and continued to flourish with his subsequent purchases of the *Mechanics Magazine* in 1869 and the first halfpenny newspaper, *The Echo*, in 1876. Passmore Edwards then embarked on a remarkable charitable spree, endowing art galleries, museums, hospitals and convalescent homes, and, above all, public libraries. Netherhall Gardens, developed in the 1870s, was his home for the last three years of his life.

SIDNEY WEBB (1859–1947)
BEATRICE WEBB (1858–1943)

social scientists and
political reformers

Fitzjohns Mansions,
10 Netherhall Gardens **40**

THE Webbs occupied 'a cosy little flat' here for about a year after their marriage in July 1892, before moving to a more permanent home in Pimlico (since demolished). Sidney Webb was an early member of the Fabian Society* and made his name as a London County Councillor; in 1895, he helped to found the London School of Economics, and in 1913, with Beatrice and others, he launched the *New Statesman*. Beatrice was the daughter of a railway magnate, and brought private means to their partnership, as well as an equally determined commitment to social justice and applied research: she sat on the 1905 Royal Commission on the Poor Laws while beginning their nine-volume *English Local Government* (1906–29). Sidney entered national politics, serving as President of the Board of Trade in the first Labour government in 1924 and as Colonial Secretary (1929–31), having been raised to the peerage as Lord Passfield in 1929. The Webbs became increasingly interested in Russia, and a long visit in 1932 led to the writing of *Soviet Communism: A New Civilisation?* (1935). Their ashes were interred in Westminster Abbey.

SIGMUND FREUD

(1856–1939) psychiatrist
and founder of psychoanalysis

20 Maresfield Gardens **41**

DRIVEN out of Vienna after the *Anschluss*, Freud arrived in London in June 1938 – a move facilitated by his dedicated disciple, Ernest Jones* – and moved to this spacious house that September. It was here that Freud spent his final year before succumbing to his 16-year struggle with cancer. Freud brought much furniture from his Vienna consulting room, including various antiquities and his

renowned couch; what had hitherto been a relatively ordinary detached house was thereby transformed into what, since its opening in 1986, has become one of London's most intriguing historic house museums.

ANNA FREUD
(1895–1982) pioneer of child psychoanalysis   20 Maresfield Gardens

ANNA Freud lived and worked here for 44 years, up to her own death. She supported her father, both domestically and professionally, and served for many years as the General Secretary of the International Psychological Association. A highly significant figure in her own right, Anna helped to establish modern approaches to child behaviour; in 1947, she founded the Hampstead Child Therapy Courses, and added the associated clinic five years later.

CECIL SHARP
(1859–1924) collector of
English folk songs and dances   4 Maresfield Gardens

SHARP lived at this semi-detached house from 1918 until his death, sharing it with his wife, Constance, and his assistant, Maud Karpeles. A sometime Principal of the Hampstead Conservatoire, Sharp became a dedicated collector and promoter of folk music, seeking out vernacular music through a series of study tours, and in 1902 published *A Book of British Song for Home and School*. In 1911, Sharp was instrumental in establishing the English Folk Dance Society, the spearhead of the morris dancing revival. Cecil Sharp House in Camden, a centre for English folk dance, music and singing, opened in 1930.

MARTINA BERGMAN ÖSTERBERG
(1849–1915) pioneer of physical
education for women   1 Broadhurst Gardens

MARTINA Bergman was born in Sweden and was an early champion of 'Swedish drill', an approach to physical education that attracted considerable attention from the London School Board, which in 1879 appointed her countrywoman Concordia Löfving to develop this aspect of teaching. Bergman took over in 1881, and soon embarked on the development of a course of instruction for teachers attached to the fast-expanding network of Board Schools. This house, a substantial building of 1880 then known as Reremonde, was acquired in 1885 to serve as her Hampstead Physical Training College for women; to its rear, visible from Greencroft Gardens, is the structure, dated 1885, which probably served as the gymnasium. The College, the first of its kind in England, opened with just four students, but by 1895 had 27 trainee teachers and had outgrown its premises. In that year, Madame Bergman Österberg – as she was known after her marriage in 1886 – and her flourishing institution transferred to Dartford, Kent.

DAVID BOMBERG

(1890–1957) artist · 10 Fordwych Road

BORN in Birmingham to Polish-Jewish parents, Bomberg studied at the Slade; he developed a powerful style akin to Vorticism. The outbreak of the First World War – in which he served – interrupted a fast-rising career. After a spell in Hampshire, Bomberg spent the mid-1920s in Palestine working for a Zionist organisation; this political engagement affected his painting, which moved away from abstraction towards expressionistic realism. In November 1928, not long after his return, he moved to this unassuming late-Victorian house in West Hampstead, sharing it with the painter Lilian Mendelson – later his wife – and her daughter Dinora. From here, he set out on numerous painting trips to Scotland, Russia and Spain; this last destination led to some of his most admired landscapes. Bomberg was a respected teacher too; both Leon Kossoff and Frank Auerbach were pupils.

DAME IDA MANN

(1893–1983) ophthalmologist · 13 Minster Road

BORN a short distance from the commemorated address, at 67 Fordwych Road, Ida Mann spent her first 41 years in West Hampstead. She became a worldwide authority on ophthalmology (the scientific study of the eye) and was the first female professor at the University of Oxford in any discipline. Mann promoted new diagnostic methods, wrote a standard text, *The Development of the Human Eye*

(1928), and, having helped to spring the contact lens pioneer Josef Dallos from the Nazi threat in Budapest, encouraged the adoption of this new optical technology. She lived in Minster Road during her early career, sharing the house with her parents who, in her own words, 'made my masculine, dedicated life secure and possible'; while at her training hospitals, she recalled that any spare moments were spent 'tearing up the Edgware Road in a No 16 bus to get a good meal from Mother'. Among her childhood memories of home were the antics of her pet canary, Spotty: 'I was interested in his reflexes and remember his frenzied aggression before a mirror.' Ida Mann later married and lived in Australia after 1949. Under the name of Caroline Gye, she wrote travel books.

ALFRED HARMSWORTH, VISCOUNT NORTHCLIFFE

(1865–1922) journalist and newspaper proprietor   31 Pandora Road

HARMSWORTH moved to this late-19th-century terraced house immediately after his marriage to Mary Milner in April 1888 and lived here until 1891. During this time, working from the attic, he launched his first successful publishing venture, the magazine *Answers to Correspondents* (1888); he also established *Comic Cuts* and *Chips*, published by the Pandora Publishing Co., which he founded in 1890. Harmsworth and his brother Harold – later Lord Rothermere – went on to found the *Daily Mail* (1896) and the *Daily Mirror* (1903).

SIR ADRIAN BOULT, CH

(1889–1983) conductor   Flat 78, Marlborough Mansions, Cannon Hill

THE son of a Chester oil merchant, Boult studied at Oxford and joined the Royal Opera House, Covent Garden, in 1914. He conducted the first (private) performance of *The Planets* by Holst* in 1918, but the most important phase of his career opened in 1930, when he became Director of Music at the fledgling BBC, in which capacity he helped to create the BBC Symphony Orchestra. Knighted in 1937, he acquired an international reputation; in a field renowned for extroverts, Boult was a modest man and a restrained conductor. During the 11 years he lived in this ground-floor flat from 1966, he conducted the London Philharmonic Orchestra in a number of notable recordings for EMI.

LEONARD HUXLEY (1860–1933)
JULIAN HUXLEY (1887–1975)
ALDOUS HUXLEY (1894–1963)
men of science and letters   16 Bracknell Gardens

LEONARD – the son of T. H. Huxley*, whose biography he wrote – entered publishing and became the long-serving editor of the *Cornhill Magazine*, living in this conventional turn-of-the-century semi-detached house from 1916 until his death.

His son Julian was a pioneer in the field of animal behaviour, and advanced theories of evolution through his own knowledge of genetics, statistics and behavioural analysis. He was appointed in 1946 the first Secretary-General – and later Director-General – of UNESCO and lived from 1943 to his death at nearby 31 Pond Street.

Another son, the near-blind Aldous, was one of the most illustrious writers of the 20th century. *Point Counter Point* (1928), *Brave New World* (1932) and *Eyeless in Gaza* (1936) are his best-known works. Aldous lived here intermittently from 1917 until his marriage in 1919; he spent much of his later life abroad, mostly in the United States.

JOHN MCCORMACK
(1884–1945) lyric tenor   24 Ferncroft Avenue

THE son of an Athlone labourer, McCormack won Ireland's gold medal for tenors in the 1903 Feis Ceoil, and trained in Italy. He sang with Nellie Melba* and became a naturalised US citizen in 1919. After his last operatic performance in 1923, he devoted himself to recitals and recordings, particularly of folk songs: his rendition of 'The Rose of Tralee' was hugely popular on both sides of the Atlantic. This was McCormack's first permanent home – which he named Rosaleen House and lived in from 1908 to 1913 – after finding initial success.

E. H. GOMBRICH
(1909–2001) art historian   19 Briardale Gardens **51**

GOMBRICH'S reputation as a populariser and interpreter of art was made by *The Story of Art*; this book first appeared in 1950, and has since been translated into 34 languages, with worldwide sales estimated at over six million. Born in Vienna to a family of Jewish heritage, he came to live in London in 1936 to escape the Nazi menace. Ernst Gombrich went on to hold several professorial chairs and the directorship of the Warburg Institute; declaring that all design was 'rooted in man's biological inheritance', he was among the first art historians to link artistic creativity to human psychology. He came to live here with his family in 1952, and died here nearly half a century later. Briardale Gardens is the work of builder George Washington Hart and architect Charles H. B. Quennell. According to his granddaughter, Gombrich and his wife Ilse 'loved that house, as did we all'.

SIR RONALD AYLMER FISHER

(1890–1962) statistician and geneticist

Inverforth House (formerly Hill House and The Hill), North End Way

FISHER, whose father was a fine art dealer, lived here as a boy between 1896 and 1904, when finances forced the family to move to Streatham. Knighted in 1952, he is remembered as the most significant British statistician of the 20th century. Fisher's early work was carried out at the Rothamsted Experimental Station in Harpenden, Hertfordshire; his classic texts are *Statistical Methods for Research Workers* (1925) and *The Genetical Theory of Natural Selection* (1930). He left Rothamsted to succeed Karl Pearson* as Galton Professor at University College London, and later moved on to Cambridge.

WILLIAM HESKETH LEVER, 1ST VISCOUNT LEVERHULME

(1851–1925) soap-maker and philanthropist

Inverforth House (formerly Hill House and The Hill), North End Way

THE son of a Bolton grocer, Lever moved into manufacturing, making his fortune from soap. He made his soap from vegetable oil rather than animal fats and understood the value of packaging and advertising, registering his brand as Sunlight soap. This approach enjoyed prodigious success – Lever Brothers was one of the largest British companies of the time – and he was able to develop his interests in architecture and collecting art. Port Sunlight, near the Lever soapworks on the Wirral, ranks as one of England's great experiments in town planning. The Hill, as this house was then called, was the London home of Lever and his wife Elizabeth after 1904. Lord Leverhulme was a great philanthropist, and a trust continues to spread his largesse.

MICHAEL VENTRIS
(1922–56) architect and decipherer of Linear B script 19 North End

VENTRIS'S achievement was to demonstrate that Linear B, an ancient script uncovered in Crete by Arthur Evans, was indeed the earliest known writing in ancient Greek. This was a major breakthrough in establishing the connection between Minoan civilisation and the subsequent development of cultures in mainland Greece. Ventris's crucial 1953 article in the *Journal of Hellenic Studies*, co-authored with John Chadwick, drew on cryptographical techniques developed in wartime intelligence. Tragically, he died in a car crash before the publication of his key work (jointly written with Chadwick), *Documents in Mycenaean Greek* (1956). The house was built in 1952–3 to designs by Ventris and his wife Lois. Fittings by Marcel Breuer* from the family flat at 47 Highpoint, Highgate – Michael's home from 1936 until 1953 – were incorporated into the interior.

SIR NIKOLAUS PEVSNER
(1902–83) architectural historian 2 Wildwood Terrace **55**

PEVSNER founded the near-comprehensive county histories *The Buildings of England,* originally published by Penguin, and popularly known as 'Pevsners'. Research for these volumes was undertaken on a punishing schedule: driven around by his wife Lola and later by graduate students, Pevsner – who once visited 19 churches and around 40 other buildings in a single day – wrote up the entries immediately, every evening – 'with iron determination; otherwise all would go dim and dead'. Somehow he found time to teach at Birkbeck College and also to work as a broadcaster. The first Pevsner volumes, full of their founder's pungently opinionated writing, came out in 1951 and the series, which has informed many a conservation campaign, continues today under Yale University Press. The founder of this English bookshelf essential came from a Russian-Jewish family and was born in Leipzig, arriving in London in 1934 after the Nazi race laws drove him out of the University of Göttingen. He and his family settled here in 1936 and he died at the house 47 years later; the terrace is described in the most recent Pevsner edition as 'surprisingly urban Gothic'.

JOHN LINNELL* (1792–1882) painter
WILLIAM BLAKE (1757–1827)
poet and artist Old Wyldes, North End

LINNELL lodged at Old Wyldes – then known as Collins' Farm or Heath Farm – in 1823 and, more permanently, from March 1824 to c.1828; he rented the western half of the house, which dates from the 17th century, for himself and his family. He was utterly captivated by the visionary poet and artist William Blake, who visited Linnell frequently here, walking the seven miles uphill from Lambeth. Blake was often joined by Linnell's future son-in-law Samuel Palmer* who, together with Linnell and Edward Calvert, would form the group of intensely lyrical painters of nature known as 'The Ancients', or the 'Shoreham Group', after the Kent village to which they gravitated from 1826 onwards. On the eastern half of the house, a private plaque of 1957 commemorates the architect and town planner Raymond Unwin (1863–1940), who lived here from 1906 until his death.

THOMAS SMITH TAIT
(1882–1954) architect Gates House, Wyldes Close

THE Scottish-born architect Tommy Tait, as he was usually called, is best known for St Andrew's House in Edinburgh (1934), which now houses the office of the Scottish First Minister, and for his work on the British Empire Exhibition of 1938, held in Glasgow. He spent most of his working life in London, however, and lived in this large detached house of 1915 from the late 1920s until 1950, and was responsible for the single-storey rear extension. Other rather larger projects in London included the *Daily Telegraph* office on Fleet Street (1927–8), and, in collaboration, Unilever House, near Blackfriars (1933). The partnership with which he worked – Burnet, Tait and Lorne – also built some fine houses in Art Deco style in Wells Rise, St John's Wood, and Tait was, alone, the designer of the piers for Sydney Harbour Bridge (opened 1932).

DAME HENRIETTA BARNETT

(1851–1936) founder of Hampstead Garden Suburb

CANON SAMUEL BARNETT

(1844–1913) social reformer   Heath End House, Spaniards Road

HENRIETTA Barnett, 'pretty, witty and well to do', devoted her life, as did her husband, to social reform; she was the key figure behind the foundation of the Hampstead Garden Suburb Trust in 1906 and was insistent that the new settlement be made up of mixed social classes. Her husband Samuel Barnett became priest in charge of the deprived parish of St Jude's, Whitechapel, in 1873. His awareness of the vast and growing chasm that separated the East End from better-off areas prompted him, together with his wife, to found in 1884 the university settlement Toynbee Hall. The couple also campaigned for poor law reforms and pensions. The Barnetts lived between 1889 and 1913 at Heath End House, built in about 1788, and which they renamed St Jude's Cottage after their Whitechapel parish; here, Whitechapel girls would come and learn how to become servants, while 'rest-rooms' were provided for 'tired Toynbee men or workers'. The novelist Hall Caine largely rebuilt Heath End House in 1923.

SIR RALPH RICHARDSON

(1902–83) actor   Bedegar's Lea, Kenwood Close

'**A**CTING is merely the art of keeping a large group of people from coughing,' Richardson once said, by way of self-deprecation. Be that as it may, with Sir John Gielgud* and Sir Laurence Olivier, he formed a trio of theatrical knights who not only dominated the mid-20th-century British stage, but made their mark in cinema too. In the 30s and 40s Richardson was associated with the Old Vic Theatre, where he gave memorable performances as Caliban, Sir Toby Belch and Bottom. Latterly he joined the company at the National Theatre, where he initiated the custom of firing a rocket from the roof to mark a play's first night; there and elsewhere, Richardson excelled in modern plays by the likes of Orton and Pinter. His many films included *Anna Karenina* (1947), produced by Alexander Korda*, *Dr Zhivago* (1965) and *Time Bandits* (1980). He lived at Bedegar's Lea, a 1930s neo-Georgian house, from 1944 until 1968; famously eccentric, he kept a pet ferret named Eddie in the attic and rode big motorbikes into his 70s.

KNIGHTSBRIDGE AND QUEEN'S GATE

ONCE a hamlet, and a favourite spot for duelling and highway robbery, Knightsbridge was said by 1840 to be 'as much London as Tottenham Court Road'. Its present appearance and its social cachet owe much to the mid-19th-century development of estates adjoining Hyde Park that were designed with an exclusive market in mind; the lack of connecting roads to the older builds in Brompton was a deliberate policy. Westwards along Kensington Road, the area around Queen's Gate was developed at about the same time. Architecturally, it is much of a part with Knightsbridge, with generous proportions and much stucco in evidence. The wealth of the inhabitants in general is reflected in the plaques: some of the writers and painters honoured may have suffered for their art, but the cause of their suffering – at least while they lived in this district – was not poverty.

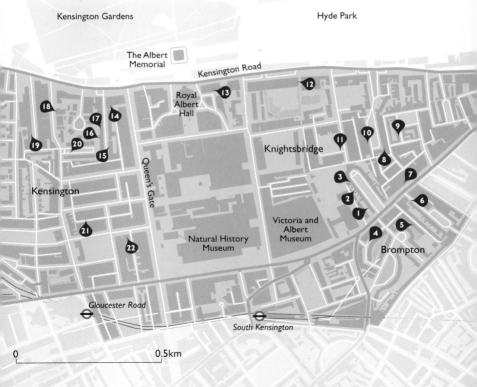

STÉPHANE MALLARMÉ

(1842–98) poet   6 Brompton Square ❶

THE French symbolist poet stayed here during the spring and summer of 1863, when the building was a boarding house. Born in Paris in 1842 and orphaned at the age of seven, Mallarmé was a disciple of Baudelaire, but his work was also influenced by Keats*, Shelley* and Coleridge*. He came to London in autumn 1862, at the age of 20, in order to learn English – partly to enable him to read the works of Edgar Allan Poe. As it transpired, he made a living – reluctantly – teaching English for most of his life. He considered London in the fog to be

'English men, like the rooms of the Grand Hotel, strike me as being all alike.'

Mallarmé, dismissing one half of London's inhabitants

'a town without peer', but loathed it in hot weather. When Mallarmé met Marie Gerhard, a German governess and another alienated émigré, he hoped that 'from our two melancholies we could perhaps make a single happiness'. They were duly married at a Catholic chapel in Kensington in August 1863, and left the country soon afterwards.

FRANCIS PLACE

(1771–1854) political reformer   21 Brompton Square ❷

FOR many years Place was known as the 'radical tailor', his shop at 16 Charing Cross doubling as a library and a meeting place for reformers. His move to Brompton in 1833 coincided with his second marriage (opposed by his family) to Louisa Simeon Chatterley (b.1797), an actress many years his junior who was then residing at 15 Brompton Square; he took a lease on number 21, a move in part prompted by financial considerations, Place having lost thousands of pounds through his lawyer's incompetence. He found the house to be 'sadly out

of condition', and spent £360 that he could ill afford on its refurbishment. Place had a hand in the reform of municipal corporations enacted in 1835 – the legislation that laid the foundations for modern local government. In 1838 he co-drafted the People's Charter, the founding document of Chartism, but became disillusioned with the movement and undertook little political activity after suffering a stroke in 1844. Seven years later, he separated from his wife and went to live with his daughter Annie in Hammersmith.

E. F. BENSON

(1867–1940) writer

BENSON, known as 'Fred', was the son of Edward White Benson, Archbishop of Canterbury (1883–96), and his brothers R. H. Benson and A. C. Benson were also writers; the latter wrote the words to 'Land of Hope and Glory' (1902). Fred's first novel, *Dodo* (1893), published when he was working in Athens, proved an overnight success, and he soon dedicated himself to writing full-time. In 1915 he took a lease on 25 Brompton Square, which remained his London home until his death. His move here is described in *Up and Down* (1918), and the house – which Steven Runciman described as 'overcrowded with objects' – formed the setting for *Lucia in London* (1927), *Secret Lives* (1932) and a short story, 'Aunts and Pianos' (1928). A talented pianist, he once accompanied Nellie Melba* in his large drawing room-study on the first floor; here, Benson 'poured tea for his guests out of a fine silver teapot, and loved to discuss, above all things, antiques'. From 1918 he spent much time in Rye, Sussex – the Tilling of the Mapp and Lucia novels for which he is best known.

SIR PATRICK ABERCROMBIE

(1879–1957)
pioneer of town and country planning

ALTHOUGH he hailed from north-west England and lived for some time on Merseyside, Abercrombie's most notable achievements as a planner were in London and the south east. His *County of London Plan* (1943) and *Greater London Plan* (1945) envisaged a post-war London cleared of slums and enhanced by open spaces; among his chief legacies were the Green Belt, the ring of 'New Towns' beyond it – including Harlow, Crawley and Stevenage – and the M25 orbital motorway. Abercrombie's original plans would have involved much more road building – and therefore demolition – than actually took place. Yet he was a conservationist, having been instrumental in the founding of what is now the Campaign to Protect Rural England. Abercrombie came to London in 1935 on becoming Professor of Town Planning at University College and settled in Egerton Gardens with his wife Maud; he left not long after her death in February 1942. Later he lived and worked in Welbeck Street, Marylebone.

WELLS COATES

(1895–1958) architect and designer

18 Yeoman's Row **5**

COATES was an outstanding exponent of modern design and architecture in the 1930s: his buildings include Lawn Road Flats in Hampstead (1934) and 10 Palace Gate in Kensington (1939). His industrial designs included the famous EKCO AD 65 radio set of 1934. Born Wells Wintemute Coates in Tokyo, the son of Canadian missionaries, he settled in London in the early 1920s, working initially as a journalist. He lived in a top-floor flat here, originally built as an artist's studio in the 1890s, from 1936 until he moved to Canada 20 years later. Coates's office was here too, on the first floor. The flat's interior, now lost, set a new standard for the optimal use of small urban spaces; one feature was a 'window garden', set between two panes of the double-glazed front window. Dressed in a kaftan, Coates dispensed hospitality in this self-designed shrine to Japanese minimalism, including expertly cooked Japanese food.

ELISABETH WELCH

(1904–2003) singer

1 Ovington Court, Ovington Gardens **6**

IN St Cyprian's evangelical church choir in her native New York, Elisabeth Welch was known as 'the loud alto': in Paris she metamorphosed into a smooth cabaret singer, and in 1933 she came to London, where she stayed for the rest of her long life. Cole Porter wrote the song 'Solomon' with Welch in mind, and 'Stormy Weather' became her signature tune; she revived it, 40 years later, in the Derek Jarman* film *The Tempest* (1979). Ovington Court was her home for her first two or three years in the capital; she shared the flat, which was then almost new, with a maid and a 'perky' fox-terrier. A *Melody Maker*

Elisabeth Welch died in 2003, aged 99, which came as news to all those who had attended her 80th birthday party – in 1989!

journalist who came to interview her (in 'a tiny, congested room') found her preparing to sing in a broadcast with Lou Preager and his Orchestra. In a flash of the diva, she gave him short shrift, and threw him out after four and a half minutes. After a career encompassing stage musicals, films, television and even her own radio show, Welch made her final professional appearance in 1996.

SIR BENJAMIN THOMPSON, COUNT RUMFORD

(1753–1814) inventor and adventurer

168 Brompton Road (formerly 45 Brompton Row)

THOMPSON made important modifications to the design of cooking-stoves and chimneys, invented a percolating coffee-pot, and enjoyed military and political escapades in more than one country. Born in Massachusetts, he was loyal to the Crown and sailed for England in 1776. Here, his experiments in cannonball ballistics led him to conclude that heat was not, as was then believed, a fluid; he was elected a Fellow of the Royal Society at the age of 26. He entered the military service of the Elector of Bavaria in 1783, and became a leading minister in the German state and a count of the Holy Roman Empire. Count Rumford was back in London in 1798, where – after George III refused him ambassadorial accreditation – he co-founded the Royal Institution. He bought this house in summer 1798, and double-glazed the front windows using projecting glass cases, in which there was space for ornamental plants. Rumford's study, on the third floor at the rear, enjoyed a view of open country. Having fallen out with his Royal Institution colleagues, he left this house and this country in 1802.

BRUCE BAIRNSFATHER

(1888–1959) cartoonist

1 Sterling Street

BAIRNSFATHER was born in the Punjab and set up as an artist in earnest after an early stint in the Army. He is widely remembered for the First World War cartoon of two beleaguered Tommies in a shell-hole, captioned, 'Well, if you knows of a better 'ole, go to it,' which first appeared in *The Bystander* in 1915. Much of his work featured an archetypal soldier, the moustachioed, pipe-smoking 'Old Bill'; this salt-of-the-earth character became a household name, but was at first viewed as insulting, with questions raised in Parliament. Bairnsfather – a machine-gun officer, later given a special rank of officer-cartoonist – was injured at the Second Battle of Ypres. He lived and worked in this mid-1840s terrace from 1919 until 1921, the year of his marriage. He was later involved in films and early television transmissions, and served as an artist for the US military during the Second World War.

SIR FRANCIS GALTON

(1822–1911) explorer, statistician and founder of eugenics   42 Rutland Gate   **9**

AFTER studying mathematics and medicine at Cambridge, in 1850 Galton set off to explore uncharted areas in south-west Africa. His encounters with indigenous people fired his interest in the extent to which traits and talents are inherited. This became his life's work, as summarised in *Natural Inheritance* (1889); inter alia, he contributed to the field of biostatistics and disproved the theory of pangenesis – that hereditary elements are carried in the bloodstream – as promulgated by his cousin Charles Darwin*. The plaque (of 1931) lauds Galton's foundational role in eugenics – he coined this term, meaning the scientific 'improvement' of the human race. The association of these ideas – which once had many adherents – with Nazi race science has forever tainted this aspect of his legacy. Galton moved to this newly built house with his wife Louisa in 1858, and lived here until his death.

LORD LUGARD

(1858–1945) colonial administrator   51 Rutland Gate   **10**

BORN in Madras, Lugard served in the Afghan, Sudan and Burmese wars before becoming High Commissioner of Northern Nigeria (1900–06); from 1907 to 1911 he was Governor of Hong Kong and from 1912 to 1919 served as Governor-General of Nigeria, the role for which he is best known; the country's provinces were amalgamated during his tenure, in 1914. During this period, on three-month furloughs, Lugard lived at Rutland Gate. His wife, Flora Louise – the first woman on the permanent staff at *The Times*, and its sometime colonial editor – found the house for them, being determined that when on home turf her husband should 'find his relations with the

London world in proper trim'. She had bought the lease on 51 Rutland Gate for £5,000, and spent nearly half that amount again on interior renovations; such was her reputation for hospitality that the house was dubbed 'The Lugard Arms'. On Lugard's return from his posting in 1919, they sold Rutland Gate and moved full-time to their country home, Little Parkhurst, in the Surrey Hills. Lugard was known for his advocacy of gradual independence for African countries, though his attitude to Africans showed the condescension common to that era.

AVA GARDNER
(1922–90) film star   34 Ennismore Gardens

A NORTH Carolina native, Ava Gardner first visited London in 1951, on her way to Spain to film *Pandora and the Flying Dutchman*. She liked the city: 'So it rains sometimes. It rains everywhere sometimes. And I happen to like the rain.' Her fame and her relationship with Frank Sinatra made her the object of press hounding, and it was for privacy that she came to live in London in 1968. Four years later Gardner moved into a spacious, laterally converted flat on the first floor of what had been numbers 34 and 35 Ennismore Gardens. The building is part of a development from around 1870 that reused stone from the 18th-century Blackfriars Bridge. Gardner continued to make films, notably *Earthquake* (1974) and *The Blue Bird* (1976), and was a guest star on *Knots Landing*, the TV soap. With her personal assistant Mearene Jordan, she furnished the flat in an eclectic 'oriental' style, and once said that the place 'suits me so well, I hate to leave it even for a park bench'. Even so, she was sometimes seen in the nearby Ennismore Arms, now gone. To mark the plaque unveiling, the BFI screened a film from her heyday, the political thriller *Seven Days in May* (1964).

JUNIUS S. MORGAN (1813–90) & JOHN PIERPONT MORGAN (1837–1913)
international bankers   14 Princes Gate 12

J UNIUS Spencer Morgan came to London from New England in the 1850s, and entered into partnership with the banker and philanthropist George Peabody*. His negotiation of a loan to France during the Franco-Prussian War of 1870–71 put the firm, by then known as J. S. Morgan & Co., at the forefront of international investment banking. Renamed Morgan, Grenfell & Co., the firm acted for both the British and American governments during the First World War, and was later absorbed into Deutsche Bank. Junius first took a lease on 13 Princes Gate – the eastern half of the present house – in 1858, ten years after it had been completed by John Elger, the developer also responsible for Rutland Gate. Morgan bought the freehold in 1870 and came here regularly until retiring to Monte Carlo, where he died in a carriage accident. His son and successor John Pierpont Morgan bought the adjacent number 14 in 1904 and threw the two houses into one; this was in part to hold his growing art collection. Many

'He would collect anything from a pyramid to Mary Magdalene's tooth.'

Frances Morgan on her husband Pierpont's collecting mania

transatlantic social and business links were forged here; Edward VII and Queen Alexandra headed many guest lists and Pierpont shared a mistress with the monarch – the actress Maxine Elliott. The present front door dates from 1925–6, when the house was remodelled as the United States ambassador's residence, a purpose it served until 1955; the young John F. Kennedy stayed here during his father Joseph's spell in that post, as is commemorated by a private plaque. More recently the building was the HQ of the Royal College of General Practitioners.

SIR MALCOLM SARGENT

(1895–1967) conductor   Flat 9, Albert Hall Mansions, Kensington Gore **13**

S CHOOLED at Stamford, Lincolnshire, and trained as an organist and composer, Sargent moved to London in 1923 on being appointed professor and conductor of orchestral classes at the Royal College of Music. A champion of contemporary classical music, he premiered works by, among others, Ralph Vaughan Williams* and William Walton*, and became a highly successful conductor, especially of choral music. In 1947 – the year of

his knighthood – Sargent settled in a flat in this imposing block designed by Richard Norman Shaw* (1880–87). Having conducted his first Prom concert in 1921, he went on to become as indelibly identified with the famous summer season as Henry Wood*. He also became known to the wider public for his contributions to BBC Radio's *Brains Trust*. Sargent's name is perpetuated by the cancer charity founded in his memory, CLIC Sargent.

ROBERT BADEN-POWELL

(1857–1941)
'Chief Scout of the World'

9 Hyde Park Gate
(formerly 1 Hyde Park Gate South)

THIS was Baden-Powell's boyhood home, where he lived with his siblings and their widowed mother, Henrietta, from the early 1860s until 1877 or 1878. Built between 1845 and 1847 by J. F. Hanson, the building's ornate stucco decoration and Corinthian pilasters are consistent with Henrietta's social pretensions; for spurious reasons, she added Baden to the family name in 1869. The young Baden-Powell – known as 'Stephe', pronounced 'Stevie', from his middle name of Stephenson – attended a dame school in Kensington Square before going on to prep school and Charterhouse. During school holidays, he enjoyed long walking tours and sailing expeditions on his eldest stepbrother's small yacht – the kind of healthy outdoor activities that he would later advocate in *Scouting for Boys* (1908). The youth organisation Baden-Powell started soon grew into a worldwide phenomenon.

SIR LESLIE STEPHEN

(1832–1904) scholar
and writer

22 Hyde Park Gate
(formerly 13 Hyde Park Gate South)

STEPHEN was the founding editor of the *Dictionary of National Biography*, begun in 1882. He was born at 42 Hyde Park Gate and lived at number 20 (then 11 Hyde Park Gate South) – in June 1876, following the death of his first wife Minny, the daughter of the author Thackeray*. Two doors away lived a widow, the noted beauty Julia Duckworth; their friendship blossomed, and they set up house together here after marrying in spring 1878. A (rather ugly) two-storey upward extension was constructed, which contained Stephen's book-lined study on the fourth floor and extra accommodation above. Seven maids were crammed into the 'dark insanitary' basement, according to the recollection of their daughter, Virginia Woolf*. She, like her sister, the artist Vanessa Bell, was born in a first-floor bedroom, and both have unofficial plaques here. Later, with their brothers Thoby and Adrian, the daughters produced a family newspaper, the *Hyde Park Gate News*. Apart from the *Dictionary* – on which he often worked at home – Stephen's works included *An Agnostic's Apology and other Essays* (1893) and *The English Utilitarians* (1900). He died here in 1904.

SIR WINSTON CHURCHILL, KG

(1874–1965) Prime Minister 28 Hyde Park Gate

Churchill and his wife Clementine on the doorstep of their Hyde Park Gate home, 1945.

CHURCHILL bought this house as his London base following his shock defeat at the general election of 1945, and had it redecorated at once. Although the general election of 1951 saw him return to 10 Downing Street, he resigned in 1955 and returned to Hyde Park Gate, buying number 27, next door, as office accommodation. Out of government, Churchill travelled and lectured, took up painting again and revised his monumental *History of the English-Speaking Peoples* for publication (1956–8). A crowd sang 'Happy Birthday' to him here on his 90th birthday in November 1964 and Churchill replied with his familiar victory sign from the window. Having suffered a series of strokes, he died at the house the following January. As well as being the London house where Churchill lived the longest, numbers 27 and 28 possess intrinsic interest as late-Georgian survivals amid a sea of Victorian stucco.

ENID BAGNOLD

(1889–1981) novelist and playwright 29 Hyde Park Gate

BORN in Rochester, Bagnold first achieved literary notice with *A Diary without Dates* (1917). The frankness of this record of her experiences as a nurse during the First World War earned her a summary dismissal from the profession. She and her husband Roderick Jones, the chairman and managing director of Reuters news agency, acquired this imposing three-storey stuccoed house dating from

Following Jones and Bagnold's purchase of the house, Edwin Lutyens* remodelled the interior. On the second floor, he fashioned an enormous nursery for their children, which doubled as a lecture hall and a square drawing room at garden level. For Enid there was a writing room 'like a ship's cabin'; this was approached by a short staircase, the newel of which was topped with a swivelling copper knob – the whimsical notion being that if inspiration struck during the night, she could run downstairs and vault straight to her desk.

the early 1840s in 1926. Her book *National Velvet* (1935) was an early success for Elizabeth Taylor in its screen adaptation (1944). Later, she turned to writing plays, including *Lottie Dundass* (1941) and *The Chalk Garden* (1955); the title of the latter derived from the couple's country home on the Sussex Downs at Rottingdean. Widowed in 1962, she sold the London house in 1970.

SIR JOHN EVERETT MILLAIS, BT

(1829–96) painter   2 Palace Gate

THE house was designed by P. C. Hardwick and built by Cubitt & Co. for Millais but although it was substantially complete by April 1876, he does not appear to have lived in it until 1878. A member of the Pre-Raphaelite Brotherhood*, Millais – once the scourge of the artistic establishment – was President of the Royal Academy by the time he died here. He shared the house with his wife Euphemia ('Effie'), who was previously married to John Ruskin*; it was, he declared 'all that he desired', with the exception of there being no garden. The large first-floor studio, hung with tapestries on three walls and with Van Dyck's *Time Clipping the Wings of Cupid* on the fourth, welcomed many distinguished sitters, including – in the single year of 1881 – Tennyson*, Disraeli* and Cardinal Newman*; the last was rated by Millais as 'the most interesting sitter, except Mr Gladstone, who ever entered his studio'.

HENRY JAMES
(1843–1916) writer   34 De Vere Gardens

AN American by birth, James is famous for his novels and short stories – and for his elaborate prose style. He moved to the recently built fourth-floor flat here in March 1886; his domestic needs were attended to by a live-in servant couple, and the writer jokingly vowed to be as 'bourgeoise as my means will permit, and have large fat sofas'. To an aunt he proclaimed that 'my new quarters work beautifully and haven't a flaw,' though with bachelor fastidiousness he complained of 'some romping little wretches of children overhead'. James nonetheless enjoyed a productive spell here; among his successes were the novels *The Reverberator* (1888) and *The Tragic Muse* (1890) and in 1891 a dramatisation of his early novel *The American* (1877). From 1896 he based himself mostly in Rye, Sussex, where he settled permanently two years later. He sublet the London flat, and gave up the lease in 1902.

SIR BENJAMIN BAKER
(1840–1907) civil engineer
and designer of the Forth Bridge   3 Kensington Gate

TOP of Baker's enviable civil engineering CV is the Forth Bridge (built 1882-9), the 2.5 km (1.5 mile) cantilever railway bridge for which he shares the design credits with John Fowler. In London, the Somerset-born Baker was involved in engineering the Metropolitan, District, Northern and Central Underground railway lines, as well as the extension of the London to Brighton line across the Thames to Victoria. He also co-designed the unusual iron cargo vessel that was used to bring Cleopatra's Needle from Egypt to London in 1877, and was later consulting engineer on the Aswan Dam. Baker's plaque marks the mid-19th-century terraced house where he lived at the height of his career (1881-94), with his mother, sister, niece and servants.

SIR DOUGLAS BADER

(1910–82) RAF fighter pilot 5 Petersham Mews **21**

BADER was commissioned in 1930 but the following year, crashed when attempting a stunt, suffering near-fatal injuries that led to the amputation of both legs. 'Bad show' was his laconic comment in the logbook, and six months later, he was walking unaided on artificial limbs. Discharged from service in 1933, Bader was never reconciled to civilian life and was eventually allowed to return to the cockpit in 1940; he was soon promoted to squadron leader. The 'big wing' formation attacks on German bombers that he advocated were controversial, though many regard them as a vital component of the Battle of Britain victory. After his plane was downed in August 1941, Bader spent the rest of the war a prisoner, latterly in Colditz. Kenneth More's sympathetic portrayal of Bader in the 1956 film *Reach for the Sky* has ensured that his remarkable life story is an ongoing source of inspiration. This 1860s mews house was his London home after 1955.

TONY HANCOCK

(1924–68) comedian 20 Queen's Gate Place **22**

IN *Hancock's Half Hour*, the radio and television programme that made him famous, Tony Hancock lived at 22 Railway Cuttings, East Cheam. In reality, at the time the programme first went out (on the radio in 1954, and on television two years later), home for Hancock was a fourth-floor flat in a mid-19th-century building in Queen's Gate Place, which he shared with his first wife Cicely Romanis. It was his longest-standing London address, and the six years he spent there were prosperous and, by the standards of his troubled life, reasonably stable and happy. Although he raised the bar for broadcast comedy

'There was an old leather club armchair with the stuffing coming out, a few other odd chairs and a put-you-up settee. There was an underfelt on the floor but no carpet … There were piles of fan letters behind the lavatory pan.'

Producer Dennis Main Wilson describes the less-than-pristine interior of Tony Hancock's flat

with his *Half Hour*, Hancock never hit such heights again himself; tortured by self-doubt, he succumbed to alcoholism, and eventually took his own life in Sydney, Australia.

CHELSEA

DURING the 16th and 17th centuries, people came to Chelsea to 'take the air' and to enjoy boating, bathing and other riverside activities. The 18th and 19th centuries saw considerable development on both sides of King's Road, the loss of some of the early mansions that had dominated the banks of the Thames, and a dramatic increase in population. Still, for much of the 1800s, Chelsea retained its village atmosphere, and the picturesque, quiet streets stretching along and north of the river became a refuge for lovers of solitude and calm. The

'There is only one place in the world wherein to live, and that is Chelsea!'

George Gissing * *to his sister, 15 September 1883*

area's special connection with artists and writers began in the 1830s and lasted until after the Second World War, when property prices rose and the bohemian atmosphere was lost. The biggest change, however, came in 1874, with the construction of the Embankment and the loss of many historic landmarks, including the ancient river wall.

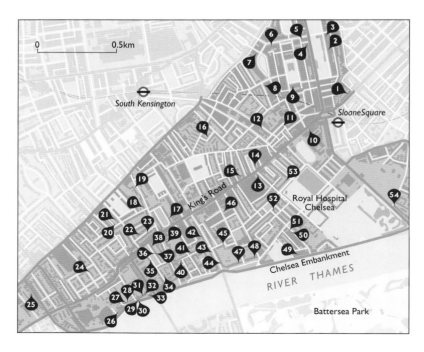

ANEURIN 'NYE' BEVAN (1897–1960)
JENNIE LEE (1908–88)
politicians

23 Cliveden Place

NYE Bevan and Jennie Lee both came from mining backgrounds – in south Wales and central Scotland respectively. They married in 1934 and lived here for the decade after 1944 – a period that encompassed Bevan's spell as Minister for Housing and Health in the post-war Labour government and the establishment of the National Health Service in 1948. As Arts Minister, Lee oversaw the creation of the Open University in 1971. At first they lived in the basement of this 19th-century terraced house, while the four storeys above were renovated after bomb damage. Lee's sense of style ensured that this was done with panache: their friend Michael Foot wrote that 'it was hard to tell whether the dwellers ... had devised the rooms or whether somehow subtly the process had happened the other way round'.

WILLIAM WILBERFORCE*
(1759–1833) opponent of slavery

44 Cadogan Place **2**

SUFFERING the after-effects of a severe bout of influenza, Wilberforce came to London from Bath in order to consult a doctor. He arrived at this house, lent to him by his cousin, Mrs Lucy Smith, on 19 July 1833. Ten days later – on 29 July – he died here. Although Wilberforce's greatest work – his leadership of the campaign against slavery – was carried out while he was living in Battersea Rise, it culminated with the bill abolishing slavery in British territories passed on 26 July 1833, just days before his death. He is said to have exclaimed, 'Thank God that I should have lived to witness [this] day.'

DOROTHY BLAND (MRS JORDAN)
(1762–1816) actress

30 (formerly 3) Cadogan Place **3**

BORN in Ireland, Dora Bland began her acting career in 1779 in Dublin, where she acquired a reputation for playing 'breeches' (meaning male) roles. In 1782, under the stage name of Mrs Jordan, she came to England and entered the limelight in 1785, on her engagement at the Theatre Royal, Drury Lane; her forte was comedy.

'Her face, her tears, her manners were irresistible. Her smile had the effect of sunshine, and her laugh did one good to hear it.'

William Hazlitt* on Mrs Jordan

In 1790 she became the mistress of the Duke of Clarence, later William IV, bearing him ten children, all given the surname FitzClarence.

The couple lived together as husband and wife, mainly at Bushy House in Bushy Park, Surrey, of which William was Ranger, until they separated in 1811. Mrs Jordan moved here the following year. Her final years were marked by tragedy: suffering increasingly from ill health, she retired from the theatre in 1815, and left Cadogan Place for France, where she died alone and in poverty.

SIR CHARLES WENTWORTH DILKE

(1843–1911) statesman and author   76 Sloane Street

DILKE was born in this house and died here at the age of 67. One of the great Liberal thinkers of his time, his first book, *Greater Britain* (1868), was published in the year that he entered Parliament as Liberal MP for Chelsea. He played a key part in the introduction of universal male suffrage, the legalisation of the position of trade unions and the limitation of hours of work. But for the fact that Dilke

was cited – it appears unjustly – in divorce proceedings in 1885, he might well have gone on to become Liberal leader in the House of Commons. Dilke – whose second wife was Emilia Francis, a prominent art historian and trades unionist – was extremely well connected: 'I have known everyone worth knowing from 1850 until my death,' he said confidently, when he knew his own demise was imminent.

LILLIE LANGTRY

(1853–1929) actress   21 Pont Street **5**

BORN Emilie Charlotte Le Breton, the 'Jersey Lily' initially made her name as a 'professional beauty' and as the mistress of the future Edward VII before taking up acting in 1881. Although never regarded as a great actress, Langtry

was immensely popular. During the 1880s she made extensive tours of the United States, and in 1900 took over the management of the Imperial Theatre, Westminster, which she rebuilt in magnificent style. She lived in this elaborate building from

1891 until 1897, when she moved to Cadogan Gardens – sharing the house with Jeanne-Marie, her daughter by Prince Louis of Battenberg – and decorated it sumptuously. On her marriage in 1899 to Hugo de Bathe, who was 18 years her junior, Langtry went to live in Monaco. In 1925, the house was incorporated into the Cadogan Hotel, and Langtry was welcomed to stay in her old room whenever she was in London.

SIR GEORGE ALEXANDER

(1858–1918) actor-manager   57 Pont Street

GEORGE Alexander Gibb Samson was born in Reading; he made his professional stage debut in 1879 and was engaged by Henry Irving* soon after. 'Five or six hours of rehearsing with Irving,' we are told, 'often left [Alexander] on the brink of tears.' In 1890, he signed the lease of the St James's Theatre, King Street, Covent Garden, where he built up a reputation for his casting of talented actors and for promoting the work of British dramatists. Oscar Wilde's* *Lady Windermere's Fan* (1892) and *The Importance of Being Earnest* (1895) both premiered at the St James's. Alexander and his wife Florence – who helped him in his work and acted as his fashion and artistic director – lived at this large late-19th-century red-brick house from 1895 until 1918.

COUNT EDWARD RACZYŃSKI

(1891–1993) Polish statesman   8 Lennox Gardens **7**

THE struggle for Polish independence was the cause to which Raczyński dedicated his life. He was appointed Ambassador to Britain in November 1934 and was closely involved in the assistance pact that effectively brought Britain into the Second World War. After the fall of France in 1940, the Polish government-in-exile fled to London, and for 50 years Raczyński was one of its key figures; he was never again to return to his native land, though he lived to see Poland liberated from Soviet domination. Between 1954 and 1972, Raczyński was one of the members of the Council of the Three, the presidential body of the Polish government-in-exile, and served as the exiled government's President from 1979 until his retirement in 1986. Raczyński – who lived for 22 years in Golders Green – moved to a flat here in 1967, which remained his home until his death here at the age of 101.

ELIZABETH DAVID

(1913-92) cookery writer   24 Halsey Street **8**

THE aristocratic Elizabeth Gwynne, as she then was, left home unable to make a cup of tea, but did more than anyone to bring Mediterranean colour and flavour to British home cooking. With a glass of wine in one hand and a Gauloise cigarette in the other, she cooked, entertained and wrote in the kitchen of this Chelsea house, part of an 1840s terrace. Having spent time in Greece as a young woman, David moved here in 1947 and died at the house 45 years later, leaving behind such culinary classics as *French Provincial Cooking* (1960).

ARNOLD BENNETT

(1867–1931) novelist   75 Cadogan Square **9**

BORN in Staffordshire, Bennett spent his early life in the Potteries; these, described as the 'Five Towns', were to form the setting for many of his novels. In 1891 Bennett moved to Chelsea, where he spent some of his formative years with the Marriott family, who introduced him into literary and musical circles and encouraged him as a writer. When he returned to Chelsea from France in the 1920s he lived in a flat here, where he continued to write novels – including *Riceyman Steps* (1923) – as well as his weekly column for the *Evening Standard*, which had made him into one of the most influential critics of his day.

PERCY GRAINGER

(1882–1961) Australian composer, folklorist and pianist   31A King's Road

GRAINGER grew up in Melbourne, where he made his debut as a pianist in 1894; in 1901 he settled in London with his mother, Rose. The quality of Grainger's innovatory compositions – his experiments in natural and synthetic sound were well ahead of their time – was quickly recognised. He was also a pioneering folk-song collector and arranger. From late 1907 until autumn 1914 – the period of his most intense activity as a composer – Grainger lived above a tobacconist's shop here; composing, among other works, *Mock Morris* (1910) and *Handel in the Strand* (1911-12). At the outbreak of the First World War, he and his mother moved to the United States, where he later settled.

EARL JELLICOE, OM

(1859–1935) Admiral of the Fleet

25 Draycott Place **11**

JOHN Rushworth Jellicoe was born in Southampton into a Hampshire seafaring family. He joined the Royal Navy in 1872, and was quickly recognised as a capable leader with a sound grasp of technology. During his time at this substantial late-19th-century house, which lasted from about 1906 to 1908, he served as Director of Naval Ordnance and Controller at the Admiralty, and was promoted Rear-Admiral (1907) and knighted (1908). On the outbreak of the First World War, he was made Commander-in-Chief of the Grand Fleet. Jellicoe is remembered especially for his direction of the British forces at the Battle of Jutland (31 May 1916), the principal naval engagement of the war. Criticised in some quarters for his tactics, Jellicoe was promoted away from active command to First Sea Lord in December 1916; he was made Admiral of the Fleet in 1919, and served as Governor-General of New Zealand in 1920–24.

SIR ARCHIBALD MCINDOE

(1900–60)
reconstructive surgeon

Flat 14, Avenue Court, Draycott Avenue **12**

MCINDOE trained and worked as an abdominal surgeon in his native New Zealand and in the United States, before coming to London in 1930. His cousin Harold Gillies* helped him make the transition to the field of reconstructive surgery, and he gained an appointment at the Hospital of Tropical Diseases and established a practice in Harley Street. Early in the Second World War, McIndoe was appointed consultant plastic surgeon to the RAF. Based at East Grinstead Hospital in Sussex, his unit carried out extensive surgery on some 3,600 airmen who had suffered severe burns. McIndoe undertook a series of painstaking operations, remodelling faces and reshaping limbs, but his work went beyond the physical; he also restored morale, and through encouragement gave his patients the strength to cope with civilian life – even lending money to some to set themselves up. Wisely, he refused an RAF rank, meaning he could pester the top brass for resources on a peer-to-peer basis. In 1941, McIndoe's grateful patients formed the Guinea Pig Club. He lived in a flat in this 1930s building from about 1949 to 1955.

P. L. TRAVERS

(1899–1996) author of *Mary Poppins*

50 Smith Street

AUSTRALIAN-born Pamela Lyndon Travers created the nanny-paragon Mary Poppins in the eponymous novel of 1934, which launched a series of books. Emma Thompson played Travers in the 2013 film *Saving Mr Banks*, which portrayed the author's fraught negotiations with Walt Disney over the film adaptation of 1964. She lived and worked at the Smith Street address from 1946 to 1962 – a period that encompassed the initial part of these talks – and took a photo of the house to Hollywood 'so they could see the Banks house was quite like hers, except with more to the garden'. Travers managed to ensure that most of the characters in the film were played by British actors, with the memorable exception of Dick Van Dyke.

DAME MAUD MCCARTHY

(1858–1949) army Matron-in-Chief

47 Markham Square

AS army Matron-in-Chief, Maud McCarthy was responsible for the entire nursing operation involving British, Imperial and American nurses on the Western Front; by 1918 she was in charge of more than 6,000 staff, and dealing with nursing challenges that – in a conflict that involved mechanised artillery, air attacks and the use of poison gas – were unprecedented in scale and scope. After the war she was created a Dame and moved to a five-storey townhouse in Markham Square, dating from around 1850. She retired in 1925: ex-soldiers, recognising her from field hospital visits, often hailed her in the street. Originally from Australia, McCarthy had trained at the London Hospital in Whitechapel, knocking several years off her age to enhance her prospects of admission and future employment. Perhaps she need not have worried: her trainee reports noted that she had 'an exceptionally nice disposition', being 'most lady-like and interested in her work'.

PRINCESS SERAPHINE ASTAFIEVA

(1876–1934) ballet dancer

152 King's Road (The Pheasantry)

THE daughter of Prince Alexander Astafiev, Seraphine (otherwise Serafina) Astafieva was born in Russia, where she attended the St Petersburg Imperial Ballet School. In 1910 she came to England with Serge Diaghilev's Ballets Russes. Three years later, Astafieva retired from the stage to teach ballet, establishing her first school in England in 1915. The following year, her dancing school – the Anglo-Russian Ballet – moved to a studio on the first floor here. The building was the former showroom (1881–1914) of Joubert's, a firm of cabinetmakers and decorators, who subsequently adapted The Pheasantry, an extravagant French-style building, for use as studios. Here, Astafieva was to live and teach until her death, influencing countless ballet dancers; her students and visitors included Serge Diaghilev, Margot Fonteyn*, Alicia Markova, Anna Pavlova, Anton Dolin and Marie Rambert*.

SIR FREDERICK ASHTON

(1904–88) choreographer

8 Marlborough Street

WIDELY considered to be Britain's finest choreographer, Ashton was key to the flowering of British ballet through his work with such stars as Nureyev* and Fonteyn*, and he defined a style described as 'lyrical rather than dramatic, preferring nuance over statement'. He was instrumental in the founding of the Ballet Rambert and the Royal Ballet, of which he was chief choreographer and, from 1963, director. Ashton lived in Marlborough Street from 1959. The house, being Georgian pastiche, was then new: one visitor found it 'very tiny, rather cold ... crammed with furniture, pictures and ornaments'.

DAME SYBIL THORNDIKE

(1882–1976) actress

6 Carlyle Square

THORNDIKE'S stage career spanned six decades, during which time she became an outstanding figure in British theatre. In 1908 – the year she married the actor and director Lewis Casson – Thorndike first worked with George Bernard Shaw*, who wrote the part of St Joan for her in 1923; it became her best-known role.

While living in this house of c.1860, from 1921 to 1932, the celebrated thespian couple managed the New Theatre, St Martin's Lane. Thorndike rehearsed in a specially extended drawing room on the first floor. In later life they lived at 98 Swan Court, a short distance away.

WILLIAM DE MORGAN
(1839–1917) ceramic artist and novelist
EVELYN DE MORGAN
(1855–1919) artist

127 Old Church Street

FAMED as a ceramicist for his richly coloured glazes, William De Morgan was born in Gower Street, Bloomsbury, and was admitted to the Royal Academy Schools in 1859. In 1871 he moved to Cheyne Row where he established the pottery that made his name; it was later sited at Merton Abbey and in Fulham, before closing down in 1907. De Morgan moved to Old Church Street in 1910 with his wife Evelyn, converting two houses of c.1804 into a single property, and stayed for the rest of their lives. At second-floor level there was a large studio, above a study in which William turned out his literary works; these included the novels *A Likely Story* (1911) and *Ghost Meets Ghost* (1914). Evelyn, meanwhile, continued to paint, producing – among other works – a series of 15 'war pictures' from her pacifist perspective, which included *The Red Cross* (1916).

JOHN F. SARTORIUS
(c.1779–1831) sporting painter

155 Old Church Street
(formerly 3 Upper Church Lane and 3 Upper Church Street) **19**

BORN in London, John Francis was the last of four generations of the Sartorius family to enjoy popularity as a painter of racehorses, hunters and other sporting subjects. He followed the style and subject matter of his father, John Nost Sartorius, which belongs in the tradition of such painters as George Stubbs and Edwin Landseer. Of the 16 pictures Sartorius exhibited at the Royal Academy, the best known is *Coursing in Hatfield Park* (1806). He seems to have moved to Chelsea soon after the death of his grandfather, Francis Sartorius, in 1804. For certain he was living at this newly built house by 1807, two years after his marriage to Zara Adamson, and left some time after 1812.

SIR STAFFORD CRIPPS

(1889–1952) statesman

32 Elm Park Gardens **20**

IN this square of tall terraced houses, which were laid out from 1875 to designs by George Godwin*, Stafford Cripps was born into a political family: his father, Charles Alfred Cripps, served in the 1924 and 1929 Labour governments, while his maternal uncle and aunt were Sidney and Beatrice Webb*. This house was the Cripps family home from 1883 until 1900; Stafford's later life was spent mostly in official lodgings and in Gloucestershire. Cripps joined the Labour Party in 1929 and, having been found a safe seat, became Solicitor-General the following year. After serving with distinction in this and other positions – including British Ambassador to the Soviet Union (1940–42) – he was made President of the Board of Trade in the 1945 government of Clement Attlee* and two years later became Chancellor of the Exchequer. The stringent measures he enforced saddled him with the nickname of 'Austerity' Cripps. Ill health forced his resignation in 1950, and he died two years later.

JOYCE GRENFELL

(1910–79) entertainer and writer

34 Elm Park Gardens **21**

THE only daughter of the architect Paul Phipps and Nora Langhorne, sister of Nancy Astor*, Joyce (who married Reginald Pascoe Grenfell, a chartered accountant, in 1929) was deeply attached to Chelsea and lived in the area for most of her life. Her public career as an entertainer began in the late 1930s and was cemented after the war with a series of revues and a radio programme, and films that included *The Million Pound Note* (1953) and the St Trinian's series. In 1954 she launched her own hugely successful show, *Joyce Grenfell Requests the Pleasure,* which featured some of her finest comic monologues.

'Nothing would make me live in Elm Park Gardens ... where the Victorian houses, built at just the wrong period, are made of what I think of as public-lavatory yellow brick.'

Joyce Grenfell, on first viewing the street

In 1957 Joyce and Reggie moved here, where they remained for the rest of their lives. The flat occupied the third and attic floors of what had been two separate houses; on viewing the interior Joyce 'liked it at once', and enlisted the help of her second cousin, Elizabeth Winn, an interior decorator.

AUGUSTUS JOHN

(1878–1961) painter   28 (formerly 5) Mallord Street **22**

JOHN came from Wales – his sister was the painter Gwen John – and studied at the Slade. He defied social convention, and in the interwar years he carved a niche as the bohemian painter *par excellence*; the studio here was the setting for parties that typically ended in 'the most dreadful' orgies. Designed by the architect Robert Van t'Hoff, the house and studio were completed in 1914. John lived here with Dorothy (Dorelia) McNeill, his model and wife in all but name. By 1934 he had tired of the 'damned Dutch shanty', and sold it to Gracie Fields*.

A. A. MILNE

(1882–1956) author   13 (formerly 11) Mallord Street **23**

ALAN Alexander Milne made his name at *Punch*, for which he worked from 1906 until the outbreak of the First World War. He published his first children's book while still in the Army, though after demobilisation first devoted himself to stage comedy. Milne and his wife Daphne moved here in summer 1919. Having previously lived in flats, Milne was thrilled to live in 'the prettiest little house in London', with its 'outside personality as well as an inside one'. Their son Christopher Robin was born here; 'Billy', as he was known, occupied a nursery on the top floor of the house with his nanny, Olive Rand. While living here Milne wrote *When We Were Very Young* (1924), *Winnie-the-Pooh* (1926), *Now We Are Six* (1927) and *The House at Pooh Corner* (1928); illustrated by E. H. Shepard*, these starred Christopher Robin and his toys, which became Pooh, Piglet, Eeyore, Kanga, Roo and Tigger.

GEORGE MEREDITH, OM

(1828–1909) poet and novelist   7 Hobury Street **24**

BORN in Portsmouth, Meredith was articled to a London solicitor before turning to journalism. In 1849, he wed Mary Ellen Nicolls – the widowed daughter of the novelist and poet Thomas Love Peacock – but the marriage was not happy, and the couple separated in 1857. By the later part of that year, Meredith and his young son Arthur were living in Hobury Street, where they remained until moving to

Esher, Surrey, in 1859. During this period he penned his first major novel, *The Ordeal of Richard Feverel* (1859); *The Egoist* (1879) and *Diana of the Crossways* (1885) were among his later successes. Appointed to the Order of Merit in 1905, Meredith was admired by writers such as Oscar Wilde* and Thomas Hardy*, and had a formative influence on the next generation, including James Joyce* and E. M. Forster*.

JOHN IRELAND
(1879–1962) composer   14 Gunter Grove **25**

AT the age of 17, Ireland became the youngest person ever to be awarded a fellowship of the Royal College of Organists. From 1904 to 1926, he was organist and choirmaster at St Luke's, Sydney Street, Chelsea. Having discovered it through one of the choirboys, Ireland rented a studio and a flat in Gunter Grove from 1908 and in 1915 he bought the whole house; two years later he wrote the piano miniature 'Chelsea Reach', the first of his *London Pieces* for piano.

For Ireland, an intensely private person, the detached studio was perfect for teaching and composing. Other works dating from his time here include *Songs Sacred and Profane* (1929–31), *A London Overture* (1936) and *These Things Shall Be*, a choral work composed to celebrate the 1937 coronation of George VI. Ireland was Professor of Composition at the Royal College of Music (1923–39), and his pupils included Benjamin Britten*.

SYLVIA PANKHURST
(1882–1960) campaigner for women's rights   120 Cheyne Walk **26**

SYLVIA was the second daughter of Richard Pankhurst, a Manchester lawyer and social reformer, and his wife Emmeline* who was – with Sylvia and her elder sister Christabel* – to become a major figure in the women's suffrage movement. In the early 1900s, Sylvia combined work for the Women's Social and Political Union, founded in 1903 by Emmeline and Christabel,

with training as an artist: between 1903 and 1906 she studied at the Royal College of Art in Kensington. Sylvia was known for her campaigning militancy – she was imprisoned for the first of many times in 1906, the year she began her three-year stay in Cheyne Walk. In 1913 she founded the East London Federation of Suffragettes, and the following year launched a newspaper, the

Woman's Dreadnought; unlike her mother and sister, she opposed the First World War. Later she authored several books, among them *The Suffragette Movement* (1931). In 1924 she moved to Woodford, Essex, where she ran a tearoom with her partner, Silvio Corio. Her refusal to marry, and the birth of a child out of wedlock widened the rift with Emmeline and Christabel, and contact was never re-established.

PHILIP WILSON STEER

(1860–1942) painter   109 Cheyne Walk **27**

STEER moved here in 1898 and it remained his home until his death; a bachelor, he was looked after for much of this period by his devoted nurse and housekeeper, Margaret Raynes, whose portrait he painted in 1922.

He worked from a first-floor room with three tall windows which served as 'sitting and painting-room combined', and the room can be glimpsed in the background of many of his paintings.

Steer's work was first exhibited at the Royal Academy in 1883. He was a central figure in the New English Art Club, and – together with Walter Sickert* – formed the nucleus of the 'English Impressionist' school. Steer became highly respected in the art world, and taught at the Slade for nearly 40 years. He spent his summers painting landscapes and his winters at his Chelsea home, working on portraits or studies from models.

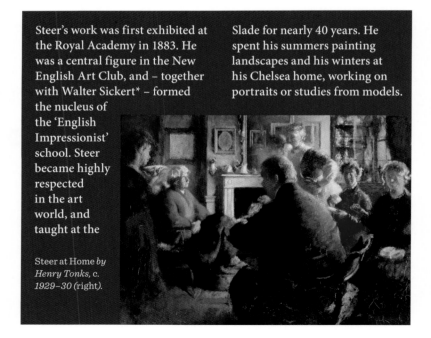

Steer at Home *by Henry Tonks*, c. *1929–30* (right).

JOHN TWEED

(1863–1933) sculptor   108 Cheyne Walk

BORN in Glasgow, Tweed studied in London and in Paris, where he met and became friends with Auguste Rodin, who was a frequent guest in Cheyne Walk. Tweed's career was characterised by a steady stream of portrait statues, and busts of soldiers and statesmen both living and dead, including Joseph Chamberlain*,

Lord Kitchener* and Clive of India*. In 1912, he completed the monument to the Duke of Wellington in St Paul's Cathedral, which had been begun by Alfred Stevens*. Tweed lived here with his wife Edith Clinton, Secretary to the Women's Suffrage Society, from 1896 until shortly before his death; for a time, he had a studio nearby at 14A Cheyne Walk.

WALTER GREAVES

(1846–1930) artist   104 Cheyne Walk (formerly 10 Lindsey Row)

THE son of a boat builder, Walter and his brother Henry decorated the prows of the City barges as boys, and their father encouraged them to paint river scenes in their spare time. In 1847 the Greaves family moved to 9 Lindsey Row and in 1855 – in need of more space – they took on the neighbouring property. In 1863, after Whistler* became a neighbour, the brothers

became the artist's assistants. On occasion, they were allowed to exhibit their own work, labelled 'by pupils of Whistler'. At first, Walter – always acknowledged as the more talented of the brothers – was dismissed as an imitator of 'the master', but an exhibition of 1911 brought him overnight success. The Greaves brothers lived here until 1897, when they moved to Fulham.

HILAIRE BELLOC

(1870–1953) poet, essayist and historian   104 Cheyne Walk **30**

IN 1896, Belloc published the collection *Sonnets and Verse*, as well as *The Bad Child's Book of Beasts*, characteristic of the comic and satirical verse for which he is best known. He wrote on many subjects,

gaining a reputation as a polemical apologist for Roman Catholicism: *The Path to Rome* (1902) was, he claimed, 'the only book I ever wrote for love'. G. K. Chesterton* was a close associate; their reputations have suffered owing to the anti-Semitic tone of some of their works. Belloc and his wife Elodie moved here in the winter of 1899–1900; one of Belloc's additions to number 104 was a telephone, the first in the street. In 1906 he was elected to Parliament and moved to Sussex.

SIR MARC ISAMBARD BRUNEL (1769–1849)
ISAMBARD KINGDOM BRUNEL (1806–59)
civil engineers 98 Cheyne Walk (formerly 4 Lindsey Row)

SIR Marc designed and built the first tunnel under the Thames, between Wapping and Rotherhithe, now part of the London Overground. This, the world's first underwater tunnel through soft ground, was begun in 1825 and finally completed in 1843. While living here with his wife Sophia, Brunel formed a company to finance the job, ran a mill at Battersea and supervised the education of his son Isambard, who had learnt the rudiments of arithmetic and geometry by the age of four. While living here Isambard assisted his father and developed the engineering skills that enabled his greatest achievements: the Great Western Railway (built from 1833), the Clifton Suspension Bridge, Bristol (1836–64), and a series of vast steamships. The Brunels moved to Blackfriars in 1824 to be closer to the tunnel works.

JAMES ABBOTT MCNEILL WHISTLER
(1834–1903) painter and etcher 96 Cheyne Walk (formerly 2 Lindsey Row)

AN American by birth and an advocate of 'art for art's sake', Whistler came to London in 1859. Of his homes in the capital, this one – to which he moved in late 1866 – was the most significant; it was here that he held his Sunday 'breakfasts', attended by fellow artists. Assisted by Walter Greaves* and his brother Henry, Whistler painted murals in the stairway and in some rooms. His studio, to the rear of the second floor, appears in the background of paintings such as the portrait, *Arrangement in Grey and Black* (1871–2), of his mother Anna, who lived with him. Among other works Whistler completed here were his Thames Nocturnes. John Ruskin* denounced one of these as a 'pot of paint flung in the public face'; the ensuing dispute reached court in November 1878, at which point Whistler had just moved to Tite Street. He died at 74 Cheyne Walk.

MRS GASKELL

(1810–65) novelist

93 Cheyne Walk
formerly 1 Belle Vue and then 12 Lindsey Row)

ELIZABETH Stevenson was born here; in early 1811 her family moved around the corner to 3 Beaufort Row (later 7 Beaufort Street, now demolished). Later that year – with Elizabeth still barely a year old – her mother died, and she was taken to live with her maternal aunt, Hannah Lumb, in Knutsford, Cheshire, the town later immortalised as Cranford in the novel of that name. Gaskell returned to Chelsea to nurse her father in his last illness in 1828–9. Her stories began to appear in 1847, 15 years after her marriage to the Revd William Gaskell, and her first novel, *Mary Barton* (1848), with its depiction of the problems of industrial Manchester, brought its author rapidly to fame.

SIR ALEXANDER FLEMING

(1881–1955) discoverer of penicillin

20A Danvers Street

FLEMING was born in Scotland, the son of a farmer, and qualified as a doctor in 1906. His crucial work was carried out after the First World War, when he worked under Almroth Wright as a bacteriologist in the inoculation department of St Mary's Hospital, Paddington. Fleming was living in a flat in this large 1840s house with his wife Sareen and their son when he made his first notable discovery in 1922; he found and isolated a remarkable enzyme with the power to attack bacteria, which he named lysozyme. Six years later, by a fortunate accident, Fleming discovered penicillin but its practical application was not developed until clinical tests were done in 1941 by Howard Florey and Ernst Chain*, with whom Fleming shared a Nobel Prize in 1945. Fleming continued to work in the inoculation department – renamed the Wright-Fleming Institute of Microbiology – until his retirement in 1948. Fleming also had a home in Suffolk, but died in Danvers Street.

HENRY WATSON FOWLER

(1858-1933) grammarian and lexicographer

14 Paultons Square

AFTER education at Rugby and at Balliol College, Oxford, Fowler tired of life as a schoolmaster in the Scottish Borders and came to London in 1899, eventually finding lodgings behind the mid-19th-century stucco of Paultons Square. Here, cushioned by a legacy, he worked as a freelance writer and bathed daily in the Serpentine. With his brother, Francis George Fowler, who he moved to join in Guernsey in 1903, he wrote *The Concise Oxford Dictionary of Current English* (1911), featuring such neologisms as motorist, aeroplane, radioactive and rag-time. *A Dictionary of Modern English Usage* (1926) was a solo effort, which Fowler aimed squarely at 'the half-educated Englishman of literary proclivities who wants to know "Can I say so-&-so?"'.

SAMUEL BECKETT

(1906–89) dramatist and author   48 Paultons Square **36**

ALTHOUGH more readily associated with Dublin – his birthplace – and Paris, his later home, Beckett had a significant sojourn in London during the 1930s, while undergoing psychoanalytical treatment. His friend Tom Mc-Greevy found him lodgings in Paultons Square with a Ralph and Doris Cheeseman, and he stayed from January to July 1934. While here he enjoyed concerts, art galleries and frequenting two local pubs with Mc-Greevy, the Six Bells and the World's End. In May 1934, *More Pricks than Kicks*, Beckett's collection of short stories about an indolent Irish intellectual, was published.

PATRICK BLACKETT

(1897–1974) physicist and scientific adviser   48 Paultons Square **37**

BLACKETT moved here in 1953 together with his wife Constanza and two children. At Birkbeck College he accomplished important work in detecting cosmic rays using giant electromagnets, which brought him the Nobel Prize in 1948. Later, while based at Imperial College, his work on rock magnetism was used to buttress the theory – now generally accepted – of continental drift. As an officer cadet, Blackett had served in the First World War at the Battle of Jutland; during the Second World War, his appliance of science to the anti-U-boat campaign was rated crucial to winning the war in the Atlantic. Afterwards his leftist views – he opposed the nuclear alliance with the United States – were sometimes held against him, but he became a scientific adviser to Harold Wilson's first government. Blackett left this three-storey 1840s terraced house in the late 1960s.

JEAN RHYS

(1890–1979) writer

BORN and raised on the West Indian island of Dominica to a Welsh father and white Creole mother, Ella Gwendoline Rhys came to 'Beautiful, hideous, romantic London' – as she later called it – to attend RADA. After dropping out, she went onstage as a chorus girl, setting the tone for a rackety life demarcated by drinking bouts and depressive episodes. 'Jean Rhys' – it was originally one of her stage names – found success as a writer with *Wide Sargasso Sea* (1966), a prequel-cum-response to Charlotte Brontë's *Jane Eyre*.

At Paultons House she shared an apartment in the then-new block with her second husband and literary agent, Leslie Tilden Smith, in 1936–8. There – mostly in the mornings, while sitting up in bed – she wrote *Good Morning, Midnight* (1939), since recognised as one of her finest works. Tilden Smith – the only one of her three husbands not to spend time in prison – died in 1945, after which Rhys wrote almost nothing for 20 years and was briefly behind bars herself after a dispute with neighbours in suburban Beckenham got out of hand.

CHARLES KINGSLEY

(1819–75)
writer

KINGSLEY was born in Devon, and spent his adolescence and formative years at St Luke's Rectory (built *c.*1725 but subsequently much altered), his father being rector of St Luke's, Sydney Street; it was the family home from 1836 until 1860. He met his future wife Fanny Grenfell at the end of his first year at Cambridge and resolved upon ordination into the Anglican priesthood in 1841. The couple settled at Eversley, Hampshire, where Charles was rector for over 30 years. A

Christian Socialist who believed in the possibility of reconciling religion and science, Kingsley published a number of controversial works, and clashed with John Henry Newman* over the latter's conversion to Catholicism. He was also Regius Professor of Modern History at Cambridge (1860–69). It is, however, for his fiction that Kingsley is chiefly remembered, notably *Westward Ho!* (1855) and *The Water-Babies* (1863), which was partly written as an attack on child labour.

CHELSEA CHINA manufactured 1745 to 1784
TOBIAS SMOLLETT
(1721–71) novelist   16 Lawrence Street (formerly Monmouth House) **40**

SMOLLETT was one of London's leading literary men of his day. Scottish by birth and a doctor by training, he became famous as the author of works such as *The Adventures of Roderick Random* (1748) and *The Adventures of Peregrine Pickle* (1751). He lived in the western portion of long-demolished Monmouth House, while the Chelsea China factory was based mainly in the eastern part of the building.

CHELSEA CHINA
The factory – famous for its soft-paste porcelain – was based mainly in the eastern part of Monmouth House, but also spread into kilns and warehouses in the vicinity. It made its name under the management of Nicholas Sprimont (*c*.1715–71) from *c*.1744 to 1769. By the early 1750s, the workforce comprised about 100 people; some of the floral patterns used in their designs were inspired by plants in the nearby Chelsea Physic Garden. The factory was closed and the firm wound up in 1784.

LEIGH HUNT
(1784–1859) essayist   22 (formerly 4 and then 10)
and poet   Upper Cheyne Row **41**

JAMES Henry Leigh Hunt was born in Southgate, Middlesex, to parents originally from the US, and turned to literature at an early age. In 1808 he became editor of *The Examiner*, set up by his brother John. He became part of the group that included Byron, Shelley*, Keats* and Lamb*; his own creative oeuvre included the narrative poems *The Story of Rimini* (1816) and 'Abou Ben Adhem' (1825). Often in debt, Hunt moved regularly; he lived in this building of *c*.1716 with his wife Marianne from 1833 until 1840. He liked Chelsea –'where the air of the neighbouring river was so refreshing ... I felt for some weeks as if I could sit still for ever, embalmed in the silence.' The house, too, pleased him, being 'of that old fashi-noned sort that I have always loved best ... [with] a small third room on the first floor, of which I made a *sanctum*'. While here Hunt wrote the play *A Legend of Florence* (1840).

JANE FRANCESCA, LADY WILDE, 'SPERANZA'

(1821–96) poet and essayist   87 (formerly 146) Oakley Street **42**

DUBLIN-BORN, Jane Elgee contributed prose and verse to the Irish journal *The Nation* as 'Speranza'. At the age of 30, she married William Wilde, a distinguished surgeon and folklorist; the couple – who had two sons, Oscar* and William – were famed for their literary salons in Dublin. Lady Wilde kept up the tradition after she moved to London in 1879 following her husband's death; she lived here from 1887 and 'Lady Wilde's crushes', as they were termed, were regularly attended by her son Oscar.

Another visitor, the painter Herbert Schmalz, told how her rooms were 'made more mysterious by pastilles burning on the mantelpiece and by large mirrors being placed between the floor and the ceiling, with curtains at the edges, so that when crowded with people you could not see where the actual room left off'. Lady Wilde – who, like her famous son, was known for epigrammatic witticisms – published essay collections while in Oakley Street, where she died in straitened circumstances during her son's imprisonment.

BOB MARLEY

(1945-81) singer and songwriter   42 Oakley Street **43**

DESCRIBED as the first global superstar, Marley stayed in this house in Chelsea in the first half of 1977 following an assassination attempt in his native Jamaica. Thanks to earlier visits he had already come to regard London 'as a second base', and along with his

band the Wailers (who lived here too) set about recording the *Exodus* album at Basing Studios in Notting Hill, which included 'Jamming', 'Three Little Birds' and 'One Love'. During downtime, Marley and the band hung out with The Clash and played football in Battersea Park.

ROBERT FALCON SCOTT

(1868–1912) Antarctic explorer   56 Oakley Street **44**

SCOTT became a naval officer while still in his teens; in 1900 he was placed in command of the

National Antarctic Expedition. In August 1901 Scott left England on the *Discovery*, leading the first extensive land investigation of Antarctica. On his return in 1904 he was acclaimed as a hero and promoted to captain. The following year he moved to this Victorian terraced house with his mother, Hannah, and his sisters. It is thought that part of Scott's classic book *The Voyage of the 'Discovery'* (1905) was written here. At around the same time he was courting his future wife, the artist Kathleen Bruce, who lived nearby at 133 Cheyne Walk. By January 1908, when he left Oakley Street, Scott was already thinking of a further Antarctic expedition – this, being that of 1910–12, turned out to be his last.

GEORGE GISSING

(1857–1903) novelist   33 Oakley Gardens (formerly 17 Oakley Crescent)

BORN in Wakefield, Yorkshire, Gissing made his name in London with a series of novels depicting the struggles of the lower-middle and working classes, including *Demos* (1886), subtitled 'A Story of English Socialism'. While renting two rooms in a lodging house here run by a Mrs Coward from September 1882, Gissing revised *Mrs Grundy's Enemies* (unpublished in his lifetime) and began *The Unclassed* (1884). The lodging house soon proved to be too noisy, and he moved to a flat in Regent's Park in May 1884. Latterly he lived mostly outside London, and spent his final years in France.

EDWARD MCKNIGHT KAUFFER (1890–1954) & MARION DORN (1896–1964)

designers   Swan Court, Chelsea Manor Street

MONTANA-BORN Edward – or Ted – McKnight Kauffer is renowned for the posters he produced for the London Underground and for Shell, which rendered multifarious modern artistic influences into accessible form – and prompted John Betjeman* to observe that 'there is no such thing as commercial art. People are either artists or they are not.' Kauffer's life partner – they eventually married in 1950 – was the Californian Marion Dorn, who is best known for her distinctive geometric rug designs: an outstanding example may be seen at Eltham Palace in London. They lived in a duplex flat – numbered 139 and 141, on the top (eighth) floor of what was then a brand-new block – from 1931 until July 1940, when they left in a hurry for the United States on embassy advice. It was a smart apartment for a smart couple: Dorn's rugs graced a white linoleum floor; the furniture, mostly built-in, was of a natural wood finish and there was room enough for Kauffer's 1,000-disc record collection, which ranged from Sibelius* to Bing Crosby.

DANTE GABRIEL ROSSETTI* (1828–82) poet and painter
ALGERNON CHARLES SWINBURNE*
(1837–1909) poet

16 Cheyne Walk

ROSSETTI, who in 1848 helped to found the Pre-Raphaelite Brotherhood*, moved here on 24 October 1862, after the death of his wife and model, Elizabeth Siddal. Some of his finest work was produced here, including the paintings *Beata Beatrix* (1864–70), and his collected *Poems* (1870), which established his reputation as a writer. During the 1860s and 1870s, Rossetti held regular dinner parties and the house, filled with antiques and works of art, became a meeting place for poets and artists. He left Cheyne Walk in early 1882, shortly before his death.

Swinburne took rooms with Rossetti for just over a year – from late 1862 until 1864 – though he was often away from home. This was a productive time for him; he started work on a novel, *Lesbia Brandon* (unfinished), and on the play *Atalanta in Calydon* (1865), which was among his most successful works.

GEORGE ELIOT*
(1819–80) novelist

4 Cheyne Walk

MARY Ann (later Marian) Evans, born in Warwickshire, moved in 1851 to London, where she wrote for the *Westminster Review* and began her first novel, *Adam Bede* (1859); as 'George Eliot', she was soon established as a writer of the first rank. She moved here with her new husband, the banker John Walter Cross (1840–1924) – more than 20 years her junior – on 3 December 1880. The couple were impressed by the view from the house, which had 'an outlook on the river and meadows beyond'. Within days, the Crosses were holding 'little feasts of music' in the evenings, and were becoming reconciled to 'the loss of country quiet light and beauty'. This calm was, however, to be short-lived; Eliot suddenly and rapidly fell seriously ill, and died here on 22 December 1880. The imposing Queen Anne building dates from 1718.

GEORGE FREDERICK SAMUEL ROBINSON, MARQUESS OF RIPON

(1827–1909) Viceroy of India   9 Chelsea Embankment **49**

GEORGE Robinson was born at 10 Downing Street, the son of Viscount Goderich, Prime Minister in 1827–8. He entered Parliament as an advanced Liberal in 1853 and succeeded to his father's title as Earl of Ripon in 1859, and to that of his uncle, Earl de Grey; he was elevated to a marquessate in 1871. In 1880 Gladstone* appointed him Viceroy; in this role, which he held until 1884, he initiated administrative, educational and political reforms to prepare India for self-government, which won him widespread support among the Indian people. On his return to England, he served as First Lord of the Admiralty, as Colonial Secretary and lastly as Lord Privy Seal (1905–8). With his wife, Henrietta, this was his London residence from 1890 until his death.

OSCAR WILDE

(1854–1900) wit and dramatist   34 (formerly 16) Tite Street **50**

WILDE and his wife Constance moved into this newly built house in January 1885, and their two sons were born here. During Wilde's ten years at the house he wrote *The Happy Prince and Other Tales* (1888), followed by *The Picture of Dorian Gray* (1891), and a series of plays including *Lady Windermere's Fan* (1892) and *The Importance of Being Earnest* (1895). The front door, entrance hall, staircase and dining room were predominantly painted white – 'My eye requires in a room a resting-place of pure colour,' Wilde wrote – while the drawing room had a ceiling by E. W. Godwin and James Whistler*. Wilde wrote in his ground-floor library but he also worked in the exotic smoking room on the first floor. It was at this house that the 8th Marquess of Queensberry – incensed by Wilde's association with his son Lord Alfred Douglas (Bosie) – appeared in 1894; after a row, he was thrown out, and Oscar sued him for libel. The action, which failed, resulted in Wilde's prosecution for homosexual offences, and a two-year prison sentence. At the insistence of Wilde's creditors, chief among them Queensberry, the entire contents of the Tite Street house were sold; William Rothenstein* described how the house 'was filled with a jostling crowd, most of whom had come out of curiosity'. After his release from Reading Gaol in 1897 Wilde was a broken man, and lived abroad thereafter.

PHILIP ARNOLD HESELTINE (PETER WARLOCK)

(1894–1930) composer

BORN in the Savoy Hotel, Warlock was early influenced by Delius*, who became a lifelong friend. After Eton, he took up music journalism during the First World War. Despite the success of his songs, books and editions of early English music, and especially of his own compositions – Warlock's masterpiece, the song-cycle *The Curlew* (1915–22), was followed by *An Old Song* (1917–23) and the *Capriol* suite (1927) – he was haunted by a lack of creative self-confidence and was prone to bouts of depression. Warlock moved in 1930 to this flat where he wrote that September: 'I am full of hope for the future of my work if I can only manage to settle down in a quiet and secluded spot where I shall be undisturbed – and the flat I have found is just such a place.' His spirit of optimism soon seemed to wither, however, and the end came abruptly: he was found dead in his gas-filled flat in December; it is generally believed that he committed suicide.

SAMUEL L. CLEMENS, 'MARK TWAIN'

(1835–1910) writer

23 Tedworth Square **52**

THE Florida-born Samuel Langhorne Clemens tried his hand at various occupations – he was a steamboat pilot on the Mississippi for a time – before turning to journalism. As Mark Twain, he first achieved literary fame with *The Innocents Abroad* (1869). This was followed by a string of successful books, including *The Adventures of Huckleberry Finn* (1884). Between 1891 and 1900 Twain went on an extended lecture tour of Europe, and was in London for a good part of that period. Distressed at the death of his daughter Susy in August 1896, Twain maintained

'Perhaps not a dozen people in London knew their address and the outside world was ignorant of it altogether.'

Albert Bigelow Paine, Twain's biographer

'complete seclusion' in Chelsea – where he lived with his wife Olivia. Still, his time here was productive; Clara Clemens, who recalled that her family 'had loved that little house and all the surrounding region', described how her father 'used to rise sometimes as early as four or five o'clock in the morning. Never did he write more continuously.'

BRAM STOKER
(1847–1912) writer and impresario

18 St Leonard's Terrace **53**

BORN in Dublin, Abraham Stoker was invited to London in 1878 by Henry Irving* and took up work as business manager of the Lyceum Theatre. Stoker worked closely with Irving in establishing the theatre's success, only leaving the job when the theatre went into receivership in 1902. His many administrative innovations included the numbering of seats and promotion of advance reservations. While living here Stoker published his famous vampire story; originally named *The Un-Dead*, the title *Dracula* was substituted shortly before its publication in 1897. The book went through 11 editions in Stoker's lifetime and is acknowledged as a classic.

JEROME K. JEROME
(1859–1927) author

91–104 Chelsea Gardens, Chelsea Bridge Road **54**

BORN in Walsall, Staffordshire, Jerome Klapka Jerome worked successively as a railway clerk, schoolmaster and actor, before finding work as a journalist. His masterpiece, *Three Men in a Boat* (1889), a comic description of a Thames riverboat trip, was written in Chelsea Gardens. It was also while here that Jerome co-founded *The Idler*, a monthly magazine of wit; contributors included Israel Zangwill* and Mark Twain*. Flat 104, on the sixth floor – 'up ninety-seven stairs' – consisted of two reception rooms, three bedrooms and a kitchen. Jerome and his wife Georgina moved here in June 1888 and remained until about 1894, when they moved to St John's Wood.

A modern view of the flat lived in by Jerome K. Jerome.

SOUTH AND CENTRAL KENSINGTON

THE greater part of the area known as South Kensington (the name was coined by Henry Cole*) is an invention of the later 19th century. Central Kensington, just south of the High Street, has earlier buildings, but most of this fashionable suburb sprang up in the wake of the hugely successful Great Exhibition of 1851, held in Hyde Park, which bankrolled the development of the great museums on land to the south. Previously regarded as part of Brompton and better known for its nurseries and market gardens, the rebranded South Kensington rapidly gained a social prestige previously attached only to Mayfair. Its houses were mostly large, stuccoed and Italianate, and their inhabitants almost invariably well off.

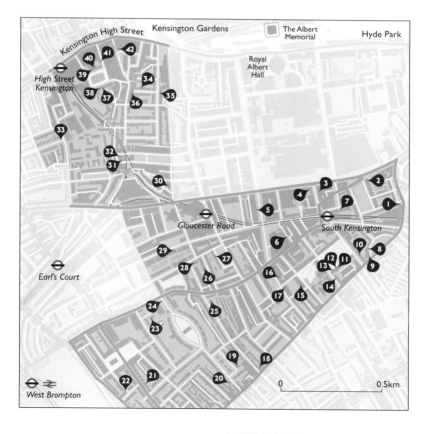

GEORGE GODWIN

(1813–88) architect, journalist and social reformer   24 Alexander Square

GODWIN learned his trade in the office of his father, George Godwin senior, and collaborated on many buildings with his brother Henry. Almost all were in Kensington, where Godwin lived for most of his life; his works include Redcliffe Square (1869–76) and its church, St Luke's (1872–3). His wider significance owes more to his editorship of *The Builder* (1844–83), which campaigned for improved housing and public health; in this capacity, Godwin was also an early supporter of what became the blue plaques scheme. His vivid accounts of the evils of slum overcrowding were collected in three volumes, among them *Town Swamps and Social Bridges* (1859), which he wrote while living in this yellow-brick and stucco terrace of the late 1820s, his home from about 1850 until 1873.

SIR HENRY COLE

(1808–82) campaigner and educator; first Director of the Victoria and Albert Museum   33 Thurloe Square **2**

COLE began his career in 1823 as a government clerk in the record commission; it was he who secured the building of the Public Record Office, begun in 1851, in Chancery Lane (now used by King's College). The Great Exhibition in Hyde Park, held in the same year, was largely organised by Cole, who spent the next 20 years working on the development of the museums precinct in South Kensington; such was his dominance of this project, which aimed to create a national centre for the arts and sciences, that he was dubbed 'King Cole'. He could indeed be imperious, but once noted that 'if he had waited for orders he would never have got anything done'. Among Cole's directorial responsibilities was the South Kensington Museum, opened in 1857 (renamed the Victoria and Albert Museum in 1899; one of its wings is now named after him). He retired in 1873, and in December of that year came to live here, staying until 1877. The house, at the northeast corner of the square, facing the V&A, forms the end of a terrace dating from about 1840, built to designs by George Basevi*. While here, Cole promoted the opening nearby of the National Training School for Music (1876), the predecessor of the Royal College of Music. Much earlier, in 1843, Cole had commissioned the very first Christmas card.

SIR JOHN LAVERY

(1856–1941) painter 5 Cromwell Place ❸

AVERY was born in Belfast; he had lost both parents by the age of four. He moved to London in 1896 and was living here by 1899. Having trained in Glasgow, he became associated with the impressionist-inspired 'Glasgow Boys'. Lavery developed a sharp business sense to accompany his artistic flair. Much of his work was in the lucrative field of portrait painting: those who sat for him ranged from Winston Churchill* to Shirley Temple. For one of his most successful genre paintings, *The Tennis Party* (1885), he chose a subject calculated to appeal to aspirational would-be patrons. With his second wife, the American-born society hostess Hazel Jenner Lavery, he had strong links with the cause of Irish self-determination; his painting *The Court of Criminal Appeal* (1916) depicted the trial of Roger Casement, and in 1922 he painted Michael Collins – a visitor here, and the object of infatuation for Hazel Lavery – on his deathbed. After Hazel's death in 1935 he spent much time in the United States, but kept the house on until May 1940, when he left war-ravaged London for Kilkenny.

SIR CHARLES JAMES FREAKE

(1814–84) builder and patron of the arts 21 (formerly 1) Cromwell Road

FREAKE became one of London's most successful speculative builders, employing nearly 400 men by 1867. Early on, he worked with George Basevi* whose stylistic influence was apparent in Freake's subsequent developments, which were notably spacious. The terrace on which he is commemorated was one of his own undertakings; he moved into the double-fronted house on its completion in 1860. According to the census 11 years later, he lived here with his wife, daughter, three other female relations and ten servants. Freake financed the

> The house was remarkable for its private theatre-cum-ballroom, contained within a large two-storey wing; the shows held here were attended by, among others, Edward, Prince of Wales, and Henry Cole*.

construction of the National Training School for Music (1874–5) and also contributed to the construction of churches including St Paul's, Onslow Square (1859–60). Created a baronet in 1882, Freake never lost his cockney accent.

DENNIS GABOR

(1900–79) physicist
and inventor of holography

THE inventor of holography and developer of the flat television tube, Dénes Gábor (as his name was originally spelt) was born in Budapest. He came to England from Berlin in 1934 (his background was Jewish), at first settling in the Midlands. He and his wife Marjorie lived at Flat 1, on the first floor of 78 Queen's Gate, from 1949, following his appointment to a readership at Imperial College. In the early 1960s they moved to a larger flat next door, at number 79. In 1971, nearly a quarter of a century after the event, Gabor was awarded the Nobel Prize

'First you have to know the answer, logic comes afterwards.'

Dennis Gabor on his scientific method

for the discovery of holography – the combination of two electron images to create a three-dimensional image. Laser technology, which Gabor narrowly missed out on developing himself, enabled the widespread application of holography. When appointed a professor at Imperial in 1958, his inaugural lecture was on 'Electronic inventions and their impact on civilization'.

FRANCIS BACON

(1909-92) painter

ONE of the most celebrated artists of the 20th century, Bacon's dramatic and disturbing paintings are exemplified by his series of Velázquez-inspired 'screaming popes'. His rackety social life, much of it lived out at the notorious Colony Club in Dean Street, Soho, is well captured in the biopic *Love is the Devil* (1998). The Dublin-born artist based himself in London from the late 1920s, mostly in Chelsea and Kensington. Reece Mews, built as a stable block in about 1874 by Charles Freake*, was his main home

and workplace from 1961 until his death 31 years later. The chaos of the studio was a spur to creativity, and he found it hard to work elsewhere: among the works completed here were *Three Studies for a Crucifixion* (1962) and *Portrait of George Dyer Talking* (1966). The latter is a study of the man who was Bacon's lover for several years until he took his own life; apocryphally, they met after Dyer bungled a burglary of the studio. After Bacon's death, the studio interior was transported and recreated at Dublin City Gallery.

DR MARGERY BLACKIE

(1898–1981)
homoeopathic physician

18 Thurloe Street
(formerly Alfred Place)

BLACKIE – the niece of the leading homoeopath James Compton Burnett and cousin of the novelist Ivy Compton-Burnett* – trained at the London School of Medicine for Women, and set up as a homoeopathic practitioner in 1926. She moved here three years later, and lived and worked in this mid-19th-century stuccoed terraced house until 1980. In her consulting room at the rear of the ground floor, patients were put at their ease by a blazing log fire and beautiful flower arrangements created by her long-term professional partner Dr Helena Banks. Blackie – described by an admirer as being 'like a wee bird whose eyes shone with an artless love of life' – played a major part in establishing the modern popularity of homoeopathy. She held several senior posts at the London Homoeopathic Hospital and encapsulated her medical ideas in a book, *The Patient, not the Cure* (1975). Her clients included several members of the royal family.

FRANÇOIS GUIZOT

(1787–1874) French politician and historian

21 Pelham Crescent

A CELEBRATED professor of history at the University of Paris, Guizot was appointed Education Minister in 1832 by King Louis-Philippe. He was briefly Ambassador to England in 1840, and his later spell as Foreign Minister was notable for a thaw in relations between the two countries. Guizot became Prime Minister in 1847 but, like his royal master, was forced to flee with his family by the revolution of 1848. He took a lease on this house, which was let furnished. Having had his French property sequestered, Guizot made a living from writing,

'I have found, close to London – at Brompton – a little house, which is almost in the country; it is good enough for us, and inexpensive.'

François Guizot

and produced several volumes on 17th-century England. He returned to France in 1849, having – so said his landlord – clocked up an impressive list of damages, including the knob from a bedstead pole, a dustpan handle, and numerous items of crockery and glassware.

SIR NIGEL PLAYFAIR

(1874–1934) actor-manager · 26 Pelham Crescent · **9**

EDUCATED at Harrow and Oxford, Playfair became a leading member of the University Dramatic Society, and proceeded to make his name as a versatile character actor with a reputation for 'good-humoured comedy, dry as the driest sherry'. He lived in Pelham Crescent from about 1910 to 1922, during which time he made the transition to theatre management. The adventurous interior décor was, according to his son Giles, widely admired – especially the dining room, 'with its red carpet, its black table and sideboard, its yellow ceiling and walls'. In 1918, together with Arnold Bennett* and his friend Alistair Tayler, Playfair bought the Lyric Theatre in Hammersmith. They transformed it from near dereliction to great prosperity, notably with a Playfair-directed revival in 1920 of John Gay's *The Beggar's Opera*. After 1925, he lived at 24 Upper Mall, Hammersmith.

BÉLA BARTÓK

(1881–1945) Hungarian composer · 7 Sydney Place · **10**

BARTÓK often stayed here at the home of Sir Duncan Wilson, sometime Chief Inspector of Factories, when performing in London. He visited Britain on at least 16 occasions, his first visit being to Manchester in 1904, and stayed with his friend Sir Duncan at least a dozen times between 1922 – when he gave his first London performance – and 1937. With Hungary's leaders allied to the Nazis, to whom Bartók was implacably opposed, he left his homeland for the US during the Second World War, and died in New York at the age of 64. Peter Warlock* was a leading British admirer of Bartók's music and it was the Peter Warlock Society that proposed the Bartók plaque.

BARON CARLO MAROCHETTI

(1805–67) sculptor · 32 Onslow Square · **II**

TURIN-BORN Marochetti's family moved to France when he was a child: his title was a Sardinian barony, bestowed in gratitude for a dramatic depiction of a 16th-century duke of Savoy on horseback that he had donated to his native city. This house in

Marochetti's best-known work in London, where he relocated after the revolutions of 1848, is the equestrian statue of Richard I, 'Coeur de Lion' (1860), that stands outside Parliament. His representations of Isambard Kingdom Brunel* and Robert Stephenson* are, respectively, on the Victoria Embankment and outside Euston Station. Landseer's Trafalgar Square lions were also cast in his workshop.

Onslow Square was Marochetti's home from 1851 until his death. He produced some of his most famous works in the workshop and foundry to the rear, and received visitors including Queen Victoria – who once called him 'very agreeable, gentlemanlike and unassuming'.

WILLIAM MAKEPEACE THACKERAY*

(1811–63) novelist   36 Onslow Square

THACKERAY'S move here in May 1854 was, he later recalled, 'awful to behold', thanks to the volume of possessions he had accumulated. The brick and stucco terraced house – one of the superior speculations of Charles Freake* – was then barely five years old. Here Thackeray completed *The Newcomes* (1853–5) and wrote *The Virginians* (1857–9), with the able assistance of his daughter Anne, later Lady Ritchie, who was his literary secretary and went on to become a respected writer in her own right. Thackeray's mother and stepfather, Major and Mrs Carmichael-Smyth, also lived here for a spell in 1857; Thackeray was not persuaded to make the arrangement permanent. With the exception of the fourth floor, added in 1907, the house remains much the same as when Thackeray left in March 1862. The plaque is sited low on the building.

ADMIRAL ROBERT FITZROY

(1805–65) hydrographer and meteorologist 38 Onslow Square **13**

A GRANDSON of the 3rd Duke of Grafton, FitzRoy entered the Navy in 1819 and commanded HMS *Beagle* for the expedition of 1831–6 on which Charles Darwin* formulated his theory of evolution – an association that gave the devoutly creationist FitzRoy 'the acutest pain'. He was the second Governor of New Zealand (1843–5), and briefly superintended the Woolwich naval dockyard before being appointed Meteorological Statist (statistician) at the newly established government meteorological department in 1854. As set out in his *Weather Book* (1863), FitzRoy advocated the use of the barometer to predict storms, and the rapid dissemination of this information by semaphore. He was careful to warn that such 'forecasts' – the notion of which, when first mentioned in the House of Commons, raised a hearty laugh – were not 'prophesies or predictions'. He lived here from 1854 – the year of his second marriage – until shortly before his death.

JOSEPH ALOYSIUS HANSOM

(1803–82) architect, founder-editor of *The Builder* 27 Sumner Place
and inventor of the hansom cab (formerly 8 Sumner Terrace) **14**

B ORN in York, where he trained as an architect, Hansom was declared bankrupt following the building of Birmingham Town Hall (1832–4), which he designed with Edward Welch. When he registered a patent for a 'safety cab', in December 1834, it was with the aim of recovering solvency. Unwisely, he sold the rights to the invention – though what became known to posterity as the hansom cab, with large wheels and driver's seat at the back, bore scant resemblance to his original design. Nor did Hansom benefit much financially as founder and editor of *The Builder* (1842–3); it was George Godwin* who set the magazine on a secure footing. Hansom did, however, enjoy success as an architect of churches, working in partnership with various members of his family and, for a time, Edward Welby Pugin. One notable later commission was St Philip Neri (1870–73), now known as the Cathedral Church of Our Lady and St Philip Howard, at Arundel, West Sussex, a magnificent building in the French Gothic style. By the year of its completion Hansom was living at Sumner Place with his wife Hannah; they stayed here for four years.

JAMES ANTHONY FROUDE

(1818–94) historian and man of letters 5 Onslow Square

FROUDE made his reputation with a monumental 12-volume history of Tudor England, published between 1856 and 1870, and cemented it in the 1880s with volumes dedicated to the life and works of his friend Thomas Carlyle*, which set a new standard for candour in biography. In Onslow Square, with his second wife Henrietta, he held dinner parties 'famous for their brilliance and charm'. Froude ceased to reside here permanently in 1892, when he was appointed Regius Professor of Modern History at Oxford; as a young scholar, he had been effectively hounded out of the university for his opposition to compulsory ordination, as expressed in his work of thinly disguised autobiographical fiction, *The Nemesis of*

> 'With a recklessness of consequence that cannot be too deeply deplored … he has thrown a new brand of discord into the smouldering embers of Irish discontent' – Lecky reviews *The English in Ireland* by J. A. Froude, his near neighbour. Despite their differences, they attended the funeral of Thomas Carlyle* together.

Faith (1849). When the LCC decided to commemorate Froude with a plaque in 1933, it was admitted that his reputation 'cannot be said to be based on his historical accuracy'; rather, it was for the literary merit of his work. At that stage, the house still belonged to Froude's son Ashley.

W. E. H. LECKY

(1838–1903) historian and essayist 38 Onslow Gardens **16**

WILLIAM Edward Hartpole Lecky, whose paternal family was Irish, moved to Onslow Gardens on his marriage to Elisabeth Boldewina van Dedem, a lady-in-waiting to Queen Sophia of the Netherlands, in 1871. Much of his time here was spent toiling on the eight-volume *History of England in the Eighteenth Century* (1878–90), which was, in spite of its title, most notable for its material on Ireland. Lecky was elected to Parliament for Dublin University, his alma mater, in 1895. His later works included *Democracy and Liberty* (1896), a discursive perspective on the issues of the day. Lecky, who turned down the Oxford chair later taken by his neighbour Froude, died in his study in Onslow Gardens.

ANDREW BONAR LAW

(1858–1923) Prime Minister

BORN and raised in New Brunswick – he never completely lost his Canadian accent – Bonar Law made his fortune as an iron merchant in Glasgow. A teetotaller who disliked music and dancing, he entered Parliament in 1900 and in 1911 was elevated to the leadership of the Conservative Party. His move here in September 1921 was supposed to signal his retirement; he had just returned from a trip to convalesce in France after relinquishing the leadership of his party and resigning from the coalition Cabinet of Lloyd George*, in which the highest office he held was Chancellor of the Exchequer. In October of the following year, however, Bonar Law returned to Downing Street as Prime Minister. Ill health drove him to relinquish the premiership in May 1923 after just 209 days in office and he returned to Onslow Gardens, where he died that October. At his funeral in Westminster Abbey, Herbert Asquith* quipped: 'It is fitting that we should have buried the Unknown Prime Minister by the side of the Unknown Soldier.'

ROSALIND FRANKLIN

(1920–58) pioneer of the study of molecular structures

Donovan Court, Drayton Gardens **18**

ROSALIND Franklin was born in Notting Hill into a rich Anglo-Jewish family. After being educated at St Paul's Girls' School, she read natural sciences at Newnham College, Cambridge, and went on to carry out groundbreaking work in the emerging fields of molecular chemistry and biology. Having worked for a time in Paris, she returned to England in 1951 to take up a fellowship at King's College London, and moved into Flat 22 of this 1930s apartment block. Franklin isolated two forms of the DNA molecule (deoxyribonucleic acid) before moving to Birkbeck College in 1953, where her supervisor was J. D. Bernal*. She remained here until her death at the Royal Marsden Hospital in Chelsea, her life having been cut tragically short by cancer. Her work was crucial to the discovery of the structure of DNA by Francis Crick and James Watson, for which they – and Maurice Wilkins, her superior at King's – won the Nobel Prize in 1962. The extent to which Franklin was subsequently written out of the story has since become a matter of controversy.

FRANK DOBSON

(1886–1963) sculptor 14 Harley Gardens **19**

THE London-born Dobson started out as a painter, and spent much of his early career in Cornwall. He was linked with the younger members of the Bloomsbury Group; among his better-known works is a brass head of Osbert Sitwell (1922); in the same year, he designed the curtain for *Façade*, the performance collaboration between Edith Sitwell* and the composer William Walton*. Dobson lived at this house – which was attached to a spacious studio – from 1945 (when he was appointed to a professorship at the Royal College of Art) until January 1961. While living here Dobson completed the curvilinear statue *London Pride*, executed for the Festival of Britain in 1951; it was recast in bronze and set up outside the National Theatre.

ROBERT FORTUNE

(1812–80) plant collector 9 (formerly 1) Gilston Road **20**

FORTUNE is famous – or notorious – for having covertly brought tea out of China, along with the secrets of cultivating it. He also introduced the rhododendron and kumquat to Britain. Formerly curator of the Chelsea Physic Garden (1846–8), Fortune lived in Gilston Road with his wife Jane and two children from 1857 when the house, built by George Godwin*, was almost new. While here he published travelogues including *A Residence among the Chinese* (1857); his later years were blighted by illness associated with the privations of his travels. Fortune died here, and is buried in Brompton Cemetery.

SYDNEY MONCKTON COPEMAN

(1862–1947) immunologist and developer
of the smallpox vaccine 57 Redcliffe Gardens **21**

BORN in Norwich, where his father was a clergyman, Copeman trained at St Thomas's Hospital in London and spent his career in public health, working first for the Local Government Board and later for the Ministry of Health. Once a mass killer, smallpox was eradicated worldwide in 1977, an achievement for which Copeman is entitled to much credit, even though he built on the work of others, most notably Edward Jenner. Copeman's chief innovation, which he first publicly advocated in 1893, was the use of glycerine to keep the calf-lymph vaccine sterile: hitherto, vaccination had carried a risk of bacterial infection. Joseph Lister took an avuncular interest, and financed his early research. Copeman lived in Redcliffe Gardens with his wife Ethel and their young family between about 1903 and 1909.

AUSTIN DOBSON
(1840–1921) poet and essayist   10 Redcliffe Street **22**

DOBSON was born in Plymouth, and had a day job as a clerk at the Board of Trade for 45 years; appropriately, his first prose work was entitled *The Civil Service Handbook of English Literature* (1874). He had moved here the year before, when the house was barely three years old. Dobson later wrote a well-regarded series of biographies of 18th-century figures, beginning with William Hogarth in 1879. In 1880 he moved to Ealing. A modest man, Dobson wrote in 1906: 'Fame is a food that dead men eat / I have no stomach for such meat.'

SIR WILLIAM ORPEN
(1878–1931) painter   8 (formerly 5) South Bolton Gardens **23**

ORPEN was primarily a painter of portraits – among his best-known works is the self-portrait *Orpsie Boy* (1924). He is also renowned for his work as an official war artist, notably the contentious *To the Unknown British Soldier in France* (1922–7). Born in County Dublin, but trained at the Slade, he spent much of his career in London. In 1906 he took a studio here, which he sublet from 1907 to 1909 to his fellow Irishman Hugh Lane, later Director of the National Gallery of Ireland. Their next-door neighbours were the artists Charles

'Every decent man in London has to be drunk by seven o' clock.'
William Orpen

Ricketts* and Charles Shannon*. Orpen later bought their property, and remodelled the houses as a single unit in 1929; the striking white stucco frontage and large first-floor windows, which made the vast studio 'as light as an operating theatre', date from this time. Orpen had family homes nearby but as his drinking estranged him from his wife Grace and their children, his studio became his principal residence too.

JENNY LIND, MADAME GOLDSCHMIDT

(1820–87) singer   189 Old Brompton Road (formerly 1 Moreton Gardens)

LIND was born in Sweden, where she made her first stage appearance at the age of ten. At the height of her fame, the 'Swedish Nightingale' enjoyed international celebrity, with sell-out concerts, legions of fans and an extensive range of merchandise; her face and name appeared on everything from soap to snuffboxes. In 1858, having retired from the stage, Lind settled in England with her husband Otto Goldschmidt, a former pupil of Jenny's friend Felix Mendelssohn*.

They moved into this substantial, newly built house in 1874 on Otto's appointment as Vice-Principal of the Royal Academy of Music. In 1883 Jenny became the first Professor of Singing at the Royal College of Music, and took classes at her home, which had good-sized ground-floor rooms well suited to the purpose. In the drawing room were held early soprano rehearsals of the Bach Choir, of which Otto was the first Musical Director; it continues to flourish.

MERVYN PEAKE

(1911–68) author and artist   1 Drayton Gardens

PEAKE was born in China, the son of a Congregationalist missionary doctor. His artistic gifts became apparent during his schooling in Kent, and he went on to paint and draw professionally, as well as to write poetry, plays and – most famously – novels and children's books, which he illustrated in his own appealingly grotesque style. Peake is best known for the 'Gormenghast' trilogy, a gothic fantasy that has been filmed and adapted for television. The final part, *Titus Alone* (1959), was finished by the time he moved here with his artist wife Maeve and their family in May 1960: the house had 'enough large

rooms for the paintings' and was 'near enough to the Fulham Road and other centres of creative activity to be alluring'. Unfortunately, Peake was already exhibiting signs of the debilitating illness – eventually diagnosed as Parkinson's disease – which brought a premature end to his professional career, though while living here he did manage to illustrate his earlier poem *The Rhyme of the Flying Bomb* (1962) and completed a commission from the Folio Society. After 1965, Peake was cared for in nursing homes, though his family preserved his ground-floor study at Drayton Gardens as he had left it.

SIR HERBERT BEERBOHM TREE

(1853–1917) actor-manager

31 Rosary Gardens

BORN Herbert Draper Beerbohm to a London corn merchant of German-Lithuanian descent and a British mother, his younger half-brother was Max Beerbohm*. He and his supportive actress wife Maud, with whom he had three daughters and who greatly contributed to his success, lived in this newly built brick terrace between spring 1886 and 1888, a period that saw his first foray into theatre management and a revival of his acting career. He took over the Comedy Theatre in Panton Street in April 1887 and moved on to the Haymarket Theatre that autumn, where he enjoyed great success. He opened Her Majesty's Theatre, also in Haymarket, in 1897. A noted champion of Shakespeare, his productions were famous for their spectacular scenery and effects, and brought the plays before a wide audience. He also founded the Royal Academy of Dramatic Art in 1904. Tree kept a second household in Wandsworth with May Pinney (later Reed), the daughter of a clergyman, and their six children, who included the film director Carol Reed and Peter, father of the hell-raising actor Oliver Reed.

GEORGE BORROW

(1803–81) author

22 Hereford Square **27**

ORIGINALLY from Norfolk, Borrow travelled widely in Europe and mastered many languages. His particular affinity with Romany peoples was reflected in the subject matter of two of his best-known books, *Lavengro* (1851) and its sequel, *The Romany Rye* (1857). Borrow's earthy tales were written in conscious contrast to 'genteel' novels; by the time he moved to Hereford Square in 1860, this was not in vogue. Hence the travelogue *Wild Wales* (1862) was little noticed, but was later hailed as a classic. A genuine eccentric, Borrow found plenty to inspire him in London, where (in the words of his biographer) 'odd characters were far more numerous than in East Anglia, or Wales, or Cornwall', and he enjoyed frequent trips to the 'countryside' of Wimbledon Common and Richmond Park. He felt keenly the loss of his wife Mary in 1869 and moved back to his wife's small estate at Oulton, Suffolk, in 1872. Their London home – which is part of a stuccoed terrace dating from about 1850 – suffered bomb damage in the Second World War, and was reconstructed behind the facade in 1949.

FIELD MARSHAL VISCOUNT ALLENBY

(1861–1936) senior army officer

EDMUND Henry Hynman Allenby saw active service in the Boer War, and commanded the Third Army in the First World War on the Western Front, in which theatre he lost his only son Michael. It is for his dynamic leadership of the Egyptian Expeditionary Force that Allenby is chiefly celebrated; this was instrumental in the capture of Jerusalem in December 1917 and the victory of the Battle of Megiddo in autumn 1918. He was made a field marshal and viscount in 1919; the worsening of his temper as he ascended the ranks led to his being nicknamed 'the Bull', though as High Commissioner for Egypt from 1919 to 1925 he displayed a sensible pragmatism. In retirement, he and his wife Mabel lived first at Deal Castle in Kent, but, finding it 'too cold', moved in 1928 to this 'conveniently sized and comfortable house' with its elaborately decorated porch. He died here shortly after returning with supplies for the aviary that he had constructed in the back garden.

SIR W. S. GILBERT*

(1836–1911) dramatist

TRADITION has it that William Schwenck Gilbert, the librettist for the Savoy Operas, written with Arthur Sullivan and promoted by Richard D'Oyly Carte*, used the proceeds from *Patience* (1881) to finance the construction of this magnificent dwelling in the Flemish style, with its enormous stepped gable. Ernest George and Harold Peto designed the row of six to which it belongs, and Gilbert informed the contractors, Stephens and Bastow, that he would take up residence in October 1883 regardless of progress; accordingly, the finishing touches were applied around him. He completed the libretto for *The Mikado*

The ship on top of the gable commemorates Gilbert's ancestor, the Tudor explorer Humphrey Gilbert. 'Sir, I do not put my trademark on my house,' Gilbert barked at one unfortunate visitor who assumed it alluded to *HMS Pinafore* (1878).

(1885) here and wrote those for *The Yeoman of the Guard* (1888) and *The Gondoliers* (1889). Gilbert preferred to work between the hours of 11pm and 3am, when 'no one can interrupt you, unless it be a burglar'. With his wife Lucy, he left here in 1890.

CHARLES BOOTH

(1840–1916) pioneer in social research   6 Grenville Place **30**

BOOTH moved here in 1875 and carried out his trailblazing social studies while living here, beginning his fieldwork in the winter of 1887–8. The first of the 17 volumes of his *Life and Labour of the People in London* (completed 1902), with its colour-coded maps showing the relative prosperity of districts, appeared in April 1889 – the year Booth and his family moved out of Grenville Place. The house, a speculative new build, suffered from smoking chimneys and faulty drains, and Booth's niece Beatrice Webb* recalled it as 'dark and airless' (and her uncle, rather unsparingly, as having 'the complexion of a consumptive girl'). It was Booth who coined the phrase 'poverty line'.

SIR TERENCE RATTIGAN

(1911–77)   100 Cornwall Gardens
playwright   (formerly 3 Cornwall Mansions) **31**

RATTIGAN was born in this opulent house of 1877–9 (named Lanarkslea after his grandfather's Lanarkshire constituency). His parents were abroad on diplomatic postings and he and his elder brother Brian were brought up by his formidable widowed grandmother. The young Rattigan's passion for the stage was first awakened in November 1918 by the pantomime *Cinderella*; he is said to have announced his wish to be a playwright shortly afterwards. In 1920 he was sent to a prep school in Surrey; after Oxford, he had his first West End hit with *French Without Tears* (1936). Twenty years of stage success followed, including hits such as *The Winslow Boy* (1946) and *Separate Tables* (1954). He also wrote and co-wrote screenplays, including those for *Brighton Rock* (1947) and *The Prince and the Showgirl* (1957).

DAME IVY COMPTON-BURNETT

(1884–1969) novelist   5 Braemar Mansions, Cornwall Gardens **32**

COMPTON-BURNETT moved into Flat 5 here in 1934 with her companion Margaret Jourdain, a furniture expert. The following year saw the publication of her sixth novel, *A House and its Head* (1935) – one of her characteristic tales of domestic power struggles, reflecting her own torrid upbringing: her mother was an overbearing social climber, and four siblings died young, including two sisters in a suicide pact. Compton-Burnett liked to write in one of the armchairs that sat on either side of the Adam fireplace that she and Jourdain had imported from their previous home in Bayswater. Their first-floor flat was otherwise spartan in its furnishings, and grew still less homely after Margaret's death: one visitor described it as 'bare, shabby and dark'. By contrast, the window boxes on the balcony were always colourfully planted out; Compton-Burnett favoured 'little twopenny petunias from Woolworths'. The landlord was, she said, 'frightfully friendly ... I believe it's because of the enormous rent I pay him'.

MICHAEL FLANDERS (1922–75)
DONALD SWANN (1923–94)
writers and performers of comic songs   1 Scarsdale Villas **33**

FLANDERS and Swann's many animal-themed airs included 'The Gnu Song' (Flanders talks about Scarsdale Villas in its spoken introduction) and 'The Hippopotamus Song' ('Mud, mud, glorious mud!'). Their work also featured a searing anti-war song ('20 tons of TNT') and a mournful paean to lost rural railways ('The Slow Train').

They shared the garden studio (then numbered 1A) for a period around 1953-4, writing songs here and performing them to friends. Flanders, who was disabled by polio, stayed until 1962: it suited him, Swann recalled, 'because it was enormous, all on one floor, and devoid of furniture which meant he could whizz around on his wheelchair'.

SAMUEL PALMER
(1805–81) artist   6 Douro Place **34**

PALMER was one of The Ancients, a group of artists associated with William Blake* and in particular with the village of Shoreham in Kent. There he lived between 1826 and 1832, producing the distinctive pastoral scenes with which his name is most readily associated. Palmer moved to the 1846 house in Douro Place with his wife Hannah, the daughter of the artist John Linnell*, in 1851. City life clearly did not suit the asthmatic Palmer, who complained that he had to lean out of an attic window in order to get a breath of fresh air. As there was no studio, he worked in the south-facing drawing room, an arrangement he actually preferred.

Palmer left London in 1861 and eventually settled in a Gothic villa at Mead Vale, Redhill, Surrey.

RUDOLF NUREYEV
(1938–93) ballet dancer

27 Victoria Road

A GLOBAL star of ballet, Nureyev fundamentally altered perceptions about the role of the leading man. In Britain he is most readily recalled for his partnership with Margot Fonteyn* at the Royal Ballet, notably in *Giselle* (1962): they danced, he said, as 'one body. One soul'. They were rumoured to be lovers, too, though most of Nureyev's relationships were with men. After defecting from the Soviet Union in 1961, Nureyev lived a peripatetic, globe-trotting existence. He owned a house next to Barnes Common, but when in London – partly owing to his fear of KGB snatch squads – preferred to seek sanctuary here in a self-contained flat in the impressive late-19th-century house owned by the dance critics Nigel and Maude Gosling – and did so on many occasions between the early 1960s and the late 1980s.

T. S. ELIOT, OM
(1888–1965) poet

3 Kensington Court Gardens

B ORN in St Louis, Missouri, Thomas Stearns Eliot married his first wife Vivien Haigh-Wood and settled in London in 1915, becoming a naturalised Briton – and an enthusiastic Anglican convert – in 1927. His reputation was established by *The Waste Land* (1922), and reinforced by the drama *Murder in the Cathedral* (1935) and the poetry collection *Four Quartets* (1943). Eliot moved to a ground-floor flat in this unremarkable apartment block, built in 1887–9, in April 1957, shortly after he had married his erstwhile secretary Valerie Fletcher. The marriage was a happy one, and when he died here, it was with Valerie's name on his lips. Eliot wrote almost no poetry while living here, but did complete the play *The Elder Statesman* (1958), and continued to work for three afternoons a week as an editor at Faber & Faber in Russell Square. Among the dinner guests at Kensington Court Gardens, in June 1964, was Groucho Marx: Eliot was apparently a devotee of Marx Brothers films.

HUBERT PARRY

(1848–1918) composer and musician 17 Kensington Square

PARRY maintained this 17th-century house as his London establishment (he inherited a country house, Highnam Court, on the outskirts of Gloucester) from 1886 until his death, and christened his new drawing room 'with a Brahms song'. Parry's choral music has remained enduringly popular, while the rest of his oeuvre, including symphonic and chamber music, songs and oratorios, has enjoyed something of a revival since the 1990s. In Kensington Square he composed his most famous work, 'Jerusalem' (1916), a setting of the poem by William Blake*, to be sung at a rally of Fight for Right – a movement that saw the First World War as a moral necessity, with which Parry later fell out. The campaign for female suffrage and the Women's Institute then took it up, and it has since become an unofficial anthem, sung at the last night of the Proms and at sporting events. Parry, who was Director of the Royal College of Music from 1895, was knighted in 1898 and made a baronet in 1902. The title was left off the plaque at the wish of his daughter, who was living at the house when it went up. Its square design was chosen to fit the narrow space.

JOHN STUART MILL*

(1806–73) philosopher 18 Kensington Square **38**

MILL moved to this house of 1686–7 with his mother Harriet and eight younger brothers and sisters in 1837, following the death of his father, the philosopher James Mill*. Here, John Stuart Mill continued to tutor his siblings according to the demanding curriculum prescribed by his father, and it was here that he wrote two of his most important works, *A System of Logic* (1843) and *Principles of Political Economy* (1848), the overarching themes of which were social progress and the relation of the individual to society. A visitor, Caroline Fox, recalled his 'charming library and … immense herbarium'. The close-knit family was blown apart in 1851 when Mill became engaged to the recently widowed Harriet Taylor, with whom he had been in love for more than 20 years, and the couple moved to Blackheath Park. Mill took umbrage at, as he saw it, his family's failure to acknowledge his new bride: the drawing room here was the scene of a painful, and unsuccessful, attempt at a family reconciliation.

SIR JOHN SIMON

(1816–1904) pioneer of public health　　　　40 Kensington Square **39**

SIMON moved to the square partly to please his wife Jane, an inveterate social animal who was not enjoying life in far-flung Blackheath. Simon was the inaugural appointment as Medical Officer of Health to the City of London in 1848; in 1855, following the retirement of Edwin Chadwick*, he was appointed Chief Medical Officer to the Board of Health. In Simon's time the interior of the 1680s house was decorated in the taste of the advanced artistic circles in which he moved, with William Morris* wallpaper and paintings by Turner* and Ruskin*. The atmosphere was said to be 'overwhelmingly cerebral', and Simon's young nieces and nephews were 'cowed by Aunt Jane's formidable appearance and ferocious intelligence, and amazed by Uncle John who quoted poetry at such length'.

SIR EDWARD BURNE-JONES*

(1833–98) artist　　　　41 Kensington Square **40**

IN 1860 – the year after Burne-Jones left the address in Red Lion Square where he is also commemorated – he married Georgiana Macdonald. 'Ned' and 'Georgie' moved here in January 1865 with their young son Philip. The house dates from 1804–5, and required extensive restoration after bomb damage in the Second World War; the garden – today much reduced – was once 'just large enough for a game of bowls'. During his time here Burne-Jones worked hard on his technique, the fruits of which can be seen in such paintings as *The Lament* (1865–6) and *Cupid Delivering Psyche* (1867). The Burne-Joneses moved in June 1867 after the house was sold from under them, decamping to The Grange in Fulham (now demolished).

WILLIAM MAKEPEACE THACKERAY*

(1811–63) novelist　　　　16 (formerly 13) Young Street **41**

THACKERAY moved here in August 1845; his wife Isabella, who had become mentally ill, had been in a private asylum since 1842. In autumn 1846 he was joined here by his two surviving daughters, Anne and Minny; three servants and a small black cat completed the household. Thackeray credited this family reunion with inspiring him to complete the novel that made his name: *Vanity Fair*, published serially between January 1847 and July 1848. The house, a yellow-brick survivor of semi-rural Kensington, dates from about 1815.

The projecting segmental bays reminded Thackeray of a feudal castle: 'I'll have a flagstaff put over the coping of the wall, and I'll hoist a standard up when I'm at home!' he joked. He moved to Onslow Square in 1854.

COLONEL R. E. B. CROMPTON

(1845–1940) electrical engineer   48 Kensington Court **42**

ROOKES Evelyn Bell Crompton formed a company in 1886 to supply electricity to the new housing development of Kensington Court. The firm, later the Kensington and Knightsbridge Electric Supply Company, laid cables in subterranean conduits that led from a purpose-built electricity generating station – now 46 Kensington Court – and carried direct current (DC), a system that eventually lost out to the rival alternating current (AC) system promoted by Sebastian Ziani de Ferranti, with whom Crompton enjoyed a friendly professional rivalry. The architect of the power

station was John Slater, who also built (in 1888–9) the house adjacent at number 48 for Crompton, using a steel-frame construction. Crompton moved here in 1891 with his wife Elizabeth, naming it Thriplands after a beautiful spot on his family's Yorkshire estate. The upper two floors served as his laboratory, 'the scene of a great variety of experimental works'. Crompton – who was an enthusiastic early motorist, and advised the War Office on the development of mechanical transport – remained at the house until 1939; he then returned to his native Yorkshire, where he died the following year.

EARL'S COURT AND WEST KENSINGTON

EARL'S Court, a hamlet in 1820 and mostly given over to market gardening, was entirely built over by the 1880s. The District and Metropolitan railways had by this time arrived, as had the exhibition centre. The earliest residential developments in neighbouring West Kensington, such as Edwardes

Square and Addison Bridge Place, were undertaken in the early 1800s, close to the arterial Kensington High Street and Hammersmith Road. Despite the name, much of West Kensington lies in the borough of Hammersmith and Fulham.

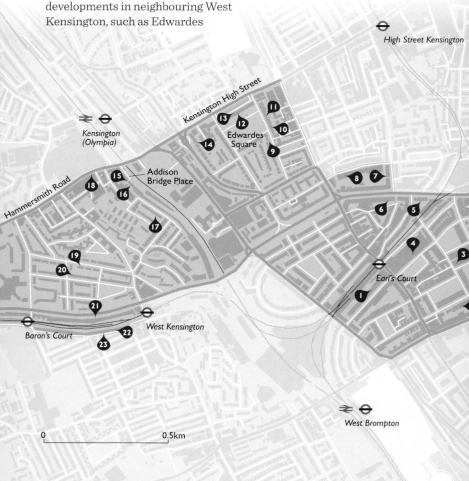

SIR NORMAN LOCKYER

(1836–1920) astronomer,
physicist and founder of *Nature*

16 Penywern Road **1**

IT was as an amateur scientist, while working as a civil servant at the War Office, that Lockyer made his groundbreaking discovery of helium. A year later, in 1869, he became the founding editor of *Nature*, which still flourishes as a leading scientific journal. In 1876, the year after Lockyer was seconded to the Department of Science and Art, then based in South Kensington, he moved into the newly built 16 Penywern Road, paying the astronomical price of £2,700. Created Director of the Royal College of Science's Solar Physics Observatory in 1890, he kept this house, which is now part of a hotel, for the rest of his life; he died at his country home (and observatory site) in Salcombe Regis, Devon.

SIR EDWIN ARNOLD

(1832–1904) poet and journalist

31 Bolton Gardens **2**

A PROLIFIC poet, Arnold is chiefly known for *The Light of Asia* (1879), an account in luxuriant verse of the life and teachings of the Buddha. This went through scores of editions and was a crucial element in the growth of interest in Buddhism in the West. Arnold drew on his experience of India from his time as principal of a college in Poona (1857–61). On his return to England he worked at the *Daily Telegraph*; he was vice-president of a vegetarian society of which a young Gandhi* was secretary. Arnold moved here in 1898; the following year his novel *The Queen's Justice* was published, a story set in the Indian subcontinent and dedicated to his Japanese third wife, Tama Kurokawa, who was 40 years his junior. He died at the house in 1904.

HOWARD CARTER

(1874–1939) Egyptologist and discoverer
of the tomb of Tutankhamun

19 Collingham Gardens **3**

CARTER, the son of an artist, was trained as a draughtsman, in which capacity he first went to Egypt in 1891. Having been inspired to take up archaeological excavation while working under Flinders Petrie*, Carter was appointed as the first Inspector-in-

Chief of the monuments of Upper Egypt and Nubia at the age of just 26. It was after leaving this post – and through the private patronage of his friend the 5th Earl of Carnarvon – that Carter made the discovery that in 1922 brought him to international attention: the treasure-filled 'lost' tomb of the boy-pharaoh Tutankhamun in the Valley of the Kings. This house, which belonged to Carter's brother Samuel, was his London base for much of the 1920s, and for some time he had a self-contained flat here, numbered 19B. Fraternal relations did not always run smooth, and a breach occurred in August 1930 after Samuel broke into Howard's drinks cabinet, lamely insisting that he needed brandy for his sick wife. Soon afterwards, Howard moved to a flat in Kensington Gore.

DAME ELLEN TERRY

(1847–1928) actress   22 Barkston Gardens 4

B ORN in Coventry, Terry was the daughter of actors, and a seasoned theatrical performer by the age of 12. She lived here at the height of her stage career, between 1889 and 1902, with a lady companion, Mrs Rumball, a bullfinch called Prince and a fine collection of theatrical ephemera. Much of Terry's work was performed at the Lyceum under Henry Irving*; by 1881 she had two failed marriages behind her – she wed her first husband, the artist G. F. Watts, at the age of 16 – and she and Irving were widely assumed to be lovers. Tall and graceful with a great sense of fun, she was adored by her public and played many leading roles with distinction, including most of the Shakespearean canon. She died at her 15th-century farmhouse in Smallhythe, Kent.

SIR ALFRED HITCHCOCK

(1899–1980) film director   153 Cromwell Road

H AILING from Leytonstone, Essex, Hitchcock made his debut as a director of feature films with *The Pleasure Garden* (1925); four years later he directed *Blackmail*, the first British full-length 'talkie', in which he made one of his trademark cameo appearances. Over the years, Hitchcock cemented his reputation for cinematic innovation and suspense-filled plotlines with film successes such as *The Thirty-Nine Steps* (1935). He moved to this modest two-bedroom flat on the top floor of a mid-Victorian terrace after his marriage in December 1926 to the film editor Alma Reville – they held their wedding reception here. Hitchcock designed the furniture and fittings for the flat, which he retained as his London base despite his rising fortune and fame; 'I never felt any desire to move out of my own class,' he once remarked. In March 1939, disillusioned with the lowly artistic standing of the cinema in Britain, Hitchcock and Alma left for Hollywood. He took US citizenship in 1955 and died at his home in Los Angeles.

BENJAMIN BRITTEN, OM

(1913–76) composer   173 Cromwell Road

THE Suffolk-born Britten lived here while studying composition at the Royal College of Music. He moved here in September 1931 with his sister Beth, who was training to be a dressmaker. They had adjacent rooms on the top floor of what was then a boarding house; Paul Wright, a fellow singer in the New Madrigal Choir, recalled listening to his ingenious musical improvisations while seated in one of the 'uncomfortable, rickety armchairs' in his eyrie. Britten spent many hours here practising and composing at the piano, occasionally to the irritation of fellow lodgers. He returned to Suffolk in autumn 1932, but was back at these lodgings a year later, on landing a job with the GPO Film Unit* in which capacity he provided the soundtrack for *Night Mail* (1936), to accompany verse written by W. H. Auden. In November 1935 Britten and Beth moved to a flat in West Hampstead: 'Anything to get away from boarding houses,' he told a friend.

ANDREW LANG

(1844–1912) man of letters   1 Marloes Road

SCOTTISH by birth, and a one-time fellow of Merton College, Oxford, Lang wrote poetry, fiction, history, biography, newspaper leader columns and literary criticism – 'a la-dy, da-dy, Oxford kind of Scot', in the words of his friend Robert Louis Stevenson. He translated Homer's *Odyssey* (1879);

'Walk up the Cromwell Road until you drop – and then turn right.'

Lang's directions for finding his house

he was also a pioneering anthropologist: his two-volume *Myth, Ritual and Religion* (1887) drew links between folk customs and beliefs in disparate parts of the globe, and he was a founder member of the Folk-Lore Society in 1878. Lang lived at Marloes Road with his wife Leonora, also a writer and translator, from 1876 until his death. He often walked home from his journalistic assignments in the City of London, which took him an hour and a half. The house is at the end of a terrace built by Samuel Juler Wyand, one of the most prolific builders in the area, and was new when the Langs moved in.

SIR LEARIE CONSTANTINE

(1901–71) West Indian cricketer and statesman   101 Lexham Gardens

THE Trinidad-born Learie Constantine came to public notice playing cricket for the West Indies; against Middlesex at Lord's in 1928, he took seven wickets and hit 103 runs in an hour, in one of the most outstanding all-round innings ever recorded. He played professionally for the Lancashire club of Nelson and later, in 1961, became Trinidad and Tobago's first High Commissioner in London. Eight years later, Constantine, who had already been knighted, became the first black member of the House of Lords. With his wife Norma and daughter Gloria, he moved into a maisonette at the substantial 1870s house at Lexham Gardens in 1949, and stayed for five years. By then retired from professional cricket, he turned out for the village team in Chalfont St Peter, Buckinghamshire, and worked as a broadcaster. It was while living here that Constantine wrote *Colour Bar* (1954), a frank and fearless assessment of race relations in the UK at that time.

SIR WILLIAM ROTHENSTEIN

(1872–1945) painter and writer   1 Pembroke Cottages

BORN in Bradford of German parents, Rothenstein studied art at the Slade and in Paris, and made his name as a portraitist with the illustrations he produced for the book *Oxford Characters* (1896). He became a leading member of the New English Art Club, with a wide circle of acquaintances in literary and artistic London. On his marriage in 1899 to Alice Knewstub, he moved to this 1840s semi-detached villa. That year he began perhaps his best-known painting, *The Doll's House*, for which the models were his wife and their friend Augustus John*. John and his sister Gwen borrowed the house for a while;

being forgetful of house keys, John fell into the habit of entering through a window. The Rothensteins moved in 1902 from their 'delectable cottage' to a larger house in Hampstead. From 1912 they lived principally in Gloucestershire, where Rothenstein suffered abuse for his slight German accent and name, which, unlike his brothers, he chose not to anglicise. He was Principal of the Royal College of Art from 1920 to 1935.

UGO FOSCOLO
(1778–1827) Italian poet and patriot   19 Edwardes Square

BY the time he was exiled to London in 1816, Foscolo had already made a name in Italy as a writer and dissident who opposed the Austrian occupation of Italy. The son of a Venetian physician and Greek mother, he lived far beyond his means, and moved frequently to avoid his creditors; his stay here from September 1817 to April 1818 was, by his standards, a settled spell. While here, Foscolo produced the first of a significant pair of essays on Dante for the *Edinburgh Review*, and collaborated on a controversial essay on Italian literature with the Whig politician John Cam Hobhouse. The fusion of poetry, polemic and romantic patriotism in Foscolo's work – his best-known poems are *I Sepolcri* (1807) and the unfinished *Le Grazie* (1822) – has led to comparisons with Byron; another point in common was their attractiveness to women. Foscolo died in poverty at Turnham Green.

G. LOWES DICKINSON
(1862–1932) author and humanist   11 Edwardes Square

A PROLIFIC writer and commentator on history and politics, Goldsworthy 'Goldie' Lowes Dickinson was a great influence on the Bloomsbury Group. He opposed the First World War as a needless bloodbath, a view he expounded in such works as *War: Its Nature, Cause and Cure* (1923) and *The International Anarchy, 1904–14* (1926). He had held a fellowship of King's College, Cambridge, since 1887, and also taught at the London School of Economics from 1896; he used the Edwardes Square address as a London pied-à-terre from 1912 until he retired from lecturing in 1920. Only weeks after the outbreak of the war, Dickinson called for the establishment of a 'league of nations'. He may have been the first to use this term, and travelled abroad to promote the scheme; in the 1920s he advised the Labour Party on international affairs. E. M. Forster* wrote his biography in 1934, a discreet affair compared to Dickinson's own disarmingly frank autobiography, which did not appear until 1973. The revelation that he was homosexual caused no great surprise; that he freely admitted to a masochistic boot fetish certainly raised a few eyebrows.

WALTER PATER
(1839–94) aesthete and writer   12 Earls Terrace **12**

BORN in Stepney, Pater was elected in 1864 to a fellowship in classics at Brasenose College, Oxford, where his writings stirred controversy on account of their religious scepticism and their implicit apologia for homosexuality. He became a leading Aesthete: his credo, 'art for art's sake', had a considerable influence on Oscar Wilde* and the younger Decadents. Pater moved here in August 1885, a few months after the appearance of his novel *Marius the Epicurean*; he hoped to find fresh stimulus in London literary circles, though he remained in Oxford during term-time. Visitors were struck by 'the extreme barrenness of the house, for there was in it neither ornament nor attempt at ornament'. While here, Pater wrote *Imaginary Portraits* (1887), four short stories and *Appreciations: With an Essay on Style* (1889). He returned to Oxford in July 1893 and died there suddenly a year later.

THOMAS DANIELL
(1749–1840) artist   14 Earls Terrace **13**

AS the first European landscape artist to work in India, Daniell was a pioneer. He was born at Kingston-upon-Thames and was apprenticed to a coach-builder before finding work with Charles Catton, coach-painter to George III and a founder member of the Royal Academy. It was at the Academy that Daniell first exhibited in 1772. He is best known for the serially published *Oriental Scenery* (1795–1808), which features aquatints derived from the drawings made with his nephew William Daniell* during his lengthy travels in India (1785–94). He moved to Earls Terrace in 1819, permanently tanned by the Indian sun, and while living here worked up his drawings into full-scale oil paintings. It was here that Daniell died.

GILBERT KEITH CHESTERTON

(1874–1936) poet, novelist and critic   11 Warwick Gardens

FROM the age of three or four, 'G. K.' – the son of Edward Chesterton, an estate agent, and his wife Marie Louise – spent a happy childhood in this stuccoed semi-detached early 1850s villa with Italianate features. His sister-in-law speculated that Chesterton's preference for writing in enclosed spaces could be traced to his childhood play in tiny upstairs 'cubbyholes'.

Chesterton published two collections of poems while here; one early verse, 'The Donkey', became an anthology favourite. Following his marriage in June 1901, he and his wife Frances moved a short distance away to 1 Edwardes Square. Chesterton was a high-profile Roman Catholic and recent moves to canonise him have fed the debate about the anti-Semitic content of some of his work.

HAROLD LASKI

(1893–1950) teacher and political philosopher   5 Addison Bridge Place

MANCHESTER-BORN Laski lived in this early-19th-century terraced house with his wife Frida from autumn 1926 until his death. Laski was an intellectual prodigy who taught politics and government at the London School of Economics from 1920, becoming Professor of Political Science in his early thirties; he remained at the LSE until his death. He became a

leading member of the Fabian Society* and theoretician for the Labour Party, of which he was Chairman in 1945–6. Together with John Strachey and Victor Gollancz, he started the Left Book Club in 1936. Laski's political thought tacked between liberal socialism and Marxism, his interest in which brought him into conflict with the party leader Clement Attlee*.

SAMUEL TAYLOR COLERIDGE*

(1772–1834) poet
and philosopher

7 Addison Bridge Place
(formerly 7 Portland Place)

COLERIDGE stayed here intermittently as a guest of John Morgan, a lawyer friend from Bristol, between late 1810 and

autumn 1811. He continued to live mostly with the Morgan family after they moved from here to Berners Street, off Oxford Street. Coleridge was then at a creative and personal nadir: ravaged by opium addiction – according to Robert Southey, he was consuming a pint of laudanum a day – he was deeply wounded to hear that his friend William Wordsworth had privately expressed no hope for him. In this state, Coleridge was able to put pen to paper only to denounce Wordsworth and to justify his own Christian faith, though he did manage to lecture at the London Philosophical Society. During 1811 he also worked for the *The Courier* newspaper, stating that he would save on carriage fares by walking to the paper's office in the Strand. A reconciliation with Wordsworth took place in 1812, and Coleridge entered a more positive phase.

SIR EDWARD ELGAR

(1857–1934) composer   51 Avonmore Road

ELGAR lived here from March 1890 to June 1891 with his wife Alice, who sold her pearls in order to secure the tenancy. While here, he composed the overture *Froissart*, which was first performed at the Worcester festival in September 1890, conducted by Elgar himself. This piece marked a step-change in his development as a composer. Although it was a significant time in his career and the place where his daughter Carice was born, Elgar was not particularly happy here: he described the winter of 1890 as 'truly awful: the fogs here are terrifying and they make me very ill'. The Elgars moved to Malvern – where the *Enigma Variations* (1899) and 'Land of Hope and Glory' (1901) were written – and thence to Hereford, before returning to London for another spell from 1912 to 1920. During that period they lived in a house in Netherhall Gardens, Hampstead, designed by Richard Norman Shaw* and now demolished.

SIR JOSEPH LYONS

(1847–1917)   11A Palace Mansions,
pioneer of mass catering   Hammersmith Road

JOSEPH Nathaniel Lyons was the name behind the Lyons tea shops and 'corner houses' that were once the last word in light refreshment. Backed by the mercantile families of Gluckstein and Salmon, the Southwark-born Lyons was not only the front man, but Managing Director of the firm from 1889. His blue plaque marks a flat he occupied with his wife Psyche for a couple of years from 1894 – the year the first Lyons tea shop opened in Piccadilly. Not far away, at 66 Hammersmith Road, was Cadby Hall, the main Lyons food factory: demolished in 1983, it could turn out 40 miles of swiss roll every day in its pomp.

THE GOOSSENS FAMILY
musicians 70 Edith Road

THE family was of Belgian origin, and came to England in the late 19th century. Eugène Goossens senior (1867–1958) – a violinist and conductor – moved here with his wife Annie Cook (1860–1946), an opera singer, and their family from Liverpool in 1912; they stayed until 1927. Léon (1897–1988) was an internationally known musician who was noted for his courageous – and successful – efforts to relearn his instrument after his face muscles were damaged in a car accident in 1962. Léon had survived the First World War thanks to a fortuitously placed silver cigarette case that deflected a bullet; his brother Adolphe (1896–1916), a promising horn player, was not so lucky, and perished at the Somme. Their sisters Marie (1894–1991) and Sidonie (1899–2005) were both harpists; all the Goossens siblings attended the Royal College of Music, where Léon and Sidonie later held professorships. Eugene Aynsley Goossens (1893–1962) was a conductor and composer who conducted the first London performance of Stravinsky's *Rite of Spring* in 1921, the same year in which Sidonie made her professional debut at a Prom concert; almost exactly 70 years later she became the oldest person to perform at the Last Night.

SIR HENRY RIDER HAGGARD
(1856–1925) novelist 69 Gunterstone Road

HAGGARD served in the colonial service in South Africa and later, following a romantic disappointment, became an ostrich farmer. Having married Louisa (Louie) Margitson, who, like him, came from a Norfolk gentry background, he returned to London and qualified as a barrister in 1885. He found the work stultifying and took to writing to alleviate the boredom. Challenged by his brother to write a boys' adventure tale as good as Robert Louis Stevenson's *Treasure Island*, Haggard wrote *King Solomon's Mines* (1885) in six weeks at this 1880s Gothic-style house, to which he had recently moved with his young family. By the end of that same year he had completed *Allan Quatermain* (largely written in Norfolk) and *Jess*. Both were published in 1887, together with *She*, which Haggard wrote during February and March 1886 'almost without rest ... it came faster than my poor aching hand could set it down'. He was able to abandon the legal profession in 1887 and move his family to Redcliffe Square, West Brompton, in May 1888. Later, following the death of his only son in 1891, Rider Haggard retired to Ditchingham, Norfolk, where he established himself as an authority on agriculture and rural life.

MARCUS GARVEY

(1887–1940) Pan-Africanist leader 53 Talgarth Road **21**

MARCUS Mosiah Garvey was born in Jamaica, where he founded the Universal Negro Improvement Association in 1914, soon after making his first visit to London. He moved to New York in 1916, where he established the Black Star Line steamship corporation, a pioneering black business enterprise, and started a militant weekly, *Negro World*. Garvey was later found guilty of fraud arising from the promotion of Black Star, and served time in a US prison. He was deported to Jamaica in 1927 and, after making another short visit to London in 1928, moved to the capital permanently in 1935, even though he found that the damp climate worsened his bronchitis and asthma. A regular at Speakers' Corner in Hyde Park, he had offices in Hammersmith, and lived here from around 1937, initially with his wife Amy Jacques and their children, and later with his secretary and nurse, Daisy Whyte; it was here that he died on 10 June 1940. Garvey remains a controversial figure – not least for his separatist assumptions – but his encouragement of black pride and self-confidence was an inspiration to many, and in Jamaica he is regarded as a national hero.

MAHATMA GANDHI*

(1869–1948) 20 Baron's Court Road **22**

MOHANDAS Karamchand Gandhi – the designation 'Mahatma', meaning 'great soul', came later – lived here as a law student in the late 1880s. He arrived in London in autumn 1888, aged 19, and was formally admitted to the Inner Temple on 6 November of that year. Board and lodging here cost him 30 shillings a week; his widowed landlady, Elizabeth Fanny Turner, had herself lived in India, but struggled to cater for his meatless diet; her meals were, he recalled, 'third rate', often leaving him hungry. While here, he took lessons in dancing, elocution and French and dressed in the garb of an aspiring lawyer, complete with top hat. Gandhi moved after about eight or nine months, for reasons of economy and dietary preference. Returning to India in June 1891, he came back to England on four occasions, and once said that 'next to India, I would rather live in London than anywhere else in the world'.

SIR GEOFFREY DE HAVILLAND

(1882–1965) aircraft designer   32 Baron's Court Road

D E Havilland lived in Flat B here from March 1909 – the year he married Louise Thomas – until January 1911. The house was conveniently close to the workshop in Bothwell Street, off Fulham Palace Road, where he and Frank Hearle, an engineer and his future brother-in-law, constructed their first aeroplane in 1908–9, with some assistance from Louise. From an early age, de Havilland was obsessed with mechanical engineering, and taught himself to fly in 1910.

From his beginnings at Bothwell Street, de Havilland (*right*) went on to become chief designer of the Aircraft Manufacturing Company (Airco), which provided almost a third of British and American aircraft during the First World War. In 1920 he founded the De Havilland Aircraft Company, which – at its factory at Stag Lane, Hendon – produced the Moth series of planes, including the Tiger Moth.

NOTTING HILL AND LADBROKE GROVE

TWO hundred years ago, the Notting Hill area – with the exception of the small settlement of Kensington Gravel Pits, now Notting Hill Gate – was farmland. Development in the area began in the early 1820s, when the arterial route of Ladbroke Grove was first delineated; the name is now applied to the northern part of this district. By 1875 the area was almost entirely built-up. A number of speculators were ruined along the way, as the supply of houses outstripped middle-class demand, and much of the stock was soon subdivided. The penurious condition of many of the inhabitants is reflected in the stories behind several of the area's plaques. Today Notting Hill is a byword as much for its smartness as for its carnival.

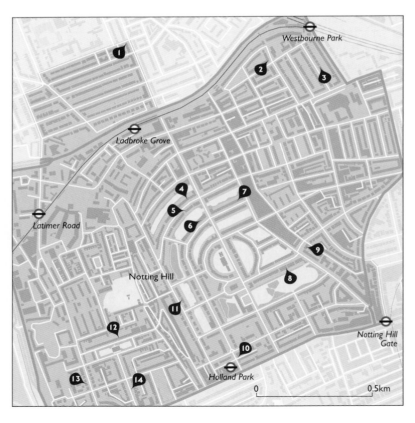

HABLOT KNIGHT BROWNE, 'PHIZ'

(1815–82) illustrator of Dickens's novels 239 (formerly 99) Ladbroke Grove

BORN in Kennington and apprenticed as a line engraver, Browne was soon producing etchings and watercolours on his own account. He made his name when Dickens* engaged him to illustrate *The Pickwick Papers* (1836–7), taking the monicker 'Phiz' – signifying a depicter of physiognomies – as a counterpart to Dickens's 'Boz'. Browne used it for most of his professional work thereafter, and went on to draw the pictures for nine more of Dickens's novels. Browne moved here in 1874, together with his wife Susannah and their children. The bow-fronted five-storey house was then new; Phiz wryly dubbed it 'Bleak House' from its end-of-terrace location. By this time, his commissions were few and his health was failing, though in 1875 he published under the pseudonym 'Damocles' the ribald *All About Kisses*, which offered helpful advice about where, how and whom to kiss. An annuity granted to Phiz by the Royal Academy facilitated his move in 1880 to Hove, East Sussex, where he died two years later.

W. H. HUDSON

(1841–1922) naturalist and writer 40 St Luke's Road **2**

ALTHOUGH his parents were from New England and he was born at Quilmes, near Buenos Aires, William Henry Hudson regarded England as his spiritual home and became a naturalised British citizen in 1900. He arrived by steamer in 1874, and moved here when his wife, Emily, inherited the property in 1888. He lived in Tower House, as it was then called, for the rest of his life, writing the works that brought him to prominence as an early environmentalist during his time here, including *Idle Days in Patagonia* (1893), the novel *Green Mansions* (1904), numerous books on the countryside and wildlife – especially the bird life of both England and Argentina – and an autobiography, *Far Away and Long Ago* (1918). Hudson and his wife let out the lower floors of the house, which was said to be 'dim with ancient paper and paint', and lived in the attic flat. Emily moved to Worthing in 1914 for health reasons, but Hudson died in St Luke's Road, leaving his entire fortune to the RSPB. The unusual bronze plaque, featuring a relief illustration of his birthplace on the Pampas, was commissioned by a body of his Argentine admirers and put up under the aegis of the LCC.

SARDAR VALLABHBHAI JAVERBHAI PATEL

(1875–1950) Indian statesman   23 Aldridge Road Villas   **3**

PATEL came to England to read for the Bar in 1910; after an initial burst of sightseeing, he threw himself wholeheartedly into his studies and lived an ascetic existence. After a short spell in a hotel, Patel moved to what was then 'a moderately priced boarding-house', from where he walked the four miles to the Middle Temple every day. He distinguished himself there, winning several prizes and completing his course of study early, and in 1912 he returned home to Gujarat, where he set up in legal practice. Patel went on to become Gandhi's* chief lieutenant and, like him, spent time in prison for civil disobedience. He participated in the negotiations leading to independence in 1947, played a leading role in the Indian National Congress, and later served as Minister for Home Affairs and Deputy Prime Minister under Nehru*.

JAWAHARLAL NEHRU

(1889–1964) the first Prime Minister of India   60 Elgin Crescent   **4**

NEHRU was educated at Harrow and Cambridge before going on to study law at the Inner Temple. In contrast to Patel* and Gandhi*, Nehru lived what he later described as 'a soft and pointless existence' during his time at London's Inns of Court, developing expensive tastes and playing cards for money; a typical evening included a trip to the theatre followed by a champagne supper at the Savoy. 'Joe' Nehru – as his Harrovian friends called him – lived in this mid-19th-century Italianate villa from July 1910 to January 1911, and returned here when he was called to the Bar in the summer of 1912. Back in India, he joined Gandhi's campaign of civil disobedience in 1919, and became a leading figure of the Indian National Congress; presiding over its annual session in 1929, he declared himself a republican and a socialist. Like Gandhi and Sardar Patel, Nehru was frequently imprisoned by the British, but in 1947 became independent India's first Prime Minister, holding this office until his death.

SIR OSBERT LANCASTER

(1908–86) cartoonist and writer

79 Elgin Crescent **5**

LANCASTER drew some 10,000 cartoons for the *Daily Express* between 1938 and 1941, and published books about fictitious English towns – Pelvis Bay and Drayneflete – with strong satirical intent, describing the ruination of their built heritage in the banal tones of a promotional brochure. His pet hate was pastiche architecture: 'Stockbroker's Tudor' and 'Banker's Georgian' were phrases of his coining. One of Lancaster's most famous architectural cartoons was of 79 Elgin Crescent – his birthplace – which he encountered on a night-time walk around his old haunts during an air raid. He described his childhood memoir *All Done From Memory* (1963) as 'a small memorial plaque to a vanished world'; in its pages, he described the muffin men, lamplighters, organ-grinders and crossing sweepers of pre-1914 Notting Hill, where he lived with his parents, a cook, a housemaid, a nurse and a bootboy – all on £600 a year. Lancaster spent most of the rest of his life within a few miles of his birthplace.

HOWARD STAUNTON

(1810–74) British world chess champion

117 Lansdowne Road **6**

WHILE the idea of a 'world chess champion' was then notional, Staunton was regarded as such in the years following his defeat of the French master Pierre Saint-Amant in 1843. A prolific writer on the game, Staunton owned and edited the monthly *Chess Player's Chronicle* (1840–54), and from *c.*1844 until his death edited the chess column of the *Illustrated London News*. Among the reference works he authored was *The Chess Player's Handbook* (1847). After 1854 Staunton played little chess, devoting himself instead to critical studies of Shakespeare. He lived

The English Opening (given in chess notation as 1. c4) was named in Staunton's honour after he used it with great success. He also gave his name to the 'Staunton pattern' of chess pieces, designed by his friend Nathaniel Cook in 1835, which is still the set most commonly used in the English-speaking world.

here from late 1871 until spring 1874, shortly before his death; the distinctive terrace has Dutch gables and a pierced parapet, and is unlike any other building in the area.

SIR WILLIAM RAMSAY

(1852–1916) chemist, discoverer of the noble gases   12 Arundel Gardens **7**

GLASGOW-BORN Ramsay accomplished his pioneering discoveries of the noble gases – the family of gases that are odourless, colourless, and do not readily combine with other elements – while a professor at University College London, where he was affectionately called 'the Chief' by his students. He moved to Arundel Gardens in 1887 with his wife and two young children, and spent 15 years at this 1860s stuccoed terraced house; later, he lived in greater splendour near Regent's Park. With Lord Rayleigh, Ramsay discovered argon in 1894; the isolation of helium – previously identified among the sun's component gases by Norman Lockyer* – followed the next year. With his student Morris Travers, Ramsay went on to isolate krypton, neon and xenon. In 1904 he became the first Briton to be awarded the Nobel Prize for Chemistry. Neon lights, photographic flash bulbs and supermarket barcode scanners are among the technological advances to have flowed from Ramsay's scientific work.

SIR WILLIAM CROOKES

(1832–1919) scientist   7 Kensington Park Gardens **8**

THE son of a Yorkshire tailor, Crookes attended the Royal College of Chemistry as a pupil and assistant of A. W. Hofmann*. He was elected Fellow of the Royal Society two years after his discovery of the metallic element thallium in 1861. He moved to this stuccoed mid-Victorian house, with elaborate porch and balustrades, which he shared with his wife Ellen, in 1880 – and died here nearly 40 years later. 'When one visited him ... one felt that here was a workshop from which phenomena of stimulating novelty might at any time emerge,' recalled fellow scientist Oliver Lodge. Crookes worked here on the development of an incandescent lamp; the house was reputed to be one of the first in the country to be lit by electricity. His work on cathode rays, and attendant success in producing a vacuum tube, was an important precursor for the discovery of X-rays and electrons; Crookes's endeavours effectively laid the ground for the entirely new fields of nuclear physics and electronics. Later, his work on anti-polarising glass provided the basis for the development of sunglasses.

LOUIS KOSSUTH

(1802–94)
Hungarian patriot

39 Chepstow Villas
(formerly 11 Kensington Park Terrace) **9**

L AJOS (Louis) Kossuth – leader of the revolution of 1848 – was Governor of Hungary in 1849, after the country briefly threw off Habsburg rule. He was defeated and exiled later that year and came to England in October 1851. Kossuth made a three-week tour of the country and was officially entertained by London's Lord Mayor, and at Copenhagen Fields in Islington addressed a gathering of thousands representing the trades unions. He then visited the United States before returning to England in July 1852. Kossuth lived at what is now 39 Chepstow Villas from this date until March 1853; widely fêted by English liberals, some sections of the political establishment regarded him as a dangerous agitator. He made his living as a journalist before leaving in 1859 for Italy, where he spent the rest of his life.

LANSDOWNE HOUSE

Lansdowne Road **10**

B UILT as studio flats for artists thanks to the munificence of Edmund Davis, Lansdowne House was completed in 1904. Ricketts, a painter, book and stage designer who worked with Oscar Wilde* and George Bernard Shaw*, lived here with his lifelong partner Charles Shannon, a lithographer and painter, between 1904 and 1923. Despite their relative poverty, they built an art collection that passed to the Fitzwilliam Museum and the British Museum after their deaths. Philpot, a portraitist and sculptor who, like Ricketts, drew inspiration from the Old Masters, variously lived and worked here from 1923 to 1935 with his friend Vivian Forbes, another portrait painter, who

Artists included on the plaque:
Charles Ricketts (1866–1931)
Charles Shannon (1863–1937)
Glyn Philpot (1884–1937)
Vivian Forbes (1891–1937)
James Pryde (1866–1941)
F. Cayley Robinson (1862–1927)

tragically killed himself after Philpot's sudden death in 1937. James Pryde, a Scottish artist who had a studio here for nearly 25 years after 1915, was an innovative poster designer. Frederick Cayley Robinson, a Symbolist painter, was commissioned by Davis to paint four murals of the Acts of Mercy for the entrance hall of the Middlesex Hospital; the first was completed in 1915. He lived here for a decade from 1914.

EMMELINE PANKHURST (1858–1928)
DAME CHRISTABEL PANKHURST (1880–1958)
campaigners for women's suffrage   50 Clarendon Road

EMMELINE Goulden was born in Manchester, and attended her first women's suffrage meeting at the age of 14. In 1879 she married Richard Pankhurst, a barrister and radical, who in 1870 had drafted the first women's suffrage bill in Britain. The couple had five children; the two eldest – Christabel and Sylvia* – became leading figures in the fight for women's rights. In 1903 Emmeline and Christabel founded the Women's Social and Political Union, a militant group whose motto was 'Deeds, not words' and whose members were known as 'suffragettes'. While Emmeline played an active role, staging rallies and suffering repeated arrests, Christabel was a remarkable organiser. The hardships took their toll on Emmeline; by 1916, when she moved here, she had transferred her energies to the care of 'war babies'

The Pankhursts (centre) after being released from prison in 1908.

– children born out of wedlock as a result of wartime social upheaval. Four of these she adopted and brought to live with her at this stuccoed semi-detached house of the mid-1800s, which she loved, and which was her home until her move to Canada in autumn 1919. Christabel lived here intermittently for periods between 1917 and 1919.

LAO SHE
(1899–1966)   31 St James's Gardens
Chinese writer   (formerly St James's Square) 12

LAO She is the pen name of Shu Qingchun; born in Beijing, he was one of the outstanding Chinese writers of the 20th century, whose humorous satire has been compared to Charles Dickens*. A

Christian convert, Lao She came to England in 1924 to teach Chinese at London University's School of Oriental Studies. His experiences resulted in the novel *The Two Mr Mas* (1929), an evocative account of London life in the 1920s from the viewpoints of a Chinese father and son. Lao She lodged here between 1925 and 1928 with the scholar Clement Egerton, whom he assisted in his translation of *The Golden Lotus*, eventually published in 1939, one of the best-known Chinese erotic novels. His plaque is unique in featuring Chinese characters.

ALBERT CHEVALIER
(1861–1923) music-hall comedian   17 (formerly 21) St Ann's Villas

AT the age of eight Chevalier took part in 'penny readings' at a local hall, but his parents, who blessed him with the middle names of Onésime Britannicus Gwathveoyd Louis, wanted him to enter the priesthood. His father, a language teacher, dabbled in spiritualism; for a time, Chevalier later recalled, the house 'became a happy hunting-ground for mystic waifs and strays. We held seances nightly.' Chevalier made his professional stage debut in London in 1877, and spent 14 years as an actor before turning to the music hall. His costermonger routine was soon a hit all over the country: such was his popularity that he performed at as many as five venues in a single night. Chevalier represented the respectable face of music-hall entertainment, and it was said that he 'never sang an offensive song'. Born in this semi-detached house (built in 1852) he had left it by 1894, the year that he married Florrie, the daughter of George Leybourne*, another star of the music hall. Chevalier later lived – and died – in Stoke Newington.

SIR HUGH CARLETON GREENE
(1910-87) journalist and Director-General of the BBC   25 Addison Avenue

AS the BBC Director-General during the 1960s, Greene fomented a change in culture that saw the commissioning of social realist dramas like *Cathy Come Home*, milestone comedies such as *Till Death Us Do Part* and the groundbreaking satirical news show *That Was The Week That Was*. BBC2, Radio 1 and colour television were all launched under his stewardship. Some – notably the campaigner Mary Whitehouse – linked his liberalisation to moral decline – yet *Songs of Praise* was his own programming idea. Greene and his family moved into this house, which was built in about 1850, in 1956 and stayed for 11 years. Graham Greene* was his older brother.

HOLLAND PARK AND CAMPDEN HILL

HOLLAND Park and Campden Hill lie on the rising ground between Kensington High Street and the old Uxbridge Road. Their names derive from two important early-17th-century buildings: Holland House – the partly surviving mansion of Walter Cope (d. 1614), which was surrounded by an estate that was developed from the 1820s – and Campden House, built for Baptist Hicks (d.1629), later Viscount Campden, and demolished in about 1900. To the east, the wider

'swarming with artistic types'
Ezra Pound on Holland Park

area is dominated by Kensington Palace, a royal residence since 1689. Mass development of housing aimed largely at the prosperous middle classes came in the 19th century. By the early 1900s, this part of Kensington – and especially Holland Park – had become a favoured place of residence for painters and writers; Ford Madox Ford* called it 'a high class Greenwich Village'.

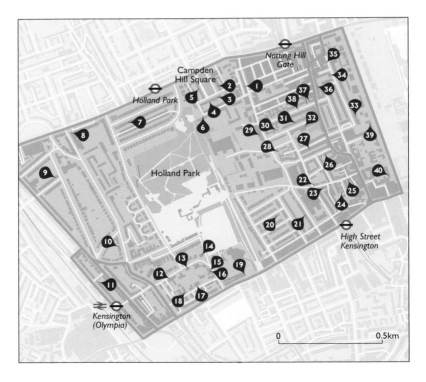

DAME MARIE RAMBERT

(1888–1982) the founder of Ballet Rambert

19 Campden Hill Gardens ❶

BORN Cyvia Ramberg in Warsaw, Rambert is said to have been inspired to take up dance after watching a performance by Isadora Duncan. In 1909 she moved to Geneva, where she studied eurhythmics with Émile Jaques-Dalcroze. During this period Rambert met Serge Diaghilev, founder of the Ballets Russes, with whom she subsequently collaborated. In 1914, she settled in London, where she studied, performed and worked as a dance teacher for the rest of her life. She opened her first school in Bedford Gardens, Kensington, in 1920 and, six years later, founded a company which performed as Ballet Rambert from 1935; it is now known simply as Rambert. Rambert herself nurtured a generation of dancers and choreographers, including

Rambert in her home, 1978.

Alicia Markova. She lived in Campden Hill with her husband, the writer Ashley Dukes, from 1920 until her death; they initially rented the top floor here and gradually took possession of the whole house.

JOHN MCDOUALL STUART

(1815–66) the first explorer to cross Australia

9 Campden Hill Square (formerly Notting Hill Square) ❷

BORN in Fife, Stuart qualified as a civil engineer before emigrating in 1838 to South Australia, where he worked as a surveyor and soon became involved in exploration, undertaking six journeys into the unknown. On Stuart's first expedition (1858), which aimed to find pasture country, he discovered around 40,000 square miles of new territory, including Chambers (now Stuart) Creek. Two years later, Stuart – a capable and caring leader – reached the centre of the continent, and in July 1862 finally set foot on its northern shore; for this remarkable achievement, he was awarded the Patron's Medal of the Royal

Geographical Society. The route he opened across Australia was used for the overland Adelaide–Darwin telegraph, and in 1942 formed the path of the Stuart Highway. Stuart never fully recovered from the privations he suffered during his journeys of discovery. In 1864 he returned to Britain on medical advice, and in that year moved into this early- to mid-19th-century house, where he died at the age of 50.

CHARLES MORGAN

(1894–1958) novelist and critic · 16 Campden Hill Square **3**

MORGAN joined the Navy in 1907, but resigned six years later to pursue a literary career, which was only interrupted by the First World War. In 1921, he joined the staff of *The Times*, and was the newspaper's drama critic (1926–39). His energies, however, were chiefly focused on novels, from *The Gunroom* (1919) to *Challenge to Venus* (1957). Many of his books – including *Sparkenbroke* (1936), *The Voyage* (1940) and *The River Line* (1949) – were written during his time at this house, which was

He 'did not suffer young children lightly and found the boisterous family next door to be unacceptably disturbing to the process of creation; remonstrances followed and we all had to keep quiet'.

Charles Morgan, recalled by a neighbour

bought largely with the proceeds of *The Fountain* (1932). Morgan was described by a neighbour as 'intensely private ... rarely exchanging words over the party-fence wall'.

SIEGFRIED SASSOON

(1886–1967) writer · 23 Campden Hill Square **4**

BORN in Kent, Sassoon lived the life of a country gentleman until the outbreak of the First World War, when he was commissioned into the Royal Welch Fusiliers; his exceptional courage earned him the MC and the nickname 'Mad Jack'. Recuperating from wounds in 1917, Sassoon spoke out in his writings against the futility of the slaughter on the Western Front and threw the ribbon of his MC into the River Mersey. Soon after, at Craiglockhart War Hospital near Edinburgh, he met the young poet Wilfred Owen, on whom he was to prove a formative influence. In 1918 he returned to fight but, later that year, a serious wound ended his military career. His war poems were first published as a collection in 1919 and he continued to write verse for the rest of his life, winning the Queen's Medal for Poetry in 1957. He is also celebrated for his fictionalised autobiographical works – *Memoirs of a Fox-Hunting Man* (1928) and *Memoirs of an Infantry Officer* (1930) – which were almost certainly written at the flat here. Sassoon leased the flat from the house's owner, the artist Harold Speed, from 1925 until 1932, when he moved to Heytesbury, Wiltshire, his home thereafter.

EVELYN UNDERHILL

(1875–1941) Christian philosopher and teacher   50 Campden Hill Square **5**

UNDERHILL was born in Wolverhampton but spent her childhood – and almost all of her life – in Kensington. She was inspired to study medieval Christianity by a series of holidays in Italy, and by 1907 had become a convinced Christian. Her first major book, *Mysticism: A Study of the Nature and Development of Man's Spiritual Consciousness* (1911), was a pioneering study that asserted the continuing relevance of the Christian mystics; the work brought her into contact with Baron Friedrich von Hügel* who became her spiritual director. Underhill moved here on her marriage in 1907 to Hubert Stuart Moore, a barrister and childhood friend, and it remained her home until summer 1939. Her biographer called it 'the friendliest of houses'.

AUBREY HOUSE

Aubrey Walk **6**

AUBREY House (formerly Notting Hill House) – which occupies the site of Kensington Wells, an early-18th-century spa – was built mainly in the mid-1700s by Edward Lloyd; it stands in substantial grounds to the west of Aubrey Walk, adjacent to Holland Park. The earliest notable resident of the house was Sir Richard Grosvenor, 7th baronet, who lived here briefly c.1767; a famous breeder

Residents included on the plaque:
Sir Edward Lloyd (d.1795)
Richard, 1st Earl Grosvenor
(1731–1802)
Lady Mary Coke
(1727–1811) diarist
Peter (1819–91) & Clementia
Taylor (1810–1908)
philanthropists
William Cleverly Alexander
(1840–1916) art lover

of racing stock, he was created an earl in 1784; the names of Lloyd and Grosvenor have been misleadingly elided in the plaque inscription.

In June 1767 the house was taken, and subsequently altered, by Lady Mary Coke, who lived here until 1788, and makes many references to the house in her celebrated journal. After a long period as a school it became the home of Peter Alfred Taylor and his wife Clementia, who took up residence in 1860 and remained here until 1873, when Peter's ill health prompted a move to Brighton. The couple held advanced liberal views; 'P. A. T.', who was MP for Leicester (1862–84), was said by his detractors to be 'anti-everything', while Clementia, who founded the Ladies' London Emancipation Society, the first national women's anti-slavery society, in 1863, was an activist for women's rights. The first meeting of the Committee of the London National Society for Women's Suffrage was held here on 5 July 1867. The Taylors opened an educational establishment, the Aubrey Institute, in the grounds in 1869; the house was known to be 'open to all, friend and stranger, black and white, rich and poor'. William Cleverly Alexander lived here next; he was a collector and connoisseur of pictures and *objets d'art* and a patron of Whistler*.

MAHARAJAH DULEEP SINGH

(1838–93) the last ruler of Lahore
53 Holland Park

AT the age of five Duleep Singh was declared Maharajah of the Punjab; his country was soon at war with the British, which culminated in the Sikh surrender of 1849. Duleep Singh was dethroned, but allowed to retain his title and granted a pension on the condition of obedience to the British government; his property, including the Koh-i-noor diamond, was confiscated. In 1854 Duleep Singh – newly converted to Christianity – arrived in England. He became a favourite of Queen Victoria, and lived the life of an English country squire at Elveden Hall, Suffolk. In April 1881 he took a lease on this 1862 house, where he planned to reside 'with my family as economically as possible'. Duleep Singh began to agitate against the British, claiming that their annexation of the Punjab was illegal and demanding his reinstatement as Maharajah; in 1886 he attempted to return to his homeland to lead the Sikh people; he was arrested on reaching Aden, where he was received back into the Sikh faith, and spent the rest of his life in Paris. Number 53 remained the home of his children and his wife, Bamba, née Müller (1849–87), until her death, and was sold in about 1890.

EUGEN SANDOW

(1867–1925) bodybuilder
and promoter of physical culture

BORN Friedrich Wilhelm Müller in Königsberg (now Kaliningrad) to a German father and a Russian mother, Sandow made a prosperous career out of his teenage obsession with bodybuilding. With his risqué posed photographs, he not only shifted public perceptions of male beauty, but also popularised the practice of exercising for health and fitness. He first came to England in 1888, performing as a strongman novelty act. In 1897 he opened an Institute of Physical Culture just off Piccadilly, offering tailored exercise programmes to a fashionable clientele; he also sold fitness products, including Health and Strength Cocoa and the Symmetrion, an exercising device for women. Appointed Professor of Scientific Physical Culture to George V in 1911, Sandow went on to work with army recruits during the First World War. In 1906 he bought the lease on this imposing 1820s house in Holland Park, and died here 19 years later aged just 58. The underlying cause was probably syphilis, and it seems that it was Sandow's philandering that provoked his widow, Blanche, into refusing to fund a marker for his grave in Putney cemetery.

JOHN RAE

(1813–93)
Arctic explorer

JOHN Rae was the Orkneyborn explorer whose explorations in the Canadian Arctic, while working for the Hudson's Bay Company, filled in some of the last blank spaces in the world map. It was Rae, in 1854, who identified the longsought North-West Passage later navigated by Roald Amundsen, and he who first discovered the terrible fate of John Franklin's expedition to find the same elusive route. Rae's subsequent report to the Admiralty

'Hairy and disagreeable'

Lady Franklin on the man who bore the bad news of her husband's expedition

included reports from local Inuit that Franklin's starving crew had, at the end, resorted to cannibalism. For accepting the word of 'savages', Rae found himself at the centre of a 19th-century media storm, though his respect for the Inuit and adoption of their winter survival techniques, such as building igloos, was crucial to his success as an explorer. For their part, the Inuit paid tribute to Rae's speed over frozen terrain by calling him Aglooka, or 'he who takes long strides'. Rae lived in Holland Park in retirement after 1869, but thought nothing of walking from here to the West End bases of the learned societies, where he lectured on the Arctic.

CHAIM WEIZMANN

(1874–1952) scientist and statesman, and first President of the State of Israel

67 Addison Road

BORN in Pinsk, then part of the Russian Empire, Weizmann began his career as a chemist; he first came to England in 1904, taking up a lecturing post at Manchester University, and six years later became a naturalised British citizen. In 1915 he moved to London, where he was appointed Admiralty adviser on acetone supplies, which were essential to the wartime manufacture of explosives. In October the following year, Weizmann and his wife Vera took up residence in Addison Road and remained until about the end of 1919; from 1920 to 1939 he lived at 16 Addison Crescent. During this time he became a major figure in the Zionist movement; he described his home during these years as 'a centre not only for the Zionists, but for a great many British political figures'. As President of the World Zionist Organisation for much of the period 1920–46, Weizmann continued to be a figure of prominence in the later part of his life. When the State of Israel was proclaimed in 1948, he was invited to become its President, a position he held for life.

MOHAMMED ALI JINNAH

(1876–1948) founder of Pakistan

35 Russell Road

JINNAH was born in Karachi and came to England in 1892 to study law at Lincoln's Inn; he was called to the Bar four years later, at the age of just 19. He occupied lodgings belonging to a Mrs Page-Drake in this modest terraced house near the railway. By the time Jinnah returned to Bombay in 1896 he was already a convinced nationalist, and in the second decade of the 20th century came to the forefront of Indian politics, playing an important part in founding the All India Home Rule League in 1916. In 1947 he was made the first Governor-General of Pakistan, the country he had played a huge part in founding.

SIR HAMO THORNYCROFT

(1850–1925) sculptor

THORNYCROFT collaborated in the design of a pair of semi-detached houses in Melbury Roadwith the architect John Belcher. He and his family of artists and sculptors (his parents and three of his sisters) moved into number 2 (4 was built for sale or let) in May 1877. They called their home, which contained a complex of studios, Moreton House after Little Moreton Hall, Cheshire, where the family had been tenants in the 1700s, and decorated it with their various work. In 1892 Belcher added a new studio house – now 2B Melbury Road – to which Thornycroft then moved. During his time here, he enjoyed a reputation as one of Britain's leading sculptors. His works include the *Mower* (1884), the *Sower* (1886), and portrait statues such as that of Oliver Cromwell in Old Palace Yard (1899).

'He is always in his studio at half-past eight, and has, before now, held on to his mallet until two the next morning.'

Thornycroft's dedication to work described in Strand *magazine, 1893*

MARCUS STONE

(1840–1921) artist

THE son of the artist Frank Stone, Marcus was educated and trained at home. The first of his works to attract attention was *On the Road from Waterloo to Paris* (1863), a depiction of the defeated Napoleon. This was followed by a series of paintings, almost all of which are historical tableaux or picturesque costume pieces; he was also active as a book illustrator. Stone lived in this house, designed for him by Norman Shaw*, from early 1877 until his death. He worked in a first-floor studio, 'one of the largest in London', lit by three huge oriel windows; there was a winter studio to the east, while the ground floor was a haven of domestic comfort. In 1896, it was said that 'few artists' houses could pretend to serve to anything like the same extent the double purpose of a delightful dwelling and an ideal working place'. The house was divided into flats in about 1950.

SIR LUKE FILDES

(1843–1927) artist

31 (formerly 11) Melbury Road **14**

FILDES commissioned Norman Shaw* to design his home in 1876–7. He began his artistic career as a book and magazine illustrator, and in 1870 collaborated with Dickens* in producing illustrations for his last, unfinished novel, *The Mystery of Edwin Drood*. Fildes's first major success came with his social-realist painting *Applicants for Admission to a Casual Ward* (1874). This was followed by works in a similar vein, including *The Widower* (1876) and *The Doctor* (1891). Fildes became a popular portrait painter: his sitters included Edward VII who, on visiting Fildes's Melbury Road studio, declared it to be 'one of the finest rooms in London'. Contrary what the plaque says, Fildes moved here in autumn 1877, and died here 50 years later.

WILLIAM HOLMAN HUNT, OM

(1827–1910) painter

18 Melbury Road **15**

BORN in the City of London, Holman Hunt – despite what is on the plaque, the name is not usually hyphenated – met and befriended Millais* and Dante Gabriel Rossetti* in the 1840s, and was a founder of the Pre-Raphaelite Brotherhood* in 1848. The works for which he is best remembered – many of them inspired by his frequent visits to Jerusalem – include *The Light of the World* (1851–3); this has been described as 'arguably the most famous religious image of the 19th century'. Holman Hunt's artistic output ended with his completion of *The Lady of Shalott* (*c*.1888–1905), by which time he was suffering from glaucoma. He moved here in 1903 and dedicated himself to literary activities: he worked on his memoirs and on *Pre-Raphaelitism and the Pre-Raphaelite Brotherhood* (1904-5), an account intended to propagate the principles of the group he had helped to start. Holman Hunt was awarded the Order of Merit in 1905.

CETSHWAYO

(*c*.1832–84) King of the Zulus 18 Melbury Road **16**

WHEN British forces instigated the Anglo-Zulu War in 1879 they came up against the formidable figure of Cetshwayo kaMpande, King of the Zulu nation since 1872. The Zulus inflicted defeat on the British at Isandlwana, but Cetshwayo was eventually captured, exiled and brought to London in 1882. He was lodged in Melbury Road, where to suit his needs, the beds were lowered to floor level. *The Times* described how 'at times the ex-king would appear for a moment at one of the windows, and he was invariably greeted with cheers'. While here Cetshwayo met Queen Victoria and the PM, William Gladstone*. Eventually he was allowed to return to South Africa and to rule again.

LORD LEIGHTON

(1830–96) painter 12 (formerly 2) Holland Park Road **17**

BORN in Scarborough, Frederic Leighton studied art on the Continent, and had his first success with *Cimabue's Madonna*, exhibited at the Royal Academy in 1855, and snapped up by Queen Victoria. Thereafter he had a triumphant career; *Flaming June* (1895) was his final masterpiece. Leighton was President of the Royal Academy (1878–96), created a baronet in 1886 and raised to the peerage the day before his death, which took place at his Holland Park home.

Leighton collaborated closely with George Aitchison in designing this house in Holland Park, and he moved there in late 1866. The plain brick exterior belies what Pevsner* has declared 'the most sumptuous and colourful 19th-century artist's house in London'. It features a vast studio at the rear of the first floor and a domed Arab Hall, added 1877–9.

PHIL MAY

(1864–1903) illustrator   20 (formerly 3 The Studios) Holland Park Road **18**

MAY, who was born in Leeds, came to public attention in London, where he worked for the *St Stephen's Review* and, from the 1890s, for *Punch*, among other magazines. He made his name with his sympathetic comic delineations of low life – especially 'guttersnipes'. So successful was he that Whistler* pronounced that 'modern black & white art could be summed up in two words – Phil May'. May, whose simple, vigorous style influenced artists such as Walter Crane*, David Low* and Bert Thomas, lived and worked at number 20 from 1896 to 1899, having previously been based elsewhere in Holland Park Road. He died at his later home in St John's Wood.

SIR DAVID LOW

(1891–1963) cartoonist   33 Melbury Court, Kensington High Street **19**

LOW lived on the top floor of the building from about 1956 until the time of his death seven years later. He was born in New Zealand, where – strongly influenced by the style of Phil May* – he developed a talent for satirical political cartoons and caricatures. In 1919 he moved to London and eventually joined the *Evening Standard* where he worked until 1949. Low's depictions of Hitler and Mussolini led to a ban on the *Standard* in both Germany and Italy. He also invented imaginary characters, of which Colonel Blimp – created in 1934 – is perhaps the best known. From 1952, Low worked for the *Manchester Guardian*.

KENNETH GRAHAME

(1859–1932) author   16 Phillimore Place (formerly 16 Durham Villas) **20**

THROUGHOUT the most important years of his life, Grahame, a Scot, enjoyed two careers: one, as an employee of the Bank of England – he was appointed Secretary in 1898 – and another as a writer. His lasting fame rests on *The Wind in the Willows* (1908). Supposedly based on a series of bedtime stories told by Grahame to his only child, Alastair, he wrote the book in this house, where he lived from the time of his marriage to Elspeth Thomson in July 1899 until June 1908, when he retired from the Bank of England.

SIR HENRY NEWBOLT

(1862–1938) poet   29 Campden Hill Road **21**

NEWBOLT is best remembered for his ballads, above all 'Drake's Drum' (1896) and 'Vitaï Lampada' (1892) – with its famous refrain 'Play up! play up! and play the game!' – in which he recollected his happy schooldays at Clifton College, Bristol. After the outbreak of the First World War, his literary output declined as he took on a succession of official posts such as chairing the government committee that produced the innovative Newbolt Report (1921) on the teaching of English in England. For many years, Newbolt was part of a remarkable *ménage à trois*: he and his wife Margaret shared a lover, Margaret's cousin Ella Coltman. Number 29 was Ella's home, and was used as a pied-à-terre by Newbolt from at least 1915. In autumn 1934 Newbolt and his wife moved in permanently. Margaret described how 'the Room of his Own in London which H. N. had used so constantly for twenty years past expanded into several rooms of our own. This was made possible by an ingenious architect who extended the little house for us – only a few feet – into its back garden.' Newbolt died here in April 1938.

SIR CHARLES STANFORD

(1852–1924) musician   56 Hornton St. (formerly part of 50 Holland St.) **22**

BORN in Dublin, Stanford was interested in music from childhood and went to Cambridge as a choral scholar in 1870. His musical output included seven symphonies, nine operas – of which the most popular was *Shamus O'Brien* (1896) – and a large body of songs and choral works. Stanford was influential as conductor of the London Bach Choir (1885–1902) and at the Leeds Festival (1901–10), as a writer on musical composition, and as a collector and editor of Irish folk music. He was also a great teacher: a professor both at the Royal College of Music and at Cambridge, Stanford's pupils included Ralph Vaughan Williams*, Samuel Coleridge-Taylor*, Arthur Bliss*, Frank Bridge*, Gustav Holst* and John Ireland*. Stanford settled in London in 1882, and occupied this distinctive corner house from 1894 to 1916, at which period it was combined with its neighbour in Holland Street.

RADCLYFFE HALL

(1880–1943) novelist and poet

37 Holland Street **23**

MARGUERITE Radclyffe-Hall began her literary career writing verse, but it was the fifth of her seven novels, *The Well of Loneliness* (1928), together with her unconventional lifestyle and masculine appearance, that has since made her an iconic figure. Hall wrote the novel while living here; it is a largely autobiographical work in which a lesbian heroine, Stephen Gordon, searches for fulfilment and acceptance in the post-Victorian age. The book was quickly banned in Britain; it remained largely unavailable until 1949. Hall – known as 'John' to her friends – lived with Una, Lady Troubridge, from 1916 until her death. The couple – both women of considerable means – were inveterate movers-of-house, flitting from flat to flat with remarkable speed. This 'charming house' as Una described it, part of an early-20th-century terrace, was their home from autumn 1924 'for four years. Something of a record for us, wandering Gentiles that we were.'

EZRA POUND

(1885–1972) poet

10 Kensington Church Walk **24**

BORN in Idaho, Pound arrived in London in 1908, spending the formative years of his career in this city before his departure for Paris in 1921. Pound lived in a top-floor bed-sitting room here from 1909 until his marriage in 1914. The house was owned by a Mr and Mrs Langley, who he described as 'positively the best England can produce at ANY level'. Here, he received visitors including Ford Madox Ford*, D. H. Lawrence* and Henri Gaudier-Brzeska*. Pound published *Personae* (1909), *Exultations* (1909), *Canzoni* (1911) and *Ripostes* (1912) while living here, and also helped to promote other writers such as James Joyce* and T. S. Eliot*. In 1912 he invented the label 'imagism': imagist poetry stressed clarity, precision and economy of language, and was to have a profound influence on 20th-century literature. Two years later he was a founder of the Vorticist group of artists and writers, giving the group their name. The later period of Pound's career was spent in Italy; his support for fascism led to his being indicted for treason in the United States, but he was instead certified insane and confined. It was partly these unsavoury associations that led to him dying a semi-recluse in Italy.

WALTER CRANE

(1845–1915) artist

The Old House, 13 Holland Street **25**

THE son of a portrait painter, Crane first exhibited his work at the age of 16, but came to public notice from 1865 for his illustrations of a series of children's books, known as 'Toy Books'. In the 1870s he also designed textiles, stained glass, tiles, wallpapers and plasterwork. In 1884 he was a founder member of the Art Workers' Guild and, four years later, founded the Arts and Crafts Exhibition Society, of which he served as President for many years; in 1898, he was appointed Principal of the Royal College of Art. The walls of The Old House (of c.1760), where he lived from autumn 1892 until the year of his death, were decorated with some of his celebrated wallpapers and textiles, while the collections it contained reflected the eclectic tastes of Crane and his wife Mary. Visitors here included William Morris* and Burne-Jones*.

JAMES JOYCE

(1882–1941) author

28 Campden Grove **26**

JOYCE was working on the first draft of *A Portrait of the Artist as a Young Man* when, in 1904, he met a chambermaid from Galway, Nora Barnacle (1884–1951). The couple eloped, and were to spend much of the rest of their lives in Trieste, Zurich and Paris. The success of his early work won him the support he needed to complete *Ulysses* (1922), among the greatest literary masterpieces of the time and one which brought him both acclaim and infamy; its scatological wit meant that it was banned in the US until 1934 and in Britain until 1936. He lived in a flat at 28B Campden Grove from early May until early September 1931, during which time he was occupied with *Finnegans Wake* (1939); the sojourn was considered, in Joycean terms, to be remarkably settled. He intended to make London his permanent home, and on 4 July married Nora Barnacle – long his wife in all but name – at Kensington Registry Office. Hounded by the press, however, Joyce's view of London soured and he took to calling his street 'Campden Grave'; the flat was let, and the writer was never to set foot in England again.

JEAN SIBELIUS

(1865–1957) composer   15 Gloucester Walk **27**

BORN in Hämeenlinna in southern Finland, Sibelius studied music in Helsinki, Berlin and Vienna; he began his musical life as a violinist but soon turned to composition, enjoying his first major success with his *Kullervo* symphony (1892), which became a keystone of the romantic nationalist movement in his homeland. After 1900 his fame spread abroad and he paid the first of five visits to Britain in 1905, largely to conduct.

His longest stay was in 1909, when Rosa Newmarch – writer (she wrote programmes for Henry Wood* and his Proms) and champion of Russian and Czech music – found him accommodation here. Sibelius lived here from February to March, during which time he composed his only published string quartet, *Voces Intimae*. Between 1910 and 1925, the composer concentrated on symphonies, before giving up composition for the last three decades of his life.

FORD MADOX FORD

(1873–1939) novelist
and critic

80 (formerly South Lodge)
Campden Hill Road **28**

BORN Ford Hermann Hueffer to a German father and English mother – he adopted the name Madox and in 1919 changed his surname to Ford – his first important publications were biographies of Ford Madox Brown* (1896), his grandfather, and D. G. Rossetti* (1902). Later he co-authored books with Joseph Conrad* and founded the *English Review* in 1908. This 'unpretentious semi-detached villa' of 1848–9 was the home of the author Violet Hunt (1862–1942) with whom he lived – scandalously – as her 'paying guest' (Ford's wife refused to divorce him) from 1913 until August 1915 when, their affair

more or less over, Ford joined the Army. He and Violet – as 'Mr and Mrs Ford Hueffer' – held a series of salons here that attracted, among others, Ezra Pound*, Wyndham Lewis* and D. H. Lawrence*. Ford's relationship with Violet gave rise to one of his greatest works, *The Good Soldier* (1915); this was followed in 1924–8 by four outstanding novels, known collectively as *Parade's End*, which drew on Ford's wartime experiences. Ford's pictures, books and furniture remained here until after Violet's death, causing a friend to comment that 'in a queer, unaccountable way, he still dominated the house'.

BILL BRANDT

(1904–83) photographer 4 Airlie Gardens **29**

BORN in Hamburg, Brandt studied with the surrealist Man Ray in Paris before settling in London in the early 1930s; he became so thoroughly assimilated that in later life he claimed to have been born in south London. Flat 4C Airlie Gardens belonged to Brandt's girlfriend (later his second wife) Marjorie Beckett, and was their home together from about 1959 onwards. Some of Brandt's nude shots of her and other models – 'my favourite pictures', he once said – were taken here, and appropriately, it now houses his photographic archive.

As a photographer and photojournalist, Brandt documented the high life, low life and landscapes of his adopted land in periodicals, notably *Picture Post*, and in books such as *A Night in London* (1938). Some of his most memorable images were taken during the Second World War, when the Ministry of Information commissioned him to record scenes in the London Underground stations that were used as

air-raid shelters. Brandt also took portrait photographs of many leading figures in the arts and literature.

DAME AGATHA CHRISTIE

(1890–1976) detective novelist and playwright 58 Sheffield Terrace **30**

DEVON-BORN Christie produced, between 1920 and 1965, one book every year, containing characters such as Hercule Poirot and Miss Marple. She shared this mid-19th-century detached house with her second husband, the archaeologist Max Mallowan, from 1934 until 1941, when they were driven out by bombing; she described it as 'a happy house'. It was the only home at which Christie had her own workroom; she declared that the room would contain 'a grand piano; large, firm table; a comfortable sofa or divan; a hard upright chair for typing; and one armchair to recline in, and there was to be nothing else'. Here, on the second floor, she completed *Murder on the Orient Express* (1934) and *Death on the Nile* (1937), among other titles.

PREBENDARY WILSON CARLILE

(1847–1942) founder of the
Church Army
34 (formerly 15) Sheffield Terrace **31**

BORN in Brixton, Carlile was ordained a priest in 1881, and from 1880 to 1882 was curate at the parish church of St Mary Abbots, Kensington. Concern about the lack of contact between the established Church and the working classes led him to set up the Church Army in 1882. Its aim was to encourage and enable working people to carry out evangelical work; a training college for men was opened in Oxford in 1884, and one for women – run by Carlile's sister, Marie Louise – in west London in 1887. Carlile lived in this terrace, built in *c*.1850, until 1891, when he became rector of St Mary-at-Hill in the City.

SIR EDWARD HENRY (1850–1931)

Metropolitan Police Commissioner and
pioneer of fingerprint identification
19 Sheffield Terrace
(formerly 29 Campden House Court) **32**

BORN in London, Henry entered the Indian Civil Service and by 1891 had risen to become Inspector-General of Police in Bengal. Building on the work on fingerprint identification carried out by Francis Galton*, he developed a new reference method for tracing individuals, and in 1900 published *Classification and Uses of Fingerprints*. The Henry system enabled, for the first time, fingerprints to be filed, searched, traced and compared with ease. In 1901 he was appointed Assistant Commissioner of Scotland Yard in charge of the Criminal Investigation Department, and set up the first fingerprint bureau in Britain; his system was soon adopted in countries around the world, and continues to be a vital element in police investigations today. In 1903 Henry became Commissioner, and moved to this tall, red-brick house of *c*.1898. Having survived an attempt on his life on the front steps here in 1912, he retired in 1920 to Ascot.

JAMES CLERK MAXWELL

(1831–79) physicist 16 (formerly 8) Palace Gardens Terrace

BORN in Edinburgh, Maxwell was already an accomplished scientist by the time he went to Cambridge in 1850. Ten years later, he was appointed Professor of Natural Philosophy at King's College London and moved here soon afterwards. This recently built house (c.1859) was to be his and his wife Katherine's home until March 1866. Maxwell experimented here and produced some of his most valuable papers; these included 'A Dynamical Theory of the Electromagnetic Field' (1865) and 'On the Dynamical Theory of Gases' (1867).

SIR MAX BEERBOHM

(1872–1956) artist and writer 57 Palace Gardens Terrace

THE youngest child of Julius and Eliza Beerbohm– and the half-brother of Herbert Beerbohm Tree*– he was born in this stuccoed house of c.1860. Having attended a day school in nearby Orme Square, Beerbohm went to Charterhouse and then Oxford, where he met Oscar Wilde* and William Rothenstein* and, through them, Aubrey Beardsley*. He came to public attention with the launch in 1894 of *The Yellow Book*, to which he contributed essays and drawings. He was a prolific writer and artist – publishing *Zuleika Dobson*, his best-known literary creation, in 1911 – but was known above all for his caricatures.

PERCY WYNDHAM LEWIS

(1882–1957) painter and writer 61 Palace Gardens Terrace **35**

BORN at sea off the coast of Nova Scotia, Lewis had a furnished room here from May 1923 until March 1926. Having studied at the Slade, Lewis gained prominence in the London art world in the period before the First World War; he was closely associated with the Camden Town Group, and was – with Ezra Pound* – a founder of Vorticism in 1914. After the war, during which he served as a war artist, he turned increasingly to writing: his first novel was *Tarr* (1918). Lewis later became art critic of *The Listener* and was based for the last 20 years of his life in a studio at 29 Notting Hill Gate (demolished), an area he described as 'Rotting Hill', reflecting its post-war decline.

MUZIO CLEMENTI (1752–1832)

composer 128 Kensington Church St.(formerly 1 High Row)

BORN in Rome, Clementi came to England at the age of 14, under the patronage of the businessman and politician Peter Beckford. In 1774 he moved to London, where his Sonatas, Op. 2 (1779) established his musical reputation. A subsequent continental sojourn featured a musical 'competition' against Mozart*; staged by Emperor Joseph II in Vienna in 1781, it resulted in a draw. From the 1790s he turned his attention to composition, teaching and business, becoming involved with music publishing and piano manufacture. Perhaps Clementi's most important musical work was his three-volume collection of études for the piano, *Gradus ad Parnassum* (1817–26), many of which were written during his time at 1 High Row (*c*.1818 to 1823), a house built in the 1730s and altered in the mid-19th century.

FRANK BRIDGE

(1879–1941) composer and musician 4 Bedford Gardens **37**

BRIDGE studied under Charles Stanford* at the Royal College of Music, and initially made his name as a viola player. He was active as a composer from 1900, producing chamber music and songs as well as orchestral works including *Dance Rhapsody* (1908) and *The Sea* (1910–11). He was also a noted conductor – admired by, among others, Henry Wood*. Bedford Gardens was Bridge's London home from 1914 until his death, which took place at his country house in Friston, East Sussex. From the early 1920s, he virtually gave up instrumental work to concentrate on composition, producing works such as his Piano Sonata (1921–4), Piano Trio (1929) and Violin Sonata (1932). A popular teacher, Bridge's most famous pupil was Benjamin Britten*, on whom he exerted a strong and lasting influence.

SIR WILLIAM BEVERIDGE

(1879–1963) architect of the welfare state 27 Bedford Gardens **38**

THE 'Beveridge Report' of 1942 proposed a system of universal social insurance 'from the cradle to the grave', supported by a comprehensive health service and family allowances – such as were later enacted. Its author was an economist, civil servant and senior academic administrator, who kept returning to the question of poverty and its elimination. Beveridge lived at three houses in this locality, and was at number 27 from 1914 to 1921 – during which time, as an early motoring enthusiast, he drove a two-cylinder Riley and a Citroën nicknamed 'Thomson'. His own nickname, pinned on him by his brother-in-law, the historian R. H. Tawney*, was – inevitably – 'Drink'.

KING HAAKON VII

(1872–1957) leader of the Norwegian government-in-exile, 1940–45

10 Palace Green

PRINCE Carl of Denmark – as Haakon was originally known – joined the Danish Navy at the age of 14, and in 1896 married his first cousin, Princess Maud, daughter of Edward VII. In 1905, he was invited to become constitutional monarch, taking the name Haakon VII. When the Germans invaded Norway in April 1940 he escaped capture, arriving in London in June 1940, and set up a base for the Norwegian Legation in Palace Green: from here he made broadcasts and chaired Cabinet meetings. Haakon's contribution had a major impact on the war effort – by 1945, some 25,000 Norwegians were fighting on behalf of the Allies – and his achievements ensured his long-term popularity. The house was designed by E. N. May and built in 1905.

WILLIAM MAKEPEACE THACKERAY*

(1811–63) novelist

2 Palace Green

THIS house, which Thackeray bought in May 1860 with money 'made out of the inkstand', was his last, and favourite, home. He had it completely rebuilt at a cost of over £8,000 to designs by the architect Frederick Hering, with his own input. Thackeray was delighted with his handsome new neo-Georgian dwelling, in spite of disapproval from friends and family who suggested he name it 'Vanity Fair' (the title of his most successful book) on account of its lavishness. The house nonetheless became 'his principal pleasure'. Thackeray's last works, written in the study here, included *The Adventures of Philip* (1861–2) and *Denis Duval* (1864). He died here on Christmas Eve 1863; the house, which was altered in the 1880s, is now the Israeli Embassy.

HAMMERSMITH AND FULHAM

THE borough of Hammersmith and Fulham stretches from Putney Bridge and Wandsworth Bridge in the south to Wormwood Scrubs, Old Oak Common and Kensal Green Cemetery – the final resting place of many eminent Londoners – in the north. Until 1834, Hammersmith was part of the parish of Fulham and the whole area was mainly agricultural, with built development along King Street and on the riverside. Well into the 19th century, Fulham was still full of orchards and market gardens, with a scattering of older settlements at New King's Road, Parsons Green and Walham Green, and a chain of substantial riverside mansions sitting in large gardens: Fulham Palace and Hurlingham House are the only survivors. Most of the borough's blue plaques and many of its most charming streets can be found in the strip running beside the Thames west of Hammersmith Bridge.

SIR FRANK BRANGWYN

(1867–1956) artist   Temple Lodge, 51 Queen Caroline Street

SUCH was Brangwyn's fame in his prime that Gerald Kelly*, President of the Royal Academy, felt able to say that 'no painter has been so internationally famous in his lifetime'. Brangwyn, who was born in Bruges, first leased Temple Lodge, a stuccoed Regency villa standing in a large garden, in 1900. In about 1908, having failed to persuade his alcohol-dependent wife Lucy to move to the country, he built a double-height studio projecting forward to the right of the house (it is now a chapel with a vegetarian restaurant on its former mezzanine floor). In his studio Brangwyn entertained eminent guests and produced some of his most important works; of special note are the British Empire Panels (1925–32), intended as murals for the House of Lords but rejected as being too colourful and flamboyant, and now on display in Swansea's Guildhall. In 1930 he moved permanently to his Sussex home at Ditchling.

The studio was overlooked by a gallery from Lucy's first-floor sitting room, where she sat (in the words of Brangwyn's great-nephew and biographer) 'feeling neglected, reading, sewing, or watching through a window her husband at work below'; she died in 1924.

GEORGE DEVINE

(1910–66) actor   9 Lower Mall **2**

DEVINE lived at this early-19th-century house, with tall French windows leading from the first-floor drawing room to the balcony, from 1954 until his separation from his wife, Sophia, in 1960. Born in Hendon, he began his theatrical career at Oxford University, where he appeared with John Gielgud* and Peggy Ashcroft in a celebrated performance of *Romeo and Juliet* (1932). He went on to revolutionise stage training and production at the London Theatre Studio in Islington, which he ran with the French actor-director Michel Saint-Denis. As Artistic Director of the English Stage Company at the Royal Court Theatre, Devine encouraged a new generation of actors, directors and writers, and brought that theatre to international prominence. Between 1956 – when *Look Back in Anger* was first produced – and 1965, he staged 150 plays, two-thirds of them by young playwrights, such as John Osborne, Edward Bond and Arnold Wesker.

THOMAS JAMES COBDEN-SANDERSON

(1840–1922) founder of the Doves Bindery and Doves Press   15 Upper Mall **3**

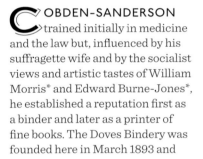

COBDEN-SANDERSON trained initially in medicine and the law but, influenced by his suffragette wife and by the socialist views and artistic tastes of William Morris* and Edward Burne-Jones*, he established a reputation first as a binder and later as a printer of fine books. The Doves Bindery was founded here in March 1893 and from 1909 this early-18th-century house was also home to the Doves Press, which he established with Emery Walker* in 1900. Cobden-Sanderson did not live here permanently until 1917, by which time he had destroyed the press: having fallen out with Walker, he tipped the distinctive type into the river to prevent him making use of it.

ERIC RAVILIOUS

(1903–42) artist   48 Upper Mall **4**

RAVILIOUS lived in the lower flat of this end-of-terrace house of 1880–83 with his wife and fellow artist Tirzah Garwood between 1931 and 1935, when they moved to Essex. Born in Acton, Ravilious trained at the Royal College of Art, where his tutor was Paul Nash*. Like Nash, he became a war artist, but was also commissioned captain in the marines and died at the age of 39 in an air-sea rescue mission off Iceland. In addition to his landscapes – which included *The Stork at Hammersmith* (1932) – Ravilious produced wood engravings for the Golden Cockerell Press and designs for Josiah Wedgwood & Co., including a series based on his paintings of the Oxford and Cambridge Boat Race as seen from the Hammersmith riverside.

EDWARD JOHNSTON

(1872–1944) master calligrapher   3 Hammersmith Terrace **5**

JOHNSTON was born in Uruguay and trained initially in medicine, a career he abandoned in favour of the practice and teaching of lettering and illumination, in which he was encouraged by W. R. Lethaby*. In 1899 he started teaching at the Central School of Arts and Crafts; his students included Eric Gill and Thomas James Cobden-Sanderson*, for whose Doves Press he designed initials and headings.

With his lectures and publications he proved influential in Europe and the United States, and created a school of calligraphy in Britain. Gill – who lived nearby from 1905 to 1907 – later said of Johnston: 'He profoundly altered the whole course of my life and all my ways of thinking.' In 1912 Johnston moved to Ditchling, Sussex, where Gill had settled five years earlier and where Frank Brangwyn* was later to live.

SIR EMERY WALKER

(1851–1933) typographer and antiquary   7 Hammersmith Terrace **6**

HAVING supposedly decided as a young boy that he wished to live 'in one of those tall old houses that look upon the river', Walker moved here in 1903. He stayed for the rest of his life; the house has been preserved much as he left it, and may be visited. In 1883 he met William Morris*, and the pair became friends and associates,

with shared interests in design and socialism. With Walker's advice and help, Morris founded the Kelmscott Press in 1890, which was run successively from three addresses in Upper Mall. In 1900 Walker set up the Doves Press in partnership with Cobden-Sanderson*, but increasingly suffered the consequences of his colleague's paranoia.

SIR ALAN HERBERT (A. P. H.)

(1890–1971) author, humorist and reformist MP   12 Hammersmith Terrace **7**

HERBERT signed the lease on this house in January 1916 while on leave from military service in France, and moved in with his wife Gwendolen the following

month. He was called to the Bar in 1918, joined the staff of *Punch* – for which he wrote the notable series of articles 'Misleading Cases in the Common Law' – in 1924, and was elected as an Independent MP for Oxford University in 1935. Herbert's novel *Holy Deadlock* (1934) took as its theme the antiquated state of the law of divorce, and was instrumental in influencing public opinion, to the extent that his reforming Matrimonial Causes Bill became law in 1937. His novels include *The House by the River* (1920) and *The Water Gipsies* (1930), both

> Herbert loved swimming in the Thames and preferred to commute to the House of Commons on his boat, *Water Gipsy*.

clearly influenced by the area in which he lived. Herbert also wrote lyrics, including those for the 1950 musical *Bless the Bride*.

'OUIDA' (MARIE LOUISE DE LA RAMÉE)

(1839–1908) novelist   Bessborough House, 11 Ravenscourt Square   **8**

ENERALLY known by her pen name Ouida, a childish corruption of her name Louise, Marie de la Ramée was born in Bury St Edmunds, the only child of the Frenchman Louis Ramé and his English wife. (She romanticised her often-absent father as a French spy, and changed her name to Marie de la Ramée to hint at aristocratic roots.) In 1857, she moved to London with her mother and grandmother and by 1859 they were living in this early-Victorian semi-detached villa. It was while here that she published her first story, 'Dashwood's Drag' (1859). She made her reputation with *Under Two Flags* (1867), which sold millions of copies, earning the author a small fortune. A satirical attack by Lord Strangford in the *Pall Mall Gazette* in 1867 had the unintended consequence of establishing a vogue

> 'Dressed in green silk, with a clever, sinister face, her hair let down, small hands and feet, and a voice like a carving-knife'
>
> *The poet William Allingham describes Ouida*

for her stories, which were admired for their fast pace and romantic heroes. After her grandmother's death in 1866, she and her mother moved to Welbeck Street, Marylebone. By the following year Ouida was living at the newly opened Langham Hotel, where she entertained on a lavish scale and gleaned information for her novels from her guests, who were almost all men. Ouida's extravagance, however, outran her income, and in 1871 she and her mother moved to Italy, where she declined into increasing eccentricity and poverty.

CHRISTOPHER WHITWORTH WHALL

(1849–1924)
stained-glass artist

19 Ravenscourt Road
(formerly Shaftesbury Road)

WHALL entered the Royal Academy Schools in 1867, where he was influenced by Frederic (later Lord) Leighton*. He converted to Roman Catholicism in 1879, and in the same year designed windows for the Rosminian Order of Charity at the newly restored St Etheldreda's, Ely Place, Holborn. Whall went on to become the leading stained-glass artist of the Arts and Crafts period and was hugely influential through his writing, inspirational teaching and association with leading architects of the day, such as John Dando Sedding, for whom he designed glass for Holy Trinity, Sloane Street. Perhaps his outstanding achievement was the glass for the Lady Chapel and Chapter House at Gloucester Cathedral (1898–1913), which led to commissions abroad. His work is distinguished by bold use of colour and contrasts. In later years, Whall collaborated with his daughter Veronica and – despite the onset of leukaemia – continued to work right up to his death at his final home, 37 Harvard Road, Gunnersbury.

SRI AUROBINDO

(1872–1950) Indian spiritual leader

49 St Stephen's Avenue

AUROBINDO'S historical significance lies in several areas: he was a campaigner for Indian self-determination, who inspired, among others, Mahatma Gandhi*. He also developed his own system of yoga – which he first began to practise while imprisoned under the British Raj on a charge of sedition in 1907 – and wrote on spiritual and philosophical subjects: the key text is *The Life Divine* (1939–40). In Pondicherry, the French enclave in India where Aurobindo took refuge after 1909, he founded an ashram that continues his work today. Educated in England, he lived in St Stephen's Avenue with a 'long suffering' landlady – along with two of his brothers and a guardian – for nearly three years from 1884, having won a scholarship to St Paul's School, then located in Hammersmith. It was while living here, at the age of 14, that Aurobindo Ackroyd Ghose – as he was then known – experienced the first stirrings of resentment at British rule in India; in his school studies, he made heroes of figures of resistance and rebellion, such as Joan of Arc and Giuseppe Mazzini*.

THE SILVER STUDIO

THE Silver Studio, run by Arthur Silver and later his sons Rex and Harry, was founded here in 1880 and produced nearly 30,000 designs, mainly for furnishing textiles and wallpapers, but also for complete interiors, dress fabrics, plasterwork, metalwork, furniture and advertisements. Its major customers were Liberty and Sanderson. Under the direction of Arthur – a friend and contemporary of William Morris* and Walter Crane* – the Silver Studio became a major exponent of British Art Nouveau. To accommodate the firm's increasing production, Arthur added a studio in 1886,

Arthur Silver (1853–96)
Rex Silver (1879–1965)
Harry Silver (1881–1971)
designers

and in 1893 Rex bought the property immediately behind, 3 Haarlem Road. The studio moved to the Corner House, 1 Haarlem Road, in 1912, where it remained until its closure in 1963. This last address was also Rex's home, where he continued to live until his death. Middlesex University holds the studio archive.

A trade card probably by Arthur Silver, 1885.

SIR FRANK SHORT

(1857–1945) engraver and painter

56 Brook Green **12**

AFTER working initially as an engineer, Short studied at the National Art Training School (later the Royal College of Art), South Kensington, where he was encouraged by Ruskin* to revive the art of mezzotint engraving. His superb prints of works by Turner* quickly established his reputation, and regular visitors to his studios – first at Wentworth Studios, Manresa Road, Chelsea, and finally at Brook Green – included Whistler*, who sought his advice on the technical aspects of etching and printing. Short often engraved outdoors, producing works such as *The Night Picket Boat at Hammersmith* (1916) and *Ebb Tide, Putney Bridge* (1925). From 1910 to 1938, he was President of the Society of Painter-Etchers, and for many years served as the Director of the Etching and Engraving School of the Royal College of Art.

GUSTAV HOLST

(1874–1934) composer

St Paul's Girls' School, Brook Green **13**

BORN in Cheltenham of Swedish ancestry, Holst was brought up in a musical environment. At the Royal College of Music, where he studied composition, his fellow students included Ralph Vaughan Williams*. Needing an income to support his work as a composer, Holst became a teacher and was appointed in 1905 Director of Music at St Paul's Girls' School, which had opened just two years previously. At the school, he composed music for his pupils to perform, such as his well-known *St Paul's Suite* for strings (1912–13). In 1913 the Holst Wing was added to the right of the main building. It was here – in a specially constructed soundproof music room, a haven of peace and solitude – that Holst composed most of his works from c.1914 to 1933, including his masterpiece, *The Planets* (1914–17).

ISLINGTON

THE present-day borough of Islington stretches from the northern edge of the City of London to the slopes of Highgate Hill and Crouch Hill some four miles to the north. The old village of Islington and neighbouring Clerkenwell were once renowned as spas and places of rural recreation, but the entire area was built up over the course of the 19th century, by which time offices and workshops had begun to displace dwellings in the southern reaches of the borough, next to the City. When Islington was 'redis-covered' in the 1960s, a process of gentrification began; this is particularly noticeable in the area around Islington Green, where many blue plaques can be found.

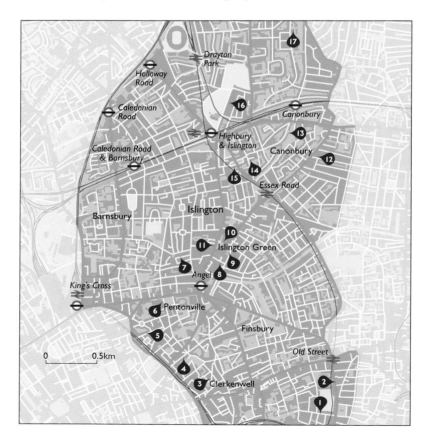

WILLIAM CASLON

(1692–1766) typefounder   21–23 (formerly 62) Chiswell Street **1**

A TYPE foundry stood on this site between 1737 and 1909, when the business transferred across the road: both buildings were lost during the Second World War. The foundry belonged to William Caslon, whose name was associated with distinctive and highly readable Hebrew, Italic and roman fonts that were very widely used for printed books until about 1780. Versions of them have been revived since, and several digital 'Caslon' fonts are available. Originally from Worcestershire and first apprenticed as an engraver, Caslon lived as well as worked in Chiswell Street, in what was a large, plain four-storey building covering two plots. A chamber-music enthusiast, he had an organ installed at the house, and his parties were fuelled by home-brewed ale. He retired in 1750, after which the business was taken on by his son, William Caslon the younger (1720–1778).

JOHN WESLEY

(1703–91) founder of Methodism   47 City Road **2**

O NE of the few elaborate, highly coloured Doulton plaques to survive commemorates Wesley's home from 1779 to 1791. The fine four-storey Georgian townhouse has been preserved as a memorial to him and is open to visitors. Next door is Wesley's chapel (1777–8), the mother church of Methodism. Wesley, who was ordained an Anglican priest in 1728, was influenced by the Moravian sect he encountered in North America. Assisted by his brother Charles Wesley*, he founded an evangelical movement – based around his charismatic preaching, often in the open air – that emphasised the role of personal salvation and appealed especially to poorer

people. Wesley laid the foundation stone of the new City Road chapel, which was designed by George Dance the Younger*, in April 1777 and spent his first night at the newly completed number 47 in October 1779. He died here at the age of 87 and is buried in a small graveyard behind the adjacent chapel.

JOHN GROOM

(1845–1919) philanthropist

8 Sekforde Street 3

A DEVOUT Anglican, John Alfred Groom started his first charity for destitute and disabled girls – the Watercress and Flower Girls' Christian Mission – in 1866, engaging the girls in the manufacture of artificial flowers, then a big local industry. At first they worked from houses in Sekforde Street, but in 1908–10 a purpose-built 'flower factory' was built at numbers 1–7. By 1913 it employed nearly 260 girls; jarringly to modern sensibilities, it was known as the 'New Crippleage'. In the last decade of his life, Groom moved to an orphanage he had founded at Clacton, Essex; in his leisure time, he swapped his top hat for a flat cap to watch Chelsea FC. The charity he founded retained its head office in Sekforde Street until 1967; its work continues today, under the name Livability. Maud Waterer and Ruth Siddell, two former Groom's flower girls, attended the unveiling of the plaque in 1997.

JOSEPH GRIMALDI

(1778–1837) clown

56 Exmouth Market (formerly 8 Braynes Row) 4

T HE shopfront has been added to this 18th-century house since Grimaldi lived here. Born into a family of entertainers originally from Italy, 'Joey' Grimaldi became the unchallenged 'king of clowns' after eclipsing his rival and sometime sidekick, John Baptist Dubois. A vital figure in shaping pantomime as we know it, Grimaldi shone in serious roles too. He lived in Exmouth Market, then known successively as Braynes Row and Exmouth Street, from 1818 to 1829. The ailing clown gave his farewell performance in 1828 at the Myddleton's Head, a pub close to Sadler's Wells Theatre that he liked to frequent, after which he

Mr J.S. GRIMALDI.

wept 'with an intensity of suffering that it was painful to witness and impossible to alleviate'.

AMELIA EDWARDS

(1831–92) Egyptologist and writer

19 Wharton Street **5**

THIS is the house where Edwards lived in the 1850s with her family, while writing novels and travelogues. Built by the Somerset-born builder Thomas Herridge between 1835 and 1839, it is an example of the distinctive Greek revival design that distinguishes the immediate area, which is known as the Lloyd Baker estate. Born at a now-vanished address in Hoxton, Edwards is best known for her foundational role in the discipline of Egyptology. Her account of her first visit to Egypt in 1873, *A Thousand Miles up the Nile* (1877), was a major legacy; another was the chair in Egyptology that she endowed at UCL, and which was first held by her protégé Flinders Petrie*. Edwards also co-founded the Egypt Exploration Fund in 1882: as the Egypt Exploration Society, its work – which she conceived as both 'protective and exploratory' – continues today.

EDWARD IRVING

(1792–1834) founder of the
Catholic Apostolic Church

4 Claremont Square **6**

AS a Church of Scotland minister Irving first preached in London in 1822, and his fiery and charismatic sermons on the imminence of Christ's second coming attracted a fashionable congregation, including the Foreign Secretary George Canning*. Members of Irving's flock, known as 'Irvingites', were later reported to swoon and speak in tongues. Irving lived at what was then 4 Myddleton Terrace – a newly built house at the edge of the metropolitan area – from 1824 to 1827. From this address, Irving attended the first of the Albury conferences in Surrey, which ultimately led to the establishment of the Catholic Apostolic Church in 1835; by this time Irving himself was dead, but is generally credited as the new denomination's originating spirit, having been expelled from the Church of Scotland for heresy in 1833. Believing that Armageddon was imminent, the Catholic Apostolic Church made no provision for ordinations after the last of its founders died in 1901 and, as a consequence, gradually disappeared, though its influence may be traced in modern Pentecostalism. The large church in Gordon Square, Bloomsbury, now dedicated to Christ the King, was its 'cathedral'.

THOMAS HOSMER SHEPHERD

(1793–1864) artist
'who portrayed London'

26 Batchelor Street
(formerly Chapman Street) **7**

BOTH Shepherd and his brother, George Sidney, showed artistic talent from an early age, and Thomas became known for his lively drawings and watercolours of Regency and early Victorian London. His first and greatest published success as a topographical artist was *Metropolitan Improvements; or, London in the Nineteenth Century...* (1827), with text by James Elmes; his views also covered Bristol, Bath and Edinburgh. Shepherd lived at number 26 from about 1819 to 1842 and advertised his services as a drawing master from the address, confirming that he worked as well as lived in the yellow-brick Regency terraced house. Shepherd spent most of his life in Islington, dying at 5 Cloudesley Street, just north of Batchelor Street.

CHARLES LAMB*, 'ELIA'

(1775–1834) essayist

64 Duncan Terrace **8**

IN 1823, the essayist Lamb – a leading figure in literary London who counted Samuel Taylor Coleridge* and William Hazlitt* among his intimates – moved to Duncan Terrace, then a part of Colebrooke Row. He lived here with his sister Mary*, with whom he had written *Tales from Shakespeare* in 1807. Lamb described their home as 'a cottage ... with six good rooms ... You enter without passage into a cheerful dining-room ... and above is a lightsome drawing-room, three windows, full of choice prints'. Beside it runs the New River – now

'I feel like a great lord, never having had a house before'

Charles Lamb, on his Islington 'cottage'

underground, but in Lamb's time, uncovered – and into which one of his visitors, the myopic writer George Dyer, once tumbled. On the house, now named Colebrooke Cottage and much altered since Lamb's time here, the terracotta-coloured plaque includes the pen name 'Elia', which was used by Lamb for his contributions to the *London Magazine*.

CAROLINE CHISHOLM

(1808–77) philanthropist,
'the emigrants' friend'

32 Charlton Place
(formerly 3 Charlton Crescent)

AN 'army wife', Chisholm opened a school for the daughters of British soldiers in Madras and a home and employment agency for destitute girls in Sydney before she and her husband Archibald returned to England in 1846. They lived at this house, part of an elegant, sweeping terrace, between 1849 and 1852; from it Caroline ran the Family Colonisation Society, which encouraged women to emigrate to Australia in order to redress the gender imbalance. Caroline, 'a sedate, matronly lady,

with ... a fascinating manner that at once seizes upon you', interviewed prospective migrants here, showing them models of the berths in which they would sleep on the long voyage. Charles Dickens* – a supporter – was a visitor to the house. Rather unflatteringly, it has been suggested that Caroline partly inspired the character of Mrs Jellyby in *Bleak House* (1852–3), who neglects her own family in fervent pursuit of philanthropic projects abroad. Caroline Chisholm's portrait has adorned Australian banknotes.

COLLINS MUSIC HALL

10–11 Islington Green

ON the north side of Islington Green, a rectangular blue plaque records that Collins Music Hall, an early and famous example of its kind, once stood here. The first music hall on the site was built as the annexe to the Lansdowne Arms in 1861–2, and was acquired shortly afterwards by the singer and occasional bankrupt Samuel Thomas Collins Vagg (1826–65), who performed as Sam Collins. Though death cut short his proprietorship after barely 18 months, the venue – which was completely rebuilt in 1897 – continued to bear his name. From the 1930s, as the popularity of music hall declined,

it was used variously for revue (*above in 1941*), repertory and strip shows, until it was gutted by a fire in 1958; the hall itself was destroyed, but the façade is authentic.

GRACIE FIELDS

(1898–1979) singer and entertainer 72A Upper Street

AMONG those who trod the boards at Collins Music Hall* in its heyday were Charlie Chaplin*, Marie Lloyd* and Gracie Fields; appropriately, her plaque lies just across Islington Green from the hall. Here she lived with her first husband, the comedian Archie Pitt, from 1926 to 1929, a period that encompassed her first appearance at the Royal Command Variety Performance in 1928 and the release of her first 78 rpm discs the same year. Although Fields (real name Grace Stansfield) is more readily associated with Lancashire, London was her home for most of the inter-war period – she had homes in Finchley Road and Hampstead – during which time she enjoyed big box-office hits with films such as *Sally in our Alley* (1931) and *Sing as we Go* (1934), the titles of which were taken from her biggest hit songs.

Sally, Sally …
Don't ever wander
Away from the alley and me.

Though Gracie Fields, born above a fish-and-chip shop in Rochdale, was billed as the ultimate Lancashire lass, she lived for many years in London.

Fields (left) in 1929 while appearing in The Show's the Thing *at the Lyceum Theatre.*

GEORGE LEYBOURNE

(1842–84) 'Champagne Charlie', music-hall comedian   136 Englefield Rd **12**

THE Gateshead-born Leybourne's breakthrough came with the 1866 song 'Champagne Charlie', which he performed as a 'swell' in a sensationally subversive imitation of upper-class dress and manners. Corporate sponsorship followed (from champagne makers, of course), as did other hits, including 'The Daring Young Man on the Flying Trapeze'; like Gracie Fields* he was a regular at Collins Music Hall*. Leybourne, who has been described as Britain's first pop star, became disillusioned with the emptiness of the celebrity lifestyle and died at the house at the age of 42, most probably from the effects of heavy drinking. A newspaper report stated that he had been living for some time in Englefield Road, where he rented rooms. His daughter Florence was married to another star of the music hall, Albert Chevalier*.

LOUIS MACNEICE

(1907–63) poet

52 Canonbury Park South **13**

BORN in Belfast into a family originally from Galway, MacNeice spent most of his life in England, a hybrid heritage that was reflected in his poetry. The MacNeice household – his wife, the singer and actress Hedli Anderson (1907–90), their two children and an Italian maid, Teresa – moved from Essex to Canonbury in 1947, while MacNeice himself was on a production assignment in India with the BBC: his day job. At number 52, MacNeice worked on a new translation of Goethe's *Faust* (1951), his rudimentary knowledge of German, he maintained, making for a freer, more readable rendition. The poetry collection *Ten Burnt Offerings* (1952) was mostly written while MacNeice was working in Athens (1951–2). On his return the family moved to Clarence Terrace, overlooking Regent's Park.

SIR BASIL SPENCE

(1907–76) architect

1 Canonbury Place **14**

THE large Georgian house, dating from the 1760s, makes for a contrast with many of Spence's own modernist buildings. Some of these, like the Knightsbridge Barracks (1967–70), continue to be controversial, but Coventry Cathedral (1962), the University of Sussex (1975) and the 'beehive' extension to the New Zealand parliament (1979) are widely regarded as classics. Spence moved to number 1 in 1956 with his wife Joan – 'the reinforcement in the concrete', as he called her – and their two children. The house functioned as a home and office, and by 1965 the expansion of his practice prompted Spence to acquire number 2, next door; connected by an internal door, they remained his domestic and professional London base for the rest of his life.

SAMUEL PHELPS
(1804–78) tragedian　　　　　　　　8 Canonbury Square

BORN in Devonport, Phelps made his London stage debut in 1837. He lived in Canonbury Square, in part of a terrace dating from around 1845, until 1867, during which time he was the successful actor-manager of Sadler's Wells Theatre (1844–62), emerging from the shadow of William Macready. Offstage, Phelps was noted for his 'retiring manner and modest mode of living', but neither his fame nor his modesty overcame snobbish contemporary attitudes towards thespians, and his daughter was refused admission to a nearby private school. The appeal of his Shakespeare productions,

however, succeeded in crossing class boundaries and brought commercial success to Sadler's Wells, a venue hitherto known for lowbrow entertainment.

JOSEPH CHAMBERLAIN*
(1836–1914) statesman　　　　　　　25 Highbury Place **16**

BEST remembered for his social reforms and for his stint as Colonial Secretary during the Boer War, Chamberlain lived at this address from 1845 to 1854, and went to school in nearby Canonbury Square before going on to University College School, then based in Gower Street. After leaving the latter – where he excelled at mathematics, and picked up a dislike of sport – he worked in the office of his father's shoemaking business in Milk Street in the City. Not long after turning 18, Chamberlain moved to Birmingham, where the family held an interest in a screw-manufacturing firm and where he built his political career – though he demonstrated his continued affection for the backdrop to his boyhood by naming his home there 'Highbury'.

DAVID GESTETNER

(1854–1939) developer of
office copying machinery

FAMOUSLY, Islington was home to many city clerks (hence 'Clerkenwell') including Mr Pooter of Holloway Road, from *The Diary of a Nobody*. Manual copying of documents – the chief occupation of the clerk – is now a thing of the past, partly thanks to the copying machines designed and made by Gestetner. Restlessly inventive, he also filed the first UK patent for nail clippers. Gestetner, who was of Hungarian-Jewish extraction, established himself and his family in Highbury New Park in 1898, and it remained his home for the rest of his life. The opulent Italo-Romanesque villa, built by Charles Hambridge in about 1860, was then known as 'Norselands'.

Gestetner's big breakthrough came in 1881 with the 'cyclostyle' – a pen with a tiny sharp-toothed wheel at the end, used to perforate a stencil through which ink could be forced. Later, this technology was adapted for use with typewriters; the Gestetner No. 3 model, which appeared in 1902, allowed copies to be run off by the turn of a handle. Based latterly at Tottenham Hale, the Gestetner company's earlier premises (of *c.*1900) are another Islington survival, at 30–32 Cross Street.

HACKNEY

MODERN Hackney consists of the former metropolitan boroughs of Stoke Newington, Shoreditch and Hackney. Shoreditch lies just outside the boundaries of the City and from medieval times was a place of recreation for Londoners. Hackney and Stoke Newington were both notable centres of religious dissent: several sects set up meeting houses and colleges as they were close enough to the City to be convenient, yet beyond its jurisdiction. In the 19th century, speculative development covered the whole of modern Hackney with homes for clerks, artisans and small tradesmen.

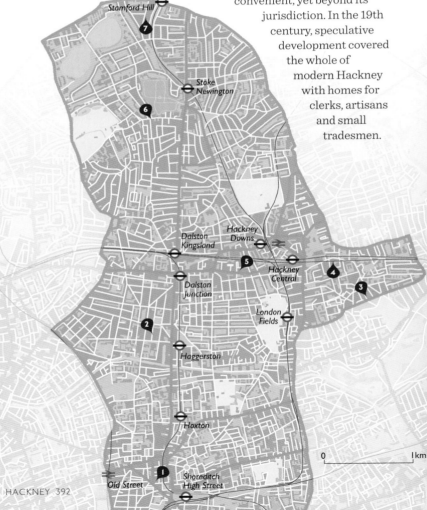

SITE OF
'THE THEATRE'

86–90 Curtain Road, Shoreditch **1**

AT the corner with New Inn Yard, a plaque of rectangular metal on a showroom-warehouse building of c.1892 commemorates the site of The Theatre, the first London building specifically devoted to the performance of plays, which from 1577 to 1598 stood – as excavations in 2008 showed – a little way to the east. Holywell (or Haliwelle) Priory, founded in the mid-12th century in fields north of London, was dissolved in 1539 and the land sold off. In 1576, a northern portion of its former precinct was leased to the actor James Burbage (d.1597) who built a theatre here – beyond the jurisdiction of the City authorities – in partnership with his brother-in-law John Brayne (d.1586). It was probably built of timber and polygonal in shape, with an open courtyard. Some of Shakespeare's early plays may have been staged, and it is more than likely that Shakespeare would have appeared here in the Lord Chamberlain's company of players. Burbage's lease expired in 1597, and the following year the theatre was broken up, and used in the construction of the Globe Theatre, Southwark.

PHILIP HENRY GOSSE (1810–88) zoologist
SIR EDMUND GOSSE

(1849–1928) writer
and critic

56 Mortimer Road
(formerly 13 Trafalgar Terrace), De Beauvoir Town **2**

P. H. Gosse was a self-trained naturalist and a great populariser of natural history. In November 1848, he married Emily Bowes, a writer of Christian tracts and fellow member of the Plymouth Brethren. 'Without a single day's honeymoon', the couple came to live in this modest terraced house, built a few years before. It belonged to Philip's formidable mother Hannah, who removed herself to nearby lodgings soon after. The couple's only child, Edmund, was born here the following year. ('E. delivered of a son. Received green swallow from Jamaica,' Gosse recorded in his diary.) In May 1853 Gosse helped to establish the world's first public aquarium at London Zoo, and in autumn of that year the family decamped to a larger house in Islington. Edmund Gosse enjoyed a successful career as a biographer, literary critic and journalist. His most enduring work is the autobiographical *Father and Son* (1907), subtitled 'A Study of Two Temperaments'.

MARIA DICKIN

(1870–1951) promoter of animal
welfare and founder of the PDSA

41 Cassland Road
(formerly 1 Farrington Terrace) **3**

WHILE carrying out charitable work among the poor
residents of London's East End, Maria Dickin noticed the sorry condition of many of their animals. On 17
November 1917 she opened her first
'People's Dispensary for Sick Animals of the Poor' in a Whitechapel
basement; the sign on the door read:
'Bring your sick animals. Do not let
them suffer. All animals treated. All
treatment free.' Dickin later toured
the country in a converted gypsy
caravan to promote her aims. Today,
her foundation, now known by the
initials PDSA, provides 2.3 million
free treatments every year. Dickin
was born at this mid-19th-century
end-of-terrace house; her father
was a Methodist preacher at a
church that then stood nearby.

Known as the 'animals' Victoria
Cross', the Dickin Medal is
awarded to animals for gallantry
and devotion to duty in service
with the armed forces or
civil defence authorities.
Its roll of honour
currently features
34 dogs, 32 pigeons,
4 horses and a cat
called Simon.

JOSEPH PRIESTLEY

(1733–1804) scientist,
philosopher and theologian

8 Chatham Place (formerly the
Old Gravel Pit Chapel, Ram Place) **4**

YORKSHIRE-BORN Priestley
was a major figure of the British Enlightenment, now remembered primarily for his discovery of
oxygen, but better known in his day
for his controversial views on theology and politics. He was minister
at a Presbyterian chapel here, the
remains of which are embedded in a

building now used as a factory outlet
by a clothing company: the plaque
lies along the alley to the north of
the building, and is not readily open
to public view. Priestley arrived in
Hackney in 1791, a refugee from
Birmingham, driven from his home
by riots caused by his nonconformist views and support for the

French Revolution. In London, his notoriety caused him to be shunned by most members of the Royal Society – though he was dined by the leading Whig parliamentarians Richard Brinsley Sheridan* and Charles James Fox*. Priestley settled in Clapton and continued to publish theological and scientific pamphlets, lecturing on history and natural philosophy at Hackney New College. When England went to war with revolutionary France his situation became 'unpleasant', and – having preached his last sermon on 30 March 1794 – he decamped with his family to the United States, where he spent the remainder of his life.

MARIE LLOYD

(1870–1922) music-hall artiste   55 Graham Road, Dalston ⑤

BORN Matilda Wood in Hoxton, in a house now demolished, Marie Lloyd made her stage debut at the age of 14. During her career she inspired enormous affection, performing songs such as 'My Old Man' and 'A Little of What you Fancy Does you Good'. In 1887, aged 17, she married a racecourse tout, Percy Courtenay, by whom she was already pregnant, and they moved here the following year. Lloyd typically performed in three shows a night in London; she also made long tours of the provinces, and played in New York in the autumn of 1890. Generous and gregarious, Lloyd filled her home with family, friends and fellow performers. Courtenay felt excluded from this 'family', and tensions appeared. They moved to a larger house in Lewisham in 1891, but separated three years later and were divorced in 1905. Lloyd married twice more and died at her home in Golders Green.

Awarded a blue plaque by the GLC, Marie Lloyd (*above*) was once hauled before the Licensing Committee of its predecessor, the LCC, to answer the charge that her material was vulgar. The performer of such numbers as 'She'd Never Had Her Ticket Punched Before' managed to persuade them that it was all in the delivery.

DANIEL DEFOE

(1661–1731) novelist

95 Stoke Newington Church Street **6**

DEFOE had enjoyed a varied career as businessman, journalist, spy and political agitator by the time he took a lease on a house that stood on this site in 1708. His son-in-law Henry Baker called it 'a very handsome house', but most accounts describe a nondescript building in the Queen Anne style, to which Defoe's addition of two flat-roofed wings did no favours. Here he wrote his first and most famous novel, *Robinson Crusoe* (1719), followed by *Captain Singleton* (1720) and *Moll Flanders* (1722), among others. In his spare time, Defoe experimented with pruning and grafting in his kitchen garden, beyond which a 1.6ha (four-acre) pleasure ground provided grazing for horses and – in 1709 – a place of encampment for Protestant refugees from Louis XIV, whose cause Defoe publicly pleaded. He remained here until 1730, when, pursued for political reasons over a long-forgotten debt, he made over the lease of the house to Baker as a dowry for his daughter Sophia, and ended his days unhappily in City lodgings.

EBENEZER HOWARD

(1850–1928) pioneer of the garden city movement

50 Durley Road, Stamford Hill **7**

HOWARD moved to this 1880s house in 1899, the year in which he formed the Garden City Association as a vehicle to promote his dream of a new form of settlement. This was intended to combine the best of town and country, and – more importantly – to embody service to community rather than self-interest, as Howard explained in *Tomorrow: A Peaceful Path to Real Reform* (1898), reissued as *Garden Cities of Tomorrow* (1902). In 1903, Howard's Garden City Pioneer Company purchased land at Letchworth, Hertfordshire, on which to build the first garden city: he moved there after the death of his wife Lizzie in the autumn of 1904. Other garden cities developed according to his principles included Welwyn Garden City (Howard's home from 1920), Wythenshawe, near Manchester, and Radburn, New Jersey. Howard was knighted a year before his death.

TOWER HAMLETS

THE borough of Tower Hamlets, situated immediately east of the City, was largely rural until the 17th century – the 'hamlets' were exactly that – when London began to evolve into Europe's greatest commercial city. Much early industry along the Thames was of a maritime nature; inland, silk weaving was a principal activity. In the 19th century the area, by then built up and racked with poverty, disease and overcrowding, became the 'East End', the 'other' or dark mirror to the prosperous West End. Wartime bombing and the closure of the docks have been countered by regeneration programmes, including the Olympics site and the Canary Wharf development, and today the borough enshrines many of the highs and lows of modern London. Despite its long-standing historical importance, Tower Hamlets has relatively few blue plaques, largely because so many of the area's older buildings have been demolished or lost to war damage.

REVEREND P. T. B. 'TUBBY' CLAYTON

(1885–1972) the founder of Toc H 43 (formerly 42) Trinity Square

PHILIP Thomas Byard Clayton was born in Australia and grew up in the City of London; he was nicknamed 'Tubby' during his university years, despite being no such thing. As an army chaplain during the First World War, he established Talbot House, a rest house at Poperinghe, Belgium, to give soldiers respite from the horrors of the Front. Abbreviated to TH, which became Toc H in Morse signallers' slang, this wartime brotherhood transferred to peacetime London and, thanks to Clayton's magnetic personality, grew into a highly successful movement with 1,000 British branches, and many more overseas. In 1922 Clayton was offered the living of All-Hallows-by-the-Tower, then in a state of 'unrelieved decay', and the church quickly became the spiritual focus for Toc H. Six years later, Charlotte Tetley presented All-Hallows with this large late-18th-century house; it was renamed Talbot House and became the headquarters of Toc H's Overseas Commissioners as well as Clayton's home. After wartime bomb damage, Clayton also devoted himself to seeing the church rebuilt.

ISAAC ROSENBERG

(1890–1918) poet 77 Whitechapel High Street
and painter (formerly Whitechapel Public Library) **2**

THE son of poor Russian Jewish immigrants, Rosenberg moved in 1897 from Bristol to London, where he studied at the Slade. He lived at a number of addresses in and around Stepney, all now demolished. Rosenberg, who left school at 14 and was apprenticed to a firm of engravers, came here to read and write poetry. His interests and abilities were encouraged by the librarian, Morley Dainow. It was, he told a friend, his greatest joy 'to run off to the library whenever he could, to read ... anything he could find about poets and poetry'. The library also became the meeting place for his circle of friends, known as the 'Whitechapel Group', which included David Bomberg* and Mark Gertler*. Next door was the Whitechapel Gallery (of which the library is now a part) where Rosenberg exhibited. Despite a pacifist upbringing, poverty drove him to enlist in 1915. While serving in the trenches, Rosenberg wrote his finest poetry, most notably 'Daughters of War' and 'Dead Man's Dump'; he was killed on a night patrol at the age of 27.

DR JIMMY MALLON, CH

(1874–1961) Warden of Toynbee Hall
and a champion of social reform

BORN in Manchester of Irish parents, Mallon moved here in 1906, when he was appointed Secretary of the National League to Establish a Minimum Wage. In October 1919 he became Warden of Toynbee Hall, the university settlement house, a position he held for 35 years. Mallon strengthened the institution's community and educational roles, helping to establish it as 'the poor man's university'. Jimmy (never James) had an effervescent character and was remembered as 'the most popular man east of Aldgate Pump'. Toynbee Hall was founded in 1884 in memory of Arnold Toynbee* by Canon Samuel Barnett* and Henrietta Barnett*, to promote the understanding and remedy of social problems. Originally it was screened from the road by a range of buildings; these were destroyed in the war.

ANNA MARIA GARTHWAITE

(1688–1763) designer of
Spitalfields silks

BROUGHT up a rector's daughter in Lincolnshire, Garthwaite came to London in her early forties, settling in this substantial corner house of *c*.1722 with her sister, the widowed Mary Dannye, and their niece Mary Bacon; it remained Anna's residence and workplace until her death. Here, she established herself as a designer of fashionable fabrics, with a flair for botanical forms (*right*). At her peak she was producing 80 designs for brocaded silks a year, and helped to introduce the 'principles of painting' into the loom. Garthwaite kept meticulous records of her designs, the greater part of which are now in the V&A.

BUD FLANAGAN
(1896–1968) comedian
and leader of the 'Crazy Gang'

12 Hanbury Street, Spitalfields **5**

BUD was born and brought up here as Reuben Weintrop, the youngest of ten children of Polish-Jewish immigrants, who ran a fried fish shop at this refronted house of *c.*1712–13. He described the street as 'a patchwork of small shops, pubs, church halls, Salvation Army hostels, doss houses, cap factories and sweat shops'. Having anglicised his name to Bud Robert Winthrop, he walked to Southampton, aged 14, and worked his passage to New York, where he played in vaudeville. He returned in 1915 to join the Royal Field Artillery; at the rest house founded by 'Tubby' Clayton* in Belgium, Bud met Chesney Allen, with whom in 1926 he formed a comedy double act, taking the name Flanagan as revenge on a sergeant major of that name who had persecuted him for being Jewish. In 1932

'Who Do You Think You Are Kidding, Mr Hitler?'

The title song of the television series Dad's Army, *recorded by Flanagan*

the duo formed part of the Crazy Gang at the London Palladium. Songs like 'Underneath the Arches' (1937), 'We're Gonna Hang Out the Washing on the Siegfried Line' (1939) and 'Run, Rabbit, Run' (1939) made Flanagan a household name.

MARK GERTLER
(1891–1939) painter

32 Elder Street **6**

GERTLER was born in Spitalfields, the son of poor East European Jewish immigrants, and found his way to the Slade where his talent shone. In April 1912 he moved here with his brother and sister-in-law, and based himself in two rooms on the top floor of this then-dilapidated house until January 1915, when he moved to Hampstead. While here Gertler produced original and powerful work, concentrating on Jewish subjects, including *Rabbi and Rabbitzin* (1914). Later inspirations were the artist (Dora) Carrington, with whom he was in love, and the First World War. Through Lady Ottoline Morrell*, Gertler came into contact with the Bloomsbury Group, but from 1920 he struggled with tuberculosis; depressed and isolated, he gassed himself at the age of 47. A coal-hole cover on the pavement below the plaque bears a representation of *The Merry-Go-Round* (1916).

SIR THOMAS FOWELL BUXTON

(1786–1845) anti-slavery campaigner

91 Brick Lane **7**

BUXTON had been leading the parliamentary campaign against slavery for ten years when, in 1833, it was finally abolished in British-ruled territories – 'a victory of moral principle over economic power' according to his most recent biographer. 'With ordinary talents and extraordinary perseverance, all things are attainable,' was Buxton's own self-effacing comment. He went on to press for military enforcement of the ban and to campaign against slavery in other jurisdictions. Buxton lived at the Directors' House at the family brewery, Truman, Hanbury and Buxton, from 1808 to 1815, and it was his workplace and occasional residence for long after that. In June 1831, as part of his lobbying endeavours, Buxton treated members of Lord Grey's Cabinet to a dinner of steaks and porter: Henry Brougham, the future Lord Chancellor, was in such high spirits that he mounted a brewery horse and rode it around the yard. Buxton was also active in local philanthropy; it was his forceful speech at a meeting for the relief of distressed Spitalfields weavers that first brought him to the attention of his predecessor as leader of the anti-slavery campaign, William Wilberforce*.

MARY HUGHES

(1860–1941) 'friend of all in need'

71 Vallance Road **8**

IN 1926 Hughes converted what had once been a notorious pub into the teetotal 'Dewdrop Inn: For Education and Joy', which she lived in and ran as a refuge for any in need of a roof over their heads. Known simply as 'Comrade', Mary was the daughter of Thomas Hughes, the author of *Tom Brown's Schooldays* (1857) and an early Christian Socialist. She was born into comfortable circumstances in Mayfair and brought up to believe that service to the poor was an obligation. In 1896 she began to work as a voluntary social worker in Whitechapel, and from 1915 chose to live in solidarity with the outcast. The Dewdrop's glass windows were 'pasted up with every sort of political and religious propaganda', the basement was a recreation room, the former bar a canteen and meeting room, and Mary Hughes had a ground-floor scullery near the main door converted into a tiny unheated room for herself: 'indignation keeps me warm!' she professed. After her death, the Dewdrop was renamed Mary Hughes House.

EDITH CAVELL

(1865–1915) pioneer of modern nursing
in Belgium and heroine of the Great War

Royal London Hospital **9**

CAVELL came to nursing late, at the age of 30, having been brought up as the daughter of a Norfolk clergyman; nurses were then commonly on duty around 12 hours a day, had few holidays and little social life. She entered the London Hospital on 3 September 1896; at the end of her two years' training, Cavell had not impressed the Matron, Miss Eva Lückes, who recommended she join the Private Nursing Staff. Cavell thus spent her third year elsewhere, but returned to 'the

London' in autumn 1899 as a junior staff nurse before leaving for the St Pancras Infirmary in January 1901. She then went to Brussels in 1907 and in 1914 she took sole charge of the St Gilles hospital, which became a centre of resistance to the German occupation. Arrested and court-martialled, Cavell was executed by the Germans on 12 October 1915. This sparked outrage and Cavell became a heroine, a martyr, and an instrument of propaganda for military recruitment.

SIR JACK COHEN

(1898–1979) entrepreneur
and founder of Tesco Stores

91 Ashfield Street
(formerly 91 Rutland Street) **10**

FOLLOWING demobilisation from the Royal Flying Corps after the First World War, Jack Cohen sold foodstuffs on London street markets, where his relentless undercutting of competitors earned him the nickname of 'Jack the Slasher'. An early foray into wholesale trading involving a consignment of tea supplied by T. E. Stockwell spawned the name 'Tesco' – a hastily contrived conjunction of Stockwell's initials and the beginning of Jack's surname. 'Tesco Stores' was registered in 1932, with the first outlets in Burnt

'Pile it high. Sell it cheap.'

The business motto of Jack Cohen

Oak and Becontree; by 1939 there were 100 such shops in the London area. The first Tesco supermarket opened in 1956. Cohen's life was the success story of a second-generation immigrant: born Jacob Kohen, his father Avroam was an East End Jewish tailor, originally from Poland. Jack Cohen lived at the commemorated address from the age of about two to fifteen, and attended nearby Rutland Street elementary school.

JOHN RICHARD GREEN*

(1837–83) historian of the English people   38 Newark Street **11**

GREEN, who was vicar of the church of St Philip here from 1888–92 and lived at the church's Gothic vicarage of 1864, was among the first historians to emphasise the role of mass society and culture. Despite consumptive frailty, he spent the 1860s in the East End as a minister, learning at first hand through a 'gruelling regimen of social work' what life was like for ordinary people. 'One never realises what the monotony and narrowness of the life and thoughts of the ordinary shopkeeper is, till one spends a whole day in the midst of them,' he wrote. At Easter 1869, tired and disillusioned, Green resigned his living for the librarianship of Lambeth Palace, and moved to Marylebone.

LINCOLN STANHOPE WAINWRIGHT

(1847–1929) vicar of St Peter's, London Docks Clergy House, Wapping Lane **12**

ST Peter's church was begun in 1865–6 by Father Charles Lowder (1820-80), a seminal figure in the rise of Anglo-Catholicism. The building is screened from the street by the Sisters' House and the Clergy House, added in 1881. Wainwright was ordained a priest in 1872 and arrived in Wapping the following year to become assistant curate under Lowder; he succeeded him as vicar in 1884, never leaving the parish for a single night thereafter. Having founded the Church of England Working Men's Society, Wainwright chose to give his life to the relief of East London's poverty at a time when the state did not provide social services. His funeral procession is said to have been followed and watched by hundreds of working men and women.

RATCLIFF CROSS MARITIME HISTORY

King Edward VII Memorial Park, Shadwell **13**

THIS unusual plaque commemorates the connection between this area of the Thames, close to Ratcliff Cross, and early English maritime history. There were shipbuilding yards here by at

Sir Hugh Willoughby (d.1554)
Stephen Borough (1525–84)
William Borough (1536–98)
Sir Martin Frobisher (c.1535–94)
Navigators

least the time of Edward III – but its importance was not cemented until the later 16th century. It was from here that Willoughby's three ships – the *Bona Esperanza*, the *Bona Confidentia* and the *Edward Bonaventure*, the crew of the latter including the Borough brothers – sailed in 1553 to find a northern passage to China. Willoughby died near Murmansk the following year; the Boroughs sailed on to 'discover' Russia. In 1576 Frobisher set off from Ratcliff on the first of three north-westerly voyages that took him to Baffin Island via Greenland.

REVEREND ST JOHN GROSER

(1890–1966) priest and social reformer   2 Butcher Row, Limehouse

THIS large brick house of 1795–6 firstly belonged to a sugar merchant, later became a vicarage and is now the home of the Royal Foundation of St Katharine, a religious foundation dating from 1147 and – as a Royal Peculiar – one that survived the Reformation. Its buildings were located by the Tower of London until 1825, when they made way for St Katharine Docks and moved to Regent's Park. After the Second World War, the foundation's move here to Butcher Row – site of the bombed St James's Ratcliff – was masterminded by Father St John Beverley Groser; born in Australia, he had moved to the East End in 1922. Committed to helping the poor and homeless – he was known as 'the apostle of the unemployed' – Groser was a Christian Socialist and a friend of Mary Hughes*. He took up the position of Warden on the reopening of St Katharine's in 1948. In 1956 he became Master of the foundation, making it – to quote the *Oxford DNB* – 'a kind of early "think tank" and a centre of commitment to the health and welfare of the East End'. Groser oversaw the building of a radically furnished new chapel in 1950–54, incorporating medieval and later fittings from the foundation's earlier buildings.

THOMAS BARNARDO*

(1845–1905)   58 Solent House (formerly Hope Place),
founder of children's homes   Ben Jonson Road, Stepney

BORN and brought up in Dublin, Thomas John Barnardo came to the East End in 1866, intending to travel on to China as a missionary. While waiting, he visited and prayed with those struck down by cholera, enrolled as a student at the London Hospital, taught at the Ernest Street ragged school and preached in the streets. Barnardo started to teach poor children in an 'old, disused, and transmogrified donkey-shed' on the west side of Hope Place. By March 1868 he had raised enough funds to buy two cottages across the road; these became the East End Juvenile Mission, where he ran classes and religious services, and he soon acquired two further cottages to either side (the original buildings used by Barnardo are gone). In 1870 he opened the first of his homes for boys at nearby 18 and 20 Stepney Causeway (closed 1922). Barnardo helped some 60,000 boys and girls out of destitution, but his advocacy of 'philanthropic abduction' makes for uncomfortable reading today.

CAPTAIN JAMES COOK

(1728–79) circumnavigator and explorer

88 Mile End Road (formerly 7 Assembly Row) **16**

COOK was a Yorkshire labourer's son whose life at sea began in the North Sea coal trade. He enlisted in the Navy in 1755, and his surveys of the St Lawrence River in 1758–9 established his reputation as a navigator. Moving to London in 1762, he married Elizabeth Batts, the daughter of a Wapping publican, and found a home in the humble mariners' suburb of Shadwell. Two years later he acquired a newly built house in the more genteel district of Mile End Old Town. The property was at the end of an irregular terrace, next to a baker's shop and a cartway leading to wine-vaults. As an ambitious seaman, Cook – most famous for charting the coasts of New Zealand, the east coast of Australia and the Pacific coast of North America – was seldom at home, though he is said to have doted on his family when he was; there were 6 children in 13 years. After Cook's death in Hawaii, the widowed Elizabeth stayed on in Assembly Row until moving in 1788 to Clapham. The decayed house was demolished in 1959; the slate plaque marks its site.

ISRAEL ZANGWILL

(1864–1926) writer and philanthropist

288 Old Ford Road **17**

ZANGWILL was born in Aldgate to a family of Jewish immigrants from eastern Europe, and lived here from 1884 to 1887, while a pupil-teacher at the Jews' Free School, Bell Lane, Spitalfields.

During his final year at Old Ford Road, Zangwill collaborated with a fellow teacher, Louis Cowen, on *The Premier and the Painter* (1888), published under the pseudonym J. Freeman Bell. His *The Children of the Ghetto* (1892) offers a compelling account of East End Jewish life, and was followed by other works, including *Ghetto Tragedies* (1893). Latterly, Zangwill was a strong supporter of the Zionist cause.

FIRST FLYING BOMB
Grove Road, Mile End

ON 13 June 1944, a week after D-Day, the first Flying Bomb fell here, seriously damaging surrounding houses, destroying the train line from Liverpool Street to Stratford, killing 6 people and injuring 42. The advent of the V1, doodlebug or buzz bomb marked a significant and sinister new phase of the war for Londoners, who quickly learned to run for cover at the moment when they heard the motor cut out. More than 2,000 V1s launched from the ground or from piloted aircraft reached the London area, with Croydon the place worst affected.

THOMAS BARNARDO*
(1845–1905) founder of Dr Barnardo's homes for children   32 Bow Road

A SECOND plaque was given to Barnardo because his first (*see page 404*) marked an inauthentic building. He moved to this handsome end-of-terrace house in 1875: it was then known as 1 Olivers Terrace East. During his four years here Barnardo founded the Copperfield Road ragged school and the Girls' Village Home at Barkingside.

MAHATMA GANDHI*
(1869–1948)   Kingsley Hall, Powis Road, Bow **20**

KINGSLEY Hall was built in 1926–8 to the designs of Charles Cowles-Voysey. This Christian Socialist community centre for the East End poor was built in commemoration of Kingsley Lester; his sister Muriel was its Warden. When in 1931 Gandhi came to England to attend the Round Table Conference at St James's Palace – an enterprise that aimed (but failed) to establish a new constitution for India – he and his party were the guests of Lester, who had met Gandhi in India in

1926. Gandhi, with his spinning
wheel, occupied one of the 'four
cell-bedrooms' – that nearest the
stone staircase – on the building's
flat roof; his son Devadas stayed
in another. In the mornings, while
here, Gandhi explored the surrounding area on foot.

GREAT EASTERN
(launched 1858)   Burrell's Wharf, 262 Westferry Road, Millwall **21**

THE *Great Eastern*, the largest
steamship of the 19th century, was conceived and designed
by Isambard Kingdom Brunel*
and built by John Scott Russell
(1808–82), whose works stood on
this site. Described as 'an engineering dream, a triumph of design over
function, of ambition over common
sense', it was Brunel's 'ultimate
triumph, and his greatest folly'.
The *Great Eastern* was more than
twice the average length for a ship,
at 211m (692ft) long, with room for
4,000 passengers and 3,000 tons of
cargo; it was nearly 50 years before
another ship, the *Lusitania*, outstripped her in size. The hull of the
'monster steamer' was built
on a huge 'gridiron' of massive
beams set on piles driven
into the foreshore, remains

of which may still be seen just north
of Burrell's Wharf. Days after she
left Millwall, the *Great Eastern* was
seriously damaged by an explosion.
In 1885 the ship was moored in the
Mersey and converted for entertainment use, but in 1888 she was sold
to ship breakers; it took 200 men
two years to take the hull apart.

The Great Eastern *nearing
completion on the Thames
foreshore, 1857.*

GREENWICH

THIS borough's historical focus is the former royal palace and park in Greenwich: the Tudor palace was rebuilt for the Navy as a magnificent home for its pensioners, while Greenwich Park, with the Old Royal Observatory on top of the hill, remains one of London's most magnificent open spaces. Eastwards, across former marshes, Woolwich (which so far lacks blue plaques) had its own naval dockyard and the Royal Arsenal, long the nation's principal arms factory and a leading local employer. Blackheath was a forbidding expanse of open land on the main London–Dover road until it was developed into a genteel suburb in the later Georgian period. Charlton, and Eltham, with its medieval royal palace, are more recent suburban developments.

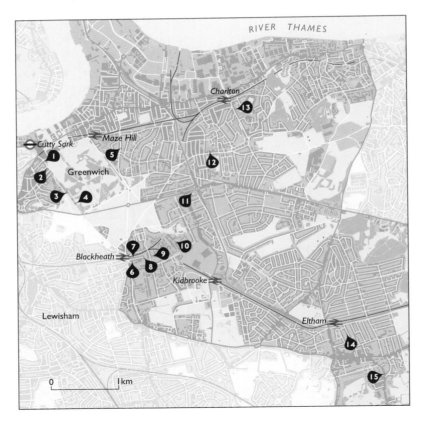

C. DAY-LEWIS

(1904–72) Poet Laureate

6 Croom's Hill

THE Irish-born Day-Lewis, who preferred 'C.' to his given name Cecil, met W. H. Auden while at Oxford, and came to prominence as a member of the left-wing 'Auden Gang'. In 1935, he published the first of 20 detective stories written under the pseudonym Nicholas Blake, and after a move to Devon in 1938 increasingly found his poetic voice. In 1951 Day-Lewis left both his wife Mary and his mistress, the writer Rosamond Lehmann, and married the actress Jill Balcon, daughter of the film producer Michael Balcon*. He moved to this house, built 1718–21, on 31 December 1957, eight months after the birth of his son, the actor Daniel Day-Lewis, and it remained his home for the rest of his life. He wrote of being 'happy, living in this place where old and new can be focused together into a historic present'.

BENJAMIN WAUGH

(1839–1908) founder of the National Society for the Prevention of Cruelty to Children

26 Croom's Hill **2**

IN 1866, the Yorkshire-born Waugh moved to Greenwich as a Congregationalist minister. He was shocked by the number of children he met who were suffering from neglect, homelessness, and desperate cruelty. Waugh's efforts to help children while he was living on Croom's Hill led to the establishment of the London Society for the Prevention of Cruelty to Children in 1884; the society became national in scope in 1889, with Waugh continuing as its director until his retirement in 1905. Unfortunately, Waugh's plaque is on the wrong building. The GLC failed to take into account that the street had been renumbered: the house in which Waugh lived in about 1874–7 is, in fact, now 62 Croom's Hill, an idiosyncratic, bow-fronted house built in 1810 by Thomas Skinner.

GENERAL JAMES WOLFE

(1727–59) victor of Quebec   Macartney House, Chesterfield Walk

WOLFE'S victory at Quebec (1759) was the battle that turned the Seven Years' War. His father, Lieutenant-General Edward Wolfe (1685–1759), moved to this house in 1751 and the younger Wolfe resided only occasionally. It was here that he learned, in October 1757, that he had been promoted colonel. Following his death at the moment of victory in Quebec, Wolfe's body was returned to his

'The prettiest-situated house in England'

James Wolfe

parents' house, where it lay in state until 20 November 1759, when he was buried beside his father at the parish church of St Alfege, Greenwich; his mother, Henrietta, lived on here until her death in October 1764. The front extension, designed by John Soane, dates from 1802–5.

PHILIP, 4TH EARL OF CHESTERFIELD
(1694–1773) statesman and author
GARNET, 1ST VISCOUNT WOLSELEY
(1833–1913) field-marshal   Ranger's (or Chesterfield) House

CHESTERFIELD inherited this villa, built in *c*.1723 for Admiral Francis Hosier (d.1727) and possibly designed by John James, on the death of his brother – John Stanhope – in December 1748, the year that he resigned as Secretary of State. It became his favourite summer residence and he called it 'Babiole', the nickname of his friend Madame de Monconseil. Chesterfield built the bow-windowed gallery wing on the south side of the 'very small' house in 1749–50, probably to designs by Isaac Ware. Gradually retreating from public life, he remained in what he called 'exile' in this

'hermitage' until autumn 1772, writing the letters for which he is chiefly remembered. The gallery housed his fine collection of art.

In summer 1888, Field Marshal Lord Wolseley was offered Ranger's House by Queen Victoria, thus becoming its last 'grace and favour' resident; he remained here until 1896. He was a reformer of army administration and training: 'all Sir Garnet' became slang for 'all in good order' and he was the inspiration for Gilbert* and Sullivan's 'very model of a modern major-general'. He led the expedition to relieve General Gordon in Khartoum (1884–5). The house is open to the public.

SIR FRANK DYSON

(1868–1939)
Astronomer Royal

6 Vanbrugh Hill
(formerly 3 Essex Villas), Blackheath **5**

DYSON was chief assistant to the Astronomer Royal when he moved here after his marriage to Caroline Best in June 1894. He left in January 1906, soon after being appointed Astronomer Royal for Scotland, but returned to Greenwich to live at the Royal Observatory in 1910 on his appointment as Astronomer Royal. Dyson's achievements included the confirmation of the deflection of starlight in the sun's gravitational field, proposed by Einstein as part of his general theory of relativity. He also constructed a free-pendulum clock of unprecedented accuracy that led the BBC in the 1920s to begin broadcasting accurate time signals from Greenwich – the origin of the 'pips'.

SIR ARTHUR EDDINGTON, OM

(1882–1944) mathematician
and astrophysicist

4 Bennett Park, Blackheath **6**

EDDINGTON worked as chief assistant to the Astronomer Royal at the Royal Observatory from 1906 until 1913, renting rooms here in what was then a boarding house. In 1913, he took up the Plumian chair of astronomy at Cambridge, where he lived for the rest of his life.

At Cambridge, Eddington devised a mathematical method of analysing stellar movements, and went on to be a leading interpreter of Einstein's theory of relativity. Eddington, who was knighted in 1930 and awarded the Order of Merit eight years later, also wrote popular scientific books.

DONALD MCGILL

(1875–1962) postcard cartoonist

5 Bennett Park, Blackheath **7**

CALLED the 'king of the saucy postcard', McGill made a speciality of double entendre, large-bottomed women and weedy men. He derived his early tag lines from jokes he heard at the Palace of Varieties, Edmonton, which belonged to his father-in-law. Having gone to school in Blackheath – where he had the misfortune to lose a foot in a rugby accident – McGill lived and worked in a flat on the top two floors of this house in Bennett Park, together with his family, from 1932 to 1939. Over his career he is said to have sold about 350 million cards; among the most popular was his depiction of a little girl being distracted from her prayers by an aggressive pet dog: 'Excuse me Lord while I kick Fido!' George Orwell* admiringly described McGill's work as a 'harmless rebellion against virtue', and it was an obvious inspiration for the writers of the *Carry On* films.

In honour of McGill's style, the plaque was unveiled in 1977 from behind a pair of frilly knickers.

DONALD
McGILL
1875–1962
Postcard
Cartoonist
lived here

GPO FILM UNIT, later CROWN FILM UNIT

(1933–43) pioneers of
documentary film-making

47 (formerly 45)
Bennett Park, Blackheath **8**

U NDER the leadership of John Grierson (1898–1972) – who is said to have coined the term 'documentary' – eloquent public-service social realism was given expression in films such as *Coal Face* (1935) and *Night Mail* (1936). Talking pictures were then in their infancy, and the General Post Office Film Unit was noted for the accomplishment of its sound editing, which is what was done at Blackheath (the unit's main offices were at 21 Soho Square). The studios were built as the Blackheath Art Club (1885), designed by John CP Higgs and Frank Rudkin and established by the philanthropist William Webster. When war broke out, the GPO unit was amalgamated under

the Ministry of Information to form the Crown Film Unit, and turned its attention to fighting fascism with a string of outstanding documentaries produced by Humphrey Jennings*. These films, all edited at Blackheath, included *Listen to Britain* (1942) and *Fires Were Started* (1943). The unit moved to Beaconsfield towards the end of the Second World War, and was disbanded in 1952.

NATHANIEL HAWTHORNE

(1804–64) American author   4 (formerly 6) Pond Road, Blackheath

HAVING written *The Scarlet Letter* (1850) and *The House of the Seven Gables* (1851) in near-isolation in Salem, Massachusetts, Hawthorne came to England with his family in 1853 to earn a living as US consul in Liverpool. The Hawthornes were invited to Blackheath to stay in the home of a friend, the poet and businessman Francis Bennoch. On arriving at the 1829 villa for a three-month stay in early July 1856, Hawthorne found 'Mr Bennoch's house not ... so big as his heart'; the author had to find rooms nearby for his children and their nurse. Hawthorne's *English Notebooks* (1870) were later edited for publication by his widow.

CHARLES GOUNOD

(1818–93)   Shirley Lodge,
composer   15 (formerly 8) Morden Road, Blackheath

BORN in Paris, Gounod made his name with the opera *Faust* (1859). Soon after the outbreak of the Franco-Prussian War, he and his family fled to England, arriving in Liverpool in September 1870. Gounod stayed at Shirley Lodge, built in 1854, shortly after his arrival in England, from early October until mid-November 1870. The composer remained mostly in London until 1874, conducting concerts at the Crystal Palace, the Royal Albert Hall and elsewhere. For much of this time he lived with the amateur soprano and litigant Georgina Weldon in Tavistock Square, Bloomsbury, until gossip drove him back to his wife in Paris. Weldon eventually sent on Gounod's manuscript scores – but not before she had written her name in crayon across every page.

WILLIAM LINDLEY (1808–1900)
SIR WILLIAM HEERLEIN LINDLEY

(1853–1917)   74 Shooters Hill
civil engineers   (formerly 10 Kidbrooke Terrace), Blackheath

THE Lindleys, father and son, constructed or advised upon water supply, drainage and sewage systems for more than 60 cities of central and eastern Europe, including Hamburg, Budapest and Warsaw. In doing so, they transformed the health and living conditions for millions of urban dwellers, and their careers present an early and an enduring example of the export of British engineering talent. Lindley senior was an early advocate of the sand filtration system to eradicate cholera, which was later widely adopted. He spent most of his career in Germany, where he married Julie Heerlein, and retired to Blackheath in 1862. William Heerlein Lindley was raised at this semi-detached house – built by a local developer in 1853 – and educated locally; he too worked mostly abroad, and his early demise was attributed to the strain of supervising the construction of a 110-mile pipeline over the Caucasus mountain range in Azerbaijan – a project that took 18 years.

WILLIAM HENRY BARLOW

(1812–1902)
engineer

145 Charlton Road
(formerly High Combe), Charlton

BORN in Woolwich, Barlow was the son of a professor of mathematics at the Royal Military Academy, and trained as an engineer in the nearby royal dockyard. In 1851 he assisted with the ironwork for the Crystal Palace, but Barlow is best known for his work for the Midland Railway, and especially the design and construction of the iron and glass train shed at St Pancras Station. When new in 1868, this was the world's largest clear-span roof, one of the great triumphs of Victorian structural engineering. Barlow moved to this villa of about 1810 in 1857 with his wife Selina Crawford, and it remained his home until his death here aged 90. High Combe, which is now the presbytery to the adjacent Roman Catholic Church of Our Lady of Grace, was also the residence of the rocket designer William Congreve (1772–1828).

ETTORE SCHMITZ, 'ITALO SVEVO'

(1861–1928) writer

67 Charlton Church Lane, Charlton

THE great Italian modernist, comic chronicler of the nature of consciousness and author of *Confessions of Zeno* (1923), lived here between 1903 and 1913. He returned to the house regularly until the year before his death, despite damning Charlton as the 'drabbest and most out-of-the-way suburb'. Svevo first came to help set up a riverside ships' paint factory, part of his father-in-law's anti-corrosion composition works. While here, he became a keen Charlton Athletic fan.

HERBERT MORRISON, LORD MORRISON OF LAMBETH

(1888–1965) Cabinet minister and Leader of the London County Council

55 Archery Road, Eltham

MORRISON lived in this modest semi-detached house from 1929, soon after it was built, until 1960, during which time he was at the centre of English politics as a leading light in the Labour Party. As the Leader of the LCC (1934–40) he implemented an ambitious programme of school building and slum clearance, and secured the construction of a new Waterloo Bridge. Having already been Minister for Transport in the 1929-31 Labour government, he went on to be Home Secretary in the wartime coalition, and Deputy Prime Minister, Leader of the

Un-named Labour MP:

'Of course the trouble with Herbie is he's his own worst enemy.'

Ernest Bevin:

'Not while I'm alive he ain't.'

Commons and Foreign Secretary in the Attlee* administration of 1945–51. Morrison, who had long schemed to replace Attlee as leader, was defeated in the leadership contest of 1955 by Hugh Gaitskell*. He counted his housing programmes and the introduction of the Green Belt among his greatest achievements.

RICHARD JEFFERIES

(1848–87)
naturalist and writer

59 Footscray Road
(formerly 14 Victoria Road), Eltham

THE son of a Wiltshire dairyman with London printing connections, Jefferies was a writer, mystic and protégé of William Morris* who came to prominence with works such as *Wild Life in a Southern County* (1879), *The Amateur Poacher* (1879), and *Bevis* (1882), which has been described as 'the best boys' book ever written'. Based on his memories of Wiltshire, these books established him as

the foremost country writer of his day. Despite increasing ill health, Jefferies kept up his literary output until his early death, at the age of 38. He lived in this semi-detached house from 24 June 1884 until April 1885; during his time here, he wrote a number of essays, collected as *The Open Air* (1885), as well as *After London* (1885), an astonishing vision of an urban relapse into primitive wilderness.

LEWISHAM

MODERN Lewisham forms a rough triangle from Thamesside Deptford to Sydenham in the south-west and Grove Park in the south-east. The site of Henry VIII's royal dockyard, Deptford had additional early significance as the first coaching stop on the road to Dover and in 1836 it became a stop on London's first railway line. Here as elsewhere, the railway gave a huge boost to suburban development, though the biggest expansion in population came in the last two decades of the 19th century. Most of the area's new inhabitants belonged to the burgeoning middle classes, with Blackheath and Sydenham being the most 'aspirational' of the new suburban centres.

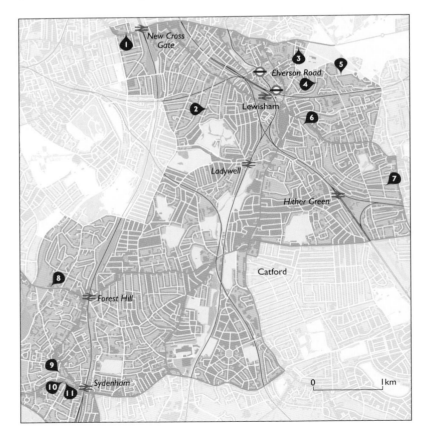

JOHN TALLIS

(1817–76) publisher of
London Street Views

233 New Cross Road,
New Cross

THE son of a Birmingham bookseller, Tallis moved the family
business in the direction of publishing, and between 1838 and 1840
released his famous *London Street
Views*. These were produced for 74
of the principal streets of the West
End and the City, and consisted of
illustrations of the elevations of
each building in the street together
with a map of the area, historical
notes, a street directory and advertisements. In the days before the
A–Z and similar directories, these
promised 'to assist strangers visiting the Metropolis, through all its
mazes without a guide'. Tallis also
produced a number of maps, atlases
and street views of other places, but
over-reached and went bankrupt in
1861. He moved to this mid-19th-
century semi-detached house in
1870, and stayed for the remaining
six years of his life, during which
time he was occasionally obliged to
take in lodgers to pay his rates.

EDGAR WALLACE

(1875–1932) writer

6 Tressillian Crescent, Brockley **2**

BORN and bred in south-east
London, Wallace tried his
hand at soldiering and journalism
before he became 'King of Thrillers'.
When he moved to this large semi-
detached house with his wife Ivy
and their two children early in 1908,
he was heavily in debt; the back door
was often left open, so that Wallace
could stealthily evade any calling
creditors. His study was at the back
of the house on the first floor; *Sanders of the River* (1911) was a notable
success to come from it. During the
First World War, the family moved
to a flat near Regent's Park.

JAMES GLAISHER

(1809–1903) astronomer, meteorologist
and pioneer of weather forecasting

20 Dartmouth Hill (formerly
1 Dartmouth Place), Blackheath **3**

THE Rotherhithe-born and
Greenwich-raised Glaisher
became interested in meteorology
while working for the Ordnance
Survey in Ireland in 1829–30.
As head of the magnetical and
meteorological department at the
Royal Observatory from 1838, he

organised a network of volunteers to make observations, which he compiled as authoritative quarterly reports on the British weather. In the 1860s he made several balloon ascents for the purpose of making meteorological observations at high altitudes. A near-fatal accident during one ascent in 1862 was widely reported – and satirised – and made Glaisher a well-known public figure. At about this time he moved to this late-18th-century house with his wife Cecilia, a noted artist and photographer; it remained his home until 1893. Glaisher retired from the Royal Observatory in 1874.

SAMUEL SMILES

(1812–1904) the author of *Self Help*   11 Granville Park, Blackheath **4**

BORN in Scotland, Smiles qualified as a doctor at Edinburgh University, but moved first into journalism and then into railway work, and relocated to London in 1854 on his appointment as Secretary to the South Eastern Railway; from Granville Park, he commuted to an office at London Bridge. Smiles also lectured and wrote, and championed the education of ordinary people. Following the publication in 1859 of *Self Help, with Illustrations of Character and Conduct*, he became a reluctant celebrity. The book preached the virtues of hard work and thrift, and warned against the

> Smiles's home, originally 6 Granville Park Terrace, is in fact across the road at number 12. The street was renumbered in 1870–72; the house that mistakenly bears the plaque was formerly 6 Granville Park.

dangers of excessive government intervention. It caught the mood of the times, selling thousands of copies around the world, and its success enabled Smiles to build a new family home, West Bank (demolished), in Dartmouth Row on the west side of Blackheath, to which he moved in 1864.

SIR JAMES CLARK ROSS

(1800–62) polar explorer   2 Eliot Place, Blackheath

ROSS joined the Navy in 1812 and served first under his uncle, John Ross, accompanying him on his first Arctic voyage in 1818. He returned to the region in four expeditions led by William

Edward Parry, and was present on the voyage – led by his uncle – that located the position of the North Pole in 1831. Having conducted a systematic magnetic survey of Britain, Ross set out in 1839 for the Antarctic, where he made a number of important observations and located, but did not quite reach, the South Pole. He did, however, discover Victoria Land and what became known as the Ross ice shelf; also named after him are the Ross Sea and Ross's gull, a native of the Arctic region. Ross rented this house after his marriage in 1843 to Ann Coulman, for whom he reputedly promised to forsake polar exploration. He started to set down his experiences on paper while living here, which were published as *A Voyage of Discovery and Research in the Southern and Antarctic Regions* (1847). In 1845 he moved to Aston Abbotts, near Aylesbury, Buckinghamshire.

JAMES ELROY FLECKER

(1884–1915) poet and dramatist 9 Gilmore Road, Lee

FLECKER was born at this newly built detached villa on a foggy 5 November 1884. His parents had moved here that August, his father, the Revd William Herman Flecker, having been appointed Headmaster of the City of London College School, as well as curate of Holy Trinity Church in Lee. The infant Flecker was baptised Herman Elroy – the second in recognition of his Jewish heritage – but adopted the name James while at Oxford University. The family moved in 1886, when his father was made Headmaster of a new school in Cheltenham. After Oxford, Flecker joined the consular service and was sent to Constantinople and later Beirut. He produced several volumes of lyrical romantic verse; his most enduring work is *The Golden Journey to Samarkand* (1913), influenced by the time he spent in the Near East. Flecker died of tuberculosis in Switzerland.

SIR STANLEY UNWIN

(1884–1968) publisher 13 Handen Road, Lee

UNWIN was born in this late-Victorian semi-detached house, the youngest of the nine children of the printer Edward Unwin and his wife, Elizabeth, whose family owned a paper firm; another relation, T. Fisher Unwin, was a successful publisher. Unwin started publishing on his own account when he formed George Allen & Unwin Ltd, just as war broke out in 1914. He was soon producing books for a serious audience – including many titles that reflected his own pacifist views – by authors such as George Lansbury, Bertrand Russell*, Leonard Woolf* and James Elroy Flecker*. Unwin's reinvigoration of the insolvent publishing house of Allen was achieved by rigorous economies on overheads and by what his nephew recalled as his 'compelling, almost mesmeric force in argument'. He became a hugely influential figure in publishing and was President of the Publishers Association of Great Britain and the International Publishers Association, and expanded his interests by taking a stake in the publishing house of Bodley Head Ltd. Unwin enjoyed great success with J. R. R. Tolkien's *The Hobbit* (1937) and *The Lord of the Rings* (1954–5). As an adult he lived in Hampstead.

FREDERICK JOHN HORNIMAN*

(1835–1906) founder of the Horniman Museum and Gardens

100 London Road, Forest Hill **8**

H|ORNIMAN was born in Somerset and in 1868 became chairman of his father's tea business, Horniman & Co., which he ran with his brother William; by 1891 it was said to be the largest tea firm in the world. In 1868 he moved to Surrey House on this site, which he filled with the natural history and anthropological specimens he had gathered on his travels abroad. In December 1890 he opened the house for three days a week to the public – without charge – as the Surrey House Museum,

Horniman and his first wife Rebekah having decamped to a nearby house, Surrey Mount, in order to escape their overstuffed abode. Such was the museum's success, and the expansion of its collections, that in 1897 he demolished his former residence and commissioned a purpose-built structure from the architect Charles Harrison Townsend, who had lately designed Whitechapel Art Gallery. Completed in 1901, the Horniman Museum incorporates elements of the Arts and Crafts and the Art Nouveau styles. Horniman gave the building and its collections to 'the people of London' in 1901.

ELEANOR MARX

(1855–98) socialist campaigner

7 Jews Walk, Sydenham

ELEANOR Marx – nicknamed Tussy – was born at the Soho flat that now bears a plaque to her father, Karl Marx*. She followed him into socialist activism, supervising the publication in English of *Das Kapital* in 1867. With William Morris*, Eleanor Marx was one of the founders of the Socialist League in 1885; she campaigned for Jewish workers in the East End and supported the gas workers' and dockers' strikes of 1889. Eleanor was present too at the founding conference of the Independent Labour Party (ILP) in 1893. She bought the house in Jews Walk two years later with a legacy from Friedrich Engels* and shared it with her partner of 11 years, the zoologist Edward Aveling, whose name she used with her own. The discovery that Aveling had secretly married his mistress was a factor in her suicide by poisoning in March 1898, aged 43. Debt added to her misery, in an echo of Flaubert's *Madame Bovary*, of which Eleanor had produced the first English translation. Aveling, who outlasted her by just four months, has been fingered for deeper culpability – by having obtained the poison for her.

SIR GEORGE GROVE

(1820–1900)
promoter of musical knowledge

14 Westwood Hill
(formerly West Hill), Sydenham

GROVE'S name has become shorthand for the *Dictionary of Music and Musicians* (1878-89) that he edited, intending it as a source 'from which an intelligent inquirer can learn, in small compass ... what is meant by a Symphony or Sonata, a Fugue, a Stretto, a Coda'. A greatly expanded 'New Grove' appeared in 1980, and is now online. From 1854, as secretary of the Crystal Palace, Grove brought classical music to a wider public with an imaginative concert programme, champion-ing – among others – Beethoven, Mendelssohn*, Schubert and Schumann. In 1852 he had moved to this house – then newly built – with his wife Harriet; it was then called 1 Church Row, West Hill. Three children were born here before the family decamped in 1860 to Grove House, Lower Sydenham, the site of which is marked by a Lewisham council plaque. Grove was the first Director of the Royal College of Music (1883-94) and was a formidable biblical scholar too. Astonishingly, his first career was as a civil engineer: he worked on the London to Birmingham railway, on Robert Stephenson's* bridge over the Menai Straits and on the construction of lighthouses in the West Indies.

SIR ERNEST SHACKLETON

(1874–1922)
Antarctic explorer

12 Westwood Hill
(formerly West Hill), Sydenham

SHACKLETON was born in County Kildare. In 1885 his father, Henry, a general practitioner, brought his family to what was then known as Aberdeen House, in this prosperous suburb. Ernest, the second of ten children, at-tended Dulwich College from 1887. At home, his chief recreation was carpentry, and he and the other chil-dren enjoyed climbing onto the flat top of the steeply sloping roof of the house. On leaving Dulwich in 1890, Shackleton was apprenticed to the White Star Line, and spent the next decade in the Merchant Navy. Two years later, on another home visit, he met his future wife Emily Dor-man, a friend of one of his sisters; they married in 1904. Shackleton's ascent to *Boy's Own* hero status began with the National Antarctic Expedition of 1901–4, on which he accompanied Captain Scott* to within 500 miles of the Pole. Later triumphs – the British Antarctic Expedition of 1907–9 and the Impe-rial Trans-Antarctic Expedition of 1914–17 – cemented his fame, and earned him a knighthood.

SOUTHWARK

THE modern borough of Southwark stretches along the south bank of the River Thames from the Oxo Tower to Rotherhithe and inland as far south as Peckham and Dulwich. From medieval times onwards, Southwark proper – at the southern end of London's oldest river crossing – was known for its inns, brothels, breweries, theatres and prisons. Later, the growth of the port of London brought development of the docks to the east, accompanied by a population explosion that spawned some of London's most notorious slums. These were gradually replaced, with some of the most intense council housing development in post-war London taking place in areas like Bermondsey and Peckham. Further south, a more rural character remained for longer; Camberwell and Dulwich were early suburbs, favoured by prosperous people.

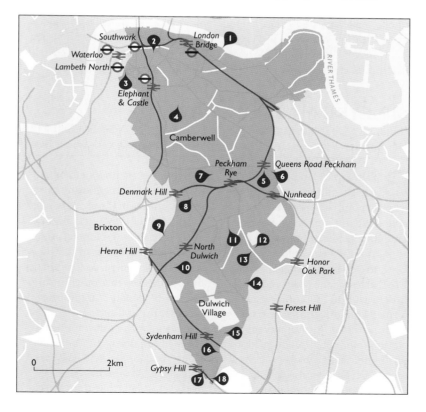

DEREK JARMAN

(1942–94) film-maker,
artist and gay rights activist

Butler's Wharf,
36 Shad Thames **1**

AS a film-maker and as an artist-activist, Jarman pushed the boundaries: *The Tempest* (1979) and *Caravaggio* (1986) brought his fantastic, disturbing and erotic visions close to the mainstream. He also worked as a set designer; painted and exhibited regularly; cultivated a famous garden on the shingle at Dungeness, Kent, and joined direct action campaigns for gay rights – and in particular against the stigmatisation of those who were (like himself) living with HIV. Born in London's north-western fringes,

Jarman spent much of his life in the capital: latterly, he had a flat on the Charing Cross Road, but in his early career he was among the pioneers of 'loft living', and stayed in four disused warehouses on the south bank of the Thames. The sole survivor of these is Butler's Wharf, where Jarman lived and worked on the third floor of block A1 for periods between May 1973 and July 1979. Here, production of his iconoclastic *Jubilee* (1978) was based. A greenhouse in the corner of the space served as a makeshift bedroom.

SIR EYRE MASSEY SHAW

(1828–1908) first Chief Officer of the
Metropolitan Fire Brigade

Winchester House,
94 Southwark Bridge Road **2**

BORN in Ireland, Shaw pursued a military career before being appointed Superintendent of police and fire services in Belfast in 1860. The following year he was appointed Superintendent of the London Fire Engine Establishment, which became the Metropolitan Fire Brigade in 1866. Shaw transformed London's fire service: under his supervision, the number of fire stations more than quadrupled, and its firemen gained an international reputation for their discipline, organisation and thoroughness. He

oversaw their attendance at many thousands of fires, suffering two major injuries in the process. Shaw lived here from 1878, and in some style, entertaining – among others – the Prince of Wales. In 1886 he was cited as a co-respondent in the famous divorce case of Lady Colin Campbell, though no impropriety was ever proved, and he retired five years later with no obvious damage to his reputation. Winchester House, built as St Saviour's Workhouse in 1777, remained the fire brigade headquarters until 1937.

GEORGE MYERS

(1803–75) builder   131 St George's Road (formerly 9 Laurie Terrace) **3**

KNOWN as 'Pugin's builder', Myers first met A. W. N. Pugin at Beverley Minster in 1827; their partnership began a decade later and Myers executed almost all of Pugin's subsequent commissions, including the Roman Catholic cathedrals in Birmingham (1839–41), Nottingham (1841–4), Newcastle (1841–4) and Southwark (1841–8). The last commission brought Myers and his wife Judith to London, and they moved to this newly built house in 1842. Myers and Pugin's last collaboration was the medieval court at the Great Exhibition (1851), and it was Myers who carved the effigy on the architect's tomb in Ramsgate (c.1853). Myers established a national contracting business and workshops at Ordnance Wharf, near Westminster Bridge, Lambeth, which did well out of the building boom of the 1850s and 1860s. Between 1837 and his retirement in 1873, it is estimated that Myers built an average of three churches a year for various denominations. His secular projects ranged from Mentmore, Buckinghamshire (1852–4), the house built for Baron Mayer de Rothschild, to Broadmoor Hospital, Berkshire (1858–63).

DR CHARLES VICKERY DRYSDALE

(1874–1961) a founder of the
Family Planning Association   153A East Street, Walworth

BOTH Drysdale's parents were ardent campaigners for birth control and women's suffrage, while his uncle, George Drysdale, was another early promoter of contraception. Drysdale junior pursued a career in engineering and was a founder member of the Men's League for Women's Suffrage in 1907. But he is best remembered as an advocate of family planning, who effectively inherited from his family the leadership of the Malthusian League. This organisation – of which he was President from 1921 to 1952 – was the first to promulgate birth control as a remedy for overpopulation and poverty. Spurred on by the success of Marie Stopes*, Drysdale opened his first clinic here in November 1921 (at the time he was Superintendent of the Admiralty Research Laboratory in Teddington). The clinic provided maternity and child welfare services as well as contraceptive advice. The committee that oversaw it morphed into the Family Planning Association.

DR INNES PEARSE (1889–1978)
DR GEORGE SCOTT WILLIAMSON
(1884–1953)
founders of the Pioneer Health Centre   142 Queen's Road, Peckham **5**

THE Pioneer Health Centre, or 'Peckham Experiment', was an initiative in holistic, preventive community health, set up by George Scott Williamson and Innes Pearse, two doctors who had met while undertaking research on the thyroid at the Royal Free Hospital (and who eventually married). About 400 people subscribed to the initial phase of the project (1926–9), which was based at this late-Georgian terraced house, in a suburb chosen for its representative social mix. In 1935 a purpose-built health centre opened nearby in St Mary's Road, equipped with what was then London's second-largest swimming pool; the striking modernist building is now converted into flats. The key finding of the Centre was that the general health of the population was rather worse than had been assumed; its ideals anticipated contemporary public health concerns about 'wellness'. But the almost anarchistic theories of self-organisation that lay behind the Peckham Experiment did not fit well into the fledgling NHS, and the centre closed in 1950.

DR HAROLD MOODY
(1882–1947) campaigner for racial equality   164 Queen's Road, Peckham **6**

MOODY came to London from Jamaica in 1904 to study medicine at King's College London. Having been denied a hospital appointment out of racial prejudice, he set up on his own as a GP, establishing a practice in King's Road (now King's Grove), Peckham, in 1913 – shortly after his marriage to Olive Mabel Tranter, 'a warm, affectionate English nurse'. He moved here in 1922, and it was where he lived, worked and died. The Moodys' house was 'open to all the travelling black people who couldn't

'A comfortable, four-storey property with a middle-floor entrance leading to a small, often cluttered hall, and beyond that, large dining and drawing rooms'

The Jamaican writer and feminist Una Marson, who lodged here

find a room or a meal elsewhere'. From here, Moody ran the League of Coloured Peoples – founded in 1931 – under which banner he published a newsletter, *The Keys*, and lobbied for the improvement of race relations and greater equality of opportunity. In 1943 Moody was appointed to a government advisory committee on the welfare of non-Europeans; a devout Congregationalist Christian, he also chaired the London Missionary Society that year.

SIR ALAN COBHAM
(1894–1973)
aviator

78 Denman Road
(formerly 4 Hetley Terrace), Peckham

COBHAM, the son of a tailor, was born and lived in this Victorian house until he was 12 years old, when the family moved to Streatham. He served with the Royal Flying Corps in the First World War, and was commissioned in the newly formed Royal Air Force as a flying instructor in 1918. Cobham was committed to promoting flight as a safe and practical mode of transport through aviation displays and, while employed by De Havilland's during the 1920s, by completing a series of long-distance flights, including a journey to and from Australia in 1926 that culminated in him landing a seaplane on the Thames. In the 1930s he began to develop practical ways of carrying out air-to-air refuelling. By the 1950s his company, Flight Refuelling Ltd, was at the forefront of this technology. Cobham died in the British Virgin Islands, where he lived after 1968.

JOSEPH CHAMBERLAIN*
(1836–1914)
statesman

188 Camberwell Grove
(formerly 3 Grove Hill Terrace), Denmark Hill

FOR the first nine years of his life Chamberlain lived with his parents in this tall late-Georgian yellow-brick house. This was then a leafy suburb; it was possible to see the Palace of Westminster – to which he was first elected in 1876 – from the upper windows of the house on a clear day. Young Joseph was educated at the school of Miss Charlotte Pace, just a few doors away; in 1845 the family moved to Highbury. As Mayor of Birmingham (1873–6), Chamberlain promoted 'municipal socialism' – the public ownership of utilities. He rose to Cabinet rank, but resigned from the Unionist government in 1903 over protectionist tariffs (which he supported); earlier, he had split from the Liberals over Irish Home Rule (which he opposed).

ARTHUR HENRY WARD, 'SAX ROHMER'

(1883–1959) creator of
Dr Fu Manchu

51 Herne Hill
(formerly 6 Danecroft Gardens) **9**

BORN in Birmingham to Irish parents, Ward started out as a newspaper reporter and ghost-writer for the music-hall comedians George Robey and 'Little Tich' (Harry Relph*). The Chinese revolution of 1911 inspired him to create his most famous fictional character, who first appeared in print in *The Mystery of Dr Fu Manchu* (1913).

Many of the Fu Manchu stories were written at this house where Rohmer moved in 1910, following his marriage to Rose Elizabeth Knox, a variety-act juggler and the sister of a member of the Crazy Gang. They were the first occupants of the house, which they shared with Sax's father, Bill. In 1919 they left for Bruton Street, Mayfair.

SCIPIO AFRICANUS MUSSABINI

(1867–1927) athletics coach

84 Burbage Road, Herne Hill **10**

IN 1913 'Sam' (so named from his initials) Mussabini was taken on by the Polytechnic Harriers athletics club as Britain's first professional 'coach' – the American term that he preferred to 'trainer'. His methods, as described in his book *The Complete Athletic Trainer* (1913), were revolutionary; one innovation was a running arm movement known as the 'Poly swing'. Six of his athletes won a total of 11 Olympic medals, including five golds; the most famous Mussabini protégé was Harold Abrahams*, whose path to the 100-metre gold in the 1924 games was depicted in the film

'Only think of two things – the gun and the tape. When you hear the one, just run like hell until you break the other.'

Sam Mussabini's simple recipe for track success

Chariots of Fire (1981). All these successes were founded on work at the Herne Hill athletics track, which lay over the back garden fence of 84 Burbage Road – the semi-detached house, then quite newly built, where Mussabini lived from about 1911 to 1916. Born in

Blackheath, of Syrian, Italian and French ancestry, he had worked as a journalist and cycling coach before starting to train athletes just after 1900. Another source of income for Mussabini was refereeing billiards matches, and the success of his athletes must have made up for the failure of a related venture – a magazine called *World of Billiards*.

HENRY COTTON

(1907–87) champion golfer 47 Crystal Palace Road, East Dulwich

AS a three-time winner of the Open during the 1930s and 40s, Cotton stood out at a time when British golfers enjoyed scant success; he won 11 other open championships elsewhere in Europe. He lived with his family in this late-19th-century detached house during the 1920s, a period that covered part of his time at Alleyn's School and his early years as a golf professional; he practised in the garage and in the garden behind, and first tasted success at the Aquarius Golf Club in Honor Oak. *Vanity Fair* called Cotton 'something of a Beau Brummel* on the links', and his silk neckerchiefs and monogrammed shirts set a style standard for future generations of golfers. He and his wife 'Toots' would invariably arrive at a tournament in a hired Rolls-Royce and with a hamper from Fortnum & Mason.

PERCY LANE OLIVER

(1878–1944) founder of the first voluntary blood donor service

5 Colyton Road, Peckham Rye

A LOCAL government officer with Camberwell Borough Council, and Honorary Secretary of the Camberwell Red Cross Division, Oliver was asked by King's College Hospital in 1921 if his division could provide a blood donor to save a stricken patient, at a time when giving blood was a novelty. Oliver and his wife, another dedicated Red Cross volunteer, were inspired to establish a London-wide panel of donors that became the world's first voluntary blood donation service. In May 1928, the Olivers moved to this more spacious house, from which he ran the Greater London Red Cross Blood Transfusion Service – as it became known – until his death. He also supported the formation in 1932 of the Voluntary Blood Donors Association; the National Blood Transfusion Service was set up in 1946.

WILLIAM HENRY PRATT, 'BORIS KARLOFF'

(1887–1969) actor   36 Forest Hill Road, Peckham Rye **13**

PRATT was born in this 1880s house, the youngest of nine children, and lived here until his family moved to Enfield in 1894. He emigrated to Canada in 1909 to pursue his acting ambitions; adopting the name Boris Karloff, he spent much of his early career in repertory theatre and, after moving to Hollywood in 1917, took minor film roles as a generic 'baddie', to which his sinister appearance was well suited. His big break came in the form of Frankenstein's monster (*right*), a part he played in the eponymous film of 1931, directed by James Whale. Karloff reprised the role in *The Bride of Frankenstein* (1935) and *Son of Frankenstein* (1939), having cemented his place in horror movie legend by his performances in *The Mummy* (1932) and *The Ghoul* (1933). In later years he lived in Sussex and Hampshire.

C. S. FORESTER

(1899–1966) novelist   58 Underhill Road, East Dulwich **14**

THE son of a schoolmaster, Cecil Lewis Troughton Smith was born in Cairo, and brought by his family to England in 1903. They moved to this late-19th-century semi in 1915 and, after Dulwich College, the young Cecil began medical training at Guy's Hospital, but soon left to try his luck as a writer; his father gave him the use of the attic here, then a claustrophobic, gloomy room with narrow windows, reached by steep stairs.

Forester – to use the pen-name he adopted in 1923 – remained at the family home long after his marriage in 1926 to Kathleen Belcher, finally moving to Sydenham in 1932. His first success was *Payment Deferred* (1926), which was partly set in Dulwich, while *The African Queen* (1935) made it to the big screen in 1951 starring Humphrey Bogart and Katharine Hepburn. Forester's popular Horatio Hornblower series was written between 1937 and 1962.

JOHN LOGIE BAIRD*

(1888–1946) television pioneer   3 Crescent Wood Rd, Upper Sydenham **15**

SCOTTISH-BORN Baird moved here in summer 1933, when his company's studios, workshops and offices moved to the Crystal Palace (which was destroyed by fire three years later); the company built aerials atop the 87m (284ft) high South Tower to transmit high-resolution pictures. Baird's wife, Margaret, a concert pianist, described their detached mid-19th-century home as 'vast, with acres of bare floors and windows high out of reach'; it was also set in a large plot of land. To Baird, its most attractive feature was its capacity to accommodate a private laboratory. This, centred on the former stables, coach house and kitchen, was the scene of numerous experiments and discoveries. Being unfit for military service, Baird continued to live and work here during the Second World War, though he regularly joined his family in Cornwall and – with the increasing dilapidation of the Sydenham property – began to stay in hotels nearby. In late 1945 he joined his family at a rented house in Bexhill, Sussex, though the house in Crescent Wood Road was kept on until his death.

SIR FRANCIS PETTIT SMITH

(1808–74) pioneer of the screw propeller   17 Sydenham Hill, Sydenham **16**

BEFORE the advent of flight, in terms of transport innovations that shrank the world, the development of the screw propeller was second to none. The idea had been around for a while, but it was Smith – a farmer originally from Romney Marsh, whose youthful passion had been toy boats – who established its technical superiority to the paddle as a means of steamboat propulsion. The key challenge, which Smith met successfully, was to pass the propeller shaft through the hull without creating a leak. But having taken out a patent for screw propulsion in 1836, he found that shipbuilders were reluctant to invest in it; a notable exception was the innovation-hungry Isambard Kingdom Brunel*, who used a propeller to drive the giant SS *Great Britain* (launched 1843), and the technology then passed into general use. In 1860 Smith was made curator of the Patent Office museum in Kensington; four years later, he bought a plot for a new house on Sydenham Hill. He named it Centra House (Fountain House is its present name) and cultivated an expansive shrubbery here before moving out in 1870.

ANNIE BESANT

(1847–1933) social reformer 39 (formerly 26) Colby Road, Gipsy Hill

ANNIE Wood was born in the City into a rich family, and married Frank Besant, a clergyman, in 1867. She separated from him in 1873 following a loss of faith and moved into this small house early in 1874, with her daughter Mabel, her ailing mother Emily and their maid. A friend and neighbour, Thomas Scott, introduced her to Charles Bradlaugh, sometime President of the National Secular Society, and she began to contribute to the society's paper and to lecture.

Besant left the house in October that year. In July 1888 Besant famously organised a strike by the female matchmakers – 'matchgirls' – employed by Bryant and May. She was also a member of the London School Board, and secured its adoption of a policy only to purchase goods made under trade-union-approved conditions. In the late 1880s Besant converted to theosophy, and lived mostly in India from 1893, becoming a strong advocate of self-determination for that country.

LESLIE HOWARD

(1893–1943) actor and film director 45 Farquhar Road, Upper Norwood **18**

LESLIE Howard is most famous for playing Ashley Wilkes in *Gone with the Wind* (1939) though he thought the character 'a dreadful milksop' and himself too old for the part. Other silver screen highlights include *Of Human Bondage* (1934) and *The Petrified Forest* (1936), in both of which Howard starred opposite Bette Davis, and *Pygmalion* (1938). Born Leslie Steiner in Forest Hill, he first crept the boards at the Stanley Halls in Norwood. When he later told his children about his 'long hours daydreaming in the high attic room that overlooked all of London', he was most likely referring to the house in Farquhar Road, where

'Terrible lot of nonsense – heaven help me if I ever read the book.'

Leslie Howard on Gone with the Wind

he lived with his family in about 1907–11. Howard's father was originally from Hungary and the family lived in Vienna for a time, returning to England after experiencing anti-Semitism. During the Second World War, Howard directed and starred in *Pimpernel Smith* (1941) and *The First of the Few* (1942), a biopic of the Spitfire designer R. J. Mitchell. He died when a civilian aircraft on which he was travelling was shot down over the Channel.

LAMBETH

LAMBETH is today one of the most densely populated parts of Britain, yet in the mid-18th century the area covered by the modern borough was largely uninhabited. The opening of new bridges across the Thames at Westminster (1750) and Blackfriars (1769) made the south side of the river more accessible. Ribbon development followed the main roads to Kennington, Wandsworth, Clapham and Brixton, while those keen to benefit from peace and fresh air built villas on the higher ground of Herne Hill, Streatham and Norwood. In the Victorian period North Lambeth descended to the state of a slum, overshadowed by industry. The 20th century brought vast amounts of new public housing, especially after the Second World War. This process of regeneration was epitomised by the Festival of Britain in 1951, which swept away the industrial buildings on the south bank of the Thames and began the transformation of the site into a centre for the arts.

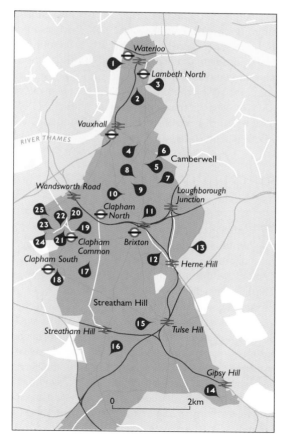

COUNTY HALL

Westminster Bridge Road, Lambeth ❶

A NGRY at the manner of the authority's abolition, the GLC approved the County Hall plaques 'to leave some permanent record which it will be virtually impossible for the successor authority to obliterate'. Designed by Ralph Knott, County Hall was begun as a purpose-built headquarters for the LCC in 1909, and was opened 13 years later by George V, although the original building was only completed in 1933 and extensions were built after that. The tradition of London-wide local government was ended – at least temporarily – by the abolition of the GLC in 1986, and the dispersal of its responsibilities, which included the erection of blue plaques.

> **London County Council** (1889–1965)
> **Greater London Council** (1965–86)
> **Inner London Education Authority** (1965–90)

Also commemorated is the Inner London Education Authority, also housed in County Hall, which oversaw schooling in the 12 inner-London boroughs from 1965. ILEA thus inherited the educational responsibilities of the LCC, which had taken over in 1904 from the London School Board. ILEA was abolished in 1990, when its duties passed to individual boroughs.

SIR PHILIP BEN GREET

(1857–1936) actor-manager

160 Lambeth Road ❷

T HE son of a naval captain, Philip Barling Ben Greet was born on board his father's ship *Crocodile* while it was moored on the Thames, and educated at the Royal Naval School in New Cross. After a brief spell as a schoolteacher, he became an actor and then, in 1886, entered theatre management. Greet made his name staging open-air performances of Shakespeare in Oxford and Cambridge colleges. In 1914 he went into partnership with Lilian Baylis*, the manager of the Old Vic Theatre in Waterloo, where he introduced thousands of school-children to Shakespeare through his innovation of matinee performances. 'B. G.' – as he was generally known – began staying with his friend John William Keys and his family at this tall brick house of *c*.1800 during the early years of the First World War, when air raids prevented him from travelling to his parental home. He lived here permanently from 1920 – together with the Keys family – until his death 16 years later.

WILLIAM BLIGH

(1754–1817)
commander of the *Bounty*

100 Lambeth Road
(formerly 3 Durham Place)

BLIGH was born in Plymouth and took part in Captain Cook's* second voyage around the world (1776–80). In 1787 he took command of the *Bounty* for an expedition to the South Seas to export breadfruit – intended as high-energy food for slaves – from Tahiti to the British West Indies. It was during this voyage that Fletcher Christian led his famous mutiny in 1789, apparently incited by Bligh's violent temper and authoritarian leadership. Set adrift in an open boat, with the 18 men who had remained loyal, Bligh managed to navigate 3,600 miles across the Pacific to Timor, while the mutineers either settled on Pitcairn Island or were arrested. In 1806 Bligh became Governor of New South Wales, where he was embroiled in another mutiny; this led to his imprisonment on board a ship at Hobart, Tasmania, and he returned to England in 1810. Bligh kept this house of about 1794 as his London base until about 1813, when, following the death of his wife Elizabeth, he moved to Farningham, Kent; he died at a house in Bond Street and was buried at St Mary's, Lambeth.

FIELD MARSHAL VISCOUNT MONTGOMERY OF ALAMEIN

(1887–1976) army officer

Oval House, 52–54 Kennington Oval

BERNARD Law Montgomery was born in this substantial mid-19th-century villa; at the time his father was vicar of St Mark's, and this was the vicarage. When in 1889 his father was appointed Bishop of Tasmania, the family left Kennington for Hobart. Montgomery, who returned with his family to England in 1901, entered the Army in 1908 and proved an outstanding, if idiosyncratic, leader of men during the First World War. It is for his achievements during the Second World War that 'Monty' is largely remembered. As commander of the British Eighth Army in North Africa, he was responsible for the Allied victory at the Battle of El Alamein (1942), a vital turning point, and went on to be the senior British officer in command of the D-Day landings at Normandy in 1944. Montgomery served as Chief of the Imperial General Staff from 1946 – the year he was raised to the peerage – until 1948; on retiring ten years later, he moved to Hampshire.

CHARLIE CHAPLIN

(1889–1977) actor and film-maker   15 Glenshaw Mansions, Brixton Road **5**

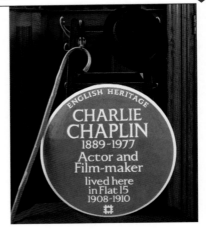

One of the biggest stars of the first age of film, Chaplin was an actor, director and producer – and even wrote the musical score for *Limelight* (1952). His poverty-stricken childhood in south London is clearly referenced in *The Kid* (1921), while his 'little tramp' persona was based on a local character in Kennington. With his brother Sydney, a fellow performer, Chaplin settled in a top floor flat here in 1908. They spent £40 on second-hand furnishings, which included a fretwork Moorish screen, lit from behind by a yellow bulb, and a tasteful female nude portrait. The effect, Chaplin wrote, was 'a combination of a Moorish cigarette shop and a French whore-house'. As his first proper independent home, this was his 'cherished haven'. It was to tour the United States with the Fred Karno troupe that Chaplin left the flat for the last time – at dawn on 20 September 1910, leaving a note for Sydney on the table.

DAVID COX

(1783–1859) artist   34 (formerly 9) Foxley Road, Camberwell **6**

COX, now recognised as one of the great English watercolourists, was born in Deritend, near Birmingham, and led a peripatetic life, often working as a drawing master in order to supplement his earnings as a painter. He first came to London in 1804, finding work as a scene painter for Astley's Theatre in Lambeth and taking lodgings nearby. He exhibited for the first time at the Royal Academy in 1805 and – immediately after his marriage in 1808 to his landlady's daughter, Mary Agg – moved to Dulwich Common. From 1814 Cox worked as drawing master in Hereford, but returned to London in spring 1827, when he and his family took up residence here. The fine row of linked houses, in which Cox and his family resided until summer 1841, was built in 1824.

DAN LENO

(1860–1904) music-hall comedian
56 Akerman Road, Camberwell 7

BORN George Wild Galvin into a family of entertainers, Leno took to the stage at the age of four as a tumbler and contortionist, and in his teens became an expert clog dancer, winning the world championship in 1880 and 1883. After his triumphant London debut as a solo artist in 1885 at the Foresters' Music Hall, Mile End, he specialised in the role of pantomime dame.

While living here between 1898 and 1901 he also started to make films with his comedy partner Herbert Campbell. Leno performed at Sandringham in 1901 at the request of Edward VII. Within three years he was dead; the cause – syphilis – was not then made public. Thousands attended his funeral, and Leno's work influenced, among others, Charlie Chaplin*.

VINCENT VAN GOGH

(1853–90) artist
87 Hackford Road, South Lambeth 8

VAN Gogh took lodgings in this terraced house of about 1840 while working at the London branch of his employers, the Dutch art dealer Goupil & Co., in 1873. He liked his landlady Mrs Sarah Loyer and her daughter Eugenie, but his happiness was marred by his unrequited love for Eugenie; he eventually left the house in summer 1874 after declaring his feelings and discovering that she was already engaged. Van Gogh moved to Ivy Cottage, 395 Kensington New Road, where he remained until he was recalled to the firm's Paris branch the following May. In April 1876 he returned to England, teaching at a school in Ramsgate and moving with it to Isleworth; he left England for the last time at

'I now have a room such as I always longed for without a slanting ceiling and without blue paper with a green border. I live with a very amusing family now.'

Van Gogh to his brother, September 1873

Christmas 1876. Only 20 when he first arrived in London, Van Gogh had not yet found his vocation as a painter; the works for which he became famous, including *Sunflowers* (1888) and *Starry Night* (1889), date largely from the last years of his life. He was, however, influenced by the works published in the *Illustrated London News* and other such journals, and carried a sketchbook on his walks around south London.

LILIAN BAYLIS

(1874–1937) manager of the Old Vic
and Sadler's Wells theatres 27 Stockwell Park Road, Stockwell

BORN in Marylebone, Baylis established the Old Vic's reputation for high-quality theatrical performance, and, together with Ben Greet*, is credited with restoring Shakespeare to the heart of the English repertoire. Performances continued throughout the First World War, despite Zeppelin attacks, which she dismissed with characteristic bravado. In the 1920s

'What's an air raid when my curtain's up!'

Lilian Baylis

Baylis raised funds to turn Sadler's Wells Theatre into a home for her ballet and opera companies. She lived here from 1914 until her death, sharing this double-fronted house of c.1850 with her aunt, Ellen Cons, a governor of the Old Vic.

VIOLETTE SZABO, GC

(1921–45) secret agent 18 Burnley Road, Stockwell **10**

BORN Violette Bushell in Paris to an English father and a French mother, she moved here (to accommodation comprising the basement, ground floor and a room on the first floor) with her family in 1935 and attended a local school in Stockwell Road. When war broke out, she was working in the perfume department of the Bon Marché store in Brixton. In 1940 she met and married a French officer of Hungarian parentage, Étienne Szabo, who joined the Free French forces in North Africa. Violette continued to live in Burnley Road with her parents until early 1942, when she moved to Notting Hill; her daughter

Tania was born in June 1942. After her husband was killed in action in October that year, Szabo was recruited into the French section of the Special Operations Executive (SOE). Known as a crack shot, as well as for her striking good looks, she was sent into occupied France on two missions in 1944. In June she was captured by the Germans; refusing to speak under interrogation, she was executed with two SOE colleagues at Ravensbrück concentration camp. Szabo was posthumously awarded the George Cross. Her life was the subject of the film *Carve Her Name with Pride* (1958), which featured scenes shot in Burnley Road.

HENRY HAVELOCK ELLIS

(1859–1939) pioneer in the
scientific study of sex

Flat 14, Dover Mansions,
Canterbury Crescent, Brixton

ELLIS'S groundbreaking seven-volume series *Studies in the Psychology of Sex* (1897–1928) brought him international fame. He focused particularly on the biological origins of human behaviour, asserting that nothing based in nature could be considered inherently wrong (homosexuality, for instance). Ellis lent his support to campaigns to reform attitudes, and gave advice to the people who wrote to him about sexual matters. Born in Croydon, he spent his teenage years in Australia before returning to London to train as a doctor at St Thomas's Hospital. He kept the flat in Dover Mansions from autumn 1909 to 1928, sharing it with his bisexual wife – the lecturer and writer Edith Oldham Lees – until her death, though Ellis was often at their Cornish home in Carbis Bay. In 1928 he moved to Herne Hill with Françoise Lafitte-Cyon, known as Delisle – his partner since 1918 – and her two sons, but by the time of his death he had moved to Suffolk. In the 1880s, he had an intense – though possibly platonic – liaison with Olive Schreiner*.

C. L. R. JAMES

(1901–89) Trinidadian writer
and political activist

Second Floor Flat,
165 Railton Road, Brixton **12**

CYRIL Lionel Robert James lived here from 1981 until his death. He first came to England in 1932 at the invitation of his fellow Trinidadian, the cricketer Learie Constantine*, and made his name reporting on cricket matches for the *Manchester Guardian*. While living in London, James wrote his most famous publication, *The Black Jacobins* (1938), a history of Haitian independence. In 1938 he moved to the United States, returning to London in 1953, and spent five years in Hampstead and Willesden before returning to Trinidad, where he became involved in the island's independence movement. By the 1980s, when James returned to London, he was internationally renowned, enjoying iconic status among the West Indian community. As he became increasingly housebound, his cramped flat in Brixton – located above the offices of the journal *Race Today* – became a place of pilgrimage for students, journalists and politicians.

JOHN RUSKIN

(1819–1900) critic, artist and man of letters

26–28 Herne Hill **13**

A PLAQUE on a post here marks the site of number 28, Ruskin's family home from 1823 to 1842. The only child of a prosperous sherry merchant, Ruskin was born in Bloomsbury but his family moved to this more salubrious spot when he was four. A substantial semi-detached house dating from the late 18th century, its large gardens looked south to the hills of Norwood and north to the valley of the Thames. Ruskin recalled it as a sort of paradise, in which he passed a happy but sheltered childhood. After Oxford,

he returned here to embark on his earliest major work, the first volume of *Modern Painters* (1843), a passionate defence of J. M. W. Turner*. In autumn 1842 his family moved to a larger house – 163 Denmark Hill (demolished) – where Ruskin was based until 1872; he lamented that 'we never were so happy again'.

Ruskin's drawing of his Herne Hill home.

MARGARET LOCKWOOD

(1916-1990) actress

14 Highland Road, Upper Norwood **14**

H aving made her name in *The Lady Vanishes* (1938) – an Alfred Hitchcock* production – Lockwood went on to be one of Britain's biggest stars of the 1940s, starring in films such as *The Man in Grey* (1943) and *The Wicked Lady* (1945). As a small child, she lived in an upstairs maisonette in this 1880s house with her formidable mother and brother Lyn, having not long arrived in England from India, her

birthplace. From the rear windows, she first looked out over 'the great greyness of London'. The family's residence is proved by directories and electoral registers: oddly, Lockwood named a different address in her memoirs. The family later lived in numbers 18 and 30 Highland Road, both lost to bombing. Lockwood first went to the cinema nearby: she was, she once said, 'only a little suburban girl from Norwood'.

ARTHUR MEE (1875–1943)
journalist, author and topographer

27 Lanercost Road, Tulse Hill

BORN in Nottinghamshire to Baptist parents, Mee served his apprenticeship on the *Nottingham Daily Express*. He moved to London in late 1896 as editor of a new weekly, *Home Magazine*, and was soon a staffer at the *Daily Mail*. By 1899 he and his wife Amy had become the first occupants of this semi-detached villa, called Redcot. They moved in 1902 to a larger house in West Norwood before leaving London for good in 1905. Mee later authored educational works for children, most notably the *Children's Encyclopedia* (1908–10) and the *Children's Newspaper*, begun in 1919, and was the editor of the series of guidebooks *The King's England*, published from 1936. He was a patriot, an imperialist, and a temperance campaigner.

SIR ARNOLD BAX
(1883–1953)
composer

13 Pendennis Road
(formerly Heath Villa, Angles Road), Streatham

BAX'S parents married in 1882 and this house, part of an 1870s development, was their first home; their eldest child, Arnold, was born here on 8 November 1883. The family moved next door the following year and eventually settled in 1896 at Ivy Bank, Haverstock Hill, Hampstead (demolished). Encouraged by his mother, Bax discovered an early talent for music, and studied at the Hampstead Conservatoire and the Royal Academy of Music, where he was taught the piano by Tobias Matthay*. Although best known for his orchestral tone poems, most notably *Tintagel* (1917–19), Bax wrote seven symphonies and a wide variety of chamber music and piano pieces. He was appointed Master of the King's Music in 1942 and, in his later years, composed music for films including David Lean's *Oliver Twist* (1948).

ARTHUR HENDERSON
(1863–1935) statesman

13 Rodenhurst Road, Clapham

BORN in Glasgow, Henderson became involved in the trade union movement while working in the iron-founding industry in Newcastle. In 1903 he was elected MP for Barnard Castle and, together with Keir Hardie and Ramsay MacDonald*, was instrumental in leading the newly created Labour Party. Henderson was Party Secretary from 1912 to 1934, a period during which Labour became established as a political force and formed its first two governments, in which he served as Home Secretary (1924)

and Foreign Secretary (1929–31). 'Uncle Arthur', as he was known, moved to this house, then not long built, in 1909 and lived here until 1921. While here, he served in the wartime Cabinets of both H. H. Asquith* and Lloyd George*; he also led the Labour Party for the second of the three terms that he held the post, between 1914 and 1917.

SIR JACK HOBBS
(1882–1963) cricketer   17 Englewood Road, Clapham ⬢**18**

JOHN Berry Hobbs was born in Cambridge; he played cricket for Surrey from 1905 to 1934 and for England from 1908 to 1930. His accomplished and seemingly effortless batting earned him the sobriquet 'The Master'. Hobbs, his wife Ada and their children lived here between 1912 and 1927, the years of his greatest achieve-

ment and fame. From here, it was a short journey up Clapham Road to Surrey's home ground at the Oval. By his retirement in 1934, Hobbs – whose sports shop in Fleet Street brought him a more reliable income than cricket ever did – had scored more first-class runs (61,237) and more first-class centuries (197) than any other cricketer.

ZACHARY MACAULAY (1768–1838) philanthropist
THOMAS BABINGTON MACAULAY
(1800–59)
historian and man of letters   5 The Pavement, Clapham Common ⬢**19**

SCOTTISH by birth, Macaulay senior first moved to this late-18th-century house in Clapham in 1800 with his wife Selina. His political and moral opinions were strongly influenced by his experiences as overseer of a plantation in Jamaica (1784–9) and

then as Governor of Sierra Leone (1794–9). Zachary committed to the campaign for the abolition of slavery, and between 1802 and 1816 edited the *Christian Observer,* the journal of the Clapham Sect*. The family moved to a smarter address near Sloane Square in 1818.

Thomas Babington Macaulay – the eldest of Zachary and Selina's nine children – took an early interest in literature and in nature, as observed on long walks around the then-wild Common. He attended Mr Greaves's Academy at 14 Clapham Common North Side, then Trinity College, Cambridge. An MP for more than 20 years, it was his *History of England* (5 vols, 1848-61) that brought lasting fame. Unusually, this plaque is white, rectangular and made of stone.

JOHN FRANCIS BENTLEY

(1839–1902) architect   43 Old Town, Clapham **20**

BENTLEY moved to this handsome house of *c.*1706 with his wife Margaret in 1876, after the house had been thoroughly renovated and furnished with a mixture of antique pieces and an oak dining suite designed by Bentley himself. He moved in August 1894 to another house (demolished) in the Old Town. Born in Doncaster, Bentley set up in practice as an architect in 1860, and two years later converted to Roman Catholicism. His work was mostly confined to churches, principally of his own denomination; Westminster Cathedral (1895–1903) – its Byzantine style inspired by a visit to St Mark's, Venice – was his magnum opus. Our Lady of Victories in Clapham Park Road (1895) is another of his works.

WILLIAM WILBERFORCE* (1759–1833) AND THE 'CLAPHAM SECT'

Holy Trinity Church, Clapham Common North **21**

THE church, built in 1774–6 by Kenton Couse, became – while John Venn (1759-1833) was its rector – the centre of a group of evangelical Anglicans known as the Clapham Sect. Led by William Wilberforce and later Thomas Fowell Buxton*, they campaigned to abolish slavery in the British Dominions, and were finally successful in 1833. The 'Saints' – as they were known– were also concerned to improve moral standards in Britain and to spread the Christian message abroad. The group – composed largely of people living in Clapham, including Charles Grant (1746-1823), Director of the East India Company, and Zachary Macaulay* – was also involved in the founding of the Church Missionary Society (1799) and the Bible Society (1804), and set up its own evangelical journal, the *Christian Observer*, in 1802. From 1792 until 1797 Wilberforce lived nearby at Battersea Rise, as did fellow Saint, the banker Henry Thornton (1760–1815). The church is the only building where the Sect could be commemorated together – hence this very exceptional plaque.

GRAHAM GREENE
(1904–91) writer 14 Clapham Common North Side

ONE of the few 20th-century writers to have enjoyed critical acclaim as well as mass popularity, Greene was delighted to rent this 'most beautiful Queen Anne house ... done up like a museum piece' in 1935, and lived in it for five years with his family. It was while here that he wrote *Brighton Rock* (1938), worked as a film critic for *The Spectator*, and founded the short-lived weekly magazine *Night and Day*. This folded after Greene lost a libel action arising from his criticism of the 'dubious coquetry' of the child star Shirley Temple. His time here also encompassed the writing of *The Power and the Glory* (1940) and his early war work for the Ministry of Information. Fortunately, his wife Vivien and their two children were not at home when the house was bombed (and rendered uninhabitable) in October 1940; Greene meanwhile was with his mistress Dorothy Glover in Bloomsbury. This messy finale to the marriage partly inspired *The End of the Affair* (1951).

SIR CHARLES BARRY
(1795–1860)
architect Trinity Hospice (formerly The Elms), 29 Clapham Common North Side

BARRY was born in Westminster, the son of a bookbinder, and served his apprenticeship with a firm of surveyors in Lambeth. After touring Italy, Greece, Egypt and Syria, he set up his architectural practice and home in Ely Court, Holborn. Barry's work included the Travellers Club (1829–32) and the Reform Club (1838–41) in Pall Mall, but is exemplified by the Houses of Parliament, the building of which dominated the last 20 years of his life. His wife Sarah laid the foundation stone in 1840, and he made his home in Westminster in order to supervise his greatest project at close hand. The Houses of Parliament were opened by Queen Victoria in 1852, and he moved to The Elms – a large three-storey house built in 1754 but with many later additions, including some by Barry himself – the following year. He died here after a sudden seizure following a day out at the Crystal Palace.

EDVARD GRIEG

(1843–1907)
composer

47 Clapham Common North Side
(formerly 5 The Cedars)

BORN in Bergen, Grieg established his reputation as the leading Norwegian composer of his day with works such as his Piano Concerto in A Minor (1868) and the incidental music for Henrik Ibsen's *Peer Gynt* (1874–5); his work was often based on the melodies and rhythms of Norwegian folk songs. This was the home of Grieg's publisher George Augener, who played host to the composer and his wife, the singer Nina Hagerup, on their visits to England in the 1880s and 1890s. In those years Grieg was in great demand among English audiences as both conductor and performer, making his first public appearance in London at the Philharmonic Society Concert at St James's Hall in May 1888. At his Clapham 'home from home' he could rehearse, relax between engagements, and entertain visitors such as George Grove*, compiler of the famous dictionary of music. Grieg loved to travel by tram from Clapham into the West End.

NATSUME SOSEKI

(1867–1916) Japanese novelist

81 The Chase, Clapham

BORN in Tokyo, Soseki was sent to London in 1900 by the Japanese Ministry of Education to study English literature, at a time when Japan was opening up to the West. Although he suffered from homesickness for much of his stay, it was in London that Soseki conceived the idea of writing fiction. The knowledge he gained of Shakespeare would be a key influence on his work and one critic has noted that 'without his restricted but intense experience of London, Soseki would not have become so great a writer'. He lived in a room here at the rear of the second floor, the paying guest of the sisters Priscilla and Eliza Leale. Soseki's stay in the capital inspired a number of short stories, including *Rondon To* ('The Tower of London', 1905).

WANDSWORTH

THIS large London borough extends from the Thames south to Tooting and, from Battersea, west as far as Wimbledon Common and Richmond Park. These expanses of open land, together with Battersea Park and Clapham and Wandsworth commons, give the borough a flavour of the countryside. The 19th century, however, saw the area's transformation from a largely agricultural settlement, with industrial activities centred on the Thames and the River Wandle, to built-up London suburbs. The borough's character and history are varied: Battersea, in the north, was long associated with the skilled working classes, while the mansions and villas of Roehampton and Clapham provided retreats for the prosperous.

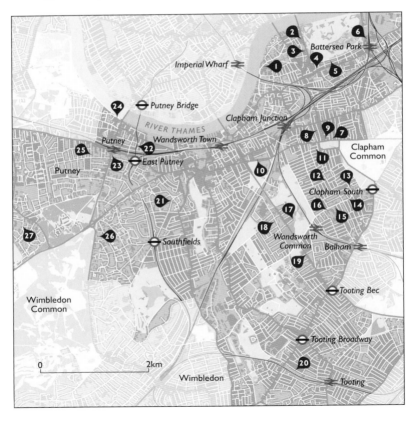

EDWARD ADRIAN WILSON

(1872–1912) Antarctic explorer and naturalist
St Mary's Vicarage, 42 Vicarage Crescent (formerly Caius House), Battersea

BORN in Cheltenham, Wilson read natural sciences at Cambridge before embarking on medical training in London. In November 1896, he came to live at this mission house – housed in a handsome 18th-century building – which was run jointly by his old Cambridge college, Gonville and Caius, and St Mary's Church, Battersea. Wilson spent his evenings 'talking, praying and singing in a positive reek of Battersea children'; it was here in the drawing room, he met his future wife, Oriana Souper. Having recovered from a bout of tuberculosis, Wilson joined the National Antarctic Expedition (1901–4) under Captain Scott*, as

'Living here in Battersea is really a good healthy change for me, as I hate Society, and here I shall have to learn to put up with a certain amount every day.'

Wilson, writing in his journal, 1896

junior surgeon, zoologist and artist, and accompanied Scott and Shackleton* to the 'Farthest South'. In 1910 he joined Scott's new expedition as chief of the scientific staff; the party reached the South Pole in January 1912, after Amundsen, and Wilson perished with his colleagues by March the same year.

NORMAN DOUGLAS

(1868–1952)
writer

Flat 63, Albany Mansions, Albert Bridge Road, Battersea

NORMAN Douglas was five when his father died in a mountaineering accident in Austria – Douglas was of mixed English-Austrian descent – and he was then sent to school in Lancashire. In the 1890s he worked for the Foreign Office before taking up writing professionally in 1907. The period 1910–17 – spent mainly in London – saw the publication of three works on southern Italy and Tunisia: *Siren Land*

(1911), *Fountains in the Sand* (1912) and *Old Calabria* (1915). Douglas's most famous work, *South Wind*, was completed in Capri in 1917. Much of the author's life was spent abroad, where his notorious pederasty was less subject to censure. Douglas chose the flat, in an imposing block of *c.*1910, for its location facing Battersea Park and lived here for nearly four years – the longest he spent at any one residence in London.

CHARLES SARGEANT JAGGER

(1885–1934) sculptor 67 Albert Bridge Road, Battersea **3**

UNLIKE many war memorial artists, Jagger experienced life on the Western Front at first hand: he joined the Artists' Rifles at the outbreak of the First World War, abandoning an already promising career as a sculptor, and went on to win the Military Cross. While convalescing he heard that the British War Memorials Committee was employing sculptors; Jagger's first commission was for a relief, the *First Battle of Ypres* (1918–19), for a proposed Hall of Remembrance. Other commissions followed, including *No Man's Land* (1919–20), the Great Western Railway Memorial (1922) at Paddington Station (*above right*) and, Jagger's masterpiece, the Royal Artillery Memorial (1921–5) at Hyde Park Corner. By autumn 1923 Jagger was living at Anhalt Studio, Anhalt Road, to the rear of 117 Albert Bridge Road, a building that continued to be his home following his marriage in 1925 to Evelyn Isabel Wade. In 1930 the couple moved to number 67, where Jagger died four years later. He was productive until the end, sculpting works for a wide circle of private patrons.

JOHN RICHARD ARCHER

(1863–1932) Mayor of Battersea who fought social and racial injustice 55 Brynmaer Road, Battersea **4**

THE first black or mixed-race Briton to achieve high office in London – or in any sizeable UK city – John Archer was born in Liverpool; his father was from Barbados, his mother from Ireland. He was a Battersea resident from about 1897 and soon after that date was established here in this 1880s terrace. Nearby, on Battersea Park Road, Archer ran a photographic business, and moved 'over the shop' after the First World War. He was active in progressive and Labour politics and, having served as a local councillor since 1906, was chosen as Mayor of Battersea in November 1913 – a widely reported event. Archer's interests extended beyond local concerns: in 1918 he used an address to the London-based African Progress Union to give notice that 'we have given up the idea of becoming hewers of wood and drawers of water'.

SEAN O'CASEY
(1880–1964)
playwright

49 Overstrand Mansions, Prince of Wales Drive, Battersea **5**

BORN in Dublin into a Protestant family, O'Casey worked mainly as a casual labourer before writing his first plays in his thirties. He is best known for his earlier work, including *Juno and the Paycock* (1924). In 1927 O'Casey moved to England, following the controversial production of *The Plough and the Stars*, set at the time of the 1916 Easter Rising; his rift with his native land was confirmed after the publication of his experimental anti-war play *The Silver Tassie* (1928), which was rejected by the Abbey Theatre. This five-room mansion flat of *c*.1900 on the third floor was O'Casey's home from late 1934 until September 1938, when he moved to Devon. Here, O'Casey – who 'had the trick of singing a good deal' when considering an idea for a new play – completed *The Flying Wasp* (1937) and worked on the first volume of his autobiography, *I Knock at the Door* (1939), and his play *The Star Turns Red* (first performed in 1940).

THE SHORT BROTHERS
aeronautical engineers

Railway Arch 75, Queen's Circus, Battersea **6**

EUSTACE (1875–1932) and Oswald Short (1883–1969) rented arches 75 and 81 (further to the north) from the London, Brighton and South Coast Railway in 1906, and in them constructed hot-air balloons for, among others, Thomas Sopwith* and C. S. Rolls*. In 1908, they were joined in Battersea by their brother Horace (1872–1917), often considered the engineering genius of the trio, for their first experiment in heavier-than-air flight. *Short No. 1* was largely built under the arches and, though it barely got airborne, convinced Wilbur and Orville Wright to place an order with them in 1909, giving Short Brothers – as the company became known – good claims to be regarded as

Britain's first aircraft manufacturers (C. S. Rolls piloted one of their first planes across the English Channel). The company soon acquired more spacious premises on the Isle of Sheppey, but retained the Battersea arches until circa 1918; all three brothers lived with their mother Emma, in nearby Prince of Wales Mansions, for much of the intervening period. The company has been based in Belfast since 1948.

FRED KNEE
(1868–1914) London Labour Party pioneer and housing reformer

24 Sugden Road, Clapham

RAISED in Somerset, Knee moved to London in 1890, and joined the Fabian Society* and the Social Democratic Foundation. By the time he became an Alderman on Battersea Council in 1900 he was already prominent, having founded the Workmen's National Housing Council in 1898, and campaigned to extend the public provision of housing. He played a central role in founding the London Labour Party in 1914; on 28 November, just before his death, Knee was confirmed as Secretary of the Party's provisional committee. He moved to this newly built house in 1898 with his wife Annie and their young family, and remained here until moving to Hertfordshire in late 1901.

G. A. HENTY
(1832–1902) author

33 Lavender Gardens, Clapham **8**

GEORGE Alfred Henty was born near Cambridge, where he went on to study Classics; on the outbreak of the Crimean War, he was commissioned into the Army and from 1865 he found work as a war correspondent. Henty's accounts of the Franco-Prussian War and the Spanish Civil War were published in the *Illustrated London News* and other journals, and brought him to widespread public attention. Such experiences fed into the works for which Henty is best remembered, his historical adventure stories for boys, including *In Times of Peril* (1881) and *With Moore at Corunna* (1898). Lavender Gardens, then a new development, was Henty's home after 1894, shared with his second wife Elizabeth, and where he wrote three of his best-selling novels: *With Buller in Natal* (1901), *With Roberts in Pretoria* (1902) and *With Kitchener in the Soudan* (1903).

JOHN WALTER

(1739–1812) founder of
The Times

Gilmore House,
113 Clapham Common North Side

WALTER was born in the City of London, where he carried on his father's business as a coal merchant before venturing into insurance in 1781. Two years later, bankruptcy forced him to give up both his town house in Bloomsbury, and his house here in Clapham – then about 20 years old – where he had lived with his wife Frances since 1773. By this time, Walter had become interested in typography, and in 1782 bought the patent to the logographic system, which was said to speed up the printing process. Walter had also conceived the idea of a news-sheet, the *Daily Universal Register*. The first issue appeared on 1 January 1785, the name being changed to *The Times* three years later. Walter's son and namesake became its longtime editor.

JOHN BURNS

(1858–1943) politician and statesman

110 Clapham Common North Side

LAMBETH-BORN Burns was the 16th child of a Scottish engineer and endured a childhood of relative poverty. His apprenticeship in public speaking was served on Clapham Common, and he came to notice as one of the organisers of the London dock strike of 1889. The same year, he was elected to represent Battersea on the new LCC – the only councillor with truly working-class origins. Three years later he became MP for Battersea and in 1905 joined the Cabinet of Campbell-Bannerman* as President of the Local Government Board. In 1914, in protest at the war with Germany, Burns left public life and moved here with his wife Martha. He spent his remaining years collecting books on Shakespeare, Thomas More and London.

EDWARD THOMAS

(1878–1917) essayist and poet

61 Shelgate Road, Clapham

ALTHOUGH much of his work was inspired by the countryside, Thomas spent the greater part of his life in London.

Born in Stockwell – the son of a clerk at the Board of Trade – he lived in Battersea from the age of two. This was his family home from 1889 until November 1900, when, having recently graduated from Oxford, he moved with his wife Helen and their young son to Earlsfield; in 1901 he moved to Kent and later to Hampshire. Thomas wrote his first book, *The Woodland Life* (1896), during his time here. His later country books included *The Heart of England* (1906) and *The South Country* (1909). From 1914 Thomas focused on poetry; he enlisted in the Artists' Rifles in summer 1915, and by the time of his death – he was killed during the first hour of the Battle of Arras – he had written nearly 150 poems.

WILLIAM WILBERFORCE*

(1759–1833) opponent of slavery

111 Broomwood Road
(the site of Broomwood House, formerly Broomfield) **12**

WILBERFORCE entered Parliament as Member for Hull, the town of his birth, in 1780. Seven years later he took up the anti-slavery cause, with which he remained intimately concerned for the rest of his life. In 1797, the year of his marriage to Barbara Spooner, he began to use Broomfield – newly built by his colleague Henry Thornton in the grounds of Battersea Rise House and demolished in the early 20th century – as an 'occasional retreat'. He spent much time here over the next 11 years, which saw Wilberforce dedicate himself to the abolition of the slave trade and eventually see this enacted by Parliament in 1807. He also became the leading light of the Clapham Sect*.

GUS ELEN

(1862–1940)
music-hall comedian

Edith Villa, 3 Thurleigh Avenue
(formerly Thurleigh Road) **13**

ERNEST Augustus Elen was born in Pimlico and, according to his own account, 'grew up singing'. Professionally, he started out at 'sing songs' in public houses such as the Magpie and Stump in Battersea, and by 1884 was appearing as a black-face singer. Elen made his name with his coster character, adopting a persona that was closer to the real-life costermonger (fruit and vegetable seller) than the idealised routine of Albert Chevalier*. He became a huge music-hall star from the 1890s until his retirement during the First World War. Elen was living at this late-19th-century semi by 1900 and it was his home until his death 40 years later; he bred poultry and took up photography as a hobby.

H. M. BATEMAN

(1887–1970) cartoonist   40 Nightingale Lane

AUSTRALIAN-BORN
Henry Mayo Bateman came
to England as a child, in 1888. He
was declared unfit for service in
the First World War and devoted
himself instead to his earliest
ambition, 'to draw and make people
laugh'. A shy man, Bateman was an
acute observer of social absurdi-
ties and basic human failings. He
is best known for 'The Man Who...'
series, which illustrated agonising
social gaffes and goggling witnesses
to them; these were published in
The Tatler from 1922, culminating
in 'The Guest who Called "Pâté de
Foie Gras" Potted Meat' (*illustrated*).

Bateman lived here for about four
years from 1910, during which time
he had his first one-man show at
the Brook Street Gallery (1911), and
published *Burlesques* (1916); his
observations of Clapham informed
works such as *Suburbia* (1922).

CHARLES HADDON SPURGEON

(1834–92)
preacher

Queen Elizabeth House (formerly Helensburgh House),
99 (formerly 59) Nightingale Lane

SPURGEON was born in
Essex and became a Baptist
preacher at Waterbeach, Cambridgeshire, in 1852. Two years
later, aged only 19, he was appointed
to the New Park Street congregation
in Southwark, where great crowds
were soon drawn to his ministry.
Larger premises were needed,
and the (surviving) Metropolitan
Tabernacle at Newington Butts (Elephant and Castle) was duly opened
in 1861. Spurgeon ministered at
the tabernacle until his death. He

moved to what was then Helensburgh House in 1857 with his wife
Susannah and their twin sons. Soon
finding it 'altogether too small and
inconvenient for a man whose work
needed a very large library',
in 1869 he had it rebuilt – largely at
the expense of his devoted admirers – by William Higgs, the builder
of the Metropolitan Tabernacle,
to plans by his eldest son, another
William Higgs. Spurgeon remained
here until summer 1880. The family
then moved to Upper Norwood.

TED 'KID' LEWIS

(1893–1970) world champion boxer   105 Nightingale Lane

BORN Gershon Mendaloff to a Jewish cabinetmaker's family in the East End, Lewis took up boxing in 1909 at the suggestion of a policeman who had seen him in a street brawl. He made his debut as 'Kid' Lewis at the Judaean Club, Whitechapel, and in 1913, aged 19, became the youngest-ever British featherweight champion. Between 1914 and 1922 he won numerous titles, including European featherweight, British, Empire, European and World welterweight, and British, Empire and European middleweight. In 1929 Lewis fought the last of nearly 300 bouts, winning by a knockout. He lived at Nightingale House, then known as the Home for Aged Jews, from 1966.

DAVID LLOYD GEORGE

(1863–1945) Prime Minister   3 Routh Road

LLOYD George was born in Manchester and brought up in Wales, where he took an early interest in politics. In 1890 he was elected to Parliament as a Liberal and represented Caernarfon Boroughs for the next 55 years. Lloyd George was appointed Chancellor of the Exchequer in 1908; his achievements included the 'People's Budget' of 1909 and the National Insurance Act of 1911. In 1916, on the resignation of Asquith*, he was appointed Prime Minister and formed a new coalition government. He guided the war effort for the remaining two years, and retained the premiership until 1922. Lloyd George and his wife Margaret moved here in 1903, and it was while living at this large late-Victorian house that he was appointed to his first political office as President of the Board of Trade in December 1905; it was here also that, in November 1907, Lloyd George's 17-year-old daughter Mair died. Lloyd George's grief was such that he left the house shortly afterwards, and in January 1908 moved with his family to Chelsea.

SIR KENNETH MACMILLAN

(1929–92) choreographer   14 Lyford Road, Wandsworth

ONE of the leading ballet choreographers of his generation, MacMillan was born in Scotland and raised in Norfolk. The psychological drama *The Burrow* (1958) was an early success with the Royal Ballet, of which MacMillan became artistic director in 1970. He lived in Lyford Road from about 1974 to 1980; highlights of that period included *Mayerling* (1978), its double-suicide plotline exemplifying MacMillan's risk-taking approach. He created over 40 ballets and discovered, among others, Lynn Seymour and Darcey Bussell.

THOMAS HARDY*

(1840–1928)
poet and novelist

172 Trinity Road (formerly The Larches, 1 Arundel Terrace)

ARTICLED at the age of 16 to an architect in Dorchester, Hardy left Dorset in 1862 to seek his fortune in London, where he entered the offices of the architect Arthur William Blomfield. In his spare time he wrote his first novel, *The Poor Man and the Lady* (1867). He turned to writing full-time in 1873, publishing *Far From the Madding Crowd* the following year. Hardy moved here on 22 March 1878 and, with his wife Emma, settled down to a London literary life; his residence saw the publication of *The Return of the Native* (1878), *The Trumpet-Major* (1880) and *A Laodicean* (1881). In the capital, however, he complained of an oppressive feeling of proximity to 'a monster whose body had four million heads and eight million eyes', and, after a period of serious illness, left Tooting for Dorset in late May 1881.

SIR HARRY LAUDER

(1870–1950)
music-hall artiste

46 (formerly Athole House, 24) Longley Road, Tooting

LAUDER was born near Edinburgh and showed an early talent for singing and comedy; having played the Scottish music halls, he came at the age of 30 to London, where he made his debut at Gatti's. In 1908 he gave a command performance before Edward VII, and during the First World War took part in many troop concerts. Lauder's act consisted of songs – almost all his own – with a Scottish flavour, interspersed with comic patter; they included 'Roamin' in the Gloamin'', 'Stop Yer Tickling, Jock' and 'I Love a Lassie'. Lauder and his wife Annie lived here, in what he called 'a very modest villa out Tooting way', from 1903 until 1911.

GEORGE ELIOT*
(1819–80) novelist   Holly Lodge, 31 Wimbledon Park Road **21**

BORN Mary Ann Evans in Warwickshire, Eliot published her first full-length novel – *Adam Bede* – in 1859, and by the 1860s enjoyed a flourishing literary career, accepted as one of the greatest writers of her time. This semi-detached house of the mid-19th century was Eliot's home between February 1859 and September 1860, and it was here that she wrote one of her most celebrated novels, *The Mill on the Floss* (1860). She lived here openly with the critic George Henry Lewes, despite his being already married. Eliot expected Holly Lodge – 'a tall cake, with a low garnish of holly and laurel' – to be their home 'for years to come' but soon became restless, feeling it to be overlooked by 'houses full of eyes', and its location 'inconvenient'. By late September 1860, she was living in Marylebone.

HENRI GAUDIER-BRZESKA
(1891–1915) sculptor and artist   25 Winthorpe Road, Putney **22**

THE subject of the Ken Russell film *Savage Messiah* (1972), Gaudier-Brzeska is renowned for geometric-primitive sculptures such as *Red Stone Dancer* (1913-14), now at Tate Britain. This railway arch served as Gaudier-Brzeska's spartan studio from September 1913 until his return to France 12 months later to enlist; during this time he signed the Vorticist manifesto and sculpted a representation of Ezra Pound*. Born Henri Gaudier near Orléans , he hyphenated his name with that of his companion, the Polish writer Sophie Brzeska. He was killed in action at Neuville-Saint-Vaast, aged just 23.

ALGERNON CHARLES SWINBURNE*
(1837–1909) poet
THEODORE WATTS-DUNTON
(1832–1914) poet, novelist and critic   11 (formerly The Pines, 2) Putney Hill

SWINBURNE developed his literary tastes at Eton and Oxford and in London mixed in a circle that included D. G. Rossetti* and Edward Burne-Jones*. He suffered from ill health and alcoholism and in 1879 was taken in by his friend (Walter) Theodore Watts-Dunton who encouraged discipline, and abstention, in the poet's life. The pair lived in this 'large double block of a building' of c.1870 from September 1879 until their respective deaths; even Theodore's marriage in 1905 'did not change the quiet, ordered life at The Pines'. Swinburne occupied 'one room on the first floor, looking out upon the beautiful back garden ... and a bedroom on the floor above, with a "commanding view" of Putney Hill'. While here Swinburne enjoyed a creative period which saw the publication of works including the verse collections *Songs of the Springtides* (1880) and *Astrophel* (1894) and a novel, written by 1862, *Love's Cross-Currents* (1904). Watts-Dunton produced *The Coming of Love, and Other Poems* (1897) and the novel *Aylwin* (1898).

FRED RUSSELL

(1862–1957)
father of modern ventriloquism

71 Kenilworth Court,
Lower Richmond Road, Putney

FRED Russell was the name adopted by Thomas Frederick Parnell, who – with his performances with a single hand-held puppet, Coster Joe – created the modern ventriloquist act. He toured the music halls with Coster Joe, who was based on the contemporary star Albert Chevalier*, from 1896 and made his last live appearance on television in 1952. Russell also published *Ventriloquism and Kindred Arts* (1898) and helped to establish the first trade union for variety

'Cor, lumme, where would Fred Russell be without me? Up the bloomin' pole ... long ago!'

Coster Joe on his puppet master

performers. Born in Poplar, he spent his earlier life in east London and for a time edited the *Hackney and Kingsland Gazette*. None of his addresses in that area survive, so his plaque adorns the Thames-side block of 1903 where he lived during the First World War and in the years immediately following.

DR EDVARD BENEŠ

(1884–1948) President of Czechoslovakia

26 Gwendolen Avenue, Putney

BORN in what was then Bohemia, Beneš became, during the First World War, a diplomat and an advocate of the cause of Czech nationalism. From 1918 to 1935 he was Foreign Minister of the new Czechoslovak state and served as its premier between 1921 and

1922, before assuming the office of President in 1935. In autumn 1938, after the Munich Agreement ceded the Sudetenland to Germany, Beneš went into exile in London, where in 1940, he became President of Czechoslovakia-in-exile.

He was confirmed in office on his return home in 1945, and continued as President until the year of his death. This was Beneš's home from October 1938 until November 1940, when the Blitz forced his Cabinet to move to Buckinghamshire.

SIR EDWIN SAUNDERS

(1814–1901) dentist   Fairlawn, 89 Wimbledon Park Side, Putney Heath

SAUNDERS was born in London, and first came to notice in 1837, when he published *The Teeth, a Test of Age*, in which he demonstrated that the age of children could be determined by observation of their teeth. From 1839 to 1854 he worked as a dental surgeon and lecturer at St Thomas's Hospital, and in 1840 co-founded an institution for the dental treatment of the poor. Six years later he took over the practice of Alexander Nasmyth in Hanover Square and thus acquired the position of dentist to Queen Victoria, which he held for almost 40 years. Saunders played a key role in the development of dentistry; the Odontological Society was formed at his Mayfair home in 1856 and he was a trustee of the Dental Hospital of London. Saunders also helped to found the British Dental Association in 1880 and became the first dentist to be knighted in 1883. Fairlawn was built for him in 1853, and was his permanent home from about 1894, after he retired.

GERARD MANLEY HOPKINS, SJ

(1844–89)   Parkstead (formerly Manresa) House,
poet   Holybourne Avenue, Roehampton

HOPKINS was born into a High Anglican family of comfortable means. At Oxford, he converted to Roman Catholicism and entered the Jesuit order in 1868 as a novice. Hopkins came to this training college (now part of the University of Roehampton), resolving 'to write no more, as not belonging to my profession'. Ten years later, he produced his most famous work, the ode 'The Wreck of the *Deutschland*' (1875); Hopkins continued to write, though little work was published until a collected volume was brought out by his friend Robert Bridges in 1918.

OUTER LONDON WEST – HOUNSLOW TO HARROW

THE boroughs of Hounslow, Ealing, Brent and Harrow – formerly in Middlesex – were incorporated into the new Greater London authority in 1965. Older centres of population include Chiswick, Brentford, Acton, Ealing and Pinner, but most development in this area – especially the infill – dates from the last 150 years.

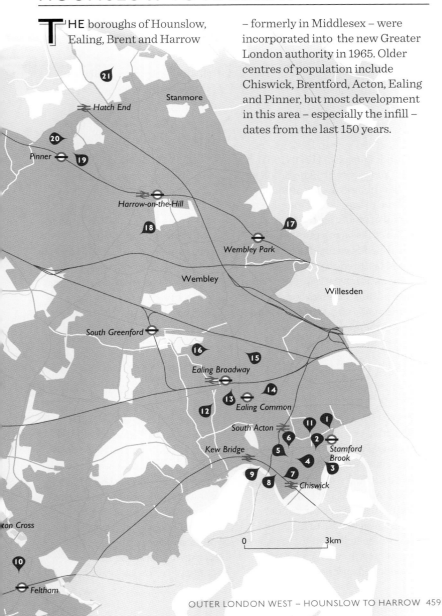

Stanmore

Hatch End

Pinner

Harrow-on-the-Hill

Wembley Park

Wembley

Willesden

South Greenford

Ealing Broadway

Ealing Common

South Acton

Kew Bridge

Stamford Brook

Chiswick

ton Cross

Feltham

0   3km

LUCIEN PISSARRO

(1863–1944) painter, printer
and wood engraver

The Brook, 27 Stamford Brook Road,
Ravenscourt Park

PISSARRO was born in Paris, the eldest son of the impressionist painter Camille Pissarro. During the Franco-Prussian War the family fled to England. Having returned, the Pissarros retained links with their country of exile and Lucien settled here in 1890, marrying Esther Bensusan (1870–1951) in 1892 and moving to The Brook in 1902. The house was the headquarters of the Eragny Press, founded in 1894 and named after the Normandy home of Pissarro's family; it published 31 books, many illustrated by him, and featured a typeface named 'The Brook' after the house. After its closure in 1914, Pissarro concentrated increasingly on painting. He was a founder member of the Camden

'... having been attracted by a derelict 18th-century farmhouse behind a little green overshadowed by some ugly tall flats ...
they turned the stable into a printing room, [and] the "brewhouse" into a studio.'

Lucien Pissarro's daughter Orovida on The Brook

Town Group (1911) and the London Group (1913), and in 1919 co-founded the Monarro Group to represent artists inspired by the work of the French impressionists Monet and Camille Pissarro. A naturalised British citizen from 1916, Pissarro died in 1944 at Hewood, Dorset.

PRIVATE FREDERICK HITCH, VC

(1856–1913) hero of Rorke's Drift

62 Cranbrook Road, Chiswick **2**

HITCH'S outstanding bravery achieved popular recognition through the 1964 film *Zulu*. A builder's labourer, Hitch enlisted at the age of 20 and – as a private in the 24th Regiment of Foot – was sent to South Africa. There, in January 1879, he saved the life of his commanding officer, helped to keep the enemy at bay while a field hospital was evacuated and, despite having

a shoulder shattered by a bullet, continued to pass ammunition to his comrades. Hitch received one of 11 Victoria Crosses presented for the defence of Rorke's Drift. Back in civilian life, he worked as a labourer, a publican and a cab driver. From 1909, Hitch lodged at this modest two-storey terraced house of the 1880s; it was here that he died of pneumonia at the age of 56.

ALEXANDER POPE

(1688–1744)
poet

Mawson Arms public house,
110 Chiswick Lane South, Chiswick **3**

POPE lived at Mawson's Buildings, a terrace of five houses built in *c.*1715, from 1716 to 1719 'under the wing of my Lord Burlington' of nearby Chiswick House. Also resident here were his parents and his old nurse Mary Beach. The house in which they lived is thought to have been the end building, converted in 1897 to a public house. Born in the City of London, Pope's early poetic successes were the *Pastorals* (1709) and *The Rape of the Lock* (1712). His time here saw the publication of his *Works* (1717), including 'Elegy to the Memory of an Unfortunate Lady' and 'Eloisa to Abelard'. Meanwhile, he was hard at work on his translation of Homer's *Iliad*, the proceeds of which enabled him to acquire, in 1719, land at Twickenham for his villa.

TOMMY COOPER

(1921–84) comedian

51 Barrowgate Road, Chiswick **4**

AFTER honing his skills as a comedian during wartime army service and in the clubs, Tommy Cooper made his television debut in 1952, and his routine of meticulously bungled conjuring tricks and deadpan humour became a small-screen favourite. Visually, his trademark was a fez – the legacy of an army posting in Cairo. A typical Cooper joke ran: 'So I rang up a local building firm, I said "Can I have a skip outside my house?". He said "I'm not stopping you."' He moved to Barrowgate Road – once a Royal Horticultural Society garden – in 1955 and stayed for the rest of his life, along with his wife Gwen, their two children, and a housekeeper. Cooper died after collapsing onstage at Her Majesty's Theatre, following several years of poor health.

PATRICK HAMILTON

(1904–62) novelist and playwright

2 Burlington Gardens, Chiswick **5**

PATRICK Hamilton is celebrated for his pungently observed portrayals of mid-20th-century English life – especially London life, and even more especially the 'bottly glitter' of saloon bars. He lived in Burlington Gardens off and on between 1914 and 1928, and here completed *Craven House* (1926), his first major novelistic success: the eponymous shabby-genteel boarding house of the title was plainly based on his family home here. *Rope* (1929), the play that made his fortune and was adapted for the big screen by Alfred Hitchcock*, was conceived while Hamilton was here. And it was just before he finally flew the nest that Hamilton became infatuated with a West End prostitute, Lily Connolly – inspiring his London trilogy *Twenty Thousand Streets Under the Sky* (1935), in which characters based on his parents also feature.

E. M. FORSTER
(1879–1970)
novelist

9 Arlington Park Mansions, Sutton Lane North, Turnham Green **6**

EDWARD Morgan Forster kept a London flat from 1925. He moved here in October 1939, partly to escape central London following the outbreak of war, and partly to be closer to his lover Bob Buckingham in Shepherd's Bush. The block was built in 1905, and Forster occupied a top-floor flat 'with a lovely view over Turnham Green'. During his time here he wrote reviews and articles, was a regular broadcaster and dedicated himself to causes such as the National Council for Civil Liberties. Forster also co-wrote the libretto for the Benjamin Britten* opera *Billy Budd* (1951). In 1945 he was elected a Fellow of King's College, Cambridge, but retained the flat here as a pied-à-terre until his death; he invariably commuted to and from it with his small Gladstone bag by bus and train, since he regarded taxis as 'a vulgar extravagance'.

JACK BERESFORD
(1899–1977) Olympic rowing champion   19 Grove Park Gardens, Chiswick

JACK Beresford Wiszniewski, the son of a Polish émigré furniture manufacturer – himself a keen oarsman who won a silver medal in the 1912 Olympics – moved here with his parents in 1903. He remained in this large detached property until his marriage in 1940. Beresford – the name he used – won silver in the rowing event at Antwerp in 1920, missing gold by a second in a legendary race against the Irish American, Jack Kelly. In all, he competed at five consecutive Olympic Games, winning medals at all of them, a record for rowing surpassed only in 2000 by Steve Redgrave. The third of his golds was won in the double sculls at the infamous Berlin Olympics of 1936. In front of Adolf Hitler, Beresford and his colleague Dick Southwood beat the highly fancied German team, who nicknamed their veteran English rival 'The Old Fox'. For Beresford's part, he proclaimed it 'the sweetest race I ever rowed in'. He also won the Wingfield Sculls, the amateur sculling championship of Great Britain, every year from 1920 to 1926.

JOSEPH MICHAEL GANDY

(1771–1843)
architectural visionary

58 Grove Park Terrace
(formerly 9 Grove Terrace), Chiswick **8**

JOSEPH Gandy is renowned for the extraordinary perspective drawings and watercolours he produced of John Soane's architecture, of which his depiction of the Bank of England in ruins is probably best known. His artwork – including a surviving item from a series called *Comparative Architecture*, which he exhibited at the Royal Academy in 1836 – may be seen at the Soane Museum in Lincoln's Inn Fields. Some three years before that, Gandy had moved from central London to this semi-detached house, part of a recently built group of ten that then stood in open fields. Sadly for Gandy – whose own architectural practice had never flourished, partly because of his unwillingness to bend the knee to patrons – he was in a Devon asylum by 1841, and died there two years later. One of his last drawings was of plans for a 'cast iron necropolis' – a dystopian vision of future burial arrangements rendered all the bleaker by the fact that Gandy's own final resting place is unknown.

JOHANN ZOFFANY

(1733–1810) painter

65 Strand-on-the-Green, Chiswick **9**

BORN near Frankfurt as Johannes Josephus Zauffaly, Zoffany first came to England in the late 1760s. He won the patronage of the actor David Garrick*, became renowned as a master of the 'conversation piece' and commissions from the royal family followed. Zoffany and his wife Mary settled in 1790 at this house, which dates from the early 18th century. Known since as Zoffany House, it was here that the artist died 20 years later. Among the works he executed while living here was *The Plundering of the King's Cellar at Paris* (1794), an expression of his horror at the violence of the French Revolution.

FREDDIE MERCURY

(1946–91) singer and songwriter

22 Gladstone Avenue, Feltham

AS the singer of Queen, Mercury fronted one of the most successful rock bands in the world. He also wrote some of their most memorable songs, including the epic 'Bohemian Rhapsody' (1975), 'Killer Queen' (1974 – their first major hit) and 'Crazy Little Thing Called Love' (1979). Born Farrokh Bulsara to a Parsi family in Zanzibar and schooled in India, he came to England – and to this inter-war terraced house in Feltham – with his family in 1962. At that point he was already using the name Fred – the formal change to 'Freddie Mercury' came in 1970, the year that Queen were formed. By this time Mercury, who studied graphics at art college in Ealing, was living in shared flats, mostly in Kensington.

EALING

JOHN LINDLEY

(1799–1865) botanist and
pioneer orchidologist

Bedford House,
The Avenue, Acton Green

THIS house, much altered since Lindley's day, was built in about 1793 to designs by John Bedford. Lindley lived here from 1836 until his death. Born in Norfolk, the son of a nurseryman, he gained a helpful introduction to Joseph Banks*, then the country's leading botanist, who in 1819 made Lindley his assistant librarian at his house in Soho Square. Lindley became the first Professor of Botany at the University of London in 1829 and was the author of numerous books on botany and horticulture. With works such as *The Genera and Species of Orchidaceous Plants* (1830–40) and *Orchidacae Lindenianae* (1846), he laid the foundations of modern orchidology and named many species. While living here with his wife Sarah and their family, Lindley lectured at the Chelsea Physic Garden and was closely involved in the Horticultural Society, to which his library was left.

SIR MICHAEL BALCON

(1896–1977)
film producer

White House building,
Ealing film studios **12**

THE identification of Ealing with a certain film genre owes plenty to Balcon, who came to London from Birmingham in the early 1920s and co-founded Gainsborough Pictures; he gave Alfred Hitchcock* his first break as a director. Following stints with Gaumont-British and MGM, Balcon became Head of Production at Ealing Studios in 1938 – with an office in the rear part of the White House – and oversaw the studio's wartime productions. After the war – having secured a distribution deal with the Rank Organisation – he set out to make films 'reflecting Britain and the British character'. The result was such classic comedies as *Passport to Pimlico* (1949), *Kind Hearts and Coronets* (1949) and *The Lavender Hill Mob* (1951) as well as the occasional epic such as *Scott of the Antarctic* (1948). When the studios were sold to the BBC in 1956, Balcon led his team into exile at the Borehamwood studios of MGM. He died at Upper Parrock, East Sussex, his country home since the Second World War.

DOROTHEA LAMBERT CHAMBERS

(1878–1960) lawn tennis champion

7 North Common Road, Ealing **13**

DOROTHEA 'Dolly' Douglass made her Wimbledon debut in 1900 and won the singles title seven times between 1903 and 1914. This remains the British record and, overall, puts her behind only Helen Wills Moody and Martina Navratilova. Between 1903 and 1910, she also won the Wimbledon ladies' doubles twice, the mixed doubles on three occasions and the Olympic ladies' singles gold medal in 1908. A badminton champion, she also played hockey for Middlesex. Dorothea lived here at the vicarage where her father, the Revd Henry Charles Douglass, had moved with his family in 1887 – the outside walls are said to have been used by her for hitting practice. She moved out 20 years later on her marriage – conducted by her father at nearby St Matthew's – to Robert Lambert Chambers, a merchant. In 1919, at the age of 40, Chambers narrowly lost a legendary final to Suzanne Lenglen, a Frenchwoman half her age. She went on to captain the British Wightman Cup team and to work as a coach.

RICHARD TITMUSS

(1907–1973) social scientist · 32 Twyford Avenue, Acton **14**

TITMUSS is generally credited as the founder of the academic discipline of social policy; in the words of one commentator, it was he who 'wrenched social work away from psycho-analysis to a serious concern with actual social problems'. A professor at LSE, he moved to this large semi-detached house in 1951 with his wife Kay and stayed for the rest of his life.

Titmuss wrote *The Social Division of Welfare* (1956) and *Essays on 'the Welfare State'* (1958), which were part defences and part critiques of the welfare state. His belief that self-interest should not be the prime motive force was expressed in *The Gift Relationship* (1970), which compares the commercial market in human blood that operates in the US with the UK's voluntary system.

ALAN DOWER BLUMLEIN

(1903–42) electronics engineer and inventor · 37 The Ridings, Ealing **15**

BORN in Hampstead to a German father and a Scottish mother, Blumlein undertook pioneering work on the development of television, and in sound recording and reproduction; the significance of his work on stereophonic sound only became apparent years later. From 1939, he was co-opted to work on radar – in particular on-board

technology for aircraft, which enabled pinpoint raids on key German industrial targets. He was killed on a test flight in June 1942, aged 38, but so effective was his prototype that the technology was put into service within months. Blumlein had settled in Ealing on his marriage to Doreen Lane in 1933, and this was his home until his untimely death.

FRED PERRY

(1909–95) tennis player · 223 Pitshanger Lane, Ealing **16**

FRED Perry's hat-trick of Wimbledon wins – in 1934, 1935 and 1936 – was hung around the neck of every subsequent British male player until Andy Murray's triumph in 2013. Perry

also won the French, Australian and US championships and skippered the British Davis Cup team to four consecutive victories; if that was not enough, he also took the world table tennis title in 1929.

Being, in his own words, 'a rebel from the wrong side of the tennis tramlines', Perry was not, however, fêted by the game's establishment: notoriously, his Wimbledon club tie was left draped over a chair rather than formally presented to him. Born in Stockport, Perry lived in Brentham Park from the age of ten, honing his shots in the garden – with some damaging consequences for his father's greenhouse – and sometimes practising with an umbrella, clipping the tops of hedges on his way to the Tube. This corner house, built in 1906, remained Perry's London base until he turned professional and moved to the US in 1936. During Wimbledon fortnight, it was his habit to be 'always in bed ... by ten o'clock, with the phone off the hook so I wouldn't be disturbed'.

'I just point to the statue and tell the gateman "That's me."'

Fred Perry, on how to secure admission to Wimbledon without a ticket or pass

BRENT

ARTHUR TOWLE, 'ARTHUR LUCAN'

(1885–1954) entertainer and creator of the character 'Old Mother Riley'

11 Forty Lane **17**

TOWLE'S family's disapproval of his theatrical endeavours forced him to leave his native Lincolnshire for Ireland, where he was adopted by the comedians Danny and Vera Clifton. In 1910 Towle cast the 13-year-old singer and actress Kitty McShane in the title role of *Little Red Riding Hood*, in which he was playing Granny. Three years later – after Arthur had taken his stage name from the village of Lucan, near Dublin – the couple were married. 'Lucan and McShane', as they were billed, performed together for the next 40 years as 'Old Mother Riley and her daughter Kitty'. The knockabout routine of an elderly washerwoman and her sophisticated daughter was popular on stage, film and radio. Offstage, their relationship was notoriously volatile, and Lucan was touring alone when he died in the wings of Hull's Tivoli Theatre. The couple were living at the house here – a substantial detached property dating from the early 1920s – by 1946, though Lucan may have moved out a couple of years before his death.

R. M. BALLANTYNE

(1825–94) author   Duneaves, Mount Park Road, Harrow on the Hill

BORN in Edinburgh into a family of prominent printers and publishers, Robert Michael Ballantyne spent five years working for the Hudson's Bay Company in Canada. His experiences inspired the autobiographical *Hudson's Bay, or, Every-day Life in the Wilds of North America* (1848) and a number of adventure stories. Ballantyne actually lived with Scottish lighthouse keepers on Bell Rock as research for *The Lighthouse* (1865); *The Coral Island* (1858) was perhaps his best-known book. For

the sake of the health of his family, he left Edinburgh for Europe in 1873; he settled in Harrow six years later, where his two sons attended the public school as day boys. With the aid of a bank loan, Ballantyne bought land in what is now Mount Park Road, and had Duneaves – a large detached house, now divided into five flats – built on the gently sloping site. With his tall, dark features, neat beard and silk top hat, Ballantyne became a well-known local figure, and lived here until shortly before his death.

SIR AMBROSE HEAL

(1872–1959) furniture designer   The Fives Court,
and retailer   Moss Lane, Pinner **19**

HEAL'S great-grandfather, John Harris Heal, founded the family firm and his grandfather established a shop in Tottenham Court Road in 1840. It was Ambrose Heal, however, who built the firm's reputation for simple, elegant furniture, which has had an enduring influence upon domestic design. Born in Crouch End, Heal trained at the Slade and was apprenticed to a cabinetmaker in Warwick. In 1900 he bought a plot of land opposite his father's house in Pinner and commissioned his cousin, the architect Cecil Brewer,

to build him a house on it in a vernacular style. Brewer went on to design Heal & Co.'s present shop in Tottenham Court Road (1913–16) and to introduce Heal to the Arts and Crafts luminaries William Lethaby* and C. F. A. Voysey*. Heal moved into The Fives Court, so named because of his love for the game, in March 1901; sadly his wife Alice died of cancer soon afterwards. Heal's second wife Edith hosted meetings of the Pinner branch of the Women's Social and Political Union here; they moved out to Buckinghamshire in 1917.

W. HEATH ROBINSON

(1872–1944) illustrator
and comic artist

Moy Lodge,
75 Moss Lane, Pinner **20**

WILLIAM Heath Robinson belonged to an artistic family and attended the Royal Academy Schools in the 1890s. He found a niche as an illustrator of children's books, including two of his own composition: *The Adventures of Uncle Lubin* (1902) and *Bill the Minder* (1912). It was for his humorous drawings for weekly magazines, featuring complicated and improbable 'contraptions' with whimsical applications – such as for peeling potatoes or testing artificial teeth – that Heath Robinson became celebrated:

their appeal has endured, and his name is still used to describe an unlikely mechanical arrangement. He and his wife Josephine lived in this detached house – dating from the turn of the 20th century – from 1913 to 1918. Much of his output during these years related to the First World War, and relied upon deadpan absurdist humour, as indicated by the title of the collection *The Saintly Hun: A Book of German Virtues* (1917). In 1918, desiring greater peace and quiet, Heath Robinson moved to Surrey.

R. NORMAN SHAW* (1831–1912) architect
FREDERICK GOODALL (1822–1904) painter
W. S. GILBERT* (1836–1911) playwright and librettist

Grim's Dyke, Old Redding, Harrow Weald **21**

THIS house is a fine example of the 'Old English' style for which Richard Norman Shaw was renowned. He built it for the painter Frederick Goodall, known especially for his Egyptian landscapes; hailed as 'an artistic house by an artist for an artist', it took its name from a nearby prehistoric earthwork, but was first known by the daintier variant of Graeme's Dyke. Goodall moved here on its completion in 1872, shortly after his marriage to his second wife Alice, a fellow artist. She, together with their daughter

Rica, were the models for *Palm Sunday* (1876), which was posed in one of the house's oriel windows. Goodall laid out 30 acres of landscape garden but, feeling isolated, moved to Swiss Cottage in 1883. William Schwenck Gilbert* bought Grim's Dyke – as he redesignated it – in 1890. Two of his later works with Arthur Sullivan were produced during his time here: *Utopia (Limited)* (1893) and *The Grand Duke* (1896). Unfortunately, Gilbert suffered a fatal heart attack after diving into the lake to save a girl who he believed was drowning.

OUTER LONDON NORTH –
BARNET, HARINGEY AND ENFIELD

THE three northernmost London boroughs formerly lay in Middlesex and, in their farthest reaches, Hertfordshire. They were brought within the Greater London boundary – and the remit of the London-wide blue plaques scheme – in 1965, but had mostly succumbed to the capital's urban sprawl some while before then.

Initial development came along road and railway corridors, followed by infill, with older settlements like Chipping Barnet being gradually enveloped. A good number of blue plaques have gone up across this area in recent years, mostly commemorating figures active in the twentieth century.

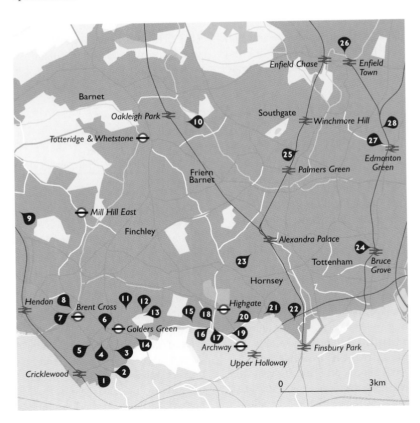

HENRY HALL

(1898–1989) dance band
leader and broadcaster

38 Harman Drive, Cricklewood **1**

PECKHAM-BORN Hall started as a pianist at the Midland Hotel in Manchester. By 1931 he was in charge of all the bands in the 32 hotels owned by the LMS Railway. In 1932, the BBC invited Hall to become resident dance band leader and form a new orchestra; his best-known hits included 'The Sun Has Got His Hat On' and 'The Teddy Bears' Picnic'. In 1934, he founded *Henry Hall's Guest Night*: the 'first chat show on British radio'. Hall left the BBC in 1937 to concentrate on touring with his band, and he later moved successfully into the new medium of television, hosting the show *Face the Music*. Hall lived here with his wife and two children from 1932 – when the house, known as Rutland, was new – until 1959, when he moved to Maida Vale.

AMY JOHNSON

(1903–41)
aviator

Flat 15, Vernon Court,
Hendon Way, Cricklewood **2**

JOHNSON moved in 1927 from her native Hull to London, where she worked as an assistant in a legal firm. In her spare time, she pursued her passion for flying, and in 1927 she joined the London Aeroplane Club at Stag Lane, Edgware; two years later, she had become the first woman in Britain to qualify as a ground engineer. On 5 May 1930, Johnson set off from Croydon in a second-hand De Havilland Gipsy Moth, *Jason*. Nineteen days later she arrived in Darwin, Australia, and as the first woman to complete this journey solo, she was hailed a model of courage and determination. In November that year Johnson –

dubbed 'Queen of the Air' – moved to newly built Vernon Court, located within easy reach of Stag Lane Aerodrome. She lived here until shortly before her marriage in July 1932 to fellow aviator and record-breaker, Jim Mollison. Soon after the outbreak of the Second World War, Johnson became a pilot with the Air Transport Auxiliary. On a routine flight in January 1941, poor weather conditions forced her to bail out over the Thames estuary; her body was never recovered.

HAROLD ABRAHAMS

(1899–1978) Olympic athlete   2 Hodford Road, Golders Green

AT the 1924 Olympic Games in Paris, Harold Abrahams won the 100m gold medal, matching the record of 10.6 seconds and becoming the first European to hold the title. This triumph, depicted (with some artistic licence) in the film *Chariots of Fire* (1981), was masterminded by his coach, 'Sam' Mussabini*, who suggested the 'drop' finish of the torso on to the tape used by Abrahams – at that time an innovation. A second-generation Jewish immigrant, Abrahams moved to this inter-war semi-detached house with his widowed mother Esther in the autumn before his Paris triumph; he lived here full-time until 1930 (and sporadically for six years after that). After his athletic career came to an end in 1925, when he broke a leg while attempting to improve on his British long jump record, he captained the British athletic team at the 1928 Olympics, and wrote books such as *Training for Athletics* (1928). Later, Abrahams worked as a broadcaster and rewrote the rules of the Amateur Athletics Association.

ABRAM GAMES

(1914–96) poster artist and designer   41 The Vale, Golders Green 4

A PHILOSOPHY of 'maximum meaning, minimum means' lay behind Games's sparse and impactful posters. During the Second World War he produced designs for everything from recruitment campaigns to public exhortations to 'dig for victory'. Games's commercial campaigns included the Guinness 'G', but his best-known design is the arresting symbol he produced for the Festival of Britain in 1951, featuring a modernistic, minimalist Britannia. He also invented a type of Cona coffee maker. Born Abraham Gamse in Mile End to Jewish parents who had fled the Russian pogroms, Games lived at this early-20th-century detached house with his wife Marianne and family from 1948, and set up his studio on the ground floor to the rear.

J. R. D. 'BOB' BRAHAM

(1920–74) RAF fighter pilot

139 Hendon Way, Childs Hill **5**

WITH his regular navigator 'Sticks' Gregory, Braham formed the most formidable RAF night-fighting team of the Second World War. He flew 316 missions, downing 29 enemy planes, and survived five crash landings; eventually, his luck ran out in June 1944 when he was forced down onto a Danish beach, and he spent the rest of the war in a prisoner-of-war camp. John Robert Daniel Braham (his RAF nickname of 'Bob' came about owing to a surfeit of Johns in his cohort) was born in Somerset, and had a peripatetic early existence thanks to his father's calling as a Methodist minister. He lived here on this busy arterial road with his parents from 1931-3, almost certainly as the first occupants of this classic inter-war semi-detached house, and was educated at a nearby preparatory school called Belmont. During the war Braham commanded 141 Squadron at Ford, West Sussex, becoming the youngest airman to be promoted to wing commander. Afterwards he lived with his wife Joan in Leicester and Hertfordshire before emigrating to Canada. There, Braham wrote his autobiography, *Scramble!* (1961).

MARY MACARTHUR

(1880–1921) trade unionist
and campaigner for working women

42 Woodstock Road,
Golders Green

GLASGOW-BORN Macarthur championed the rights of women workers, most famously the chainmakers of Cradley Heath in the West Midlands, whose demands for improved pay she supported in her capacity as General Secretary of the National Federation of Women Workers (NFWW). Of particular concern for her were the conditions endured by women homeworkers in 'sweated' industries: she contracted diphtheria while investigating the privations of Northamptonshire lacemakers. An early supporter of a legal minimum wage and a founder member of the Anti-Sweating League, Macarthur backed universal suffrage, as distinct from voting rights for propertied women. She lived in London from 1903, and is commemorated at the house, then quite new, that she moved to in 1919 with her infant daughter Anne. Shortly before, Spanish flu had claimed the life of her husband (and sometime Labour MP) Will Anderson, and Macarthur's own untimely death from cancer took place here on New Year's Day, 1921.

HARRY RELPH, 'LITTLE TICH'

(1867–1928) music-hall comedian · 93 Shirehall Park, Hendon · **7**

AS a child, Relph – who never grew past 137cm (4ft 6in) – was nicknamed 'Young Tichborne', after his supposed resemblance to the celebrated Tichborne claimant. Soon after making his London debut in 1884, he adopted an abbreviated version as his stage name, and became so famous in music hall and comic theatre – especially for his 'Big Boot Dance' – that his name entered the English language as a way of referring to a small person. Relph and his second wife, Winifred Emma Ivey, moved into this newly built house in October 1925, and it was here that he died, after a stroke.

HERBERT CHAPMAN

(1878–1934) football manager · 6 Haslemere Avenue, Hendon · **8**

CHAPMAN was born near Sheffield and became a professional footballer in 1901. During his five years (1907–12) as Manager of Northampton Town, Chapman led the club to the top of the Southern League. This success continued at Huddersfield Town, which he managed between 1921 and 1925, a period that saw an FA Cup and two League Championship victories. As Manager of Arsenal he moved into this newly built house in 1926 with his wife Annie. Chapman was responsible for a number of footballing innovations, including rubber studs on boots, numbers on players' shirts and floodlights; he also improved the club's Highbury ground, and in 1932, arranged for the name of the closest Underground station to be changed to Arsenal – a public relations coup. On the pitch, Arsenal won the FA Cup in 1930 and the League Championship in 1930–31 and 1932–3. After Chapman's untimely death (at the house here) – probably hastened by overwork – the team he built went on to win two further League titles in succession.

GRAHAM HILL

(1929–75) racing driver

GRAHAM Hill drove his first Formula One race for Team Lotus at Monaco in 1958. Two years later, he transferred to British Racing Motors (BRM) and in 1962 won his first Grand Prix; later that year, after a tense battle with the Lotus driver Jim Clark, Hill emerged as world champion, the first British driver to achieve this success in an all-British car. Having returned to Lotus, Hill won his second world championship in 1968 and he went on to win his 14th, and last, Grand Prix the following year. By the time of his retirement as a driver in 1975, Hill had competed in a record-breaking 176 races, and had also achieved the 'triple crown' of victory at Formula One (1962, 1968), Indianapolis (1966) and Le Mans (1972); he remains the only driver to have done so. In November 1960, Hill moved into this five-bedroom house, with its large garden, with his wife Bette and their children (including Damon, who also became a world champion racing driver). They moved to Hertfordshire in 1972 – three years before Hill's untimely death, with members of his Embassy Hill team, in a flying accident.

SIR KARL POPPER

(1902–94) philosopher

POPPER'S best-known book, *The Open Society and Its Enemies* (1945) – a strong attack on totalitarianism of the left and right – was written in New Zealand, where he went as a Jewish refugee from Vienna. The year after it came out, he accepted a post at the LSE and moved to this modest 1930s terraced house in what his wife Hennie unflatteringly described as 'a semi-proletarian suburb'. Neither of them enjoyed living here, feeling hemmed in by the proximity of their neighbours and bothered by the noise of their radios. One amenity that Popper did enjoy, however, was door-to-door milk deliveries, not a feature of Austrian life. The four years that he spent here were vital in the establishment of his academic reputation, and saw him become a British citizen in 1949. It was while here that Popper clashed with Ludwig Wittgenstein at a Cambridge seminar: holding a poker, the latter asked Popper to cite a 'moral rule': 'Not to threaten visiting lecturers with pokers,' he retorted. Later, Popper lived in Buckinghamshire and at Kenley, on Greater London's extreme southern fringe.

ROBERT DONAT

(1905–58) actor   8 Meadway, Hampstead Garden Suburb **11**

THE son of a civil engineer of Polish descent, Donat studied drama in his native Manchester. He had his first theatrical triumph playing Gideon Sarn in a 1931 adaptation of Mary Webb's *Precious Bane*, and went on to enjoy a number of other stage successes. Donat played the lead role in *The Count of Monte Cristo* (1934), which established him as a major film star. Soon after being offered the part, Donat moved into this house of 1908 – which was built to designs by M. H. Baillie Scott – with his first wife Ella. Donat's time here, from 1934 to 1937, saw him star in the Hitchcock* classic *The Thirty-Nine Steps* (1935). Soon after moving out, he scored his greatest screen hit – and his first Oscar – with the title role in *Goodbye, Mr Chips* (1939).

FRANK PICK

(1878–1941) pioneer of good design for London Transport   15 (formerly 8) Wildwood Road **12**

FRANK Pick joined the Underground Electric Railways Company of London in 1906, and became Vice-Chairman and Chief Executive of the newly created London Passenger Transport Board from 1933 until his retirement in 1940. In collaboration with Lord Ashfield*, he changed the face of the capital's transport, merging the Underground, the London General Omnibus Company and more than 150 independent transport undertakings into the largest and – at the time – most efficient urban transport system in the world. Pick was passionately interested in design: he set new standards for poster art, being responsible for the imaginative commissioning of work from Edward McKnight Kauffer*. In 1916 he set Edward Johnston* the task of designing a new typeface for use on the Underground, and worked with the architect Charles Holden, whose designs for stations on the outlying extensions of the Piccadilly and Northern lines remain moderne models of their kind. Between 1932 and 1934, Pick served as President of the Design and Industries Association, and in 1934 was also the first Chairman of the Council for Art and Industry. He lived in this detached red-brick house from about 1914 and died here 27 years later. The classic sans serif typeface Pick commissioned from Johnston was used for the plaque's lettering.

DAME MYRA HESS

(1890–1965) pianist

48 Wildwood Road **13**

HESS was born in West Hampstead into a prosperous Jewish family. She made her official London debut in a 1907 concert conducted by Thomas Beecham*, and during her long and successful career, built up a large repertoire, though she specialised in works by Mozart*, Beethoven and Schumann. She is perhaps best remembered for her role as the organiser of the daily chamber music concerts held at the National Gallery, the only regular performances of music in London during the Second World War. These made a vital contribution to keeping up public morale, earning Hess a DBE in 1941. Unmarried, she worked from this neo-Georgian house of c.1912 which was her home from 1936 until 1953, when she moved to St John's Wood.

EVELYN WAUGH

(1903–66) writer

145 North End Road, Golders Green **14**

DESCRIBED by Waugh as a 'typical unpretentious house of its period', the house – originally named Underhill – was built in 1907 for the writer's father, the publisher and editor Arthur Waugh. It was the family home from September 1907 until 1931, and although Evelyn came to dislike the house, he spent much time here, even after his marriage to Evelyn Gardner ('She-Evelyn') in 1928. Waugh's time here saw the publication of his biography of D. G. Rossetti* (1928), his first novel, *Decline and Fall* (1928), and his first major success, *Vile Bodies* (1930), which satirised the 'bright young things' of the day. He later lived in grander surroundings; Waugh's son, Auberon, explained the 'profound effect' number 145 had exerted on his father in his twenties, 'chiefly in the desire to get away from it into the elegant salons of Brideshead'.

Auberon Waugh unveiling the plaque to his father, 1993.

A. V. HILL

(1886–1977) physiologist   16 Bishopswood Road, Highgate **15**

ONE of the founding fathers of sports medicine and the first Briton to win the Nobel Prize for Physiology, Hill was also a highly respected independent MP during the Second World War and, as a founder member of the Academic Assistance Council, helped more than 900 academics escape persecution by the Nazis. The Nobel Prize, shared with Otto Meyerhof, was awarded in 1923 for Hill's work on the production of heat during muscular function; news of the honour came to him from his wife Margaret – the sister of the economist John Maynard Keynes* – who read about it in a newspaper. Just before this, Hill and his young family had moved into this detached house of 1878, where he lived for nearly 44 years; appropriately, perhaps, it backs onto the playing fields of Highgate School. A. V. Hill (he hated his first name of Archibald) was a keen amateur athlete and undertook vital research on the body's uptake of oxygen and the effect of air resistance on running. He also sat on the committee that oversaw the development of radar, alongside Patrick Blackett*.

A. E. HOUSMAN

(1859–1936) poet and scholar   Byron Cottage, 17 North Road, Highgate **16**

ORIGINALLY from Worcestershire, Alfred Edward Housman studied at Oxford, and moved to London in 1882 to take up a clerkship at the Patent Office. He returned to academia in 1892, when he took up the chair of Latin at University College London. Later, from 1911 until the time of his death, he held a comparative professorship at Cambridge. Although Housman anticipated that his greatest memorial would be his work as a classical scholar – he produced editions of Ovid (1894), Manilius (1903–30), Juvenal (1905) and others – it is as a poet that he is best remembered. During the time that he lived in this fine early-18th-century terraced house (named after a governor of Highgate School, situated opposite), from 1886 until 1905, Housman wrote *A Shropshire Lad* (1896), *Poems by Terence Hearsay* (1896) and the majority of the works published in *Last Poems* (1922). A bachelor, he was served devotedly by his landlady, Mrs Trim; when in November 1905 she moved to Pinner, Housman moved with her, remaining there until he transferred to Cambridge in 1911.

MARY KINGSLEY

(1862–1900) traveller and ethnologist

22 Southwood Lane, Highgate **17**

MARY Henrietta Kingsley was born in Islington, the niece of the novelist Charles Kingsley*. She grew up in this detached villa of c.1830 largely in the company of her mother and brother, and caused minor domestic disasters here by experimenting with gunpowder and the household plumbing. Following the death of her parents in 1892, the self-educated Kingsley made two pioneering voyages to West Africa, where she gathered information about indigenous religious beliefs and practices. She returned to England in 1895 and published *Travels in West Africa* (1897) and *West African Studies* (1899). As a volunteer nurse in the South African War, she contracted typhoid and died.

ARTHUR WALEY

(1889–1966) poet, translator
and orientalist

50 Southwood Lane, Highgate **18**

THE Kent-born Waley became an assistant in the new sub-department of Oriental Prints and Drawings at the British Museum in 1913. He taught himself Chinese and Japanese in order to catalogue the paintings in the collection and began to publish translations, including *A Hundred and Seventy Chinese Poems* (1918), *The Nō Plays of Japan* (1921) and *Tale of Genji* (1925–33), which won him a strong scholarly reputation. Alison Grant Robinson, to whom Waley had been romantically attached for years, moved into this house when Waley – a long-time Bloomsbury resident – acquired it in 1960. Following the death in 1962 of his long-term partner Beryl de Zoete, Waley joined Alison here. The couple finally married in 1966, a month before Waley's death.

VINAYAK DAMODAR SAVARKAR

(1883–1966) Indian patriot
and philosopher

65 Cromwell Avenue, Highgate **19**

SAVARKAR came to England on a scholarship supported by Lokamanya Tilak*. He entered Gray's Inn and was called to the Bar in 1910; his four years in London were critical to his development as a Hindu nationalist and revolutionary leader. While living at this hostel for

Indian students set up by Krishna-varma, and known as India House, Savarkar mixed with other fighters for Indian independence, among them Gandhi*. In 1907, Savarkar translated into Marathi the auto-biography of Mazzini*, and carried out research for *The Indian War of Independence of 1857* (published in 1909 but banned in India until 1946). Savarkar was implicated in the 1910 murder of a British official in Nasik, near his birthplace, and later con-victed. While in prison, he wrote the influential pamphlet *Hindutva: Who is a Hindu?* (1923). Later, Savarkar was cleared of having co-organised the assassination of Gandhi in 1948.

V. K. KRISHNA MENON

(1896–1974) campaigner for
Indian independence   30 Langdon Park Road, Highgate **20**

KRISHNA Menon was one of the leading London-based campaigners for Indian independ-ence during the 1930s and 40s . He was also the St Pancras Labour councillor responsible for intro-ducing the loan of gramophone records and a 'children's corner' to the borough libraries. Another literary achievement was Menon's (seldom credited) founding role in Pelican books, the non-fiction arm of Penguin. Being close – politi-cally and personally – to India's first Prime Minister, Jawaharlal Nehru*, Menon was appointed as the coun-try's first High Commissioner in London in 1947; his major achieve-ment was to keep India in the Com-monwealth, of which – despite his opposition to the British *raj* – he was a supporter. It was on first coming to London in 1929, to study law and political science at the LSE, that Menon lived – for around two and a half years – at this late-Victorian ter-raced house in Highgate. Tall, spare and ascetic, he subsisted for several years on a meagre diet of toast, buns and tea – up to 30 cups a day.

FRANK MATCHAM

(1854-1920) theatre architect   10 Haslemere Road, Crouch End **21**

THE Devon-born Matcham built or rebuilt over 150 thea-tres, including the Hackney Empire (1901), the London Coliseum (1905) and the Palladium (1910); his stylistically eclectic and exuberant interiors earned him the nickname 'Matchless Matcham'. He lived here between 1895 and 1904, the period in which he did much of his best work.

LAURIE CUNNINGHAM

(1956–1989)
England international footballer

A FLEET-FOOTED winger who, it was said, 'could run on snow without leaving footprints', Cunningham became the first black player to represent England in a competitive international, in May 1979 against Wales. The son of Jamaican immigrants, he hit the heights as a club player while with West Bromwich Albion and Real Madrid. But it was at Leyton Orient that Cunningham first came to prominence, and in Stroud Green that he spent his formative years; born at the Whittingham Hospital, he attended Highgate Wood School.

Cunningham's former teammates Peter Allen and Cyrille Regis at the unveiling.

THE WORLD'S FIRST REGULAR HIGH-DEFINITION TELEVISION SERVICE

(2 November 1936)
Alexandra Palace, Wood Green **23**

THE BBC needed a site on high ground close to central London from which to pilot their first television transmissions, and chose Alexandra Palace. Built in 1873–5 to the designs of Alfred Meeson and John Johnson and known originally as the 'People's Palace', it was intended to rival the Crystal Palace as a public recreation and entertainment centre. The BBC constructed offices and two studios here, and a 67m (220ft) transmission mast was raised above the existing corner tower – from which, in November 1936, the world's first television programme was broadcast. The transmission range was some 25 miles; all of London was covered, though at that date only a tiny fraction of the population owned television sets on which to view the two separate hours of broadcasting on offer each day (using, alternately, the rival Baird and Marconi-EMI systems, of which the latter was eventually preferred). Alexandra Palace ceased to be used by the BBC in 1981, though the transmitter remains in use as a relay.

LUKE HOWARD

(1772–1864) namer of clouds

7 Bruce Grove, Tottenham

THE son of a Quaker tinsmith, Howard enjoyed a successful career as a manufacturing chemist. He was one of the founders, in 1796, of the London-based philosophical group, the Askesian Society, to which he presented his paper 'On the Modification of Clouds' in 1803. This indicated the nature and height of clouds, and set out a system of classification and nomenclature – cirrus, stratus, cumulus and nimbus – which remains in international use today. Howard's work was much admired: Goethe was so impressed that he wrote a poem, 'Howard's Ehrengedächtnis' (1817), in his honour. In 1818–20, Howard published further meteorological findings in *The Climate of London* and later wrote *Seven Lectures on Meteorology* (1837). Luke Howard lived from 1837 at 4 Bruce Grove, next door to his sister Elizabeth. In 1852, on the death of his wife Mariabella, he moved to number 7, a house of the 1790s which had been in his ownership since at least the mid-1820s and was the home of his eldest son Robert. Luke Howard remained at this address until his death, which took place here.

ENFIELD

STEVIE SMITH

(1902–71) poet

1 Avondale Road, Palmers Green **25**

FLORENCE Margaret Smith – known as 'Stevie' from the 1920s – was born in Hull. In 1906, she moved with her family to Palmers Green, then a rural village near London. She lived in this 'house of female habitation' – described in her poem 'A House of Mercy' (1966) – from then until the time of her death 65 years later. Smith shared this end-of-terrace house with her elder sister Molly, her mother Ethel and, most enduringly, her aunt, Margaret Spear (d.1968). 'The Aunt' cared for Stevie for much of her life, and appeared in her writings as the

'Lion of Hull'. Smith's first work of fiction, *Novel on Yellow Paper* (1936), was written on the copying paper of the firm where she worked as a personal secretary until 1953. Her verse – witty, bizarre, sad, sometimes caustic, and illustrated with her own line drawings – reached a wide audience and brought her immense success; *Not Waving but Drowning* (1957) is her best-known collection. Smith died on a visit to Devon. The plaque was unveiled by the Poet Laureate, Andrew Motion.

JOSEPH WHITAKER
(1820–95) publisher
and founder of *Whitaker's Almanack*

White Lodge,
68 Silver Street, Enfield

WHITAKER was a well-established religious and theological publisher and the editor of the *Gentleman's Magazine* when, in 1858, he founded *The Bookseller*, a monthly book trade journal that continues today. Ten years later, he launched the work that made his name familiar – *Whitaker's Almanack*, a comprehensive reference book that has been published annually since 1868. Whitaker took a lease on this handsome weatherboarded house, which may date from the 17th century, in June 1862, before purchasing the property in 1875, and lived here until his death. The editorship of the *Almanack* passed to his twelfth child, Cuthbert.

CHARLES LAMB* (1775–1834)
MARY LAMB (1764–1847)
writers   Lamb's Cottage (formerly Bay Cottage), Church St., Edmonton

THE London-born writer Charles Lamb and his sister Mary collaborated on *Tales from Shakespear* [*sic*] (1807) and *Poetry for Children, Entirely Original* (1809). Behind this lies tragedy: in 1796, Mary killed their ageing mother with a table knife; found insane, she was entrusted to her brother's care. In May 1833 – the year Charles's *The Last Essays of Elia* appeared – he moved from Enfield with the deteriorating Mary to Bay Cottage, an early-18th-century house kept as a discreet private asylum by a Mr and Mrs Walden. Here, Charles witnessed her decline 'in a half-way purgatory' and, just before Christmas 1834, suffered a fall and died shortly afterwards. Mary lived until 1847, and was buried alongside her brother in the nearby churchyard of All Saints.

CHARLES COWARD

(1905–76) rescuer of
prisoners from Auschwitz

COWARD'S wartime experiences – partially brought to the screen in *The Password is Courage* (1962), starring Dirk Bogarde – earned him widespread recognition, especially in Israel, where he has a tree at Yad Vashem, the Holocaust memorial in Jerusalem. He joined the Army in 1937, and in 1940 was captured at the fall of Calais. Coward vowed to make himself a nuisance to the Nazis and to help his fellow prisoners. Posted to labour camp E715, next to the I.G. Farben plant at Auschwitz, he was appointed Red Cross Trustee responsible for British prisoners of war, which allowed him to operate more freely. He risked his life in order to smuggle reputedly hundreds of prisoners out of Auschwitz; he also brought in arms and sent coded letters to the British government. On one occasion, the inaptly named Coward exchanged places with a concentration camp inmate and had a night-long experience of the horrific conditions. He moved to Chichester Road in 1945 where he lived with his wife Florence and their five children. While living here, in 1947, he gave crucial – and, at the time, sensational – testimony at the Nuremberg trials.

OUTER LONDON EAST – WALTHAM FOREST TO BARKING

THE London boroughs to the east of the River Lea were historically part of Essex, and have only been covered by the blue plaques scheme since 1965. The area was home to much of the capital's industry and suffered heavily from bombing in the Second World War: in some districts, even the streetplan is entirely changed. The relatively poor survival rate for historic buildings is one reason for the relative scarcity of blue plaques. The borough of Barking and Dagenham got its first in 2016, marking the boyhood home of footballing legend Bobby Moore.

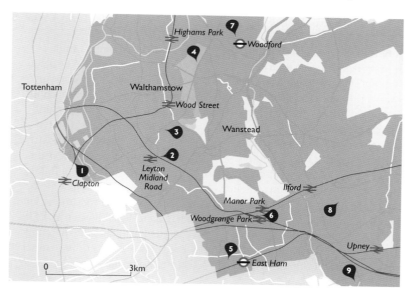

WALTHAM FOREST

ALLIOTT VERDON ROE

(1877–1958) aircraft designer
and manufacturer

Walthamstow Marsh
Railway Viaduct

BORN in Manchester, Roe in 1907 won a prize for a model aeroplane. A full-scale version tested at Brooklands the following year, but it was only in 1909 that Roe managed a substantial flight.

Beneath two arches here, he built his *Avro No. 1* triplane, which flew 30m (100ft) on 13 July 1909 – the first all-British powered flight. In 1910 he set up A. V. Roe & Co. with his brother, H. V. Roe, in Manchester. The firm's first great triumph was the Avro 504, the leading military plane of the First World War. Roe sold his share in his company to Armstrong Siddeley in 1928; his later years were dedicated to flying boats, such as the Saunders-Roe Princess (launched 1952).

HARRY BECK

(1902–74) designer of the London Underground map

14 Wesley Road, Leyton

I N 1931, Harry Beck produced the first diagrammatic map of the London Underground network; he was working as a freelancer and is thought to have been paid just five guineas (£5.25) for it. He took the conventional map then in use and straightened the distinctive coloured lines – the 'vermicelli', as Beck called them – to verticals, horizontals or 45-degree diagonals. The only topographical feature shown was a similarly idealised River Thames; the font was a variant of that designed for the Underground by Edward Johnston*. Similar lettering is used on the blue plaque that marks Beck's birthplace in Leyton – a house then newly built. The Underground management initially thought Beck's map too revolutionary, but the very positive public reaction to an initial print run of pocket 'diagrams' in 1933 persuaded them to adopt it. Beck, whose later London addresses were in Highgate, Finchley and Mill Hill, continued to update the map, and it has spawned imitations in other countries, and parodies too.

SOLOMON T. PLAATJE

(1876–1932) writer and campaigner for African rights

25 Carnarvon Road, Leyton **3**

P LAATJE was born into the Setswana-speaking Barolong people in the Orange Free State, South Africa. In 1902, he became a newspaper editor, and in 1912 he was one of the founders of what became the African National Congress. He arrived in London in May 1914 as a member of a deputation sent to protest against the Natives'

Land Act of 1913, which deprived Africans of the right to acquire non-African land. Shortly after his arrival, Plaatje found lodgings with a Mrs Timberlake here, and this remained his home until mid-to-late 1915, when he moved to Acton.

While here, Plaatje wrote most of *Native Life in South Africa* (1916). *Mhudi* (1930) was largely completed in London in 1920, during a second visit; this was the first novel in English known to have been written by a black South African.

JAMES HILTON

(1900–54) novelist and scriptwriter   42 Oak Hill Gardens, Woodford Green

BORN in Leigh, Lancashire, Hilton moved in 1902 with his family to London, where his father John – one of the models for Mr Chips – was employed as a master by the Walthamstow School Board. While an undergraduate at Cambridge, Hilton published his first novel, *Catherine Herself* (1920). After university, he moved to his parents' new home here – which they had named Leigh – and dedicated himself to writing. It was not until 1933 that Hilton found fame, about a year after leaving his parents' house, when he published *Lost Horizon*. Soon after came *Goodbye, Mr Chips,* written in four days and published in 1934. Soon after, Hilton went to Hollywood to work on film versions and lived for the rest of his life in California, though he often returned to visit his widowed father, who lived here until the 1950s.

NEWHAM

WILL THORNE

(1857–1946) trade union leader and Labour MP   1 Lawrence Rd, West Ham **5**

THORNE was born in Birmingham; in the early 1880s, a few years after his marriage to Harriet Hallam, the daughter of a fellow gasworker, he took up work at Beckton Gasworks, London, and joined the Social Democratic Federation. With the help of Ben Tillett, in 1889, Thorne established the National Union of Gasworkers and General Labourers, which persuaded gas companies to introduce the eight-hour day. Thorne was a member of West Ham Council from 1891 until his death, and was MP for the area from 1906 to 1945. He lived in Lawrence Road, at the heart of his constituency, from 1907 to 1946.

STANLEY HOLLOWAY

(1890–1982) actor and humorist · 25 Albany Road, Manor Park

HOLLOWAY'S most celebrated screen role was as Alfred Doolittle in *My Fair Lady* (1964); at the age of 73, he was the film's only lead actor to do his own singing. He also starred in the West End and Broadway versions of the show, which was based on *Pygmalion* by George Bernard Shaw*. Holloway's other films included *Brief Encounter* (1945), *The Lavender Hill Mob* (1951) and *The Titfield Thunderbolt* (1952). Earlier, he was known for his comic monologues, notably the self-penned 'Sam, Sam, Pick Opp Tha Musket' (1928) and 'Albert and the Lion' (1930), both delivered with consummate timing in a flat Lancashire accent. Yet Holloway was an east Londoner; his birthplace, in an early 1880s terrace, bears his blue plaque, and he lived at two other addresses in the Manor Park neighbourhood during his youth, when he cut his teeth performing as a boy soprano.

REDBRIDGE

CLEMENT ATTLEE

(1883–1967) Prime Minister · 17 Monkhams Avenue, Woodford Green ❼

ATTLEE was the son of a solicitor and was born and brought up in Putney. After witnessing deprivation in the East End, he joined the Stepney branch of the Independent Labour Party in 1908 and devoted himself to advancing democratic socialist politics. Attlee was elected MP for Limehouse in 1922, and in 1931 became Deputy Leader of the Labour Party; four years later, he published *The Will and the Way to Socialism*, the same year that he became party leader. In 1940, Attlee joined Winston Churchill* in the War Cabinet and two years later became Deputy Prime Minister, playing a major part in the wartime government. The surprise Labour victory of 1945 brought him to power as premier and he implemented a massive programme of nationalisation; abroad, he granted full independence to India in 1947. Attlee remained leader of the party until 1955, when he retired and was elevated to the peerage. He moved here shortly after his marriage to Violet Millar in January 1922, and lived here until October 1931 when, to cater for the needs of his growing family, he moved to Stanmore.

ALBERT MANSBRIDGE

(1876–1952) Workers' Educational Association founder   198 Windsor Rd., Ilford

MANSBRIDGE moved from Gloucester to London with his family in 1880 and grew up in Battersea. In his twenties, he became closely involved in the co-operative movement. He founded the WEA with his wife Frances (née Pringle) in 1903, the year before they moved here from Clapham. Their late-19th-century end-of-terrace house here served as the association's central office until late 1906. The WEA – originally the Association to Promote the Higher Education of Working Men – had great impact. By the outbreak of the First World War, there were nearly 180 WEA branches, with over 2,500 affiliated societies, organising lectures, courses and tutorials in order to raise standards of education. After his retirement as Secretary in 1915, Mansbridge involved himself in other bodies committed to adult education at home and abroad.

BARKING AND DAGENHAM

BOBBY MOORE

(1941–1993) captain of the World Cup-winning England football team

43 Waverley Gardens, Barking

THE on-pitch leader in 1966 of England's most successful international football team, Moore was a classy defender – the epitome of composure under pressure. His haul of 108 international caps stood as the English record for many years and, having first been given the job aged 22 and 47 days, he remains the youngest ever England captain. The plaque graces the end-of-terrace house in Barking where Moore lived as a boy, until his marriage in 1962. Nearby, he honed his ball skills in Greatfields Park, and played for his school teams (Westbury Primary and Tom Hood Grammar) before winning the London-wide Crisp Shield with the Barking Schools Association District team in 1951. Fifteen years later, as the World Cup final headed into extra time, his father Bob watched the game on television here, while his mother Doris (Doss) pottered with her plants in the back garden, unable to watch. Normally more voluble, she could be heard urging on her son – 'Unload him!' – from the stand at West Ham, the club where Moore spent most of his career. Curiously, one of his middle names was 'Chelsea'.

OUTER LONDON SOUTH-EAST –
BEXLEY AND BROMLEY

FORMERLY part of Kent, Bexley and Bromley were brought under the Greater London Council in 1965. Some of the – so far, relatively few – blue plaques in this area mark houses that were once country retreats, and despite rampant development, the outer districts here still retain something of their former rural character.

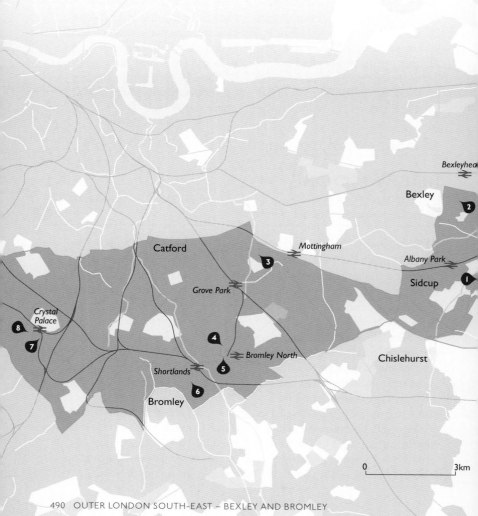

VISCOUNT CASTLEREAGH

(1769–1822) statesman　　　Loring Hall, 8 Water Lane, North Cray, Sidcup ❶

ASTLEREAGH took a life-long lease on this mid-18th-century farmhouse – then known as North Cray Farm or Cottage – in the summer of 1810. He enlarged it, and bred Merino sheep while his wife Amelia kept a small zoo. Born in Dublin, he began his career as Chief Secretary for Ireland (1798–1801), and played a key role in the passage of the Act of Union between Britain and Ireland (1801). In 1812, in the midst of the Napoleonic Wars, he became Foreign Secretary and was responsible for negotiating the peace treaties of 1814 and 1815. Castlereagh was also Leader of the House of Commons; in 1822, after a difficult parliamentary session, he retreated here for the summer recess, feverish and delusional. His pistols and razors were taken away lest he harm himself, but on the morning of 12 August 1822, he committed suicide by cutting his throat with a penknife. Castlereagh was so unpopular that his funeral cortège was jeered en route to Westminster Abbey.

PHILIP WEBB (1831–1915) architect
WILLIAM MORRIS*

(1834–96) poet and artist　　　Red House, Red House Lane, Bexleyheath ❷

RED House was conceived by Morris in summer 1858, the year before his marriage to Jane Burden, as a retreat, away from the smoke and dirt of London in what was then the remote hamlet of Upton. Designed by his friend the architect Philip Webb, the house was essentially the prototype of all domestic architecture in the Arts and Crafts style. The early days at Red House fitted Morris's ideal of friends living, working and playing together in an idyllic rural setting – into which, in 1861 and 1862, his daughters Jenny and May were born. Soon, however, Morris's

'More a poem than a house ... but an admirable place to live in.'

D. G. Rossetti* on Red House

London-based furnishing firm of Morris, Marshall, Faulkner & Co. – in which Webb and Burne-Jones* were also involved – was taking up most of his time, and in 1865 he moved to Queen Square, Bloomsbury. He left behind much of his monumental furniture, it being too heavy to shift, and could never bring himself to revisit Red House, which was sold. It survives intact, and is cared for by the National Trust.

W. G. GRACE

(1848–1915) cricketer Fairmount, Mottingham Lane, Mottingham **3**

IN his 40-year career, William Gilbert Grace helped to elevate cricket to a national institution. A doctor by profession, he moved to London from Bristol in 1898. The following year, he played his last test match for England and transferred to the new London County Club, based at Crystal Palace, of which he also became manager. In 1909, the year after he retired from first-class cricket with a career total of nearly 55,000 runs, 'W. G.' moved here with his wife Agnes from Sydenham. Grace – affectionately known as 'The Old Man' – remained a keen sportsman, playing golf, bowls and curling as well as cricket. In October 1915 he suffered a stroke while working in the garden – in which he grew the choicest asparagus – and died at home a few days later. It was said that Zeppelin raids contributed to his demise; Grace complained that, unlike fast bowlers, it was a threat that he could not see coming.

PRINCE PETER KROPOTKIN

(1842–1921) theorist of anarchism 6 Crescent Road, Sundridge Park **4**

SCION of an aristocratic Russian family, Kropotkin became a committed anarchist after a visit to western Europe in 1872. Having been imprisoned for his political activities in both Russia and France, he took refuge in England in 1886 and worked as a scientific journalist while living a life of blameless respectability on the fringes of London. In the summer of 1894, Kropotkin moved here from Acton and wrote a number of influential books here, including *Fields, Factories and Workshops* (1899); his autobiography, *Memoirs of a Revolutionist* (1899); and *Mutual Aid: A Factor of Evolution* (1902), which expounded a peaceful, gradualist theory of anarchism. He also tended his small garden with skill and care. Although they had little money, Kropotkin and his wife Sofiya entertained friends every Sunday afternoon at their vine-covered house, which was then called Viola. In the front room, the chief adornments of which were natural science specimens, Kropotkin would entertain his guests at the piano with renditions of revolutionary songs; his playing was said to be 'atrocious'. The Kropotkins left Bromley in the autumn of 1907. He returned to Russia in the wake of the February Revolution of 1917.

RACHEL MCMILLAN (1859–1917)
MARGARET MCMILLAN (1860–1931)
pioneers of nursery education   51 Tweedy Road ❺

THE McMillan sisters founded the 'Deptford Camp School' in 1911, in which nursery children were taught under rudimentary shelters, and in which particular attention was paid to nutrition and physical development: the sisters had previously run early school clinics in Deptford and elsewhere. The school, which was educating 350 children by 1927, had various sites before being established in what is now McMillan Road, formerly Church Road. Rachel McMillan first moved to Bromley in 1895, settling at the large corner house in Tweedy Road, then of quite recent construction, as a lodger of Miss Ilott. Margaret joined her in 1902 and they lived together here for another six years. A Christian Socialist and active propagandist for the Independent Labour Party, Margaret later set up a training college for nursery teachers next to the school, in memory of her sister Rachel.

ALEXANDER MUIRHEAD
(1848–1920) electrical engineer   20 Church Road, Shortlands ❻

MUIRHEAD enjoyed an outstanding academic career at University College London, where he studied chemistry. At St Bartholomew's Hospital he undertook pioneering work on the electrocardiogram, before joining his father's firm of telegraph engineers; later he set up his own business making electrical equipment, Muirhead & Co., which moved to Bromley in 1896. With his wife Mary, Muirhead lived at this house, then known as The Lodge, from 1893 until his death here. In 1901 he formed the Lodge-Muirhead Wireless Syndicate, a business that was bought by Marconi* in 1911.

IRA ALDRIDGE, 'THE AFRICAN ROSCIUS'

(1807–67) Shakespearean actor

DESCRIBED as the first major African-American actor, Aldridge had to come to England from his native New York to carve out a career. Under the name 'Mr Keene' he made his London stage debut playing Othello, in 1825, and came to prominence when he reprised the role eight years later at the Covent Garden Theatre, taking over from Edmund Kean, who was mortally ill. Aldridge played in theatres around Britain, Ireland and Europe, earning the sobriquet of 'The African Roscius', and by the time he returned to the West End in 1848 his notices were fulsome. He took on the parts of Macbeth, Shylock and King Lear, and extended his repertory to some of Shakespeare's less performed plays, such as *Titus Andronicus*. The house, which he named Luranah Villa after his mother, was his last base in London. Enjoying great acclaim on the Continent, Aldridge died while on tour in Łódź, Poland, in August 1867. Adrian Lester played Aldridge in Lolita Chakrabarti's 2012 play about his life, *Red Velvet*.

MARIE STOPES

(1880–1958) promoter of
sex education and birth control

THE early publications of Marie Stopes – chief among them *Married Love* (1918), written after the failure of her first marriage – had an enormous impact in promoting birth control and shaping the modern notion of sex being for pleasure. Some of Stopes's other views are less palatable: she fell out with her only son because his wife was myopic and therefore fell short – in her view – as breeding stock. Stopes was, however, remarkable in many ways: the first woman to gain a PhD in botany, she developed a classification for the components of coal that, with modifications, is still used. She spent her first 12 years at this 1870s house, then called Kenwyn, and recalled being 'brought up in the rigours of the stern Scottish old-fashioned Presbyterianism ... special books were kept for Sunday reading; no toys were allowed'. It was underneath a quince tree in the heavily sloping back garden that questions about her own origins first occurred to her, to which she received no satisfactory answer. A seed had been sown in Cintra Park.

OUTER LONDON SOUTH – CROYDON TO MERTON

THE London boroughs of Croydon, Sutton and Merton were in Surrey until 1965, when they were drawn under the Greater London banner. Wimbledon, Sutton and – especially – Croydon, were considerable towns in their own right but all had been effectively subsumed into the capital's outward spread by that point. The area is home to an eclectic variety of plaques, with writers well represented.

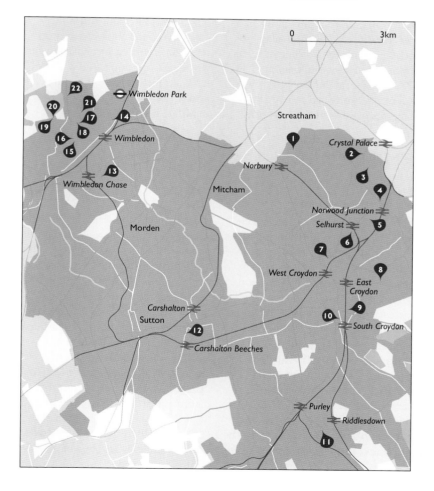

WILL HAY

(1888–1949) comic actor and astronomer   45 The Chase, Norbury ❶

WILLIAM Thomson Hay had a peripatetic childhood, but returned to the north of England (he was born in County Durham) in his twenties. Following his marriage in 1907 to Gladys Perkins, he embarked on a music-hall career, taking inspiration from his sister's teaching anecdotes to develop his schoolmaster comedy persona. His routine – above all, his sketch 'The Fourth Form at St Michael's' – was soon widely enjoyed, as were his lampoons of blustering authority figures, notably in the police and prison service. Hay acted in 19 films in the 1930s and 1940s, a few of which he also directed; these are epitomised by *Oh, Mr Porter!* (1937) and *My Learned Friend* (1944). He had long been interested in astronomy and while living in Norbury, using his home-made observatory in the back garden, he discovered a white spot on Saturn in 1933. Hay left this house after his marriage broke down in 1934 and later lived in Mill Hill and Chelsea.

EMILE ZOLA

(1840–1902)   Queen's Hotel,
French novelist   122 Church Road, Upper Norwood ❷

IN 1897, this great French novelist's literary career was interrupted by the Dreyfus Affair: Captain Alfred Dreyfus, a French-Jewish army officer, was tried for treason, and Zola was among those who protested his innocence, publishing a fierce denunciation of the French general staff, 'J'Accuse' (1898), as an open letter in the newspaper *L'Aurore*. Zola was found guilty of libel, and while awaiting retrial on appeal he fled to England in July 1898. By October, he was living here incognito as M. Jean Richard, firstly in rooms overlooking the garden and then in a suite at the front on the raised ground floor. He was visited in turn by his wife, Gabrielle, and by his mistress, Jeanne Rozerot – the latter accompanied by their two young children. Here, Zola wrote *Fécondité* (1899), one of the series of novels known as *Les Quatres Evangiles*, and in his leisure time cycled around Upper Norwood and took photographs, especially of the Crystal Palace. When he heard that Dreyfus was to be retried, he returned to his homeland in June 1899 and received a pardon from the government in 1900. He died from carbon monoxide poisoning, caused by a blocked chimney, two years later.

RAYMOND CHANDLER

(1888–1959) writer   110 Auckland Road, Upper Norwood **3**

ONE of the originators of the 'hardboiled' school of detective fiction and, via numerous big screen adaptations, a pioneer of film noir, Chandler achieved worldwide acclaim for novels such as *The Big Sleep* (1939) and *The Long Goodbye* (1953), and for the private detective character he created, Philip Marlowe. Chicago-born, Chandler came to London with his mother in 1900, and was accommodated in rental property owned by his uncle, Ernest Thornton. From about 1901 to 1907, Chandler – together with his mother, aunt and grandmother – lived at this house, then called Mount Cyra; a double-fronted red-bricked villa of 1883, it was among some 70 put up by the south London builder Charles Pawley on the former estate of Lord Auckland. Until 1905, when he was sent abroad to learn languages, Chandler was educated at Dulwich College; he later acknowledged the influence of his schooling – especially in the classics – on his fiction. He recalled composing his first published poem in an upstairs bathroom at the age of 19; this may have been here, but more likely at a subsequent address.

W. F. R. STANLEY

(1829–1909) inventor, manufacturer and philanthropist   Stanley Halls and Technical Trade School, 12 South Norwood Hill **4**

THE son of a mechanic, William Ford Robinson Stanley grew up in Hertfordshire, and his natural aptitude for mathematics and science soon led to a career designing scientific instruments. In 1854 he set up a small shop at 3 Great Turnstile, Holborn (demolished), where he sold drawing instruments and, later, tools for surveying. A year later he moved to South Norwood and two years after that he established his own factory in Belgrave Road, where it remained until a business merger in 1926 brought about a move to Eltham. A visionary thinker and polymath, Stanley produced a blueprint for an ideal community – Stanleyton – in *The Case of the Fox: A Political Utopia* (1903), which was set in 1950. In keeping with his principles, he invested hugely in Stanley Halls which he intended should serve as a secular meeting place and a technical education centre, and which he founded and designed between 1901 and 1909. Described by Pevsner* as 'the most memorable buildings in South Norwood', the halls remain in use.

SIR ARTHUR CONAN DOYLE

(1859–1930) creator of Sherlock Holmes   12 Tennison Rd, South Norwood   **5**

CONAN Doyle studied medicine at Edinburgh, the city of his birth, and moved to London from Hampshire in spring 1891 with his wife Louise and their daughter Mary. He set up in practice at 2 Upper Wimpole Street as an eye specialist but had already published *A Study in Scarlet* (1887) and its sequel *The Sign of the Four* (1890), which introduced the characters of Sherlock Holmes and Dr Watson. By the end of summer 1891, he had moved to this 'prettily-built and modest-looking red-brick residence' dating from *c*.1887 – and begun to write full-time. In his study, to the left of the front door, he wrote 3,000 words a day, turning out 18 Holmes stories, including 'The Boscombe Valley Mystery' (1891); the area inspired later tales such as 'The Norwood Builder' (1903). As the fame of his literary creation grew, Conan Doyle became uneasy and decided to kill off his detective in 'The Final Problem' (1893). He left Tennison Road the following year, and settled in Hindhead, Surrey, before – under pressure from his publisher – reviving Holmes and Watson for *The Hound of the Baskervilles* (1902) and subsequent works.

SAMUEL COLERIDGE-TAYLOR

(1875–1912) composer   30 Dagnall Park, South Norwood   **6**

COLERIDGE-TAYLOR was the son of a Sierra Leonean father who returned home from England, possibly unaware that he had left Alice Hare Martin pregnant. Brought up in Croydon by his English mother, Coleridge-Taylor studied the violin at the Royal College of Music and showed early promise as a composer. In 1898 he premiered *Hiawatha's Wedding Feast* at the College; its success inspired him to complete a three-part cantata, *Scenes from 'The Song of Hiawatha'*, by 1900. He moved here early that year, after his marriage to Jessie Fleetwood Walmisley; the couple and their son Hiawatha remained here until 1901. Coleridge-Taylor taught at Trinity College of Music (1903–10) and the Guildhall School of Music (1910–13), and was a conductor in London and New York. His interest in African folk music spawned works including *24 Negro Melodies* (1905). Pneumonia, brought on by overwork, led to his untimely death at the age of 37 at his later home in Duppas Hill, Waddon.

C. B. FRY

(1872–1956)
all-round sportsman

CHARLES Burgess Fry was a top-class long jumper, sprinter and hurdler, a fine swimmer, golfer and horseman, ventured into rugby, played football for England in 1901 and was an FA Cup finalist with Southampton the following year. But it was as a cricketer that Fry rose to international prominence. He played in 26 Tests for England, often – and famously – partnered with K. S. Ranjitsinhji. Over the course of his career in first-class cricket – which came to a close in 1922 – Fry reached an aggregate of 30,886 runs and made 94 centuries. He was also a sports journalist, and from 1904 to 1911 edited *Fry's Magazine of Sports and Outdoor Life*. He spent over 40 years in Hampshire, but it was his birth and brief residence here that qualified 'C.B.' to join the Surrey County Cricket team in 1891.

FREDERICK GEORGE CREED

(1871–1957) electrical engineer
and inventor of the teleprinter

CREED was born in Nova Scotia, Canada, the son of a Scotsman, and settled in Glasgow in 1897 with his wife Jeannie; while working for the *Glasgow Herald* he developed a tape-perforating machine adapted from a typewriter keyboard, and equipment to record and print incoming signals. The first transmission, in 1898, reached a speed of 60 words per minute; by 1912 Creed's 'high speed automatic printing telegraphic system' was in use across the globe and could transmit up to 200 words per minute, an invention that revolutionised the diffusion of news. Creed and his business partner, Harald Bille, moved to Croydon in 1909 in order to be nearer to the Post Office – a key client. In 1923 he produced the first teleprinter, which recorded and printed incoming signals directly as letters, rather than as dots and dashes. A strict Evangelical, Creed insisted on abstinence from his employees, and resigned from the board of Creed & Co. – acquired in 1928 by the International Telephone and Telegraph Corporation – over the use of company sports fields on Sundays. He devoted his retirement to ship design; in 1939 he moved to this detached villa of 1863 and remained here until his death.

JOHN HORNIMAN (1803–93)
FREDERICK JOHN HORNIMAN*

(1835–1906) tea merchants, collectors
and public benefactors

Coombe Cliff,
Coombe Road, Fairfield

JOHN Horniman started out as a grocer and is generally credited with selling the first sealed packets of tea in 1826. In 1852 he settled in Croydon with his wife Ann and their family; having acquired land in Coombe Road in 1850, he commissioned this imposing Italianate villa from E. C. Robins. His son Frederick entered his father's firm at the age of 14 and, on his father's retirement in 1868, took over the business with his elder brother William. Shortly after his marriage to Rebekah Emslie, Frederick moved to Forest Hill, where his extensive collections became the core of the Horniman Museum*. Frederick inherited Coombe Cliff, which he owned until 1902. A large conservatory was built in 1894 to house his rare and exotic plants; this was dismantled in the 1980s and re-erected adjacent to the Horniman Museum. Coombe Cliff's extensive gardens, now part of Park Hill, are open to the public.

ALFRED RUSSEL WALLACE

(1823–1913)
naturalist

44 St Peter's Road (formerly Pen-y-Bryn),
South Croydon

BORN near Usk, Monmouthshire, Wallace explored the wildlife of the Amazon basin (1848–52) and between 1854 and 1862 carried out research in the Malay Archipelago, where he identified the delineation between oriental and Australian fauna, known subsequently as the Wallace Line. He formulated an evolutionary theory on 'the survival of the fittest' that was comparable with Darwin's theory of natural selection. Wallace and Darwin* corresponded about their ideas, and presented their papers jointly to the Linnean

Society* in 1858. Darwin's *On the Origin of Species* was published the following year, while Wallace is known principally for his 1876 work *The Geographical Distribution of*

Animals. Wallace moved to Croydon in 1878 with his wife Annie and took up residence at the newly built Pen-y-Bryn in 1880 – the year that *Island Life* appeared. He left the area a year later. Wallace also wrote on spiritualism, land nationalisation and the anti-vaccination movement.

PETER CUSHING

(1913–94) actor   32 St James' Road, Purley

CUSHING'S name is indelibly associated with 'Hammer horror' films; among the roles he took on were Sherlock Holmes and Baron Frankenstein. He also played Dr Who and Grand Moff Tarkin in *Star Wars* (1977). Born in nearby Kenley, Cushing spent his formative years in St James' Road, Purley (*c*.1925–36), making his first stage appearances and enrolling at the Guildhall School of Music and Drama as a part-time student. The house is a striking one of the interwar period: with its flat roof and angular moderne styling, it boasts the architectural equivalent of its former occupant's high cheekbones.

SUTTON

WILLIAM HALE WHITE, 'MARK RUTHERFORD'

(1831–1913) novelist   19 Park Hill, Carshalton

FROM a Nonconformist family, White was born and educated in Bedford and began training for the ministry at St John's Wood. His unorthodox views on the Bible ensured he was expelled in 1852 and he afterwards pursued parallel careers as a writer and civil servant. White commissioned this house in the 1860s from Charles Vinall, a pupil of Philip Webb*; his father and brother-in-law also lived on the same street. While living here, he wrote his best-known works – *The Autobiography of Mark Rutherford: Dissenting Minister* (1881), *Mark Rutherford's Deliverance* (1885) and *The Revolution in Tanner's Lane* (1887), all semi-autobiographical novels, which traced the agonies of a man losing his faith. His honest and candid self-analysis, and the quality of his writing – exhibited in these and later works – ensured that his reputation continued beyond his lifetime.

JOHN INNES

(1829–1904) founder of the
John Innes Horticultural Institution

Manor House, Rutlish School,
Watery Lane **13**

INNES had the Manor House, an old farmhouse, rebuilt according to his eclectic tastes between *c.*1870 and 1900 by the architect H. G. Quartermain. With Quartermain, Innes undertook the development of the Merton Park estate as an early garden suburb, with generous plots and a profusion of trees and holly hedges. The settlement was built between the 1870s and 1904 and reflected Innes's political and social outlook – it had a temperance house rather than a pub, a masonic hall and a boys' club. On his death here in 1904, Innes left his home and estate for charitable purposes, in particular horticultural research. In 1910, the John Innes Horticultural Institution was founded, which, in the 1930s, developed the now-famous Innes compost.

GEORGETTE HEYER

(1902–74) novelist

103 Woodside, Wimbledon **14**

HEYER'S historical romances, mostly set in the 18th century and Regency periods, were selling a million copies a year in Britain alone by the 1970s, and most of her 56 novels remain in print. Their appeal lies in entertaining plots, strong characters and credible dialogue, but what set her apart was her meticulous historical research: her account of the Battle of Waterloo in *An Infamous Army* (1937) was recommended to students at Sandhurst. Heyer's plaque marks her birthplace and home for the first four years of her life. The semi-detached house – then newly built – was one of seven in the area that she lived in. Heyer was also educated locally and met and married her husband Ronald Rougier in Wimbledon. Two of her novels – *Pastel* (1929) and *Behold, Here's Poison* (1936) – were set in the district.

DAME MARGARET RUTHERFORD

(1892–1972) actress

4 Berkeley Place, Wimbledon

IN 1895, following the suicide of her mother in India, Rutherford was sent to live with her maternal aunt, Bessie Nicholson, at this late-19th-century house, which remained her home until 1920. Her aunt died in 1925, leaving a small income which enabled Rutherford to give up teaching music and join the Old Vic Company as a trainee actress. In 1933, aged 41, she made her West End debut; her big break came as Miss Prism in *The Importance of Being Earnest* (1939). She went on to appear in films such as *Passport to Pimlico* (1949), and *The VIPs* (1963), for which she won an Oscar, and to portray Miss Marple too.

ROBERT GRAVES
(1895–1985) writer 1 Lauriston Road, Wimbledon

THE house, where Graves was born, was built in 1893–4 and designed to the specifications of his German mother, Amy. From Charterhouse school, Graves joined the Royal Welch Fusiliers upon the outbreak of the First World War and formed a friendship with fellow poet Siegfried Sassoon*; his first volume of poems were collected as *Over the Brazier* (1916). In 1918 he married Nancy Nicholson, sister of the artist Ben Nicholson*. Following the publication of his autobiography, *Goodbye to All That*, in 1929 – written while living in Hammersmith – he moved to Majorca, where *I Claudius* was written.

SISTER NIVEDITA
(1867–1911) educationalist and campaigner for Indian independence 21A High Street, Wimbledon

MARGARET Noble hailed from County Tyrone and ran schools in Wimbledon on progressive educational lines. She became a disciple of Swami Vivekananda* after meeting him in 1895, and she devoted herself to the campaign for Indian independence; Vivekananda named her Nivedita, meaning 'the dedicated'. She stayed in Wimbledon High Street with her mother and sister in the years around 1900.

ARTHUR SCHOPENHAUER
(1788–1860) philosopher Eagle House, High Street, Wimbledon 18

THIS fine gabled building of 1613 served as Wimbledon School from 1789 to 1805 and continued in educational use until 1887, when it was bought and restored by the architect T. G. Jackson. Schopenhauer was one of the school's most celebrated pupils. Born in Danzig (now Gdańsk), Schopenhauer accompanied his parents on an extensive European journey in 1803, arriving at Dover in May of that year. His six-month stay in England was to prove an important formative experience, especially the three months from 30 June until 20 September that he spent at Wimbledon School, then run by the Revd Thomas Lancaster – although he found the regime miserable and the curriculum tedious. Schopenhauer – who entered the University of Göttingen in 1809 –was later known as the 'philosopher of pessimism'.

SIR ERNST CHAIN

(1906–79) biochemist and developer of penicillin   9 North View, Wimbledon

OF German-Jewish origins, Chain came to Britain from Berlin in 1933; two years later he joined Oxford's anti-bacterial research team, headed by the Australian scientist Howard (later Lord) Florey. Around 1938, he and Florey began to work on the isolation and concentration of pure penicillin. Although penicillin had been discovered by Alexander Fleming* in 1928, it was of little practical value until Chain and Florey demonstrated its enormous medical benefits. Chain became Professor of Biochemistry at Imperial College London in 1961. He moved here on his retirement 12 years later, but spent much time at the home he built in Mulranny, Co. Mayo, and it was there that he died.

JOSEPHINE BUTLER

(1828–1906) champion of women's rights   8 North View, Wimbledon

BORN in Northumberland into a wealthy family of political reformers – the Whig Prime Minister Earl Grey was a relative – Josephine Grey was mostly educated at home. In 1852 she married the academic and Anglican clergyman Dr George Butler. Together, in 1864, they moved to Liverpool, where Josephine became increasingly involved in promoting higher education for women and supporting women's suffrage. She became particularly concerned with the plight of prostitutes and lobbied vigorously for reform. After her husband's death in 1890, Butler moved to this 1880s end-of-terrace house with her son George Grey Butler. After her son's marriage in 1893, she lived in Wandsworth, Cheltenham, and back in Northumberland.

LIONEL TERTIS

(1876–1975) viola soloist

TERTIS is celebrated as the man who turned the viola from an orchestral also-ran into a solo instrument, thereby effectively becoming its first virtuoso player. Among the distinguished composers who wrote music for him were Arnold Bax*, Ralph Vaughan Williams*, Frank Bridge* and Gustav Holst*. Tertis designed his own viola, of oversize dimensions to improve the resonance – the 'Tertis model' was 42.5cm (16.75in) long, which was the most he reckoned could be comfortably tucked under the chin. He grew up in Princelet Street, Spitalfields, but is commemorated at this large detached house, dating from 1900, where Tertis and his second wife Lilian had a flat after 1961. This was the home of his retirement, but Tertis continued to promote the 'Tertis model', and gave his last public performance in spring 1964, at a meeting of the London Philharmonic Society club.

JOSEPH TOYNBEE (1815–66) surgeon
ARNOLD TOYNBEE

(1852–83)
social philosopher

LINCOLNSHIRE-BORN Joseph Toynbee was apprenticed to a London surgeon. In 1851 he was appointed aural surgeon and lecturer on ear diseases at St Mary's Hospital, Paddington, and distilled his experiences into the highly regarded textbook *Diseases of the Ear: Their Nature, Diagnosis and Treatment* (1860). He and his wife Harriet moved into this large Italianate villa in 1854, and stayed until his death in 1866. Arnold was the second of Toynbee's four sons and, having grown up at Beech Holme, went up to Oxford in 1873. He taught at Balliol College but also gave extramural lectures, specialising in industrial history, and undertook educational work among east London's poor. Following his early death, Arnold's friends Canon Samuel Barnett* and Henrietta Barnett* founded the first university settlement – in modern terms, an outreach centre in a deprived area – which they named Toynbee Hall in his honour. Toynbee's reputation as a historian rests on his *Lectures on the Industrial Revolution in England* (1884) – the first serious study of the social and economic changes brought about by technological advances in the 18th and 19th centuries.

OUTER LONDON SOUTH-WEST – RICHMOND AND KINGSTON

RICHMOND and Kingston are both ancient towns with royal connections, the latter being the historic county town of Surrey. The wider area was taken into Greater London in 1965; Richmond now includes Twickenham and Teddington, north of the Thames and formerly in Middlesex. This district has seen a rise in the number of blue plaques in recent years, reflecting its enduring popularity as an attractive place of residence within easy reach of central London.

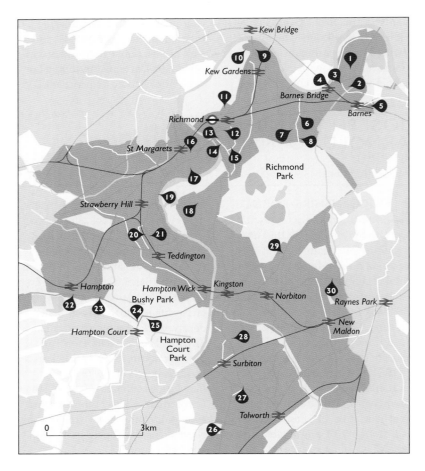

KURT SCHWITTERS

(1887–1948) artist   39 Westmoreland Road, Barnes ❶

IN 1919, Schwitters formulated his own interpretation of Dada – Merz – which involved the assembly of pieces of discarded ephemera into collages, applied to canvas and to buildings. Labelled 'degenerate' by the Nazi regime, Schwitters left his native Germany for Oslo in 1937 and, three years later, fled Norway for Britain, where he was initially interned on the Isle of Man. On his release, Schwitters came to London and from August 1942 until June 1945, he shared this house with his son Ernst and an émigré friend, Gert

'English people don't understand art at all,'
mused Schwitters

Strindberg, a great-nephew of the Swedish writer and artist August Strindberg. Here, using the garden shed as a studio, he covered the walls with paintings and the loft with collages made from material collected from London's streets and the River Thames. In 1944 Schwitters suffered a stroke, and with a friend, Edith Thomas, moved to Ambleside in the Lake District in 1945.

HERBERT HOWELLS

(1892–1983) composer and teacher   3 Beverley Close, Barnes ❷

HOWELLS has been described as the last of the great English Romantic composers, and his canticle settings, anthems and motets are considered among the greatest contributions to Anglican church music of the 20th century. He succeeded Gustav Holst* as Director of Music at St Paul's Girls' School in 1936 and was given a chair in music at London University in 1950. Born in Gloucestershire, Howells lived at four addresses in Barnes after 1917, having first come to the area to convalesce after a life-threatening illness. It was in this locality too that he and his wife

Dorothy lost their nine-year-old son Michael to polio, a traumatic event that prompted Howells to write the large-scale choral work *Hymnus Paradisi* (1938). The Howellses moved to this 'Tudorbethan' 1930s house in Beverley Close in 1946; it backs directly onto Barnes Common. After Dorothy died in 1972, he remained here until the year before his own death. *Stabat Mater* (1963) was among the works Howells completed while in residence; he was also commissioned to write a motet for President Kennedy's memorial service, his work being particularly appreciated in the United States.

HENRY FIELDING*

(1707–54) novelist   Milbourne House, 18 Station Road, Barnes **3**

SOMERSET-BORN Fielding earned his living as a dramatist before turning to a legal career in 1737. He continued to write, however, publishing his acknowledged masterpiece, *Tom Jones*, in 1749. As Magistrate of Middlesex, based in Bow Street, Fielding watched 'the long parade of wretchedness and villainy' pass before him, and did much to reduce crime in the metropolis. While this work demanded his presence in town, his fragile health – he suffered from gout, asthma and dropsy – led him to seek the fresh air and tranquillity of the countryside. After living in what is now Holly Road, Twickenham, he took Milbourne House in *c*.1750–52, dividing his time between Bow Street and Barnes; the house, re-fronted in the 18th century, was conveniently situated to be near his sisters in Turnham Green. While here, Fielding worked on his last and best-selling novel, *Amelia* (1752), which depicts a London of corrupt courts and squalid prisons. By February 1753 he and his second wife, Mary, had moved to Fordbrook, Ealing (demolished); a year later he left for Portugal, where he died.

DAME NINETTE DE VALOIS, OM

(1898–2001) founder of the Royal Ballet   14 The Terrace, Barnes **4**

DE Valois returned in 1925 from a two-year stint in Paris with Diaghilev's Ballets Russes, determined that Britain should have its own ballet. Thanks to Lilian Baylis*, she was able to found the Vic-Wells ballet in 1931; this moved from Sadler's Wells to the Royal Opera House in 1946 and was awarded a royal warrant a decade later. De Valois's transformational role in British ballet was buttressed by her skills as a choreographer; *Job* (1931) was a key production. Born Edris Stannus to an Anglo-Irish family, Ninette de Valois took her name at the suggestion of her mother – based on a tenuous family connection to the medieval French royal house. During her early career, she lived in Earl's Court and Bloomsbury; the move to this part-18th-century house in The Terrace came in 1962, when she was on the point of retirement. With her husband Arthur, a general practitioner, de Valois stayed here for 20 years, and spent the rest of her life at an address nearby. Her Order of Merit was not won without struggle; in her early career she appeared in a 'jazz-zaganza' entitled *You'd be Surprised*.

JAMES HENRY GREATHEAD

(1844–96) railway and tunnelling engineer   3 St Mary's Grove, Barnes **5**

GREATHEAD came to England from South Africa. In 1869, aged only 24, he was entrusted with building the Tower Subway, a pedestrian tunnel under the Thames; this he completed in 1870, with the use of a cylindrical boring device of his own design – the 'Greathead Shield' – which enabled tunnels to be driven through soft ground. From 1886, Greathead worked on the City and South London Railway, the world's first underground electric railway; opened in 1890, it is now part of the Northern Line. He was also involved in the construction of the Blackwall Tunnel (opened 1897) and the Waterloo and City Line (opened 1898). In 1885, he and his wife Blanche came to live at St Mary's Grove, remaining until their move to Streatham in 1889.

RICHARD DIMBLEBY

(1913–65) broadcaster   20 Cedar Court, Sheen Lane, East Sheen **6**

A COMMENTATOR, Dimbleby once said, 'must *feel* without letting his emotions run away with him', and his ability to strike this balance saw him become one of the leading broadcasters of the immediate post-war era. He is most famed for his commentaries on public events, ranging from Elizabeth II's coronation to Winston Churchill's funeral in 1965 – by which time he was himself mortally ill. Cedar Court, then a new block, was Dimbleby's home for two years from 1937; his first as a married man. Having cut his teeth on newspapers – including the family's own, the *Richmond and Twickenham Times* – Dimbleby joined the BBC; he had been with the corporation for about a year when he moved in. While living here, he covered the Munich crisis and the last stages of the Spanish Civil War in 1939.

KATHLEEN 'KITTY' GODFREE

(1896–1992) lawn tennis champion   55 York Avenue, East Sheen **7**

'KITTY' Godfree – her press nickname stuck, though she disliked it – was twice Wimbledon champion, in 1924 and 1926. In the latter year she also triumphed in the mixed doubles alongside her new husband, Leslie Godfree: they remain the only married couple to have won the title. Godfree's haul of five Olympic medals, including gold in the women's doubles in 1920, stands as a record for tennis; she was also four times all-England champion at badminton. Born Katherine McKane in Bayswater, Godfree moved to this late-1920s suburban villa with her husband in

'Competitors today are so competitive, aren't they?'

Godfree harks back to the amateur era, 1984

1936 and lived here until just before she died. She played competitive tennis until 1988; two years earlier, Godfree had been asked to present the trophies at Wimbledon.

SIR ROBERT WATSON-WATT
(1892–1973) pioneer of radar   287 Sheen Lane **8**

RADAR, or 'RAdio Detection And Ranging', was developed by a team led by Watson-Watt in the late 1930s, based on the Suffolk coast at Bawdsey. The original brief was to develop a 'death ray' to fry the occupants of enemy aircraft; the location of such aircraft by bouncing radio waves off them proved more realistic. Thus, in the view of

A. J. P. Taylor*, Watson-Watt 'laid the foundations for victory' in the Second World War. The plaque marks the early-20th-century house that he occupied during the 1940s, while he was working for the Air Ministry. A Scot, born in Brechin, he later lived in Canada, where he suffered the indignity of being caught for speeding by a radar gun.

ARTHUR HUGHES
(1832–1915) Pre-Raphaelite painter   Eastside House, 22 Kew Green, Kew **9**

IN the early 1850s, while a student at the Royal Academy Schools, Hughes was inspired by the work of the Pre-Raphaelite Brotherhood*. Among his best-known works are *The Long Engagement* (1853–9) and *April Love* (1856), which was acquired by William Morris*. From the 1860s, Hughes established himself as an illustrator, providing designs for – most notably – the works

of George MacDonald*, Tennyson's* *Enoch Arden* (1865) and Thomas Hughes's *Tom Brown's School Days* (1869). Hughes, his wife Tryphena and their children moved house frequently; it was in 1891 that they moved to this early-19th-century house on Kew Green, by which time Hughes's popularity had declined, though he continued to exhibit. He died here at the age of 83.

SIR WILLIAM HOOKER (1785–1865)
JOSEPH HOOKER (1817–1911)
botanists and directors of Kew Gardens   49 Kew Green, Kew

THE Hookers – father and son – served successively as directors of Kew Gardens for a period of 70 years, and created a public-facing institution of scientific excellence and enquiry. When William Hooker was appointed Director of Kew in 1841, it was just after the site – formerly an exotic garden on the royal estate – had been adopted as a national botanic garden. Kew Gardens was greatly expanded and altered during Hooker senior's 24 years at the helm, but his most important innovation was to open it to the public; by the time of his death in 1865, the number of visitors had reached half a million a year. The baton then passed to William's son Joseph, an associate of Charles Darwin* and author of *Flora of British India* (1872-97). After 1851, father and son occupied 49 Kew Green in turn; of brown brick, it is a curious amalgam of late-18th- and early-19th-century buildings.

JAMES THOMSON
(1700–48) poet and author of 'Rule, Britannia'   Richmond Royal Hospital, Kew Foot Road (formerly Lane) **11**

THOMSON came to London from Scotland in 1725, where in 1730 he staged his first play, *Sophonisba,* and published his most successful poetical work, *The Seasons,* which made him one of Britain's most widely admired poets in the century after his death. In 1739, Thomson acquired this substantial house next to Richmond Gardens; and it was while here that he wrote 'Rule, Britannia' – first performed in Thomson's *Alfred: A Masque* in 1740, with music by Thomas Arne*.

LEONARD WOOLF (1880–1969) writer and political activist
VIRGINIA WOOLF*
(1882–1941) writer   Hogarth House, 34 Paradise Road **12**

THE Woolfs 'fell in love with' Hogarth House, which dates to c.1748, at the end of 1914; it was, wrote Virginia, 'far the nicest house in England'. Her mental health improved in 'the tranquil atmosphere' and she wrote her second novel *Night and Day* (1919), *Jacob's Room*

(1922) and much of *Mrs Dalloway* (1925) here; Leonard meanwhile worked on international relations for the Fabian Society* and later the Labour Party. In 1917, they set up the Hogarth Press here, publishing 32 books at this house, many of which were printed and bound by the Woolfs. In March 1924, the couple moved to Bloomsbury – Virginia having begun to feel 'tied, imprisoned, inhibited' in Richmond – taking the press with them (it was eventually acquired by Chatto & Windus in 1946). From 1919, they spent much time in Rodmell, Sussex, where Virginia took her own life in 1941, and where Leonard also died.

BERNARDO O'HIGGINS

(1778–1842) general, statesman and liberator of Chile

Clarence House, 2 The Vineyard

O'HIGGINS was sent to England by his father, Ambrosio O'Higgins – then Governor of Chile – to learn English and to finish his education – which he did in this building of 1696, then a Roman Catholic boarding school (1795–8). While here, he met Francisco de Miranda* and José de San Martín*; he left England in 1799, and on his return to Chile three years later, joined their fight for South American independence from Spanish rule. Victorious at the Battle of Chacabuco on 12 February 1817, O'Higgins was declared Supreme Director and led his country for six years, before being deposed in a coup in January 1823 and exiled to Peru, where he died.

DAME CELIA JOHNSON

(1908–82) actress

46 Richmond Hill (formerly 3 Ellerker Gate)

CELIA Johnson's most celebrated role is in the film classic *Brief Encounter* (1945), an adaptation of a Noël Coward* play, in which she plays a repressed housewife who falls in love with a married doctor (played by Trevor Howard); they meet by chance in a station buffet when she gets 'something in my eye'. This has served to obscure the breadth of Johnson's career, which ranged from West End comedy in the 1930s to television drama four decades later. Born at this Richmond terraced house, then recently built, Celia Johnson lived here for the first 20 years of her life. Her first public performance – at the age of six – was as the beggar maid in *King Cophetua and the Beggar Maid* (1916), a benefit for soldiers wounded in the First World War. After her marriage to Peter, the brother of Ian Fleming*, Celia Johnson lived in Chelsea.

SIR EDWIN CHADWICK

(1800–90) public-health reformer

5 Montague Road (formerly Montague Villas), Richmond

AS a boy Chadwick moved from Lancashire to London. He was active as a reformer from 1832, when he became involved with the Royal Commission on Poor Laws; he was appointed a Commissioner and was also instrumental in seeing the Factory Act become law in 1833. It is, however, for sanitary reform of urban areas that Chadwick is remembered; his *Report on the Sanitary Condition of the Labouring Population of Great Britain* (1842) created a sensation and led to the first Public Health Act of 1848. In that year, the government created the General Board of Health, and Chadwick was made a Commissioner, but his combative nature led to him being eased out. He moved to this Italianate house of c.1840 in 1855, with a pension of £1,000 per annum. Chadwick spent his long retirement advocating various initiatives for the public benefit, such as the state ownership of railways, and made several unsuccessful attempts to win a seat in Parliament. In 1869 he moved to East Sheen, where he died.

J. M. W. TURNER, RA

(1775–1851) painter

40 Sandycombe Road

JOSEPH Mallord William Turner entered the Royal Academy Schools at the age of 14, and was soon recognised as an artist of genius. In 1807, he bought for £400 a plot of land in Twickenham and worked on the design of the house over the next five years. Construction began in 1812 and Solus Lodge – soon renamed Sandycombe Lodge – was completed the following year. Here Turner – whose main base remained in Marylebone – entertained friends from the art world, while his father William, with whom he shared the house, enjoyed working in the garden. Turner painted many local scenes, but – being often away on long painting tours – came to regard the house as 'an act of folly', and sold it in 1826.

WALTER DE LA MARE

(1873–1956) poet   South End House, Montpelier Row, Twickenham **17**

THE two upper floors of this fine house of c.1720 were de la Mare's home from 1940 until his death here 16 years later. Born in Charlton, south-east London, he came to public attention with the poetry collection *The Listeners* (1912), and achieved immense success with his collection of children's verse, *Peacock Pie* (1913). De la Mare was deeply attached to South End House and its garden, continuing to live here through the war and after the death of his wife Elfrida. Works he produced here included the anthology *Love* (1943) and the long poems *Traveller* (1946) and *Winged Chariot* (1953).

JOHN HENRY NEWMAN, CARDINAL NEWMAN

(1801–90)   Grey Court (now part of Grey Court School), Ham Street, Ham **18**

GREY Court was the country home of Newman's parents – the banker John Newman and his wife Jemima – from before his birth until September 1807; the other home of Newman's childhood was in Bloomsbury. Ordained in 1824, Newman came to prominence in the Oxford Movement, a group of High Church Anglicans, several of whom later converted to Catholicism. Newman himself joined the Roman Catholic Church in 1845, established the Birmingham Oratory in 1848 and that in London in 1849, and was made a Cardinal in 1879. His influential writings included *Apologia Pro Vita Sua* (1864), which set out the motivation for his conversion. He recalled his first home vividly, including his family's celebration of the victory at Trafalgar (1805), when candles were placed in the house's windows.

HENRY LABOUCHERE

(1831–1912)   Pope's Villa (Radnor House Independent School),
radical MP and journalist   19 Cross Deep, Twickenham **19**

LABOUCHERE lived here with his wife, the actress Henrietta Hodson, from 1881 until they moved to Florence in 1903. They used the sprawling mansion, built in 1842–3, mainly in summer. Born in London to a Huguenot family, Henry Du Pré Labouchere became a highly successful journalist; in 1876 he founded the journal *Truth*, which exposed corruption and hypocrisy in the Establishment. In Parliament, 'Labby' was a leading radical, but was behind the clause in the Criminal Law Amendment Act of 1885, known as 'Labouchere's Amendment', which made sexual activity between men explicitly illegal. This was the Act that led to the downfall of Oscar Wilde*, and remained in force until 1967: Labouchere's responsibility for it was seemingly not appreciated at the time he was approved for a blue plaque.

SIR NOËL COWARD

(1899–1973) actor, playwright and songwriter

131 (formerly 5) Waldegrave Road, Teddington

COWARD'S parents met in the church choir of nearby St Alban's church where Coward was christened, but 18 months after his birth they left this house, then called Helmsdale, for another house nearby: 'An unpretentious abode/ Which, I believe,/ Economy forced us to leave/ In rather a hurry,' wrote Coward many years later. A child prodigy, he later established himself as a playwright and composer with works such as *Hay Fever* (1925) and *Private Lives* (1930). During the Second World War, he wrote and co-produced a number of classic films including *In Which We Serve* (1942), *Brief Encounter* (1945) and *Blithe Spirit* (1945). In later years, he remained the epitome of pre-war style and glamour while reinventing himself as a cabaret singer, introducing his own songs – among them 'Mad Dogs and Englishmen' – to a new audience. Coward lived in Belgravia from 1930 until 1956, and spent the last 25 years of his life largely in Jamaica.

EDWARD WHYMPER

(1840–1911) mountaineer

82 Waldegrave Road, Teddington

MOUNTAINEERING was the Victorians' extreme sport and Whymper was one of its leading exponents. In July 1865, he led the first expedition to conquer the Matterhorn, the famous Swiss peak, but the death of three of his party on the descent – after a rope snapped – left him devastated, and racked by insomnia for the rest of his life. Whymper came from a Lambeth-based family of wood engravers but – as all built trace of his earlier life in London has gone – he is commemorated at the home of his last four years. In that period he remained active, travelling to Canada in 1909 and continuing to make an annual trip to the Alps to update and promote his guidebooks to Chamonix and Zermatt. The large detached house, dating from around 1895 and then called Holmwood, was also the scene of Whymper's late bid for domestic bliss with Edith Lewin, who was some 45 years his junior. A solitary, irascible man, Whymper gave her an ice axe as a wedding present; perhaps inevitably, they were legally separated in 1910.

JOHN BEARD (c.1717–91) singer
WILLIAM EWART*
(1798–1869) promoter of
public libraries

Rose Hill (now Hampton Library),
off Rosehill and Upper Sunbury Road

BEARD made his name in Handel's opera company at Covent Garden. A successful actor, he appeared regularly at Drury Lane and Covent Garden, and was perhaps best known for playing Macheath in John Gay's *The Beggar's Opera*, revived in 1737. In 1761 he took over the patent for the Covent Garden Theatre from his late father-in-law, John Rich. He sold it six years later for £60,000 and retired to Hampton, living close to his friend David Garrick*. Beard acquired this house in April 1774 and died here 17 years later. From 1838 to 1842, Rose Hill, as it was named from the 1820s, was the home of recently widowed William Ewart, the Liberal MP who was the spark of inspiration behind the London plaques scheme; he is also remembered for the Libraries Act of 1850, which established what became a national system of free libraries. Appropriately, Rose Hill has been a public library since 1902.

DAVID GARRICK*
(1717–79)
actor

Garrick's Villa (formerly Fuller House),
Hampton Court Road

FROM his debut in 1741, Garrick made a sensational impact on the London stage with his dynamic and expressive acting; he was also a successful manager, running the Drury Lane theatre from 1747 until his retirement in 1776. Garrick and his Austrian wife Eva Maria bought the property in 1754; Robert Adam* was employed to make alterations, including the building of the facade with its central portico facing the river. The gardens, sloping down to the Thames, featured 'a grateful temple to Shakespeare', whose reputation Garrick did much to foster. The Garricks entertained lavishly here – their 'night fêtes' were famous – and the grounds were thrown open one day every year.

SIR CHRISTOPHER WREN

(1632–1723) architect, mathematician and astronomer

Old Court House, Hampton Court Road, East Molesey

WREN, the Surveyor-General of the King's Works, took charge of rebuilding the City of London after the Great Fire, designing numerous churches and St Paul's Cathedral, his crowning achievement, between 1675 and 1711. He was granted a lease from the Crown on this then-decayed building in Hampton Court Road in 1708 and carried out major alterations, some of which survive. The house was by turns the home of Wren, his son Christopher and his grandson Stephen. When he retired from the Office of Works in 1718, Wren left his home in Scotland Yard, Whitehall (demolished), and came to live here more permanently; 'free from worldly affairs' and passing his time 'in contemplation and studies', before dying at his son Christopher's house in St James's Street, off Piccadilly, at the age of 90.

LANCELOT 'CAPABILITY' BROWN

(1716–83) landscape architect

Wilderness House, Moat Lane, Hampton Court

BROWN'S name is synonymous with naturalistic but well-ordered English park design: some outstanding examples of his landscapes are at Stowe, Buckinghamshire (begun 1741), Petworth, Sussex (1753), and Blenheim, Oxfordshire (1764). The Northumberland-born Brown earned his distinctive sobriquet because, in surveying a property for a client, he would invariably speak of its 'capabilities'. In 1764, he was appointed Chief Gardener at Hampton Court; Wilderness House, which lies within the walls of the Palace and dates from about 1700, came with the job. At Hampton Court, Brown resisted the temptation to tear up the garden of William III – his habit elsewhere with formal gardens – but incurred wrath from some for neglecting the topiary. The Great Vine was planted during his tenure here.

ENID BLYTON

(1897–1968) writer   207 Hook Road (formerly Southernhay), Chessington **26**

BLYTON started writing in her teens but decided in 1915 to train as a teacher. In January 1920, she was engaged as a governess by Horace and Gertrude Thompson – who had lived at this late-Victorian house since their marriage – to care for their four sons, David, Brian, Peter and John. Blyton described her time here as 'the foundation of all my success'. Her charges were quickly joined by other local children, forming a small 'school', and it was on this group that she practised, writing and reciting plays, poems and songs for their education and enjoyment. In her small room at the back of the house when her day's duties were done, Blyton wrote her first success, the poetry collection *Child Whispers* (1922). From 1924, the year she left Southernhay, Blyton became a full-time writer; that year, she married Hugh Pollock, an editor who worked at Newnes, her first publisher. Blyton was extraordinarily prolific, her many best-sellers including the *Secret Seven*, the *Famous Five*, the *Faraway Tree* and the *Malory Towers* series. Most were written at her later home in Beaconsfield, Buckinghamshire.

COOPER CAR COMPANY

winners of the Formula One World Championships in 1959 and 1960

Hollyfield Road, Surbiton **27**

At its peak, the Cooper Car Company was the world's largest specialist racing car manu-facturer. The firm, led by the father and son team of Charlie Cooper (1893-1964) and John Cooper (1923-2000), won both the drivers' and the constructors' Formula One World Championships in 1959 and 1960, with the Australian-born Jack Brabham (1926-2014) at the wheel. They also pioneered the rear engine layout of the modern Formula One car. All this was accomplished with a full-time team that never exceeded 35 people, working from a stylish purpose-built workshop and offices in suburban Surbiton (*above, right*), completed not long before that first Formula One victory. Its curved frontage mirrors the curved chassis that was a distinctive design feature of Cooper racing cars. Proto-types of the Mini-Cooper, a popular road-car collaboration, were also made here. John Cooper sold the business in 1965; not long after that, operations moved to Byfleet, Surrey.

ALFRED BESTALL

(1892–1986)
illustrator of Rupert Bear

Stavordale,
58 Cranes Park, Surbiton

BORN in Burma, Bestall came to England at the age of five. He studied art in Birmingham and London and worked as a full-time illustrator, after active service on the Western Front, for *Punch* magazine and on children's books. Bestall had his big break in 1935 when he succeeded Mary Tourtel as writer and artist of the Rupert Bear strip, which was published in the *Daily Express*. Tourtel had created her 'Little Bear Lost' – with his distinctive checked trousers and scarf – in 1920, and Bestall developed Rupert's adventures in Nutwood, watching him rise to international stardom in the 30 years he produced the strip. (He continued to illustrate the Rupert Annuals until 1973.) Bestall moved to this detached 1920s house on his father's death in December 1936, living here with his mother and sister, and working in an attic room at the front of the house. After his mother's death in 1966, he sold the house but remained in Surbiton – a much-loved member of the local community – until 1980, when he moved permanently to North Wales.

SIR MALCOLM CAMPBELL (1885–1948)
DONALD CAMPBELL (1921–67)
speed record holders   Canbury School, Kingston Hill

BETWEEN them, the Campbells – father and son – set 10 world speed records on land and 11 on water – all in crafts named *Blue Bird*. Malcolm Campbell, who sold cars for a living but preferred to race them, first broke the land speed record in 1924; by the time he set it for a ninth time, in 1935, he had taken it over 300mph. Donald Campbell, not to be outdone, managed 403mph in July 1964, and set six records on water – as against his father's four, though his attempt to exceed 300mph in January 1967, on Coniston Water, had fatal consequences. Campbell senior had moved to Canbury – a substantial late-19th-century house now in use as a school – in 1919 and was joined by his new wife Dorothy the following year. Donald was born there in March 1921; Malcolm, notoriously, spent the evening of Dorothy's labour helping a neighbour to build a dog kennel. Having disposed of his collection of inferior china, the family were on the move in 1922, living thereafter at a succession of addresses in east Surrey.

DAME NELLIE MELBA
(1861–1931)   Coombe House (formerly Coombe Cottage),
singer   187 Coombe Lane West **30**

BORN Helen Mitchell, and known as 'Nellie' from childhood, Melba is said to have coined her stage name in honour of Melbourne, her native city. She trained under the celebrated Mathilde Marchesi and made her operatic debut in Brussels aged 26, first appearing in London in 1888. For the next 20 years, she reigned supreme as the prima donna of Covent Garden, and also enjoyed a brilliant career in Europe and the US. Melba was so successful that the chef Auguste Escoffier created Peach Melba in her name, a dessert of peaches, vanilla ice and raspberry sauce first served in London in 1892. Her fame allowed her to move in exalted social circles, and she gained a reputation as a shameless name-dropper. In 1906 she rented Coombe Cottage (built in 1863 for the banker E. C. Baring and altered 1870–74) from her friend Admiral Lord Charles Beresford. As her country retreat, it provided the name and inspiration for the house she built in Coldstream, Australia, which became her principal base after 1909.

ACKNOWLEDGEMENTS

THIS books stands on the shoulders of a giant – namely *Lived in London: blue plaques and the stories behind them*, edited and introduced by Emily Cole (Yale, 2009). This covered the first 800 plaques, and its text has been distilled and updated for the present work by Bronwen Riley, Henry Howard, Charlotte Fairbairn and myself. Most of the work for *Lived in London* was undertaken by Emily Cole, Susan Skedd and myself. Other contributing authors were Roger Bowdler, Nick Chapple, Peter Guillery, Timothy Jones, Chris Sumner, Sarah Vidler and Simon Wartnaby. Thanks are also due to others who have worked on blue plaques, including Esther Godfrey, Allison Sharpe, Cathy Power, Alison Frappell, Libby Wardle, Caroline Howarth, Jane Biro, Stephanie Jenner, Sarah Whittingham, Johanna Roethe, Lesley Hoskins, Rebecca Preston, Fiona Fisher and Cathy Benson, who expertly proofread this editon, as well as to the Blue Plaques Panel and all the donors to the scheme. Jeremy Ashbee and Anna Eavis enabled me to take the time to write the new entries for this new, compact guide; Clare Loughlin offered timely assistance with the maps. And I would like to thank my partner Matt for his support and forbearance.

The book is dedicated to everyone who has ever worked on the blue plaques scheme, and to my late father John, whose enthusiasm for history helped to fire my own.

Howard Spencer

PICTURE CREDITS

INDEX